WINDSOR SECONDARY SCHOOL
931 BROADVIEW DRIVE
NORTH VANCOUVER, BC V7H 2E9

011215

MATHPOWER™ Eight

Western Edition

Authors

George Knill, B.Sc., M.S.Ed.
Hamilton, Ontario

Dino Dottori, B.Sc., M.S.Ed.
North Bay, Ontario

Enzo Timoteo, B.A., B.Ed.
Edmonton, Alberta

Eileen Collins, B.A., M.Ed.
Hamilton, Ontario

Mary Lou Forest, B.Ed., M.Ed.
Edmonton, Alberta

Mary Lou Kestell, B.Math.
Ancaster, Ontario

Archie Macdonald, B.A., B.Ed.
Dartmouth, Nova Scotia

Consultants

Laurie Birnie
Green Timbers Elementary School
Surrey, British Columbia

Bruce Christie
Garden City Collegiate
Winnipeg, Manitoba

Sylvia Coverdale
Colonel Irvine Junior High School
Calgary, Alberta

Katie Donnachie
Father Whelihan Elementary School
Calgary, Alberta

Carol Jaap Klass
Louis St. Laurent School
Edmonton, Alberta

Richard Kopan
R. T. Alderman Junior High School
Calgary, Alberta

Peter Luongo
Glenwood Elementary School
Langley, British Columbia

Diane Malecki
Cardinal Leger Junior High School
Edmonton, Alberta

John Macnab
Grandview Heights School
Edmonton, Alberta

Betty Morris
Consultant, Edmonton Catholic
School District
Edmonton, Alberta

Susan Schroeder
Windsor Park Collegiate
Winnipeg, Manitoba

Harold Wardrop
Princess Margaret School
Surrey, British Columbia

McGraw-Hill Ryerson Limited

Toronto   Montreal   New York   Auckland   Bogotá   Caracas
Lisbon   London   Madrid   Mexico   Milan   New Delhi
San Juan   Singapore   Sydney   Tokyo

*COPIES OF THIS BOOK
MAY BE OBTAINED BY
CONTACTING:*

McGraw-Hill Ryerson Ltd.

WEBSITE:
http://www.mcgrawhill.ca

E-MAIL:
Orders@mcgrawhill.ca

TOLL FREE FAX:
1-800-463-5885

TOLL FREE CALL:
1-800-565-5758

**OR BY MAILING
YOUR ORDER TO:**
McGraw-Hill Ryerson
Order Department,
300 Water Street
Whitby, ON L1N 9B6

Please quote the ISBN and
title when placing your
order.

MATHPOWER™ 8
Western Edition

Copyright © McGraw-Hill Ryerson Limited, 1996.

All rights reserved. No part of this publication may be
reproduced or transmitted in any form or by any means,
or stored in a data base or retrieval system, without the
prior written permission of McGraw-Hill Ryerson Limited.

ISBN 0-07-552650-6

10   TRI   5 4 3

Printed and bound in Canada

Care has been taken to trace ownership of copyright
material contained in this text. The publishers will gladly
accept any information that will enable them to rectify any
reference or credit in subsequent editions.

Canadian Cataloguing In Publication Data

Main entry under title:

Mathpower eight

Western ed.
Includes index.
ISBN 0–07–552650–6

1. Mathematics.   2. Mathematics – Problems,
exercises, etc.   I. Knill, George, date.

QA107.M376474 1996   510   C95-932899-8

Publisher: Andrea Crozier
Editorial Consulting: Michael J. Webb Consulting Inc.
Associate Editors: Sheila Bassett, Mary Agnes Challoner, Jean Ford
Senior Supervising Editor: Carol Altilia
Copy Editors: Dianne Brassolotto, Debbie Davies
Permissions Editor: Tina Dell
Production Coordinator: Yolanda Pigden
Cover and Interior Design: Pronk&Associates
Electronic Assembly: Pronk&Associates
Art Direction: Pronk&Associates/ Joe Lepiano
Production: Pronk&Associates/ Technical Art and Page Assembly,
     Linda Stephenson, Chris Trubela; Production Coordinator, Nelly Toomey;
     Production Assistant, Nancy Cook; Art Assistant, Caren Thomas;
     Typesetting, Stanley Tran, Craig Swistun
Cover Illustration: Doug Martin
Photo Researcher: Lois Browne/In a Word Communications Services

This book was manufactured in Canada using
acid-free and recycled paper.

CONTENTS

USING MATHPOWER™ 8

Each chapter contains a number of sections.
In a typical section, you find the following features.

2.3 Subtracting Fractions

About $\frac{3}{10}$ of Canadians live in the 4 western provinces. About $\frac{1}{10}$ of Canadians live in Alberta. The fraction of Canadians in the other 3 western provinces is $\frac{3}{10} - \frac{1}{10}$.

To subtract 2 fractions with the same denominator, subtract the numerators.

$\frac{3}{10} - \frac{1}{10} = \frac{2}{10}$ or $\frac{1}{5}$

So, the fraction of Canadians who live in British Columbia, Saskatchewan, or Manitoba is about $\frac{1}{5}$.

Activity: Use the Information

Before the school picnic, the gauge on the barbecue's propane tank showed it was $\frac{3}{4}$ full. At the end of the day, the gauge showed the tank was $\frac{1}{8}$ full.

Inquire

1. Read the gauge. What fraction is equivalent to $\frac{3}{2}$?

3. Describe a method of subtracting fractions with different denominators.

2. What fraction of the tank was used at the picnic?

4. Use diagrams to show that $\frac{5}{12} - \frac{1}{4}$ does not equal $\frac{4}{8}$.

Example

Subtract.   **a)** $\frac{4}{5} - \frac{1}{2}$ **b)** $3\frac{1}{2} - 1\frac{2}{3}$

Solution

To subtract fractions with different denominators, write equivalent fractions with the lowest common denominator.

a) The LCD of $\frac{4}{5}$ and $\frac{1}{2}$ is 10.

$\frac{4}{5} = \frac{8}{10}$ $\frac{1}{2} = \frac{5}{10}$

$\frac{4}{5} - \frac{1}{2} = \frac{8}{10} - \frac{5}{10}$
$= \frac{8-5}{10}$
$= \frac{3}{10}$

EST $1 - \frac{1}{2} = \frac{1}{2}$

b) The LCD of $\frac{1}{2}$ and $\frac{2}{3}$ is 6.

$3\frac{1}{2} - 1\frac{2}{3}$ $4 - 2 = 2$
$= 3\frac{3}{6} - 1\frac{4}{6}$ $3 < 4$, so rewrite the first mixed number.
$= 2\frac{9}{6} - 1\frac{4}{6}$ Subtract whole numbers, then fractions.
$= 1\frac{5}{6}$

50

Practice

Express all answers in lowest terms.

Find the difference.

1. $\frac{5}{12} - \frac{4}{12}$ **2.** $\frac{3}{4} - \frac{1}{4}$
3. $\frac{7}{9} - \frac{4}{9}$ **4.** $\frac{5}{8} - \frac{3}{8}$

Subtract. Use diagrams to explain your method.

5. $\frac{5}{8} - \frac{1}{2}$ **6.** $\frac{2}{5} - \frac{1}{10}$ **7.** $\frac{5}{6} - \frac{1}{3}$
8. $\frac{2}{3} - \frac{1}{2}$ **9.** $\frac{1}{2} - \frac{1}{6}$ **10.** $\frac{3}{4} - \frac{2}{3}$

Estimate, then subtract.

11. $2\frac{3}{5} - \frac{1}{2}$ **12.** $4\frac{7}{8} - \frac{5}{8}$
13. $5\frac{3}{4} - 1\frac{1}{4}$ **14.** $3\frac{1}{6} - 1\frac{5}{6}$

Estimate, then subtract. Use diagrams to explain your method.

15. $2\frac{3}{5} - \frac{1}{2}$ **16.** $1\frac{3}{8} - \frac{1}{4}$
17. $2\frac{1}{6} - \frac{2}{3}$ **18.** $4\frac{1}{4} - 1\frac{1}{2}$
19. $1\frac{1}{2} - \frac{2}{3}$ **20.** $3\frac{1}{2} - 1\frac{1}{5}$
21. $2\frac{1}{4} - 1\frac{2}{3}$ **22.** $3\frac{1}{6} - 1\frac{1}{4}$

Problems and Applications

23. About $\frac{1}{4}$ of the world's motor vehicles are built in Canada or the United States. About $\frac{1}{5}$ of the world's motor vehicles are built in the United States. What fraction of the world's motor vehicles are built in Canada?

24. a) Describe how you would find the answer to this problem.
$\frac{2}{3} + \blacksquare = 1\frac{5}{6}$
b) Calculate the answer.

Find the missing value.

25. $\frac{9}{10} - \blacksquare = \frac{1}{2}$ **26.** $\blacksquare - \frac{3}{4} = \frac{2}{3}$
27. $1\frac{3}{4} - \blacksquare = \frac{5}{8}$ **28.** $\blacksquare - \frac{5}{6} = 2\frac{1}{4}$

29. Daniel ran $2\frac{2}{5}$ laps of the track. Carol ran $2\frac{3}{4}$ laps.
a) Who ran farther?
b) How much farther?

30. Interprovincial Pipeline stock prices varied one day from $\$29\frac{3}{4}$ to $\$30\frac{1}{2}$. By how much did the price change?

31. About $\frac{1}{3}$ of Canada is covered in forest, and about $\frac{1}{12}$ is covered in fresh water. What fraction of Canada is not covered in either forest or fresh water?

32. Write two fractions
a) with a difference of $\frac{1}{4}$
b) with a difference of $\frac{3}{8}$
c) that have different denominators and a difference of $\frac{1}{2}$

33. Write a problem that involves the subtraction of fractions or mixed numbers. Have a classmate solve your problem.

PATTERN POWER

Look for the pattern, then draw the fourth diagram.

51

---

1 You start with an activity to generate your own learning.

2 The inquire questions help you learn from the activity.

3 The example shows you how to use what you have learned.

4 The EST logo in a solution indicates an estimate.

5 These questions let you practise what you have learned.

6 These questions let you apply and extend what you have learned.

7 These logos indicate special kinds of questions.

The pencil logo tells you that you will be writing about math.

The critical thinking logo indicates that you will need to think carefully before you answer a question.

The working together logo shows you opportunities for working with a class-mate or in a larger group.

8 The power questions are challenging and fun. They encourage you to reason mathematically.

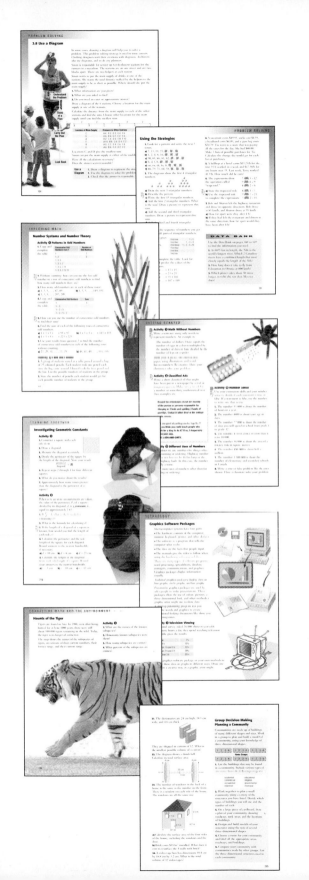

In the first 4 chapters of the book, there are 12 PROBLEM SOLVING sections that help you to use different problem solving strategies.

At or near the end of each chapter is a page headed PROBLEM SOLVING: Using the Strategies. To solve the problems on this page, you use the strategies you have studied. In each chapter, this page ends with DATA BANK questions. To solve them, you need to look up information in the Data Bank on pages 360 to 369.

There are 13 EXPLORING MATH pages before Chapter 1. The activities on these pages let you explore 13 mathematical standards that will be essential for citizens of the twenty-first century.

A GETTING STARTED section begins each chapter. This section reviews, in a fun way, what you should know before you work on the chapter. Each GETTING STARTED section includes Mental Math questions.

In LEARNING TOGETHER sections, you learn by completing activities with your classmates.

The TECHNOLOGY sections show you some uses of technology and how you can apply technology to solve problems.

Some sections are headed CONNECTING MATH AND…. In these sections, you apply math to other subject areas, such as art, language, science, and the environment.

Each chapter includes sets of questions called REVIEW and CHAPTER CHECK, so that you can test your progress.

At the end of each review is a column headed GROUP DECISION MAKING. Here, you work with your classmates to research careers and do other projects.

Chapters 4, 8, and 10 end with sets of questions headed CUMULATIVE REVIEW. These three reviews cover the work you did in Chapters 1–4, 5–8, and 9–10. In addition, a CUMULATIVE REVIEW covering Chapters 1–10 follows Chapter 10.

The GLOSSARY on pages 394 to 400 helps you to understand mathematical terms.

On pages 370 to 393, there are ANSWERS to most of the problems in this book.

A Problem Solving Model

The world is full of mathematical problems. A problem exists when you are presented with a situation and are at first unable to make sense of it. To solve any problem, you must make decisions.

MATHPOWER™ 8 will help you to become actively involved in problem solving by providing the experiences and strategies you need.

George Polya was one of the world's best problem solvers. The problem solving model used in this book has been adapted from a model developed by George Polya.

The problem solving model includes the following 4 stages.

Understand the Problem

First, read the problem and make sure that you understand it. Ask yourself these questions.
- Do I understand all the words?
- What information am I given?
- What am I asked to find?
- Can I state the problem in my own words?
- Am I given enough information?
- Am I given too much information?
- Have I solved a similar problem?

Think of a Plan

Organize the information you need. Decide whether you need an exact or approximate answer. Plan how to use the information. The following list includes some of the problem solving strategies that may help.
- Act out the problem.
- Manipulate materials.
- Work backward.
- Account for all possibilities.
- Change your point of view.
- Draw a diagram.
- Look for a pattern.
- Make a table.
- Use a formula.
- Guess and check.
- Solve a simpler problem.
- Use logical reasoning.

Carry Out the Plan

Choose the calculation method you will use to carry out your plan. Estimate the answer to the problem.
Carry out your plan, using paper and pencil, a calculator, a computer, or manipulatives.
Write a final statement that gives the solution to the problem.

Look Back

Check all your calculations.
Check your answer against the original problem. Is your answer reasonable? Does it agree with your estimate?
Look for an easier way to solve the problem.

Problem Solving

The ability to solve problems is an important skill that can be learned.

Solve the following problems. Compare your solutions with your classmates'.

1. Suppose June 1 is a Monday. If you start counting days on June 1, how many days will you count to reach the first Monday in October?

2. Divide the numbers from 1 to 12 into 2 groups. One group must have twice as many numbers as the other. The sum of the numbers in the larger group must be twice the sum of the numbers in the smaller group.

3. Draw a 3-by-3 grid. Colour 3 of the small squares red, 3 of them blue, and 3 of them green to meet these conditions.

• Every red square touches at least one green square along a complete side.

• Every green square touches at least one blue square along a complete side.

• Every blue square touches at least one red square along a complete side.

4. Professional basketball, hockey, and baseball championships are decided on the best 4 out of 7 games. The first team to win 4 games wins the championship. One way in which a team could win the first game and then go on to win a best-of-7 championship series is as follows.

Game	1	2	3	4	5	6	7
Result	W	L	L	W	W	W	

In how many other possible ways could the team win the championship series after winning the first game?

5. Two cars are travelling along a highway in the same direction toward a service centre. Car A is travelling at 20 m/s and is 100 m from the service centre. Car B is travelling at 25 m/s and is 125 m from the service centre.

Will car B draw level with car A before, at, or after the service centre?

Communication

Activity ❶ Communicating Information

Ideas can be represented and communicated in many ways.
Here are 4 ways of communicating information about 3 dogs.

A

B

Age

CT •   • CS

• GR

Height

C

Age: CS > CT > GR

Height: CT < CS < GR

D

The golden retriever is 60 cm high at the shoulder and is 10 months old.

The cocker spaniel is 39 cm high at the shoulder and is 3 years old.

The cairn terrier is 25 cm high at the shoulder and is 2 years old.

1. a) Which communication method gives the most complete
information?

b) Which method is the most efficient way to present
a lot of information?

c) What mathematical symbols are used in the
algebraic method? What do these symbols mean?

d) When would each method of communication
be the most helpful?

2. Gather information about the pets owned by some
classmates. Communicate the information in 4 different
ways.

Activity ❷ Interpreting Conditions

List as many answers as possible that satisfy each condition.

1. even numbers between 30 and 50 that are multiples of 5

2. plane figures with 4 sides and at least 2 right angles

3. square numbers greater than 40 and less than 150

4. solid figures with exactly 4 flat faces

5. ways to represent $\frac{1}{2}$, other than with equivalent fractions

6. pairs of whole-number factors whose product is 36

Reasoning

Reasoning is the process of drawing conclusions from given facts or pieces of information. Reasoning often involves looking for a pattern.

Activity ❶ A Number Pattern

1. Start with 5×5, 15×15, and so on, until you think you have found the pattern in the products.

5×5	15×15	25×25	35×35	45×45
55×55	65×65	75×75	85×85	95×95

2. Predict the rest of the products and check them with a calculator.

3. Describe the pattern in words.

4. Use the pattern to predict each of the following products. Check your answers with a calculator.
a) 150×150 **b)** 450×450
c) 125×125 **d)** 195×195

Activity ❷ A Tile Pattern

The floor of a rectangular room is covered with square tiles. The tiles around the outside are red, and the tiles in the middle are white. In the diagram, the room is 6 tiles by 5 tiles. There are 18 red tiles and 12 white tiles.

Find the dimensions of a rectangular room in which the number of red tiles equals the number of white tiles.

Activity ❸ Dividing a Grid

Here are 2 ways to divide a 4-by-4 grid into 2 identical halves, with 8 small squares in each half.

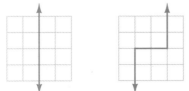

There are 4 other ways of dividing the grid into 2 identical halves, so that each half contains only complete squares. Find these 4 other ways.

Connections

Mathematics is used in many fields, including sports, music, and design. What other fields can you think of?

Activity ❶ Strike Zones in Baseball

In baseball, a player's official strike zone is a rectangle. The width is 43 cm, the width of home plate. The length is the distance from the knees to the armpits when the player is in a batting stance.

1. Find the distance from the knees to the armpits for players in a batting stance, if they have these official strike zones.

a) 3440 cm²   **b)** 3655 cm²   **c)** 3827 cm²

2. With a classmate, find the area of your official strike zone.

3. In major league baseball, the length of the strike zone used by umpires is the distance from the player's knees to the waist. If you played major league baseball, what would be the area of your strike zone?

4. Find the difference in the areas of your 2 strike zones.

Activity ❷ Musical Notes

Music is written in notes that have different values.

Whole note $\frac{1}{2}$ note $\frac{1}{4}$ note $\frac{1}{8}$ note $\frac{1}{16}$ note

1. Write one note that has the equivalent value to each group of notes.

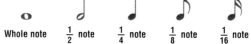

a)   **b)**   **c)**

2. Each group of notes is equivalent to one whole note. Write the missing note.

a)   **b)**

3. What is the total value, in whole notes, of all the notes in this piece of music?

Activity ❸ Flag Designs

Geometric figures are used to design flags.

1. Name the figures used in the flag of each country.

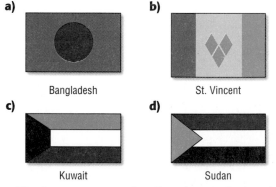

a)   **b)**

Bangladesh   St. Vincent

c)   **d)**

Kuwait   Sudan

2. Design a rectangular flag that includes the following.

a) at least 4 triangles

b) a hexagon and a circle

c) a kite, a square, and at least 2 rectangles

Number and Number Relationships

Numbers can be expressed in a variety of forms, including fractions, decimals, integers, and percents.

Activity ❶ Using a Floor Plan

Scale drawings are often used to shrink or enlarge diagrams. This scale drawing shows the floor plan of a 3-bedroom apartment.

1. What fraction of the apartment does each room occupy?

2. What percent of the apartment does each room occupy?

3. Express your answers to question 2 as decimals.

4. Which form of the numbers you found in questions 1, 2, and 3 is most helpful in describing the plan? Explain.

5. If the actual dimensions of the apartment are 12 m by 12 m, does the fraction occupied by each room change?

6. Decide on the fraction of an apartment you think each of the following should occupy. Then, draw a floor plan.

Living Room   Kitchen   2 Bedrooms   Laundry Room

Bathroom   Hallway   Dining Room

Activity ❷ Interpreting a Graph

Larisa sells books to bookstores. On one sales trip, she drove from Ancaster to Evergreen through the towns of Blinky, Chad, and Devon. The graph shows the time of day and the distance she was from Ancaster every hour. Write a description of her trip using the information on the graph. Your description should give the following facts, plus any others you wish to provide.

a) the time she started, the times at which she stopped, and the time she arrived in Evergreen

b) the total distance she travelled

c) her speed at various times during the trip

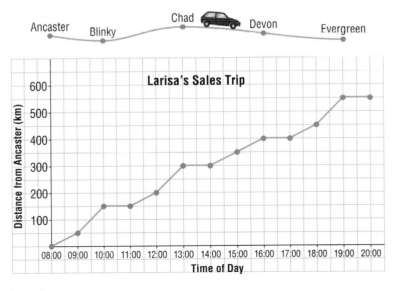

Number Systems and Number Theory

Activity ❶ Patterns in Odd Numbers

1. Copy and complete the table.

Consecutive Odd Numbers from 1	Number of Odd Numbers
1	1
1, 3	2
1, 3, 5	
1, 3, 5, 7	
1, 3, 5, 7, 9	
1, 3, 5, 7, 9, 11	

2. Without counting, how can you use the last odd number in a row of consecutive odd numbers to find how many odd numbers there are?

3. How many odd numbers are in each of these rows?
a) 1, 3, 5, ... , 87, 89   **b)** 1, 3, 5, ... , 149, 151
c) 1, 3, 5, ... , 207, 209

4. Copy and complete the table.

Consecutive Odd Numbers	Sum
1	1
1 + 3	
1 + 3 + 5	
1 + 3 + 5 + 7	

5. How can you use the number of consecutive odd numbers to find their sum?

6. Find the sum of each of the following rows of consecutive odd numbers.
a) $1 + 3 + 5 + \cdots + 95 + 97$ **b)** $1 + 3 + 5 + \cdots + 113 + 115$
c) $1 + 3 + 5 + \cdots + 223 + 225$

7. Use your results from question 2 to find the number of consecutive odd numbers in each of the following rows without counting.
a) 27, 29, 31, ... , 77, 79   **b)** 45, 47, 49, ... , 333, 335

Activity ❷ Pass the Pencils

1. A group of students seated at a table passed around a bag of 25 coloured pencils. Each student took one pencil each time the bag came around. Chantal took the first pencil and the last. List the possible numbers of students in the group.

2. State the number of pencils each student would get for each possible number of students in the group.

Computation and Estimation

You estimate to check or to make sense of an answer you have computed. Practising mental math helps you to make good estimates.

Activity ❶ Adding from the Left

One way to add mentally is to *add from the left*.

To add 45 + 38, think: "40 + 30 is 70,
5 + 8 is 13,
70 + 13 is 83."

Add mentally.

1. 24 + 63   **2.** 56 + 32   **3.** 64 + 87

4. 93 + 68   **5.** 426 + 339   **6.** 135 + 826

7. 7.3 + 8.2   **8.** 61.7 + 85.2

Activity ❷ Adding in Expanded Form

Another way to add mentally is to break up numbers into expanded form. This method can be called *bridging*.

To add 247 + 78, you can add 247 + 70 + 8.

Think: "247 + 70 is 317,
317 + 8 is 325."

To add 8.5 + 5.6, you can add 8.5 + 5 + 0.6.

Think: "8.5 + 5 is 13.5,
13.5 + 0.6 is 14.1."

Add mentally.

1. 120 + 75   **2.** 846 + 92   **3.** 634 + 95

4. 460 + 135   **5.** 309 + 168   **6.** 123 + 159

7. 2.5 + 2.6   **8.** $0.25 + $0.58

Activity ❸ Checking Your Change

After you buy something, it is a good idea to check your change. You can decide how much change you should have by subtraction. Another way is to use *adding on*.

Suppose you spend $3.68 and hand over a $10 bill.

To check the change,
you think: "$3.68 + $0.02 gives $3.70,
$3.70 + $0.30 gives $4.00,
$4.00 + $6.00 gives $10.00.
So, the change is $6.32."

Calculate the change from $20.00.

1. $12.50   **2.** $15.75   **3.** $16.97

4. $14.32   **5.** $17.69   **6.** $13.52

7. $7.55   **8.** $4.74

Patterns and Functions

In mathematics, we often study patterns and use them to make predictions.

Activity ❶

1. A small village had 3 roads passing through it, one going north–south (N–S) and 2 going east–west (E–W).

There was a stop sign at each corner of each intersection. How many stop signs were there?

2. As the village grew larger, new roads were built. Each time a new intersection was created, a stop sign was placed at each corner. How many stop signs were needed for the following numbers of roads?

a) 2 N–S, 2 E–W   **b)** 2 N–S, 3 E–W

c) 3 N–S, 3 E–W   **d)** 3 N–S, 4 E–W

3. Assume that the next street added will run N–S, the one after that E–W, and so on. Use your results from question 2 to predict how many streets there will be when the total number of stop signs is 120.

Activity ❷

1. Look for patterns. Copy and complete the table.

Large Cube	Number of Small Cubes	Dimensions of Each Face of Large Cube	Number of Small Cube Faces Showing
	1	1×1	6
	8	2×2	24
	27	3×3	
	64		
	125		
	216		

2. Describe the patterns in words.

3. Predict the number of small cube faces showing on a large cube with the dimensions of each face 10×10.

Algebra

Algebra uses numbers and symbols to communicate ideas.
Algebra is the language of mathematics.

Activity ❶

The first diagram shows how you can use 16 toothpicks to make a square with a perimeter of 16. Call the perimeter p. The second diagram shows 16 toothpicks arranged as 5 identical squares connected along entire sides. The perimeter is 12 or $p - 4$. Draw diagrams to show how you can use 16 toothpicks to make the following.

1. three different rectangles with a perimeter of p

2. two rectangles connected along entire sides to give a perimeter of $p - 4$

3. three rectangles connected along entire sides to give a perimeter of $p - 2$

Activity ❷

1. The statement ▲ + ▲ = ▲ + ■ + ■ is not true for ▲ = 1 and ■ = 2, because 1 + 1 does not equal 1 + 2 + 2. The statement is true for ▲ = 4 and ■ = 2, because 4 + 4 does equal 4 + 2 + 2. Find 3 other pairs of whole numbers that make the statement true.

2. Find 3 pairs of whole numbers that make each of these statements true.

a) ▲ + ▲ = ■
b) ■ + ■ + ■ = ▲
c) ▲ + ▲ = ■ + 2
d) ▲ + ▲ − ■ = 1
e) ▲ + ■ + ■ = ■ + 4

Activity ❸

1. Find a value of ■ to make each number sentence true.
a) ■ + 3 = 7   **b)** ■ + ■ = 10   **c)** ■ + ■ + 3 = 19

2. Find a value of n to make each number sentence true.
a) $n - 3 = 6$ **b)** $2 \times n = 8$ **c)** $3 \times n - 1 = 8$

3. Write each of the following as a number sentence, using n to represent the unknown number. Then, find the value of n.
a) A number plus three equals eight.
b) Four times a number equals twelve.
c) A number decreased by seven equals 4.

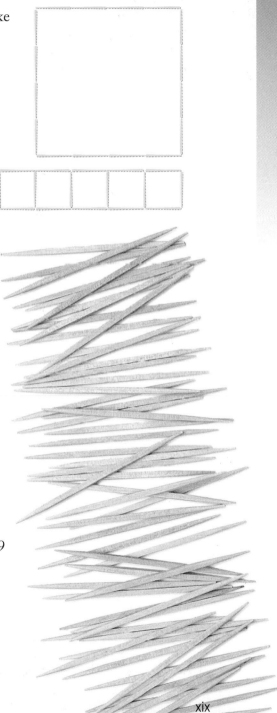

Statistics

Statistics is the science of collecting facts and making predictions based on the facts.

Activity ❶ A Sampling Experiment

Work in pairs.

1. Student A places 20 cubes in a paper bag, without showing them to student B. The cubes are of 2 different colours. Student B must predict the number of cubes of each colour by sampling.

2. Student A mixes the cubes. Student B takes a sample of 5 cubes from the bag and records the number of each colour in a table. Student B then returns the cubes to the bag.

3. Student A again mixes the cubes, and student B draws 5 more. The students carry out the process a total of 10 times. If the colours are red and blue, the table looks like this.

Trial	1	2	3	4	5	6	7	8	9	10	Totals
Number of Red Cubes											
Number of Blue Cubes											

4. Student B uses the totals to predict the number of cubes of each colour in the bag. The students compare the prediction to the actual number of each colour. They then switch roles and repeat the experiment.

Activity ❷ Phone Book Statistics

Each of the last 2 digits of a telephone number can be any digit from 0 to 9. If you add the last 2 digits, the sum can be any number from 0 (the last two digits are 0 and 0) to 18 (the last two digits are 9 and 9).

1. Without looking in a phone book, predict whether certain sums occur more often than others.

2. Test your prediction for one column of numbers from a phone book. Find the sum of the last 2 digits in each number, make a tally, and record the results on a bar graph.

3. Compare your graph with the graphs of other students. Explain the results.

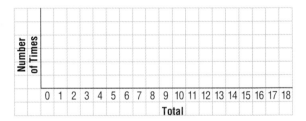

Probability

Probability is the mathematics of chance. Probabilities do not give you the exact answers to questions, but they tell you what you can expect to happen, on the average. When you think of tossing a coin 10 times, you might expect it to land "heads" 5 times, but you will not know how it will land until you actually toss it.

Activity ❶ Number Tiles

There are 10 number tiles, numbered from 1 to 10, in a paper bag.

1. You pick one tile from the bag without looking. The probability, or chance, of getting the tile with the 3 on it is $\frac{1}{10}$. Why?

2. What is the probability of picking an odd number?

3. What is the probability of picking an even number?

4. What is the probability of picking a number greater than 6?

Activity ❷ Birthdays

Do you think there is a good chance that two students in a grade 8 class have the same birthday?

1. If there are 30 students and 365 possible birthdays, you might think the chance is about 1 in 10. Why?

2. In fact, if there are 23 students, the chance is about 1 out of 2, or 50%, that two students have the same birthday. For 42 students, the chance is about 9 out of 10, or 90%, that two students have the same birthday. For 57 students, there is a 99% chance that two have the same birthday.
Divide 57 slips of paper among the members of your class. Have each person secretly write a different birthday on each of the slips he or she has. Collect the slips of paper and see if 2 birthdays are the same.

3. Canada has 104 senators. The probability that two of them have the same birthday is almost 100%. Use an almanac to find out how many senators have the same birthday.

Geometry

A knot design is one way of making
pictures on a flat page look
three-dimensional. The woodcut
Snakes, by M.C. Escher, is a knot
design.

© 1994 M.C. Escher/Cordon Art - Baarn - Holland.
All Rights Reserved

Activity ❶

Draw a knot design with squares by
following these steps.

1. Start with 9 squares.
Make the sides of the
squares double lines.

2. Erase the 4 centre
sections on the outside
of the design.

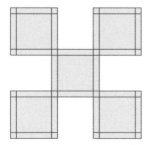

3. Erase the parts of
double lines that
overlap with other
double lines.

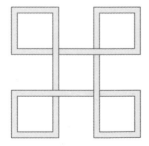

Now, start with 16 squares and make a knot design.

Activity ❷

Knot designs can be made from circles. The
logo for the Olympic Games has 5 circles in
a knot design.

1. Draw the Olympic logo.

2. Make 2 different knot designs with 4 circles
in each.

Measurement

Measurement is all around us.

Activity ❶ Using Measurements

1. List as many situations as possible in which each of the following types of measurement is required.

a) speed   **b)** depth   **c)** height

d) mass   **e)** volume   **f)** temperature

2. Describe ways in which people in each of the following occupations use measurement.

a) police officer   **b)** mail carrier

c) disc jockey   **d)** meteorologist

e) nurse   **f)** truck driver

3. Sports coaches must deal with many measurements. Choose a sport and list the types of measurement that the coach must be aware of.

Activity ❷ Designing a Room

An interior designer decorates rooms in homes and businesses.

1. List all the measurements an interior designer must know in order to decorate a room.

2. What units of measurement are used to measure each of the following?

a) carpeting   **b)** floor tiles   **c)** wallpaper

d) window blinds   **e)** curtains   **f)** paint

3. Using catalogues, magazines, and advertising flyers, choose materials to furnish and decorate a room used by your family. Write a report in which you describe your plan and estimate the cost of decorating the room.

Activity ❸ Earth Measurements

Through the ages, humans have explored and measured the highest, widest, longest, and deepest features of the Earth. Use an almanac or other reference source to name these features of the Earth and find their dimensions.

a) longest river   **b)** largest desert

c) highest mountain   **d)** deepest ocean

e) coldest continent   **f)** largest lake

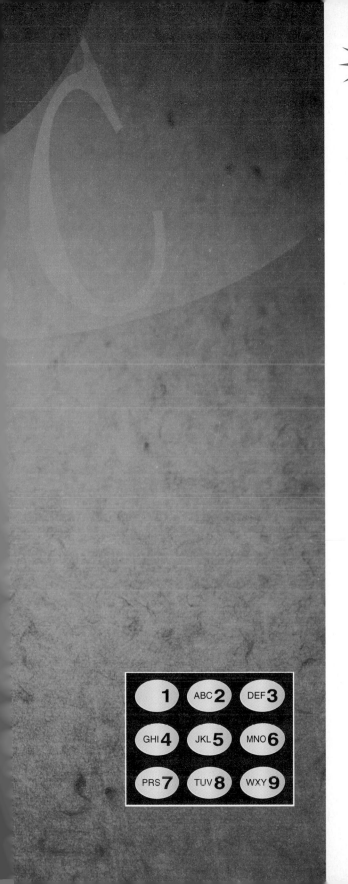

CHAPTER 1

Number Connections

The object is to spell out a word on a telephone keypad according to these rules:

1. Start on any button with letters and choose one of the letters on that button. This is the first letter of your word.

2. Move horizontally, vertically, or diagonally to a second button that is next to your first button. Choose one of the letters on the second button. This is the second letter in your word.

3. Continue moving to the buttons that are next to each other until you have spelled a word.

4. You cannot stay on a button and take 2 letters from it, but you can come back to a button as often as you like.

5. If you use the same button more than once, you can choose the same letter each time, if you wish.

6. The score of your word is found by adding the numbers on the buttons for the letters that you use. The best word has the highest score.

1

Activity ❶ Math Without Numbers

Write a sentence using only words to represent numbers. An example is:

> The number of dollars I have equals the number of eggs in a dozen multiplied by the number of days in June divided by the number of legs on a spider.

Show your sentence on construction paper, using illustrations and words but no numbers. Be creative. Have your classmates solve your problem.

Activity ❷ Classified Ads

Write a short classified ad that might have been put in a newspaper by a real or imaginary person. Make sure your ad has a number or something mathematical in it. Two examples are:

> **Reward for information about the identity of the person or persons responsible for sleeping in 3 beds and spoiling 3 bowls of porridge. Contact Father Bear in the cottage in the woods.**
>
> **Are you good at putting puzzles together? Do you think you could teach people who work for a king to do it? If so, I desperately need your help.**
> **Call 1-800-HMD-DMTY.**

Activity ❸ Different Uses of Numbers

Sometimes we use numbers for things other than counting or ordering. Highway number 56 does not have to be 56 km long or the 56th highway built. In this case, the number is really a name.

List 3 more uses of numbers other than for counting or ordering.

Activity ❹ Number Sense

Use your estimation skills and your number sense to decide if each statement is true or false. If a statement is false, use the number to write one that is true.

1. The number 53 000 is about the number of hours in a year.

2. The number 4800 is about your age in days.

3. The number 22 000 is about the number of days you will spend in school from grade 1 to grade 12.

4. The number 4700 is closer to 1000 than it is to 10 000.

5. The number 56 000 is about the area of a hockey rink in square metres.

6. The number 490 000 is about half a million.

7. The number 1 500 000 is about the number of elementary and secondary schools in Canada.

8. Write a true or false problem like the ones shown. Have a classmate solve your problem.

Activity ❺ Time

1. a) Work in pairs. You will need a digital watch or a watch with a second hand.

Person 1: Tap your finger for what you think is 10 s.

Person 2: Use the watch to time Person 1. Then, calculate how close Person 1 was to 10 s. If Person 1 did not tap close to 10 s, have him or her try the experiment again until he or she can tap between 9 s and 11 s. Switch roles and repeat the experiment.

b) Repeat the experiment, but this time try to tap for 100 s. Compare your results with your classmates'.

2. Calculate.

a) How many minutes are there in 1000 s?

b) How many hours are there in 10 000 s?

c) How many days and hours are there in 100 000 s?

Activity ❻ How Big Is a Million?

1. a) How many days, hours, and minutes are in 1 000 000 s?

b) What age were you when you had lived for 1 000 000 min?

c) Can a person live to be 1 000 000 h old?

2. a) About what distance would 1 000 000 cars stretch if they were parked bumper to bumper?

b) How many lengths of an Olympic swimming pool equal 1 000 000 m?

c) How many new pencils laid end to end measure 1 000 000 mm?

3. a) Does an average household television screen have an area of more or less than 1 000 000 mm²?

b) How many students could stand in an area of 1 000 000 cm²?

c) How many pages of a telephone book are needed to hold 1 000 000 names and numbers?

Mental Math

Calculate. Add the tens and then the ones.

1. $54 + 32$ **2.** $77 + 81$ **3.** $19 + 99$

4. $44 + 88$ **5.** $127 + 73$ **6.** $238 + 85$

7. $15 + 65 + 45$ **8.** $109 + 56 + 22$

9. $34 + 56 + 73$ **10.** $182 + 40 + 34$

11. $71 + 13 + 42$ **12.** $88 + 13 + 54$

13. $115 + 127 + 86$ **14.** $77 + 105 + 19$

Calculate. Subtract the tens and then the ones.

15. $369 - 42$ **16.** $48 - 26$ **17.** $173 - 64$

18. $81 - 37$ **19.** $600 - 58$ **20.** $129 - 38$

21. $528 - 65$ **22.** $733 - 46$ **23.** $366 - 27$

24. $208 - 19$ **25.** $188 - 96$ **26.** $500 - 68$

27. $1000 - 15$ **28.** $562 - 91$ **29.** $199 - 175$

Calculate.

30. 6×12 **31.** 3×80 **32.** 4×90

33. 9×90 **34.** 12×50 **35.** 12×600

36. 15×7 **37.** 11×29 **38.** 8×55

39. 49×3 **40.** 99×2 **41.** 16×12

42. 19×7 **43.** 105×4 **44.** 9×23

Calculate.

45. $720 \div 9$ **46.** $8100 \div 9$ **47.** $240 \div 6$

48. $720 \div 80$ **49.** $360 \div 6$ **50.** $150 \div 10$

51. $560\ 000 \div 700$ **52.** $150 \div 15$

53. $15\ 000 \div 300$ **54.** $960 \div 80$

55. $1080 \div 12$ **56.** $840 \div 70$

57. $1050 \div 70$ **58.** $800 \div 25$

1.1 Exponents

All organisms, regardless of how complicated they are, begin with a single cell. This cell splits to form 2 new cells. The 2 new cells split, and the process continues until the organism develops into an adult containing trillions of cells.

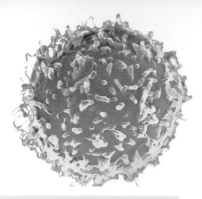

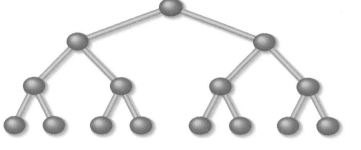

Number of Cells		
Standard Form	Factors	Exponential Form
2	2	2^1
4	2×2	2^2
8	$2 \times 2 \times 2$	2^3
16	$2 \times 2 \times 2 \times 2$	2^4

The product $2 \times 2 \times 2 \times 2$ can be written as 2^4, which is called a **power** of 2. It is read as "2 to the exponent 4" or "2 to the fourth." The **exponent**, 4, is the number of times the **base**, 2, is multiplied.

power → 2^4 ← exponent
base

Activity: Look for the Patterns

Copy and complete the table.

Expression	Factored Form	Exponential Form
$2^3 \times 2^2$	$(2 \times 2 \times 2) \times (2 \times 2)$	2^5
$3^2 \times 3^4$	$(3 \times 3) \times (3 \times 3 \times 3 \times 3)$	
$4^4 \times 4^3$		
$5^6 \times 5^1$		
$3^4 \times 3^4$		
$2^5 \div 2^2$	$\frac{2 \times 2 \times 2 \times 2 \times 2}{2 \times 2}$	2^3
$3^6 \div 3^4$	$\frac{3 \times 3 \times 3 \times 3 \times 3 \times 3}{3 \times 3 \times 3 \times 3}$	
$5^3 \div 5^2$		
$2^3 \div 2^1$		
$4^5 \div 4^3$		

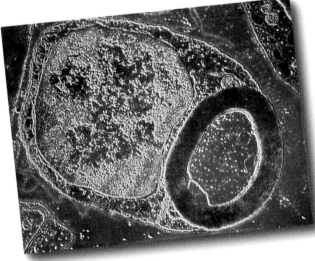

Inquire

1. For the multiplications, how are the exponents in the first column related to the exponents in the last column?

2. For the divisions, how are the exponents in the first column related to the exponents in the last column?

3. Write a rule for multiplying powers with the same base.

4. Write a rule for dividing powers with the same base.

4^2 is read as "four squared."

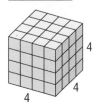

4^3 is read as "four cubed."

Example 1

Simplify.

a) $3^4 \times 3^2$

b) $4^5 \div 4^2$

Solution

a) To multiply powers with the same base, add the exponents.

$$3^4 \times 3^2 = 3^{4+2}$$
$$= 3^6$$

b) To divide powers with the same base, subtract the exponents.

$$4^5 \div 4^2 = 4^{5-2}$$
$$= 4^3$$

Example 2

Evaluate $2^5 \times 2^3$.

Solution

$$2^5 \times 2^3 = 2^{5+3}$$
$$= 2^8 \quad \boxed{C} \; 2 \; \boxed{Y^x} \; 8 \; \boxed{=} \quad \boxed{256.}$$
$$= 256$$

Example 3

Evaluate $(2^3)^2$.

Solution

$$(2^3)^2 = 2^3 \times 2^3$$
$$= 2^{3+3}$$
$$= 2^6$$
$$= 64$$

Practice

Copy and complete the table.

	Power	Base	Exponent	Standard Form
1.	2^5			
2.	4^3			
3.	5^2			
4.	6^1			
5.	7^3			

Write in exponential form.

6. $3 \times 3 \times 3 \times 3 \times 3$

7. $10 \times 10 \times 10 \times 10 \times 10 \times 10 \times 10 \times 10$

8. $(5 \times 5 \times 5) \times (5 \times 5)$

9. $(2 \times 2 \times 2 \times 2 \times 2 \times 2 \times 2) \times (2 \times 2 \times 2)$

Write as a power of 2.

10. 32 **11.** 2 **12.** 128

13. 256 **14.** 1024 **15.** 8

Problems and Applications

Simplify. Leave your answer in exponential form.

16. $2^5 \times 2^2$ **17.** $3^2 \times 3^3$

18. $5^4 \div 5^3$ **19.** $2^7 \div 2^6$

20. $1^4 \times 1^5$ **21.** $1^6 \div 1^3$

22. $5^5 \div 5^2$ **23.** $7^4 \div 7$

Simplify. Leave your answer in exponential form.

24. $5^2 \times 5 \times 5^4$ **25.** $2^8 \times 2^4 \div 2^9$

26. $6^5 \div 6^4 \times 6^3$ **27.** $4^3 \times 4 \times 4^2$

28. $2^2 \times 2^2 \times 2^4$ **29.** $5^4 \times 5 \div 5^2$

30. $4^6 \div 4 \times 4^2$ **31.** $10^2 \times 10^4 \times 10^2$

Evaluate.

32. $(2^2)^2$ **33.** $(3^2)^2$ **34.** $(10^2)^3$

35. $(2^4)^2$ **36.** $(1^5)^6$ **37.** $(3^2)^3$

CONTINUED ▶

38. The mass of Neptune is about 10^{26} kg. The mass of the moon is about 10^{23} kg.

a) About how many times greater is the mass of Neptune than the mass of the moon? Write your answer in standard form.

b) The mass of the sun is about ten million times greater than the mass of the moon. What is the approximate mass of the sun? Write your answer in exponential form.

39. The number of bacteria in a culture doubles every 6 min. Starting with one bacterium, how many bacteria will the culture contain after 1 h?

40. A patch of algae on the surface of a pond doubled in size every day. It took 30 days for the algae to cover the pond. How long did it take the algae to cover half of the pond?

41. A drop of water contains about 10^{21} water molecules. If a billion people could share these molecules equally, how many molecules would each person get? Write your answer in standard form and in words.

42. The expression $3^2 \div 3^2$ can be evaluated in two ways.

$$3^2 \div 3^2 = \frac{3 \times 3}{3 \times 3} \qquad \text{or} \qquad 3^2 \div 3^2 = 3^{2-2}$$
$$= \frac{9}{9} \qquad\qquad\qquad\qquad = 3^0$$
$$= 1$$

What is the value of 3^0?

43. a) Complete each pattern.

1, 3, 9, 27, ▨, ▨, ▨

1, 2, 4, 8, ▨, ▨, ▨

1, 4, 16, ▨, ▨, ▨

1, 10, 100, ▨, ▨, ▨

b) Rewrite each sequence using powers.

c) How will you express the 1 in each sequence as a power?

d) What is the value of any power with exponent zero?

44. a) Take a piece of paper and fold it once. Open it up and count the number of regions formed by the fold lines. Repeat this a second time, then a third, and so on. Complete a chart to keep track of the number of regions you have created after each fold. Continue until you can fold no more.

Number of Folds	Number of Regions
0	1
1	2

b) How many times did you fold the paper before you could not physically fold it any more times?

c) Compare your results with a classmate's.

45. Write a problem that requires the use of an exponent. Have a classmate solve your problem.

PATTERN POWER

1. Describe the following pattern in words.

$$2^2 = 3 \times 1 + 1 = 4$$
$$3^2 = 4 \times 2 + 1 = 9$$
$$4^2 = 5 \times 3 + 1 = 16$$
$$5^2 = 6 \times 4 + 1 = 25$$

2. Write the next 3 lines of the pattern.

3. The pattern allows you to use mental math to square some numbers.

$$19^2 = 20 \times 18 + 1$$
$$= 360 + 1$$
$$= 361$$

Use mental math to evaluate the following.

a) 21^2 **b)** 31^2 **c)** 99^2

1.2 Integral Exponents

Activity: Look For a Pattern

The table at the right shows the masses of different animals relative to the mass of a Barbary ape. For example, the mass of a moose is one hundred times the mass of a Barbary ape.

Animal	Standard Form	Exponential Form
African Elephant	1000	10^3
Moose	100	10^2
Cougar	10	10^1
Barbary Ape	1	$10^?$
Rabbit	$\frac{1}{10}$	$10^?$
Dwarf Weasel	$\frac{1}{100}$	$10^?$
Pygmy Mouse	$\frac{1}{1000}$	$10^?$

Inquire

1. What pattern do you see in the values of the exponents in the first 3 lines of the table?

2. Use the pattern to predict the exponential form of the number 1.

3. Use the pattern to complete the final 3 rows of the table.

4. Write a rule for expressing a multiple of 10 less than one as a power of 10.

5. What is the exponential form of 10 000? $\frac{1}{10\ 000}$?

6. How do the patterns help you to write 3^{-2} and 5^{-1} in standard form?

Example 1
Express in standard notation.

a) 10^0 **b)** 10^{-7}

Solution

a) $10^0 = 1$ **b)** $10^{-7} = \frac{1}{10^7}$

$= \frac{1}{10\ 000\ 000}$

Example 2
Write each number in exponential form.

a) $\frac{1}{100\ 000\ 000}$ **b)** 0.1 **c)** $0.000\ 001$

Solution

a) $\frac{1}{100\ 000\ 000}$

$= \frac{1}{10^8}$

$= 10^{-8}$

b) $0.1 = \frac{1}{10}$

$= \frac{1}{10^1}$

$= 10^{-1}$

c) $0.000\ 001$

$= \frac{1}{1\ 000\ 000}$

$= \frac{1}{10^6}$

$= 10^{-6}$

Practice

Write each number in exponential form.

1. 100 000   **2.** 10 000 000

3. $\frac{1}{100\ 000}$ **4.** $\frac{1}{10\ 000\ 000}$

5. 0.000 01   **6.** 0.000 000 001

Express in standard form.

7. 10^4 **8.** 10^5 **9.** 10^{-4}

10. 10^{-1} **11.** 10^{-9} **12.** 10^1

Problems and Applications

13. The Yukon's Ivvavik National Park covers about $\frac{1}{1000}$ of the area of Canada. Write this fraction in exponential form.

Replace each ● with >, =, or < to make each statement true.

14. 10^2 ● 1000   **15.** $\frac{1}{10}$ ● 10^0

16. 10^{-3} ● 0.0001   **17.** 10^{-4} ● $\frac{1}{10\ 000}$

18. 10^2 ● $\frac{1}{100}$ **19.** 0.000 01 ● 10^{-5}

20. a) How many times larger is 0.1 than 0.0001?
b) How many times smaller is 0.001 than 1?

1.3 Look for a Pattern

It has been said that *mathematics is a search for patterns.*
Patterns are used in many kinds of work. Astronomers look for
patterns in signals from outer space and in the way comets
move. Managers of fast-food restaurants use patterns to decide
how many employees they need at certain times. Patterns help
you make predictions.

Sue works at the Dunlop Horse Stables. She must buy
brass numbers for the 99 horse stalls. The stalls are to
be numbered from 1 to 99. How many brass numbers
should she buy for each digit from 0 to 9?

Understand the Problem

1. What information are you given?

2. What are you asked to find?

3. Do you need an exact or approximate answer?

Think of a Plan

Use a table to organize the information.
Then, look for a pattern in the first few rows.

Stall Numbers	Brass Digits Needed									
	0	1	2	3	4	5	6	7	8	9
1 – 9		1	1	1	1	1	1	1	1	1
10 – 19	1	11	1	1	1	1	1	1	1	1
20 – 29	1	1	11	1	1	1	1	1	1	1
30 – 39	1	1	1	11	1	1	1	1	1	1
40 – 49										
50 – 59										
60 – 69										
70 – 79										
80 – 89										
90 – 99										

Carry Out the Plan

There are 10 rows in the table.
The zeros column will show 9 brass zeros.
The ones column will show 9 + 11 or 20 brass ones.
The twos column will show 9 + 11 or 20 brass twos.

Sue should buy 9 brass zeros and 20 brass numbers for
each digit from one to nine.

Look Back

Does the answer seem reasonable?
Can you think of another way to solve the problem?

Look for a Pattern	**1.** Use the given information to find a pattern.
	2. Use the pattern to solve the problem.
	3. Check that the answer is reasonable.

Problems and Applications

Look for a pattern, then write the next 3 terms in each sequence.

1. 5, 9, 13, 17, ■ , ■ , ■

2. 81, 74, 67, 60, ■ , ■ , ■

3. 40, 39, 37, 34, ■ , ■ , ■

4. 3, 6, 12, 24, ■ , ■ , ■

5. a, d, g, j, ■ , ■ , ■

6. a, c, f, j, ■ , ■ , ■

Find the pattern, then copy and complete each table.

7.

4	10
6	12
9	15
11	
	33

8.

8	5
12	9
17	14
21	
	26

9.

4	8
5	10
7	
9	
	26

10.

21	7
9	3
24	
33	
	15

11. Find the pattern in the first 5 rows of Pascal's triangle. Then, write the next 4 rows.

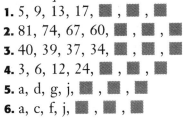

First row				1				
Second row			1		1			
Third row		1		2		1		
Fourth row	1		3		3		1	
Fifth row	1		4	6		4		1

12. The figures show the acute angles formed by 2, 3, 4, and 5 rays.

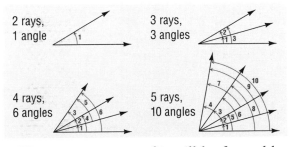

2 rays, 1 angle

3 rays, 3 angles

4 rays, 6 angles

5 rays, 10 angles

a) How many acute angles will be formed by 6 rays? 7 rays?

b) Describe the pattern in words.

13. a) How many small triangles are in the 8th figure? the 12th figure? the 25th figure?

b) Describe the pattern in words.

14. The table gives the sums of even numbers.

First two	2 + 4 = 6
First three	2 + 4 + 6 = 12
First four	2 + 4 + 6 + 8 = 20
First five	2 + 4 + 6 + 8 + 10 = 30

a) What is the sum of the first 6 even numbers? the first 20? the first 100?

b) Describe the pattern in words.

15. The following expressions show the operation called "triangle."

$$2 \triangle 3 = 7$$
$$3 \triangle 2 = 8$$
$$5 \triangle 4 = 14$$

a) State the "triangle rule."

b) Copy the following. Use the triangle rule to complete them.

$$4 \triangle 5 = ■$$
$$6 \triangle ■ = 14$$
$$■ \triangle 3 = 17$$

16. The following expressions show the operation called "rectangle."

$$3 \square 5 = 16$$
$$4 \square 2 = 12$$
$$6 \square 1 = 14$$

a) State the "rectangle rule."

b) Copy the following. Use the rectangle rule to complete them.

$$7 \square 5 = ■$$
$$2 \square ■ = 22$$
$$■ \square 5 = 20$$

17. Write a problem similar to question 15 or question 16. Have a classmate solve your problem.

1.4 Scientific Notation: Large Numbers

Activity: Study the Examples

Scientists often deal with very large numbers. To make notation easier, they use a short form that involves decimals and powers of ten. This short form is called **scientific notation**.

Study the numbers in standard form and scientific notation.

a) Cirrocumulus clouds are more than 5000 m high or 5×10^3 m high.

b) The interior temperature of the sun is about 15 000 000°C or 1.5×10^7°C.

c) The area of Hudson Bay is approximately 822 000 km² or 8.22×10^5 km².

Inquire

1. a) In scientific notation, how many digits are written to the left of the decimal point?

b) What determines the value of the exponent in the power of 10?

2. Write a rule for expressing a large number in scientific notation.

Practice

Write the value of the exponent.

1. $8700 = 8.7 \times 10^{\blacksquare}$

2. $150\ 000 = 1.5 \times 10^{\blacksquare}$

3. $3\ 250\ 000 = 3.25 \times 10^{\blacksquare}$

4. $12\ 600\ 000 = 1.26 \times 10^{\blacksquare}$

5. $75\ 000 = 7.5 \times 10^{\blacksquare}$

6. $4\ 000\ 000 = 4 \times 10^{\blacksquare}$

Find the value for each ■.

7. $28\ 000 = \blacksquare \times 10^4$

8. $360\ 000 = \blacksquare \times 10^5$

9. $1\ 200\ 000 = \blacksquare \times 10^6$

10. $6300 = \blacksquare \times 10^3$

11. $94\ 500 = \blacksquare \times 10^4$

12. $70\ 000\ 000 = \blacksquare \times 10^7$

Write each number in scientific notation.

13. 43 000   **14.** 825 000   **15.** 1 500 000

16. 9000   **17.** 36 000 000   **18.** 980

19. 8450   **20.** 340 000   **21.** 10 000

Problems and Applications

Write each number in standard form.

22. 5.8×10^4 **23.** 9×10^7

24. 4.25×10^5 **25.** 1.7×10^3

26. 6×10^2 **27.** 2.63×10^8

28. 7.5×10^6 **29.** 5.45×10^9

Express each number in scientific notation.

30. The area of Manitoba is about 650 000 km².

31. The Jurassic period lasted from about 210 000 000 to 140 000 000 years ago.

32. The length of the Yukon Territory coastline is 343 km.
a) Write this number in scientific notation.
b) Express the length of the Yukon Territory coastline in metres. Write the result in scientific notation.

33. Find a method of calculating the following. Compare your method with a classmate's.
a) $9 \times 10^3 + 8.2 \times 10^3$ **b)** $6 \times 8.2 \times 10^4$
c) $5 \times 10^5 - 7 \times 10^4$ **d)** $8.1 \times 10^2 \times 7.4 \times 10^6$

1.5 Scientific Notation: Small Numbers

Activity: Study the Examples

Scientific notation is used as a short form for small numbers as well as for large numbers.

Study the small numbers written in standard form and in scientific notation.

a) The mass of an electron is about 0.000 54 of the mass of a proton or 5.4×10^{-4} of the mass of a proton.

b) One millimetre equals 0.000 001 km or 1×10^{-6} km.

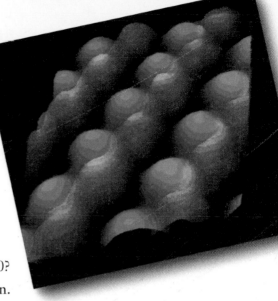

These highly magnified atoms contain protons, electrons, and other particles.

Inquire

1. What determines the value of the exponent in the power of 10?

2. Write a rule for expressing small numbers in scientific notation.

Practice

Write the value of each exponent.

1. $0.027 = 2.7 \times 10^{\blacksquare}$

2. $0.000\ 08 - 8 \times 10^{\blacksquare}$

3. $0.54 = 5.4 \times 10^{\blacksquare}$

4. $0.0037 = 3.7 \times 10^{\blacksquare}$

5. $0.000\ 625 = 6.25 \times 10^{\blacksquare}$

6. $0.000\ 009 = 9 \times 10^{\blacksquare}$

7. $0.000\ 000\ 12 = 1.2 \times 10^{\blacksquare}$

Find the value for each $\blacksquare$.

8. $0.0046 = \blacksquare \times 10^{-3}$

9. $0.000\ 053 = \blacksquare \times 10^{-5}$

10. $0.024 = \blacksquare \times 10^{-2}$

11. $0.99 = \blacksquare \times 10^{-1}$

12. $0.000\ 000\ 73 = \blacksquare \times 10^{-7}$

13. $0.0004 = \blacksquare \times 10^{-4}$

14. $0.000\ 008\ 7 = \blacksquare \times 10^{-6}$

Write each number in scientific notation.

15. 0.000 46

16. 0.000 003

17. 0.0124

18. 0.000 078

19. 0.0001

20. 0.000 000 27

Problems and Applications

Write each number in standard form.

21. 5.8×10^{-4}

22. 2.03×10^{-2}

23. 7.96×10^{-9}

24. 4.5×10^{-7}

25. 1.03×10^{-5}

26. 3.45×10^{-3}

Express each number in scientific notation.

27. The diameter of some cells is 0.005 mm.

28. The percent of neon in dry air at sea level is about 0.0018.

29. Fresh water covers 0.019 of the area of British Columbia.

30. Victoria gets 0.37 times as much snow fall as Edmonton.

Work with a partner to find a method of calculating the following.

31. $8 \times 4.2 \times 10^{-4}$

32. $2.3 \times 10^{-3} + 5.6 \times 10^{-5}$

33. $9.3 \times 10^{-6} - 7 \times 10^{-8}$

34. $4.6 \times 10^{-2} \times 3.8 \times 10^{-7}$

11

Designing for the Future: The Multi-Purpose Vehicle

Some people prefer cars in two- or four-door models. Other people drive vans or pickup trucks. If you lived on Moose Factory Island, you would travel to the mainland by boat. Some wilderness camps can be reached only by aircraft.

There are many examples of technology in the above modes of transportation. These range from the speedometer in a car to the depth finder in a boat to the altimeter in an airplane, as well as the engine in each type of vehicle.

Today, some people own several vehicles. Will this situation be possible in the future? Will environmental and cost concerns lead to the development of multi-purpose vehicles (MPVs)?

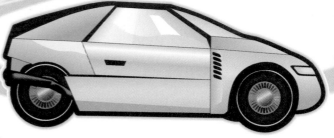

Activity ❶

1. Design an MPV to run on land and on water.

2. What changes would you make so that the MPV could also run under water?

3. Change your design so that the MPV could fly.

4. Would you steer the vehicle with a steering wheel, joystick, or trackball, or would you design something new?

Activity ❷

The personal vehicle of the future may be equipped as a mobile office.

1. List the equipment to be included.

2. Design the interior of an MPV as an office, showing where you would place the equipment.

Activity ❸

The personal vehicle of the future will have to be environmentally friendly.

1. How would you power the MPV? Gas? Solar energy? Batteries? Another form of energy?

2. If the MPV needs to refuel, how far should it travel before refuelling?

3. What special parts should the MPV have to protect the environment?

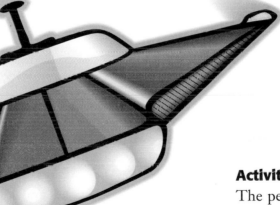

Activity ❹

The personal vehicle of the future will need to be equipped with an onboard computer, as well as a communication system.

1. What jobs will the onboard computer have?

2. Should the communication system use an antenna, a dish, or some other kind of technology?

1.6 Rational Numbers

You have already found the quotient of 2 integers.

$$\frac{8}{2} = 4 \qquad \frac{-6}{3} = -2 \qquad \frac{12}{-4} = -3 \qquad \frac{-18}{-9} = 2$$

The quotient of 2 integers is not always another integer.
$2 \div 5 = \frac{2}{5}$ (a fraction) or 0.4 (a decimal)

Activity: Use a Number Line

The table shows the high temperatures in winter for several Canadian cities. Plot the temperatures on a number line, like the one below.

City	Temperature (°C)
Charlottetown	−3
Halifax	−1.6
Calgary	−3.6
St. John's	−0.5
Toronto	−2.5

Inquire

1. Which 2 integers are closest to the Calgary temperature?

2. Which 2 integers are closest to the Toronto temperature?

3. Here are 2 ways to write the Charlottetown temperature as the quotient of 2 integers.

$$\frac{-6}{2} \qquad\qquad \frac{9}{-3}$$

Give 2 other ways.

4. Write the St. John's temperature as the quotient of 2 integers in 2 ways.

5. Write the Toronto temperature as the quotient of 2 integers in 2 ways.

Rational numbers are numbers that can be written as the quotient of 2 integers, that is, in the form $\frac{a}{b}$, where a is any integer, and b is any integer except 0.

All fractions and mixed numbers are rational numbers. $2\frac{1}{2} = \frac{5}{2}$

All integers are rational numbers. $8 = \frac{8}{1} \quad -4 = \frac{-4}{1}$

All terminating and repeating decimals are rational numbers.
$0.7 = \frac{7}{10} \quad 0.\overline{3} = \frac{1}{3}$

Rational numbers can be written in many equivalent forms.

The rational number −2 can be written as
$\frac{2}{-1}, \frac{-4}{2}, \frac{-2}{1}, -\frac{2}{-1}$, and so on.

The rational number 3 can be written as
$\frac{3}{1}, \frac{-3}{-1}, \frac{-6}{-2}$, and so on.

Numbers that cannot be written as the quotient of two integers are called **irrational numbers**. These numbers are non-repeating, non-terminating decimals. Examples of irrational numbers are $\sqrt{2}$, $\sqrt{3}$, and π.

Real numbers include all of the rational and irrational numbers. This diagram shows the relationships among the sets of numbers.

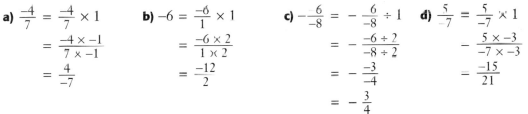

```
              Real Numbers
         ┌─────────┴─────────┐
  Rational Numbers    Irrational Numbers
      Integers
   Whole Numbers
  Natural Numbers
```

Example 1

Express each rational number in an equivalent form.

a) $\frac{-4}{7}$ **b)** -6 **c)** $-\frac{-6}{-8}$ **d)** $\frac{5}{-7}$

Solution

a) $\frac{-4}{7} = \frac{-4}{7} \times 1$

$\quad = \frac{-4 \times -1}{7 \times -1}$

$\quad = \frac{4}{-7}$

b) $-6 = \frac{-6}{1} \times 1$

$\quad = \frac{-6 \times 2}{1 \times 2}$

$\quad = \frac{-12}{2}$

c) $-\frac{6}{-8} = -\frac{6}{-8} \div 1$

$\quad = -\frac{6 \div 2}{-8 \div 2}$

$\quad = -\frac{-3}{-4}$

$\quad = -\frac{3}{4}$

d) $\frac{5}{-7} = \frac{5}{-7} \times 1$

$\quad -\frac{5 \times -3}{-7 \times -3}$

$\quad = \frac{-15}{21}$

The results of Example 1 suggest the following general statement.
$\frac{-a}{b} = \frac{a}{-b} = -\frac{a}{b} = -\frac{-a}{-b}$, where $b \neq 0$.

Rational numbers may be located on a number line.

Recall that numbers increase in value as you go from left to right on the number line.

For example, $-1\frac{3}{4}$ is less than -1.

Example 2

Which is larger, $\frac{-2}{3}$ or $\frac{-4}{5}$?

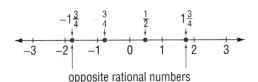

opposite rational numbers

Solution

Method 1

The LCD of $\frac{-2}{3}$ and $\frac{-4}{5}$ is 15.

$\frac{-2 \times 5}{3 \times 5} = \frac{-10}{15}$ $\frac{-4 \times 3}{5 \times 3} = \frac{-12}{15}$

Compare numerators. $-10 > -12$

Therefore, $\frac{-2}{3} > \frac{-4}{5}$

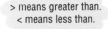
> means greater than.
< means less than.

Method 2

You can use your calculator to compare numbers.

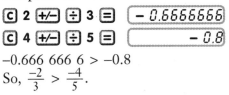

$-0.666\,666\,6 > -0.8$

So, $\frac{-2}{3} > \frac{-4}{5}$.

CONTINUED ▶

15

Example 3

Write each of the following as the quotient of two integers in lowest terms.

a) $1\frac{1}{2}$ **b)** -0.8 **c)** 3 **d)** -2.51

Solution

a) $1\frac{1}{2} = \frac{3}{2}$

b) 0.8 means 8 tenths.

So, $-0.8 = -\frac{8}{10}$

$\quad\quad\quad = -\frac{4}{5}$

c) $3 = \frac{3}{1}$

d) 2.51 is $2\frac{51}{100}$ or $\frac{251}{100}$.

So, $-2.51 = -\frac{251}{100}$

Practice

State which are rational numbers.

1. $\frac{1}{2}$ **2.** $\frac{2}{5}$ **3.** $-\frac{1}{3}$ **4.** $\frac{-3}{0}$

5. $\frac{-0}{4}$ **6.** 0 **7.** -7 **8.** $2\sqrt{2}$

9. π **10.** $\frac{-8}{-1}$ **11.** $\frac{18}{-19}$ **12.** $\frac{7}{0}$

Express each rational number in an equivalent form.

13. $\frac{-2}{5}$ **14.** 7 **15.** $\frac{-6}{12}$ **16.** $\frac{8}{-3}$

17. $\frac{-3}{4}$ **18.** -5 **19.** $\frac{2}{-3}$ **20.** $\frac{-2}{-5}$

Write each rational number in lowest terms.

21. $\frac{4}{8}$ **22.** $\frac{-3}{6}$ **23.** $\frac{-2}{8}$ **24.** $\frac{-14}{2}$

25. $\frac{-18}{21}$ **26.** $\frac{-8}{10}$ **27.** $\frac{-3}{9}$ **28.** $\frac{12}{15}$

Write each of the following as the quotient of two integers in lowest terms.

29. $2\frac{3}{4}$ **30.** 0.4 **31.** -7 **32.** -1.2

33. $-3\frac{1}{2}$ **34.** 2.25 **35.** -0.3 **36.** $\frac{-12}{18}$

Which is larger?

37. $\frac{-1}{2}$ or $\frac{3}{4}$ **38.** $\frac{3}{5}$ or $\frac{8}{3}$

39. $\frac{-3}{4}$ or $\frac{5}{-4}$ **40.** 0 or $\frac{-4}{-5}$

Replace each ● by <, >, or = to make each statement true.

41. $\frac{1}{2}$ ● $\frac{3}{4}$ **42.** $\frac{-3}{5}$ ● $\frac{-2}{5}$

43. $\frac{8}{3}$ ● $2\frac{2}{3}$ **44.** $\frac{-2}{3}$ ● $\frac{-3}{4}$

45. $\frac{11}{12}$ ● $\frac{5}{6}$ **46.** $\frac{3}{-4}$ ● $\frac{-1}{8}$

Use a number line to arrange the rational numbers in order from largest to smallest.

47. $\frac{1}{2}$, $\frac{4}{5}$, $1\frac{2}{5}$, 0, -0.5, $\frac{-7}{-10}$, 2

48. $1\frac{7}{8}$, $1\frac{1}{2}$, $1\frac{2}{3}$, $\frac{5}{4}$, $\frac{11}{6}$, $\frac{9}{4}$

49. $\frac{-5}{3}$, $\frac{11}{9}$, $\frac{-11}{-9}$, $\frac{4}{-3}$

50. $\frac{7}{4}$, -2, -0.75, $\frac{9}{2}$, -2.6, -3, $-3\frac{1}{2}$

Problems and Applications

51. Write an example of a rational number
a) with a numerator of 1 and a denominator greater than 5
b) with a numerator less than −3 and a denominator greater than 0
c) with a denominator of −16 and a numerator that makes a rational number in lowest terms

52. How many times more provinces are there to the east of Manitoba than there are to the west of Manitoba? Write your answer as a quotient of two integers in lowest terms.

53. Divide the number of consonants by the number of vowels in each name. Express each answer as a quotient of two integers in lowest terms.
a) Montreal   **b)** Red Deer
c) Nanaimo   **d)** Saskatoon
e) Barrie   **f)** Truro
g) Fredericton   **h)** Gander

54. a) List your answers from question 53 in order from largest to smallest.
b) Which name has the greatest quotient?

55. The following game report was published by the operators of an animal safari.

Safari Game Report

	Population 5 Years Ago	Population Now
Elephants	18	14
Monkeys	6	12
Giraffes	14	19
Rhinoceroses	3	1
Hyenas	8	8

The growth factor for each type of animal can be calculated using the following formula.

$$GF = \frac{\text{Pop. now } - \text{ Pop. 5 years ago}}{\text{Pop. 5 years ago}}$$

Calculate the growth factor for each type of animal. Express each answer as the quotient of 2 integers in lowest terms.

56. Between 1951 and 1966, the Canadian population increased from about 14 000 000 to about 20 000 000. How many times greater was the population in 1966 than it was in 1951? Express your answer as a quotient of two integers in lowest terms.

57. Is $\frac{-3}{4}$ the opposite of $\frac{-4}{3}$? Explain.

58. Since $4 \times 2 = 8$, $\frac{8}{2} = 4$. Use this idea to show why $\frac{8}{0}$ is not possible.

59. State whether each statement is always true, sometimes true, or never true. Explain.
a) The quotient of two integers has a value greater than 1 if the numerator is greater than the denominator.
b) The value of the quotient of two integers decreases as the denominator increases.
c) An integer is a rational number.
d) A rational number is a real number.
e) A real number is a rational number.

LOGIC POWER

Assume that there are no cubes missing from the back of this stack.

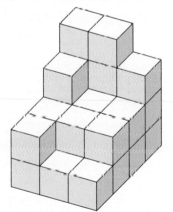

1. How many cubes are in the stack?

2. If you painted the outside of the stack green, including the bottom, what fraction of the cubes would have the following numbers of green faces?
a) 1   **b)** 2   **c)** 3   **d)** 4

1.7 Use a Data Bank

A data bank is a collection of information organized so that the information can be easily retrieved. A telephone book is one example of a data bank. A data bank can provide you with the information you need to solve a problem.

A plane leaves Vancouver for Montreal at 08:00 and flies at 820 km/h. At about what time will the plane land in Montreal, Montreal time?

1. What information are you given?

2. What are you asked to find?

3. What information do you need?

4. Where could you find the missing information?

5. Do you need an exact or approximate answer?

Understand the Problem

Find the flying distance from Vancouver to Montreal and the time zone each city is in. An atlas or an almanac gives this information. You can also use the Data Bank on pages 360 to 369 of this book.

Think of a Plan

Divide the flying distance by 820 to determine how long the flight will take. Find the time the plane will land in Montreal, Vancouver time. Then, allow for the change in time zones.

The flying distance from Vancouver to Montreal is 3679 km. The time the flight will take is

$$\frac{3679}{820} \doteq 4.49$$

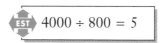

EST $4000 \div 800 = 5$

Carry Out the Plan

The flight will take about 4.5 h.
The plane will land in Montreal at about 12:30, Vancouver time. Montreal is 3 h ahead of Vancouver, so the plane will land in Montreal at about 15:30, Montreal time.

Look Back

Does the answer seem reasonable?

Use a Data Bank	1. Find the missing information.
	2. Use the information to solve the problem.
	3. Check that the answer is reasonable.

Problems and Applications

Use the Data Bank on pages 360 to 369 of this book to solve these problems.

1. Which distance is longer, the driving distance from Regina to Saint John or the length of the Mackenzie River?

2. Which feels colder —an outside temperature of –29°C with a wind speed of 48 km/h, or an outside temperature of –32°C with a wind speed of 40 km/h?

3. About how long does it take to fly from Winnipeg to Ottawa at a speed of 800 km/h?

4. What is the difference between the flying distance and the driving distance from Toronto to Halifax?

5. What is the total number of known moons in the solar system?

6. A plane flies from Ottawa to Edmonton at 850 km/h. If it leaves Ottawa at 15:00, at about what time will it land in Edmonton, Edmonton time?

7. The area of Alberta is 661 190 km². How many of the world's islands have a bigger area than Alberta?

8. One year on Earth is how many years on Mercury? Round your answer to the nearest one hundredth.

9. Wei phoned her friend in Victoria from Hong Kong on Saturday at 11:00, Hong Kong time. What was the day and the time in Victoria?

10. The Alaska Highway runs for 2400 km from Dawson Creek, B.C., to Fairbanks, Alaska. How many round trips, from Dawson to Fairbanks and back, equal the distance from the sun to the Earth?

11. The Lebrun family left Winnipeg at 08:00 on a Saturday morning. They drove to Regina, then Calgary, then Edmonton, and back to Winnipeg. They averaged 90 km/h on the trip and drove for no more than 9 h/day. They spent 2 nights in Regina, 2 nights in Calgary, and 2 nights in Edmonton. They left each city at 08:00, local time.
a) On what day of the week and at about what time did they arrive back in Winnipeg?
b) State any assumptions you made.

12. With a classmate, use your research skills to write an itinerary for a class trip from Montreal to see a Canadian astronaut lift off from the Kennedy Space Center in Florida. Go by bus, averaging 80 km/h and travelling 10 h/day. Plan to spend 3 full days and 4 nights at the Space Center.

13. Newfoundland's time zone is $-3\frac{1}{2}$. Use the Data Bank and your research skills to list other places that have fractional time zones. Compare your list with a classmate's.

14. Use the Data Bank to write a problem. Have a classmate solve your problem.

1.8 Ratios

Activity: Use the Information

A professional baseball team has 25 players. Some teams
have 10 pitchers, 3 catchers, 6 outfielders, and 6 infielders.

Inquire

1. What is the ratio in lowest terms of
a) catchers to outfielders?
b) outfielders to infielders?
c) infielders to catchers?
d) pitchers to all players?

2. What is the ratio in lowest terms of
a) catchers to outfielders to infielders?
b) outfielders to infielders to pitchers?

Example 1

Write each ratio.
a) circles to triangles
b) triangles to squares
c) squares to circles to triangles
d) squares to the total number of shapes

□ ○ △ △ ○
□ ○ ○ □
○ △ ○ △ ○

Solution

There are 7 circles, 4 triangles, 3 squares, and 14 shapes in all.
a) circles to triangles = 7:4
b) triangles to squares = 4:3
c) squares to circles to triangles = 3:7:4
d) squares to the total number of shapes = 3:14

Example 2

Write the ratio of dimes to quarters to nickels
in lowest terms.

Solution

There are 2 dimes, 4 quarters, and 6 nickels.
The ratio is 2:4:6. Divide each number by 2.
The ratio in lowest terms is 1:2:3.

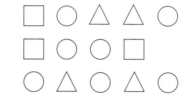

✏ The ratios in Example 2 are called **equal ratios** or **equivalent ratios**. Explain.

Practice

Express all ratios in lowest terms.

Use the diagram to write the following ratios.

1. red squares to black squares to yellow
squares

2. yellow squares to red squares to all squares

Write each ratio in lowest terms.

3. 10:25:15

4. 35:14:49

5. 16:32:12

6. 100:150:225

Problems and Applications

7. State the ratio of AB to BC to AC in △ABC.

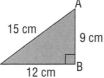

8. The annual numbers of days of frost at 3 Canadian airports are as follows.

Quebec City 180, Ottawa 165, Winnipeg 195

Write the ratio of days of frost in Winnipeg to days of frost in Quebec City to days of frost in Ottawa.

9. The table shows the numbers of Members of Parliament (MPs) elected to the House of Commons from the four Western Provinces.

Province	Number of MPs
British Columbia	32
Alberta	26
Saskatchewan	14
Manitoba	14

Write the following ratios.
a) MPs from Saskatchewan to MPs from Manitoba
b) MPs from Alberta to MPs from British Columbia
c) MPs from British Columbia to the total number of MPs from Saskatchewan and Manitoba
d) MPs from Alberta to MPs from Saskatchewan to MPs from British Columbia

10. State each ratio.
a) length to width
b) width to height
c) length to width to height

11. The power used by a light bulb is indicated by the power rating in watts (W). Express the following power ratings as ratios.
a) 100 W to 60 W   **b)** 40 W to 60 W
c) 40 W to 150 W   **d)** 150 W to 100 W
e) 40 W to 60 W to 100 W
f) 100 W to 60 W to 150 W

12. A cash register contains 12 $2 bills, 10 $5 bills , and 6 $10 bills.
a) What is the ratio of $2 bills to $5 bills to $10 bills?
b) What is the ratio of the value of the $2 bills to the value of the $5 bills to the value of the $10 bills?
c) Why are the answers to parts a) and b) different?

13. Write as a ratio in simplest form.
a) 1 min to 45 s   **b)** 2 kg to 250 g
c) 73 days to 1 year   **d)** 1.5 L to 750 mL
e) 35¢ to $1.05 to 14¢ **f)** 1 m to 175 cm to 250 mm

14. One term of a two-term ratio is a prime number. What can you state about the other term if it is possible to write the ratio in simpler form?

15. a) Without looking at a newspaper, estimate as a group the ratio of advertising space to non-advertising space in a local newspaper.
b) Get a copy of the local paper and determine the ratio of advertising space to non-advertising space. You need to estimate and add fractions of pages to get this ratio.
c) Compare your solution and your strategy with those of other groups.
d) Is the ratio different for a national newspaper?
e) Is the ratio different for a magazine?

Percent

A percent is a useful way to convey information and to make comparisons.

A percent is a ratio that compares a number to 100. Percent means "per hundred," "out of one hundred," or "for every 100."

You can think of a percent as a fraction with a denominator of 100. So, 45% means $\frac{45}{100}$.

A mark of 21 out of 25 on a test is $\frac{21}{25}$ or $\frac{84}{100}$ or 84%.

Reprinted by permission: Tribune Media Services

Activity ❶ Some Uses of Percent

1. Work with a classmate to list how percent is used in the examples shown on this page.

2. Collect examples of how magazines, newspapers, radio and television commercials, and almanacs use percent.

NHL Playoff Scoring Leaders			
Player	Shots	Goals Scored	Percent
Ferraro	47	13	27.7
Francis	26	6	23.1
Damphousse	52	11	21.2
Lemieux	40	8	20.0
Gretzky	76	15	19.7

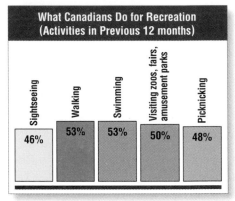

What Canadians Do for Recreation (Activities in Previous 12 months)

Sightseeing 46%; Walking 53%; Swimming 53%; Visiting zoos, fairs, amusement parks 50%; Picknicking 48%

Activity ❷ Percents Less than 100%

1. a) Work with a classmate. Fold a hundred grid into 4 equal sections.

b) What percent of the hundred grid does each section represent?

2. Fold another hundred grid into 4 equal sections with different shapes from those in step 1. What percent of this hundred grid does each section represent?

3. Use hundred grids to shade, in 2 different ways, areas that represent each percent.
a) 10%   **b)** 30%   **c)** 50%   **d)** 75%

4. a) Fold a hundred grid into 8 equal sections.
b) What percent of the grid does each section represent? Explain.
c) How can you use a hundred grid to shade an area that represents $37\frac{1}{2}$%? $62\frac{1}{2}$%? $87\frac{1}{2}$%?

Activity ❸ Percents Greater Than 100%

1. If a hundred grid represents 100%, what percent does the shaded part of these hundred grids represent?

2. Shade the same area in step 1 on hundred grids in another way.

3. Use hundred grids to shade the following percents in 2 different ways.
a) 125%   **b)** 250%   **c)** $137\frac{1}{2}$%

Activity ❹ Percents on a 4-by-4 Grid

Write the fraction of the grid that is shaded in each case.
Then, write each fraction as a percent.

1. **2.** **3.** **4.**

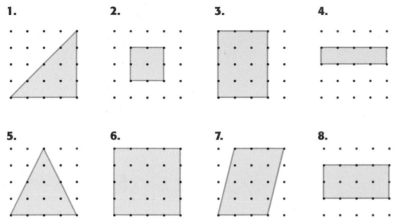

5. **6.** **7.** **8.**

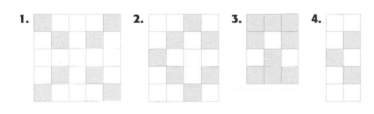

Activity ❺ Percents on Other Grids

Write the fraction of each grid that is shaded. Then, write
each fraction as a percent.

1. **2.** **3.** **4.**

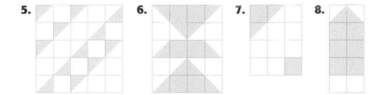

5. **6.** **7.** **8.**

9. **10.**

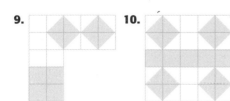

Activity ❻ Percents of Geometric Figures

1. On dot or grid paper draw
5 different geometric figures.
Shade a different percent of
each figure.

2. Exchange figures with a
classmate. Determine the
percents of your classmate's
figures that have been shaded.

1.9 Percents

A **percent** is a fraction with a denominator of 100.

Activity: Study the Information

Wetlands have many benefits. They are flood plains, swamps, or marshes that provide a habitat for wildlife and plants. They also collect sediment that would pollute rivers and streams. Coastal wetlands protect the mainland from damaging waves. Canada has $\frac{1}{4}$ of the world's wetlands. These wetlands cover nearly $\frac{1}{5}$ of the country. At one time, $\frac{7}{25}$ of the world's wetlands were in Canada.

Inquire

1. Write each of the fractions with a denominator of 100.

2. What percent of the world's wetlands are in Canada now?

3. What percent of the country do they cover?

4. What percent of the world's wetlands did Canada once have?

5. What is the difference in the percent of the world's wetlands that Canada once had and the percent that Canada now has?

6. How does a country lose its wetlands?

Example

About $\frac{1}{25}$ of the United States, $\frac{13}{20}$ of Canada, and $\frac{1}{50}$ of Mexico is wilderness. What percent of each country is wilderness?

Solution

For the United States	For Canada	For Mexico
$\frac{1}{25} = \frac{1 \times 4}{25 \times 4}$	$\frac{13}{20} = \frac{13 \times 5}{20 \times 5}$	$\frac{1}{50} = \frac{1 \times 2}{50 \times 2}$
$= \frac{4}{100}$	$= \frac{65}{100}$	$= \frac{2}{100}$
$= 4\%$	$= 65\%$	$= 2\%$

So, 4% of the United States, 65% of Canada, and 2% of Mexico is wilderness.

Practice

Express the shaded part of each figure as a percent.

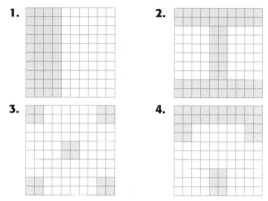

1.

2.

3.

4.

What percent of each figure is shaded?

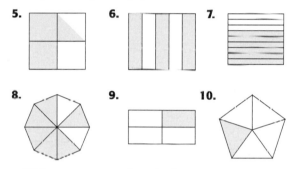

5.

6.

7.

8.

9.

10.

11. What percent of each figure in questions 5–10 is not shaded?

Draw each of the following.

12. a circle with 50% shaded in 2 different ways

13. a square with 25% shaded in 3 different ways

14. a rectangle with 75% shaded in 2 different ways

15. Estimate the percent shaded.

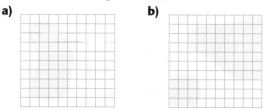

a)

b)

Copy and complete the following.

16. $\frac{3}{20} = \frac{\blacksquare}{100} = \blacksquare\%$ **17.** $\frac{7}{5} = \frac{\blacksquare}{100} = \blacksquare\%$

18. $\frac{\blacksquare}{50} = \frac{\blacksquare}{100} = 88\%$ **19.** $\frac{\blacksquare}{25} = \frac{\blacksquare}{100} = 44\%$

20. $\frac{\blacksquare}{25} = \frac{\blacksquare}{100} = 164\%$ **21.** $\frac{\blacksquare}{200} = \frac{\blacksquare}{100} = 35\frac{1}{2}\%$

Write as a percent.

22. $\frac{7}{10}$ **23.** $\frac{1}{50}$ **24.** $\frac{24}{25}$

25. $\frac{9}{20}$ **26.** $\frac{3}{4}$ **27.** $\frac{1}{3}$

28. $\frac{5}{4}$ **29.** 1 **30.** $\frac{3}{8}$

Write each fraction in lowest terms. Then, write it as a percent.

31. $\frac{12}{15}$ **32.** $\frac{9}{12}$ **33.** $\frac{7}{14}$

34. $\frac{30}{18}$ **35.** $\frac{9}{24}$ **36.** $\frac{7}{35}$

Problems and Applications

37. Around the world, 17 people out of 20 have brown eyes. What percent of the world's population has brown eyes?

38. The area of Manitoba is about $\frac{4}{3}$ of the area of the Yukon Territory. Express this fraction as a percent.

39. About $\frac{9}{25}$ of Canada is covered by forests. What percent of Canada is covered by forests?

40. Explain how the word "percent" can help you remember what it means.

41. a) Twenty-two out of 25 Canadians put on their right shoe first. What percent of Canadians put on their right shoe first?
b) About what percent of your classmates put on their right shoe first?

42. List the ways percent is used, other than with money. Share your list with your classmates.

1.10 Ratios, Fractions, Decimals, and Percents

Activity: Use the Information

In the television and movie industries, a shooting ratio is the ratio of the length of film shot to the length of film used. A well-produced movie has a shooting ratio of 5:1.

Inquire

1. What fraction of the film is used?

2. Write the fraction with a denominator of 100.

3. What percent of the film is used?

4. What percent of the film is not used?

5. Some television commercials have shooting ratios of 50:1. What percent of the film or tape is used?

Example 1

A 30-min television show has 6 min of commercials. What percent of the show is commercials?

Solution

The fraction of the show that is commercials is $\frac{6}{30}$.

Method 1
Express the fraction with a denominator of 100.

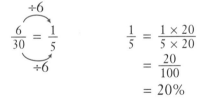

$$\frac{1}{5} = \frac{1 \times 20}{5 \times 20}$$
$$= \frac{20}{100}$$
$$= 20\%$$

Method 2
Express the fraction $\frac{6}{30}$ as a decimal.

$$\frac{6}{30} = 6 \div 30$$
$$= 0.2$$
$$= \frac{20}{100}$$
$$= 20\%$$

So, 20% of the show is commercials.

Example 2

Write as percents.   **a)** 0.235   **b)** 8:5   **c)** $\frac{2}{3}$

Solution

a) $0.235 = \frac{23.5}{100}$
$= 23.5\%$
or $0.235 = 0.235 \times 100\%$
$= 23.5\%$

b) $8:5 = \frac{8}{5}$
$= \frac{160}{100}$
$= 160\%$

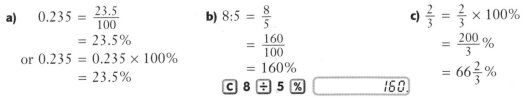

c) $\frac{2}{3} = \frac{2}{3} \times 100\%$
$= \frac{200}{3}\%$
$= 66\frac{2}{3}\%$

Example 3

Write as decimals.
a) 7%
b) 143.2%
c) $5\frac{1}{2}\%$

Solution

a) $7\% = \frac{7}{100}$
$= 0.07$

b) $143.2\% = \frac{143.2}{100}$
$= 1.432$

c) $5\frac{1}{2}\% = 5.5\%$
$= \frac{5.5}{100}$
$= 0.055$

Practice

Express as a percent.

1. 0.4
2. 1:4
3. 3:8
4. $\frac{6}{25}$
5. $\frac{22}{20}$
6. 9:45
7. 0.125
8. $\frac{98}{1000}$
9. $\frac{27}{40}$

Express as a percent. Round each answer to the nearest tenth, if necessary.

10. $\frac{1}{3}$
11. 2:11
12. 0.5
13. $\frac{4}{7}$
14. $\frac{11}{200}$
15. 9:5

Write as a decimal.

16. 18%
17. 85.9%
18. $6\frac{3}{4}\%$
19. 3%
20. 33.3%
21. 5%

Replace each ● with >, <, or = to make each statement true.

22. 0.01 ● 10%
23. $\frac{3}{5}$ ● 65%
24. $\frac{35}{50}$ ● 35%
25. 0.05 ● 50%
26. 17:20 ● 85%
27. 1.8 ● 178%

Problems and Applications

28. About $\frac{1}{50}$ of the Earth's water is frozen in ice caps and glaciers. Write this fraction as a percent.

29. The pull of gravity on the surface of Earth is 2.62 times the pull of gravity on the surface of Mars. Write this decimal as a percent and as a fraction in lowest terms.

The table shows the make-up of the human body, by mass. Copy and complete the table.

	Part	Fraction (lowest terms)	Decimal	Percent
30.	Muscles	$\frac{11}{25}$		
31.	Fat		0.12	
32.	Bones			16%
33.	Internal Organs	$\frac{1}{5}$		
34.	Blood		0.08	

35. The ratio of British Columbians who live in the city of Vancouver to the total number of people in the province is about 1:7.
a) Write this ratio as a decimal.
b) Express the ratio to the nearest percent.

36. Some schools use a 4-point scale instead of percents for student marks.
a) A grade of 3 on a 4-point scale is $\frac{3}{4} \times 100\%$ or 75%. What percent is a grade of 2? 3.2? 2.4?
b) The following calculation shows how to write 65% as a grade on a 4-point scale.

$\frac{65}{100} = \frac{n}{4}$

$\frac{65 \div 25}{100 \div 25} = \frac{n}{4}$

$\frac{2.6}{4} = \frac{n}{4}$

$2.6 = n$

So, 65% is a grade of 2.6.
On a 4-point scale what grade is 25%? 70%? 85%?

37. What percent is the reciprocal of 50%? Explain.

Estimating Square Roots

The square root of a number is the value that, when multiplied by itself, gives the original number.

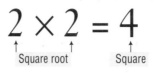

$$2 \times 2 = 4$$

↑ Square root   ↑   ↑ Square

Activity ❶

1. Here are 9 square tiles. Assume that each has a side length of 1 unit.

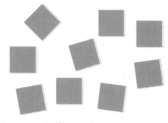

Arrange them into a square.
What is the length of the side of the square?

2. Write a multiplication statement to describe the area of your square.

■ × ■ = 9

3. What is the square root of 9?

4. Repeat steps 1 to 3 for
a) 16 tiles   **b)** 25 tiles

Activity ❷

Use 1-cm grid paper to draw your diagrams.

1. To find the square root of 12, think of the largest square you can make from 12 squares. How many squares do you have left over?

Divide the left-over squares into halves and add them to the two sides of your large square to make a larger figure.

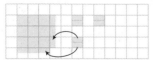

2. What is the length of each of the two longer sides of your larger figure?

3. What is your estimate of the square root of 12?

4. a) Calculate the square of your estimate. Does the result equal 12? If not, explain why the result does not equal 12.

5. Use grid paper to estimate the square root of
a) 20   **b)** 6   **c)** 30   **d)** 42

Activity ❸

Use 1-cm grid paper to draw your diagrams.

1. Suppose you want to find the square root of 18. What is the largest square that you can make from 18 squares? How many squares do you have left over?

2. You want to divide the left-over squares into pieces, and to fit the pieces along 2 sides of the larger square to make a larger figure. How should you do this?

3. What is the length of each of the two longer sides of your figure?

4. What is your estimate of the square root of 18?

5. Use steps 1 to 3 to estimate a value for the square root of each of the following.
a) 5   **b)** 7   **c)** 22   **d)** 39

6. Use a calculator to check your estimates in question 5. Explain the difference between the square of your estimate and the number you began with. Use your diagrams in your explanations.

7. Use steps 1 to 3 to estimate a value for the square root of each of the following. Round your answer to 2 decimal places, if necessary.
a) 11   **b)** 13   **c)** 27   **d)** 38

1.11 Squares and Square Roots

At the Olympic Games in Barcelona, Spain, Jeff Thue from Port Moody, B.C., won a silver medal in the Super Heavyweight division of the wrestling competition.

A wrestling mat is in the shape of a square. The area of the mat is 64 m². The length of each side is 8 m.

Since $8^2 = 64$, 8 is the number whose square is 64. So, 8 is called the **square root** of 64.

Activity: Complete the Table

Mathematicians studied square numbers or perfect squares over 2500 years ago. Square numbers could be shown as squares of pebbles.

They can also be shown as squares on a grid.

Area of Square	Area in Exponential Form	Length of Each Side
1	1^2	1
4	2^2	
9		

Draw squares to represent the next three square numbers. Then, copy and complete the table.

Inquire

1. The length of each side of a square is the square root of its area. What is the square root of each of the areas in the table?

2. How does the exponential form of the area compare to the length of the side and the area of the square?

3. A SCRABBLE® board is a square made up of 225 small squares. What is the square root of 225?

4. The square roots of some numbers are not whole numbers. Which two whole numbers does the square root of 90 lie between? Explain.

CONTINUED ▶

The square root of a number, say 49, is the number that, when multiplied by itself, gives 49. Since $7 \times 7 = 49$, then $\sqrt{49} = 7$.

The symbol $\sqrt{}$ means the positive or **principal square root** of a number.

A number, such as 49, which has a whole number as its principal square root, is called a **perfect square**.

The number 4.41 is not a perfect square, but it does have a square root. Since $2.1 \times 2.1 = 4.41$, then $\sqrt{4.41} = 2.1$.

Example 1

Evaluate.

a) $\sqrt{121}$ **b)** $\sqrt{900}$ **c)** $\sqrt{0.09}$

Solution

a) $11 \times 11 = 121$ **b)** $30 \times 30 = 900$ **c)** $0.3 \times 0.3 = 0.09$
So $\sqrt{121} = 11$ So $\sqrt{900} = 30$ So $\sqrt{0.09} = 0.3$

Some numbers have square roots that are not exact. Suppose a square has an area of 12 cm². Since $3 \times 3 = 9$ and $4 \times 4 = 16$, the square root of 12 is between 3 and 4.

You could measure the length of a side and find that it is about 3.5 cm. So, $\sqrt{12}$ has an approximate value of 3.5. If you check, $3.5 \times 3.5 = 12.25$, which is close to 12.

A calculator also gives approximate values of square roots that are not exact.

12 cm²

Example 2

Estimate. Then, evaluate using a calculator. Round answers to the nearest tenth. Check each answer by multiplication.

a) $\sqrt{73}$ **b)** $\sqrt{411}$ **c)** $\sqrt{0.5}$

Solution

a) $\sqrt{73}$ is close to $\sqrt{81}$, which is 9.

| c | 73 | √ | 8.5440037 |

$\sqrt{73} \doteq 8.5$
Check: $8.5 \times 8.5 = 72.25$

b) $\sqrt{411}$ is close to $\sqrt{400}$, which is 20.

| c | 411 | √ | 20.273135 |

$\sqrt{411} \doteq 20.3$
Check: $20.3 \times 20.3 = 412.09$

c) $\sqrt{0.5}$ is close to $\sqrt{0.49}$, which is 0.7.

| c | 0.5 | √ | 0.7071068 |

$\sqrt{0.5} \doteq 0.7$
Check: $0.7 \times 0.7 = 0.49$

Practice

Evaluate. Check your answer by multiplication.

1. $\sqrt{144}$ **2.** $\sqrt{400}$ **3.** $\sqrt{256}$ **4.** $\sqrt{625}$

5. $\sqrt{4.84}$ **6.** $\sqrt{0.81}$ **7.** $\sqrt{1.69}$ **8.** $\sqrt{0.25}$

Find a number with a square root between the given numbers.

9. 7 and 8 **10.** 11 and 12 **11.** 4 and 5

12. 9 and 10 **13.** 1 and 2 **14.** 3 and 4

Write the two whole numbers closest to each of the following square roots.

15. $\sqrt{60}$ **16.** $\sqrt{30}$ **17.** $\sqrt{20}$

18. $\sqrt{45}$ **19.** $\sqrt{75}$ **20.** $\sqrt{110}$

Estimate. Then, evaluate to the nearest tenth with your calculator. Check each answer.

21. $\sqrt{92}$ **22.** $\sqrt{802}$ **23.** $\sqrt{1000}$

24. $\sqrt{10}$ **25.** $\sqrt{0.8}$ **26.** $\sqrt{0.08}$

Problems and Applications

27. a) List the perfect squares from 1 to 400.
b) Examine the last digit in each perfect square. Write a rule that will help you to identify a perfect square from its last digit.
c) Use your rule to decide which of the following numbers might be perfect squares. Then, use your calculator to check.

1983	551	961	3481	987
2025	3175	1296	1896	1022

28. a) Prince Edward Island is Canada's smallest province. It has an area of 5660 km². If Prince Edward Island were square, what would be the length of each side, to the nearest whole number of kilometres?
b) Canada's largest province, Quebec, has an area of 1 540 680 km². If it were square, what would be the length of each side, to the nearest whole number of kilometres?
c) About how many Prince Edward Island squares could fit into a Quebec square?

29. A square has an area of 81 cm². What is the length of one side? What is the radius of the largest circle you can fit inside it?

30. a) Draw each square on 1-cm grid paper. Count squares to find the area of each figure.

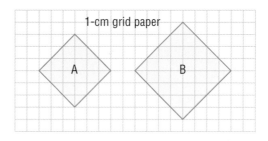

1-cm grid paper

A   B

b) Measure the length of a side to find the square root of each area.

31. Is each statement always true, sometimes true, or never true? Explain.
a) The square of a number is larger than the number.
b) The square of an even number is even.
c) The principal square root of an even number is even.
d) The principal square root of a number is half the number.
e) The principal square root of a perfect square is less than 1.

PATTERN POWER

The quotient $96 \div 32 = 3$.
Reverse the digits. $69 \div 23 = 3$

1. Divide $48 \div 24$. Then, reverse the digits and divide again.

2. Describe the pattern in the pairs of digits.

3. Find 2 more pairs of 2-digit numbers with the same property. Do not include pairs of numbers with the same digits, such as 44.

The Voyageurs

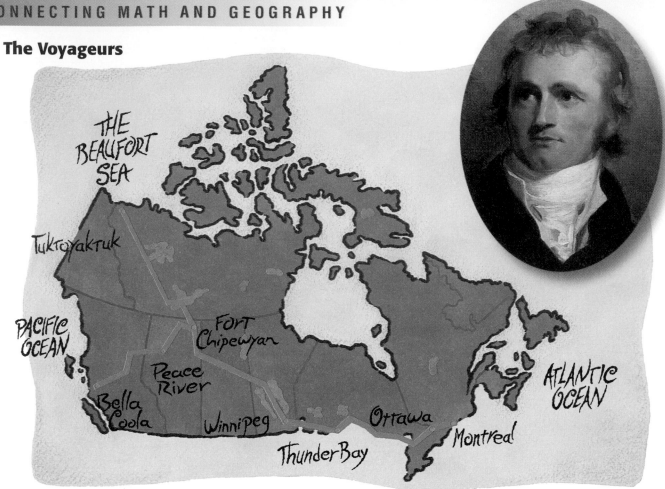

Alexander Mackenzie was a *voyageur* and one of Canada's most famous explorers. The *voyageurs* were fur traders who travelled across the continent by canoe.

Mackenzie was a partner with the North West Company, which had its headquarters in Montreal. He travelled west from Montreal many times. With the help of First Nations guides, Mackenzie's expeditions reached the Arctic Ocean and the coast of British Columbia.

In 1789, Mackenzie's group travelled about 3500 km from Fort Chipewyan, in northern Alberta, down the Big River to its mouth at the Arctic Ocean. This river is now called the Mackenzie River. However, Mackenzie was not looking for the Arctic Ocean. He returned to England in 1791 to go to school and improve his navigational skills. In 1793, Mackenzie led an expedition about 2000 km up the Peace River and over the Rockies to the British Columbia coast.

Two hundred years later, four groups of students from Lakehead University, led by Dr. Jim Smithers, paddled and portaged along Mackenzie's historic 12 000-km route across the country. This adventure took place in four summers from 1989 to 1993.

In each part of the expedition, students spent some days paddling. Other days were spent interacting with local communities and presenting a "Stay in School" program. At full speed, the Lakehead students paddled an average of 54 strokes/min. There were many portages, the longest being the Methye Portage at 19 km and the Grand Portage at 14 km.

Part 1, 1989:

Fort McMurray, Alberta, to Kendall Island, Beaufort Sea

The first part of the expedition started on May 25 in Fort McMurray and ended 3235 km later at Kendall Island on July 27. Dr. Smithers' students paddled for 31 of those days. When Mackenzie travelled this route, he averaged 120 km a day going downstream and 50 km a day going upstream.

Part 2, 1991:

Montreal to Winnipeg

This leg started on May 20 and ended 3400 km later on August 23. The students paddled for 55 days.

Part 3, 1992:

Winnipeg to Peace River, Alberta

In the third summer, the students started on June 5 and ended 3200 km later on August 29. The total number of days spent paddling on this leg was 64.

Part 4, 1993:

Peace River, Alberta, to Bella Coola, British Columbia

The final leg of the expedition started on May 16 and ended 2000 km later on July 22. There were 57 days of paddling. Mackenzie averaged 35 km per day on this part of his trip.

Activity ❶

1. How many days did the students take to complete each part of the expedition?

2. How many days of paddling did it take the students to complete the entire expedition?

3. How many days did the students spend on community interaction and presenting?

4. Draw a double bar graph to show the number of days spent on each part and the number of days paddling.

Activity ❸

1. How many strokes would the paddlers take in 1 h at full speed?

2. The average speed of a canoe was about 7 km/h in still water. How many hours would it take to complete the entire 12 000-km route at this speed?

3. How many strokes of the paddle would be needed to complete the entire route at the average speed?

Activity ❷

1. a) Use the fraction $\frac{\text{kilometres travelled}}{\text{days of paddling}}$ to calculate the average distance travelled per day on each part of the expedition.

b) Calculate the average distance travelled per day for the entire expedition.

2. a) In part 1 of the expedition, along the Mackenzie River, were the students travelling upstream or downstream?

b) Compare the students' rate of travel with Mackenzie's rate of travel for this part of the expedition.

3. Compare the students' and Mackenzie's rates of travel on part 4 of the expedition.

4. Draw a bar graph to show the students' average rate of travel for each part of the expedition.

Activity ❹

1. In your group, decide what you would expect to learn if you were one of the students on the expedition.

2. a) List the things you would bring on the expedition.

b) Identify the 10 most important things and give a reason for including each one.

1.12 Sequence the Operations

Global Fitness Centre is open from 06:00 to 22:00 from Monday to Friday, and from 09:00 to 18:00 on Saturday and Sunday. When open, it is staffed by a manager, a receptionist, and 2 instructors. Managers earn $21.75/h, instructors $18.25/h, and receptionists $13.50/h. Two cleaners each work 2 h/day after the centre closes. They each earn $11.15/h. How much does the fitness centre pay in wages each week?

Understand the Problem

1. What information are you given?

2. What are you asked to find?

3. Do you need an exact or approximate answer?

Think of a Plan

Find the number of hours the centre is open each week.
Find the total staff pay per hour, then per week.
Find the number of hours of cleaning each week.
Find the total cleaners' pay per hour, then per week.
Find the total paid each week in wages.

Hours of operation

Monday to Friday:	06:00 to 22:00 is 16 h	$5 \times 16 = 80$
Saturday and Sunday:	09:00 to 18:00 is 9 h	$2 \times 9 = 18$
Total hours per week:	$80 + 18 = 98$	

Carry Out the Plan

Staff wages per hour

1 manager: $21.75
2 instructors: $2 \times \$18.25 = \$36.50$
1 receptionist: $13.50
Total: $71.75

> EST $20 + 40 + 10 = 70$

Staff wages per week $98 \times \$71.75 = \$7031.50$

> EST $100 \times 70 = 7000$

Hours of cleaning per week $7 \times 2 = 14$
Cleaners' wages per hour $2 \times \$11.15 = \$22.30$
Cleaners' wages per week $14 \times \$22.30 = \$312.20$

> EST $14 \times 20 = 280$

Total wages per week $\$7031.50 + \$312.20$
$= \$7343.70$

> EST $7000 + 300 = 7300$

Look Back

The fitness centre pays $7343.70 in wages each week.

Does the answer seem reasonable? Is there another way to solve the problem?

Sequence the Operations	**1.** List the given facts.
	2. Decide on a correct solution sequence.
	3. Complete the calculations.
	4. Check that your answer is reasonable.

Problems and Applications

1. The football stadium has 32 560 seats. For the last game, 4500 tickets were given away. The rest were sold at $9.50 each. How much money was received from ticket sales?

2. The school library had a used book sale. Paperback books were 25¢ each, and hardcover books were $1.25 each. There were 54 paperbacks and 163 hardcover books sold. How much money did the library raise?

3. Paula repairs swimming pools and earns $14.50/h for the first 35 h she works in a week. For hours over 35 h, she earns 1.5 times as much. If she works 48 h in a week, how much does she earn?

4. Tamara has to go on a business trip. Including taxes, her round trip airfare is $398.60, and her room costs $115.70 per night. The cab fare from the airport to the hotel is $40.00. If Tamara stays for 2 nights, how much does the trip cost, excluding the cost of food?

5. Brazil is the country with the largest number of species of mammals, birds, and reptiles and amphibians. Brazil has 394 species of mammals, 1573 species of birds, and 970 species of reptiles and amphibians. The United States has 346 species of mammals, 650 species of birds, and 122 species of reptiles and amphibians. Altogether, how many more species of mammals, birds, and reptiles and amphibians does Brazil have than the United States?

6. Tides are caused by the sun and moon pulling on the Earth. The greatest tides happen in the Bay of Fundy, where they can rise and fall over 15 m. The ground you walk on also rises and falls, but by only 50 cm a day. What is the difference in the heights of these tides?

7. You can buy a bicycle for $399.95 cash, or pay $34.90/month for 12 months. If you exclude taxes, which price is less and by how much?

8. When he started his job, Terry earned $8.75/h and worked 8 h a week. After 2 months, he got a raise to $9.30/h. How much more a week did he earn? What assumption have you made?

9. Wolfgang Amadeus Mozart started writing music at age 4. He wrote about 1000 pieces of music before he died at age 35. About how many pieces of music was that a year? What assumptions have you made?

10. In 1991, the population of Nova Scotia was 900 000. On the average, the population increased by 4500 per year from 1891 to 1991. What was the population in 1891?

11. Ribbon costs $2.50/m. Find the cost of the ribbon for this present. Allow 80 cm for the bow.

12. Three grade 8 classes decided to raise money for 2 charities by selling boxes of greeting cards. A box of cards cost $3.80 from the supplier and sold for $6.00. One class sold 150 boxes, the second 175, and the third 225. If the proceeds were divided equally between the 2 charities, how much did each receive?

13. Write a problem in which operations must be sequenced. Have a classmate solve your problem.

Review

Write in standard form.

1. $4 \times 2 \times 8$ **2.** 5^4

3. $2 \times 2 \times 2 \times 2 \times 3 \times 3$ **4.** $3^4 \times 5^2$

Write in order from smallest to largest.

5. 3^4, 5^3, 10^2 **6.** 11^2, 4^3, 2^6

Simplify. Leave your answer in exponential form.

7. $5^2 \times 5^3 \times 5$ **8.** $3^9 \div 3^3$ **9.** $2^4 \times 2^2 \div 2^3$

Rewrite each number in scientific notation.

10. 24 000 **11.** 360 000 **12.** 5 800 000

Rewrite each number in standard form.

13. 2.6×10^4 **14.** 8.31×10^7 **15.** 1.7×10^5

Rewrite each number in scientific notation.

16. 0.0063 **17.** 0.000 052

18. 0.047 **19.** 0.000 000 046

Rewrite each number in standard form.

20. 4.3×10^{-3} **21.** 8.902×10^{-6}

22. 2×10^{-4} **23.** 5.13×10^{-5}

Write each of the following as the quotient of two integers in lowest terms.

24. 0.6 **25.** $-2\frac{4}{5}$ **26.** -1.7 **27.** $1\frac{2}{3}$

Write in order from least to greatest.

28. 155.7, -175, -99.2, 101.9, 50.2

29. $\frac{5}{4}$, -1.5, 2.9, $1\frac{5}{6}$, 0, -0.91, 15.8

Use the diagram to express each ratio in lowest terms.

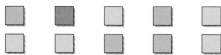

30. yellow squares to red squares

31. red squares to green squares to yellow squares

32. all squares to red squares to yellow squares

33. Make 5 copies of the diagram in your notebook. Colour the small squares red or blue to obtain the following ratios.

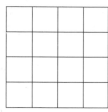

a) red squares to blue squares, 3:1

b) blue squares to red squares, 5:3

c) red squares to blue squares, 7:1

d) blue squares to all small squares, 1:2

e) red squares to all small squares, 1:4

Express in lowest terms.

34. 3:9 **35.** 3:3 **36.** 4:8

37. 40:5 **38.** 12:3 **39.** 50:10

40. 14:35:7 **41.** 16:24:12 **42.** 30:15:40

Draw each of the following in 2 different ways.

43. a square with 50% shaded

44. a circle with 75% shaded

45. Estimate the percent that is shaded.

a) **b)**

Express as a decimal.

46. 20% **47.** 168% **48.** 35.8% **49.** 0.5%

Express as a fraction in lowest terms.

50. 10% **51.** 60% **52.** 12.5%

53. 188% **54.** 0.6% **55.** 2%

Write as a percent.

56. $\frac{2}{5}$ **57.** $\frac{11}{20}$ **58.** 25:24 **59.** $\frac{7}{4}$

60. 0.83 **61.** 0.015 **62.** $1\frac{7}{8}$ **63.** 1.32

Express to the nearest tenth of a percent.

64. $\frac{2}{3}$ **65.** $\frac{4}{9}$ **66.** $1.\overline{5}$

Evaluate.

67. $\sqrt{121}$ **68.** $\sqrt{0.49}$ **69.** $\sqrt{900}$

70. $\sqrt{0.04}$ **71.** $\sqrt{441}$ **72.** $\sqrt{1.96}$

Estimate. Then, evaluate to the nearest tenth.

73. $\sqrt{150}$ **74.** $\sqrt{8.5}$ **75.** $\sqrt{1700}$

76. A microsecond is 0.000 001 s.

a) Write this number in scientific notation.

b) How many microseconds are in 1 min?

c) Write your answer to part b) in scientific notation.

77. Edmonton is Alberta's biggest city, with an area of 670 km². If you could fit the whole of Edmonton into a square, what would its side length be to the nearest tenth of a kilometre?

78. A light year is the distance that light travels through space in a year. It equals about 10^{13} km. The Milky Way Galaxy is about 10^5 light years across. Express this distance in kilometres.

79. The number of wet days per year is 108 in Saskatoon, 120 in Winnipeg, and 156 in Fredericton. Write each ratio.

a) wet days in Saskatoon to wet days in Winnipeg

b) wet days in Winnipeg to wet days in Fredericton to wet days in Saskatoon

Write the next three numbers.

80. 3, 9, 27, … **81.** 128, 64, 32, …

82. 54, 61, 68, 75, … **83.** 98, 87, 76, 65, …

Group Decision Making
The SCAMPER Technique

The mnemonic SCAMPER was first used by the writer B. Eberle to help people expand their thinking when they are brainstorming. It is one way of producing "what if" questions.

S: Substitute — What if a person or a thing takes another's place?

C: Combine — What if you put things together? combine purposes?

A: Adapt: — What if you adjust something? What else can it be?

M: Modify, Magnify, Make Smaller — What if you change the purpose? the size? the colour? the sound? the speed?

P: Put to Other Uses — What are new ways of using something?

E: Eliminate — What if you get rid of a part? a whole?

R: Rearrange — What if you change the order? turn it around? turn it backward? turn it upside down?

1 2 3 4 6	1 2 3 4 5	1 2 3 4 5
	Home Groups	
1 2 3 4 5	1 2 3 4 5	1 2 3 4 5

1. In your home group, use the SCAMPER technique to design a town. Here are some ideas to get you started.

a) What if you *substitute* parks for parking lots?

b) What if you *combine* parks, schools, zoos, and aquariums?

c) What if you *adapt* sidewalks into moving treadways?

d) What if you *modify* building roofs to become a dome over the town?

e) What if you *put* water in the streets so that boats could use them?

f) What if you *eliminate* cars and trucks, except for emergency vehicles?

g) What if you *rearrange* the buildings so they go down instead of up?

2. Present your design to the class and explain how you used the SCAMPER technique.

Chapter Check

Write as a power and then in standard form.

1. $4 \times 4 \times 4 \times 4 \times 4$

2. $10 \times 10 \times 10 \times 10 \times 10 \times 10$

3. $2 \times 2 \times 2 \times 2 \times 2 \times 2 \times 2 \times 2 \times 2$

4. $3 \times 3 \times 3 \times 3$　　　**5.** $6 \times 6 \times 6$

Write in scientific notation.

6. 52 000　　　　　**7.** 270 000

8. 6 150 000　　　　**9.** 0.058

10. 0.000 07　　　　**11.** 0.001 13

Write in standard form.

12. 2.7×10^3　　　**13.** 7.9×10^4

14. 1.65×10^7　　　**15.** 3.2×10^{-2}

16. 6.13×10^{-6}　　　**17.** 2.8×10^{-5}

18. Arrange the numbers in order from least to greatest.

$-0.5, \frac{3}{4}, 5.01, -5, 1\frac{1}{2}, 1.11, -3.022$

Use the diagram to write each ratio in lowest terms.

19. red tiles to blue tiles

20. white tiles to red tiles

21. red tiles to white tiles to blue tiles

22. white tiles to all of the tiles

23. blue tiles to red tiles and white tiles

What percent of each figure is shaded?

24.　　　　　　　　**25.**

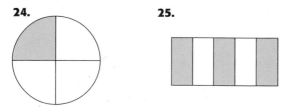

Express as a percent.

26. $\frac{41}{100}$　　**27.** 0.5　　**28.** 3:5　　**29.** $1\frac{1}{4}$

30. $\frac{8}{200}$　　**31.** 0.095　　**32.** 2.55　　**33.** 0.125

Express each percent as a decimal and as a fraction in lowest terms.

34. 45%　　**35.** 62.5%　　**36.** 120%　　**37.** 0.5%

Estimate the percent of each figure that is shaded.

38.　　　　　　**39.**

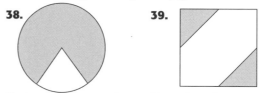

Estimate, then evaluate. Round to the nearest tenth, if necessary.

40. $\sqrt{256}$　　**41.** $\sqrt{6.4}$　　**42.** $\sqrt{88}$　　**43.** $\sqrt{0.16}$

44. The number of bacteria in a culture doubles every minute. From each bacterium in the culture, how many bacteria are produced in 6 min?

45. The mass of the Milky Way Galaxy is about 10^{42} kg. The mass of the sun is about 10^{30} kg. About how many times greater is the mass of the Milky Way Galaxy than the mass of the sun?

46. The largest mammal is the blue whale. It can grow to about 150 000 kg. Write this number in scientific notation.

47. Which number is the largest? Write each in standard form to compare.

100^4　　　1000^3　　　$10\ 000^2$

48. There are 6 cities in New Brunswick, 12 cities in Saskatchewan, and 16 cities in Alberta. Write each ratio in lowest terms.
a) cities in Saskatchewan to cities in New Brunswick
b) cities in New Brunswick to cities in Alberta
c) cities in Alberta to cities in Saskatchewan to cities in New Brunswick

Using the Strategies

1. Look for a pattern and write the next 3 terms.

a) 7, 13, 19, 25, ■ , ■ , ■
b) 1, 2, 4, 8, 16, ■ , ■ , ■
c) 90, 85, 86, 81, 82, ■ , ■ , ■
d) b, d, f, h, ■ , ■ , ■
e) on, tw, th, fo, fi, ■ , ■ , ■
f) 88, 79, 71, 64, 58, ■ , ■ , ■

2. The diagrams show the first 4 triangular numbers.

a) Draw the next 3 triangular numbers.
b) Describe the pattern.
c) Write the first 15 triangular numbers.
d) Add the first 2 triangular numbers. What is the sum? Draw a picture to represent this sum.
e) Add the second and third triangular numbers. Draw a picture to represent this sum.
f) Add the third and fourth triangular numbers.
g) Describe the sequence of numbers you get when you add pairs of triangular numbers.

3. The table gives the sums of odd numbers.

First one	1 = 1
First two	1 + 3 = 4
First three	1 + 3 + 5 = 9
First four	
First five	
First six	

Copy and complete the table. Look for patterns and predict the values of the following sums.

a) 1 + 3 + 5+ ... + 13 + 15
b) 1 + 3 + 5+ ... + 23 + 25
c) 1 + 3 + 5+ ... + 99 + 101
d) 1 + 3 + 5+ ... + 107 + 109

4. A sweatsuit costs $49.95, socks cost $4.59, a headband costs $4.09, and a gym bag costs $24.79. Tia went to a store that was paying all the taxes for the day. She had $80.00. Make 3 lists of possible purchases for Tia. Calculate the change she would get for each list of purchases.

5. A bellhop at a hotel earns $15.25/h for the first 35 h worked in a week and $17.50/h for any hours over 35. Last week, Terry worked 41.5 h. How much did he earn?

6. The expressions show the operation called "trapezoid."

$$7 \; \diagdown\diagup \; 3 = 12$$
$$9 \; \diagdown\diagup \; 6 = 9$$
$$4 \; \diagdown\diagup \; 2 = 6$$

a) State the trapezoid rule.
b) Use the trapezoid rule to complete the expressions.

$$8 \; \diagdown\diagup \; 1 = ?$$
$$9 \; \diagdown\diagup \; ? = 21$$
$$? \; \diagdown\diagup \; 2 = 15$$

7. Bob and Sharon left the highway restaurant and drove in opposite directions. Bob drove at 85 km/h, and Sharon drove at 95 km/h.
a) How far apart were they after 4 h?
b) If they had left the restaurant and driven in the same direction, how far apart would they have been after 4 h?

DATA BANK

Use the Data Bank on pages 360 to 369 to find the information you need.

1. At 6695 km in length, the Nile is the world's longest river. Which 2 Canadian rivers have a combined length that most closely equals the length of the Nile?

2. How long does it take to fly from Edmonton to Ottawa at 800 km/h?

3. Which planet takes about 50 times longer to orbit the sun than Mercury does?

CHAPTER 2

Operations with Rational Numbers

Sperm whales near the Galapagos Islands seem to use clicking sounds to communicate.

Linda Weilgart and Hal Whitehead, Dalhousie University biologists, have found these 23 patterns of clicking sounds the whales use. A vertical line represents a click. A space between two lines gives the time between clicks.

1. Which pattern has the greatest number of clicks?

2. Which patterns have the smallest number of clicks?

3. In which of the patterns are the clicks evenly spaced?

4. Which pattern has the longest length of time between 2 clicks?

5. Which pattern is the longest? About how long does it last?

6. Which pattern is the shortest? About how long does it last?

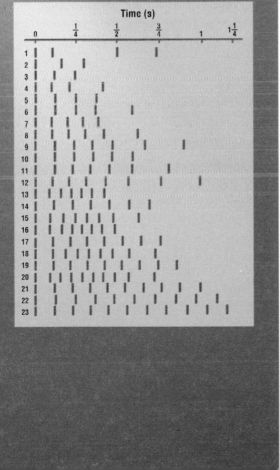

41

Pattern Blocks

Activity ❶ Shapes

The value of a yellow hexagon is one whole or 1.

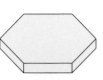

Two red trapezoids cover 1 hexagon.

Three blue rhombuses cover 1 hexagon.

Six green triangles cover 1 hexagon.

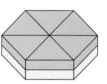

1. What fraction of a hexagon is covered by 1 triangle?

2. What fraction of a hexagon is covered by 3 triangles? Write the answer in 2 different ways.

3. What shape can be used to replace 3 triangles?

4. What fraction of a hexagon does 1 rhombus cover?

5. What fraction of a hexagon do 2 rhombuses cover?

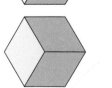

6. How many triangles are needed to cover 2 rhombuses?

7. What fraction of a hexagon do 4 triangles cover? Write your answer in 2 ways.

Activity ❷ More Shapes

1. Write the fraction of the hexagon that is covered.

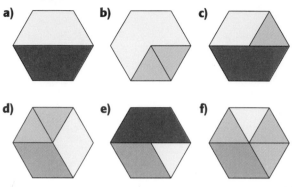

a)   b)   c)

d)   e)   f)

2. How would you use the shapes to show that these statements are true?

a) $\frac{1}{2} = \frac{3}{6}$ **b)** $\frac{1}{3} = \frac{2}{6}$ **c)** $\frac{4}{6} = \frac{2}{3}$

3. What is the total number of hexagons covered in each of the following?

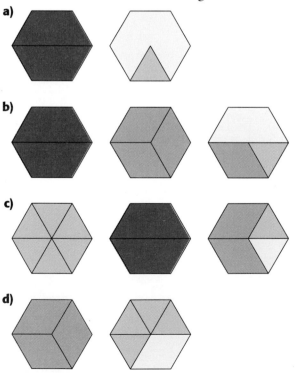

a)

b)

c)

d)

Warm Up

1. Which of the following are divisible by 3?
62, 87, 455, 612, 315, 433, 616

List the prime factors of each number.

2. 35   **3.** 48   **4.** 21

5. 16   **6.** 51   **7.** 144

Find the greatest common factor.

8. 6, 8   **9.** 8, 3   **10.** 5, 10

11. 12, 15   **12.** 8, 24   **13.** 6, 5, 2

14. 18, 12   **15.** 24, 28

List 5 multiples of each number.

16. 8   **17.** 6   **18.** 2   **19.** 4

Find two common multiples for each pair.

20. 3, 4   **21.** 16, 8

Find the lowest common multiple of each group.

22. 4, 6   **23.** 3, 6, 8

24. Name the fractions shown on the number line by the letters.

```
|----+----+----+----+----+----+----+----|
0    A         B    C    D              1
```

25. Write 8 as a fraction.

26. Which numbers are mixed numbers?

$2\frac{1}{2}$ $\frac{11}{5}$ $1\frac{4}{5}$ $3\frac{1}{4}$ $\frac{5}{6}$ $6\frac{2}{3}$

27. What is an improper fraction? Give an example.

Determine whether each fraction is closest to 0, $\frac{1}{2}$, or 1.

28. $\frac{7}{8}$ **29.** $\frac{3}{5}$ **30.** $\frac{1}{8}$

Round each of the following to the nearest whole number.

31. $\frac{4}{5}$ **32.** $2\frac{1}{8}$ **33.** $3\frac{3}{8}$ **34.** $4\frac{5}{6}$ **35.** $1\frac{1}{4}$

Mental Math

Add.

1. $\frac{1}{2} + \frac{1}{2}$ **2.** $\frac{1}{5} + \frac{3}{5}$

3. $\frac{5}{6} + \frac{1}{6}$ **4.** $\frac{1}{3} + \frac{2}{3}$

5. $2 + 3\frac{1}{4}$ **6.** $1 + 2\frac{1}{2}$

7. $3\frac{2}{5} + 1\frac{1}{5}$ **8.** $2\frac{1}{4} + 1\frac{3}{4}$

Find the remainder.

9. $12 \div 5$ **10.** $8 \div 3$

11. $15 \div 4$ **12.** $16 \div 5$

13. $27 \div 5$ **14.** $32 \div 6$

Subtract.

15. $\frac{2}{3} - \frac{1}{3}$ **16.** $\frac{5}{8} - \frac{1}{8}$

17. $\frac{11}{4} - \frac{7}{4}$ **18.** $\frac{23}{5} - \frac{11}{5}$

19. $2\frac{3}{5} - \frac{1}{5}$ **20.** $1\frac{1}{4} - \frac{3}{4}$

Calculate.

21. $\frac{1}{2}$ of 20   **22.** $\frac{1}{3}$ of 24

23. $\frac{1}{4}$ of 36   **24.** $\frac{1}{2}$ of 16

25. $\frac{1}{5}$ of 25   **26.** $\frac{1}{6}$ of 18

Evaluate.

27. $2 \times 3 + 1$ **28.** $3 \times 4 + 3$

29. $2 \times 5 + 4$ **30.** $2 \times 6 + 5$

31. $3 \times 5 + 2$ **32.** $4 \times 2 + 3$

Evaluate.

33. 2^2 **34.** 3^2 **35.** 2^3

36. 4^2 **37.** 5^2 **38.** 6^2

2.1 Solve a Simpler Problem

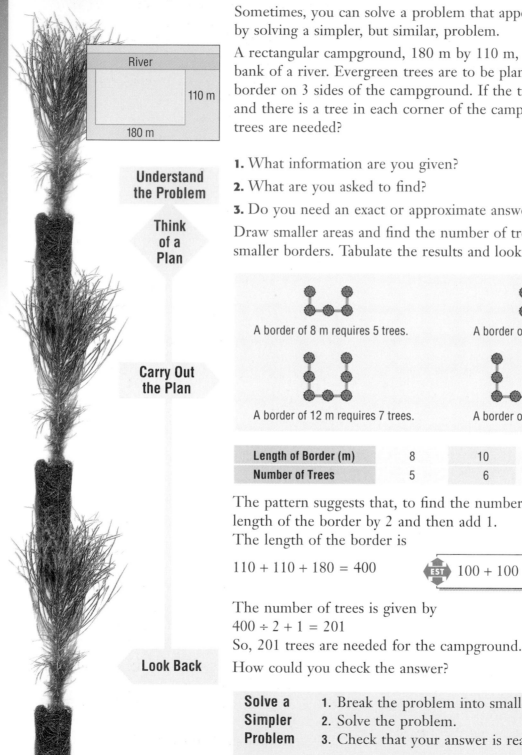

Sometimes, you can solve a problem that appears to be difficult by solving a simpler, but similar, problem.

A rectangular campground, 180 m by 110 m, is located on the bank of a river. Evergreen trees are to be planted to form a border on 3 sides of the campground. If the trees are 2 m apart, and there is a tree in each corner of the campground, how many trees are needed?

Understand the Problem

1. What information are you given?

2. What are you asked to find?

3. Do you need an exact or approximate answer?

Think of a Plan

Draw smaller areas and find the number of trees needed for smaller borders. Tabulate the results and look for a pattern.

Carry Out the Plan

A border of 8 m requires 5 trees.

A border of 10 m requires 6 trees.

A border of 12 m requires 7 trees.

A border of 20 m requires 11 trees.

Length of Border (m)	8	10	12	20
Number of Trees	5	6	7	11

The pattern suggests that, to find the number of trees, divide the length of the border by 2 and then add 1.
The length of the border is

$110 + 110 + 180 = 400$

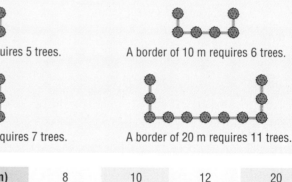

EST $100 + 100 + 200 = 400$

The number of trees is given by
$400 \div 2 + 1 = 201$
So, 201 trees are needed for the campground.

Look Back

How could you check the answer?

Solve a Simpler Problem
1. Break the problem into smaller problems.
2. Solve the problem.
3. Check that your answer is reasonable.

Problems and Applications

1. A horizontal line through the letter N divides the N into a maximum of 4 parts.

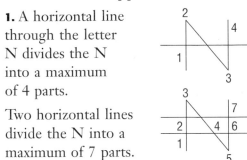

Two horizontal lines divide the N into a maximum of 7 parts.

What is the maximum number of parts when 50 horizontal lines divide the N?

2. One horizontal line divides the letter V into a maximum of 3 parts.

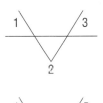

Two horizontal lines divide it into a maximum of 5 parts.

What is the maximum number of parts when 100 horizontal lines divide the V?

3. You are planning your time for spring break. You have to read a 210-page book during the 7 days. How can you estimate the number of hours it will take you to read the book?

4. You are making a schedule for a volleyball league with 10 teams. Every team is to play every other team once. How many games do you have to schedule?

5. There are 12 teams in a hockey league. Every team is to play every other team twice. How many games will be played?

6. A rectangular field measures 620 m by 440 m. The field is to be fenced with fence posts placed 10 m apart and with one post in each corner. How many fence posts will be needed?

7. a) Describe how you would find the approximate number of breaths you take in 1 week. Then, find the number.
b) Your lungs hold about 5.5 L of air. Each time you breathe out, about 1.5 L of air is left in your lungs. About how many litres of air do you breathe in a week?

8. Evaluate $1 \div 200\ 000\ 000$.

9. Describe how you would find the approximate number of cars that pass in front of your school in a month during school hours.

10. The foyer in a building is a 9 m by 17 m rectangle. The floor is to be tiled with square tiles that are 20 cm by 20 cm. How many tiles are needed?

11. The pool area of a hotel is in the shape of a rectangle with the dimensions shown. Two sides of the area are against the hotel. The other two sides are to have shrubs planted along them, with one shrub every metre. Shrubs are to start 1 m from the building. How many shrubs are needed?

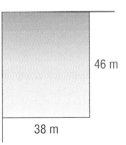

12. a) What is the ones digit of the product when one hundred nines are multiplied?
b) What is the ones digit of the product when one hundred threes are multiplied?

13. a) Work with a classmate to determine how much time each step takes when you walk at your normal walking pace. Give your answer to the nearest tenth of a second.
b) Describe the method you used.

Fraction Strips and Fractions

Activity ❶ Making Fraction Strips

Work with a partner. Use the fraction strips supplied or make a set as follows. You will need 24 strips of paper, each 16 cm long and 2 cm wide. Each strip represents 1 whole.

1. Fold 3 strips in half and label the halves.

$\frac{1}{2}$	$\frac{1}{2}$

2. Fold 3 strips in half twice. Label the quarters.

$\frac{1}{4}$	$\frac{1}{4}$	$\frac{1}{4}$	$\frac{1}{4}$

3. How can you fold a strip to represent eighths? Fold 3 strips into eighths and label the eighths.

4. Fold 3 strips into thirds and label the thirds.

$\frac{1}{3}$	$\frac{1}{3}$	$\frac{1}{3}$

5. How can you fold a strip to represent sixths? twelfths? Fold and label 3 strips to represent sixths and 3 strips to represent twelfths.

6. Fold 3 strips into fifths and label the fifths.

$\frac{1}{5}$	$\frac{1}{5}$	$\frac{1}{5}$	$\frac{1}{5}$	$\frac{1}{5}$

7. How can you fold a strip to represent tenths? Fold and label 3 strips to represent tenths.

Activity ❷ Equivalent Fractions

Line up the halves fraction strip and the quarters fraction strip.

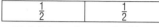

Since two quarters are the same length as one half, you can write

$$\frac{2}{4} = \frac{1}{2}$$

The fractions $\frac{2}{4}$ and $\frac{1}{2}$ are called **equivalent fractions** because they represent the same fraction of the whole.

Use fraction strips to answer the following.

1. How many sixths are equivalent to one half? Write a number statement to show the equivalent fractions.

2. How many twelfths are equivalent to one third? Write a number statement to show the equivalent fractions.

3. If we know that $\frac{1}{2}$ is equivalent to $\frac{2}{4}$ and to $\frac{5}{10}$, we can write 3 number statements to show pairs of equivalent fractions.

$$\frac{1}{2} = \frac{2}{4} \qquad \frac{1}{2} = \frac{5}{10} \qquad \frac{2}{4} = \frac{5}{10}$$

Write two fractions equivalent to each of the following fractions. In each case, write 3 number statements to show pairs of equivalent fractions.

a) $\frac{1}{3}$ **b)** $\frac{1}{4}$ **c)** $\frac{3}{4}$ **d)** $\frac{4}{8}$ **e)** $\frac{4}{6}$

Activity ❸ Adding Fractions

1. Work with a partner. Describe how the fraction strips are used to find each sum. What do you notice about the denominators in each question?

a) $\frac{1}{3} + \frac{1}{3}$

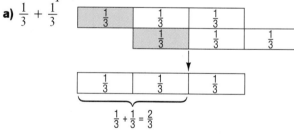

b) $\frac{2}{6} + \frac{3}{6}$

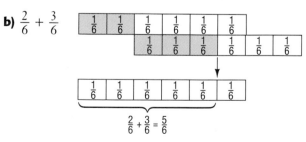

2. Use your fraction strips to find each sum.

a) $\frac{1}{5} + \frac{3}{5}$ **b)** $\frac{3}{8} + \frac{4}{8}$ **c)** $\frac{3}{10} + \frac{4}{10}$ **d)** $\frac{4}{12} + \frac{3}{12}$

3. Work with a partner. Describe how the fraction strips are used to find each sum. What do you notice about the denominators?

a) $\frac{1}{4} + \frac{1}{2}$

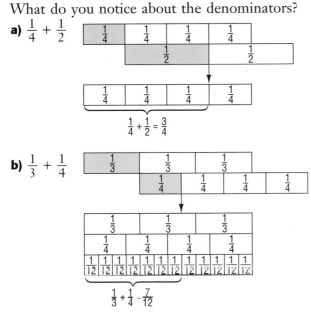

b) $\frac{1}{3} + \frac{1}{4}$

4. Use your fraction strips to find each sum.

a) $\frac{1}{2} + \frac{1}{3}$ **b)** $\frac{1}{2} + \frac{2}{5}$ **c)** $\frac{2}{4} + \frac{3}{8}$ **d)** $\frac{1}{3} + \frac{5}{12}$

Activity ❹ Subtracting Fractions

1. Work with a classmate. Describe how the fraction strips are used to find each difference. What do you notice about the denominators?

a) $\frac{3}{4} - \frac{1}{4}$

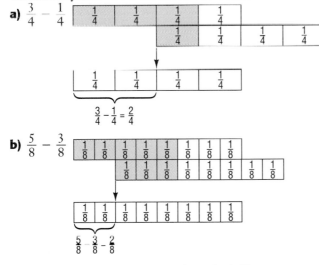

b) $\frac{5}{8} - \frac{3}{8}$

2. Use fraction strips to find each difference.

a) $\frac{3}{6} - \frac{1}{6}$ **b)** $\frac{7}{10} - \frac{3}{10}$ **c)** $\frac{4}{5} - \frac{2}{5}$ **d)** $\frac{11}{12} - \frac{5}{12}$

3. Work with a partner. Describe how the fraction strips are used to find each difference. What do you notice about the denominators?

a) $\frac{1}{2} - \frac{1}{3}$

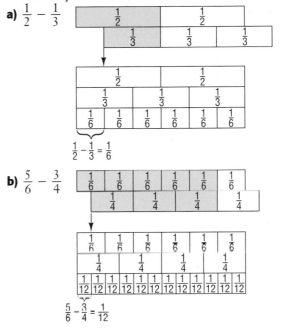

b) $\frac{5}{6} - \frac{3}{4}$

4. Use fraction strips to find each difference.

a) $\frac{7}{8} - \frac{1}{2}$ **b)** $\frac{4}{5} - \frac{1}{2}$ **c)** $\frac{3}{4} - \frac{1}{12}$ **d)** $\frac{5}{6} - \frac{1}{4}$

Activity ❺ Fractions in Lowest Terms

The fraction $\frac{9}{12}$ is not in lowest terms because it can be expressed as the equivalent fraction $\frac{3}{4}$, which contains smaller whole numbers. A fraction is in lowest terms when it contains the smallest possible whole numbers.

1. Which of the fractions supplied in Activity 2, question 3 are not in lowest terms?

2. Write each fraction from question 1 as an equivalent fraction in lowest terms.

3. Express each fraction in lowest terms.

a) $\frac{6}{10}$ **b)** $\frac{10}{12}$ **c)** $\frac{6}{12}$

2.2 Adding Fractions

Lake Michigan and Lake Huron each cover about $\frac{1}{4}$ of the area of the Great Lakes. Together, Lake Michigan and Lake Huron cover a fraction of the Great Lakes that equals $\frac{1}{4} + \frac{1}{4}$.

To add fractions with the same denominator, add the numerators.
$\frac{1}{4} + \frac{1}{4} = \frac{2}{4}$ or $\frac{1}{2}$

So, Lake Michigan and Lake Huron together cover about $\frac{1}{2}$ of the area of the Great Lakes.

Activity: Use the Diagrams

Two equal-sized pans of lasagna were used for dinner at the camp. The lasagna in one pan was cut into quarters. There was $\frac{1}{4}$ left. The lasagna in the other pan was cut into eighths. There were $\frac{3}{8}$ left. How much lasagna was left?

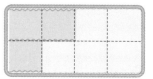

Inquire

1. Is the amount left closest to $\frac{1}{2}$ a pan, 1 whole pan, or 0?

2. If the pan with $\frac{1}{4}$ left had been cut into eighths, how much lasagna would be left in that pan?

3. What is the total amount left in the 2 pans?

4. Describe a method of adding fractions with different denominators.

5. Use the pictures of the pans to explain why $\frac{1}{4} + \frac{3}{8}$ does not equal $\frac{4}{12}$.

Example

Add.   **a)** $\frac{2}{3} + \frac{4}{5}$ **b)** $2\frac{3}{4} + 3\frac{2}{3}$

Solution

To add fractions with different denominators, write equivalent fractions with the lowest common denominator.

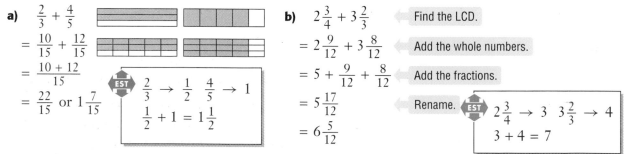

a) $\frac{2}{3} + \frac{4}{5}$

$= \frac{10}{15} + \frac{12}{15}$

$= \frac{10 + 12}{15}$

$= \frac{22}{15}$ or $1\frac{7}{15}$

EST $\frac{2}{3} \rightarrow \frac{1}{2}$ $\frac{4}{5} \rightarrow 1$
$\frac{1}{2} + 1 = 1\frac{1}{2}$

b) $2\frac{3}{4} + 3\frac{2}{3}$ Find the LCD.

$= 2\frac{9}{12} + 3\frac{8}{12}$ Add the whole numbers.

$= 5 + \frac{9}{12} + \frac{8}{12}$ Add the fractions.

$= 5\frac{17}{12}$ Rename.   EST $2\frac{3}{4} \rightarrow 3$ $3\frac{2}{3} \rightarrow 4$
$3 + 4 = 7$

$= 6\frac{5}{12}$

Practice

Express all answers in lowest terms.

Write the addition indicated by each diagram and find the sum.

1.
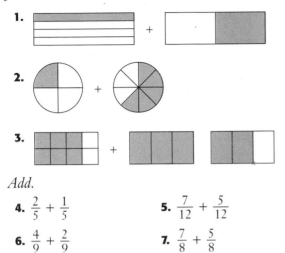

2.

3.

Add.

4. $\frac{2}{5} + \frac{1}{5}$ **5.** $\frac{7}{12} + \frac{5}{12}$

6. $\frac{4}{9} + \frac{2}{9}$ **7.** $\frac{7}{8} + \frac{5}{8}$

Add. Use diagrams to explain your method.

8. $\frac{3}{4} + \frac{1}{2}$ **9.** $\frac{5}{9} + \frac{2}{3}$ **10.** $\frac{5}{12} + \frac{1}{4}$

11. $\frac{1}{4} + \frac{2}{3}$ **12.** $\frac{1}{6} + \frac{3}{4}$ **13.** $\frac{3}{8} + \frac{3}{4}$

Estimate, then add.

14. $2\frac{1}{4} + \frac{1}{4}$ **15.** $3\frac{5}{8} + \frac{3}{8}$

16. $4\frac{1}{2} + 1\frac{1}{2}$ **17.** $3\frac{3}{5} + 2\frac{4}{5}$

Estimate, then add. Use diagrams to explain your method.

18. $1\frac{1}{2} + \frac{1}{4}$ **19.** $2\frac{3}{8} + 1\frac{1}{4}$

20. $2\frac{3}{10} + 1\frac{4}{5}$ **21.** $1\frac{1}{2} + 2\frac{1}{3}$

22. $3\frac{2}{3} + 4\frac{3}{5}$ **23.** $2\frac{1}{4} + 1\frac{1}{3}$

Estimate, then add.

24. $\frac{5}{8} + \frac{1}{2} + \frac{3}{8}$ **25.** $\frac{3}{4} + \frac{1}{2} + \frac{3}{8}$

26. $\frac{3}{7} + \frac{5}{7} + 1\frac{1}{2}$ **27.** $1\frac{1}{4} + 2\frac{1}{2} + 3$

Problems and Applications

28. Asia covers about $\frac{3}{10}$ of the area of all the continents, and Africa covers $\frac{1}{5}$. What fraction of the area of the continents do Asia and Africa cover together?

29. In a full set of permanent teeth, $\frac{1}{4}$ of the teeth are incisors, $\frac{1}{4}$ are premolars, and $\frac{3}{8}$ are molars. What fraction of all the teeth are incisors, premolars, or molars?

30. Quebec and Ontario together cover about $\frac{1}{4}$ of the area of Canada. The Territories cover about $\frac{2}{5}$, and the Prairie provinces about $\frac{1}{5}$. What fraction of the area of Canada do these regions cover together?

31. Nada made a snack by combining $\frac{1}{3}$ of a bowl of granola with $\frac{1}{4}$ of a bowl of chopped banana and $\frac{1}{2}$ of a bowl of yogurt. Did one bowl hold all the ingredients at one time? Explain.

32. In his first two hockey games of the season, Kent played about $1\frac{1}{2}$ periods and $1\frac{3}{4}$ periods. About how many periods in all did he play?

33. Write 2 different fractions
a) with a sum of $\frac{1}{2}$ **b)** with a sum of $1\frac{1}{2}$

34. Write a problem that involves the addition of fractions or mixed numbers. Have a classmate solve your problem.

2.3 Subtracting Fractions

About $\frac{3}{10}$ of Canadians live in the 4 western provinces.
About $\frac{1}{10}$ of Canadians live in Alberta. The fraction of
Canadians in the other 3 western provinces is $\frac{3}{10} - \frac{1}{10}$.

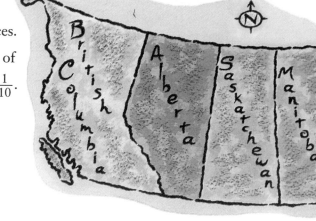

To subtract 2 fractions with the same denominator,
subtract the numerators.

$\frac{3}{10} - \frac{1}{10} = \frac{2}{10}$ or $\frac{1}{5}$

So, the fraction of Canadians who live in British
Columbia, Saskatchewan, or Manitoba is about $\frac{1}{5}$.

Activity: Use the Information

Before the school picnic, the gauge on the barbecue's
propane tank showed it was $\frac{3}{4}$ full. At the end of the day,
the gauge showed the tank was $\frac{1}{8}$ full.

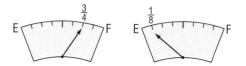

Inquire

1. Read the gauge. What fraction is
equivalent to $\frac{3}{4}$?

2. What fraction of the tank was used at
the picnic?

3. Describe a method of subtracting fractions
with different denominators.

4. Use diagrams to show that $\frac{5}{12} - \frac{1}{4}$ does
not equal $\frac{4}{8}$.

Example

Subtract.   **a)** $\frac{4}{5} - \frac{1}{2}$ **b)** $3\frac{1}{2} - 1\frac{2}{3}$

Solution

To subtract fractions with different denominators, write
equivalent fractions with the lowest common denominator.

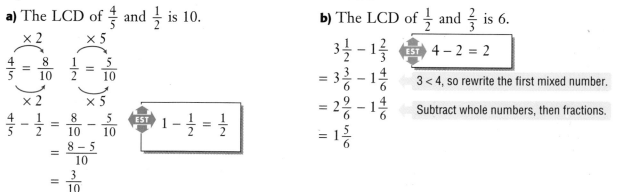

a) The LCD of $\frac{4}{5}$ and $\frac{1}{2}$ is 10.

$$\overset{\times 2}{\frac{4}{5} = \frac{8}{10}} \quad \overset{\times 5}{\frac{1}{2} = \frac{5}{10}}$$

$\frac{4}{5} - \frac{1}{2} = \frac{8}{10} - \frac{5}{10}$ **EST** $1 - \frac{1}{2} = \frac{1}{2}$

$\quad\quad\quad = \frac{8 - 5}{10}$

$\quad\quad\quad = \frac{3}{10}$

b) The LCD of $\frac{1}{2}$ and $\frac{2}{3}$ is 6.

$3\frac{1}{2} - 1\frac{2}{3}$ **EST** $4 - 2 = 2$

$= 3\frac{3}{6} - 1\frac{4}{6}$ 3 < 4, so rewrite the first mixed number.

$= 2\frac{9}{6} - 1\frac{4}{6}$ Subtract whole numbers, then fractions.

$= 1\frac{5}{6}$

Practice

Express all answers in lowest terms.

Find the difference.

1. $\frac{5}{12} - \frac{4}{12}$ 2. $\frac{3}{4} - \frac{1}{4}$

3. $\frac{7}{9} - \frac{4}{9}$ 4. $\frac{5}{8} - \frac{3}{8}$

Subtract. Use diagrams to explain your method.

5. $\frac{5}{8} - \frac{1}{2}$ 6. $\frac{2}{5} - \frac{1}{10}$ 7. $\frac{5}{6} - \frac{1}{3}$

8. $\frac{2}{3} - \frac{1}{2}$ 9. $\frac{1}{2} - \frac{1}{6}$ 10. $\frac{3}{4} - \frac{2}{3}$

Estimate, then subtract.

11. $2\frac{3}{5} - \frac{1}{5}$ 12. $4\frac{7}{8} - \frac{5}{8}$

13. $5\frac{3}{4} - 1\frac{1}{4}$ 14. $3\frac{1}{6} - 1\frac{5}{6}$

Estimate, then subtract. Use diagrams to explain your method.

15. $2\frac{3}{4} - \frac{1}{2}$ 16. $1\frac{3}{8} - \frac{1}{4}$

17. $2\frac{1}{6} - \frac{1}{2}$ 18. $4\frac{1}{4} - 1\frac{1}{2}$

19. $1\frac{1}{2} - \frac{1}{3}$ 20. $3\frac{1}{2} - 1\frac{1}{5}$

21. $2\frac{1}{4} - 1\frac{2}{3}$ 22. $3\frac{1}{6} - 1\frac{1}{4}$

Problems and Applications

23. About $\frac{1}{4}$ of the world's motor vehicles are built in Canada or the United States. About $\frac{1}{5}$ of the world's motor vehicles are built in the United States. What fraction of the world's motor vehicles are built in Canada?

24. a) Describe how you would find the answer to this problem.

$\frac{2}{3} + \blacksquare = 1\frac{5}{6}$

b) Calculate the answer.

Find the missing value.

25. $\frac{9}{10} - \blacksquare = \frac{1}{2}$ 26. $\blacksquare - \frac{3}{4} = \frac{2}{3}$

27. $1\frac{3}{4} - \blacksquare = \frac{5}{8}$ 28. $\blacksquare - \frac{5}{6} = 2\frac{1}{4}$

29. Daniel ran $2\frac{2}{3}$ laps of the track. Carol ran $2\frac{3}{4}$ laps.

a) Who ran farther?

b) How much farther?

30. Interprovincial Pipeline stock prices varied one day from $\$29\frac{3}{4}$ to $\$30\frac{1}{2}$. By how much did the price change?

31. About $\frac{1}{2}$ of Canada is covered in forest, and about $\frac{1}{12}$ is covered in fresh water. What fraction of Canada is not covered in either forest or fresh water?

32. Write two fractions

a) with a difference of $\frac{1}{4}$

b) with a difference of $\frac{3}{8}$

c) that have different denominators and a difference of $\frac{1}{2}$

33. Write a problem that involves the subtraction of fractions or mixed numbers. Have a classmate solve your problem.

PATTERN POWER

Look for the pattern, then draw the fourth diagram.

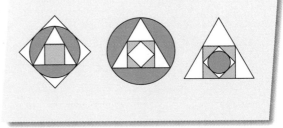

2.4 Work Backward

In some problems, you are given the end result and asked to find a fact that gives that result. For these problems, working backward is a useful problem solving strategy.

Kevin visited Calgary and spent a day in the southwest part of the city. The streets and avenues are numbered, as shown on the map. Kevin left his hotel to visit the Alberta Science Centre. He walked 5 blocks west, then 2 blocks south, then 3 blocks west, and finally 1 block south. The Science Centre is at 7th Avenue and 11th Street. Where was Kevin's hotel?

1. What information are you given?

2. What are you asked to find?

3. Do you need an exact or approximate answer?

Understand the Problem

Think of a Plan

Start at the Science Centre and retrace Kevin's walk by working backward.

Kevin's walk had 4 stages. The fourth stage was to walk 1 block south, so walk 1 block north from the Science Centre.

The third stage was 3 blocks west, so walk 3 blocks east.

Carry Out the Plan

The second stage was 2 blocks south, so walk 2 blocks north.

The first stage was 5 blocks west, so walk 5 blocks east.

Kevin's hotel was at 4th Avenue and 3rd Street.

Look Back

Does the answer seem reasonable? Is there another way to solve the problem?

Work Backward	1. Start with what you know.
	2. Work backward to get an answer.
	3. Check that the answer is reasonable.

Problems and Applications

1. A city's streets are numbered and the avenues are lettered, as shown.

```
   A B C D E F G H I
1
2
3
4
5
6
```

Angelica left the library and walked 4 blocks south, then 3 blocks east, then 1 block north, and finally 2 blocks east to reach the museum. The museum was at the corner of Avenue G and 5th Street. On what corner was the library?

2. An Italian scientist, Guglielmo Marconi, received the first transatlantic radio message in St. John's, Newfoundland. Eighteen years later, the first successful transatlantic flight left St. John's. Thirty years after that, Newfoundland became Canada's tenth province. Newfoundland joined Canada in 1949. In what year did Marconi receive the radio message?

3. The ferry leaves at 08:30. It takes 35 min on the bus from your home to the dock. You should allow 10 min to buy your ferry ticket. You need 45 min to shower and dress. You need another 20 min to eat breakfast and 15 min to walk your dog. For what time should you set your alarm?

4. Sonja had some baseball cards. She gave 7 to her sister and shared the rest equally among herself and two friends. Sonja's share was 13 cards. How many cards did she have originally?

5. The library held a used book sale. Bill went to the mystery section and bought half the books. Jason bought one-third of the remaining books. Mark bought the rest of the books. If Mark bought 12 books, how many mystery books were originally on sale?

6. Yasmina said: "If you multiply my age by 2, then add 16, then divide by 3, the result is 20." How old is she?

7. Andy asked Melissa how many teams were in the basketball tournament her team had won. "I'm not sure," Melissa answered. "I do know that all the teams started playing at 08:00, and all the winners played every 2 h. The losers dropped out as soon as they lost, and our team played 4 games." How many teams were in the tournament?

8. Before any taxes were added, a new car had a sticker price of $37 789.60. This included the base price, plus $6345.00 worth of options and $620.00 for the dealer to prepare the car. What was the base price of the car?

9. Ari had $45.67 in his account at the end of the month. During the month, he wrote cheques for $23.80, $19.35, and $167.84. He also withdrew $50.00 at a banking machine and deposited $100.00 from his pay cheque. How much was in his account at the beginning of the month?

10. You are directing the school play. The curtain will go up at 20:15. You want the cast ready 10 min before the play starts. The make-up people need 45 min to do their job. The costume people need 35 min to get the cast ready before make-up. You need a 10-min meeting with the cast when they arrive at the school. At what time should the cast arrive at the school?

11. Money invested at 7% interest per year doubles every 10 years. Cheryl's grandmother invested some money 20 years ago at 7% per year. She now has $100 000. How much did she invest 20 years ago?

12. Write a problem that can be solved with the work backward strategy. Be creative. Have a classmate solve your problem.

Multiplying Fractions Using Paper Folding

Activity ❶ Folding Fractions

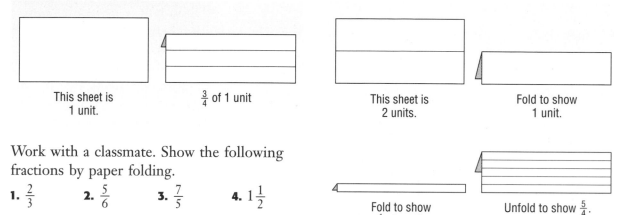

This sheet is
1 unit.

$\frac{3}{4}$ of 1 unit

This sheet is
2 units.

Fold to show
1 unit.

Work with a classmate. Show the following
fractions by paper folding.

1. $\frac{2}{3}$ **2.** $\frac{5}{6}$ **3.** $\frac{7}{5}$ **4.** $1\frac{1}{2}$

Fold to show
$\frac{1}{4}$ of a unit.

Unfold to show $\frac{5}{4}$.

Activity ❷ Multiplying Fractions Less Than 1

This folding method shows the product of $\frac{1}{3} \times \frac{2}{3}$.

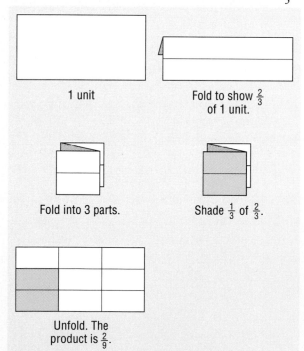

1 unit

Fold to show $\frac{2}{3}$
of 1 unit.

Fold into 3 parts.

Shade $\frac{1}{3}$ of $\frac{2}{3}$.

Unfold. The
product is $\frac{2}{9}$.

Work with a classmate. Find the products by
paper folding.

1. $\frac{1}{2} \times \frac{3}{4}$ **2.** $\frac{2}{3} \times \frac{2}{3}$ **3.** $\frac{3}{4} \times \frac{1}{4}$

4. $\frac{1}{4} \times \frac{2}{3}$ **5.** $\frac{1}{6} \times \frac{1}{2}$ **6.** $\frac{2}{3} \times \frac{1}{3}$

7. Use the example and your answer to
question 6 to compare the product of $\frac{1}{3} \times \frac{2}{3}$
with the product of $\frac{2}{3} \times \frac{1}{3}$. Does the order of
the fractions affect their product?

Activity ❸ Multiplying Fractions Greater Than 1

This folding method shows the product of $\frac{2}{3} \times \frac{5}{4}$.

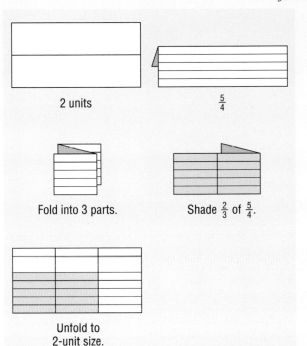

2 units

$\frac{5}{4}$

Fold into 3 parts.

Shade $\frac{2}{3}$ of $\frac{5}{4}$.

Unfold to 2-unit size.

In the unfolded result, 10 parts are shaded. There are 12 equal parts *in each unit*. So, the 10 shaded parts represent $\frac{10}{12}$.

$$\frac{2}{3} \times \frac{5}{4} = \frac{10}{12}$$

Work with a classmate. Find the products by paper folding.

1. $\frac{1}{2} \times \frac{4}{3}$ **2.** $\frac{1}{2} \times \frac{3}{2}$ **3.** $\frac{3}{4} \times 1\frac{2}{3}$

Activity ❹ A Special Case

This folding method shows the product of $\frac{1}{2} \times 2$.

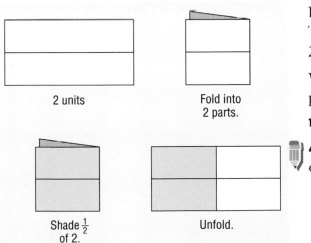

2 units

Fold into 2 parts.

Shade $\frac{1}{2}$ of 2.

Unfold.

In the unfolded result, 2 parts are shaded. There are 2 equal parts in each unit. So, the 2 shaded parts represent $\frac{2}{2}$ or 1.

Work with a classmate. Find the products by paper folding.

1. $\frac{1}{3} \times 3$ **2.** $\frac{2}{3} \times \frac{3}{2}$ **3.** $\frac{3}{4} \times \frac{4}{3}$

4. What kinds of fractions give a product of 1?

2.5 Multiplying Fractions

The area of Canada is about 10 million square kilometres. The Prairie provinces make up $\frac{1}{5}$ of Canada's area. $\frac{1}{5}$ of 10 is $\frac{1}{5} \times 10$ or 2. So, the area of the Prairie provinces is about 2 million square kilometres.

Activity: Use the Diagram

The diagram shows the fraction of Canada's area covered by the Northwest Territories. The Northwest Territories are divided into three districts: Franklin, Keewatin, and Mackenzie. The diagram also shows the fraction of the Northwest Territories covered by the Franklin District.

} Franklin District

Rest of Canada   NWT

Inquire

1. What fraction of Canada's area do the Northwest Territories cover?

2. What fraction of the Northwest Territories' area does the Franklin District cover?

3. What fraction of Canada's area does the Franklin District cover?

4. What is $\frac{1}{2}$ of $\frac{1}{3}$?

5. Describe a method of multiplying fractions.

Example 1

Multiply. **a)** $\frac{3}{4} \times \frac{2}{5}$ **b)** $1\frac{2}{3} \times 1\frac{1}{5}$

Solution

a) $\frac{3}{4} \times \frac{2}{5}$ Multiply the numerators.
Multiply the denominators.

$= \frac{6}{20}$ Write the answer in lowest terms.

$= \frac{3}{10}$ EST $1 \times \frac{1}{2} = \frac{1}{2}$

b) Write the mixed numbers as improper fractions, then multiply.

$1\frac{2}{3} \times 1\frac{1}{5} = \frac{5}{3} \times \frac{6}{5}$

$= \frac{30}{15}$

$= \frac{2}{1}$ or 2 EST $2 \times 1 = 2$

Two numbers whose product is 1 are **reciprocals**. Since $\frac{3}{4} \times \frac{4}{3}$ is $\frac{12}{12}$ or 1, $\frac{3}{4}$ and $\frac{4}{3}$ are reciprocals.

Example 2

Find the reciprocals. **a)** $\frac{2}{3}$ **b)** 6 **c)** $2\frac{1}{2}$

Solution

a) The reciprocal is $\frac{3}{2}$, since $\frac{2}{3} \times \frac{3}{2} = 1$.

b) The reciprocal is $\frac{1}{6}$, since $6 \times \frac{1}{6} = 1$.

c) Write $2\frac{1}{2}$ as $\frac{5}{2}$. The reciprocal is $\frac{2}{5}$, since $\frac{5}{2} \times \frac{2}{5} = 1$.

Practice

Write all answers in simplest form.

The diagram illustrates the statement $\frac{1}{3} \times \frac{1}{2} = \frac{1}{6}$. Draw a diagram to find each of the following products.

1. $\frac{1}{4} \times \frac{1}{2}$ **2.** $\frac{1}{3} \times \frac{2}{3}$ **3.** $\frac{1}{2} \times \frac{3}{5}$

Multiply.

4. $\frac{1}{4} \times \frac{1}{3}$ **5.** $\frac{2}{3} \times \frac{1}{5}$ **6.** $\frac{1}{2} \times \frac{3}{4}$

7. $\frac{5}{8} \times \frac{2}{3}$ **8.** $\frac{3}{5} \times \frac{5}{6}$ **9.** $\frac{3}{4} \times \frac{5}{6}$

Calculate.

10. $\frac{1}{2}$ of $\frac{1}{4}$ **11.** $\frac{3}{4}$ of $\frac{2}{3}$ **12.** $\frac{2}{3}$ of 6

Estimate, then multiply.

13. $3 \times 1\frac{1}{2}$ **14.** $2\frac{1}{4} \times 4$ **15.** $3 \times 2\frac{1}{6}$

16. $1\frac{2}{3} \times 4$ **17.** $\frac{1}{4} \times 2\frac{1}{3}$ **18.** $\frac{3}{8} \times 1\frac{1}{2}$

19. $\frac{4}{5} \times 3\frac{3}{4}$ **20.** $2\frac{3}{4} \times 3\frac{1}{3}$ **21.** $2\frac{1}{2} \times 1\frac{1}{9}$

Multiply.

22. $\frac{2}{3} \times \frac{1}{2} \times \frac{4}{5}$ **23.** $\frac{1}{4} \times 2 \times \frac{5}{6}$

24. $\frac{1}{2} \times 2\frac{1}{3} \times \frac{3}{4}$ **25.** $1\frac{1}{5} \times 2\frac{1}{2} \times 3\frac{2}{3}$

Write the reciprocal.

26. $\frac{1}{4}$ **27.** 3 **28.** $\frac{3}{5}$ **29.** $\frac{5}{4}$

30. $\frac{2}{9}$ **31.** $3\frac{1}{2}$ **32.** $2\frac{1}{3}$ **33.** $1\frac{7}{8}$

Problems and Applications

34. Insects account for about $\frac{5}{6}$ of known animal species. About $\frac{1}{4}$ of insect species are species of beetles. What fraction of all animal species are species of beetles?

35. A marsupial, such as a kangaroo, carries its young in a pouch. About $\frac{1}{25}$ of mammal species are marsupials. About 4250 species of mammals are known. How many species of marsupials are there?

36. Forests once covered $\frac{1}{3}$ of the land on Earth. Two thirds of the forested land has been cleared. What fraction of the land on Earth is now covered in forests?

37. The Bayview Bobcats play an 80-game season. They won $\frac{3}{5}$ of their games in the first half of the season and $\frac{3}{4}$ of their games in the second half of the season. How many games did they win in all?

38. Summerside has $\frac{1}{2}$ as many thunderstorms per year as Edmonton. How many times more thunderstorms per year does Edmonton have than Summerside?

39. Neptune completes $1\frac{1}{2}$ turns about its axis each day. How many turns does it complete in
a) 1 week? **b)** April? **c)** 12 h?

40. Can the reciprocal of a mixed number be another mixed number? Explain.

LOGIC POWER

The circle and the square intersect at 2 points.

Draw diagrams to show a circle and a square intersecting at 3, 4, and 5 points.

2.6 Dividing Fractions

Kenji buys grapefruit in bags of 4. He eats $\frac{1}{2}$ of a grapefruit with his breakfast each day. The 4 grapefruit last him 8 days. So, $4 \div \frac{1}{2} = 8$.

Activity: Study the Process

Dividing by fractions uses two ideas you are familiar with.

- Any number divided by 1 gives the number.

$$3 \div 1 = 3 \qquad 2.5 \div 1 = 2.5 \qquad \frac{1}{2} \div 1 = \frac{1}{2}$$

- If the dividend and divisor in a division are multiplied by the same power of 10, the value of the quotient does not change.

$0.2\,)\overline{2.32}$ becomes $0.2 \times 10\,)\overline{2.32 \times 10}$, which is $2\,)\overline{23.2}$

Now, combine these two ideas to simplify dividing fractions. Multiply the dividend and divisor by the same fraction to make the divisor 1.

Copy and complete the table. The first row is done for you.

Division	Multiplication to Make the Divisor 1	New Expression	Answer
$\frac{1}{3} \div \frac{1}{2}$	$\left(\frac{1}{3} \times \frac{2}{1}\right) \div \left(\frac{1}{2} \times \frac{2}{1}\right)$	$\frac{1}{3} \times \frac{2}{1} \div 1$	$\frac{2}{3}$
$\frac{2}{5} \div \frac{1}{3}$			
$\frac{1}{2} \div \frac{1}{4}$			
$\frac{3}{4} \div \frac{2}{3}$			
$\frac{3}{8} \div 2$			
$4 \div \frac{3}{2}$			

Inquire

1. What name is given to the fraction that multiplies the divisor to make it 1?

2. In your own words, describe a method of dividing fractions.

Example

Divide.

a) $\frac{3}{4} \div \frac{2}{5}$

b) $2\frac{2}{3} \div 1\frac{1}{2}$

Solution

To divide by a fraction, multiply by its reciprocal.

a)
$$\frac{3}{4} \div \frac{2}{5}$$

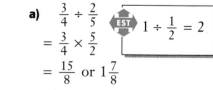
EST $1 \div \frac{1}{2} = 2$

$$= \frac{3}{4} \times \frac{5}{2}$$
$$= \frac{15}{8} \text{ or } 1\frac{7}{8}$$

b) Write the mixed numbers as improper fractions, then divide.

$$2\frac{2}{3} \div 1\frac{1}{2}$$

EST $3 \div 2 = \frac{3}{2}$ or $1\frac{1}{2}$

$$= \frac{8}{3} \div \frac{3}{2}$$
$$= \frac{8}{3} \times \frac{2}{3}$$
$$= \frac{16}{9} \text{ or } 1\frac{7}{9}$$

Practice

Write all answers in lowest terms.

The diagram shows the number of sixths in one half and illustrates the statement $\frac{1}{2} \div \frac{1}{6} = 3$. Use a diagram to find each of the following quotients.

1. $\frac{1}{4} \div \frac{1}{2}$ **2.** $\frac{2}{5} \div \frac{1}{10}$ **3.** $\frac{2}{3} \div \frac{1}{6}$

Divide.

4. $\frac{3}{8} \div \frac{1}{4}$ **5.** $\frac{3}{8} \div \frac{1}{2}$ **6.** $\frac{2}{3} \div \frac{3}{5}$

Divide. Illustrate each division with a diagram.

7. $3 \div \frac{1}{2}$ **8.** $6 \div \frac{2}{3}$ **9.** $\frac{1}{3} \div 2$

Find the quotient.

10. $2\frac{1}{2} \div \frac{1}{2}$ **11.** $2\frac{3}{4} \div \frac{1}{4}$ **12.** $\frac{3}{4} \div 1\frac{2}{3}$

13. $\frac{5}{9} \div 1\frac{2}{3}$ **14.** $2\frac{1}{4} \div 1\frac{1}{2}$ **15.** $2\frac{3}{4} \div 1\frac{1}{2}$

Problems and Applications

16. How many people can you serve with 6 pizzas if each person has $\frac{3}{4}$ of a pizza?

17. Nine tenths of a grade 8 class are in the gym. If these students are divided into 3 equal groups, what fraction of the class will be in each group?

18. Michael has a piece of tape $7\frac{4}{5}$ units long. If he cuts it into pieces each $\frac{3}{5}$ of a unit long, how many pieces will he have?

19. It takes $\frac{3}{4}$ of a minute to do a lap on your bicycle at the velodrome. How many laps could you do in $\frac{1}{2}$ hour?

20. The power used by a light bulb is measured in watts, W. If a light bulb uses $3\frac{3}{4}$ times less power than a 150-W bulb, how much power does it use?

21. The maximum life span of a leopard is 24 years. This life span is $\frac{3}{10}$ of the maximum life span of a salamander. What is the maximum life span of a salamander?

22. Without doing an actual calculation, how would you explain to someone that $6 \div 2\frac{3}{4}$ has an answer closer to 2 than to 3?

23. If you divide a number by a fraction less than 1, is the result larger or smaller than the original number? Explain.

24. a) Work with a classmate to find the quotients for the following problems.

$\frac{2}{3} \div \frac{1}{3}$ $\frac{4}{5} \div \frac{2}{5}$ $\frac{6}{8} \div \frac{3}{8}$

$\frac{2}{10} \div \frac{8}{10}$ $\frac{3}{10} \div \frac{2}{10}$ $\frac{5}{9} \div \frac{4}{9}$ $\frac{2}{5} \div \frac{4}{5}$

b) What do the divisions in part a) have in common?

c) For each division in part a), find the quotient for only the numerators.

d) Write an alternative method for dividing fractions.

e) Test your method on the following divisions.

$\frac{3}{4} \div \frac{1}{2}$ $\frac{5}{6} \div \frac{2}{3}$ $\frac{1}{2} \div \frac{1}{5}$

$2 \div \frac{1}{4}$ $1\frac{1}{4} \div \frac{1}{2}$ $2\frac{1}{2} \div 1\frac{1}{3}$

Writing and Interpreting Instructions

😀 Activity ❶ Drawing Designs

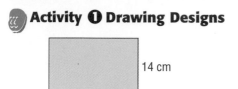

14 cm

21 cm

Work with a classmate.

Use a piece of paper with dimensions about 21 cm by 14 cm, or half the size of a sheet of notepaper. Place the paper on your desk so that the long side is across the top.

Read the instructions and sketch the figures. Read each instruction completely before making the sketch from that instruction. Do not use a ruler or a straight edge. Use your estimation skills to draw the shapes.

1. Mark point A, 6 cm from the left side of the paper and 4 cm from the top.

2. Use A as the centre and draw a circle of radius 3 cm.

3. Draw a square with sides 5 cm, so that the top left vertex of the square is at A. The other sides of the square are parallel to the edges of the paper.

4. Mark point B, 5 cm from the bottom edge of the paper and 5 cm from the right edge.

5. Use point B as the bottom left vertex of a rectangle. The sides of the rectangle are parallel to the edges of the paper. The rectangle has a length of 7 cm and a width of 3 cm. The longer side of the rectangle is parallel to the shorter edge of the paper.

Use a ruler to check how accurate you were in marking A and B. Use a ruler to check the radius of your circle and the dimensions of the square and the rectangle.

Compare your final sketch with the sketches of other pairs.

Activity ❷ Writing Instructions

Write a set of instructions that you would give to a classmate to sketch the design. Each instruction can be given only once.

Check that your instructions would allow someone to sketch the complete design.

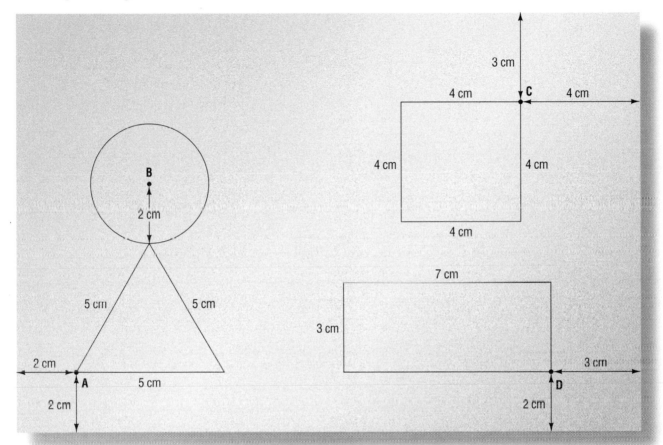

Activity ❸ Making Designs

Make a design of your own, using geometric figures. Write a set of instructions that you would give to classmates, so that they could sketch the design.

Read your instructions to 3 classmates. Have them sketch the design individually, without looking at each other's sketches.

Once you have finished reading the instructions, have the 3 classmates compare their sketches.

How are the sketches the same?

How are they different?

How could you have improved your instructions?

Fractions and Calculators

Activity ❶ Computing in Decimal Form

One way to calculate $1\frac{3}{4} \div \frac{5}{8}$ is to write each fraction as a decimal and to divide the decimals with a calculator.

$$1\frac{3}{4} \div \frac{5}{8} = 1.75 \div 0.625$$
$$= 2.8$$

[C] 1 [.] 75 [÷] 0 [.] 625 [=] 2.8

1. Complete the division $1\frac{3}{4} \div \frac{5}{8}$ without writing the fractions as decimals and without using a calculator. Does the answer in fractional form agree with the decimal answer shown above?

2. Complete each of the following calculations in 2 ways. First, leave the numbers in fractional form. Then, repeat the calculation using decimal form and a calculator. In each case, compare your answers and decide which method is faster.

a) $\frac{2}{5} + \frac{1}{4}$ **b)** $\frac{3}{4} + 1\frac{1}{2}$

c) $\frac{7}{8} - \frac{3}{8}$ **d)** $1\frac{3}{4} - 1\frac{1}{3}$

e) $\frac{2}{3} \times \frac{1}{2}$ **f)** $2\frac{1}{4} \times \frac{5}{6}$

g) $\frac{5}{8} \div \frac{3}{4}$ **h)** $\frac{9}{10} \div \frac{3}{10}$

i) $2\frac{1}{2} \div \frac{1}{4}$ **j)** $\frac{3}{5} \div 1\frac{1}{5}$

Activity ❷ Using the Order of Operations

1. Activity 1 included the example $1\frac{3}{4} \div \frac{5}{8}$.

a) What answer does your calculator give if you do not write the fractions as decimals and you try to do the calculation all at once? To find out, key in the following sequence.

[C] 1 [+] 3 [÷] 4 [÷] 5 [÷] 8 [=]

b) If your calculator has bracket keys, [(] and [)], work out a way of using them to get the correct answer. Compare your calculator sequence with your classmates' sequences.

c) How can you use the memory keys on your calculator to get the correct answer? Compare your calculator sequence with your classmates' sequences.

2. Use the bracket keys or memory keys on your calculator to evaluate the following. In each case, also complete the calculation with the numbers in fractional form. Compare your answers from each method.

a) $\frac{3}{5} + \frac{1}{4}$ **b)** $\frac{2}{5} + 1\frac{3}{4}$

c) $1\frac{1}{6} - \frac{2}{3}$ **d)** $1\frac{1}{2} - \frac{5}{8}$

e) $\frac{1}{3} \times 1\frac{1}{3}$ **f)** $1\frac{1}{8} \times 3\frac{1}{2}$

g) $2\frac{1}{6} \div \frac{3}{4}$ **h)** $\frac{1}{2} \div 1\frac{3}{8}$

i) $\frac{5}{9} - \frac{1}{3} \times \frac{3}{4}$ **j)** $\frac{1}{2} \times \frac{5}{6} + \frac{5}{12}$

2.7 Multiplying Rational Numbers

Activity: Study the Table

The value of one share of a company's stock changes depending on what other people are willing to pay. The following table shows the change in value of some stocks in one day.

Stock	Change
Sony	−1
Coca-Cola	+0.25
Nike	−0.25
Reebok	−0.75
Disney	−0.50

Inquire

1. By how much did the value of 500 shares of Coca-Cola increase?

2. By how much did the value of 1000 shares of Disney decrease?

3. By how much did the value of 400 shares of Reebok decrease?

4. Did the value of 500 shares of Nike stock increase or decrease during the day? By how much?

When multiplying rational numbers, multiply as you did with decimals and use the *sign rules* you used with integers.

Example 1

Multiply $0.67 \times (-4.3)$.

Solution

$0.67 \times (-4.3)$
$= -2.881$

EST $1 \times (-4) = -4$

+0.50

+0.25

0

−0.25

−0.50

CONTINUED ▶

63

Example 2

Multiply.

a) $\frac{1}{3} \times \frac{3}{5}$ 　　　　**b)** -0.75×3 　　　**c)** $5 \times (-1.35)$

Solution

a) 　$\frac{1}{3} \times \frac{3}{5}$

　　$= \frac{3}{15}$

　　$= \frac{1}{5}$

b) 　-0.75×3

　　$= -2.25$

　　EST $-1 \times 3 = -3$

c) 　$5 \times (-1.35)$

　　$= -6.75$

　　EST $5 \times (-1) = -5$

You can use a calculator to multiply rational numbers.

Example 3

Multiply.

a) 3.2×0.9 　　　　**b)** $8.5 \times (-0.125)$ 　　　**c)** $(-1.1) \times (-0.69)$

Solution

a) C 3 · 2 × 0 · 9 =   2.88

$3.2 \times 0.9 = 2.88$ 　　　**EST** $3 \times 1 = 3$

b) C 8 · 5 × 0 · 125 +/− =   − 1.0625

$8.5 \times (-0.125) = -1.0625$ 　　**EST** $9 \times (-0.1) = -0.9$

c) C 1 · 1 +/− × 0 · 69 +/− =   0.759

$(-1.1) \times (-0.69) = 0.759$ 　　**EST** $-1 \times (-1) = 1$

Practice

Write a multiplication sentence to represent each diagram.

1. 　　　　**2.** 　　　　**3.**

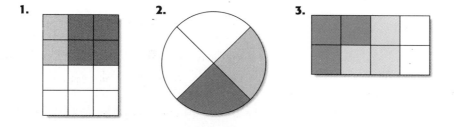

Estimate each product.

4. $-8.5 \times (-1.25)$ **5.** -6.6×3.5

6. $5\frac{1}{2} \times 2\frac{1}{4}$ **7.** $3.2 \times (-2.8)$

Calculate.

8. -0.25×0.6 **9.** $0.75 \times (-0.2)$

10. $\frac{2}{7} \times \frac{7}{2}$ **11.** $\frac{1}{8} \times \frac{1}{2}$

12. $0.3 \times (-0.25)$ **13.** -0.5×0.75

14. $\frac{18}{5} \times \frac{1}{2}$ **15.** $-0.7 \times (-0.75)$

16. $\frac{4}{4} \times \frac{1}{4}$ **17.** $0 \times \frac{3}{4}$

Calculate.

18. $1\frac{1}{2} \times 3\frac{1}{4}$ **19.** -0.75×2.5

20. $-1.5 \times (-1.67)$ **21.** $1 \times (-0.875)$

22. $\frac{7}{2} \times 1\frac{1}{4}$ **23.** $\frac{1}{10} \times 100$

24. Evaluate when $p - 0.5$, $q - 0.6$, and $r = -0.75$.

a) $p \times q$ **b)** $q \times r$ **c)** $p \times q \times r$

Problems and Applications

25. The price of General Motors stock fell by 0.35 one day. By how much did 400 shares of General Motors stock fall?

26. Martina can ride 11.5 km/h on her mountain bike. What distance can she ride in 3.25 h?

27. The temperature in Halifax changed by $-1.3°$C/h overnight. What was the temperature change from 01:00 to 06:00?

28. How many hours are there in $3\frac{1}{4}$ weeks?

29. In 1993, about 6600 satellites were orbiting the Earth. There were also about $2\frac{3}{11}$ times that number of pieces of junk in orbit. The junk included used rockets and debris from explosions in space. About how many pieces of junk were orbiting the Earth?

30. It is estimated that the loon population today is about $\frac{1}{2}$ what it was 10 years ago.

a) If the population 10 years ago was approximately one million, what is the loon population today?

b) What factors might be responsible for this decline in the loon population?

31. Decide whether each statement is always true, sometimes true, or never true. Explain.

a) The square of a non-zero rational number is negative.

b) The product of 2 negative rational numbers is greater than either of them.

c) The product of 2 rational numbers is not zero.

32. Work with a classmate. Research the cost of advertising space in your local newspaper or your favourite magazine. Determine the cost of a $\frac{1}{4}$-page, $\frac{1}{2}$-page, and $\frac{1}{8}$-page advertisement. List any factors other than size that might affect the cost of an advertisement.

DESIGN POWER

How many triangles can you find in this figure?

Make up a similar type of design using a different geometric shape. Ask a classmate to solve it.

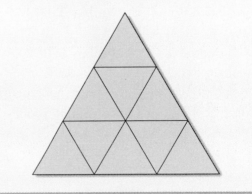

2.8 Dividing Rational Numbers

Every day, the newspaper compares the Canadian dollar with the U.S. dollar. If the Canadian dollar is quoted as 80.03¢ U.S., one Canadian dollar (100 cents) will buy approximately 80 cents of U.S. money.

Activity: Complete the Table

Suppose you want to buy some U.S. money to take on vacation. You would like to know how much Canadian money buys 1 U.S. dollar. To do this, you divide 100 Canadian cents by the number of U.S. cents they will buy.

Copy the table in your notebook and use your calculator to complete it. Round your answers to the nearest cent.

Value of 100 Canadian Cents in U.S. Cents	Division	Cost of 1 U.S. Dollar in Canadian Dollars
80.03	100 ÷ 80.03	
83.45		
91.34		
101.56		
77.34		
106.42		

Inquire

1. How much does it cost to buy $200 U.S. if the value of 1 Canadian dollar is 80.03¢ U.S.?

2. How much does it cost to buy $500 U.S. if the value of 1 Canadian dollar is 91.34¢ U.S.?

3. How much does it cost to buy $800 U.S. if the value of 1 Canadian dollar is 106.42¢ U.S.?

4. If you have $80 Canadian and the value of 1 Canadian dollar is 83.45¢ U.S., do you have enough money to buy $70 U.S.?

When dividing rational numbers, use the same *sign* rules you used to divide integers.

Example 1

Divide.

a) $\frac{1}{4} \div \frac{1}{2}$ **b)** $3 \div 0.25$ **c)** $-2.4 \div 0.8$ **d)** $-1.25 \div (-0.25)$

Solution

a) $\frac{1}{4} \div \frac{1}{2}$

$= \frac{1}{4} \times \frac{2}{1}$

$= \frac{2}{4}$

$= \frac{1}{2}$

b) $3 \div 0.25$

$= \frac{3 \times 100}{0.25 \times 100}$

$= \frac{300}{25}$

$= 12$

c) $-2.4 \div 0.8$

$= \frac{-2.4 \times 10}{0.8 \times 10}$

$= \frac{-24}{8}$

$= -3$

d) $-1.25 \div (-0.25)$

$= \frac{-1.25 \times 100}{-0.25 \times 100}$

$= \frac{-125}{-25}$

$= 5$

You can use a calculator to divide rational numbers.

Example 2

Divide.

a) $-3.5 \div 0.07$ **b)** $-1.68 \div (-1.4)$ **c)** $-2.76 \div 0.16$

Solution

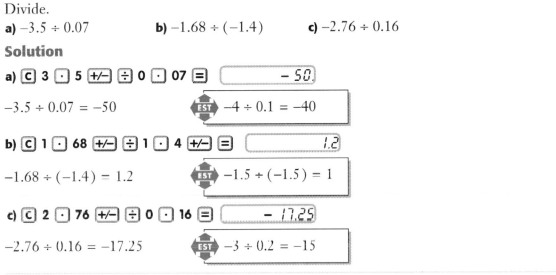

a) C 3 . 5 +/− ÷ 0 . 07 =   − 50.

$-3.5 \div 0.07 = -50$ EST $-4 \div 0.1 = -40$

b) C 1 . 68 +/− ÷ 1 . 4 +/− =   1.2

$-1.68 \div (-1.4) = 1.2$ EST $-1.5 \div (-1.5) = 1$

c) C 2 . 76 +/− ÷ 0 . 16 =   − 17.25

$-2.76 \div 0.16 = -17.25$ EST $-3 \div 0.2 = -15$

Practice

Write a division statement to represent each diagram.

1.   **2.**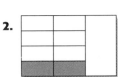

Estimate each quotient.

3. $3\frac{1}{2} \div 2\frac{1}{4}$ **4.** $4\frac{1}{4} \div 1\frac{7}{8}$

5. $1.4 \div (-5.5)$ **6.** $-2.7 \div (-1.5)$

State the reciprocal.

7. $\frac{1}{4}$ **8.** $\frac{1}{2}$ **9.** $\frac{5}{3}$ **10.** $\frac{7}{2}$

11. 3 **12.** $1\frac{3}{4}$ **13.** 0 **14.** $2\frac{1}{5}$

State whether each answer will be positive or negative.

15. $-0.25 \div 0.5$ **16.** $6 \div \frac{1}{3}$

17. $\frac{4}{5} \div 5$ **18.** $0.8 \div (-0.3)$

19. $-4.5 \div (-1.5)$ **20.** $0.4 \div (-0.15)$

CONTINUED ➤

Write a division statement and solve.

21. How many $\frac{1}{2}$s are in $\frac{3}{4}$?

22. How many $\frac{1}{4}$s are in $1\frac{3}{4}$?

23. How many $\frac{1}{3}$s are in $\frac{2}{3}$?

Simplify.

24. $2 \div 0.4$

25. $-0.875 \div (-0.25)$

26. $-10.5 \div 0.25$

27. $-50 \div 0.4$

28. $\frac{1}{2} \div 0$

29. $\frac{4}{5} \div \frac{8}{10}$

30. $2\frac{1}{3} \div \frac{1}{2}$

31. $-1.75 \div 4$

32. $-6.75 \div (-3)$

33. $6.36 \div (-0.16)$

Problems and Applications

34. Cecil had $1\frac{2}{3}$ pizzas. He wanted each person to have $\frac{1}{3}$ of a pizza. How many friends could he share with?

35. Kerry drove the 299 km from Calgary to Edmonton in 3.25 h. What was her average speed?

36. There are 100 pennies in a British pound. If a Canadian dollar is worth 49.32 British pennies, how many Canadian dollars does it cost to buy
a) a British pound?
b) 250 British pounds?

37. If the Swiss franc is worth 80.27¢ Canadian, how many Swiss francs can you buy for $100.00 Canadian?

38. A chemist is measuring the acid needed for an experiment. If she has $2\frac{1}{5}$ cylinders of acid and needs $\frac{1}{5}$ of a cylinder for each experiment, how many experiments can she do?

39. If $\frac{1}{2}$ a loaf of bread is cut into 8 equal slices, what fraction is each slice of the original loaf?

40. If a car travels 12.5 km on 1 L of gasoline, how many litres of gasoline does it use when it travels 100 km?

41. The value of an Inco share changed by -1.25 one day. If Lisa's Inco shares decreased in value by $325.00 that day, how many Inco shares did she have?

42. The national debt is the amount of money the federal government owes. The debt stood at about $465 000 000 000 in 1993. The Canadian population was about 28 000 000. If all the people in Canada had shared equally in paying off the debt, how much would each of them have paid? Round your answer to the nearest $100.

43. What is the value of the quotient of 2 opposite rational numbers? Explain.

44. Write the following numbers. Compare your answers with a classmate's.
a) 2 rational numbers with a quotient of 1.25
b) 2 rational numbers with a quotient of -0.5
c) 2 rational numbers whose quotient is an integer

45. Write a problem that requires division of rational numbers to solve it. Have a classmate solve your problem.

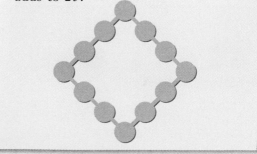

NUMBER POWER

Write the numbers from 1 to 12 in the circles so that each side adds to 25.

2.9 Adding and Subtracting Rational Numbers

The **opening price** of a stock tells you how much one share of a stock cost when the stock market opened for the day. The **closing price** of a stock tells you what one share was worth when the stock market closed for the day.

Activity: Complete the Table

The table shows the opening price for TCBY on a Monday and the daily change in price for 5 days. Copy and complete the table. The closing price on Monday becomes the opening price on Tuesday, and so on.

	Opening Price	Change	Closing Price
Monday	9	−1.50	
Tuesday		−0.75	
Wednesday		+0.25	
Thursday		−0.25	
Friday		−0.50	

Inquire

1. What was the closing price on Friday?

2. What is the sum of the Change column for the week?

3. What number do you get when you subtract the closing price on Friday from the opening price on Monday?

4. How does this number compare with the sum of the Change column?

5. What number do you get when you subtract the opening price on Monday from the closing price on Friday?

6. How does this number compare with the sum of the Change column? Explain.

When adding or subtracting rational numbers, use the *sign rules* you used for integers.

Example 1

a) Add $3.4 + 1.3$.
b) Subtract $-2.4 - (-6.7)$.

Solution

a) $3.4 + 1.3$
$= 4.7$ EST $3 + 1 = 4$

b) $-2.4 - (-6.7)$
$= -2.4 + 6.7$ EST $-2 + 7 = 5$
$= 4.3$

CONTINUED ▶

Canadian Pacific Limited

Par Value $5. each.

NANCY BELLE:COOK

This certifies that
Les présentes attestent que

TWO HUNDRED FIFTY

is the owner of
est le propriétaire de

fully paid and non-assessable shares of the Ordinary Capital Stock of Canadian Pacific Limited of the par value of Five Dollars each, transferable only on the books of the Company in person or by attorney upon surrender of this Certificate properly endorsed.

This Certificate is not valid until countersigned by the Transfer Agent and registered by the Registrar.

In Witness Whereof, the Company has caused this Certificate to be signed by its duly authorized officers.

Dated:
Daté:

MAR 1 3

SECRETARY–SECRÉTAIRE

Transferable at the offices of The Royal Trust Company in Halifax, N.S., Saint John, N.B., Montreal, P.Q., Toronto, Ont., Winnipeg, Man., Regina, Sask., Calgary, Alta., and Vancouver, B.C., at the office of the Bank of Montreal Trust Company in New York City, U.S.A., and at the office of the Deputy Secretary in London, Eng.

THE ROYAL TRUST COMPANY, COMPAGNIE TRUST ROYAL

You can use a calculator to add and subtract rational numbers.

Example 2

Simplify.

a) $1.25 - 2.375$ **b)** $-0.875 + 0.75$ **c)** $-3 - (-1.67)$

Solution

a) C 1 · 25 − 2 · 375 = | − 1.125 |

$1.25 - 2.375 = -1.125$ **EST** | $1 - 2 = -1$ |

b) C 0 · 875 +/− + 0 · 75 = | − 0.125 |

$-0.875 + 0.75 = -0.125$ **EST** | $-0.9 + 0.8 = -0.1$ |

c) C 3 +/− − 1 · 67 +/− = | − 1.33 |

$-3 - (-1.67) = -1.33$ **EST** | $-3 + 2 = -1$ |

Practice

State the lowest common denominator for each pair of fractions.

1. $\frac{1}{2}, \frac{1}{5}$ **2.** $\frac{3}{8}, \frac{1}{4}$ **3.** $1\frac{2}{3}, 2\frac{3}{4}$

Estimate.

4. $1\frac{1}{3} + 2\frac{3}{4}$ **5.** $3\frac{1}{8} - 1\frac{1}{2}$

6. $6\frac{2}{3} - 4\frac{1}{4}$ **7.** $-0.85 - 2.25$

8. $4.125 - 2.75$ **9.** $4.4 - (-2.5)$

Write true or false for each number sentence.

10. $0.25 - 0.875 = -0.625$

11. $2\frac{1}{3} - \frac{5}{6} = \frac{2}{6}$

12. $\frac{7}{10} + \frac{11}{20} = \frac{18}{20}$

13. $-0.65 - (-1.25) = 0.6$

Calculate.

14. $2\frac{1}{3} - \frac{1}{4}$ **15.** $-2.55 + 6.3$

16. $\frac{7}{9} + \frac{1}{3}$ **17.** $\frac{9}{10} - \frac{3}{5}$

18. $8.83 - 9.75$ **19.** $\frac{3}{5} - \frac{1}{4}$

20. $-1.8 + 0.7$ **21.** $2\frac{3}{16} - \frac{5}{8}$

22. $4\frac{8}{9} - 2\frac{2}{3}$ **23.** $-0.25 + 0.21$

24. $6.23 - (-3.65)$ **25.** $\frac{3}{10} + \frac{53}{100}$

26. $1 - \frac{1}{100}$ **27.** $-8.93 + (-5.63)$

28. $-4.61 - 1.84$ **29.** $-3.65 + 2.99$

30. $2.25 - (-1.5)$ **31.** $5.2 - 3.47$

Problems and Applications

32. The nightly low temperatures one week in Winnipeg were −1.5°C, +2.1°C, −3.8°C, −2.2°C, +4.3°C, −5.3°C, and −6.9°C. What was the average low temperature that week?

33. Shares of ABC Foods opened at 9.15 and closed at 7.65. What was the change that day?

34. Six friends bought 3 pizzas. Each person ate $\frac{3}{8}$ of a pizza. How much pizza was left over?

35. On their vacation, the Reikos spent $\frac{1}{4}$ of their money on gas, $\frac{1}{4}$ on food and lodging, and $\frac{1}{8}$ on tourist attractions. What fraction of their money did they spend? If they started with $840.00, how much money did they have left?

36. In February 1993, Canada's Kate Pace won the gold medal at the World Alpine Ski Championships. Her winning time was 1 min 27.38 s. She finished $\frac{28}{100}$ of a second ahead of Astrid Loedemal of Norway. What was Astrid's time?

37. About $\frac{2}{5}$ of Canada's gold production comes from Ontario. About $\frac{3}{10}$ comes from Quebec and $\frac{1}{10}$ from British Columbia. What fraction of Canada's gold production comes from the rest of the country? Write your answer in lowest terms.

38. a) If the sum of 2 different rational numbers is zero, what can you say about the numbers?

b) If the sum of 2 equal rational numbers is zero, what can you say about the numbers?

39. Decide whether each statement is always true, sometimes true, or never true. Explain.

a) The difference between 2 negative rational numbers is negative.

b) The sum of 2 non-zero rational numbers is greater than either of the numbers.

c) The difference between 2 rational numbers is an integer.

40. Write the following numbers. Compare your answers with a classmate's.

a) 2 rational numbers with a sum of −0.6

b) 3 rational numbers with a sum of −2.25

c) 2 rational numbers with a difference of $\frac{5}{8}$

PATTERN POWER

If

and

how many △ will balance the ●?

2.10 Make Assumptions

When you leave for school in the morning, you make the assumption that your journey will take about the same length of time as it did the day before. When you solve many problems, you also have to make assumptions.

Lin works Saturdays at the farmers' market. She earns $10.00 if she arrives in time to unload the truck and set up the booth. She also earns $7.25/h for selling vegetables from 06:00 to 16:00, when the market closes. Lin hopes to earn $4000 over the next year. Will she?

Understand the Problem

1. What information are you given?

2. What are you asked to find?

3. What assumptions should you make?

4. Do you need an exact or approximate answer?

Think of a Plan

Make some assumptions about Lin's work.
• Lin will work 52 Saturdays in the year.
• She will work the same hours every Saturday.
• She will always arrive in time to unload the truck and set up the booth.
• She will be paid at the same rate all year.

Then, calculate how much she will earn each Saturday and multiply by 52.

Carry Out the Plan

From 06:00 to 16:00 is 10 h.
Earnings for selling: $10 \times \$7.25 = \$72.50$
Earnings for unloading and setting up: $10.00
Total: $82.50
Earnings in 52 weeks: $52 \times \$82.50 = \$4290.00$

EST $50 \times 80 = 4000$

Lin should earn more than $4000 over the next year.

Look Back

Does the answer seem reasonable?
How could you use division and subtraction to check your answer?

Make Assumptions	1. Decide what assumption(s) to make.
	2. Use your assumption(s) to solve the problem.
	3. Check that your answer is reasonable.

Problems and Applications

1. List some assumptions you make when you
a) leave home to go to a movie
b) sit down to study for a math test

2. Michelle is in grade 8. She called a college and learned that first-year students pay $2000 to attend. She calculated that she must save $400/year for the next 5 years.
a) What assumption did she make?
b) What was wrong with her assumption?

3. Assume that each pattern continues, and write the next 3 terms.
a) 3, 5, 7, 9, ■, ■, ■
b) 22, 18, 14, ■, ■, ■
c) 1, 3, 9, 27, ■, ■, ■
d) 256, 128, 64, ■, ■, ■
e) 1, 2, 4, 7, 11, ■, ■, ■
f) 2, 5, 4, 7, 6, 9, 8, ■, ■, ■
g) a, f, d, i, g, l, ■, ■, ■

4. The distance around an island is 20 km. A patrol boat travels around it at 5 km/h.
a) How many trips can the boat make around the island from 20:00 to 08:00?
b) What assumptions did you make?

5. Jerry scored 10 points in the first basketball game of a 24-game season. He assumed that he would score 240 points altogether.
a) What assumptions did Jerry make?
b) Were his assumptions logical?

6. Thirty students are taking a ski trip. The slopes are 280 km from the school. The bus can travel at 80 km/h.
a) How long will it take to get to the slopes?
b) What assumptions have you made?

7. Five grade 8 students wrapped gifts and put them into 35 holiday baskets for the people in a hospital. The group could make 3 baskets every day before classes started.
a) How long did it take to make the baskets?
b) What assumptions have you made?

8. Frank opened a greeting card store. In the first month, the store sold 8000 cards. Frank calculated it would sell 96 000 cards a year.
a) What assumption did Frank make?
b) What was wrong with his assumption?
c) What are the best months for selling cards?

9. You are the editor of a school newspaper. It is Friday, and all the students have left for the weekend. There are 600 students in grades 6, 7, and 8 in the school. You must have the paper printed on Saturday. You need to know how many students will buy the paper on Monday, so that you can tell the printer how many papers to print.
a) How would you solve the problem?
b) What assumptions would you make?

10. In 1928, the Canadian women's team won the Olympic 4 × 100-m relay in about 48 s. In 1988, the American women's team won in about 42 s.
a) Predict the approximate winning time in the year 2108.
b) What assumptions have you made?
c) Are your assumptions reasonable?

11. Write 2 problems requiring assumptions. Have a classmate solve your problems.

WORD POWER

Lewis Carroll invented the word game "doublets." You must change one word to another by changing one letter at a time. You must form a real word each time you change a letter. Change the word TOP to the word HAT by changing one letter at a time. Compare your list of words with your classmates'. The best solution has the least steps.

Review

Express all answers in lowest terms.

1. Write 3 fractions equivalent to $\frac{3}{4}$.

Find the missing values.

2. $\frac{\blacksquare}{4} = \frac{15}{12}$ **3.** $\frac{9}{36} = \frac{\blacksquare}{4}$ **4.** $\frac{2}{5} = \frac{8}{\blacksquare}$

Estimate, then find the sum.

5. $\frac{1}{12} + \frac{5}{12}$ **6.** $\frac{3}{8} + \frac{1}{4}$

7. $1\frac{3}{4} + \frac{3}{4}$ **8.** $1\frac{1}{3} + 3\frac{2}{3}$

9. $2\frac{1}{2} + \frac{5}{6}$ **10.** $2\frac{1}{3} + 4\frac{5}{6}$

11. $\frac{3}{4} + \frac{5}{8} + 1\frac{1}{2}$ **12.** $\frac{4}{5} + 1\frac{3}{10} + 2\frac{1}{2}$

Estimate, then subtract.

13. $\frac{5}{6} - \frac{3}{6}$ **14.** $\frac{11}{12} - \frac{3}{4}$ **15.** $1\frac{1}{3} - \frac{2}{3}$

16. $2\frac{1}{5} - 1\frac{3}{10}$ **17.** $3\frac{2}{5} - 2\frac{3}{4}$ **18.** $1\frac{3}{8} - 1\frac{1}{4}$

Find the missing value.

19. $\frac{3}{4} - \blacksquare = \frac{3}{8}$ **20.** $1\frac{5}{6} - \blacksquare = \frac{2}{3}$

21. $1\frac{1}{2} - \blacksquare = \frac{5}{6}$ **22.** $\blacksquare - 2\frac{1}{4} = \frac{3}{4}$

Estimate, then multiply.

23. $\frac{2}{3}$ of 15   **24.** $\frac{1}{4} \times \frac{3}{4}$

25. $2\frac{1}{2} \times \frac{4}{5}$ **26.** $2\frac{2}{3} \times \frac{3}{5} \times \frac{1}{4}$

27. $4 \times \frac{5}{6} \times \frac{1}{3}$ **28.** $3 \times 2\frac{1}{6}$

Write the reciprocal.

29. $\frac{1}{2}$ **30.** $\frac{3}{8}$ **31.** 3   **32.** $5\frac{1}{3}$

Estimate, then divide.

33. $\frac{3}{4} \div \frac{1}{2}$ **34.** $\frac{2}{9} \div \frac{2}{3}$ **35.** $\frac{5}{6} \div 3\frac{1}{3}$

36. $1\frac{1}{10} \div \frac{4}{5}$ **37.** $2\frac{1}{6} \div 1\frac{1}{3}$ **38.** $1\frac{1}{2} \div 2\frac{3}{4}$

Evaluate.

39. 0.5×7 **40.** $-0.75 \div (-4)$

41. $18.29 - 12.5$ **42.** $\frac{3}{4} \div \frac{7}{8}$

43. $21 \div \frac{7}{3}$ **44.** $3.2 + 0.116$

45. $0.3 \div 1$ **46.** $0.833 - 0.5$

47. $-3.6 + 5.4$ **48.** -7×0.5

49. $9.1 - 3.7$ **50.** $-6 - 0.5$

51. Evaluate when $m = -0.5$, $n = 0.8$, and $p = -1$.

a) $m \times n \times p$ **b)** $n + p$

c) $m + n + p$ **d)** $n \div m \div p$

e) $m + n - p$ **f)** $m \times p + n$

52. Tien ran for $\frac{1}{2}$ an hour on Monday, $\frac{3}{4}$ of an hour on Thursday, and $\frac{1}{3}$ of an hour on Saturday. For how many hours did she run?

53. One tenth of Canadians aged 15 and over have a university degree. One fifth of the Canadians with degrees have a degree in education. What fraction of Canadians aged 15 and over have an education degree?

54. Kaitlin ate $\frac{3}{8}$ of a pizza, Michael ate $\frac{3}{4}$ of one, Nicole ate $\frac{1}{4}$, and Rob ate $\frac{1}{2}$ of a pizza. There was $\frac{1}{8}$ of a pizza left. How many pizzas were there to begin with?

55. Brad, Kim, and Damian took $1\frac{1}{2}$ hours to cut and trim the lawn. If one of them had done the job alone, how long would it have taken? What assumptions have you made?

56. If $5\frac{1}{4}$ granola bars are shared equally by 6 people, what fraction of a bar does each person receive?

57. Renee ran $3\frac{3}{4}$ laps of a track. Jean ran $4\frac{1}{2}$ laps. How many more laps did Jean run than Renee?

58. Of the national parks in Canada or the United States, about $\frac{3}{5}$ are in the United States. What fraction of the national parks are in Canada?

59. The greatest depth of snow on the ground at the Whistler Roundhouse weather station in British Columbia was about 2.5 times the greatest depth of snow at the Glenlea station in Manitoba. The greatest depth of snow recorded at Glenlea was about 180 cm. What was the greatest depth of snow at Whistler Roundhouse?

60. The average mass of a grizzly bear is about 0.8 the average mass of a polar bear. Grizzly bears have a mass of about 340 kg. Find the mass of a polar bear.

61. Janelle is paid $5.75 for each hour she works plus a base salary of $50. How much does she earn if she works
a) 3.5 h?   **b)** 11.25 h?   **c)** 21.4 h?

62. Calculate the area of each figure.
a)

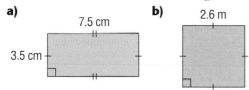

7.5 cm

3.5 cm

b) 2.6 m

63. Find today's closing price for BC Magazine Publishing stock if it closed yesterday at 64.25 and the net change today was −1.125.

64. Is each of the following situations possible? Explain.
a) Farsanah spent $\frac{1}{3}$ of the day sleeping, $\frac{3}{8}$ of the day working, $\frac{1}{12}$ of the day travelling to and from work, and $\frac{1}{4}$ of the day on other activities.
b) About $\frac{4}{5}$ of Canadians live to the east of Alberta. About $\frac{3}{5}$ of Canadians live in Ontario or Quebec.

Group Decision Making
Researching Law Enforcement Careers

1. Brainstorm with the whole class the careers you would like to investigate. They could include such careers as police officer, coast guard crew member, pathologist, judge, forensic scientist, or forensic accountant. Decide as a class on 6 careers.

2. Go to home groups. In your group, decide which career each member will investigate. Also, decide on the questions you want to answer about the careers. Include a question on how math is used in each career.

Home Groups

3. Research your career individually.

4. Form an expert group with students who have researched the same career as you. In your expert group, combine the information you have found.

Expert Groups

5. In your expert group, prepare a report on the career. The report can take any form the group chooses.

6. Present your findings to your home group. Evaluate the process and identify what went well and what you would do differently next time.

Chapter Check

1. Write two fractions equivalent to $\frac{2}{3}$.

Add.

2. $\frac{3}{10} + \frac{9}{10}$

3. $\frac{5}{6} + \frac{1}{2}$

4. $2\frac{5}{6} + \frac{2}{3}$

5. $1\frac{1}{2} + 4\frac{3}{4}$

Subtract.

6. $\frac{5}{9} - \frac{2}{9}$

7. $\frac{7}{12} - \frac{1}{4}$

8. $2\frac{1}{4} - 1\frac{2}{3}$

9. $5\frac{3}{4} - 3\frac{1}{6}$

Find the product.

10. $\frac{3}{5}$ of 10

11. $\frac{2}{9} \times \frac{3}{4}$

12. $\frac{2}{3} \times \frac{1}{4}$

13. $3\frac{2}{3} \times \frac{1}{2}$

14. What is the reciprocal of $\frac{1}{3}$? $2\frac{1}{5}$?

Divide.

15. $\frac{8}{5} \div \frac{4}{5}$

16. $\frac{3}{4} \div \frac{1}{2}$

17. $4 \div \frac{2}{5}$

18. $2\frac{1}{3} \div 1\frac{1}{2}$

Calculate.

19. $0.513 + 0.481$

20. -1.8×0.2

21. $\frac{8}{3} \div \frac{1}{3}$

22. $1.33 \div 0.07$

23. $-1.225 - 3.75$

24. $1.66 + 0.055$

25. $6.1 \times (-0.88)$

26. $255 - 37.505$

27. $-1.5 \times (-2.3)$

28. $5.6 \div (-0.7)$

29. $-4.1 - 3.5$

30. $1.2 - (-0.9)$

31. Evaluate $x + y \div z$ when $x = 0.5$, $y = 0.6$, and $z = -3$.

32. Evaluate $s \times r \div t$ when $s = 0.75$, $r = -1.3$, and $t = 2.6$.

33. The Safety Taxi Co. charges $0.125 for each kilometre travelled, plus a basic fee of $2.50. If the distance between Hyde Street and 34 Busy Road is 5.6 km, how much would the taxi fare be between these two locations?

34. Pele bought a lettuce for $1.29, a cucumber for $1.75, and a kilogram of tomatoes for $4.35.
a) What did he pay in total for his items?
b) How much change did he get from $20?

35. Jeremy estimated he used $\frac{2}{3}$ of a tank of gas one day and $\frac{3}{5}$ of a tank the next day. He thought that $\frac{3}{4}$ of the driving he did was on business. What fraction of a tank did he use on business during the 2 days?

36. On Monday morning, the value of 1 Merlin Mines share was $15.30. Sonja bought 110 shares. The following Friday the value of one share had fallen to $14.85.
a) What did it cost Sonja to buy the shares?
b) By how much had the value of all of her shares fallen by Friday?
c) What was the value of all of her shares on Friday?

37. Canada produces about $\frac{2}{3}$ of the world's maple syrup. About $\frac{9}{10}$ of Canada's production comes from Quebec. What fraction of the world's maple syrup comes from Quebec?

38. The average life span of a lynx is 0.75 of the average life span of a cougar. The average life span of a lynx is 15 years. What is the average life span of a cougar?

Using the Strategies

Look for a pattern and write the next three terms.

1. 61, 63, 65, …

2. 84, 79, 80, 75, 76, 71, …

3. z, y, x, w, …

4. az, by, cx, dw, …

5. j, f, m, a, m, …

6. Figure 1 has 6 cubes, figure 2 has 11 cubes, and figure 3 has 16 cubes.

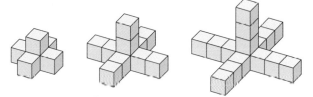

a) How many cubes are there in the fourth figure?

b) How many cubes in the 200th figure? the 3000th figure?

7. A tropical fruit salad was being prepared for brunch. The recipe called for twice as many kiwis as pineapples and 4 fewer bananas than kiwis. Twenty-one pieces of fruit were used for the salad. How many pieces of each fruit were used?

8. How would you estimate how long it would take you to complete a 20-km walk-a-thon?

9. The first week Devin cut lawns, he earned $80.
a) How much should he earn in a year?
b) What assumptions did you make?

10. The football stadium has 22 145 seats. On the sides, there are 17 800 seats that cost $23.50 each. The rest of the seats are at the ends and cost $12.25 each. If all the seats are sold for a game, how much money will be collected?

11. Sarah is saving for a telescope that costs $575, including taxes. She has already saved $205. She plans to save the rest in equal amounts for the next 5 months. How much should she save each month?

12. George is 15. He is five times as old as his sister was five years ago. How old is his sister now?

13. a) You have a red bead, a blue bead, and a yellow bead. How many different arrangements of 3 different-coloured beads in a row can you make?

b) Suppose you added a green bead. How many different arrangements of 4 different-coloured beads in a row can you make?

14. Lyndon agreed to train for 2000 h for an upcoming race. He can train for 5 h a day. How long in weeks and days will he have to train to reach his goal?

15. How would you estimate the thickness of one page of a telephone book?

16. What is the sum of the 3 largest prime numbers less than 50?

DATA BANK

1. When it is 03:00 on a Wednesday in Tashkent, Uzbekistan, what time and what day is it in Winnipeg?

2. It is possible to drive from Saskatoon to Vancouver through Edmonton or Calgary. Which route is shorter and by how much?

Life History of Nimpkish Island Firs

Fire   Fire   Parents of Present-Day Tall Trees   Potential Future Growth

Height of Trees (m)

1492
Columbus sails
to the New World.

Fire destroys all but
a few Douglas Firs
on Nimpkish Island.

Captain Cook
visits Vancouver
Island.

Year

CHAPTER 3

Ratio and Rate

The drawing on the opposite page shows the growth of the Douglas firs found in the Nimpkish Island area of British Columbia.

1. About how tall were the trees when Columbus sailed to the New World?

2. a) When Captain Cook visited Vancouver Island, about how much taller than the new trees were the trees that survived the fire?

b) Estimate the height of the new trees as a fraction of the height of the surviving trees when Captain Cook visited Vancouver Island.

3. a) About how many metres did the trees grow between 1300 and 1400?

b) About how many centimetres did they grow between 1300 and 1400?

c) About how many centimetres did they grow each year between 1300 and 1400?

Using Patterns

Activity ❶ Picture Patterns

Draw the next diagram for each of the following.

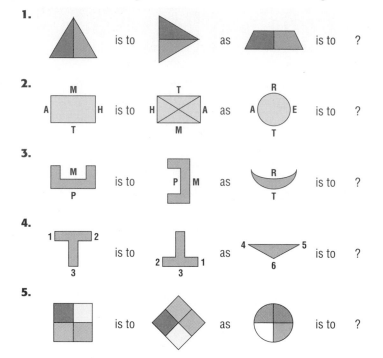

1. ⬛ is to ▷ as ⬛ is to ?

2. [M A H T] is to [T H M A] as [A R E T] is to ?

3. [M P] is to [P M] as [R T] is to ?

4. [1 T 2 / 3] is to [⊥ 2 1 / 3] as [4 ▽ 5 / 6] is to ?

5. ⬛ is to ◆ as ⊕ is to ?

Activity ❷ Analogies

Copy and complete the following analogies.

1. Car is to driver as plane is to ▮.
2. Tree is to bark as orange is to ▮.
3. Horse is to foal as dog is to ▮.
4. TV is to channels as radio is to ▮.
5. Whisper is to yell as walk is to ▮.
6. Moon is to Earth as Earth is to ▮.
7. Boat is to sails as car is to ▮.

Activity ❸ Number Patterns

Copy and complete the following.

1. 3 is to 6 as 4 is to 8 as 5 is to ▮.
2. 20 is to 10 as 8 is to 4 as 12 is to ▮.
3. 3 is to 9 as 4 is to 12 as 5 is to ▮.
4. A is to D as E is to H as I is to ▮.
5. 12 is to 4 as 15 is to 5 as 18 is to ▮.

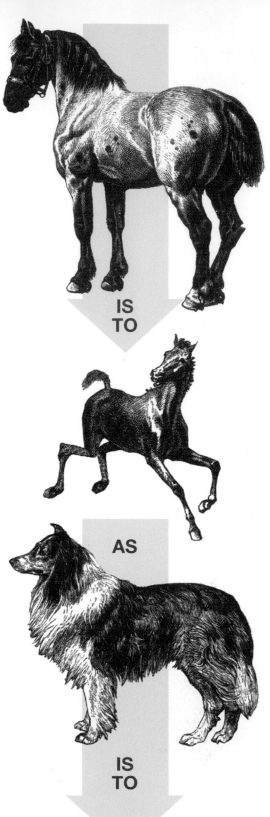

IS
TO

AS

IS
TO

Warm Up

Copy and complete.

1. In 1 h, you drive 70 km. In 4 h, you drive ▓ km.

2. In 3 h, you walk 12 km. In 1 h, you walk ▓ km.

3. In 5 h, you earn $45. In 1 h, you earn $▓. In 7 h, you earn $▓.

4. In 2 h, you read 40 pages. In 1 h, you read ▓ pages. In 6 h, you read ▓ pages.

5. Three bags have 39 rolls. Four bags have ▓ rolls.

6. Two trucks have 36 wheels. Nine trucks have ▓ wheels.

Express each fraction as a whole number or decimal.

7. $\frac{15}{3}$ **8.** $\frac{49}{7}$ **9.** $\frac{64}{8}$ **10.** $\frac{99}{11}$

11. $\frac{12}{8}$ **12.** $\frac{15}{6}$ **13.** $\frac{5}{10}$ **14.** $\frac{3}{4}$

Express each fraction with a denominator of 100.

15. $\frac{1}{2}$ **16.** $\frac{3}{10}$ **17.** $\frac{7}{10}$ **18.** $\frac{1}{4}$

19. $\frac{3}{50}$ **20.** $\frac{7}{20}$ **21.** $\frac{2}{5}$ **22.** $\frac{3}{25}$

Express each fraction as a decimal.

23. $\frac{3}{10}$ **24.** $\frac{3}{5}$ **25.** $\frac{9}{2}$ **26.** $\frac{15}{8}$

27. $\frac{7}{20}$ **28.** $\frac{11}{4}$ **29.** $\frac{64}{25}$ **30.** $\frac{5}{16}$

Mental Math

Express in lowest terms.

1. $\frac{3}{9}$ **2.** $\frac{2}{6}$ **3.** $\frac{2}{4}$

4. $\frac{5}{10}$ **5.** $\frac{2}{8}$ **6.** $\frac{8}{12}$

7. $\frac{2}{12}$ **8.** $\frac{3}{15}$ **9.** $\frac{4}{16}$

10. $\frac{12}{15}$ **11.** $\frac{10}{15}$ **12.** $\frac{6}{10}$

State an equivalent fraction.

13. $\frac{1}{2}$ **14.** $\frac{1}{3}$ **15.** $\frac{1}{4}$

16. $\frac{2}{3}$ **17.** $\frac{3}{5}$ **18.** $\frac{3}{4}$

19. $\frac{4}{7}$ **20.** $\frac{5}{6}$ **21.** $\frac{3}{8}$

22. $\frac{9}{10}$ **23.** $\frac{2}{9}$ **24.** $\frac{5}{12}$

Multiply.

25. 60×50 **26.** 30×90

27. 70×90 **28.** 14×20

29. 11×30 **30.** 12×40

31. 32×20 **32.** 32×30

Divide.

33. $1400 \div 7$ **34.** $2500 \div 5$

35. $1800 \div 3$ **36.** $3600 \div 4$

37. $1000 \div 20$ **38.** $1500 \div 30$

39. $1600 \div 40$ **40.** $2700 \div 90$

3.1 Guess and Check

The grade 8 class had a problem solving contest. One group came up with the following problem.

There were 5 bags of dried peas in a row. The total number of peas was 335.

The first bag had 7 fewer peas than the second bag, the second bag had 7 fewer peas than the third bag, and so on.

There was a prize for the first student who correctly guessed the number of peas in the first bag. How many were there?

Understand the Problem

1. What information are you given?

2. What are you asked to find?

3. Do you need an exact or approximate answer?

Think of a Plan

Guess the number of peas in the first bag. Use your guess to write the numbers of peas in the other bags.

Find the total number of peas. If your total is not 335, make another guess at the number of peas in the first bag.

Carry Out the Plan

GUESS						CHECK
Bag 1	Bag 2	Bag 3	Bag 4	Bag 5	Total	Is the total 335?
40	47	54	61	68	270	Too low
60	67	74	81	88	370	Too high
50	57	64	71	78	320	Too low
55	62	69	76	83	345	Too high
52	59	66	73	80	330	Too low
53	60	67	74	81	335	335 = 335

CHECKS!

There were 53 peas in the first bag.

Look Back

Check the answer against the given information.
Does the answer seem reasonable?
Is there another way to solve the problem?

Guess and Check	1. Guess an answer that fits one of the facts.
	2. Check the answer against the other facts.
	3. If necessary, adjust your guess and check again.

Problems and Applications

1. There are 5 bags of dried peas in a row. The second bag has 5 more peas than the first. The third bag has 6 more peas than the second. The fourth bag has 7 more peas than the third. The fifth bag has 8 more peas than the fourth. The total number of peas is 295. How many peas are in the first bag?

2. If you multiply a certain number by 11 and add 76, the result is 208. What is the number?

3. The number in each red square is found by adding the numbers in the small green squares connected to it. Find the numbers in the green squares.

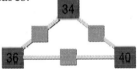

4. Heather scored 21 more points than Justin in a game of SCRABBLE®. Together, they scored a total of 333 points. How many points did each of them score?

In questions 5-8, each letter represents a different digit. Find the value of each letter.

5.
```
   I
+ M
─────
 M E
```

6.
```
  R S
×   9
─────
R R R
```

7.
```
    A 8
×   3 B
───────
2 7 3 0
```

8.
```
   C 2 D
8)X 9 Y
```

9. The length of a rectangle is twice the width, and the area is 112.5 cm². Find the dimensions of this rectangle.

10. Find 4 consecutive whole numbers whose sum is 318.

11. Find 3 consecutive odd whole numbers whose sum is 405.

12. Find 3 consecutive whole numbers such that the sum of their squares is 509.

13. In the number TT5T4, the letter T stands for the same digit. If the number is divisible by 38, find T.

14. Find 2 consecutive whole numbers whose cubes differ by 397.

15. For selling magazine subscriptions, Samira earned $20 a day, plus $4 for every subscription she sold. One day, she earned a total of $232. How many subscriptions did she sell?

16. The cube root of 8 is 2, because $2 \times 2 \times 2 = 8$. Find the cube root of 36, to the nearest tenth.

17. A total 86 of Canada's 295 Members of Parliament (MPs) are elected from the 4 western provinces. Equal numbers of MPs are elected from Saskatchewan and Manitoba. The number elected from Alberta is 12 more than the number elected from Manitoba. The number elected from British Columbia is 18 more than the number elected from Saskatchewan. How many MPs are elected from each of these 4 provinces?

18. Write a problem that can be solved using the guess and check strategy. Have a classmate solve your problem.

LOGIC POWER

One blue cube has the same mass as 3 green cubes. One green cube has the same mass as 4 pink cubes plus 1 red cube. One red cube has the same mass as 2 pink cubes. How many pink cubes have the same mass as 1 blue cube?

3.2 Equivalent Ratios and Proportions

Activity: Complete the Table

Copy and complete the table by writing the ratio of the width to the length for each flag. Do not simplify the ratios.

Flag	Ratio
Cuba	
Mongolia	
Nigeria	
Philippines	

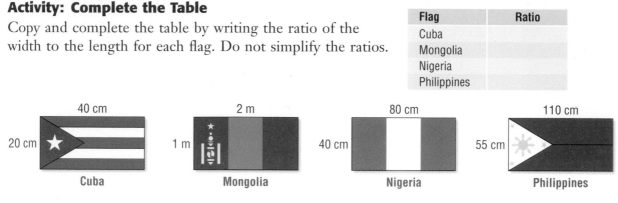

Cuba   Mongolia   Nigeria   Philippines

Inquire

1. Write the 4 ratios in fraction form.

2. Are the ratios equivalent? Explain.

3. If the width of the Mongolian flag was increased to 2 m, what would its length be?

4. If the width of the Cuban flag was increased to 60 cm, what would its length be?

5. If the length of the Nigerian flag was decreased to 20 cm, what would its width be?

Example 1

Write two equivalent ratios for the ratio 3:6:9.

Solution

Multiply each term by 2.

$3{:}6{:}9 = (3 \times 2){:}(6 \times 2){:}(9 \times 2)$
$\qquad = 6{:}12{:}18$

Divide each term by 3.

$3{:}6{:}9 = (3 \div 3){:}(6 \div 3){:}(9 \div 3)$
$\qquad = 1{:}2{:}3$

The table shows the side length, s, of an equilateral triangle and its perimeter, P. The ratios of side length to perimeter are 1:3, 2:6, 3:9, and 4:12. These are equal or equivalent ratios. A statement that 2 ratios are equal, such as $\frac{1}{3} = \frac{2}{6}$, is called a **proportion**.

s (cm)	1	2	3	4
P (cm)	3	6	9	12

Example 2

Find the missing term in each proportion.

a) $\frac{5}{6} = \frac{x}{18}$ **b)** $\frac{12}{20} = \frac{3}{y}$

Solution

a) $\frac{5}{6} = \frac{x}{18}$ Think: $6 \times 3 = 18$

$\quad = \frac{5 \times 3}{6 \times 3}$

$\quad = \frac{15}{18}$

So, the missing term is 15.

b) $\frac{12}{20} = \frac{3}{y}$ Think: $12 \div 4 = 3$

$\quad = \frac{12 \div 4}{20 \div 4}$

$\quad = \frac{3}{5}$

So, the missing term is 5.

Example 3

The ratio of width to height for a television screen is 4:3. What is the height of a screen that has a width of 32 cm?

Solution

Let the height of the screen be h. Write the proportion.

$4:3 = 32:h$ or $\frac{4}{3} = \frac{32}{h}$

$= \frac{4 \times 8}{3 \times 8}$ Think: $4 \times 8 = 32$

$= \frac{32}{24}$

So, the height of the screen is 24 cm.

Practice

Write 3 ratios equal to the ratio of circles to squares.

1. 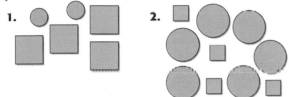 **2.**

Determine whether the ratios in each group are equivalent.

3. 2:3 and 4:9

4. 1:2 and 2:1

5. 5:8 and 15:32

6. 4:1 and 20:5

7. $\frac{12}{15}$ and $\frac{3}{5}$

8. $\frac{48}{16}$ and $\frac{3}{1}$

9. 7:2:3 and 21:6:9

10. 24:36:12 and 6:9:4

Find the unknown value in each proportion.

11. $\frac{x}{5} = \frac{4}{20}$

12. $\frac{t}{15} = \frac{3}{5}$

13. $\frac{m}{25} = \frac{1}{5}$

14. $\frac{15}{x} = \frac{45}{6}$

15. $\frac{3}{?} = \frac{15}{a}$

16. $\frac{18}{24} = \frac{m}{4}$

Find the unknown value in each proportion.

17. $x:3 = 12:18$

18. $y:5 = 15:25$

19. $2:3 = p:12$

20. $1:6 = r:24$

21. $n:4 = 3:12$

22. $4:c = 12:15$

23. $2:3 = 12:t$

24. $x:2 = 2:1$

Problems and Applications

Find the unknown values in each proportion.

25. $\frac{3}{n} = \frac{6}{14} = \frac{p}{28}$

26. $\frac{9}{15} = \frac{m}{5} = \frac{18}{y}$

27. $x:3:5 = 2:y:10$

28. $b:6:8 = 36:a:24$

29. At the Winter Olympics in Lillehammer, Norway, the ratio of Norway's medals to Germany's medals to Finland's medals was 13:12:3. If Norway, Germany, and Finland won a total of 56 medals, how many medals did each country win?

30. The ratio of the length of the human body to the length of the head is about 8:1. What is the length of the head of a person who is 168 cm tall?

31. The ratio of the length to the width of the Canadian flag is 2:1. What is the width of a 50-cm long Canadian flag?

32. The ratio of the length to the width of the Japanese flag is 3:2. What is the length of a 30-cm wide Japanese flag?

33. In Canadian federal elections, 3 out of 4 voters usually cast their votes. In a riding with 60 000 voters,

a) how many people are expected to vote?

b) how many people are not expected to vote?

c) what is the expected ratio of voters who cast their votes to voters who do not cast their votes to total number of voters?

34. Bag A contains 4 red disks and 6 blue disks. Bag B contains a total of 30 red disks and blue disks. The ratio of red to blue disks in each bag is the same. How many red disks and blue disks are in bag B?

35. Write a problem that involves a proportion. Have a classmate solve it.

85

Estimating with Ratios

Activity ❶ An Experiment with Ratios

Work with a classmate. You will need counters or cubes of 2 different colours, and a box or paper bag. The object is for one person to use ratios to estimate how many counters or cubes of one colour are in the box or bag.

1. Suppose you have red and blue counters, and a paper bag. Together, decide the total number of counters that will be put into the bag. Make it some multiple of 10 and at least 50.

2. Person A puts the agreed number of counters into the bag, without letting Person B see how many are red and how many are blue. Person A then mixes the counters in the bag.

3. Person B now takes a small handful of counters from the bag, and counts the number of blue counters and the total number of counters in this handful. Then, Person B records the results in a table, like the one shown. Person A returns the counters to the bag and mixes them.

Trial	Blue Counters	Total Counters	Ratio (Blue:Total)
1			
2			
3			
4			
5			

4. Repeat step 3 four more times.

5. Use the results in the ratio column to estimate the ratio of blue counters to the total number of counters in the bag. Use a simple ratio, with the second term less than 10.

6. Suppose there were 50 counters in the bag, and the ratio of blue counters to the total number of counters was 1:5. How many blue counters would there be?

7. Use the ratio found in step 5 to estimate the number of blue counters in the bag. Check how close the estimate is to the actual number of blue counters in the bag.

8. Switch roles and repeat the experiment.

Activity ❷ A Capture/Replacement Experiment

You will need counters of 2 different colours, say red and blue, and a box or paper bag. One person will put a number of red counters into the bag. The other person will use the blue counters and ratios to estimate how many red counters were put into the bag.

1. Person A secretly puts a number of red counters greater than 40 into the bag and records the number.

2. Person B takes some red counters from the bag and replaces the red counters with an equal number of blue counters. Person B records the number of blue counters added. Person A then mixes the counters in the bag.

3. Person B picks a small handful of counters from the bag and records the fraction of the counters that are blue.

4. Let the number of red counters in the bag at the start be n. Suppose 10 blue counters were added in step 2. Suppose also that, in step 3, 9 counters were removed, 2 of which were blue. Then,

$$\frac{\text{blue counters removed in step 3}}{\text{total counters removed in step 3}} = \frac{\text{blue counters added to the bag}}{\text{total red counters at the start}}$$

$$\frac{2}{9} = \frac{10}{n}$$

$$\frac{2 \times 5}{9 \times 5} = \frac{10}{n}$$

$$\frac{10}{45} = \frac{10}{n}$$

$$45 = n$$

There were about 45 red counters at the start.

5. Use the results from step 3 to estimate the number of red counters at the start. Check how close the estimate is to the actual number.

6. Switch roles and repeat the experiment.

7. Why is the value of n an estimate?

Activity ❸ Estimating Wildlife Populations

The capture/recapture method, used to estimate the size of wildlife populations, is like the capture/replacement experiment in Activity 2.

1. To estimate the deer population in a park, conservation officers caught and tagged 30 deer. The deer were then released. After the deer had time to mix in the park, another 20 were caught. Of these, 2 had tags.

To estimate the deer population, let n represent the number of deer in the park. Write a proportion.

$$\frac{\text{tagged deer caught}}{\text{total deer caught}} = \frac{\text{total number of tagged deer}}{\text{total number of deer in park}}$$

$$\frac{2}{20} = \frac{30}{n}$$

Find n.

2. To estimate the fish population in a lake, 250 fish were caught, tagged, and released. After sufficient time had passed for the fish to mix in the lake, 100 were caught. Five of these fish had tags. Estimate the fish population in the lake.

3. From a flock of Canada geese, 200 birds were captured and banded. After these birds had mixed with the flock, 300 birds were caught. Eight of them had been banded. Estimate the number of birds in the flock.

3.3 Draw and Read Graphs

2 km   2 km   1 km

R

1 km

H   2 km   S

Understand the Problem

Think of a Plan

Carry Out the Plan

Look Back

A graph is a useful and attractive way of displaying information. Magazines and newspapers often display information in this way. The ability to draw and interpret graphs is an important life skill.

The diagram shows the route Belen takes to get from her house, H, to the recreation centre, R.

Belen rides her bicycle at 15 km/h. She slows down to make the turns. There is a stop sign, S, 2 km from her house. Sketch a graph of Belen's speed versus the distance from her house.

1. What information are you given?

2. What are you asked to do?

Draw a horizontal axis to show Belen's distance from her house. Draw a vertical axis to show her speed. Use the map of Belen's route to sketch a graph of her speed at various distances from her house.

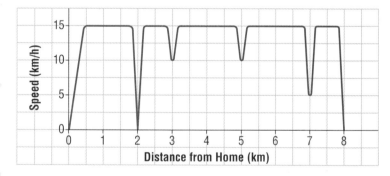

Speed (km/h) vs Distance from Home (km)

Check that the graph agrees with the given facts.

Draw a Graph	1. Draw and label the axes.
	2. Use the data to draw the graph.
	3. Check that the graph is reasonable.
Read a Graph	1. Read the necessary data from the graph.
	2. Use the data to solve the problem.
	3. Check that the answer is reasonable.

Problems and Applications

1. Karen and Isabel live near a lake. They left their house at noon to go for a walk on the beach. The graph shows their distance from home at any one time. Describe what was happening between A and B; B and C; C and D; and D and E.

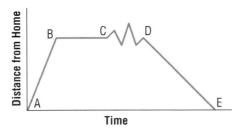

2. Sketch a graph of the number of people in your school on a school day versus the time of day.

3. Sketch a graph of the number of students in a grade 2 classroom on a school day versus the time of day. Assume that the weather is good, so the students can go out for recess.

4. Karl made 5 phone calls to his friends from a pay phone at the airport. The graph shows the friends he called, how long he talked, and the cost of each call.

a) Which calls cost the same?
b) Which calls were local?
c) Which calls were long-distance?
d) Which one of Karl's friends lived farthest from the airport?
e) Which of the people he called long-distance lived closest to the airport?

5. Mariko travels to businesses to repair photocopiers. The graph shows her distance from her office on one day. Write a story to describe Mariko's activities for the day.

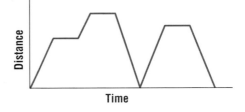

6. The diagram shows Ali's house and the grocery store. Ali drove to the store at 40 km/h along the straight sections of the road and slowed down at the corners.

Copy the following axes. Sketch a graph to show the speed of Ali's car from his house to the store.

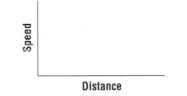

7. A playground supervisor is pushing a child on a swing. Copy the following axes. Sketch a graph of the child's height above the ground versus time for 3 complete swings.

8. Write a problem that requires a sketch of a graph. Have a classmate solve your problem.

3.4 Rate

A ratio is a comparison of numbers with the same units. The ratio 2:4 or 1:2 compares the 2-kg mass of a raven with the 4-kg mass of an eagle owl. In this 2:4 ratio, the numbers are 2 and 4, and the units are kilograms.

A **rate** is a comparison of 2 numbers with different units. A speed of sixty kilometres per hour, or 60 km/h, is a rate. It could be written as 60 km:1 h. The numbers are 60 and 1, and the units are kilometres and hours. A rate is usually written as a **unit rate**, in which the second term is 1.

Activity: Use the Information

British Columbia's Clayoquot Sound rain forest is home to a western red cedar tree that is a celebrity. It is about 1000 years old and has the special name "Hanging Garden Tree." It takes water from the soil and returns it to the atmosphere as water vapour, at about 300 L every 10 h. It is estimated that a large oak tree releases about 2100 L of water vapour every 10 h.

Inquire

1. Write a unit rate, in litres per hour, for water vapour release by the cedar tree.

2. Write a unit rate, in litres per hour, for the oak tree.

3. Write a unit rate, in litres per minute, for
a) the cedar tree   **b)** the oak tree

Example 1

Montreal's Nathalie Lambert retired from short-track speed skating as world champion in both the 1000-m and 3000-m events. She won the 1000-m event in 1 min 45.46 s. What was her average speed, to the nearest tenth of a metre per second?

Solution

Divide the distance, in metres, by the time, in seconds, to find the rate in metres per second.

Statement of fact: Nathalie skated 1000 m in
                        1 min 45.46 s or 105.46 s.

Rate for 1 s: $\dfrac{1000}{105.46} \doteq 9.5$

 $1000 \div 100 = 10$

C 1000 ÷ 105 · 46 = $\boxed{9.4822682}$

Nathalie's average speed was about 9.5 m/s.
How could you use multiplication to check the answer?

Recall the steps

Understand
the Problem

Think
of a
Plan

Carry Out
the Plan

Look Back

Rate problems can be solved using the "Rule of Three," so called because it involves only 3 steps.

Example 2

Three lemons cost $1.35. What is the cost of 7 lemons?

Solution

Use the Rule of Three.

1. Statement of fact: 3 lemons cost $1.35

2. Rate for 1: 1 lemon costs $\dfrac{\$1.35}{3} = \$0.45$ — Divide by 3 to find the cost of 1 lemon.

3. Rate for 7: 7 lemons cost $7 \times \$0.45 = \$3.15$ — Multiply by 7 to find the cost of 7 lemons.

So, 7 lemons cost $3.15.

Practice

Copy and complete each proportion.

1. $\dfrac{15}{3} = \dfrac{\blacksquare}{1}$ **2.** $\dfrac{21}{7} = \dfrac{\blacksquare}{1}$ **3.** $\dfrac{30}{5} = \dfrac{\blacksquare}{1}$

4. $\dfrac{88}{11} = \dfrac{\blacksquare}{1}$ **5.** $\dfrac{49}{7} = \dfrac{\blacksquare}{1}$ **6.** $\dfrac{80}{5} = \dfrac{\blacksquare}{1}$

Copy and complete each statement.

7. 48 bread rolls in 6 bags = ■ rolls/bag

8. 140 students on 4 buses = ■ students/bus

9. $28 for 4 hours' work = ■/h

10. 300 km in 5 h = ■ km/h

11. one dozen eggs for $1.80 = ■/egg

12. 5 pairs of socks for $25.50 = ■/pair

Write as a unit rate.

13. 1000 paper clips in 10 boxes

14. 60 m in 6 s

15. $2.40 for 6 bagels

16. $1245 for 5 plane tickets

17. 40 slices of apple pie for 20 people

18. earnings of $62.50 for 5 h

Problems and Applications

19. Sumi drove at 75 km/h. How far did she drive in 4 h?

20. Eight bus tickets cost $12. What is the cost of 5 tickets?

21. In 5 years, the average North American eats about 115 kg of fruit. How much fruit does the average North American eat in 7 years?

22. An aircraft flies 4900 km in 7 h. How far will it fly in 4.5 h?

23. The last RCMP Northern Dog Team Patrol left Old Crow in the Yukon on March 11, 1969. The team travelled 804.5 km in 26 days. What was the average rate of travel, to the nearest kilometre per day?

24. Speed is defined as $\dfrac{\text{distance}}{\text{time}}$.
a) If you increase the distance you travel in a certain length of time, do you increase or decrease your speed? Explain.
b) If you decrease the time you take to travel a certain distance, do you increase or decrease your speed? Explain.

25. a) Examine the job section of a newspaper and list 10 jobs that pay by the hour.
b) Rank the jobs from lowest paid to highest paid.
c) What kinds of jobs pay the higher wages?
d) Use your research skills to find the minimum wage for an adult and for a student.
e) Compare the minimum wages with your findings in parts a) and b).

3.5 Comparing Unit Rates and Unit Prices

Activity: Complete the Table

One way to rank hockey players is to compare the rates at which they score points or their "points per game."

The table gives the games played, goals, assists, and points for 5 players in their rookie seasons in the NHL.

Copy the table. Complete it by calculating, to the nearest hundredth, the points per game or $\frac{\text{points}}{\text{game}}$ for each player.

Player	Games Played	Goals	Assists	Points	Points Game
Joe Juneau	84	32	70	102	
Mario Lemieux	73	43	57	100	
Eric Lindros	61	41	34	75	
Joe Nieuwendyk	75	51	41	92	
Teemu Selanne	84	76	56	132	

Inquire

1. Rank the players from first to fifth according to their points per game.

2. Are the 2 players who tied still tied if you round to the nearest thousandth? If not, which one has the higher rank?

3. How does the ranking change if you rank the players by just using
a) points for the season? **b)** goals for the season?

4. What do you think is the best way to rank hockey players? Give reasons for your answer.

It is often difficult to know which size of container in a store is the best value. To make a comparison, you must read the mass or volume of the product from the containers. To help consumers decide which size is the best value, some stores show **unit prices**. These unit prices are examples of unit rates.

Example

A 250-mL jar of fruit spread costs $2.90. A 450-mL jar of the same fruit spread costs $5.40. Which size of jar is the better value?

Solution

Use a calculator to find the unit price in cents per millilitre.

Small Size
250 mL cost $2.90 or 290¢.
1 mL costs $\frac{290}{250}$
= 1.16   [C] **290** [÷] **250** [=] [1.16]
The unit price is 1.16¢/mL.

Large Size
450 mL cost $5.40 or 540¢.
1 mL costs $\frac{540}{450}$
= 1.2   [C] **540** [÷] **450** [=] [1.2]
The unit price is 1.2¢/mL.

Since 1.16 < 1.2, the 250-mL size is the better value.

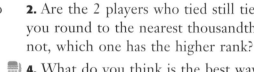

Practice

Find the unit price.

1. $4.50 for 5 pens

2. $17.80 for 10 floppy disks

3. $6.60 for 4 L of milk

4. 12 bread rolls for $2.88

5. 120 g of tuna for $2.40

6. 14 L of spring water for $12.46

Find the unit price. Round to the nearest tenth of a cent, if necessary.

7. $2.79 for 400 g of breakfast cereal

8. 24 cans of soda for $8.99

9. 10 kg of flour for $5.88

10. $2.49 for 750 g of yogurt

Find the unit rate.

11. keyboarding 520 words in 10 min

12. driving 180 km in 4 h

13. using 200 mL of toothpaste in 8 weeks

14. sharing 6 pizzas among 8 students

Problems and Applications

15. Fruit juice is advertised at $5.99 for 8 packages. Each package contains 3 boxes. What is the unit price per box, to the nearest cent?

Some stores quote unit prices in terms of 100-g or 100-mL units. Find the price of 100 g or 100 mL of each product. Round to the nearest tenth of a cent, if necessary.

16. pasta at $0.99 for 900 g

17. 1 kg of peanut butter for $3.99

18. $3.24 for 400 mL of salad dressing

19. 500 mL of olive oil for $6.49

20. Athena earned $105.00 for 12 h of cutting lawns. Brad earned $126.75 for 15 h of packing groceries. Who had the higher rate of pay and by how much?

21. In 667 games, Michael Jordan scored 21 541 points. In 1560 games, Kareem Abdul-Jabbar scored 38 387 points. Who scored points at the greater rate per game?

22. Runner Nicki Knapp became Canadian women's 800-m champion in 2 min 4.23 s. Angela Chalmers became the 1500-m champion in 4 min 15.31 s. Who ran faster?

23. At top speed, an elephant can run at about 40 km/h. The fastest human can run 100 m in about 10 s. Which can run faster, an elephant or a human?

24. If 500 people live in a village with an area of 5 km^2, the unit rate or **population density** is 100 people/km^2. Dauphin, Manitoba, has an area of 12 km^2. Swift Current, Saskatchewan, has an area of 21 km^2. When the population of Dauphin was about 9000, the population of Swift Current was about 15 000. How did the population densities of these communities compare?

Predict which is the better buy. Compare your predictions with a classmate's. Then, check your predictions by calculating which is the better buy.

25. 8 granola bars for $1.89 or 12 for $2.89

26. $13.00 for 10 bus tokens or $4.50 for 3 tokens

27. $2.19 for 48 tea bags or $3.39 for 72 tea bags

28. 1 L of orange juice for $1.99 or 1.36 L for $2.49

29. $2.75 for 283 g of curry sauce or $3.48 for 380 g

30. 200 sheets of paper for $1.98 or 500 sheets for $4.49

31. Write a problem that involves the comparison of 2 unit rates. Have a classmate solve your problem.

Computer Spreadsheets and Exchange Rates

Spreadsheets organize data in rows and columns, so that you can work with the data to produce valuable information.

Banks regularly convert from one system of money to another. The formulas in a spreadsheet can be set up to do the calculations that make these conversions.

Activity ❶

You are going to the United States, and you want to know the cost of 100 United States dollars in Canadian dollars.

1. Check a daily newspaper to compare the U.S. dollar with the Canadian dollar. What is the rate of exchange that shows the number of Canadian dollars equal to 1 U.S. dollar?

2. Use the following formula to calculate the cost of 100 U.S. dollars in Canadian dollars.

Canadian dollars = U.S. dollars × rate of exchange

Activity ❷

The following spreadsheet is set up to change foreign currencies to Canadian dollars, and Canadian dollars to foreign currencies. The column "$Cdn Per Unit" gives the exchange rates you multiply by to change from foreign currencies to Canadian dollars. You can also divide by these exchange rates to change from Canadian dollars to foreign currencies.

10 francs

	A	B	C	D	E	F	G
1	Foreign Exchange						
2							
3				Foreign to✱✱✱✱✱✱✱✱✱✱		Canadian to✱✱✱✱✱✱✱✱	
4				Canadian✱✱✱✱✱✱✱✱✱✱✱		Foreign✱✱✱✱✱✱✱✱✱✱✱✱	
5			$Cdn	Foreign	Amount	Amount	Foreign
6	Country	Currency	Per Unit	Units	in $Cdn	in $Cdn	Units
7							
8	Britain	Pound	2.0718		+D8*C8		+F8/C8
9	France	Franc	0.2427		+D9*C9		+F9/C9
10	Germany	Mark	0.8306		+D10*C10		+F10/C10
11	Japan	Yen	0.01319		+D11*C11		+F11/C11
12	Mexico	Peso	0.4132		+D12*C12		+F12/C12
13	U.S.A.	Dollar	1.3738		+D13*C13		+F13/C13

2 pesos

1. What does the formula in each of the following cells calculate?
a) E8 **b)** G10

2. Key in the computer spreadsheet, but replace the values in cells C8 to C13 with the present exchange rates.

3. Use columns D and E to change 100 units of each foreign currency to Canadian dollars.

4. Use columns F and G to change $100 Cdn to each of the foreign currencies.

Activity ❸

This spreadsheet will calculate the cost in Canadian dollars of a purchase made in a foreign currency.

	A	B	C	D	E
1	Foreign Purchases				
2					
3			$Cdn	Value of	Amount
4	Country	Currency	Per Unit	Purchase	in $Cdn
5					
6	Britain	Pound	2.0718		+D6*C6
7	France	Franc	0.2427		+D7*C7
8	Germany	Mark	0.8306		+D8*C8
9	Japan	Yen	0.01319		+D9*C9
10	Mexico	Peso	0.4132		+D10*C10
11	U.S.A.	Dollar	1.3738		+D11*C11

1. Key in the spreadsheet, but replace the values in cells C6 to C11 with the present exchange rates.

2. Find the cost of each of the following purchases in Canadian dollars.
a) a British racing bicycle that costs 2000 pounds
b) a German car that costs 50 000 marks
c) a Japanese computer that costs 95 000 yen
d) a Mexican mango that costs 2 pesos
e) a French croissant that costs 10 francs
f) a ball glove that costs 79.50 U.S. dollars

79.50 U.S. dollars

2000 pounds

95

Enlargements and Reductions

Activity ❶ Enlargements and Reductions

1. Draw a grid of squares with sides twice as long as in the grid below.

2. Make an enlargement of the whale by copying the contents of each square in the grid below into corresponding squares in the grid from step 1.

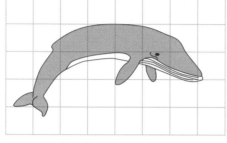

3. Repeat steps 1 and 2 for the crab and the bird, below.

4. Make a reduction of the crab and the bird by using a grid of squares whose side lengths are half as long as in the given grid.

5. a) Draw a grid of 3 cm × 3 cm squares over a picture from a magazine or a newspaper.

b) Draw a grid with 1 cm × 1 cm squares. Use this grid to make a reduction of your picture.

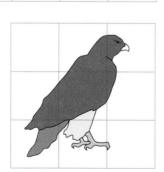

Activity ❷ Scale Factors

Triangles ABC and A′B′C′ have the same shape, but their side lengths are different. The ratio of the side lengths of △A′B′C′ to those of △ABC is 2:1.

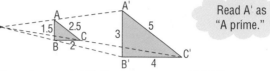

Read A′ as "A prime."

To enlarge △ABC to create △A′B′C′, we multiply each side length in △ABC by 2. We say that the **scale factor** for the enlargement is 2 and that △A′B′C′ is the **image** of the original figure, △ABC.

1.

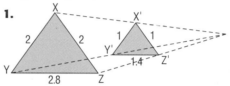

If we create △X′Y′Z′ by reducing △XYZ,
a) which triangle is the original figure?
b) which triangle is the image?
c) by what number is each side length in the original figure multiplied to give the image?
d) what is the scale factor for the reduction?

2. Draw rectangle ABCD on grid paper and use it as the original figure for each of the following.

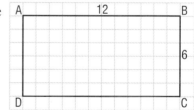

a) Draw an image rectangle using a scale factor of $\frac{1}{3}$. Is the image an enlargement or a reduction of the original figure?
b) Draw an image rectangle using a scale factor of $\frac{3}{2}$. Is the image an enlargement or a reduction of the original figure?
c) For each image you drew, describe how the image is like rectangle ABCD and how the image is different from rectangle ABCD. Compare your descriptions with a classmate's.

Activity ❸ A Viking Statue

On the Western shore of Lake Winnipeg, at Gimli, stands a large Viking statue. It is 4.5 m high and is a symbol of Gimli's Scandinavian heritage.

1. The photograph is a reduction image of the statue. Measure the height of the statue in the photograph and estimate the scale factor for the reduction. Compare your estimate with a classmate's.

2. The statue is an enlargement image of a man. Assume that the average height of a man is about 180 cm. What is the scale factor of the enlargement?

Activity ❹ Huskie the Muskie

Kenora, Ontario, is the home of Huskie the Muskie. This 13-m high statue of a muskellunge fish was constructed to symbolize Kenora's sports fishery.

1. A muskellunge fish is about 65 cm long. What scale factor was used to construct the statue?

2. a) The photograph shows a reduction image of the statue. Measure the length of the fish in the photograph and determine the scale factor for the reduction. Compare your result with a classmate's.

b) To enlarge the photograph of the fish to the same height as the statue, what scale factor would you use?

3. Use your scale factor from question 2 b) to estimate the following measures on the statue. Compare your results with a classmate's.
a) the width of the tail
b) the diameter of the eye

Activity ❺ Other Applications

1. Some photographs show enlargements, while other photographs show reductions. Give an example of each use of photographs.

2. List other examples of enlargements and reductions you see in everyday life. Compare your list with a classmate's.

3.6 Scale Drawings

When it is impossible to draw an object to its actual size, we use a **scale drawing**. Blueprints, maps, and floor plans are examples of scale drawings.

Every scale drawing has a **scale**, which is a ratio of the length of the drawing to the actual length of the real object. If an object measures 2 cm and the scale is 1:1000, the actual length of the object is 1000×2 cm or 2000 cm or 20 m.

Activity: Measure the Drawings

Inquire

1. Copy the table. Complete the first row by using the scale of each drawing to calculate the actual height of each object, in metres.

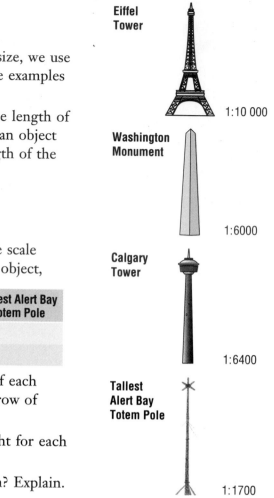

Eiffel Tower
1:10 000

Washington Monument
1:6000

Calgary Tower
1:6400

Tallest Alert Bay Totem Pole
1:1700

	Eiffel Tower	Washington Monument	Calgary Tower	Tallest Alert Bay Totem Pole
Calculated Height (m)				
Correct Height (m)				

2. Use your research skills to find the correct height of each structure, in metres. Record the values in the second row of the table.

3. Compare the calculated height and the correct height for each object.

4. Is a scale drawing of any use if the scale is not given? Explain.

Example

The estuarine or saltwater crocodile from South Asia and Northern Australia is the world's largest crocodile. The scale is 1:60. What is the actual length of the crocodile, in metres?

Solution

The scale is 1:60. This means that 1 cm on the drawing represents 60 cm on the crocodile.
Let l represent the actual length of the crocodile.

1 cm on drawing $\longrightarrow \dfrac{1}{60} = \dfrac{10}{l} \longleftarrow$ length of drawing
60 cm actual $\longrightarrow$ $\longleftarrow$ actual length of crocodile

$$\frac{1}{60} = \frac{1 \times 10}{60 \times 10}$$
$$= \frac{10}{600}$$
$$l = 600$$

The crocodile is 600 cm or 6 m long.

— 10 cm —

98

Practice

Write each ratio in lowest terms.

1. 4:12 **2.** 5:15 **3.** 10:100

4. 10:1000 **5.** 40:4 **6.** 20:2

7. 0.5:50 **8.** 0.1:1 **9.** 10:0.5

Write each scale as a ratio in lowest terms.

10. 1 cm represents 25 cm

11. 1 cm represents 1 m

12. 1 cm represents 3 m

13. 5 cm represent 50 m

14. 1 cm represents 100 km

15. 2 cm represent 250 km

16. 1 cm represents 0.5 cm

17. 1 cm represents 2 mm

Problems and Applications

18. Find the actual height of the ostrich, in metres.

2.5 cm

Scale 1:100

19. Find the actual length of the beluga whale, in metres.

Scale 1:70

6 cm

20. Find the actual length of the housefly, in millimetres.

Scale 8:1

4.8 cm

21. A Pacific leatherback turtle is about 2 m long. What is the length, in centimetres, of a drawing with a scale of 1:50?

22. A bee hummingbird's egg is 11 mm long. What is the length, in centimetres, of a drawing with a scale of 4:1?

23. Vancouver's Harbour Centre building is 130 m tall. If the height of a drawing is 6.5 cm, what is the scale?

24. The volleyball court is drawn to a scale of 1:300. Use the drawing to determine these lengths, in metres.
a) the length of the court, excluding the service areas
b) the distance between the attack lines
c) the dimensions of each service area
d) the perimeter of the court, excluding the service areas
e) the perimeter of the court, including the service areas

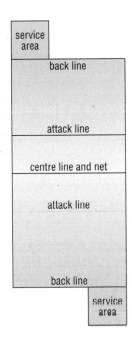

service area

back line

attack line

centre line and net

attack line

back line

service area

25. If necessary, use your research skills to determine the height of each of the following. Decide on a suitable scale you would use to make a drawing of each in your notebook. Compare your scales with a classmate's.
a) Ottawa's Peace Tower
b) Empire State Building
c) your school
d) yourself

3.7 Maps and Scales

A map is a scale drawing that represents a part of the Earth. The scale of the map is the ratio of a distance on the map to the actual distance on the Earth.

Activity:
Interpret the Map

The map of Vancouver Island is drawn to a scale of 1:1 500 000.

Measure the straight-line distance from Nanaimo to Victoria.

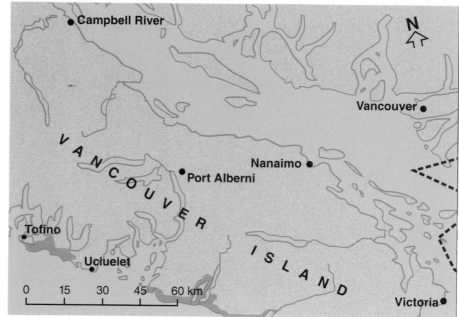

Inquire

1. Use the scale to calculate the actual distance, in kilometres, from Nanaimo to Victoria.

2. The scale is shown in 2 different ways. Show that they have the same meaning.

3. If the scale was 1:2 500 000, how could you show it in another way?

Example

Use the map to find the approximate distance, in kilometres, from Port Alberni to Victoria.

Solution

The distance from Port Alberni to Victoria on the map is about 7.8 cm. On the map, 1 cm represents 15 km on the Earth. Let d represent the distance from Port Alberni to Victoria.
Set up and solve a proportion.

1 cm on map ⟶ $\dfrac{1}{15} = \dfrac{7.8}{d}$ ⟵ 7.8 cm on the map
15 km actual ⟶   ⟵ actual distance from Port Alberni to Victoria

$$= \frac{1 \times 7.8}{15 \times 7.8}$$

$$= \frac{7.8}{117}$$

$$d = 117$$

EST: $15 \times 8 = 120$

The distance from Port Alberni to Victoria is about 117 km.

Practice

Represent each of the following scales in another way.

1. 1:500 000

2. 1:1 000 000

3.

```
0      100    200   300 km
├───────┼──────┼──────┤
```

4.

```
0       25      50    75 km
├───────┼──────┼──────┤
```

5. On a map with a scale of 1:1 500 000, what actual distance, in kilometres, is represented by 3 cm? 4.8 cm?

6. On a map with a scale of 1:30 000 000, what distance, in centimetres, represents an actual distance of 1500 km?

Problems and Applications

7. On a map, the distance from Montreal to Berlin is 7.5 cm. The scale is 1:80 000 000. Calculate the actual distance, in kilometres, from Montreal to Berlin.

8. Calgary is 520 km from Saskatoon. How far apart are they on a map with a scale of 1:10 000 000?

9. Copy the chart. Use the map of Vancouver Island on the opposite page to complete it.

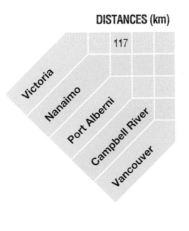

DISTANCES (km)

10. Ostia was an ancient Roman port. When archaeologists excavated the ruins, they found a complex of apartments, shops, and gardens, called the "Garden Houses." A plan of the ground floor is shown below.

The complex included 2 large, rectangular buildings inside a courtyard. Each building had 4 apartments on the ground floor. Around the courtyard were other buildings, containing shops and more apartments. What were the approximate dimensions, in metres, of

a) the courtyard?

b) each building inside the courtyard?

c) each apartment on the ground floor of these buildings?

11. Write a problem based on the plan of the Garden Houses. Have a classmate solve your problem.

From "A Roman Apartment Complex," by Donald J. Watts and Carol Martin Watts. Copyright © 1986 by Scientific American, Inc. All rights reserved.

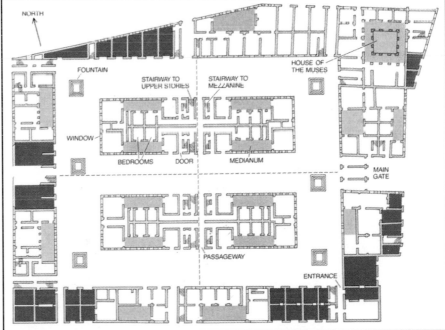

Scale 1:1300

The Footprints at Laetoli

About 3.7 million years ago, a volcano erupted near Laetoli in Tanzania. The volcano left ash deposits on the ground. Mammals and birds walked on the ash and left their footprints. Then, it rained. Because the ash had lime in it, the rain hardened it. More ash from the volcano then covered the ground and protected the footprints from erosion.

The scale diagram below shows some of the footprints discovered by archaeologists in the 1980s.

Activity ❶ Interpreting the Diagram

1. What are the actual length and width of one of the footprints of the elephant?

2. What are the actual length and width of the largest footprint of the rhinoceros?

3. a) What is the actual length of the longest track left by the giraffe?

b) What might have caused the giraffe to make the four long tracks?

4. Make an actual-size drawing of a hyena footprint.

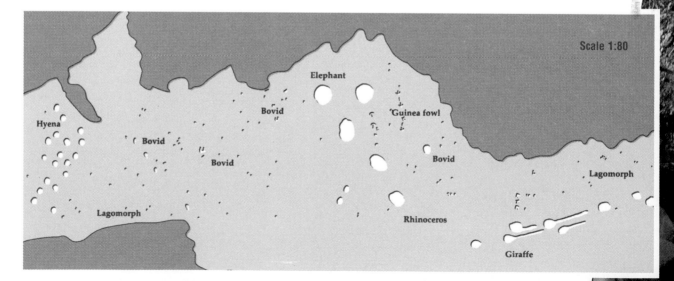

Activity ❷ Using Your Research Skills

1. Find out what a guinea fowl is.

2. What is a lagomorph?

3. Locate Tanzania on a map.

4. Use an almanac or encyclopedia to find some interesting data about Tanzania. Share your findings with your classmates.

103

3.8 Use a Diagram

In some cases, drawing a diagram will help you to solve a problem. This problem solving strategy is used in some careers. Clothing designers start their creations with diagrams. Architects also use diagrams, and so do city planners.

Susan is responsible for setting up 6 refreshment stations for the runners in a marathon. The stations are on one street and are two blocks apart. There are two helpers at each station.

Susan wants to put the main supply of drinks at one of the stations. She wants the total distance walked by the helpers to the main supply to be as short as possible. Where should she put the main supply?

Understand the Problem

1. What information are you given?

2. What are you asked to find?

3. Do you need an exact or approximate answer?

Think of a Plan

Draw a diagram of the 6 stations. Choose a location for the main supply at one of the stations.

Carry Out the Plan

Calculate the distance from the main supply to each of the other stations and find the sum. Choose other locations for the main supply until you find the smallest sum.

```
      2          2          2          2          2
 •─────────•─────────•─────────•─────────•─────────•
 A         B         C         D         E         F
```

Location of Main Supply	Distance to Other Stations	Total Distance
C	A 4; B 2; D 2; E 4; F 6	18
D	A 6; B 4; C 2; E 2; F 4	18
A	B 2; C 4; D 6; E 8; F 10	30
F	A 10; B 8; C 6; D 4; E 2	30
B	A 2; C 2; D 4; E 6; F 8	22
E	A 8; B 6; C 4; D 2; F 2	22

Locations C and D give the smallest sum.
Susan can put the main supply at either of the middle stations.

Look Back

Were all the calculations necessary?
Does the answer seem reasonable?

> **Use a Diagram**
> 1. Draw a diagram to represent the situation.
> 2. Use the diagram to solve the problem.
> 3. Check that the answer is reasonable.

Problems and Applications

1. Four identical squares can be made with 16 toothpicks.

The following diagrams show how 4 identical squares can be made with only 13 toothpicks.

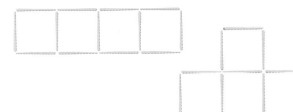

a) What is the smallest number of toothpicks needed to make 4 identical squares?
5 identical squares?

b) What is the maximum number of identical squares you can make with 22 toothpicks?

2. On a sightseeing tour, a bus left the hotel and went 3 blocks due south, 8 blocks due east, 7 blocks due north, 2 blocks due west, and 4 blocks due south. Where was the bus in relation to the hotel?

3. An elevator started on the ground floor, rose 12 floors, rose 3 more floors, descended 5 floors, descended 2 floors, rose 4 floors, and descended 6 floors. Where was the elevator in relation to the ground floor?

4. How many diagonals does a regular hexagon have?

5. Norah needed to fence an 8 m by 12 m yard. She wanted fence posts to be 2 m apart, with a post in each corner. How many posts did she need?

6. Four sticks measure 5 cm, 8 cm, 9 cm, and 13 cm. How many triangles can you make if each triangle has 3 of the sticks as sides?

7. How many isosceles triangles can you draw with a perimeter of 14 cm or less if the lengths of the sides must be whole numbers of centimetres?

8. Mike has 3 containers. One holds 3 L of water, another 5 L, and the third 8 L. How can he use the containers to measure 4 L of water?

9. How can you use 3 sticks that measure 6 cm, 10 cm, and 12 cm to mark off a distance of 8 cm?

10. Each of the 6 teams in a baseball league plays every other team 6 times. How many games are played?

11. How many different-sized squares can you make on a 4-by-4 geoboard?

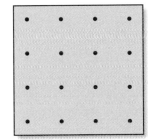

12. A soccer team has 3 different tops, red, white, and blue. There are 2 different shorts, red and blue, and 2 different socks, red and blue. How many different uniforms can the team wear?

13. As the crow flies, the distance from Appletown to Beantown is 40 km. The distance from Appletown to Corntown is 35 km and the distance from Appletown to Dairytown is 36 km. Beantown is 40 km from Corntown and 60 km from Dairytown. Corntown is 24 km from Dairytown. Draw a map that shows the possible locations of the 4 towns. Compare your map with your classmates'.

14. Write a problem that can be solved by drawing a diagram. Have a classmate solve your problem.

Review

Find the unknown value in each proportion.

1. $\dfrac{18}{y} = \dfrac{6}{5}$ 2. $\dfrac{n}{50} = \dfrac{7}{10}$

3. $\dfrac{4}{3} = \dfrac{a}{9}$ 4. $\dfrac{55}{44} = \dfrac{5}{z}$

5. $m{:}2 = 5{:}10$ 6. $4{:}x = 12{:}15$

7. $8{:}7 = 32{:}t$ 8. $40{:}25 = s{:}5$

Find the unknown values in each proportion.

9. $\dfrac{21}{a} = \dfrac{27}{9} = \dfrac{b}{1}$ 10. $\dfrac{n}{16} = \dfrac{2}{m} = \dfrac{4}{8}$

11. $\dfrac{3}{w} = \dfrac{1}{12} = \dfrac{5}{x}$ 12. $100{:}200{:}700 = 2{:}p{:}q$

13. $3{:}x{:}2 = 15{:}35{:}y$ 14. $g{:}45{:}h = 7{:}15{:}2$

Write two ratios equivalent to each ratio.

15. $9{:}15$ 16. $5{:}10{:}25$

17. The ratio of the top speed of a lion to the top speed of a hyena is 5:4. A lion's top speed is 80 km/h. What is a hyena's top speed?

18. At the Summer Olympics in Barcelona, Spain, the ratio of Canada's silver medals to Romania's silver medals was 2:3. Canada and Romania together won 10 silver medals. How many silver medals did Romania win?

19. Canada's Mark Tewksbury broke the Olympic 100-m backstroke record in 53.98 s. What was his average speed, to the nearest hundredth of a metre per second?

20. A car travels 315 km in 3 h. How far would you expect it to travel in 5 h?

21. The ratio of the number of wet days per year in Fredericton, New Brunswick, to the number in Saskatoon, Saskatchewan, to the number in Winnipeg, Manitoba, is 13:18:20. Winnipeg has 120 wet days per year. Find the number of wet days per year in
a) Fredericton   b) Saskatoon

22. Don earned $166.50 for 18 h of window washing. Whitney earned $230.40 for 24 h of painting. Who had the higher rate of pay?

23. The 15th Commonwealth Games were held in Victoria, British Columbia. Andrea Nugent of Calgary, Alberta, won a silver medal in the women's 50-m freestyle swimming with a time of 26.24 s. Express Andrea's average speed to
a) the nearest tenth of a metre per second
b) the nearest metre per minute

Calculate the unit price. Round to the nearest tenth of a cent, if necessary.

24. 10 apples for $5.50

25. $4.50 for 12 sheets of Bristol board

26. 12 m of telephone cable for $4.20

27. $4.98 for 200 vitamin C tablets

Determine the price per 100 g. Round to the nearest tenth of a cent.

28. 550 g of bread for $1.69

29. $3.49 for 2 kg of oranges

Which is the better buy?

30. 2 kg of potatoes for $1.28 or 5 kg for $2.99

31. 3 bagels for $1.29 or 8 bagels for $2.99

32. Measure the height of the diagram of the giraffe. The scale is 1:150. What is the giraffe's actual height, in metres?

33. Use the map of Vancouver Island on page 100 to find these distances, in kilometres.
a) Victoria to Tofino
b) Ucluelet to Campbell River

34. The scale of a drawing of a building is 1:2500. If the building is 100 m tall, what is the height of the drawing, in centimetres?

35. The distance between Whitehorse and Saskatoon is about 2600 km. The distance between these two locations on a map is 13 cm. Write the scale of the map in two ways.

36. Fran is charging $100 to mow the lawns and weed the gardens outside an apartment building. How can she make her rate of pay as high as possible?

37. Density is a unit rate defined as the mass of a material divided by its volume. The table shows the masses and volumes of different quantities of materials.

Material	Mass (g)	Volume (cm³)	Density (g/cm³)
Aluminum	41.85	15.5	
Steel	192.5	25	
Turpentine	34.4	40	
Western Red Cedar	275.5	725	

a) Copy the table and complete it by finding the density of each material.
b) Rank the materials from lowest density to highest density.

38. Three pieces of wood measure 4 cm, 7 cm, and 9 cm. Describe 2 ways you could use these sticks to measure a length of 15 cm.

39. The number in each circle is the average of the numbers in the squares connected to it. Find the number in each square.

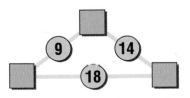

Group Decision Making
The Cannonball Run

The Cannonball Run is a famous car rally, which begins and ends in Detroit, Michigan. The course goes through these cities in this order.

Detroit, Michigan	→ Laredo, Texas
Indianapolis, Indiana	Jackson, Mississippi
Denver, Colorado	Atlanta, Georgia
Las Vegas, Nevada	Darien, Connecticut
Monterey, California	Mansfield, Ohio
Los Angeles, California	Detroit, Michigan
Tucson, Arizona ─────┘	

1. Work in home groups. Draw a map of the Cannonball Run, using the shortest possible route between cities. Mark the highway numbers on the map.

1 2 3 4	1 2 3 4	1 2 3 4

Home Groups

1 2 3 4	1 2 3 4	1 2 3 4

2. Determine the driving distance from Detroit to Indianapolis, from Indianapolis to Denver, and so on. Mark the distances on the map.

3. Find the total driving distance for the Cannonball Run.

4. The speed limit in the rally is 80 km/h. About how many hours would the rally take to complete at this speed?

5. If the rally started at noon on a Saturday, and vehicles were on the road 24 h/day, on what day and at what time would the rally finish?

6. Compare your map and driving times with those of other groups. Account for any differences.

7. Evaluate how effectively the members of your group worked together.

Chapter Check

1. Write 3 ratios equivalent to 6:4.

Find the unknown value in each of the following proportions.

2. $\dfrac{18}{x} = \dfrac{9}{11}$ **3.** $\dfrac{x}{3} = \dfrac{10}{6}$

4. $\dfrac{8}{3} = \dfrac{24}{x}$ **5.** $\dfrac{28}{16} = \dfrac{x}{4}$

Find the missing values in each proportion.

6. $5:15:10 = 25:a:b$ **7.** $m:12:8 = 16:d:32$

8. $\dfrac{4}{7} = \dfrac{p}{70} = \dfrac{400}{q}$ **9.** $\dfrac{30}{k} = \dfrac{15}{3} = \dfrac{w}{2}$

10. The Sharpshooters basketball team won 2 out of every 3 games they played in a season. They played 45 games. How many did they win?

11. Runner Camille Noel became Canadian women's 400-m champion in a time of 52.98 s. What was her average speed, to the nearest hundredth of a metre per second?

12. The ratio of cities in New Brunswick to cities in Saskatchewan to cities in Alberta is 3:6:8. There are 12 cities in Saskatchewan. How many cities are there in
a) New Brunswick?   **b)** Alberta?

13. Darcy ran 8 laps of the track in 12 min. Orly ran 5 laps of the same track in 8 min. Who ran faster?

14. If 250 g of fruit spread cost $3.75, what is the unit price?

15. If 5 apples cost $1.95, how much do 8 apples cost?

16. A case of 24 fruit drinks costs $6.99. A 6-pack of the same fruit drinks costs $1.99. Which is the better buy?

17. The height of a blue heron is 96 cm. What is the height of a drawing if the scale is 1:16?

18. Halifax is 880 km from St. John's. If these 2 cities are 4.4 cm apart on a map, what is the scale? Express your answer as a ratio in lowest terms.

19. The Calgary Tower Building is about 190 m tall. If a model of the building is 9.5 cm tall, what is the scale of the model?

Reprinted with permission—The Toronto Star Syndicate
Copyright: Tribune Media Services.

Using the Strategies

1. As you move from the top rung to the bottom rung on this ladder, the length of each rung increases by the same amount.

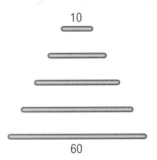

Find the lengths of the middle 3 rungs.

2. Here are 6 towns. What is the smallest number of roads that must be built between towns, so that you can start at any town and get to any other town? Assume that 1 road cannot connect more than 2 towns and that roads cannot cross.

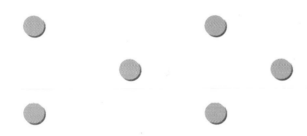

3. Joshua takes the 08:00 bus from Beeton to Carlton. The trip takes 6 h. Buses leave every hour on the hour from Carlton to Beeton. How many buses travelling from Carlton to Beeton will Joshua see on the trip?

4. You must be at work by 08:15. You take 35 min to get there on the bus. Before you leave, you need 20 min to wash and get dressed. You need 25 min to make and eat your breakfast. You have to walk the dog for 15 min before you go. For what time should you set your alarm?

5. Cut out a square and label it as shown.

What figure is formed when you make each of the following folds?
a) W is folded onto Z.
b) W is folded onto Y.
c) W is folded onto Z, then Z is folded onto Y.
d) W is folded onto Y, then Z is folded onto X.

6. The driving distance from Winnipeg to Thunder Bay is 10 km less than from Thunder Bay to Sault Ste. Marie. The driving distance from Thunder Bay to Sault Ste. Marie is 86 km less than from Sault Ste. Marie to Ottawa. The total driving distance from Winnipeg through Thunder Bay and Sault Ste. Marie to Ottawa is 2218 km. What is the driving distance from Sault Ste. Marie to Ottawa?

7. Sketch a graph of the distance you travel versus time on a normal school day, starting when you leave home for school and ending when you get back home.

DATA BANK

1. Jan lives in Windsor, Ontario. She called her friend in Sydney, Australia, at 22:00 on December 31 to wish her a happy New Year. What was the time and date in Sydney when Jan called?

2. If the mouth of the Mackenzie River were at Vancouver, and the river ran along the Canada–U.S. border, where would the river begin?

CHAPTER 4

Percent

The flags are used as international signals on ships. Each flag has a different meaning. For example, flag E means: "I am altering my course to starboard." Flag V means: "I require assistance."

All the flags are rectangles, except for flag A and flag B.

1. What fraction of the flags have 2 colours? 3 colours?

2. What colour is used the most? What fraction of the flags have this colour?

3. What colour is used the least? What fraction of the flags have this colour?

4. The length of each flag is greater than the width. There are no squares on the flags. Which flag(s) appear to have squares?

5. List all the geometric shapes you can find on the flags.

6. Which flags have triangles of the same size and shape on them?

7. Draw a set of flags to spell the name of your favourite singer or group.

Working with Squares

Activity ❶ Diagonals of Squares

When a square is drawn on a grid, the diagonals of the square cut through the grid squares. In a 2-by-2 square, each small square is cut by 1 diagonal.

In a 3-by-3 square, 4 small squares are cut by 1 diagonal, 1 small square is cut by 2 diagonals, and 4 small squares are not cut by a diagonal.

1. For 4-by-4 to 7-by-7 squares, find the number of small squares cut by 1 diagonal and 2 diagonals, and the number not cut by a diagonal. Copy and complete the table.

Side Length of Square	Number of Small Squares		
	Cut by 1 Diagonal	Cut by 2 Diagonals	Not Cut by a Diagonal
2	4	0	0
3	4	1	4
4			
5			
6			
7			

2. Describe the patterns you see in the numbers of small squares cut by 1 diagonal and 2 diagonals, and the number of small squares not cut by a diagonal.

3. Use the pattern to predict the next three lines of the table.

4. a) For a 10-by-10 square, what fraction of the small squares are cut by 1 diagonal?
b) For a 10-by-10 square, what fraction of the small squares are not cut by a diagonal?
c) Write the fractions from parts a) and b) in lowest terms.

Activity ❷ Areas of Squares on a Grid

1. The 3-by-3 square has an area of 9 square units. The red square has an area of 5 square units. Its area is $\frac{5}{9}$ of the area of the large square.

There are 3 other different-sized squares you can draw that have intersection points of the grid as vertices, are smaller than the large square, and have whole-number areas. Draw them and express the area of each as a fraction of the area of the large square.

2. The 4-by-4 square has an area of 16 square units. The red square has an area of 2 square units. Its area is $\frac{1}{8}$ of the area of the large square.

There are 6 other different-sized squares you can draw that have intersection points of the grid as vertices, are smaller than the large square, and have whole-number areas. Draw them and express the area of each as a fraction of the area of the large square.

3. The 5-by-5 square has an area of 25 square units.

There are 10 different-sized squares you can draw that have intersection points of the grid as vertices, are smaller than the large square, and have whole-number areas. Draw them and express the area of each as a fraction of the area of the large square. Then, express each fraction as a percent.

Warm Up

Estimate, then calculate.

1. $4.80 + $1.65 + $2.99
2. $64.20 + $9.40 + $102.25
3. $6.00 + $17.20 + $1114.28 + $0.72
4. $5.50 + $359.60 + $61.75 + $1.95

Estimate, then calculate.

5. $64.77 − $25.00
6. $46.25 − $18.35
7. $224.00 − $69.95
8. $75.89 − $36.05

Round to the nearest dollar.

9. $6332.49
10. $719.61
11. $99.51
12. $354.19

Write as a decimal.

13. twenty-nine thousandths
14. one hundred sixteen and thirty-two hundredths
15. one hundred nine and nine hundredths
16. forty-one and forty-one hundredths

Estimate, then calculate.

17. 6.6×4
18. 60.4×12
19. 7.5×3.5

Calculate, then round each answer to the nearest hundredth.

20. $1 \div 3$
21. $63.9 \div 7$
22. $8.2 \div 0.09$

Write as a decimal, then as a fraction in lowest terms.

23. four tenths
24. twenty-five hundredths
25. two hundred fifty thousandths
26. five twenty fifths

Write in lowest terms. Then, write as a percent.

27. $\frac{3}{6}$
28. $\frac{32}{50}$
29. $\frac{75}{250}$
30. $\frac{12}{8}$
31. $\frac{28}{80}$
32. $\frac{20}{16}$

Mental Math

Calculate.

1. 16×10
2. $16 \div 10$
3. 1.6×100
4. $1.6 \div 100$
5. 126×100
6. $126 \div 100$
7. 0.82×10
8. $0.82 \div 10$

Write as a decimal.

9. $\frac{6}{10}$
10. $\frac{2}{25}$
11. $\frac{5}{100}$
12. $\frac{8}{16}$
13. $\frac{4}{50}$
14. $\frac{7}{20}$
15. $\frac{3}{12}$
16. $\frac{150}{100}$
17. $\frac{4}{5}$

Add.

18. $\frac{1}{2} + \frac{2}{4}$
19. $\frac{1}{2} + \frac{3}{4}$
20. $\frac{1}{5} + \frac{2}{10}$
21. $\frac{1}{4} + \frac{3}{8}$
22. $\frac{1}{2} + \frac{1}{3}$
23. $\frac{1}{6} + \frac{1}{3}$

Calculate.

24. $\frac{7}{10} - \frac{2}{5}$
25. $\frac{30}{100} - \frac{3}{10}$
26. $\frac{30}{50} - \frac{14}{25}$
27. $\frac{75}{100} - \frac{10}{20}$
28. $\frac{3}{5} - \frac{1}{2}$
29. $\frac{4}{3} - \frac{1}{6}$

Multiply

30. $4 \times \frac{1}{2}$
31. $6 \times \frac{1}{3}$
32. $10 \times \frac{1}{5}$
33. $12 \times \frac{1}{4}$
34. $18 \times \frac{1}{6}$
35. $48 \times \frac{1}{8}$

Divide.

36. $1 \div \frac{1}{2}$
37. $\frac{1}{2} \div \frac{1}{2}$
38. $6 \div \frac{1}{2}$
39. $\frac{1}{2} \div \frac{1}{4}$
40. $\frac{2}{3} \div \frac{1}{6}$
41. $3 \div \frac{1}{3}$

4.1 Use a Formula

A formula is an equation that shows how quantities are related. For example, the formula for calculating the perimeter of a rectangle is $P = 2 \times (l + w)$.

Many problems can be solved using formulas.

A person's shoe size depends on the length of the foot. In North America, the sizes of some shoes are given by these 2 formulas.
For males: $S = 1.2 \times f - 22.6$
For females: $S = 1.2 \times f - 20.6$
where S is the shoe size, and f is the length of the foot in centimetres.
The length of one of Bob's feet is 28 cm. The length of one of Susan's feet is 24 cm. What are their shoe sizes?

Understand the Problem

1. What information are you given?

2. What are you asked to find?

3. Do you need an exact or approximate answer?

Think of a Plan

For Bob, use the formula $S = 1.2 \times f - 22.6$ and substitute 28 for f.
For Susan, use the formula $S = 1.2 \times f - 20.6$ and substitute 24 for f.
Use the order of operations to find each value of S.

For Bob

$S = 1.2 \times f - 22.6$
$\quad = 1.2 \times 28 - 22.6$
$\quad = 33.6 - 22.6$
$\quad = 11$

For Susan

$S = 1.2 \times f - 20.6$
$\quad = 1.2 \times 24 - 20.6$
$\quad = 28.8 - 20.6$
$\quad = 8.2$

Carry Out the Plan

Bob's shoe size is 11.
Susan's shoe size is 8.

Look Back

Do the answers seem reasonable?
How could you work backward to check the answers?

Use a Formula	1. Write the formula.
	2. Replace the letters by their values, making sure that you use the proper units.
	3. Complete the calculation.
	4. Check that your answer is reasonable.

Problems and Applications

1. a) The tallest human on record was an American called Robert Wadlow (1918–1940). His feet were about 47 cm long. Use the formula $S = 1.2 \times f - 22.6$ to calculate his shoe size. Round your answer to the nearest whole number.

b) Does one of the formulas on the opposite page work for your shoe size?

2. The formula that relates distance, time, and speed is
$$D = s \times t$$
where D is the distance travelled in kilometres, s is the speed in kilometres per hour, and t is the time in hours. Calculate the distance travelled in each car journey.

a) 3 h at 55 km/h

b) 2.5 h at 80 km/h

3. The formula gives the time, t seconds, an object takes to fall from a height of h metres.
$$t = \sqrt{\frac{h}{4.9}}$$

Calculate the time it takes an object to fall from each of these heights.

a) 19.6 m   **b)** 122.5 m

c) the top of the 92-m high Peace Tower on Canada's Parliament Buildings. Round this answer to the nearest second.

4. The formula can be used to find a dog's age in "dog years," y, from its age in human years, n.
$$y = 21 + 4 \times (n - 1)$$
Find a dog's age in dog years when the dog has the following ages in human years.

a) 1   **b)** 6   **c)** 10   **d)** 15

5. The formula for determining the number of days between water changes in a hot tub is
$$d = \frac{a}{10 \times u}$$
where d is the number of days, a is the volume of water in litres, and u is the average number of people who use the tub each day. If the tub holds 1500 L of water, and an average of 25 people use the tub each day, how many days are there between water changes?

6. Bowling handicaps make competitions fairer among bowlers with different averages. A bowler's handicap is added to the bowler's score in each game. One formula used to calculate a handicap is
$$H = 0.8 \times (200 - a)$$
where H is the bowler's handicap, and a is the bowler's average.

a) Copy the table and calculate each bowler's handicap. Round each answer to the nearest whole number, if necessary.

Bowler	Average	Handicap
Sarah	180	
Paul	155	
Kim	147	
Chung	174	

b) If a bowler's handicap is 44, what is the bowler's average? Describe your method and compare it with a classmate's.

7. State 2 careers in which formulas are used to solve problems. List all the careers suggested by members of your group.

8. Find 4 formulas used to calculate sports statistics. Write the formulas and identify the letters used in each. Write a problem using each formula. Have a classmate solve your problems.

4.2 Percent of a Number

Recall that "of" means multiply.

So, $\frac{1}{2}$ of $8 = \frac{1}{2} \times 8$ or 4, and 50% of $8 = 0.5 \times 8$ or 4.

Activity: Calculate the Costs

Feature films can cost anywhere from $500 000 to hundreds of millions of dollars to make. The table gives the motion picture industry's typical breakdown of expenses for a low-budget movie.

Copy the table. Complete it by calculating the cost of each item for a $3 000 000 movie.

Component	Percent	Cost ($)
Screenplay, Producer, Director	10%	
Cast	25%	
Studio Overhead	20%	
Crew and Materials	40%	
Unknowns	5%	

Inquire

1. What is the cost of each component?

2. How would you use addition to check your calculations?

3. Why is there an "unknowns" component when making movies?

Example

Songwriters and song publishers earn royalties when their songs are played on the radio. Radio stations pay 3.25% of their advertising income to a performing rights association. The association pays the writers and publishers. If the money received from advertisers by Canadian radio stations is about $960 000 000 a year, how much does the association receive?

Solution

To find the percent of a number, write the percent as a decimal and then multiply by the number.

$3.25\% = \frac{3.25}{100}$

$= 0.0325$

3.25% of $\$960\ 000\ 000 = 0.0325 \times \$960\ 000\ 000$

$= \$31\ 200\ 000$

The association receives $31 200 000.

C 0 · 0325 × 960 000 000

= 31200000.

EST $0.03 \times 1\ 000\ 000\ 000 = 30\ 000\ 000$

Practice

Calculate.

1. 50% of 30

2. 25% of 40

3. 15% of 60

4. 20% of 25

5. 30% of 50

6. 110% of 500

Estimate, then calculate.

7. 12% of 25

8. 14% of 22

9. 8% of 140

10. 95% of 70

11. 255% of 50

12. 14% of 85

Calculate.

13. 2.5% of 120

14. $87\frac{1}{2}$% of 400

15. 22.5% of 30

16. 6.75% of 1600

17. 66.6% of 45

18. 38.9% of 600

Estimate, then calculate.

19. 13% of 190

20. 48% of 95

21. 26% of 375

22. 62% of 210

23. 51.5% of $126

24. 83% of $565

Replace each ● with >, <, or = to make each statement true.

25. 6% of 120 ● 60% of 12

26. 25% of 150 ● 35% of 120

27. 64% of 3 ● 16% of 12

28. 68% of 500 ● 73% of 350

Problems and Applications

In questions 29–34, estimate the percent and then test with your calculator.

29. ▨% of 60 is 30

30. ▨% of 44 is 11

31. ▨% of 15 is 3.3

32. ▨% of 22 is 40.7

33. ▨% of 56 is 40.32

34. ▨% of 84 is 23.52

35. The area of Lake Winnipeg is about 85% of the area of Great Slave Lake. The area of Great Slave Lake is 28 600 km². What is the area of Lake Winnipeg?

36. Many live theatre productions are non-profit. The table shows where the money goes from their ticket sales.

Artists	33%
Promotion	17%
Administration	15%
Production	23%
Theatre	12%

If a ticket costs $40, how much of the $40 goes to each category?

37. A rule of thumb for large commercial theatre productions is that 30% of the cost of a ticket goes to salaries, rent, and production, 30% goes to the investors, and 40% goes to the producer. If a ticket costs $95, how much goes to each category?

38. The table shows how the money you pay for a CD is distributed.

Raw Materials	14%
Record Company Overhead	21%
Royalties to Artist, Composer, Publisher, and Producer	25%
Record Company Profit	8%
Store Markup	32%

Use a current price for a CD and calculate how much goes to each category.

WORD POWER

Change the word WARM to the word COLD by changing one letter at a time. Each time you change a letter, you must form a real word. The best solution has the fewest steps.

4.3 Estimating with Percent: Mental Math

Activity: Use the Information

One way to rate baseball players is to calculate the percent of the time they get on base. The season John Olerud won his first batting championship, he came to the plate 665 times, got 200 hits, and was walked 114 times.

Inquire

1. What was the total number of times he got on base because of hits and walks?

2. What fraction of the times he came to the plate did he get on base?

3. Use this fraction to estimate a simpler fraction with small whole numbers in the numerator and denominator.

4. Estimate the percent of the time he got on base.

Example	Solution

Example

Fran's bill at a restaurant was $24.75. She wanted to leave a 15% tip. Estimate the tip.

Solution

Think of 15% as 10% + 5%.
$24.75 is about $25.   10% of $25 is $2.50.
5% is $\frac{1}{2}$ of 10%, so $\frac{1}{2}$ of $2.50 is $1.25.
$2.50 + $1.25 = $3.75
The 15% tip was about $3.75.

Practice

Estimate the percent of each area that is shaded.

1.   **2.**   **3.**

Estimate the percent of each number.

4. 49% of 82

5. 110% of 63

6. 9% of $212

7. 3% of $308

Estimate the percent for each of these test marks.

8. 46 out of 52

9. 15 out of 19

10. 22 out of 33

11. 7 out of 16

Problems and Applications

12. Old Glory Mountain in British Columbia has fog 226 days a year. Estimate the percent of the days in a year the mountain has fog.

Estimate the 15% tip for each of these restaurant bills.

13. $39.50   **14.** $16.35   **15.** $9.69

16. $123.42   **17.** $19.43   **18.** $31.56

19. Commonwealth Stadium in Edmonton has a seating capacity of 60 081. Olympic Stadium in Montreal can seat 72.8% of this number. Estimate the seating capacity of Olympic Stadium.

20. The second year the Toronto Blue Jays won the World Series, Joe Carter was at bat 603 times and he got a hit 25.4% of the time. Estimate the number of hits he got.

21. Use your estimation skills to find the approximate percent of the space taken up by advertising in a newspaper or magazine.

4.4 Discount and Sale Price

Activity: Use the Information

To attract people into their stores, some store managers offer discounts on certain items. Other store managers offer a discount on a popular item, such as a CD. A store paid $14.00 for the CD shown. The store can sell 100 copies a week at the list price, or 500 copies a week at the sale price.

Inquire

1. What does the store make
a) on each CD sold at the list price of $20.00?
b) on 100 CDs sold at the list price?

2. Calculate 15% of $20.00.

3. What is the sale price?

4. What does the store make
a) on each CD sold at the sale price?
b) on 500 CDs sold at the sale price?

Example

The regular price of a CD player with an AM/FM receiver is $598.00. What is the sale price after a discount of 25%?

Solution

The discount is 25% of $598.00.
$0.25 \times 598.00 = 149.50$
The discount is $149.50.

> **EST** $\frac{1}{1}$ of $600 = 150$

> C 598 × 25 % M+

Sale price = regular price − discount
$\qquad = \$598.00 - \$149.50$
$\qquad = \$448.50$
The sale price is $448.50.

> **EST** $600 - 150 = 450$

> C 598 − MRC = [448.5]

Problems and Applications

Estimate, then calculate each discount.

1. 20% off a shirt at $39.95

2. 25% off a blank videocassette at $4.50

3. 40% off perfume at $88.00

4. 60% off designer jeans at $69.95

5. 30% off an exercise bike at $399.95

Estimate, then calculate each sale price.

6. a $2.50 binder at 25% off

7. a $1269 computer at 5% off

8. a $29.95 towel set at 15% off

9. a $449.50 TV set at 20% off

10. Jane says, "A $174.99 personal CD player at 40% off is cheaper than a $149.99 personal CD player at 25% off." Is Jane correct?

11. A Raptors T-shirt that sold for $30 was increased in price by 20%. What was the new price?

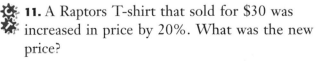

12. Write a problem that involves finding a discount or sale price. Have a classmate solve your problem.

4.5 PST and GST

Activity: Calculate the Cost

The Goods and Services Tax (GST) is a federal government tax. The rate is the same for all provinces. Each province determines a rate of Provincial Sales Tax (PST).

Inquire

1. What is the rate of GST? your provincial rate of PST?

2. Calculate the GST on the in-line skates.

3. In your province, is the PST calculated on the price of the item, or on the sum of the price and the GST?

4. Calculate the PST on the in-line skates.

5. What is the total cost of the in-line skates?

Example

A mountain bike lists for $550.00. Calculate the total cost if the GST is 7% and the PST is 8%.

Solution 1

(PST on selling price)

$$
\begin{aligned}
\text{Selling price} &= \$550.00 \\
\text{GST} = 0.07 \times \$550.00 &= \$\ 38.50 \\
\text{PST} = 0.08 \times \$550.00 &= \$\ 44.00 \\
\text{Total cost} &= \$632.50
\end{aligned}
$$

Solution 2

(PST on selling price plus GST)

$$
\begin{aligned}
\text{Selling price} &= \$550.00 \\
\text{GST} = 0.07 \times \$550.00 &= \$\ 38.50 \\
\text{Total} &= \$588.50 \\
\text{PST} = 0.08 \times \$588.50 &= \$\ 47.08 \\
\text{Total cost} &= \$635.58
\end{aligned}
$$

EST $0.07 \times 600 = 42$

EST $0.08 \times 600 = 48$

Problems and Applications

Estimate the GST and PST in your province.

	Item	Price
1.	Radio	$110.00
2.	T-shirt	$18.75
3.	Boat	$31 000.00
4.	Jeans	$55.00

Calculate the total cost, including the GST and PST in your province.

	Item	Price
5.	Portable phone	$99.95
6.	Computer	$2049.00
7.	Sunglasses	$21.75
8.	Pen	$7.90

9. The regular price of a pair of boots is $120.00. The discount is 10%. Calculate the total cost, including the GST and PST in your province.

10. A rowing machine regularly costs $240.00. It is discounted 25%. Calculate the total cost in your province, including all taxes.

11. Cut out of newspapers and magazines the pictures and prices of 6 items that you would like to buy. Glue or tape the pictures into your notebook. Calculate the total cost of each item, including the GST and PST in your province.

12. List 5 ways your province uses the money it raises from the PST.

4.6 Commission

Some salespeople earn a salary or an hourly wage, plus a **commission** on what they sell. Commission is a percent of the cost of goods sold. Some salespeople work for commission only.

Activity: Calculate the Commission

Lyndsay earns a 4% commission for selling computers. One weekend, she sold 2 at $2200.00 each and 3 at $2600.00 each.

Inquire

1. What were Lyndsay's total sales?

2. What was Lyndsay's commission?

3. What is one advantage of being paid on commission?

4. What is one advantage for an employer to pay on commission?

5. What is one disadvantage for employees? for employers?

6. List 4 jobs for which commission might be all or part of total earnings.

Example

Carlos sells sports clothes. He earns $9/h, plus 2% commission. How much does he earn for sales of $850 in 7 h?

Solution

Commission = 2% of $850
$$= 0.02 \times \$850$$
$$= \$17.00$$

$0.02 \times 1000 = 20$ **EST**

Salary = $7 \times \$9.00$
$$= \$63.00$$

Earnings = $\$17.00 + \$63.00$
$$= \$80.00$$

$20 + 60 = 80$ **EST**

C 850 × 2 % M+ 7 × 9 + MRC = [80.]

Problems and Applications

1. Omar sells real estate at 1.5% commission. Calculate his commission on the following sales.

a) $320 000.00   **b)** $120 000.00
c) $75 500.00   **d)** $93 750.00

2. Elizabeth sells new cars. Her commission is 10% of the profit on each car. Calculate her commission on sales with the following profits.

a) $2000.00   **b)** $1550.00
c) $3175.00   **d)** $1998.00

3. Marcia works in a clothing store. She earns $12.00/h, plus 2% commission. Calculate her earnings for a 35-h week in which her sales were $4695.00.

4. Ernst works in a computer store. He earns $7.50/h, plus 4% commission. One week he worked 39 h and had sales of $12 456.00. Calculate his earnings for the week.

5. Pat works in a clothing store where he is paid $650.00 a week, plus 2% commission. In the month of May, he had weekly sales of $9367.50, $7123.75, $12 680.25, and $8764.00. Calculate his earnings for the month.

121

4.7 Use Logic

Many problems require no mathematical calculations or no special skills in mathematics. You have to think through the problems logically. Sometimes, it helps to put the information in a table.

Detective Sam Diamond investigated a crime at a mansion. The 4 suspects were Amy, Bob, Colleen, and Domingo. Their jobs at the mansion were secretary, gardener, cook, and driver. Diamond was sure that the cook committed the crime, but the suspects refused to name their jobs. Diamond learned that neither Bob nor Domingo had a driver's licence, Colleen and Domingo did not know where the potatoes were kept, and Colleen worked indoors. Who was the cook?

AMY   BOB

COLLEEN   DOMINGO

Understand the Problem

1. What information are you given?

2. What are you asked to find?

Think of a Plan

Make a table and fill in the facts from the clues.

Carry Out the Plan

Neither Bob nor Domingo was the driver because neither had a licence.

	A	B	C	D
Secretary				
Gardener				
Cook				
Driver		n		n

Since Colleen and Domingo did not know where the potatoes were kept, neither was the cook.

	A	B	C	D
Secretary				
Gardener				
Cook			n	n
Driver		n		n

Colleen worked indoors, so she was not the driver or the gardener. Thus, Colleen was the secretary, and Amy was the driver.

	A	B	C	D
Secretary			y	
Gardener			n	
Cook			n	n
Driver	y	n	n	n

Complete the table.

Bob was the cook.

	A	B	C	D
Secretary	n	n	y	n
Gardener	n	n	n	y
Cook	n	y	n	n
Driver	y	n	n	n

Look Back

Check that the answer agrees with the given facts.

Use Logic
1. Organize the information.
2. Draw conclusions from the information.
3. Check that the answer is reasonable.

Problems and Applications

1. Robert, Peggy, and Jeff study painting, drama, and singing. The singer sang at Peggy's birthday party. Robert and the painter are brothers. Who is the singer?

2. Four students, Ana, Brenda, Carlos, and Devon, wrote a math quiz marked out of 10. Their marks were 8, 7, 6, and 4, but not necessarily in that order. Devon's mark was half of Brenda's. Carlos got a higher mark than Ana. What mark did each student get?

3. Mary, Harminder, and Allison each have one favourite subject. The subjects are math, history, and art. No one likes the subject that begins with the same letter as his or her name. Mary and the student who likes history are cousins. What is the favourite subject of each person?

4. Tessa, Yuri, and Jennifer had 24 books between them. Jennifer gave Tessa 2 books. Then, Tessa gave Yuri 1 book. Finally, Yuri gave Jennifer 1 book. They each ended up with an equal number of books. How many books did each person start with?

5. In a game, 1 orange marker is worth 4 red markers. One red marker is worth 5 yellow markers plus 2 blue markers. One blue marker is worth 3 yellow markers. How many yellow markers is 1 orange marker worth?

6. Francine, Donna, and Shelly finished first, second, and third in a race. Shelly was not third, Francine did not finish first, and Donna was not second. Shelly finished ahead of Donna. In what order did they finish the race?

7. On a history test, Anitha got 4 marks less than Tom. Gino got 5 marks less than Sarah. Tom got 16 marks more than Gino. How many marks more than Sarah did Anitha get?

8. Prince Edward Island, Manitoba, Alberta, and British Columbia became Canadian provinces in different years. Of these 4 provinces, Manitoba did not join second or third. British Columbia did not join first or fourth. Prince Edward Island did not join first or second. Alberta did not join second. Prince Edward Island joined before Alberta. In which order did these provinces join Canada?

9. Aaron, Jessica, Stephanie, and Roberto went to the museum to work on history projects. Each went to a different room — the Egyptian Room, the Dinosaur Room, the Aztec Room, and the Inca Room. Aaron saw Stephanie in the Aztec Room. Roberto did not see the dinosaurs. Roberto and Jessica did not see the Inca exhibit. Which room did each student visit?

10. There are 4 empty seats in the front row of the theatre. Two couples are going to sit in them, but neither couple is willing to be separated. If you were on the stage looking at the 4 people, in how many different ways could they be seated?

11. Write a problem that can be solved using a logic table. Start with a table that shows the correct answers. Then, remove some answers and write clues so that someone else can find the answers. Test the clues to make sure the problem can be solved. Have a classmate solve your problem.

PATTERN POWER

What is the ones digit of the product of one hundred sevens?

Designing Theatrical Sets

Although drama is classified as a fine art, there is probably more math involved in the theatre than most people realize. For example, a set designer is a technologist who uses math in designing the set for a production.

Long before rehearsals begin or construction starts, the director and the set designer discuss the needs of the play, what shape the set should take, and how the set will relate to the theatre. The set designer listens to the director's ideas, then mentally creates an image of the set. To communicate this image, the designer draws a *ground plan* and a *thumbnail sketch*.

The ground plan shows the physical relationships of the objects in the set, and how they relate to the theatre.

The thumbnail sketch better displays what the audience will actually see.

Activity ❶ A Box Set

Ground Plan (or top view in 2-D)   Thumbnail Sketch (or front view in 3-D)

_____   _____

1. The set shown in the above diagrams is known as a box set. Explain why.

2. You are the set designer for a play that will be performed in a box set. The scene is a dining room. Four people will be seated for dinner. Draw the ground plan and the thumbnail sketch of the set.

124

Activity ❷ A Black-Box Theatre

For more complex sets, the ability to think and draw in both two and three dimensions is more important and more difficult.

Suppose the designer decides to use scaffolds as the major pieces to define the space. The show is performed in a black-box theatre, which has the shape of an empty rectangular prism. In such a theatre, the relationship of the seating to the performing areas is very flexible. The audience may sit on scaffolding around the perimeter, with the actors performing in the centre of the room. The props for the actors may be as simple as boxes.

1. Determine the scaffold from which the designer chose to draw the thumbnail sketch. How would this sketch differ if you sketched the set from
a) the stage left scaffold?
b) the stage right scaffold?

2. The relationship of the ground plan to the thumbnail sketch is very important for showing the designer's image. For example, the ground plan contains the exact height of each scaffold, while the thumbnail sketch shows how many sections high each scaffold is. What other dimensions would you need to know before building the set?

3. The next step in the design process is to combine the information in the diagrams to create a three-dimensional scale model of the set. List other examples of the use of three-dimensional scale models.

4. Design your own black-box theatre. Draw the ground plan and the thumbnail sketch. Include dimensions.

Ground Plan

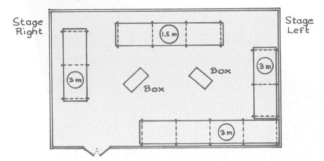

Thumbnail Sketch

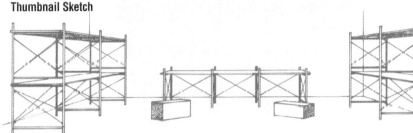

Activity ❸ Using Technology

Activities 1 and 2 could be completed with paper, a pencil, and a ruler. Answer the following questions about how newer technologies might be used.

1. Describe any advantages of using computer graphics to draw the diagrams.

2. How might you use virtual reality to help you design a set?

4.8 Finding the Percent

A cube 1 cm long, 1 cm wide, and 1 cm high has a volume of one cubic centimetre (1 cm³). A cube 1 km long, 1 km wide, and 1 km high has a volume of one cubic kilometre (1 km³). Statisticians use cubic kilometres when calculating a country's water supply.

Activity: Use the Information

The amount of water in use in Canada is about 40 km³. Three cubic kilometres are used in agriculture, 32 km³ in industry, and 5 km³ in homes and cities.

Inquire

1. What fraction of the water is used in industry?

2. Write this fraction in lowest terms.

3. Write the fraction with a denominator of 100.

4. What percent of the water is used in industry?

5. What fraction of the water is used in agriculture?

6. Express this fraction as a decimal.

7. Write the decimal as a percent to find the percent of the water used in agriculture.

8. What percent of the water is used in homes and cities?

9. Canada's renewable water supply is 2900 km³. About what percent of the supply is in use?

Example

Commercial breaks in radio broadcasting are called "islands." An island is usually 2.5 min long. Many FM stations have 3 islands every hour. What percent of the time do commercials take up?

Solution

There are 60 min in 1 h.
There are 3 × 2.5 min or 7.5 min of commercials.

The fraction of commercial time in one hour is $\frac{7.5}{60}$.

$\frac{7.5}{60} = 0.125$ **EST** $6 \div 60 = 0.1$

$0.125 \times 100\% = 12.5\%$

Commercials take up 12.5% of the time.

Practice

Write each decimal as a percent.

1. 0.8   **2.** 0.57   **3.** 0.515

4. 1.67   **5.** 0.02   **6.** 2.4

7. 0.302   **8.** 0.999   **9.** 0.007

Write as a percent.

10. $\frac{4}{5}$ **11.** $\frac{3}{10}$ **12.** 13:20

13. $\frac{8}{25}$ **14.** $\frac{11}{11}$ **15.** $\frac{90}{72}$

16. 44:200   **17.** $\frac{45}{150}$ **18.** $\frac{24}{64}$

Express as a percent, to the nearest tenth.

19. $\frac{2}{3}$ **20.** $\frac{4}{7}$ **21.** $\frac{5}{9}$

22. 1:6   **23.** $\frac{15}{11}$ **24.** 14:13

Calculate. Round to the nearest tenth, if necessary.

25. 25 is what percent of 200?

26. What percent of 75 is 45?

27. 21 is what percent of 24?

28. 60 is what percent of 45?

29. What percent of 8.6 is 5.9?

30. What percent of 0.8 is 0.12?

Problems and Applications

31. a) Canada's first 6 astronauts were chosen in 1983. The next 4 were chosen in 1992. What percent of Canada's first 10 astronauts were chosen in 1992?

b) The 2 youngest astronauts chosen in 1992 were Julie Payette, aged 28, and Chris Hadfield, aged 32. What percent was Julie's age of Chris's age?

32. In a test on percent applications, Lily answered 28 of the 35 questions correctly. What percent of the questions did Lily **a)** answer correctly?   **b)** not answer correctly?

33. Of the 19 events in which Canadians won medals at the Barcelona Olympics, 5 were rowing events, and 4 were swimming events. What percent of the events were rowing or swimming events, to the nearest tenth?

34. Agnes Macphail (1890–1954) was the first Canadian woman elected as a Member of Parliament (MP). She was elected in 1921 and served until 1940. For what percent of her life was she an MP? Round your answer to the nearest percent.

35. The price of a pair of sunglasses increased from \$120 to \$144.

a) By what percent did the price increase?
b) What percent is the new price of the original price?

36. When the Blue Jays won their second World Series, 25 Blue Jays actually played in the 6 World Series games. The Blue Jays gave out 265 championship rings. What percent of the people who received rings did not play in the World Series? Round your answer to the nearest percent.

37. Use your research skills to determine the percent of Canadians who live in each of the following provinces or cities. Round each answer to the nearest tenth of a percent.
a) Alberta   **b)** Prince Edward Island
c) Halifax   **d)** Ontario

NUMBER POWER

Find 5 different digits with a sum of 21 that make the multiplication statement true. ▩▩ × ▩ = ▩▩

4.9 100% of a Number

Activity: Study the Information

Part of the money you spend on a book goes to the author or authors as royalties. Fernand was part of an author team that wrote a book about the history of Canadian art. He receives a royalty of 1% of sales. His last royalty cheque was for $890.00.

Inquire

1. If 1% of sales was $890.00, how can you find 100% of sales?

2. Calculate 100% of sales.

3. The book publisher gave a total of 10% of sales to the author team as royalties. Calculate 10% of sales.

Example 1

The shooting time for a typical made-for-TV movie is about 40 days. This time accounts for just 20% of the total time needed to make the movie. The rest of the time is used for scripting, preproduction, and postproduction. What is the total number of days needed to make the movie?

Solution 1

20% of the time is 40 days.

1% of the time is $\frac{40}{20}$ or 2 days.

100% of the time is 100×2 days or 200 days.

Solution 2

Let x represent the total number of days needed. Write a proportion.

$$\frac{20}{100} = \frac{40}{x}$$
$$\frac{20 \times 2}{100 \times 2} = \frac{40}{x}$$
$$\frac{40}{200} = \frac{40}{x}$$
$$200 = x$$

It takes about 200 days to make the movie.

Example 2

If 7% of a number is 8.4, find the number.

Solution 1

7% of the number is 8.4.

1% of the number is $\frac{8.4}{7}$.

100% of the number is

$$100 \times \frac{8.4}{7} = \frac{840}{7}$$
$$= 120$$

The number is 120.

Solution 2

Let x represent the number. Write a proportion.

$$\frac{7}{100} = \frac{8.4}{x}$$
$$\frac{7 \times 1.2}{100 \times 1.2} = \frac{8.4}{x}$$
$$\frac{8.4}{120} = \frac{8.4}{x}$$
$$120 = x$$

Practice

Copy and complete the statements.

1. 5% of a number is 20.
1% of the number is ■.

2. 20% of a number is 60.
1% of the number is ■.

3. 15% of a number is 30.
1% of the number is ■.

4. 4% of a number is 24.4.
1% of the number is ■.

Find each number.

5. 1% of the number is 5.

6. 1% of the number is 26.

7. 1% of the number is 8.2.

8. 1% of the number is 29.7.

Copy and complete the statements.

9. 5% of a number is 25.
1% of the number is ■.
100% of the number is ■.

10. 15% of a number is 75.
1% of the number is ■.
100% of the number is ■.

11. 12% of a number is 48.
1% of the number is ■.
100% of the number is ■.

Find the value of x.

12. $\frac{40}{100} = \frac{80}{x}$ **13.** $\frac{15}{100} = \frac{45}{x}$

14. $\frac{9}{100} = \frac{54}{x}$ **15.** $\frac{8}{100} = \frac{3.2}{x}$

16. If 10% of a number is 70, find the number.

17. If 125% of a number is 15, find the number.

18. If 9% of a number is 72, find the number.

19. If 6% of a number is 5.4, find the number.

Problems and Applications

20. Susan writes mystery novels. Her royalties are 10% of sales. Her last royalty cheque was for $2300. Calculate the sales.

21. The Earth's surface is about 30% land, and the rest is water. The area of the land is 148 million square kilometres. What is the total area of the Earth, to the nearest million square kilometres?

22. Of all the animal species in North America, 200 are classified as "historic." Scientists know that these species existed at one time and believe that they still survive. Historic species represent 2% of the known North American animal species. How many North American animal species are there?

23. The original price of a camera was reduced by 20%. The selling price was $280. What was the original price?

24. a) $33\frac{1}{3}\%$ of what number is 20?

b) $66\frac{2}{3}\%$ of what number is 20?

LOGIC POWER

The 2 train cars are too big to go under the bridge, but the engine can. Either end of the engine can push or pull a car. The engine can also move both cars at once when they are joined together, or it can push one and pull the other. Show how the engine can reverse the positions of the cars and return to its starting position. (Hint: You might use different coins to represent the engine and the cars.)

4.10 Simple Interest

When you deposit money in a bank, the bank pays you **interest** for the use of your money. If you borrow money from a bank, you pay interest for the use of the bank's money. The money you deposit or borrow is called the **principal**. The total of the principal and the interest is called the **amount**.

Activity: Calculate the Interest

Francie bought $2000 worth of Canada Savings Bonds. The government paid Francie 7% interest for one year.

Inquire

1. If the interest was 7% of $2000, how much interest did Francie earn?

2. What amount of money did Francie have at the end of one year?

Example

Mark bought a $500 Canada Savings Bond that paid 6.5% interest a year for 5 years.
a) How much interest did Mark earn?
b) What amount of money did Mark have after 5 years?

Solution

a) The formula to calculate simple interest is $I = Prt$, where I is the interest earned, P is the principal, r is the rate of interest, and t is the time in years.

$I = Prt$
$= 500 \times 0.065 \times 5$
$= 162.50$

Mark earned $162.50 in interest.
b) The amount is $500 + $162.50 or $662.50. Mark had $662.50 after 5 years.

Problems and Applications

For each deposit, calculate the interest and the amount.

	Principal	Interest Rate	Time (years)
1.	$800	6%	1
2.	$1000	7%	2
3.	$2000	6.5%	3
4.	$5000	8.2%	0.5

For each loan, calculate the interest and the total amount to be repaid.

	Principal	Rate	Time (years)
5.	$7500	9%	4
6.	$10 000	7.5%	3
7.	$4500	9.2%	3.5
8.	$9000	7.8%	0.5

9. Sofia bought a $1000 Canada Savings Bond. The interest rate was 8% per year. Calculate the amount she had after 9 years.

10. If interest is compounded, the amount at the end of one year becomes the principal for the next year. Copy and complete the table.

Year	Principal	Rate	Interest	Amount
1	$100 000	5%	$5000	$105 000
2	$105 000	5%		
3				
4				
5				

Activity ❶ The Chicxulub Crater

Something big happened on the Earth 65 million years ago. Species by the hundreds, including the dinosaurs, disappeared.

One theory of their disappearance is that a meteor, about 16 km in diameter, crashed into the Earth, forming a crater with a radius of 160 km. The crater is called the Chicxulub Crater and is located in Mexico's Yucatán Peninsula.

The impact of the meteor caused a huge cloud of dust to be blown into the sky. The dust produced a thick blanket of debris that covered the Earth. The dust was so thick that it blocked out the sun.

The resulting cold, dark conditions might have lasted for months, stopping the most important food-making process — photosynthesis. In this process, plants use the sun's light to grow and to produce oxygen. Plants have produced 99% of the free oxygen added to the atmosphere since the world's beginning.

The Chicxulub Crater is underground. In this colour-enhanced computer image, the crater appears in blue to the right of the highest red peak.

1. The area of the Chicxulub Crater is about 80 000 km². What provinces have areas smaller than that of the Chicxulub Crater?

2. Locate the Yucatán Peninsula on a map. What are its latitude and longitude?

3. Why would a huge dust cloud cause hundreds of species to become extinct?

4. What kinds of species would survive? Why?

Activity ❷ Polar Ice

Millions of years ago, the Arctic and Antarctic were rain forests. This meant that the water level on the Earth was about 60 m higher than it is today.

1. Why was the water level higher when the Arctic and the Antarctic were rain forests?

2. List the provincial capitals. Without looking up their elevations, list the ones you think would have been under water when the Arctic and the Antarctic were rain forests.

3. Check your answers to question 2 by locating the elevations of the provincial capitals.

4.11 Problem Solving with Percents

Activity: Discover the Relationship

Alexi waited until the end of the ski season to buy skis. The original price of the skis was $475.00. In January, the skis were reduced to $427.50. In February, the skis were reduced again to $342.00.

Inquire

1. To what percent of the original price was the price reduced in January?

2. To what percent of the January price was the price reduced in February?

3. a) To what percent of the original price was the price reduced in February?
b) How is the percent from part a) related to the percents you found in questions 1 and 2?

In some problems, such as the inquire questions above, a number is changed *to* a percent of its value. In other problems, such as Example 1 below, a number is changed *by* a percent of its value.

Example 1

Tonya deposited $250 in her bank account. At the end of the first year, she earned 4% interest. At the end of the second year, she earned 6% interest.
a) How much money did she have at the end of two years?
b) By what percent did her money increase over the two-year period?

Solution

a) *At the end of year 1,*
Tonya's money increased by 4%.

$250 × 4% = $250 × 0.04
         = $10
$250 + $10 = $260
Tonya had $260 in the bank.

At the end of year 2,
Tonya's money increased by 6%.

$260 × 6% = $260 × 0.06
         = $15.60
$260 + $15.60 = $275.60
Tonya had $275.60 in the bank.

C 250 M+ + MRC × 4 % = M+ + MRC × 6 % = | 275.60

So, Tonya had $275.60 at the end of 2 years.

b) Over the two-year period, Tonya's money increased by $275.60 − $250.00 = $25.60
Divide to find what percent $25.60 is of $250.

$\frac{25.60}{250} = 0.1024$
      $= 10.24\%$
Tonya's money increased by 10.24% over the two-year period.

132

Example 2

Stefan had a drawing that was 8 cm long. He used a photocopier to make an enlargement to 125% of its original length. He then enlarged the copy to 140% of its length. What percent of the original length of the drawing was the length of the final copy?

Solution

First Enlargement

$8 \times 125\% = 8 \times 1.25$
$= 10$

Length of the first enlargement was 10 cm.

Second Enlargement

$10 \times 140\% = 10 \times 1.4$
$= 14$

Length of the second enlargement was 14 cm.

Divide to find what percent 14 cm is of 8 cm.

$\frac{14}{8} = 1.75$

$= 175\%$ C 8 × 125 % × 140 % ÷ 8 % 　　　　　 *175.*

The length of the final copy was 175% the length of the original drawing.

Problems and Applications

1. The regular price of a jacket was $150. For a sale, the price was reduced by 25%. A week later, the price was reduced by 10% of the first sale price.
a) What was the first sale price?
b) What was the final sale price?
c) What percent of the regular price was the final sale price?
d) By how much was the price reduced from the regular price to the final sale price?
e) By what percent was the price reduced from the regular price to the final sale price?

2. The length of the St. Lawrence River is about 150% of the length of the Columbia River. The length of the Mackenzie River is about 140% of the length of the St. Lawrence River. The length of the Columbia River is 2000 km.
a) What is the approximate length of the St. Lawrence River?
b) What is the approximate length of the Mackenzie River?
c) What percent of the length of the Columbia River is the length of the Mackenzie River?

3. Lloyd sells industrial cleaning supplies to large factories. One month his sales totalled $150 000. Lloyd earned 3% commission on the first $50 000 of sales and 6% on the next $100 000 of sales.
a) What commission did Lloyd earn on the first $50 000?
b) What commission did Lloyd earn on the next $100 000?
c) What commission did Lloyd earn in total?
d) What was Lloyd's average rate of commission for the $150 000 of sales?

4. A CD was on sale at 20% off of the regular price. The price was then increased by 20% of the sale price. Was the final price the same as the regular price? Explain.

5. Marlene needs to enlarge a quilt pattern to 180% of its original size. The photocopier allows enlargements in whole-number percents up to 155%. Work with a classmate to find how Marlene can enlarge the pattern to 180% using a combination of
a) 2 enlargements   **b)** 3 enlargements
Compare your answers with your classmates'.

133

4.12 Use a Table

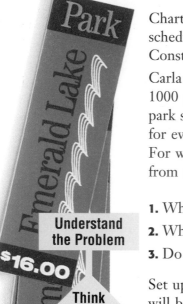

Charts and tables are efficient ways to organize information. Bus schedules, team standings, and school timetables are 3 examples. Constucting a table is a useful problem solving strategy.

Carla is the business manager of Emerald Lake Park. Ticket sales average 1000 people/day, when the cost of a ticket is $16. People who visit the park spend $4.00 each at the concession stands. Carla has learned that, for every dollar she lowers the price, sales will increase by 100 people/day. For what price should Carla sell tickets to get the greatest total receipts from tickets sales and the concession stands?

Understand the Problem

1. What information are you given?

2. What are you asked to find?

3. Do you need an exact or approximate answer?

Think of a Plan

Set up a table to show the price of a ticket, the number of tickets that will be sold at that price, the receipts from ticket sales, the receipts from concession sales, and the total receipts. Find the ticket price that gives the greatest receipts.

Carry Out the Plan

Ticket Price ($)	Number Sold	Ticket Sales ($)	Concession Sales ($)	Total Receipts ($)
16	1000	16 000	4000	20 000
15	1100	16 500	4400	20 900
14	1200	16 800	4800	21 600
13	1300	16 900	5200	22 100
12	1400	16 800	5600	22 400
11	1500	16 500	6000	**22 500**
10	1600	16 000	6400	22 400

EST $1500 \times 10 = 15\ 000$
$15\ 000 + 5000 = 20\ 000$

A ticket price of $11 gives the greatest total receipts.

Look Back

Check that the receipts are close to the estimate.
How could you use subtraction and division to check your answer?

Use a Table	**1.** Organize the given information in a table.
	2. Complete the table with the results of your calculations.
	3. Find the answer from the table.
	4. Check that your answer is reasonable.

Problems and Applications

1. The table shows the greatest depths of the Great Lakes.

Lake	Greatest Depth (m)
Erie	64
Huron	229
Michigan	281
Ontario	244
Superior	405

a) How much deeper than Lake Huron is Lake Superior?

b) Which lake is closest to 5 times deeper than Lake Erie?

c) How many times deeper than Lake Ontario is Lake Superior? Round your answer to the nearest hundredth.

2. The toll to cross the Tallahassee Bridge is 75¢ a car. In the lane for drivers with exact change, a driver must toss 75¢ into a hopper, which funnels the coins into a counter. If the total is 75¢, the car is allowed through. The hopper does not accept pennies or 50¢ pieces. Use a table to determine how many different combinations of coins can be used to make the exact change.

Number of Quarters	Number of Dimes	Number of Nickels

3. Water World Aquarium charges $15 admission. There is an average of 150 visitors a day. Researchers have suggested that, for every dollar decrease in price, the number of visitors will increase by 50 a day. Find the admission price that gives the greatest receipts.

4. The bus for the wilderness trip left the school at 08:00. The trip took 12 h at 50 km/h. Dino missed the bus and asked his father to try to catch up with it. Dino and his father left the school at 09:00. They travelled at 60 km/h. Copy and complete the table to find when Dino and his father caught up with the bus.

Time	Distance Travelled (km)	
	Bus	Car
08:00	0	0
09:00	50	0
10:00	100	60

5. The 3 teams in a soccer league are the Aces, Bisons, and Chargers. Each team has played 4 games. A win is worth 2 points, a tie 1 point. There are no points for a loss. Here is some information about the games played.

- The Bisons have 3 wins and no ties.
- The Chargers have 1 point.

Copy and complete the table to find how many wins, losses, ties, and points each team has.

Team	Won	Lost	Tied	Points

6. A concert promoter can sell 5000 tickets at $30 each. Every $2 decrease in price will result in the sale of another 500 tickets. People attending the concert will spend $10 each at the concession stands. Find the ticket price that will give the greatest total revenue from ticket sales and concessions.

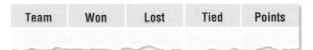

7. Write a problem that can be solved with a table. Have a classmate solve your problem.

The Misunderstood Grey Wolf

The grey wolf was once the most widely distributed mammal in the world. It has been relentlessly exterminated wherever humans have settled. It is now found in greatly reduced numbers in a small part of its original range. In some countries where it was once persecuted, there are now protection policies to prevent the wolf's extermination. However, many areas of the world still have vigorous control programs to reduce the number of wolves.

Activity ❶

1. The grey wolf stands about 75 cm at the shoulder. Name 3 objects in your classroom that are this height.

2. The many subspecies of grey wolf found in Canada range from 26 kg to 79 kg in mass. The larger subspecies live in the cold, northern regions. How does the mass of a wolf compare with the mass of an average human adult?

3. Wolves have 42 teeth. The 4 longest teeth are 5 cm long.
a) How many teeth do humans have?
b) Approximately how many times longer than your longest tooth is the wolf's longest tooth?

4. It is common for a pack of wolves to cover 75 km in a day over frozen lakes and through rugged forest. Use a map to locate places that are about 75 km from your home.

5. Wolves are often confused with coyotes, especially in areas where the wolf has disappeared. Locate information about the coyote and compare its size and appearance with those of the wolf.

Activity ❷

The table shows the estimated population of wolves in some parts of Europe and Asia.

1. It is estimated that there are 90 000 wolves left throughout Europe and Asia. What percent of this total is left in each of the countries or areas listed?

2. Approximately 2% of the wolves in Europe and Asia live in India. How many wolves live in India?

3. Researchers believe that about 30% of the wolf population is killed each year. How many wolves might be killed in Europe and Asia each year?

Country/Area	Population
Afghanistan	1000
Greece	500
Iran	1000
Israel	150
Italy	250
Mongolia	10 000
Poland	900
Spain	750
Scandinavia	100
Former U.S.S.R.	70 000

Activity 3

The map shows the estimated number of wolves living in Canada and Alaska.

Researchers believe there are approximately 1275 wolves in the rest of North America.

1. Estimate the maximum number of wolves living in Canada.

2. What percent of this number lives in each section of Canada?

3. Estimate the maximum number of wolves in North America.

4. What percent of this total lives in Alaska?

5. Between 1600 and 1950, approximately two million wolves were erased from North America. What percent of this number is left?

6. a) Why do you think the number of wolves in the Northwest Territories is so uncertain?

b) What might be the reason that there is no estimated number for Saskatchewan, Manitoba, and Labrador?

Activity 4

The wolf has been persecuted partly because of fear and misunderstanding. There is a belief that wolves are vicious killers, even though there is no record of a healthy wild wolf attacking a human.

1. Other than fear, why do some hunters and farmers want the wolf exterminated?

2. How do you think the misunderstanding about the wolf's viciousness arose?

3. Look for stories and poems about wolves. What characteristics of wolves are portrayed?

4. Read the story of Romulus and Remus. What characteristics of the wolf are portrayed in this story?

5. Read some accounts about wolves written by researchers and environmentalists. One book you might read is *Never Cry Wolf*, by the Canadian author Farley Mowat. How does the factual evidence compare with the literary images you discovered?

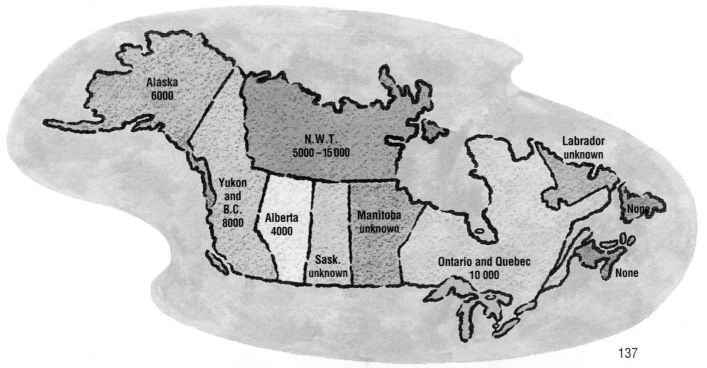

Alaska 6000

N.W.T. 5000–15 000

Labrador unknown

Yukon and B.C. 8000

Alberta 4000

Manitoba unknown

Sask. unknown

Ontario and Quebec 10 000

None

None

Review

Estimate.

1. 33% of $190
2. 78% of $42
3. 105% of $40
4. 0.5% of $50

Estimate, then calculate.

5. 25% of $39
6. 60% of $145
7. 72% of $4.50
8. $15\frac{1}{2}$% of $2500
9. 205% of $60
10. 1200% of $48
11. $107\frac{3}{4}$% of $20
12. 0.6% of $760
13. 1.5% of $70.85
14. 7.5% of $22.80

Estimate the 15% tip on these restaurant bills.

15. $15.75
16. $73.10
17. $254.88
18. $246.05

Calculate. Round your answers for questions 19 to 26 to the nearest cent, if necessary.

19. 75% of $80.50
20. 25% of $30.25
21. 60% of $345
22. 5% of $68
23. 125% of $70
24. 600% of $22.50
25. 1.3% of $25 000
26. 0.25% of $350 000
27. What percent is 35 of 56?
28. What percent of 50 is 2.5?
29. What percent is 22 of 77, to the nearest tenth of a percent?
30. What percent of 60 is 150?
31. If 15% of a number is 6, what is the number?
32. If 40% of a number is 85, what is the number?
33. If 200% of a number is 360, what is the number?
34. Jim has 4 nickels and 6 dimes.
a) What percent of his coins are nickels?
b) What percent of his coins are dimes?
c) What percent of the total value of the coins is the value of the dimes?

35. The elevation of Moose Jaw above sea level is 680% of the elevation of Kingston. The elevation of Kingston is 80 m. What is the elevation of Moose Jaw?

36. The average Canadian eats about 2.7 kg of breakfast cereal per year. The average American eats 200% of this amount. How much cereal does the average American eat per year?

37. Vanessa Monar-Enweani became Canadian women's long jump champion with a leap of 6.42 m. The world record in the women's long jump was then 7.52 m. Calculate the percent that Vanessa's winning jump was of the world record. Round your answer to the nearest tenth of a percent.

38. Mars takes 686 days to orbit the sun. What percent of this time does the Earth take to orbit the sun? Round your answer to the nearest percent.

39. If 1 cm of rain falls as snow, the depth of the snow is 1000% of the depth of the rain. How deep is the snow?

40. St. John's gets the least sunshine of the provincial capitals. It gets only 1497 h of sunshine a year. There are 4470 h in the year when the sun could shine in St. John's. Estimate, then calculate the percent of the possible time the sun is actually shining. Round your calculated answer to the nearest tenth of a percent.

41. Last year, the price of a theatre ticket was $25. This year, it is $30.
a) What is the percent increase over last year's price?
b) What percent of last year's price is this year's price?

Calculate the discount and the sale price.

42. $22.50 book at 10% off
43. $159.00 coat at 15% off

44. $79.99 shoes at 25% off

45. $234 software at $12\frac{1}{2}$% off

For each item, calculate the GST and the PST in your province.

46. $62.95 watch

47. $95.00 pair of shoes

48. $1299.00 stereo

49. $950.00 bicycle

Calculate the total cost, including the GST and the PST in your province.

50. a can of tennis balls for $3.99

51. a pair of socks at $5.99

52. 2 CDs at $17.99 each

53. a motorcycle at $1599

54. a bicycle at $299

55. A store offers pyjamas at $32.50 with a discount of 10%. What is the total cost of the pyjamas, including GST and PST in your province?

56. Mario sold a $156 000.00 house for a commission of 1.5%. How much commission did he earn?

57. If you bought $200 worth of Canada Savings Bonds at 8.5% interest per year, what amount of money would you have at the end of one year?

58. On Anita's first birthday, her height was 70 cm. Her height on her second birthday was 115% of her height on her first birthday. Her height on her third birthday was 110% of her height on her second birthday.
a) How tall was Anita on her third birthday?
b) What percent of her height on her first birthday was her height on her third birthday?
c) By what percent did her height increase from her first birthday to her third birthday?

Group Decision Making
Researching Entertainment Careers

1. As a class, list the entertainment careers you would like to investigate. They might include such careers as a disc jockey, television or radio producer, actor, singer, book publisher, song writer, instrumentalist, music publisher, director, theatre or television critic, movie theatre manager, talent agent, or set designer. As a class, select six careers and list the questions you want answered. Include a question on how math is used in each career.

2. Go to home groups. As a group, decide which career each member is going to investigate.

1 2 3 4 5 6	1 2 3 4 5 6

Home Groups

1 2 3 4 5 6	1 2 3 4 5 6

3. Do the research for your career individually.

4. Form an expert group with students who have the same career. Use the results of your research to answer the questions.

1 1 1 1	2 2 2 2	3 3 3 3

Expert Groups

4 4 4 4	5 5 5 5	6 6 6 6

5. In your expert group, decide on a format for your report and prepare a report on your assigned career. Include a description of how your career makes use of mathematics.

6. Present your report to the class.

7. Return to your home group and evaluate the group process and the reports.

Chapter Check

What percent is the first number of the second? Round your answer to the nearest tenth, if necessary.

1. 12, 25   **2.** 35, 20   **3.** 4, 22

4. 2, 500   **5.** 500, 350   **6.** 0.5, 3.5

Calculate.

7. 1% of 300   **8.** 46% of 60

9. $12\frac{1}{2}$% of 80   **10.** 2.5% of 300

11. 120% of 55   **12.** 15% of 9.6

13. Of 30 animals in a field, 25 are cows. What percent of the animals are cows? Round your answer to the nearest tenth of a percent.

14. Montreal has 16 days of blowing snow a year. Winnipeg has 25 days of blowing snow a year. What percent is the number of days of blowing snow in Winnipeg of the number of days of blowing snow in Montreal?

15. The usual number of bones in the human skeleton is 206. Twenty-nine bones are in the skull. What percent of the bones are in the skull, to the nearest percent?

16. If 5% of a number is 10, what is the number?

17. One day, 7 students were absent with colds. This was 25% of the class. How many students were in the class?

18. About a million people live in Saskatchewan. About 20% of these people live in Saskatoon. What is the approximate population of Saskatoon?

19. Estimate the 15% tip on a $65.95 restaurant bill.

20. Tony bought a $500.00 savings bond that earned 8% interest in the first year and 7% interest in the second year. What amount of money did he have at the end of the second year?

21. Calculate the total price, including taxes, of a $250.00 CD player in your province.

22. Manya sold computers for $8.00/h, plus 4% commission on sales. In one 35-h week, she sold $10 500.00 worth of computers. How much did she earn that week?

23. If a coat with a regular price of $199.00 is sold at a 25% discount, what is the sale price?

Reprinted by permission of United Feature Syndiate.

Using the Strategies

1. Complete the magic square.

2. a) What is the area of the triangle?

b) Sketch all the different figures that can be made by placing this triangle and an identical triangle together along one side.
c) What is the area of each figure?
d) Sketch all the different figures that can be made by placing the triangle and 3 identical triangles together along complete sides.
e) What is the area of each figure?

3. Use the digits and a decimal point 8 2 5 7 . to complete the following. Do not use the decimal point at the beginning or the end of a number.
a) Write the largest number possible.
b) Write the smallest number possible.
c) Write the number that is closest to 10.
d) Write the number that is closest to 100.
e) Write the number that is closest to 1000.

4. Copy and complete the patterns so that the product of the numbers in the opposite squares is the number in the circle.

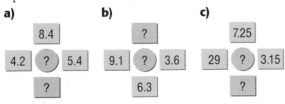

a)

| 8.4 |
| 4.2 | ? | 5.4 |
| ? |

b)

| ? |
| 9.1 | ? | 3.6 |
| 6.3 |

c)

| 7.25 |
| 29 | ? | 3.15 |
| ? |

5. The product of 2 numbers is 972. One number is 3 times the other. What are the numbers?

6. Add the numbers of letters in the names of the cards in a suit of playing cards, from ACE (3) to KING (4). What is significant about the total?

7. Calculate the perimeter of the figure.

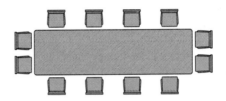

60 cm
24 cm

8. Twelve people can be seated around a table.

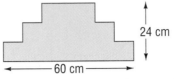

a) Using the same spacing, determine the number of people who could be seated around
• 2 tables joined along the width
• 2 tables joined along the length
• 3 tables joined along the width
• 3 tables joined along the length
b) Predict the number of people who could be seated using 8 tables joined along the width; using 8 tables joined along the length.

9. The pages of a book are numbered from 1 to 200. How many page numbers contain at least one 5?

DATA BANK

1. a) Which provincial capital has the greatest annual precipitation?
b) About how much precipitation does this capital have in September?

2. Use the Data Bank to write 2 problems. Have a classmate solve your problems.

Chapter 1

List the numbers in order from least to greatest.

1. 15.271, 15.072, 7.152, 1275, 909.001

2. 26 584, 8456, 1 000 001, 25 048, 52 846

Evaluate.

3. $(5^2)^2$ **4.** $(2^3)^2$ **5.** $(4^3)^2$

Evaluate. Write your answers in exponential form.

6. $3^2 \times 3^2 \times 3$ **7.** $6^4 \div 6^2$ **8.** $4^5 \div 4^4 \times 4^2$

Write each number in standard form.

9. $\frac{1}{10^2}$ **10.** -10^3 **11.** 10^7

Write each number in scientific notation

12. 28 000 000   **13.** 0.0008   **14.** 156 000

Write each number in standard form.

15. 8.2×10^5 **16.** 2.7×10^{-6} **17.** 5.29×10^{-4}

Write each of the following as the quotient of two integers in lowest terms.

18. $3\frac{1}{2}$ **19.** 0.8   **20.** -1.9

Express in lowest terms.

21. $\frac{4}{10}$ **22.** 40 to 20   **23.** 16:24:40

Draw in 3 different ways.

24. a rectangle with 50% shaded

25. a square with 75% shaded

Write as a percent.

26. $\frac{23}{50}$ **27.** $\frac{17}{25}$ **28.** 3:5   **29.** $\frac{5}{2}$

30. 0.6   **31.** 0.07   **32.** 2.35   **33.** 3:2

34. 0.452   **35.** 3:8   **36.** $\frac{1}{3}$ **37.** 1.2

Write as a decimal.

38. 53.6%   **39.** $4\frac{1}{2}\%$ **40.** 145%   **41.** $\frac{1}{4}\%$

Evaluate.

42. $\sqrt{361}$ **43.** $\sqrt{2.25}$

Chapter 2

Express all answers in lowest terms.

Add.

1. $\frac{3}{8} + \frac{1}{8}$ **2.** $\frac{1}{2} + \frac{2}{5}$ **3.** $\frac{2}{3} + \frac{3}{4}$

4. $2\frac{1}{2} + \frac{1}{4}$ **5.** $1\frac{1}{3} + 1\frac{1}{2}$ **6.** $3\frac{5}{6} + 1\frac{1}{2}$

Subtract.

7. $\frac{3}{5} - \frac{1}{5}$ **8.** $\frac{5}{8} - \frac{1}{4}$ **9.** $\frac{3}{4} - \frac{2}{3}$

10. $1\frac{1}{2} - \frac{1}{4}$ **11.** $2\frac{1}{6} - \frac{2}{3}$ **12.** $3\frac{1}{2} - 2\frac{3}{5}$

Multiply.

13. $\frac{1}{2} \times \frac{2}{3}$ **14.** $\frac{3}{5} \times \frac{5}{6}$ **15.** $\frac{3}{4} \times \frac{1}{2}$

16. $1\frac{1}{2} \times \frac{1}{4}$ **17.** $1\frac{3}{5} \times 2$ **18.** $1\frac{1}{3} \times 2\frac{1}{2}$

Divide.

19. $3 \div \frac{1}{2}$ **20.** $\frac{1}{3} \div \frac{2}{3}$ **21.** $\frac{3}{5} \div \frac{1}{4}$

22. $1\frac{1}{2} \div 2$ **23.** $1\frac{1}{3} \div \frac{3}{4}$ **24.** $2\frac{1}{2} \div 1\frac{1}{5}$

Evaluate.

25. -2.5×3.7 **26.** 0.125×6.9

27. $9.43 \div 2.30$ **28.** $48 \div (-0.16)$

29. $-3.6 \div (-0.45)$ **30.** $-3.1 + (-1.5)$

31. $-3.125 + 2.375$ **32.** $-4.1 \times (-0.8)$

33. $-0.05 - 0.15$ **34.** $25.22 - (-13.05)$

35. About $\frac{1}{4}$ of Canada's grizzly bears live in the Northwest Territories (NWT). About 5000 grizzlies live in the NWT. About how many live in Canada?

36. The winter high temperature is +5.2°C in Vancouver, and the winter low is −0.2°C. Find the average of these temperatures.

37. Paulo has a piece of moulding 3.6 m in length. He wishes to cut it into smaller pieces, each 0.9 m in length. How many pieces will he have?

Chapter 3

1. Write 3 ratios equivalent to 3:5.

Find the unknown values.

2. $\frac{6}{y} = \frac{12}{10}$ **3.** $\frac{32}{8} = \frac{8}{n}$ **4.** $15:18 = b:6$

5. $m:6:10 = 14:n:20$ **6.** $\frac{27}{45} = \frac{9}{p} = \frac{q}{30}$

7. Greg drove 300 km in 4 h. Claudia drove 400 km in 5 h. Who had the higher average speed?

8. The ratio of baseballs to volleyballs in a box was 7:9. The number of volleyballs was 27. How many baseballs were in the box?

9. A jar contains a total of 66 yellow cubes and green cubes. Maurice pulled out 3 cubes. He had 2 yellow cubes and 1 green cube in his hand. If the ratio of yellow cubes to green cubes is the same in the jar and in his hand, how many yellow cubes and how many green cubes are in the jar?

10. If 7 bananas cost $3.15, what is the cost of 5 bananas?

In questions 11 and 12, find the unit price.

11. $26.00 for 6 L of paint

12. 12 pencils for $1.95

13. If 175 g of yogurt costs $0.98, and 590 g costs $2.49, which is the better buy?

14. A drawing of a moose is 7 cm long. The scale is 1:40. What is the actual length, in metres, of a moose?

15. Edmonton is about 1200 km from Whitehorse. How far apart are these cities on a map with a scale of 1:20 000 000?

16. Canada's Marnie McBean and Kathleen Heddle won the women's pairs rowing event at the Barcelona Olympics by rowing 2000 m in 7 min 6.22 s. Find their average speed, to the nearest hundredth of a metre per second.

Chapter 4

Calculate

1. 21% of 350 **2.** 4.5% of 80

3. $12\frac{1}{2}$% of 88 **4.** 0.5% of 250

5. If 20% of a number is 80, what is the number?

6. If 150% of a number is 360, what is the number?

Calculate.

7. 300% of 80 **8.** 200% of 2000

9. 150% of 60 **10.** 110% of 900

Calculate what percent the first number is of the second number.

11. 32, 50 **12.** 130, 65 **13.** 2.5, 12.5

14. The regular price of a pair of jeans is $78. What is the sale price after a discount of 20%?

15. Linda sells shoes. She earns $15/h , plus a 5% commission on his sales. One week, she worked for 38 h and had sales of $690. How much did she earn?

16. A sweater sells for $84. Find the total cost, including GST and PST, in your province.

17. Luis bought a $5000 savings bond that paid 7% interest per year. What was the amount after 4 years?

18. The forested land area of the province of Saskatchewan is 178 000 km^2. This is about 31% of the total land area of Saskatchewan. What is the area of the total land area of Saskatchewan?

19. Vancouver has 55 cm of snow per year. Edmonton has 230% as much snow as Vancouver. Ottawa has 175% as much snow as Edmonton. To the nearest centimetre, how much snow does Ottawa have per year?

CHAPTER 5

Patterns and Relations

Start with any number, say 12, and write all the divisors.

12: 1, 2, 3, 4, 6, 12

Add all the digits of these numbers to get a new number.

$1 + 2 + 3 + 4 + 6 + 1 + 2 = 19$

Repeat the process for the new number 19.

19: 1, 19

$1 + 1 + 9 = 11$

Repeat the process for 11.

11: 1, 11

$1 + 1 + 1 = 3$

Continue the process for every new number formed.

1. What number eventually keeps repeating?

2. Pick another starting number and repeat the process. Does the number that repeated above always repeat?

3. Write a statement to explain what you discovered. Use mathematical language such as, "The digits of the whole numbers that divide…"

Calendar Magic

Activity ❶ Calendar Patterns

The 3-by-3 squares come from a calendar. Eight dates are missing from each square. Copy and complete the squares.

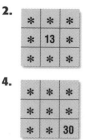

1.

4	*	*
*	*	*
*	*	*

2.

*	*	*
*	13	*
*	*	*

3.

*	*	11
*	*	*
*	*	*

4.

*	*	*
*	*	*
*	*	30

Activity ❷ Calendar Squares

A square block of 9 dates is outlined on the calendar.

S	M	T	W	T	F	S
		1	2	3	4	5
6	7	8	9	10	11	12
13	14	15	16	17	18	19
20	21	22	23	24	25	26
27	28	29	30			

1. What is the sum of the numbers on each diagonal?

2. What is the sum of the middle row of numbers?

3. What is the sum of the middle column of numbers?

4. How are the sums in questions 1–3 related to the middle number in the square?

5. Use another set of 9 dates in a square. Repeat questions 1–4. Is the relationship between the sums and the middle number in the square the same?

6. A magician's trick involves asking someone to choose a square of 9 dates and to state the sum of the middle row. The magician draws the chosen square without seeing the calendar. How is this done?

Activity ❸ Four Corners

S	M	T	W	T	F	S
	1	2	3	4	5	6
7	8	9	10	11	12	13
14	15	16	17	18	19	20
21	22	23	24	25	26	27
28	29	30				

1. What is the sum of the 4 corner numbers in the 3-by-3 square?

2. How is the sum related to the middle number?

3. The sum of the 4 corner numbers in a 3-by-3 square is 76. Draw the piece of the calendar.

Activity ❹ The Whole Square

S	M	T	W	T	F	S
1	2	3	4	5	6	7
8	9	10	11	12	13	14
15	16	17	18	19	20	21
22	23	24	25	26	27	28
29	30					

1. What is the sum of all 9 numbers in the square?

2. How is the sum related to the middle number in the square?

3. Use another set of 9 dates in a square and repeat questions 1 and 2. Is the relationship between the sum of all 9 dates and the middle number in the square the same?

4. The sum of all the numbers on a 3-by-3 square from a calendar is 162. Draw the piece of the calendar.

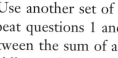

Activity ⑤ Vertical Rectangles

A vertical 3-by-2 rectangle is outlined on the calendar.

S	M	T	W	T	F	S
				1	2	3
4	5	6	7	8	9	10
11	12	13	14	15	16	17
18	19	20	21	22	23	24
25	26	27	28	29	30	31

1. What is the sum of the 6 dates?

2. How is the sum related to the sum of the 2 dates in the middle row?

3. Repeat question 1 for another 3-by-2 vertical rectangle. How is the sum of the 6 dates related to the sum of the 2 dates in the middle row?

4. If the sum of the two dates in the middle row of a vertical 3-by-2 rectangle is 37, what are the other dates in the rectangle?

5. The planet Icon has a calendar with 7 days a week and 70 days in a month. The sum of the 2 dates in the middle row of a 3-by-2 rectangle of this calendar is 99. Draw the rectangle of dates.

Activity ⑥ Horizontal Rectangles

A horizontal 2-by-3 rectangle is outlined on the calendar.

S	M	T	W	T	F	S
				1	2	3
4	5	6	7	8	9	10
11	12	13	14	15	16	17
18	19	20	21	22	23	24
25	26	27	28	29	30	31

1. Find the sum of the 6 dates.

2. How is the sum related to the sum of the 2 dates in the middle column?

3. If the sum of the two dates in the middle column of a 2-by-3 rectangle is 27, what are the other dates in the rectangle?

4. Activity 5, question 5, referred to the calendar on the planet Icon. The sum of the 2 dates in the middle column of a 2-by-3 rectangle in the planet Icon's calendar is 99. Draw the rectangle of dates.

Mental Math

Six multiples of 2 are 2, 4, 6, 8, 10, 12. State the following.

1. 8 multiples of 3   **2.** 5 multiples of 5   **3.** 6 multiples of 4   **4.** 6 multiples of 6

5. 7 multiples of 7   **6.** 5 multiples of 8   **7.** 7 multiples of 9   **8.** 6 multiples of 11

State all the factors of these numbers.

9. 4   **10.** 6   **11.** 7   **12.** 8   **13.** 10   **14.** 20   **15.** 24   **16.** 17   **17.** 16   **18.** 36

Evaluate the powers. Example: $2^3 = 2 \times 2 \times 2 = 8$

19. 3^2 **20.** 4^2 **21.** 6^2 **22.** 3^3 **23.** 2^4 **24.** 1^6 **25.** 10^3 **26.** 5^3

Calculate.

27. $2^2 \times 8$ **28.** $(5-2)^2$ **29.** $2 \times 3 + 4$ **30.** $2 \times (3+4)$ **31.** $4^2 + 2^2$

32. $(4+2)^2$ **33.** $15 \div 3 + 2$ **34.** $15 \div (3+2)$ **35.** $3^2 \div 3$ **36.** $(3 \div 3)^2$

Finding Patterns

Activity ❶

1. The large cube has dimensions 2-by-2-by-2 and is made from 8 small cubes.

If the outside of the large cube was painted blue, how many of the small cubes would have

a) 3 blue faces?   **b)** 2 blue faces?

c) 1 blue face?   **d)** 0 blue faces?

2. The large cube is made from 27 small cubes and has dimensions 3-by-3-by-3.

If the outside of the large cube was painted blue, how many of the small cubes would have

a) 3 blue faces?   **b)** 2 blue faces?

c) 1 blue face?   **d)** 0 blue faces?

3. The large cube is made from 64 small cubes. The dimensions are 4-by-4-by-4.

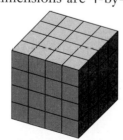

If the outside of the large cube was painted blue, how many of the small cubes would have

a) 3 blue faces?   **b)** 2 blue faces?

c) 1 blue face?   **d)** 0 blue faces?

4. The large cube is made from 125 small cubes and has dimensions 5-by-5-by-5.

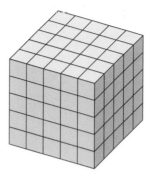

If the outside of the large cube was painted blue, how many of the small cubes would have

a) 3 blue faces?   **b)** 2 blue faces?

c) 1 blue face?   **d)** 0 blue faces?

5. a) Copy the table. Use the results from questions 1 to 4 to complete it.

Number of Small Cubes	Number of Blue Faces			
	3	2	1	0
8				
27				
64				
125				

b) Use the patterns in the table to complete the next row of the table for a large cube that has dimensions 6-by-6-by-6 and is made from 216 small cubes.

c) Complete the next row of the table for a large cube with dimensions 7-by-7-by-7.

Activity ❷

1. Cubes are stacked in the pattern shown. Assume that cubes that cannot be seen are all there.

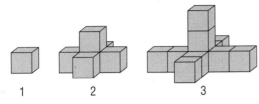

1   2   3

a) Draw diagrams of the next 3 stacks of cubes.
b) Copy and complete the table.

Diagram	1	2	3	4	5	6
Number of Cubes						

c) Describe the pattern in words.
d) How many cubes are in the 10th stack?
e) Which stack contains 146 cubes?

2. Cylindrical glass pipes are stacked as shown. Because glass is fragile, the cylinders are stacked no more than two layers high. The first 4 stacking arrangements are given.

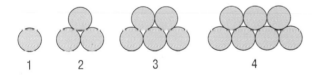

1   2   3   4

a) Draw diagrams of the next 2 stacks.
b) Describe the arrangement of the cylinders in the 15th stack.
c) How many cylinders are in the 15th stack?
d) In which stack in the pattern are there 239 pipes?
e) A plumber has to store 12 of the glass pipes. If she follows the pattern, why can she not arrange the pipes in 1 stack?
f) Draw all the possible sets of stacks for the 12 pipes.

3. In a banquet hall, small tables are arranged in 3s to seat 8 customers. For larger groups, extra tables are added to the arrangement. The first 3 possible seating arrangements are shown in the diagrams.

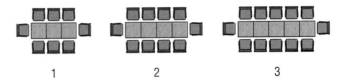

1   2   3

a) Record the number of tables and the number of seats for the first 6 arrangements.
b) Describe, in words, the pattern in the number of tables and seats.
c) How many people can be seated at an arrangement of 20 tables?
d) How many tables are in an arrangement to seat 32 people?

4. Each diagram is made up of squares of sides 1 unit.

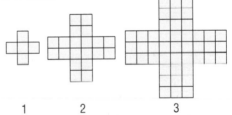

1   2   3

a) Draw the next 2 diagrams of the pattern.
b) Copy and complete the table.

Diagram	1	2	3	4	5
Area					
Perimeter					

c) Describe, in words, the pattern for the area.
d) Describe, in words, the pattern for the perimeter.
e) What is the perimeter of a shape that has an area of 320 square units?
f) What is the area of a shape that has a perimeter of 108 units?

149

Patterns in Rectangles

Mathematics is a study of patterns. Once a pattern
is found, rules can often be written to describe it.

Activity ❶ 2-by-■ Rectangles

A 2-by-4 rectangle is made up of 8 squares.
A diagonal passes through 4 squares.

A 2-by-5 rectangle is made up of 10 squares.
A diagonal passes through 6 squares.

Draw the rectangles from 2-by-1 to 2-by-10.
Draw a diagonal in each rectangle.
Copy and complete the table.

Dimensions	Squares Passed Through
2-by-1	
:	
2-by-4	4
2-by-5	6
:	
2-by-10	

1. Describe the pattern in the right-hand column of the table.

2. Extend the table for the next 4 rectangles. Complete the
"Squares Passed Through" column without drawing the
rectangles and diagonals.

3. How many squares would the diagonal pass through in
a 2-by-26 rectangle? a 2-by-31 rectangle?

4. Write a rule to find the number of squares a diagonal
passes through if the second dimension is a multiple of 2.

5. Use your rule to find the number of squares a diagonal
passes through in each of these rectangles.
a) 2-by-50   **b)** 2-by-88   **c)** 2-by-2000

6. Write a rule to find the number of squares a diagonal
passes through if the second dimension is not a multiple of 2.

7. Use your rule to find the number of squares a diagonal
passes through in each of these rectangles.
a) 2-by-53   **b)** 2-by-99   **c)** 2-by-2013

8. What are the possible values of the second dimension
of a rectangle whose diagonal passes through
a) 20 squares?   **b)** 126 squares?   **c)** 210 squares?

Activity ❷ 3-by-■ Rectangles

Draw the rectangles from 3-by-1 to 3-by-9.
Draw a diagonal in each rectangle.

Copy and
complete
the table.

Dimensions	Squares Passed Through
3-by-1	
:	
3-by-9	

1. Write a rule to find the number of squares a diagonal passes through if the second dimension is a multiple of 3.

2. Use your rule to find the number of squares a diagonal passes through in each of these rectangles.
a) 3-by-36   **b)** 3-by-45   **c)** 3-by-3000

3. What is the second dimension of a rectangle whose diagonal passes through 333 squares?

4. Write a rule to find the number of squares a diagonal passes through if the second dimension is not a multiple of 3.

5. Use your rule to find the number of squares a diagonal passes through in each of these rectangles.
a) 3-by-28   **b)** 3-by-44   **c)** 3-by-2000

6. What is the second dimension of a rectangle whose diagonal passes through 79 squares?

Activity ❸ 4-by-■ Rectangles

Draw the rectangles from 4-by-1 to 4-by-8.
Draw a diagonal in each rectangle.

Copy and
complete
the table.

Dimensions	Squares Passed Through
4-by-1	
:	
4-by-8	

1. Write rules to find the number of squares a diagonal passes through if you are given the second dimension.

2. Test your rules by drawing the next 4 rectangles and one diagonal for each.

3. Use your rules to find the number of squares a diagonal passes through in each of these rectangles.
a) 4-by-42   **b)** 4-by-55   **c)** 4-by-44

151

5.1 Variables and Expressions

A basketball court is 26 m long and 14 m wide.
The perimeter of the court is given by $2l + 2w$,
where l is the length and w is the width.

$$2l + 2w = 2 \times 26 + 2 \times 14$$
$$= 52 + 28$$
$$= 80$$

A soccer field is 100 m long and 73 m wide.

$$2l + 2w = 2 \times 100 + 2 \times 73$$
$$= 200 + 146$$
$$= 346$$

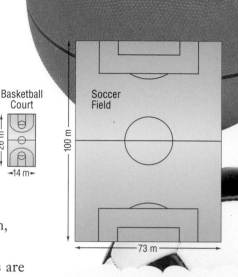

Basketball Court

Soccer Field

So, the basketball court has a perimeter of 80 m,
and the soccer field has a perimeter of 346 m.

In the **algebraic expression** $2l + 2w$, the **terms** are
$2l$ and $2w$. The letters in the expression are called
variables because they can represent many numbers.

The term $2l$ means $2 \times l$ or $l + l$.
In words, $2l$ means "two times the length."

Activity: Make a Comparison

Arithmetic	Algebra
$5 + 5$	$x + x$
$2(4) - 3$	$2x - 3$
$7(2) + 8(6)$	$7x + 8y$
3^2	x^2

 Inquire

1. How are the expressions $5 + 5$ and
$x + x$ alike? How are they different?

2. How are the expressions in each of the
other pairs alike? How are they different?

An algebraic expression can have many different values,
depending on the numbers assigned to the variables.
Replacing a variable by a number is called **substitution**.

Example 1

Evaluate.
a) $2x + 3y$ for $x = 4$ and $y = 5$
b) $x^2 - x$ for $x = 3$

Solution

a) $2x + 3y = 2(4) + 3(5)$
$= 8 + 15$
$= 23$

b) $x^2 - x = (3)^2 - 3$
$= 9 - 3$
$= 6$

Variables can also be replaced by negative numbers.

Example 2

Evaluate $3t + 5$ for $t = -2$.

Solution

$3t + 5 = 3(-2) + 5$
$= -6 + 5$
$= -1$

Practice

Write the words as an algebraic expression.

1. the length plus seven

2. three times the height minus four

3. two times the height plus four times the width

4. five times the number of dogs minus two times the number of cats

Write each expression in words.

5. $2b + 4$

6. $3w - 6$

7. $2l + 3w - 1$

8. $2d - 3c + 6$

Evaluate.

9. $x + 4,\ x = 2$

10. $4y,\ y = 3$

11. $t - 1,\ t = 7$

12. $8 - w,\ w = 2$

13. $4m + 2,\ m = 3$

14. $6t - 2,\ t = 5$

15. $9 - 2x,\ x = 4$

16. $6r + 8,\ r = 7$

Evaluate $4x$ for each value of x.

17. 3 **18.** 7 **19.** 2 **20.** 0

Evaluate $4y + 2$ for each value of y.

21. 1 **22.** 6 **23.** 3 **24.** 5

Evaluate for $x = 2$.

25. $3x$

26. $4x + 7$

27. $10 - 4x$

28. x^2

29. $x^2 - 1$

30. $2(x + 1)$

Evaluate for $y = 3$.

31. $4y$

32. $8 - y$

33. $10 - 3y$

34. $4 + y^2$

35. $y^2 - 2$

36. $2(y - 2)$

Evaluate for $x = 1$ and $y = 4$.

37. $x + y$

38. $2x + y$

39. $4x + y + 3$

40. $x + y - 5$

41. $2x + 3y - 5$ **42.** $5x - y + 1$

Evaluate for $x = 3.2$ and $y = 1.4$.

43. $x + y$

44. $x - y$

45. $x + 2y$

46. $3x - 2y$

47. $4x + y$

48. $2(x + y)$

Evaluate.

49. $2x,\ x = -2$

50. $5n,\ n = -1$

51. $y + 6,\ y = -3$

52. $4t + 3,\ t = -4$

53. $5 + 3m,\ m = -2$

54. $8 - 2n,\ n = -1$

Evaluate for $x = -2$ and $y = -3$.

55. $x + y$

56. $2x + 3y$

57. $3x - 2y$

58. $5x + 4y + 7$

Problems and Applications

59. The total cost of a banquet, in dollars, is represented by the expression $22n$, where n is the number of people. What is the cost for 37 students?

60. The points total of an NHL team is given by the expression $2w + t$, where w is the number of wins, and t is the number of ties. Copy and complete the table to find the points totals for some Canadian teams in one season.

Team	Wins	Ties	Points
Calgary	43	11	
Edmonton	26	8	
Montreal	48	6	
Ottawa	10	4	
Quebec	47	10	
Toronto	44	11	
Vancouver	46	9	

61. An expression that has 3 terms is called a **trinomial**. The prefix *tri-* means three. Find two other words that start with *tri-*.

62. Evaluate each expression.
a) $(x + 3)^2 + 2y,\ x = 2,\ y = 3$
b) $2(t - 3)^2 - 4s,\ t = 6,\ s = 2$
c) $3(d + 5) - 2e^2,\ d = -3,\ e = -2$

63. Find the whole-number values of x for which the first expression is larger than, or equal to, the second.
a) $2x,\ x^2$ b) $3x,\ x^2$

153

5.2 Developing and Working with Formulas

Activity: Complete the Table

The first figure is made up of one L-shape. It has a perimeter of 12 units. The second figure is made up of 2 connected L-shapes. It has a perimeter of 22 units.

Copy the table. Complete it by finding the perimeters of the figures with the given numbers of L-shapes.

Number of L-Shapes	Perimeter
1	12
2	22
3	
4	
5	

Inquire

1. What is the increase in the perimeter each time an L-shape is added?

2. What is the perimeter of the figure made from
a) 6 L-shapes?   **b)** 7 L-shapes?   **c)** 8 L-shapes?

3. Describe how you would find the perimeter of a figure made from 80 L-shapes.

4. Write a formula for the perimeter in the form $P = \blacktriangle \times n + \blacksquare$, where n is the number of L-shapes in the figure, and $\blacktriangle$ and $\blacksquare$ represent two different numbers.

5. Use the formula to calculate the perimeter of a figure made from 97 L-shapes.

6. How many L-shapes are in a figure with a perimeter of 272 units?

Example

Euler's formula for polyhedra states that the number of vertices plus the number of faces equals the number of edges plus 2, or $V + F = E + 2$. A certain polyhedron has 8 vertices and 12 edges. How many faces does it have?

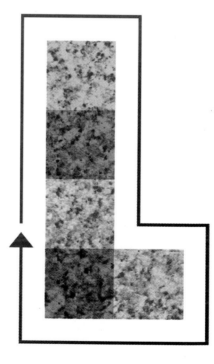

Solution

Substitute the known values, $V = 8$ and $E = 12$, into the formula and solve for the unknown value.

$$V + F = E + 2$$
$$8 + F = 12 + 2$$
$$8 + F = 14$$
$$8 - 8 + F = 14 - 8$$
$$F = 6$$

Check: L.S. $= V + F$ **R.S.** $= E + 2$
$= 8 + 6$ $= 12 + 2$
$= 14$ $= 14$

The polyhedron has 6 faces.

Practice

Copy and complete the table. State a rule for each pattern.

1.

x	1	2	3	4	5	6
y	4	8	12			

2.

s	3	5	7	9	11	13
t	8	10	12			

Copy and complete the table. Then, use the variables to write a formula for each pattern.

3.

Hours (*h*)	1	2	3	4	5	6
Wages (*w*)	9	18	27			

4.

Number of Tickets (*n*)		2	4	6	8
Cost (*c*)		42	84		

5. The formula for the area of a rectangle is $A = l \times w$.

a) Find A when $l = 9$ m and $w = 6$ m.

b) Find l when $A = 30$ m^2 and $w = 5$ m.

c) Find w when $A = 24$ m^2 and $l = 8$ m.

6. The formula for the perimeter of a rectangle is $P = 2(l + w)$.

a) Find P when $l = 11$ m and $w = 7$ m.

b) Find w when $P = 80$ m and $l = 23$ m.

c) Find l when $P = 74$ m and $w = 17$ m.

Problems and Applications

7. The first figure is made up of one T-shape. It has a perimeter of 10 units. The second figure is made up of 2 connected T-shapes, and so on.

a) Copy the table. Complete it by finding the perimeters of the figures with the given numbers of T-shapes.

Number of T-Shapes	Perimeter
1	10
⋮	
5	

b) What is the increase in the perimeter each time a T-shape is added?

c) What is the perimeter of the figure made from 6 T-shapes? 7 T-shapes?

d) Write a formula for the perimeter in the form $P = \blacktriangle \times n + \blacksquare$, where n is the number of T-shapes in the figure, and $\blacktriangle$ and $\blacksquare$ represent two different numbers.

8. a) Copy and complete the table.

Number of Triangles	Figure	Perimeter
1	△	3
2	▽	4
3	△▽△	5
⋮		
6		

b) Write a formula for the perimeter in terms of the number of triangles.

c) What is the perimeter of the figure made from 30 triangles?

d) How many triangles are in the figure with a perimeter of 42 units?

9. a) Copy and complete the table.

Number of L-Shapes	Figure	Perimeter
1		8
2		12
3		16
⋮		
6		

b) Write a formula for the perimeter in terms of the number of L-shapes.

c) What is the perimeter of the figure made from 15 L-shapes?

d) How many L-shapes make a figure with a perimeter of 88 units?

5.3 Relations as Ordered Pairs

Activity: Complete the Table

A light plane glides when the engine is turned off.
Pilots use the saying "five for one."
This means that the plane will glide 5 m for every
1 m of altitude, or 500 m for every 100 m of altitude.
Copy and complete the table of values.

Altitude (m)	Glide Distance (m)
100	500
200	
600	
1000	
1500	
2000	

Inquire

1. How many metres will a plane glide from an altitude
of 200 m? 600 m? 1500 m?

2. Write the results from the table as **ordered pairs**.
For an altitude of 100 m, the ordered pair is (100, 500),
where the first number is the altitude, and the second
number is the glide distance.

3. Write an equation in the form $d = \blacksquare \times a$ to calculate
the glide distance, d, from the altitude, a.

4. Use your equation to find the glide distance for each
of these altitudes.   **a)** 400 m   **b)** 500 m   **c)** 1250 m

The equation $x + 1 = 4$ has one variable, x.
There is one solution, $x = 3$, that makes the equation true.

There are two variables in the equation $x + y = 7$.
There are many solutions, or values of the variables, that
make the equation true.
One solution is $x = 3$ and $y = 4$, because $3 + 4 = 7$.
This solution can be written as the ordered pair (3, 4).
It is customary to write the x-value first, then the y-value.

A set of ordered pairs is known as a **relation**. A relation can also
be expressed as an equation, as a table of values, or in words.

Example 1

Use the equation $x + y = 4$.
a) Describe the relation in
words.
b) Complete a table of values
for $x = 3, 2, 1, 0, -1$.
c) Write the ordered pairs.

Solution

a) The sum of the x- and y-values is four.
b) Find the y-values. Complete the table of values.

$x + y = 4$
$3 + 1 = 4$
$2 + 2 = 4$
$1 + 3 = 4$
$0 + 4 = 4$
$-1 + 5 = 4$

x	y
3	1
2	2
1	3
0	4
−1	5

c) The ordered pairs are (3, 1), (2, 2), (1, 3), (0, 4), (−1, 5).

Example 2

Use the equation $y = 2x + 3$.
a) Describe the relation in words.
b) Complete a table of values for $x = 2, 1, 0, -1, -2$.
c) Write the ordered pairs.

Solution

a) The value of y is two times the value of x, plus 3.
b) Find the y-values. Complete the table of values.

$y = 2x + 3$
$y = 2(2) + 3 = 7$
$y = 2(1) + 3 = 5$
$y = 2(0) + 3 = 3$
$y = 2(-1) + 3 = 1$
$y = 2(-2) + 3 = -1$

x	y
2	7
1	5
0	3
-1	1
-2	-1

c) The ordered pairs are (2, 7), (1, 5), (0, 3), (–1, 1), and (–2, –1).

Practice

Use each of the following equations.
a) Describe the relation in words.
b) Copy and complete the table of values.
c) Write the ordered pairs.

1. $x + y = 6$

x	y
3	
2	
1	
0	
-1	

2. $x + y = 2$

x	y
2	
1	
0	
-1	
-2	

3. $x - y = 2$

x	y
6	
5	
4	
3	
2	

4. $x - y = 0$

x	y
3	
2	
1	
0	
-1	

5. For the equation $x + y = 9$, find the missing value in each ordered pair.
a) (3, ■) **b)** (7, ■)
c) (■, 2) **d)** (■, 0)
e) (–1, ■) **f)** (–3, ■)
g) (■, –2) **h)** (■, –7)

6. For the equation $x - y = 1$, find the missing value in each ordered pair.
a) (6, ■) **b)** (2, ■) **c)** (■, 3)
d) (■, 7) **e)** (–1, ■) **f)** (■, –2)

Use each of the following equations.
a) Describe the relation in words.
b) Copy and complete the table of values.
c) Write the ordered pairs.

7. $y = x + 3$

x	y
2	
1	
0	
-1	
-2	

8. $y = x - 1$

x	y
3	
2	
1	
0	
-1	

9. $y = 2x + 1$

x	y
2	
1	
0	
-1	
-2	

10. $y = 3x - 2$

x	y
2	
1	
0	
-1	
-2	

11. For the equation $y = x + 2$, find the missing value in each ordered pair.
a) (2, ■) **b)** (3, ■) **c)** (–1, ■)
d) (0, ■) **e)** (■, 5) **f)** (■, 0)

12. For the equation $y = x - 3$, find the missing value in each ordered pair.
a) (4, ■) **b)** (6, ■) **c)** (0, ■)
d) (–1, ■) **e)** (■, 5) **f)** (■, 0)

Write 5 ordered pairs for each relation.

13. $x + y = 5$ **14.** $x - y = 3$

15. $y = x + 4$ **16.** $y = 2x + 2$

CONTINUED ▶

Problems and Applications

Write an equation for each relation.

17.

x	y
1	6
2	5
3	4
4	3
5	2

18.

x	y
8	4
7	3
6	2
5	1
4	0

19.

x	y
4	5
3	4
2	3
1	2
0	1

20.

x	y
6	4
5	3
4	2
3	1
2	0

21. List 5 ordered pairs of a relation for which the *y*-value is always 4 more than the *x*-value.

22. List 5 ordered pairs of a relation for which the *x*-value is always two times the *y*-value.

23. List 5 ordered pairs of a relation for which the *x*-value minus the *y*-value is always 6.

24. Over long distances, the fastest animal on land is the pronghorn. It resembles an antelope and is found in rocky deserts of the western United States. The pronghorn can run at about 15 m/s for 6 min.

a) Copy and complete the table to show the distances a pronghorn can cover in different lengths of time.

Time (s)	Distance (m)
1	15
2	
3	
4	

b) Describe the pattern in the distance column.
c) How far can a pronghorn run in 5 s? 6 s?
d) Write the results from the table as ordered pairs.
e) Describe the relation in words.
f) Let *t* represent the time. Write an equation of the form $d = \blacksquare \times t$ to find the distance.

g) Use your equation to find the distance a pronghorn can cover in 12 s; 50 s.
h) What distance, in kilometres, can a pronghorn run in 6 min?
i) What is the pronghorn's average speed, in kilometres per hour, over this distance?

25. a) The figures are made up of rows of squares. Copy the table. Complete it by finding the perimeters of the figures.

Figure	Squares	Perimeter
☐	1	4
☐☐	2	6
☐☐☐	3	
☐☐☐☐	4	
☐☐☐☐☐	5	

b) Describe the pattern in the perimeter column.
c) What would the perimeter be for 6 squares? 7 squares?
d) Write the results from the table as ordered pairs.
e) Describe the relation in words.
f) Let *n* represent the number of squares. Write an equation in the form $P = \blacksquare \times n + ?$ to find the perimeter.
g) Use your equation to find the perimeter of a figure made from 13 squares; 24 squares; 300 squares.

26. Describe each relationship.
a) the speed of a train and the distance it travels
b) the number of daylight hours and the time of year
c) the number of people at the beach and the outside temperature

27. Make up your own table of values like the ones in questions 17 to 20, where there is a relationship between the values of *x* and *y*. Have a classmate write an equation for the relation.

5.4 Graphing Ordered Pairs

Activity: Use the Coordinate Grid

A French mathematician, René Descartes, developed a system for plotting ordered pairs on a grid. The horizontal number line is called the **x-axis**. The vertical number line is called the **y-axis**. The two lines meet at a point called the **origin**. For any point on the grid, such as A(2, 4), the first number in the ordered pair is the **x-coordinate**. The second number in the ordered pair is the **y-coordinate**. To plot the point A(2, 4) on the grid, start at the origin, and move 2 units to the right and 4 units up.

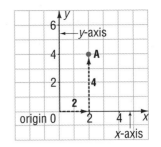

Inquire

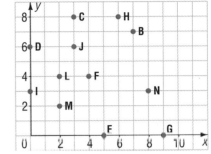

1. Name the point that has the following coordinates.

a) (4, 4) **b)** (8, 3) **c)** (3, 6) **d)** (5, 0) **e)** (0, 6) **f)** (7, 7)

2. State the coordinates of the following points.

a) C **b)** L **c)** H **d)** M **e)** G **f)** I

Practice

1. State the coordinates of each point.

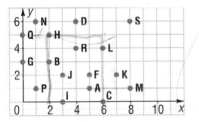

Problems and Applications

In each of the following, identify the closed figure formed by joining the points in the order given, and find the area of the figure.

2. O(0, 0), D(0, 5), E(5, 5), F(5, 0)

3. P(1, 1), Q(1, 5), R(6, 5), S(6, 1)

4. D(1, 1), E(7, 1), F(7, 5), G(1, 5)

5. W(2, 0), X(2, 5), Y(6, 5), Z(6, 0)

6. a) Plot the points P(3, 1), Q(3, 4), R(6, 7), S(9, 4), and T(9, 1) on a grid, and join the points in the order given.
b) Identify the figure.

7. a) Plot the points A(1, 2), B(3, 2), C(3, 5), and D(1, 5) to make a rectangle.
b) Find the perimeter and the area.
c) Multiply each pair of coordinates of the rectangle by 2. So, (1, 2) becomes (2, 4), and so on. Draw the new rectangle. Find the perimeter and the area.
d) How do the perimeter and the area of the new rectangle compare with those of the original rectangle?

8. The points D(8, 2), E(2, 2), and F(2, 5) are 3 vertices of a rectangle.
a) Plot the points on a grid.
b) Find the coordinates of G so that DEFG is a rectangle.
c) Calculate the perimeter and the area of the rectangle.

9. If you join the points (2, 1) and (2, 6) on a grid, you get the letter I.
a) What points would you use to represent the letter A?
b) Use positive coordinates to spell out a word. Have a classmate discover your word.

159

5.5 Graphing on the Coordinate Plane

For years, a navigator on a ship at sea used a compass, a sextant, and charts to estimate the ship's latitude and longitude. A Canadian company in Vancouver has developed an Electronic Chart Display and Information System (ECDIS). The electronic chart combines radar, satellite, and other data to display the ship's latitude and longitude on a video screen.

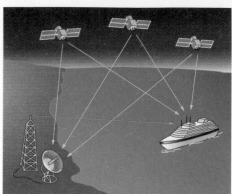

In mathematics, positions of points are given by coordinates on a grid. In this section, the coordinate plane is extended to include integers.

Activity: Study the Grid

The coordinates of point P are (3, –4).
The coordinates of point Q are (–4, –2).

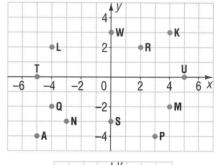

Inquire

1. State the coordinates of the following points.

a) K   **b)** L   **c)** M   **d)** N   **e)** W
f) T   **g)** R   **h)** S   **i)** U   **j)** A

2. The x- and y-axes divide the coordinate plane into 4 quadrants, as shown. In which quadrants are

a) the y-coordinates negative?   **b)** the x-coordinates negative?
c) the signs of the x- and y-coordinates opposite?

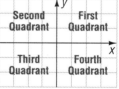

Example

a) Plot the points P(1, 2), Q(–4, 2), R(–4, –2), and S(1, –2) on a grid. Join the points in order.
b) Calculate the area of the figure.

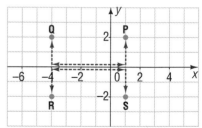

Solution

a) Start at the origin.
For P, move 1 right and 2 up. For Q, move 1 left and 2 up.
For R, move 4 left and 2 down. For S, move 1 right and 2 down.
Join the points P, Q, R, S, P, in order.
b) The figure is a rectangle.
The length is RS, so the length is 5 units.
The width is QR, so the width is 4 units.

$A = l \times w$
  $= 5 \times 4$
  $= 20$

The area of PQRS is 20 square units.

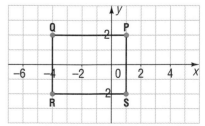

Practice

1. Write the coordinates for each point.

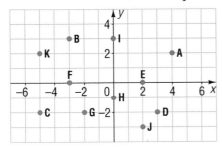

On the following grid, name the points given by these ordered pairs.

2. (2, 3) **3.** (–2, 2) **4.** (–3, –3)

5. (3, –3) **6.** (–4, –1) **7.** (–3, 4)

8. (2, 0) **9.** (0, 4) **10.** (–2, 0)

11. (0, –2) **12.** (–1, 1) **13.** (3, –1)

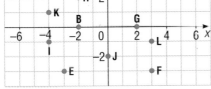

Problems and Applications

14. Plot the ordered pairs to make a word.
a) Join (–3, 0) to (–3, 1), (–3, 0) to (–5, 0), (–5, 2) to (–5, 0), (–5, 2) to (–3, 2), (–3, 1) to (–4, 1).
b) Join (–1, 2) to (1, 2), (–1, 2) to (–1, 0), (1, 1) to (1, 2), (1, 1) to (–1, 1), (1, 0) to (–1, 1).
c) Join (2, 2) to (2, 0).
d) Join (5, 1) to (4, 0), (5, 1) to (4, 2), (3, 0) to (3, 2), (3, 0) to (4, 0), (4, 2) to (3, 2).

Plot the points on a grid and join them in order. Identify each figure and find the area.

15. A(–3, 0), B(–3, 3), C(0, 3), D(0, 0)

16. E(–5, 5), F(–5, –5), G(1, –5), H(1, 5)

17. P(–2, –2), Q(–2, 2), R(2, 2), S(2, –2)

18. D(–4, 2), E(8, 2), F(8, –4), G(–4, –4)

19. a) Points A(1, 1), B(2, 4), and C(6, 4) are 3 vertices of a parallelogram. Plot the points on a grid.
b) Find three different coordinates for point D so that ABCD is a parallelogram.

20. An ant moves from point A on a grid along a straight path determined by the points A(–3, –5), B(–2, –4), and C(–1, –3). An anteater moves from point P on the same grid along a straight path determined by the points P(–2, 6), Q(–1, 5), and R(0, 4). They move at the same speed.
a) Plot the two paths on a grid.
b) What are the coordinates of the point where the paths cross?
c) Does the ant pass in front of the anteater or behind the anteater, or do they meet where their paths cross?
d) Write 3 different ant and anteater problems. In one, have them meeting at a point. In another, have the ant passing in front of the anteater. In another, have the ant passing behind the anteater. Have a classmate solve your problems.

NUMBER POWER

The expression shows one way of using four –5s and the order of operations to express the value 1.

$$-5 - (-5) + \left(\frac{-5}{-5} \right)$$

Use four –5s and the order of operations to write expressions that equal each of these values.

a) 0 **b)** 2 **c)** 9
d) 3 **e)** 7 **f)** 5

5.6 Graphing Relations

Activity: Complete the Table

Francine has 20 m of fence for a rectangular garden. This means that the sum of the length and the width must be 10 m. There are many possible dimensions for the garden. One possible garden could be 7 m long and 3 m wide. Copy and complete the table for gardens with a perimeter of 20 m and whole-number values of the length and the width.

Length, l	Width, w	Ordered Pair, (l, w)
9		
8		
7	3	(7, 3)
⋮		
1		

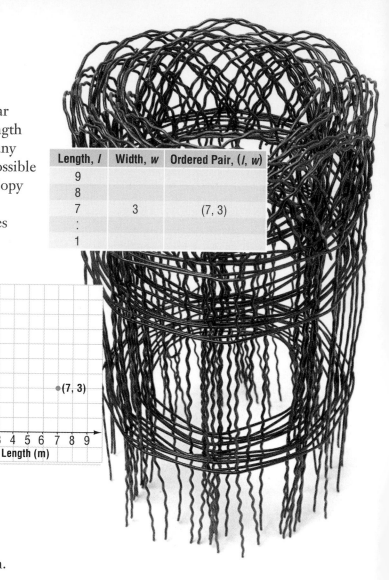

Inquire

1. Graph the relation and write the coordinates of each point on the grid.

2. What does the product of each pair of coordinates represent?

3. What are the dimensions of the garden with the largest area?

Example

Graph the relation $y = 3x + 2$ for integer values of the variable.

Solution

Find 5 ordered pairs that satisfy the relation. Graph the ordered pairs.

When $x = 2$, $y = 3(2) + 2$
$\quad = 8$
When $x = 1$, $y = 3(1) + 2$
$\quad = 5$
When $x = 0$, $y = 3(0) + 2$
$\quad = 2$
When $x = -1$, $y = 3(-1) + 2$
$\quad = -1$
When $x = -2$, $y = 3(-2) + 2$
$\quad = -4$

x	y
2	8
1	5
0	2
−1	−1
−2	−4

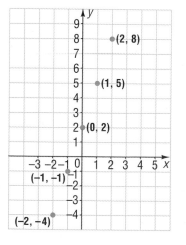

Many ordered pairs satisfy the relation.
The graph represents part of the graph of $y = 3x + 2$.

Practice

Graph each relation and express it in words.

1.
x	y
3	0
2	1
1	2
0	3
−1	4

2.
x	y
5	4
3	2
1	0
−1	−2
−3	−4

3.
x	y
3	6
1	2
−1	−2
−3	−6
−5	−10

Find 5 ordered pairs that satisfy each relation. Draw each graph.

4. $x + y = 7$ **5.** $x + y = 6$ **6.** $x - y = 1$

7. $x - y = 0$ **8.** $x + y = 0$ **9.** $y - x = 2$

Find 5 ordered pairs that satisfy each relation. Draw each graph.

10. $y = x + 4$ **11.** $y = x - 2$

12. $y = 2x + 1$ **13.** $y = 3x - 4$

Problems and Applications

14. The area of a rectangle is 12 cm^2.
a) Copy the table. Complete it for the possible values of the length and width.

Width, w	Length, l	Ordered Pair, (w, l)
1		
2		
3		
4		
6		
12		

b) Graph the relation and write the coordinates of each point on the grid.
c) For each point, what does the sum of the coordinates represent?
d) What are the whole-number dimensions of a 12-cm² rectangle that has the smallest perimeter?

15. List 5 ordered pairs of a relation for which the x-coordinate is always 3 and the y-coordinate is an integer. Plot the points on a grid. Describe the result.

16. List 5 ordered pairs of a relation for which the y-coordinate is always −3 and the x-coordinate is an integer. Plot the points on a grid. Describe the result.

17. Jo-Anna makes ceramic mugs to sell at craft shows. She has two choices to pay for the firing in the kiln.
A: $5 set-up charge, plus $1 per mug
B: $0 set-up charge, and $2 per mug
a) List the ordered pairs for 1 to 10 mugs using choice A.
b) List the ordered pairs for 1 to 10 mugs using choice B.
c) Plot the ordered pairs for each relation on the same grid.
d) Examine the graphs and decide the number of mugs for which
• both choices give the same cost
• choice A gives a lower cost
• choice B gives a lower cost

18. The manager of a supermarket has 24 m of fence available to enclose a rectangular lot for gardening supplies.

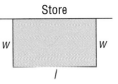

One side of the lot will be against the store wall and will not need fencing.
a) Copy the table. Complete it for the possible whole-number lengths and widths.

Width, w	Length, l	Ordered Pair, (w, l)
1		
2		
⋮		
11		

b) Graph the relation and write the coordinates of each point on the grid.
c) For each point, what does the product of the coordinates represent?
d) What are the whole-number dimensions of the rectangle that has the largest area?

Spreadsheets

Activity ❶ Spreadsheet Design

A **spreadsheet** is like a large sheet of paper divided into rows and columns. Each of the rectangles in a spreadsheet is called a **cell**. Three things can be put into cells: numbers, words that tell you what the numbers mean, and arithmetic operations that do calculations.

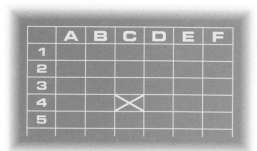

Columns are named across the top of the spreadsheet by capital letters. Rows are named by numbers down the side.

Each cell has its own name. A cell is named using the capital letter of the column the cell is in, followed by the number of the row the cell is in. The cell C4 is in column C and row 4.

1. Name the following cells.
a) 4 columns over and 3 rows down
b) 6 columns over and 2 rows down
c) 2 columns over and 5 rows down
d) 1 column over and 1 row down

2. Find out, and describe, how spreadsheets name columns after the 26 letters of the alphabet have been used.

3. Manual spreadsheets have been used for a long time. Your report card may be like a spreadsheet, if it has cells for words and numbers.
a) List 2 examples of spreadsheets that you see in a newspaper. What are they used for?
b) What are the cells that have words in them used for?
c) What are the cells that have numbers in them used for?
d) Are there any cells that have the result of an arithmetic calculation in them?

Activity ➋ A 3-by-3 Magic Square

The spreadsheet has been set up to make a 3-by-3 magic square. The arithmetic operations are shown in the cells.

On a computer, you would see them at the top of the spreadsheet when you put the cursor in the cell.

	A	B	C	D
1				@SUM(A4,B3,C2)
2	+B2 + 7	1	+B2 + 5	@SUM(A2..C2)
3	+B2 + 2	+B2 + 4	+B2 + 6	@SUM(A3..C3)
4	+B2 + 3	+B2 + 8	+B2 + 1	@SUM(A4..C4)
5	@SUM(A2..A4)	@SUM(B2..B4)	@SUM(C2..C4)	@SUM(A2,B3,C4)

1. What number is in cell B2?

2. What does the instruction in cell A2 tell you to do?

3. Draw a 3-by-3 grid to represent the magic square shown on the spreadsheet. Use the instructions to complete the square.

4. What do the instructions in column D tell you to do? Do the calculations.

5. What do the instructions in row 5 tell you to do? Do the calculations.

6. Why are the numbers in the red box called a magic square?

7. What numbers result in the square when you multiply the entry in cell B2 by 2? by 4? Are the resulting squares magic squares?

Activity ➌ A 4-by-4 Magic Square

1. The arithmetic operations for a 4-by-4 magic square are shown. Copy the spreadsheet and insert the instructions for column E and row 6.

	A	B	C	D	E
1					
2	1	+A2 + 14	+A2 + 13	+A2 + 3	
3	+A2 + 11	+A2 + 5	+A2 + 6	+A2 + 8	
4	+A2 + 7	+A2 + 9	+A2 + 10	+A2 + 4	
5	+A2 + 12	+A2 + 2	+A2 + 1	+A2 + 15	
6					

2. What is the magic number of this square?

Review

Write these words as an algebraic expression.

1. the difference between the amount and 7

2. four times the number of squares plus three times the number of triangles

Write each expression in words.

3. $3w + 2$ **4.** $\frac{2w}{3}$ **5.** $5a + b - 3$

Evaluate for x = 6.

6. $x - 5$ **7.** $\frac{x}{2}$ **8.** $x^2 - 2$ **9.** $3x - 2$

Evaluate for x = 2 and y = −3.

10. $2x + y$ **11.** $x - y$ **12.** $3x - 2y$

13. a) Copy and complete the table.

Number of Pentagons	Figure	Perimeter
1		5
2		8
3		11
⋮		
6		

b) Write a formula for the perimeter in terms of the number of pentagons.

c) What is the perimeter of the figure made from 20 pentagons?

d) How many pentagons make up a figure with a perimeter of 101 units?

14. Describe the relation, in words, between each of the following.

a) the number of birds and the time of year

b) the distance a car travels and the amount of gas it uses

15. For the equation $x + y = 5$, find the missing value in each ordered pair.

a) $(1, \blacksquare)$ **b)** $(5, \blacksquare)$ **c)** $(\blacksquare, 2)$ **d)** $(\blacksquare, 0)$
e) $(-2, \blacksquare)$ **f)** $(-1, \blacksquare)$ **g)** $(\blacksquare, -1)$ **h)** $(\blacksquare, -2)$

Use each of the following equations.

a) *Describe the relation in words.*
b) *Copy and complete the table of values.*
c) *Write the ordered pairs.*

16. $x + y = 8$

x	y
4	
3	
2	
1	
0	

17. $y = x + 5$

x	y
2	
1	
0	
−1	
−2	

18. For the equation $y = x + 6$, find the missing value in each ordered pair.

a) $(2, \blacksquare)$ **b)** $(3, \blacksquare)$ **c)** $(\blacksquare, 2)$
d) $(\blacksquare, 0)$ **e)** $(-3, \blacksquare)$ **f)** $(\blacksquare, -4)$

Write 5 ordered pairs for each relation.

19. $x + y = 4$ **20.** $x - y = 1$ **21.** $y = x + 3$
22. $y = x - 4$ **23.** $y = 2x + 5$ **24.** $y = 3x - 1$

Write an equation for each relation.

25.

x	y
1	7
2	6
3	5
4	4
5	3

26.

x	y
5	3
4	2
3	1
2	0
1	−1

27.

x	y
3	5
2	4
1	3
0	2
−1	1

28. a) Copy and complete the table for a car travelling at 70 km/h.

Time (h)	Distance (km)
1	70
2	
3	
4	

b) How far would the car travel in 5 h? 6 h?

c) Describe the pattern in the distance column.

d) Write the results from the table as ordered pairs.

e) Describe, in words, the relation between the time and the distance travelled.

f) Let t represent the time, in hours. Write an equation in the form $D = \blacksquare \times t$ to find the distance travelled in kilometres.

Name the points on the grid with the following coordinates.

29. (4, 0) **30.** (3, 2) **31.** (−4, 2)

32. (5, −3) **33.** (−2, −4) **34.** (0, 4)

35. (−3, 0) **36.** (5, 5) **37.** (−5, −1)

38. (0, −5) **39.** (−2, 4) **40.** (1, −3)

41. a) Plot and join each pair of points to form line segments.

A(−5, 3), B(5, 3) H(−2, 3), I(2, −3)

D(−3, 4), E(4, −3) J(−5, 4), K(−4, 5)

F(4, −1), G(−4, 1) L(−3, 3), M(3, −3)

b) Which line segments pass through (0, 0)?

c) For the line segments that pass through (0, 0), describe any pattern you see in the coordinates of the end points.

Plot the points on a grid and join them in order. Identify each figure and find the area.

42. P(1, 4), Q(1, −1), R(4, −1), S(4, 4)

43. A(−1, 1), B(−1, 4), C(−4, 4), D(−4, 1)

Plot the points on a grid and join them in order. Identify each figure.

44. D(0, −4), E(6, −4), F(4, −2), G(2, −2)

45. I(−8, −5), J(−3, −5), K(−1, −2), L(−6, −2)

Find 5 ordered pairs that satisfy each relation. Draw each graph.

46. $x + y = 7$ **47.** $x - y = 2$

48. $y = x + 3$ **49.** $y = x - 4$

50. $y = 2x + 3$ **51.** $y = 3x - 1$

Group Decision Making
Designing a Classroom Floor Plan

Work in home groups.

| 1 2 3 4 | 1 2 3 4 | 1 2 3 4 |

Home Groups

| 1 2 3 4 | 1 2 3 4 | 1 2 3 4 |

1. Make a rough sketch of the floor area of your classroom. Include fixtures, such as doors, windows, and counters. Do not include movable furniture, such as desks and chairs. Measure the dimensions of the floor and fixtures, and mark them on your sketch.

2. Use grid paper to draw a plan of your classroom floor. Again, include fixtures, but not movable furniture.

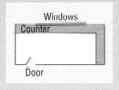

3. Measure the movable furniture and make a template for each piece. Use the same type of grid paper as you used for the floor plan. Cut out each template.

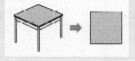

4. Experiment with different arrangements by moving the templates within the floor plan. Consider the effects of each arrangement on such issues as:
• the movement of students and the teacher
• the view of the chalkboard and screen
• the need to keep entrances clear
• the need for access to storage areas

5. Choose the plan you like best. Then, glue the templates onto your floor plan.

6. Display your floor plan with those of other groups. As a class, compare the floor plans and decide on the positive and negative points of each.

Chapter Check

Evaluate for x = 3, and y = 5.

1. $x + 2y$ **2.** $3x - y$ **3.** $2(x + y)$

4. The formula for the perimeter of a rectangle is $P = 2(l + w)$.
a) Find P when $l = 12$ m and $w = 6$ m.
b) Find l when $P = 36$ m and $w = 9$ m.
c) Find w when $P = 42$ m and $l = 14$ m.

5. In the diagrams, each small square has a side length of 1 unit.
a) Draw the next 2 diagrams in the pattern.
b) Copy and complete the table.

Diagram	1	2	3	4	5
Perimeter					

c) Describe, in words, the pattern in the perimeters.
d) What is the perimeter of the 8th diagram?
e) Which diagram has a perimeter of 24 units?

Use each of the following equations.
a) *Describe the relation in words.*
b) *Copy and complete the table of values.*
c) *Write the ordered pairs.*

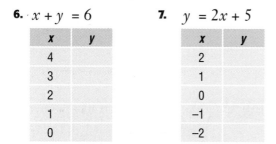

6. $x + y = 6$

x	y
4	
3	
2	
1	
0	

7. $y = 2x + 5$

x	y
2	
1	
0	
−1	
−2	

Write an equation for each relation.

8.

x	y
1	4
2	3
3	2
4	1
5	0

9.

x	y
3	5
2	4
1	3
0	2
−1	1

10. a) T-shirts at a concert cost $30 each. Copy and complete the table.

Number of T-Shirts	Cost ($)
1	30
2	
3	
4	

b) Describe the pattern in the cost column.
c) What would be the cost of 5 T-shirts? 6 T-shirts?
d) Write the results from the table as ordered pairs.
e) Describe, in words, the relation between the number of T-shirts and the cost.
f) Let n represent the number of T-shirts. Write an equation in the form $C = \blacksquare \times n$ to find the cost.
g) Use your equation to find the cost of 12 T-shirts; 50 T-shirts.

11. Write the coordinates of each letter on the grid as an ordered pair.

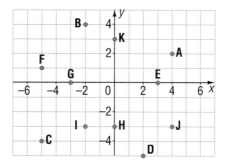

In questions 12 and 13, plot the points on a grid and join them in order. Identify the figure and find its area.

12. A(−2, 1), B(−2, −1), C(4, −1), D(4, 1)

13. E(−6, 2), F(−2, 2), G(−2, −2), H(−6, −2)

Find 5 ordered pairs that satisfy each relation. Draw each graph.

14. $x + y = 7$ **15.** $y = 2x + 1$

Using the Strategies

1. A number is multiplied by 8, increased by 4, and then divided by 3. The result is 12. What is the number?

2. How many different kinds of pizza can be made using toppings of green peppers, mushrooms, and ham if multiple toppings are allowed?

3. Ms. Nguyen wanted to arrange her students in rows, so that each row had the same number of students. She tried 5 in a row, but 1 was left over. She tried 6 in a row, but 3 were left over. Three in a row worked perfectly. What was the smallest possible number of students in the class?

4. Rosalyn went for a walk. From her home, she walked 2 blocks east, 3 blocks south, 1 block west, and 1 block north. What was the shortest route she could take to get home?

5. The graph shows the numbers of blocks from the school to the homes of 4 students and the time it takes for the students to get to school.

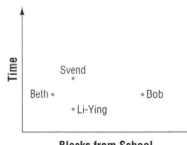

Blocks from School

a) Who lives closest to the school?
b) Who lives farthest from the school?
c) Which students live the same distance from the school?
d) Two students walk to school, and two ride bicycles. Which students do you think ride bicycles? Explain.

6. Copy the grid, then join points to make a square with an area of 5 square units.

```
· · · ·
· · · ·
· · · ·
· · · ·
```

7. Use each of the digits 1, 2, 3, and 4 once to make the smallest possible sum.

8. Four strips of wood are placed on a table, so that 2 strips are perpendicular to the other 2. Each strip is 10 cm long and 2 cm wide. What area of the table is covered by the strips?

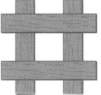

9. Palindromes, such as 777 and 1221, read the same forward and backward. Which perfect squares less than 500 are palindromes?

DATA BANK

1. Write the height of Virginia Falls as a fraction of the height of Chute Montmorency. Express your answer in lowest terms.

2. In which 5 provinces and territories is the total amount of fresh water the same as in Ontario and Quebec combined?

CHAPTER 6

Solving Equations

Sir Arthur Conan Doyle had Sherlock Holmes crack a stick figure code in a short story, "The Adventure of the Dancing Men." The coded note below was written by Holmes after he cracked the code. Each figure stands for a letter.

1. How many letters are in the note?

2. The note contains 4 words. How is the last letter of each word indicated?

3. The letter E is the most common in the English language. The stick figure used most often in the note represents an E. Draw this stick figure.

4. The next most commonly used letters in the English language are, in order, T, A, O, I, N, S, H, R, D, and L. The letter O is found twice in the note, once in the first half of the first word and once in the first half of the last word. Draw the stick figure for the letter O.

5. Use the following clues to decode the rest of the note.
- The word AT appears in the note.
- The letter C appears twice.
- H, M, N, and R are each used once.

6. Design your own code using stick figures. Write a message with your code and have a classmate try to decipher it.

Patterns

Activity ❶ Illustrating Equations

The balance shows that the mass of 2 cubes equals the mass of 1 cylinder. The mass of each object is a whole number of grams. The total mass of the 3 objects is 12 g.

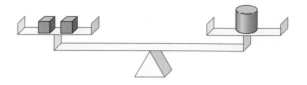

1. Find the mass of

a) a cube   **b)** a cylinder

2. Use your results from part 1 to copy and complete the table.

Number of Cubes	2	3	3	4	4	4	4
Number of Cylinders	1	1	2	1	2	3	4
Total Mass (g)	12						

Activity ❷ Listing All Possibilities

The balance shows that 1 cube, 1 cylinder, and 1 pyramid balance 2 cubes. The mass of each object is a whole number of grams. The total mass of the 5 objects is 20 g. Copy the table and use it to record the possible masses.

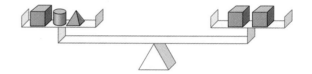

Mass of Cube (g)			
Mass of Cylinder (g)			
Mass of Pyramid (g)			

Activity ❸ Balancing the Scales

1. The balance shows that the mass of 1 cube and 3 pyramids equals the mass of 1 pyramid and 2 cylinders. The mass of each object is a whole number of grams. The total mass of the 7 objects is 20 g. Find the mass of

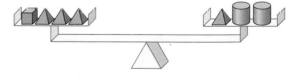

a) a cylinder   **b)** a pyramid   **c)** a cube

2. Design a problem like the one in part 1 of this activity. Have a classmate solve your problem.

Order of Operations

Simplify.

1. $3 \times 2 + 5$

2. $3 + 2 \times 5$

3. $3 \times (2 + 5)$

4. $(3 + 2) \times 5$

5. $3 + 2 \div 5$

6. $(3 + 2) \div 5$

7. $3 \times 2 - 5$

8. $3 \times 2 \div 5$

9. $3 \div 2 + 5$

10. $3 \div 5 \times 2$

11. $3^2 - 2^2$

12. $21 - 2 \times 2^3$

13. $(6 - 4)^2 + 7$

14. $4 \times 7 - 3^3$

15. $1^2 + 3^2 + 6^2$

16. $98 - 96 \div 3$

Copy the expressions in questions 17–22. Insert one pair of brackets to make each expression equal to 24.

17. $3 + 5 \times 3$

18. $2 + 4 \times 4$

19. $12 \times 8 - 6$

20. $4 + 5 \times 7 - 3$

21. $2 \times 10 + 2$

22. $6 \times 4 + 4 \div 2$

Calculate.

23. $7 \times 2 + 5 \times 2$

24. $6 \times 7 - 2 \times 11$

25. $4 \times 5 - 6 \div 3$

26. $\frac{1}{2}$ of $24 + \frac{1}{3}$ of 24

27. $\frac{1}{2}$ of $(3 + 5) + \frac{1}{4}$ of $(16 - 4)$

28. $15 \div (8 - 5) \times 6$

29. $\frac{1}{3}$ of $12.3 + 8.2 - 2.4$

30. $7 \times 0 + 5 - 0$

31. $(3 + 2) \times (6 - 4) \div (8 - 6) \times (9 - 8)$

32. $28.8 \div 4 + 96.6 \div 3$

Copy the numbers in order. Then, insert +, −, ×, and ÷ signs so that each expression simplifies to 15.

33. 4   5   2   1

34. 3   4   7   4

35. 5   2   6   1

36. 36   9   6   5

37. 4   3   4   1

38. 6   6   3   3

39. 5   5   3   3   1

40. 18   8   3   1   2

Add.

1. $45 + 10$

2. $45 + 100$

3. $625 + 5$

4. $625 + 25$

5. $350 + 50$

6. $350 + 150$

7. $350 + 250$

8. $350 + 1000$

9. $38 + 12$

10. $38 + 102$

Subtract.

11. $125 - 5$

12. $125 - 15$

13. $125 - 25$

14. $125 - 50$

15. $418 - 8$

16. $418 - 18$

17. $418 - 108$

18. $438 - 28$

19. $147 - 17$

20. $147 - 27$

Multiply.

21. 4×12

22. 40×12

23. 2×25

24. 4×25

25. 20×25

26. 40×25

27. 47×100

28. 47×1000

29. 5×80

30. 50×800

Divide.

31. $35 \div 7$

32. $3500 \div 7$

33. $3500 \div 70$

34. $3500 \div 700$

35. $3500 \div 10$

36. $3500 \div 500$

37. $72\ 000 \div 100$

38. $72\ 000 \div 12$

39. $72\ 000 \div 72$

40. $72\ 000 \div 12\ 000$

State the remainder.

41. $24 \div 5$

42. $15 \div 6$

43. $45 \div 8$

44. $36 \div 7$

45. $36 \div 5$

46. $36 \div 10$

47. $50 \div 8$

48. $55 \div 9$

49. $3002 \div 10$

Simplify.

50. $3.6 + 0.1$

51. $4.25 + 0.1$

52. $63.5 - 0.2$

53. $63.57 - 0.2$

54. 5.25×0.1

55. 5.25×0.01

56. $75.5 \div 0.1$

57. $75.5 \div 0.001$

6.1 Writing Equations

Albert Einstein's equation $E = mc^2$ is the most famous in the history of science. This equation allows scientists to understand the energy source of the sun and other stars.

Many problems can be solved by first writing the information as an equation and then solving the equation.

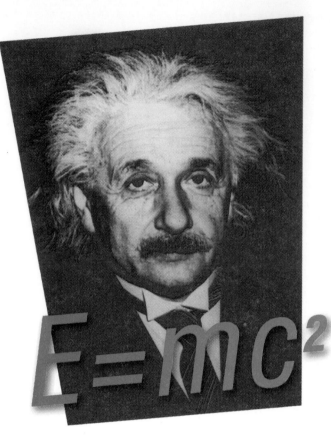

Activity: Use the Information

Heidi has two more fish in her saltwater aquarium than Jerry has. Together they have a total of 18 fish.

Inquire

1. Let n represent the number of fish Jerry has. Write an expression for the number of fish Heidi has.

2. Use numbers and variables to write an equation that gives the information about the fish.

3. Suppose Heidi bought one more fish. What would the new equation be?

Example 1

Write an equation for each sentence.
a) Five more than a number, n, is ten.
b) Six less than a number, x, is five.
c) Five times a number, y, is thirty.
d) When three is added to two times a number, n, the result is nineteen.
e) When five is subtracted from three times a number, t, the result is thirteen.

Solution

a) $n + 5 = 10$
b) $x - 6 = 5$
c) $5y = 30$
d) $2n + 3 = 19$

e) $3t - 5 = 13$

Example 2

There are 110 more species of cuckoos than species of penguins. Together, there is a total of 146 species of these birds. Write an equation to find the number of species of penguins.

Solution

Let n represent the number of species of penguins. Then, the number of species of cuckoos is $n + 110$. The sum of the numbers is 146.

So $n + n + 110 = 146$
and $2n + 110 = 146$

Practice

Describe each equation in words.

1. $x - 5 = 7$ 2. $11 = y + 2$

3. $2m = 8$ 4. $\frac{n}{4} = 3$

Describe each equation in words.

5. $m + 3 = 7 - m$ 6. $2 + 3t = 5$

7. $\frac{1}{2}w + \frac{1}{3}w = 25$ 8. $\frac{a}{3} - 2 = a - 4$

Write an equation for each sentence.

9. Four more than a number is nineteen.

10. Three less than a number is nine.

11. Four times a number is twelve.

12. Twelve decreased by a number is four.

13. One quarter of a number is three.

14. A number multiplied by four, then increased by three, is eleven.

15. A number increased by three, then multiplied by five, is twenty-three.

16. A number decreased by three, then multiplied by four, is twelve.

17. The sum of a number and five more than the number is fifteen.

18. Four less than twice a number is fifty.

19. The sum of a number and two less than the number is twelve.

Let a letter represent the unknown and write an equation.

20. Two less than one third of a number is three.

21. The length increased by four is eleven.

22. Five times the width is sixty.

23. The perimeter decreased by six is forty.

24. The area multiplied by three, then decreased by twelve, is ten.

25. A number divided by six is two.

26. One more than twice a number is seven.

Problems and Applications

Write an equation that could be used to solve each problem.

27. Three years from now, Jenny's age will be sixteen. What is Jenny's age?

28. Julio has fifteen dollars, which is ten dollars less than he needs. How much does Julio need?

29. One Sunday, Angie did math homework for one hour, which was half the total time she spent on homework that day. How much time did she spend on homework?

30. Miki wants to double her present keyboarding rate to 50 words/min. What is her present rate?

31. Maria is two years older than Sue. The sum of their ages is twenty-six. How old is Sue?

32. Vancouver has three times the annual snowfall of Tokyo. Together, they have a total of 80 cm of snow a year. What is Tokyo's annual snowfall?

33. One year, Alberta had 250 forest fires more than Manitoba. The total number of forest fires in these two provinces was 1596. How many forest fires did Manitoba have?

34. Sabi has $2.50 more than Tony. Together, they have $17.50. How much does Tony have?

35. Tatiana has a total of 25 nickels and dimes. Their total value is $2.00. How many nickels does she have?

Write a word problem that could be solved by each equation. Compare your problems with a classmate's.

36. $x + 3 = 11$ 37. $m - 9 = 14$

38. $3y = 18$ 39. $\frac{t}{2} = 6$

40. $2x + 1 = 13$ 41. $3e - 4 = 17$

42. $2(x + 1) = 6$ 43. $3(y - 2) = 9$

6.2 Solving Equations

Activity: Solve the Problem

Memorial School is having a 50-year reunion. Those who attend
will receive a commemorative pin. It costs $200 to design the pin,
plus $5 to make each pin. The Student Council has budgeted
$2200 for pins. If n represents the number of pins made, then
the expression for the cost of the pins, in dollars, is $5n + 200$.

Inquire

1. How much does it cost to make

a) 100 pins?   **b)** 200 pins?   **c)** 500 pins?

2. How many pins can be made for $2200?

3. When you answered question 2, you solved the equation
$5n + 200 = 2200$. Explain.

A sentence with an equal sign, =, is called an **equation**. Formulas
are examples of equations. Two equations are $P = 2(l + w)$ and
$A = lw$. These are also equations: $8 + 4 = 12$ and $4 \times 3 = 12$.

Equations, like other sentences, can be true or false.
The equation $7 + 6 = 13$ is true, but $7 - 6 = 2$ is false.

The equation $x + 2 = 5$ contains the variable x. The equation can
be either true or false, depending on the number you substitute
for the variable. If you replace x by 3, the equation is true. If you
replace x by any other number, the equation is false. A number
that replaces a variable to make an equation true is called a
solution of the equation.

Some equations can be solved mentally. This method is called
solving by inspection.

Example 1

Solve and check $2n - 7 = 1$.

Solution

What number gives 1 when 7 is subtracted from it?
Since $8 - 7 = 1$, $2n$ must be 8. If $2n = 8$, then $n = 4$.
Substitute $n = 4$ into the left side of the equation.
The solution is correct if the value of the left side equals
the value of the right side.

Check: **L.S.** $= 2n - 7$ **R.S.** $= 1$
$$= 2(4) - 7$$
$$= 8 - 7$$
$$= 1$$
The solution is $n = 4$.

Example 2

Solve $3x + 13 = 37$.

Solution

Use guess and check. Substitute different numbers for x until you find the solution.

Try $x = 5$. $3x + 13 = 3(5) + 13$
$= 15 + 13$
$= 28$ $3x + 13$ is less than 37.

Try $x = 9$. $3x + 13 = 3(9) + 13$
$= 27 + 13$
$= 40$ $3x + 13$ is greater than 37.

Try $x = 8$. $3x + 13 = 3(8) + 13$
$= 24 + 13$
$= 37$ The solution is $x = 8$.

Practice

Determine whether the number in brackets is a solution of the equation.

1. $n + 5 = 11$ (6)   **2.** $4n = 12$ (3)

3. $y - 8 = 12$ (20)   **4.** $u - 9 = 11$ (20)

5. $\frac{x}{3} = 5$ (8)   **6.** $\frac{y}{2} = 4$ (8)

7. $4 - n = 1$ (5)   **8.** $6 + x = 12$ (2)

Solve by inspection.

9. $x + 11 = 15$ **10.** $z + 7 = 14$

11. $u + 6 - 15$ **12.** $v + 8 = 13$

Solve by inspection.

13. $n - 10 = 15$ **14.** $x - 4 = 12$

15. $y - 12 = 0$ **16.** $u - 0 = 21$

Solve by inspection.

17. $5m = 35$ **18.** $5n = 45$ **19.** $2x = 24$

20. $4y = 24$ **21.** $8x = 56$ **22.** $9y = 72$

Solve by inspection.

23. $\frac{x}{7} = 7$ **24.** $\frac{y}{2} = 10$ **25.** $\frac{m}{2} = 5$

26. $\frac{n}{2} = 20$ **27.** $\frac{u}{4} = 8$ **28.** $\frac{v}{6} = 4$

Solve and check.

29. $12 + x = 19$ **30.** $15 - y = 8$

31. $4m = 28$ **32.** $\frac{y}{5} = 4$

Solve by guess and check.

33. $5x + 3 = 13$ **34.** $2n - 1 = 13$

35. $10 - 2n = 2$ **36.** $3n - 5 = 4$

37. $4 + 3x = 13$ **38.** $10p + 7 = 67$

39. $\frac{r}{5} - 2 = 1$ **40.** $\frac{x}{3} + 2 = 6$

Problems and Applications

Write an equation in the form shown, replacing the ■ and ▲ with numbers. The solution for x is given in the brackets.

41. $x + ■ = ▲$ (2)   **42.** $x + ■ = ▲$ (3)

43. $■x = ▲$ (5)   **44.** $\frac{x}{■} = ▲$ (10)

In questions 45 and 46, find the equation that represents the problem and solve it.

45. Five more than a number is 20. What is the number?

a) $n - 20 = 5$ b) $n + 5 = 20$
c) $n - 5 = 20$ d) $5n = 20$

46. There are 150 riders and 30 extra horses. How many horses are there?

a) $n + 30 = 150$ b) $n + 150 = 30$
c) $n - 150 = 30$ d) $30n = 150$

47. Write 2 equations with the same solution. Have a classmate solve your equations.

Algebra Tiles

Activity ❶ Expressions with Positive Tiles

Each red tile is a square, with each side 1 unit long.
The area of the square is $1 \times 1 = 1$.
Each red tile represents +1.

Each long green tile has a length of x and a width of 1.
The area is $x \times 1 = x$.
Each long green tile represents +x or x.

Each square green tile has a length of x and a width of x.
The area is $x \times x = x^2$.
Each square green tile represents +x^2 or x^2.

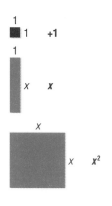

Groups of tiles represent expressions. Expressions are
made up of terms. Terms are separated by + and −.

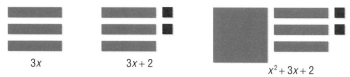

$3x$ $3x + 2$

$x^2 + 3x + 2$

1. Write the expression represented by each group of tiles.

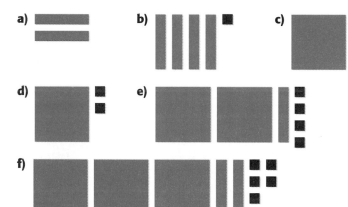

a)   b)   c)

d)   e)

f)

2. Use algebra tiles or drawings to model
these expressions.

a) $5x$ **b)** $2x + 4$
c) $x^2 + 3x + 7$ **d)** $4x^2 + 2$
e) $2x^2 + x + 1$ **f)** $x + 6$

Activity ❷ Expressions with Negative Tiles

Each small white tile represents −1.   −1   −x   −x^2
Each long white tile represents −x.
Each large white tile represents −x^2.

1. Write the expression represented by each group of tiles.

a)   **b)**   **c)**   **d)**

2. Use algebra tiles or drawings to model these expressions.

a) −3x   **b)** −x − 3   **c)** −2x^2 − 2x − 2   **d)** −x^2 − x − 1

Activity ❸ Simplifying Expressions

Each pair represents zero.

> For a pair of tiles to represent zero, they must have the same size, but different colours.

Just as ■■ simplifies to +2,   simplifies to +2x.

1. Copy and complete the table. The first row has been done for you.

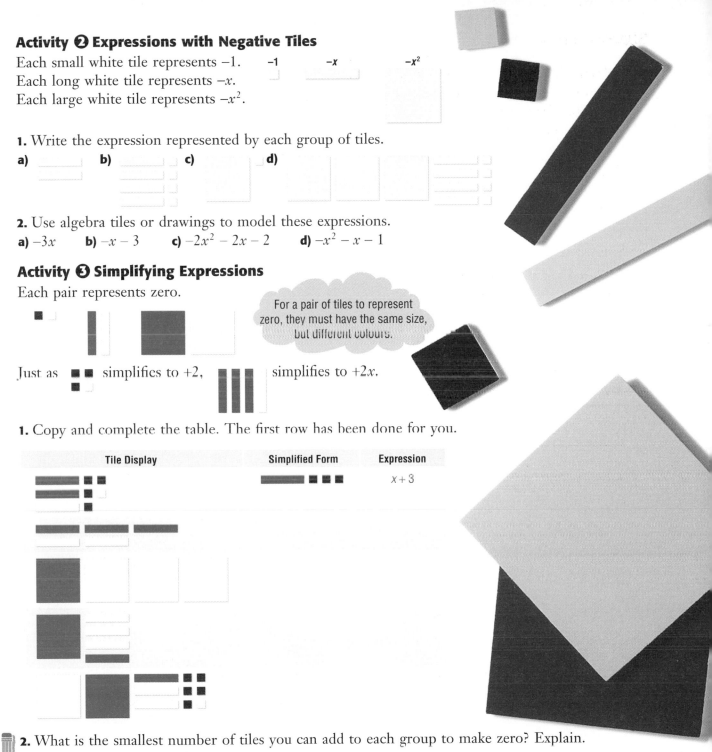

Tile Display	Simplified Form	Expression
		x + 3

2. What is the smallest number of tiles you can add to each group to make zero? Explain.

a)   **b)**   **c)**   **d)**

179

6.3 Solving Equations by Addition

Each red tile represents +1, and each white tile represents −1.
A red tile and a white tile together make 0.
The long green tile represent the variable +x or x.

Activity: Use Algebra Tiles

The tiles shown represent the equation $x - 4 = 5$.

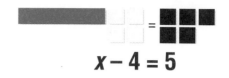

$$x - 4 = 5$$

Inquire

1. Add 4 red tiles to both sides. What is the new equation?

2. What is the value of x?

3. What must be added to both sides of $x - 5 = 12$ to solve the equation?

4. What must you add to both sides to solve each of the following equations?
a) $x - 6 = 7$ **b)** $36 = x - 12$ **c)** $-4 + x = 7$

5. Describe a method for solving equations by addition.

Activity: Use Algebra Tiles

The tiles shown represent the equation $x + 4 = 5$.

$$x + 4 = 5$$

Inquire

1. Add 4 white tiles to both sides. What is the new equation?

2. What is the value of x?

3. What must you add to both sides of $x + 11 = 35$ to solve it?

4. What integer must you add to both sides to solve each of the following equations?
a) $x + 7 = 15$ **b)** $9 + x = 24$ **c)** $15 = x + 6$

Example 1	**Solution**

Solve and check $x - 3 = 4$.

Add 3 to both sides of the equation.

$$x - 3 = 4$$
$$x - 3 \boxed{+3} - 4 \boxed{+3}$$
$$x = 7$$

The solution is $x = 7$.

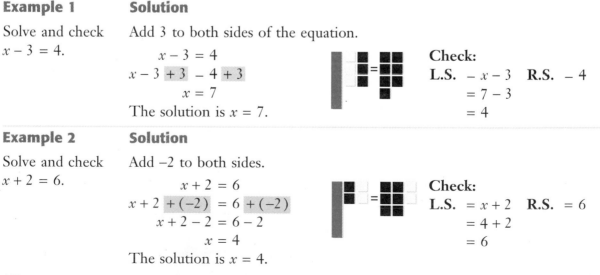

Check:
L.S. $- x - 3$ R.S. $- 4$
$= 7 - 3$
$= 4$

Example 2	**Solution**

Solve and check $x + 2 = 6$.

Add −2 to both sides.

$$x + 2 = 6$$
$$x + 2 \boxed{+ (-2)} = 6 \boxed{+ (-2)}$$
$$x + 2 - 2 = 6 - 2$$
$$x = 4$$

The solution is $x = 4$.

Check:
L.S. $= x + 2$ R.S. $= 6$
$= 4 + 2$
$= 6$

Practice

What number would you add to both sides to solve each equation?

1. $x - 8 = 10$

2. $x - 7 = 15$

3. $z - 5 = 12$

4. $y - 1 = 2$

5. $3 = x - 3$

6. $7 = y - 4$

What number would you add to both sides to solve each equation?

7. $x + 5 = 11$

8. $y + 8 = 12$

9. $z + 2 = 23$

10. $x + 15 = 45$

11. $32 = y + 7$

12. $25 = x + 7$

Solve and check.

13. $p - 3 = 6$

14. $y - 5 = 3$

15. $r - 7 = -2$

16. $4 = y - 6$

17. $x - 12 = 0$

18. $z - 10 = 10$

19. $10 = x - 5$

20. $-4 + m = 0$

Solve and check.

21. $y + 9 = 24$

22. $z + 8 = 16$

23. $q + 15 = 34$

24. $5 + x = 18$

25. $12 = x + 2$

26. $20 = 8 + m$

27. $x + 12 = 30$

28. $p + 13 = 29$

Solve and check.

29. $x - 3 = 5.2$

30. $z - 3.5 = 8$

31. $z + 4 - 6.7$

32. $r + 3 = 8.2$

33. $11 = t - 2.2$

34. $4.6 = x - 4.5$

35. $x + 2.5 = 8$

36. $5 = y + 3.7$

37. $m - 3.2 = 4.7$

38. $5.1 = s - 0.6$

39. $s + 7.2 = 10.2$

40. $8.1 = m + 5.1$

41. $x + 3.5 = 5.7$

42. $0.7 = t + 0.2$

Problems and Applications

43. Nick paid $9 for a pen. He had $7 left. Solve the equation $x - 9 = 7$ to find how much he had at the start.

44. Cape Scott, at the northern end of Vancouver Island, has hailstorms on 18 days per year. This is 11 days more than the number of days per year that Edson, Alberta, has hailstorms. Solve the equation $d + 11 = 18$ to find the number of days per year that Edson has hailstorms.

45. Montreal's Place Victoria has 15 more storeys than Winnipeg's Richardson Building. Place Victoria has 47 storeys. Solve the equation $x + 15 = 47$ to find how many storeys the Richardson Building has.

46. The average summer high temperature in St. John's, Newfoundland, is 15°C lower than in Calcutta, India. The average summer high in St. John's is 20°C. Solve the equation $x - 15 = 20$ to find the value for Calcutta.

47. Write 2 different equations that have 6 as a solution and can be solved by adding a positive integer to both sides.

48. Write 2 different equations that have 8 as a solution and can be solved by adding a negative integer to both sides.

49. What is the result when you add 0 to both sides of an equation?

Solve and check.

50. $x - 4 = -7$

51. $y - 5 = -9$

52. $x + 7 - 4$

53. $y + 6 = 3$

54. $t - 8 = -13$

55. $m - 7 = -8$

56. $t + 10 = 6$

57. $r + 7 = 6$

NUMBER POWER

On what day in which month and year will you have lived for at least 1 billion seconds?

6.4 Solving Equations by Division

Activity: Use Algebra Tiles

Recall that 2 long green tiles mean $x + x$ or $2x$. The algebra tiles represent the equation $2x = 6$.

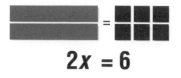

$$2x = 6$$

Inquire

1. How many equal parts are there on the left side?

2. Divide the red tiles into the same number of equal parts. How many red tiles are in each part? What is the value of x?

3. What is the new equation when you divide both sides of the equation $3x = 24$ by 3? What is the value of x?

4. By what number must you divide both sides to solve each equation?

a) $2x = 12$ **b)** $5x = 15$ **c)** $7x = 35$

5. Describe a method for solving equations by division.

Example

Solve and check
$3x = 12$.

Solution

$3x = 12$

Divide both sides by 3: $\dfrac{3x}{3} = \dfrac{12}{3}$

$x = 4$

The solution is $x = 4$.

Check: **L.S.** $= 3x$ **R.S.** $= 12$
$= 3(4)$
$= 12$

Practice

By what number would you divide both sides to solve each equation?

1. $3x = 6$ **2.** $5x = 10$ **3.** $7z = 42$

4. $4t = 20$ **5.** $9s = 27$ **6.** $10m = 60$

7. $15y = 45$ **8.** $3x = 15$ **9.** $6n = 18$

Solve and check.

10. $4x = 8$ **11.** $9y = 9$ **12.** $2r = 18$

13. $6w = 72$ **14.** $8x = 32$ **15.** $10m = 50$

16. $10 = 5x$ **17.** $24 = 8x$ **18.** $7n = 28$

19. $20 = 5t$ **20.** $25y = 75$ **21.** $60 = 15z$

Solve and check.

22. $2x = 5$ **23.** $4y = 4.8$

24. $5w = 4.5$ **25.** $2 = 4x$

26. $1.2x = 24$ **27.** $8 = 0.2n$

28. $0.4t = 0.8$ **29.** $1.2x = 3.6$

30. $3.6 = 0.6t$ **31.** $20 = 0.1m$

Problems and Applications

32. The height of a great gray owl is 5 times the height of a pygmy owl. A great gray owl can grow to 85 cm in height. Solve the equation $5x = 85$ to find the height of a pygmy owl.

33. Write 2 different equations that have 3 as a solution and that can be solved using division.

Solve and check.

34. $4x = -8$ **35.** $3x = -12$

36. $2x = -6$ **37.** $-5x = -20$

6.5 Solving Equations by Multiplication

Activity: Interpret the Diagram

The algebra tiles represent the
equation $\frac{x}{2} = 4$.

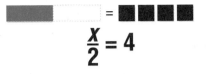

$$\frac{x}{2} = 4$$

Inquire

1. What do you multiply $\frac{x}{2}$ by to give x?

2. Multiply both sides of the equation by this number. What is the value of x?

3. By what number must you multiply both sides to solve each of these equations?

a) $\frac{x}{3} = 6$ **b)** $\frac{x}{5} = 3$ **c)** $\frac{x}{4} = 1$

4. Describe a method for solving equations by multiplication.

Example

Solve and check
$\frac{x}{6} = 2$.

Solution

$\frac{x}{6} = 2$ **Check: L.S.** $= \frac{x}{6}$ **R.S.** $= 2$

Multiply both sides by 6: $6 \times \frac{x}{6} = 6 \times 2$ $= \frac{12}{6}$

$x = 12$ $= 2$

The solution is $x = 12$.

Practice

By what number would you multiply both sides to solve each equation?

1. $\frac{x}{3} = 5$ **2.** $\frac{y}{2} = 4$ **3.** $\frac{t}{5} = 7$

4. $\frac{w}{4} = 4$ **5.** $\frac{x}{7} = 9$ **6.** $\frac{m}{6} = 0$

Solve and check.

7. $\frac{x}{4} = 8$ **8.** $\frac{y}{2} = 8$ **9.** $\frac{m}{3} = 6$

10. $\frac{y}{3} = 2$ **11.** $\frac{x}{5} = 5$ **12.** $\frac{y}{2} = 0$

13. $7 = \frac{x}{7}$ **14.** $4 = \frac{y}{2}$ **15.** $9 = \frac{t}{3}$

16. $\frac{x}{2} = 3$ **17.** $\frac{y}{8} = 1$ **18.** $\frac{y}{10} = 0$

Solve and check.

19. $\frac{x}{2} = 3.1$ **20.** $\frac{y}{4} = 0.2$ **21.** $\frac{t}{3} = 1.2$

22. $0.7 = \frac{m}{5}$ **23.** $11.1 = \frac{r}{6}$ **24.** $\frac{s}{9} = 0$

Problems and Applications

25. Chatham, New Brunswick, has blowing snow on $\frac{1}{4}$ as many days as Churchill, Manitoba. Chatham has 16 days of blowing snow a year. Solve the equation $\frac{x}{4} = 16$ to find how many days of blowing snow Churchill has in a year.

26. Write two different equations that have 7 as a solution and that can be solved using multiplication.

27. What is the result if you multiply both sides of an equation by zero?

Solve and check.

28. $\frac{x}{2} = -4$ **29.** $\frac{y}{3} = -1$ **30.** $\frac{m}{-4} = 5$

31. $\frac{n}{-5} = -3$ **32.** $-5 = \frac{w}{2}$ **33.** $-1 = \frac{t}{3}$

The Information Superhighway

The information superhighway will be a high-speed data network that will link everyone in the country to everyone else. The superhighway will bring information into homes and workplaces on expanded phone lines and cable TV lines.

Among the signals you will be able to receive and send will be sound and three-dimensional pictures. You might choose to dial up a movie and watch digitized images of yourself and your friends in the acting roles. If you wanted, you might even change the script and the ending of the movie!

Videophones, interactive games, electronic newspapers, and 500-plus TV stations will form just a small part of the information superhighway.

Activity ❶ Access to the Superhighway

To get on the superhighway, you will need a tool with extra brain-power. Four types of tools will be:

•a TV set with a box on the top, like a cable TV box today

•a PCTV, which will be a combined computer and TV set

•a screen-based phone

•a personal communicator you can carry with you

1. Which of these tools do you think will be the most popular? Why?

2. Which of these tools would you like to have? Why?

3. What other ways could be used to get onto the superhighway?

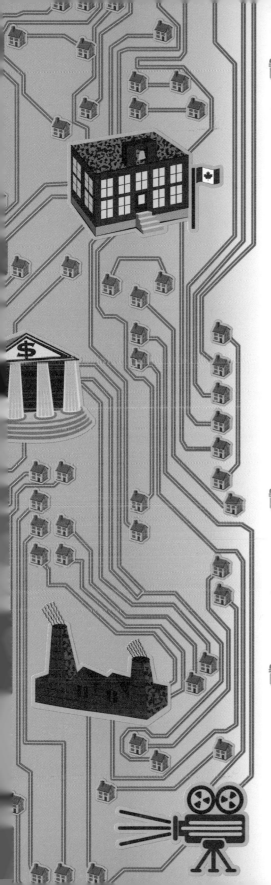

Activity ❷ Superhighway Information

Among the services supplied by the superhighway will be:
- face-to-face phone calls
- access to the world's biggest library
- news and video clips on subjects that interest you
- schools without walls
- round-the-clock pay-per-view movies, concerts, sporting events, and TV show reruns
- shopping and banking

1. What will be the advantages and disadvantages of face-to-face phone calls?

2. What do you think "access to the world's biggest library" means?

3. How do you think schools without walls will work?

4. List some advantages of having access to round-the-clock pay-per-view movies, concerts, sporting events, and TV show reruns. What could be some disadvantages?

5. How do you think shopping and banking will work on the superhighway?

6. What other services would you like to see on the superhighway?

Activity ❸ Environmental Benefits

Some environmentalists say that, once the superhighway is in place, valuable land will be freed up. It might then be restored to its natural state.

1. How might the superhighway free up valuable land?

2. Why might ground and air travel be reduced?

3. How else might the superhighway benefit the environment?

Activity ❹ Security

Concerns about the superhighway include its effects on privacy and security.

1. How could your privacy be invaded by users of the superhighway?

2. Of the information that superhighway users could access, what would you want to be kept secret?

6.6 Like Terms

Activity: Use Algebra Tiles

The area of the rectangle is the sum of the areas of the algebra tiles.
The area of each square green tile is x^2 square units.
The area of each long green tile is x square units.

Inquire

1. How many pieces make up the rectangle?

2. Use each piece to write an expression for the area of the rectangle in terms of x^2 and x.

3. Use the idea that $x + x + x = 3x$ to combine as many terms as possible in the expression you wrote in question 2. What is your new expression?

Terms that have the same variable parts are called **like terms**. The terms $3x$, $4x$, and $6x$ are like terms. The terms $5x$, $2x^2$, and $3y$ are **unlike terms**. They have different variable parts.

Like terms can be combined.
Since $2x$ means $x + x$, and $3x$ means $x + x + x$, then

$$2x + 3x = x + x + x + x + x$$
$$= 5x$$

Example

Simplify $4x + 2y - 2x - 3y$.

Solution

Combine like terms.

$$4x + 2y - 2x - 3y = 4x - 2x + 2y - 3y$$
$$= 2x - y$$

Practice

Simplify.

1. $3x + 5x$

2. $6a^2 - 3a^2$

3. $2t + 3t + 4t$

4. $7w - 2w + 3w$

5. $9c - 8c - c$

6. $y + 5y - y$

7. $6a + 9 + 7a - 3$

8. $3x + 7x + 4x^2 + 3x^2$

9. $9 + 6b - b + 4b$

10. $x + y - x - y$

11. $a + b + b + a$

12. $6w - 5w - w + 8y$

Problems and Applications

Simplify, then evaluate for $t = 2$ and $w = 3$.

13. $6t - 3t + 4t + 2w$

14. $5w + 7t - 5t + w$

15. $6t + 4w - 6t - 3w$

16. $3t - 4t + w - 2w$

17. a) Write and simplify an expression for the perimeter of the figure.
b) Find the perimeter if $s = 40$ m and $t = 30$ m.

18. Write two different expressions that simplify to $2x + 3y$. Compare your expressions with your classmates'.

6.7 The Distributive Property

Activity: Use Algebra Tiles

The area of the large rectangle is the sum of the areas of the algebra tiles.

The area of each long green tile is x square units.

The area of each red tile is 1 square unit.

Inquire

1. Write an expression for the total area of the green tiles.

2. What is the total area of the red tiles?

3. Use the results from questions 1 and 2 to write an expression for the area of the large rectangle.

4. For the large rectangle, what is the length? the width?

5. Describe a method for multiplying the width and the length of the large rectangle to give the area you found in question 3.

To **expand** an expression with brackets means to remove the brackets by multiplying. This is done using the **distributive property.**

Example	Solution
Expand $3(y + 2)$.	Multiply each term inside the brackets by 3.

$$3(y + 2) = 3(y + 2)$$
$$= 3 \times y + 3 \times 2$$
$$= 3y + 6$$

Practice

Expand.

1. $2(x + 5)$ **2.** $3(b + 3)$ **3.** $6(y - 1)$

4. $5(t - 3)$ **5.** $7(m + 1)$ **6.** $4(a - 7)$

7. $4(4 + m)$ **8.** $8(x - 4)$ **9.** $7(3 + t)$

Expand.

10. $2(3x + 4)$ **11.** $4(2y + 1)$ **12.** $3(4m - 3)$

13. $5(5t - 2)$ **14.** $6(1 + 2x)$ **15.** $7(4w - 7)$

16. $2(3x + 2y)$ **17.** $3(4a + 5b)$

18. $-3(3m - 2n)$ **19.** $-5(3s - t)$

Expand.

20. $3(2x + 4y + 1)$ **21.** $2(a + b + 1)$

22. $4(3c - 2d + 5)$ **23.** $5(x - 3 + 4y)$

24. $-6(2 + 3x + y)$ **25.** $-2(1 - x - y)$

Problems and Applications

Evaluate each expression for $x = 1$ and $y = 1$. Then, expand and evaluate the new expression for $x = 1$ and $y = 1$.

26. $3(5x + 2y + 4)$ **27.** $3(4x - 2y - 1)$

You can use the distributive property to multiply some pairs of numbers without a calculator.

20×38	30×31
$= 20(40 - 2)$	$= 30(30 + 1)$
$= 800 - 40$	$= 900 + 30$
$= 760$	$= 930$

Use this method to multiply the following.

28. 20×19 **29.** 30×28 **30.** 40×37

31. 50×22 **32.** 20×41 **33.** 30×33

6.8 Solving Equations in More Than One Step

Suppose the mass of something was measured in African elephants, instead of kilograms. A sperm whale would have a mass of about 5 elephants.

Let x be the mass of food, in elephants, a person eats in a lifetime. Then, twice this mass minus 3 elephants equals the mass of a sperm whale. This information can be represented by the equation $2x - 3 = 5$.

Activity: Use Algebra Tiles

The algebra tiles represent the equation $2x - 3 = 5$.

$$2x - 3 = 5$$

Inquire

1. How many red 1-tiles must be added to both sides so that only the value of the x-tiles remains on the left side?

2. What is the new equation after the red tiles are added?

3. How many red 1-tiles does one green x-tile represent?

4. What mass of food, in elephants, does a person eat in a lifetime?

When you solve equations, the object is to get the variable alone, or to **isolate the variable**, on one side of the equal sign.

Example 1	Solution

Solve and check
$4x + 3 = 11$.

$$4x + 3 = 11$$

Subtract 3 from both sides: $4x + 3 \boxed{-3} = 11 \boxed{-3}$

$$4x = 8$$

Divide both sides by 4: $\dfrac{4x}{\boxed{4}} = \dfrac{8}{\boxed{4}}$

$$x = 2$$

Check: L.S. $= 4x + 3$ **R.S.** $= 11$
$= 4(2) + 3$
$= 8 + 3$
$= 11$

The solution is $x = 2$.

You can also use a flow chart to solve equations. Start by isolating the variable on the left side.

START → $4x + 3$ → Subtract 3 → Divide by 4 → x → STOP

Now, apply the same steps to the right side.

START → 11 → Subtract 3 → Divide by 4 → 2 → STOP

188

Example 2

Solve and check
$3(x-1) = x+5$.

Solution

$$3(x-1) = x+5$$

Remove brackets: $\quad\quad\quad\quad\quad\quad 3x-3 = x+5$

Subtract x from both sides: $\quad 3x-x-3 = x-x+5$

$$2x-3 = 5$$

Add 3 to both sides: $\quad\quad\quad 2x-3+3 = 5+3$

$$2x = 8$$

Divide both sides by 2: $\quad\quad\quad \dfrac{2x}{2} = \dfrac{8}{2}$

$$x = 4$$

Check: **L.S.** $= 3(x-1)$ $\quad\quad$ **R.S.** $= x+5$

$= 3(4-1)$ $\quad\quad\quad\quad = 4+5$

$= 3(3)$ $\quad\quad\quad\quad\quad\quad = 9$

$= 9$

The solution is $x = 4$.

Practice

Solve and check.

1. $2x+1 = 5$ $\quad\quad$ **2.** $3y+2 = 11$

3. $4t-3 = 13$ $\quad\quad$ **4.** $5m+7 = 12$

5. $4+2e = 12$ $\quad\quad$ **6.** $16 = 3a+7$

7. $7z+1 = 18-3$ $\quad\quad$ **8.** $4b+2 = 6+4$

Solve using a flow chart.

9. $5x+2 = 17$ $\quad\quad$ **10.** $2x+3 = 9$

Solve and check.

11. $2x-4 = 2$ $\quad\quad$ **12.** $4n-3 = 5$

13. $3s-9 = 6$ $\quad\quad$ **14.** $6r-2 = 10$

15. $3y-5 = -2$ $\quad\quad$ **16.** $2b-9 = -3$

17. $5t-4 = 22-1$ $\quad\quad$ **18.** $4z-7 = 3+10$

Solve and check.

19. $2x+1.5 = 5.5$ $\quad\quad$ **20.** $3y-2.6 = 3.4$

21. $4m+0.9 = 2.5$ $\quad\quad$ **22.** $5t-1.2 = 4.3$

Solve and check.

23. $\frac{x}{2}+3 = 4$ $\quad\quad$ **24.** $\frac{n}{3}-1 = 1$

25. $4+\frac{z}{2} = 6$ $\quad\quad$ **26.** $2 = \frac{a}{4}-3$

27. $\frac{m}{5}-2 = -1$ $\quad\quad$ **28.** $-5 = \frac{t}{3}-7$

Solve and check.

29. $3x+2x = 15$ $\quad\quad$ **30.** $8y-y = 7$

31. $4t-t-6+t$ $\quad\quad$ **32.** $3w+5 = 2w+7$

33. $4c-7 = 2c-1$ $\quad\quad$ **34.** $2z+4 = 5z-8$

Solve and check.

35. $2(x+1) = 6$ $\quad\quad$ **36.** $3(m-1) = m+9$

37. $5(y-3) = y+1$ $\quad\quad$ **38.** $6+4(r-2) = r+7$

39. $4+2s = 3(s-2)+1$

40. $5(g-3)+2 = 3(g+1)$

41. $-3(n-4) = 6$ $\quad\quad$ **42.** $-3(1-b) = 2(b+1)$

Problems and Applications

43. The average mass of a lynx is 16 kg. This mass is 4 kg less than twice the average mass of an otter. Solve the equation $2x-4 = 16$ to find an otter's mass, in kilograms.

44. Canada has a river named the Mississippi. It is not as long as the Mississippi River in the United States, which is 3780 km long. Solve the equation $18x+162 = 3780$ to find the length of Canada's Mississippi River.

45. Write an equation that has the solution $x = 3$, and takes at least two steps to solve. Have a classmate solve your equation.

6.9 Using Equations to Solve Problems

National parks protect the natural beauty of parts of a country for its people to see. Both Canada and the United States have designated certain areas as national parks.

Activity: Solve the Problem

The United States has fifteen more national parks than Canada. Together they have a total of eighty-nine national parks. Answer the following questions to find out how many national parks each country has.

Inquire

1. Let n represent the number of national parks Canada has. Write an expression for the number of national parks in the United States.

2. Write an expression for the total number of national parks.

3. Write an equation with your expression from question 2 on one side, and the total number of national parks on the other.

4. Solve the equation.

5. How many national parks are in
a) Canada? **b)** the United States?

Example 1

Joanna works in a marina. Boat servicing costs $70.00, plus $4.50 for each litre of oil. Joanna serviced a boat and made out a bill for $88.00. How many litres of oil did she use?

Solution

Let n represent the number of litres of oil she used.
Then, the cost of the oil is $4.50 \times n$ or $4.50n$.
Write an equation.
Word equation: Basic service $70.00 plus $4.50n$ equals $88.00.

$$70.00 + 4.50n = 88.00$$
$$70.00 - 70.00 + 4.50n = 88.00 - 70.00$$
$$4.50n = 18.00$$
$$\frac{4.50n}{4.50} = \frac{18.00}{4.50}$$
$$n = 4$$

Joanna used 4 L of oil.

Check:
1 L of oil costs $4.50
4 L of oil cost 4 × $4.50 or $18.00
Basic service $70.00
Total charge $88.00

Example 2

The length of a rectangle is 5 m longer than the width. The perimeter of the rectangle is 82 m. Find the length and the width of the rectangle.

Solution

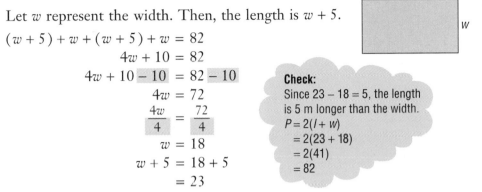

Let w represent the width. Then, the length is $w + 5$.

$$(w + 5) + w + (w + 5) + w = 82$$
$$4w + 10 = 82$$
$$4w + 10 - 10 = 82 - 10$$
$$4w = 72$$
$$\frac{4w}{4} = \frac{72}{4}$$
$$w = 18$$
$$w + 5 = 18 + 5$$
$$= 23$$

Check:
Since $23 - 18 = 5$, the length is 5 m longer than the width.
$P = 2(l + w)$
$= 2(23 + 18)$
$= 2(41)$
$= 82$

The length is 23 m and the width is 18 m.

Problems and Applications

1. Mary has 2 CDs more than Jamil. Together, they have 30 CDs. How many CDs does Mary have?

2. Film processing costs $4.95, plus $0.35 for each picture printed. Milan paid $11.95 for processing and printing. How many pictures did he have printed?

3. A store has a total of 108 full-time staff and part-time staff. There are three times as many full-time staff as part-time staff. How many of the staff are in each category?

4. The side lengths in a triangle are three consecutive whole numbers. The perimeter is 24. What is the length of each side?

5. A horse can jump 6 times farther, horizontally, than a lion can. The difference between the distances they can jump is 10 m. How far can each animal jump?

6. One week, Earla earned $75.00 more than three times as much as Murray earned. Earla earned $450.00. How much did Murray earn?

7. The two countries with the greatest areas are Russia and Canada. The area of Russia is about 1.7 times the area of Canada. The total area of the two countries is about 27 million square kilometres. Find the approximate area of each country in millions of square kilometres.

8. There are 15 seats in the front row of a theatre. Each of the other rows contains 2 seats more than the row in front of it.
a) How many people can be seated in the 2nd row? the 3rd row? the 4th row?
b) Describe the pattern in words.
c) Write an equation you can use to calculate the number of seats in the nth row.
d) Use your equation to find how many people can be seated in the 10th row.
e) If the last row seats 53 people, how many rows of seats are in the theatre?

9. Use some information of your own to write two problems that can be solved with equations. Have a classmate solve your problems.

6.10 Equations with Rational Solutions

Activity: Use Algebra Tiles

The algebra tiles represent the equation $x - 2 = -7$.

$$x - 2 = -7$$

Inquire

1. What is the new equation if you add 2 red tiles to each side?

2. What is the value of x?

Equations can have negative numbers as solutions. These equations are solved in the same ways as other equations.

Example 1

Solve and check $x + 5 = 3$.

Solution

Subtract 5 from both sides:

$$x + 5 = 3$$
$$x + 5 - 5 = 3 - 5$$
$$x = -2$$

The solution is $x = -2$.

Check: L.S. $= x + 5$ **R.S.** $= 3$
$= (-2) + 5$
$= 3$

Example 2

Solve and check $2x - 3 = -8$.

Solution

Add 3 to both sides:

$$2x - 3 = -8$$
$$2x - 3 + 3 = -8 + 3$$
$$2x = -5$$

Divide both sides by 2:

$$\frac{2x}{2} = \frac{-5}{2}$$
$$x = -2.5$$

The solution is $x = -2.5$.

Check: L.S. $= 2x - 3$ **R.S.** $= -8$
$= 2(-2.5) - 3$
$= -5 - 3$
$= -8$

Example 3

Solve $4(y - 1) + 3 = 2y - 7$.

Solution

$$4(y - 1) + 3 = 2y - 7$$

Expand:

$$4y - 4 + 3 = 2y - 7$$
$$4y - 1 = 2y - 7$$

Add 1 to both sides:

$$4y - 1 + 1 = 2y - 7 + 1$$
$$4y = 2y - 6$$

Subtract $2y$ from both sides:

$$4y - 2y = 2y - 2y - 6$$
$$2y = -6$$

Divide both sides by 2:

$$\frac{2y}{2} = \frac{-6}{2}$$
$$y = -3$$

The solution is $y = -3$.

Practice

Solve and check.

1. $x - 1 = -4$ **2.** $x + 4 = 2$

3. $z - 3 = -7$ **4.** $t + 6 = -1$

5. $4 = m + 9$ **6.** $-5 = y - 2$

7. $6 + r = 3$ **8.** $-2 = 4 + w$

9. $\frac{b}{2} = -6$ **10.** $-7 = \frac{a}{3}$

Solve and check.

11. $2x - 1 = -3$ **12.** $2y + 5 = 4$

13. $4t + 1 = -7$ **14.** $5a - 10 = -30$

15. $7 + 2r = 7$ **16.** $-17 = 6x + 1$

17. $8y - 3 = 3$ **18.** $4w + 6 = 0$

19. $9 + 4x = 1$ **20.** $-4 = 3m + 5$

Solve and check.

21. $3x + 4 = 2x - 3$ **22.** $4m - 6 = 2m - 1$

23. $8 + 4t = 13 - t$ **24.** $6y + 3 = 3y - 7 + y$

25. $3w - 9 = 4 + 7w - 1$

Solve and check.

26. $2(y - 1) = -6$ **27.** $3(m + 2) + 4 = 1$

28. $2t + 3(t - 1) = 4$

29. $5(m + 3) + 2 = 2m + 5$

30. $7x + 4 = 2(x - 3)$

31. $3(w + 2) = 2(w - 1)$

32. $6y + 7 = 3 + 2(y - 4)$

Solve and check.

33. $2(x - 1) + 7 = 4x + 3$

34. $5x - 8x = 3(x + 4)$

35. $6 - 2(m + 3) = 8$

36. $5t - 3t = 5 - 3(t + 5)$

Solve and check.

37. $x + 4.3 = -2.7$ **38.** $t - 1.3 = -5.3$

39. $y - (-1.8) = -4.8$ **40.** $m - (-2.2) = 5.4$

Problems and Applications

Solve and check.

41. $x^2 + 1 = 5$ **42.** $y^2 - 1 = 8$ **43.** $w^2 + 3 = 28$

44. $m^2 - 6 = 10$ **45.** $\frac{3x}{4} = -6$ **46.** $\frac{5w}{3} = -4$

47. $\frac{w}{6} = \frac{2}{3}$ **48.** $\frac{x}{4} = \frac{1}{2}$ **49.** $\frac{n}{4} + \frac{3}{2} = \frac{5}{2}$

50. If you multiply Canada's lowest outside air temperature by 3 and then add 19, you get −170°C. This is the lowest surface temperature on the moon. Write an equation, then solve it to find Canada's lowest outside air temperature.

51. Write two different equations that have −4 as the solution, and that must be solved using more than 1 step. Have a classmate solve your equations.

LOGIC POWER

Draw a grid and place 8 markers of 2 different colours on it, as shown. Label the markers, so that you can record your moves.

The object is to switch the positions of the markers in as few moves as possible. A move consists of sliding a marker to an empty space, as in checkers. A marker can jump only another marker of a different colour. The order of the markers at the end does not matter, as long as the blue and red markers exchange places. Making less than 20 moves is good. Making 15 moves is the best.

Haunts of the Tiger

Tigers are found in Asia. In 1900, even after being hunted for at least 1000 years, there were still about 100 000 tigers remaining in the wild. Today, the tiger is in danger of extinction.

The map shows the names of the subspecies of tigers, an estimate of their current numbers, their former range, and their current range.

Activity ❶

1. What are the names of the known subspecies?

2. How many known subspecies were there?

3. How many subspecies are extinct?

4. What percent of the subspecies are extinct?

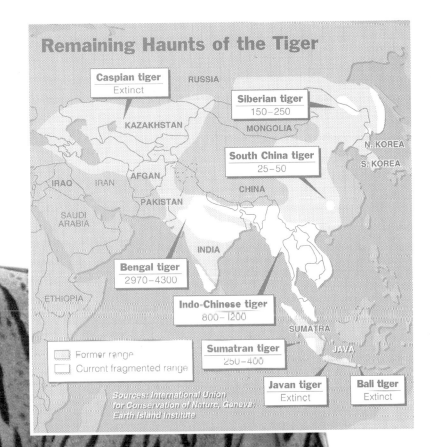

Remaining Haunts of the Tiger

Caspian tiger — Extinct

RUSSIA

Siberian tiger — 150–250

KAZAKHSTAN

MONGOLIA

N. KOREA

S. KOREA

South China tiger — 25–50

CHINA

IRAQ   IRAN   AFGAN.

PAKISTAN

SAUDI ARABIA

INDIA

Bengal tiger — 2970–4300

ETHIOPIA

Indo-Chinese tiger — 800–1200

SUMATRA

☐ Former range
☐ Current fragmented range

Sumatran tiger — 250–400

JAVA

Javan tiger — Extinct

Bali tiger — Extinct

Sources: International Union for Conservation of Nature, Geneva; Earth Island Institute

Activity ❷

1. Assume that the maximum number of tigers shown for each area is the actual number in that area.

a) About how many tigers are there?

b) What percent of the population in 1900 does this number represent?

c) About what percent of the tigers are Bengal tigers?

2. Assume that the minimum number of tigers shown for each area is the actual number in that area.

a) About how many tigers are there?

b) What percent of the population in 1900 does this number represent?

3. About what percent of its former range does the Sumatran tiger have?

Activity ❸

1. List some reasons why you think tigers are in danger of becoming extinct.

2. Use your research skills to check whether your ideas are reasonable.

Review

Describe each equation in words.

1. $x + 2 = 5$ **2.** $3x = 12$

3. $\frac{b}{4} = 3$ **4.** $3 - 2x = 1$

Write an equation for each sentence.

5. Seven less than twice a number is eleven.

6. Don has $10 less than Donna, and together they have $26.

7. Nine more than one fifth of a number is the same as twice the number.

Determine whether the number in brackets is a solution of the equation.

8. $x + 3 = 7$ (4)   **9.** $y - 4 = 3$ (1)

10. $\frac{t}{3} = 6$ (2)   **11.** $5d = 15$ (3)

12. $2s + 1 = 5$ (2)   **13.** $7 = 3n - 2$ (3)

14. $1 = 4m$ (4)   **15.** $\frac{a}{2} + 3 = 4$ (2)

The algebra tiles illustrate the equation $2x + 3 = 5$.

Describe how algebra tiles can illustrate each of the following equations.

16. $x - 2 = 5$ **17.** $2x + 1 = 3$

18. $x + 5 = -2$ **19.** $8 = 3x - 1$

Solve and check.

20. $3x = 12$ **21.** $5n = 20$

22. $\frac{y}{2} = 5$ **23.** $\frac{a}{3} = 2$

24. $x + 5 = 11$ **25.** $b - 3 = 7$

26. $4.2 = z + 1.5$ **27.** $2.6 = t - 4.5$

Simplify.

28. $5x + 3x$ **29.** $9a - 6a$

30. $-2w - 4w + w$ **31.** $2b + 3b - 5$

32. $6n + 4 - 3n - 3$ **33.** $3 + 7k + k - 2k$

Expand.

34. $4(x + 1)$ **35.** $3(2a - 2)$

36. $2(4m + 3n)$ **37.** $-6(2s - t)$

38. $3(-2p - q)$ **39.** $2(-x - 4y)$

Solve and check.

40. $2m + 1 = 9$ **41.** $5 + 3z = 14$

42. $6r - 3 = 9$ **43.** $6 = 2c - 4$

44. $3x + 2 = 7 + 1$ **45.** $3 + 17 = 8y - 4$

46. $2t - 3.5 = 1.3$ **47.** $4.6 = 3p + 0.7$

48. $\frac{n}{2} + 3 = 5$ **49.** $2 = \frac{a}{4} - 1$

Solve and check.

50. $k + 4 = 1$ **51.** $q - 3 = -7$

52. $2x + 9 = 5$ **53.** $-11 = 3y - 2$

54. $\frac{c}{3} + 4 = 2$ **55.** $-1 = 3 + \frac{q}{2}$

56. $2(x + 1) = -4$ **57.** $3 + 1 = 4(y + 2)$

58. $2(x + 4) = 3x - 1$ **59.** $4(a + 1) = 3(a - 1)$

60. $x + 1.6 = 0.5$ **61.** $y - (-4.3) = 5.4$

62. $2.7 = 3m$ **63.** $\frac{n}{4} = -1.2$

64. $4x - 1 = 2$ **65.** $7 + 5y = 1$

66. $\frac{t}{2} + 2.5 = 1.5$ **67.** $1.6 = 1.4 + \frac{w}{3}$

68. $2(a + 1) = -5.6$ **69.** $2(x + 1) = 6(1 - x)$

Solve each problem.

70. One sixth of Canada's planetariums are in Winnipeg. There are 2 planetariums in Winnipeg. How many planetariums are there in Canada?

71. At the Winter Olympics in Albertville, Canada and Italy won a total of 21 medals. Italy won twice as many medals as Canada. How many medals did each country win?

72. The number of known moons that Neptune has is two more than one third the number of known moons Saturn has. Neptune has 8 known moons. How many known moons does Saturn have?

73. The vertical drop of Panther Falls, Alberta, is 183 m. Multiplying the vertical drop of the Virginia Falls, Northwest Territories, by 2 and then adding 3 m results in the vertical drop of the Panther Falls. What is the vertical drop of the Virginia Falls?

74. Subtracting 3 m from one fifth of the elevation of Yellowknife, Northwest Territories, gives the elevation of Prince Rupert, British Columbia. If the elevation of Prince Rupert is 38 m, what is the elevation of Yellowknife?

75. Multiplying the average wind speed at Vancouver Airport by 3 and then reducing the result by 28 km/h gives the average wind speed at Regina Airport. The average wind speed at Regina Airport is 20 km/h. What is the average wind speed at Vancouver Airport?

76. Pietr has CDs and tapes. The number of tapes he has is twelve more than twice the number of CDs. If he has 42 tapes, how many CDs does he have?

77. The average annual temperature of Churchill, Manitoba, is 2°C more than the average annual temperature of Dawson, Yukon. If the average annual temperature of Churchill is −5.1°C, what is the average annual temperature of Dawson?

78. The top speed of an elk is 1.5 times the top speed of a white-tailed deer. The difference between their top speeds is 24 km/h. What is the top speed of each animal?

79. The average mass of a polar bear is 10 kg more than ten times the average mass of an Arctic wolf. If the average mass of a polar bear is 410 kg, what is the average mass of an Arctic wolf?

Group Decision Making
Researching Publishing Careers

Publishers have three major products: newspapers, magazines, and books.

1. Brainstorm with the whole class the careers you would like to investigate. They could include reporter, editor, writer, salesperson, photographer, designer, printer, distributor, reviewer, and artist. As a class, select six careers.

2. Go to home groups. As a group, decide which career each group member will research.

Home Groups

3. Form an expert group with students who have the same career to research. In your expert group, decide what questions you want to answer about the career. Include a question on how math is used. Then, research the answers.

Expert Groups

4. In your expert group, prepare a report on your career for the class. As a group, decide what form the report will take. It could be written, acted out, presented as a video, displayed on a poster, or presented in any other appropriate form.

5. Return to your home group and evaluate the process. Identify what worked well and what you could do differently the next time.

Chapter Check

Describe each equation in words.

1. $y + 2 = 7$ **2.** $2x + 1 = 5$ **3.** $\frac{m}{2} = 17$

Write an equation for each sentence.

4. A number plus eight is fifteen.

5. Half of a number is twelve.

6. Five less than twice a number is one.

Describe how algebra tiles can be used to illustrate each equation.

7. $x - 5 = 1$ **8.** $-2 = 3x - 5$ **9.** $2x + 3 = 7$

Solve and check.

10. $3x = 15$ **11.** $\frac{x}{4} = 3$

12. $13 = x + 5$ **13.** $2x + 3 = 11$

14. $3x - 5 = 4$ **15.** $\frac{x}{2} + 1 = 4$

16. $2y + 1.1 = 3.5$ **17.** $5n + 6 = 7$

18. $x + 5 = 1$ **19.** $y - 2 = -6$

20. $\frac{x}{3} = 1.7$ **21.** $\frac{m}{4} + 1.2 = 0.5$

22. $3(x - 2) = 6$ **23.** $6 - 4 = 2(y + 3)$

24. $3(b - 2) = -7.5$ **25.** $-4x - 1 = 3(2 - x)$

Simplify.

26. $4y + 2y - y$ **27.** $5t - 7 + 3t + 9$

Expand.

28. $3(n - 2)$ **29.** $2(3x + 4y)$

30. There are two parts to Niagara Falls. The American Falls are 2 m higher than the Horseshoe Falls. The American Falls are 59 m high. Use this information to write an equation in which the variable represents the height of the Horseshoe Falls.

Solve.

31. Joe has $2 more than Mona. Together they have $32. How much does Joe have?

32. The number of pets Leon has is one more than one third the number Marina has. Leon has 2 pets. How many pets does Marina have?

33. The average number of days of thunderstorms per year in Edmonton is 4 less than 5 times the average number in Vancouver. Edmonton has about 26 days of thunderstorms per year. About how many days of thunderstorms per year does Vancouver have?

34. The warmest temperature ever recorded in the Yukon was 36°C. This was 99°C higher than the coldest temperature ever recorded in the Yukon. What was the coldest temperature ever recorded in the Yukon?

35. The number of hours Jesse worked this week, multiplied by 3 and then reduced by 2, equals the number of hours he worked last week. Last week, Jesse worked 35.5 h. How many hours did he work this week?

Reprinted with permission — The Toronto Star Syndicate. Copyright: Tribune Media Services.

Using the Strategies

1. Two different types of carnations are growing in the same greenhouse. A plant of one type is 12 cm tall and is growing at 1.5 cm/day. A plant of the other type is 8 cm tall and is growing at 2 cm/day. How long will it take for the two plants to reach the same height?

2. A race car is 1200 m from the finish line. At what speed, in kilometres per hour, must it travel to reach the finish line in 0.4 min?

3. At the produce store, 3 lettuces and 2 cabbages cost $6.75. Two lettuces and 3 cabbages cost $7.00. What is the cost of a cabbage?

4. At 13:00, Kia noticed that her car's odometer reading was 34 614. She drove until 17:00, except for a 1-h rest stop. At 17:00, the odometer reading was 34 899. What was Kia's average speed, excluding the rest stop?

5. Six members of the craft club made 6 bookmarks in 6 min. How many bookmarks could 18 members make in 18 min?

6. a) Draw the next 2 figures.

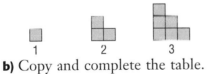

b) Copy and complete the table.

Figure	1	2	3	4	5
Area					
Perimeter					

c) Describe the patterns you see in the table.
d) Extend the table to include figures 6 and 7, without drawing them.

7. In how many ways can you put 25 identical coins into 3 identical bags, so that there is an odd number of coins in each bag, and each bag has more than 1 coin in it?

8. Each of four friends, Amanda, Brittany, Christopher, and Dalil, has a favourite sport. The sports are biking, swimming, jogging, and tennis, but not necessarily in that order. Use the clues to determine each person's favourite sport.
- Amanda and Dalil do not need a racket for their sports.
- Dalil cannot ride a bicycle.
- Dalil and Brittany can participate in their sports on the streets and sidewalks around their homes.

9. The graph describes a pushcart race between Jordan and Justin.

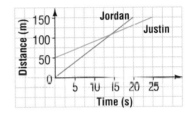

a) How far did Jordan go?
b) How far did Justin go?
c) Who won the race?
d) The lines cross. What does this show?
e) Write a paragraph to describe the race from start to finish.

DATA BANK

1. Which provincial capital is
a) warmest in January?
b) wettest in July?

2. A car uses fuel at a rate of 6.5 L/100 km. How much fuel is needed for each of the following journeys in the car? Round each answer to the nearest litre.
a) Calgary to Vancouver
b) Montreal to Winnipeg
c) Toronto to Regina
d) Halifax to Edmonton

CHAPTER 7

Measurement

The tangram puzzle is a square cut into 7 geometric shapes. They are 2 large triangles, 1 medium triangle, 2 small triangles, a square, and a parallelogram.

You can make a square from all 7 tangram pieces, as shown. You can also make slightly larger squares with holes in them from the 7 pieces.

Use the 7 tangram pieces to make squares like the ones shown.

a parallelogram missing:

a square missing:

a medium triangle missing:

two small triangles missing:

The holes do not have to be in the positions shown. Sketch your solutions.

Measuring Length

Activity ❶

1. Copy and complete the statements.

a) 1 m = ▇ mm   **b)** 1 mm = ▇ m

c) 1 m = ▇ cm   **d)** 1 cm = ▇ m

e) 1 m = ▇ km   **f)** 1 km = ▇ m

g) 1 cm = ▇ mm   **h)** 1 mm = ▇ cm

2. Write the meaning of each of the prefixes.

a) centi   **b)** milli   **c)** kilo

Activity ❷

Estimate, then measure the number of each object needed to make 1 m.

1. baseball cards laid end to end

2. quarters laid side by side

3. *MATHPOWER*™ textbooks stacked on top of each other

4. paper clips laid end to end

5. thumbtacks laid side by side

6. new pencils laid end to end

7. hockey pucks stacked on top of each other

8. sticks of chalk laid end to end

Activity ❸

Estimate, then measure to find which distance is greater and by how much.

1. the height of your classroom door or twice its width

2. the distance around the top of the classroom's wastebasket or its height

3. the distance across the face of a dollar coin or the length of a paper clip

4. twice the length of a running shoe or the length of its shoelace

5. the length of the school gymnasium or 3 times the length of your classroom

Activity ❹

Without a ruler, try to draw the length or the width, whichever is stated, of each object. Check your accuracy by measuring.

1. length of a $5.00 bill

2. length of a staple

3. width of a VHS videotape

4. length of a wire coat hanger

5. distance across the face of a dime

6. length of your foot

Activity ❺

Locate a map of your community. If you could walk at a rate of about 6 km/h, how long would it take you to walk from your school to each of the following destinations?

1. the nearest shopping centre

2. the city hall or municipal building

3. the nearest recreation centre

4. the nearest airport

5. the nearest lake or river

6. the nearest bus station

Activity ❻

1. On your school grounds, mark off 100 m.

2. With a group, take turns to count the paces needed to walk 100 m.

3. Calculate the length of the average pace for your group. Using this measurement, estimate, then determine, the following distances.

a) the length of the longest school hallway
b) the width of the gymnasium
c) the distance around the outside of the school building
d) the width of the school's main entrance
e) the distance from your classroom door to the nearest drinking fountain

Warm Up

Write in standard form.

1. four thousand twenty and five tenths

2. sixteen and forty-four hundredths

3. five hundred eighty-seven thousandths

4. six thousand eight hundred thirty-five

5. ninety-two and sixty-three hundredths

Write in words.

6. 112.7   7. 2036.08   8. 59.006

9. 0.345   10. 3.62   11. 75 264.9

Round to the given place value.

12. 14.659 to the nearest tenth

13. 425.17 to the nearest one

14. 8.427 to the nearest hundredth

15. 9574.12 to the nearest ten

16. 55.048 to the nearest tenth

Multiply.

17. 5.68×10 18. 45.03×100

19. 0.036×1000 20. 84.557×10

21. 2.73×0.01 22. 18.6×0.1

23. 4652×0.001 24. 52.09×0.01

Divide.

25. $2.76 \div 100$ 26. $38.165 \div 10$

27. $562.19 \div 1000$ 28. $2.6 \div 100$

29. $7.8 \div 0.01$ 30. $19.35 \div 0.1$

31. $246.115 \div 0.001$ 32. $42.06 \div 0.01$

Calculate.

33. $15.73 + 28.04 + 21.98$ 34. 3×49.56

35. $2 \times 12.3 + 2 \times 16.9$ 36. 4×9.86

37. $5 \times 16.2 + 8.3 \times 12.5$ 38. 3.14×12.5

39. $15.4 \times 27.6 - 9.2 \times 10.8$

40. $218.858 \div 3.14$

Mental Math

Express in millimetres.

1. 5 cm   2. 16 cm   3. 0.2 cm

4. 2 m   5. 0.3 m   6. 1.16 m

Express in centimetres.

7. 4 m   8. 25 m   9. 1.7 m

10. 0.8 m   11. 36 mm   12. 112 mm

Express in metres.

13. 240 cm   14. 516 cm   15. 24 cm

16. 9 cm   17. 1350 cm   18. 905 cm

19. 1500 mm   20. 625 mm   21. 52 mm

22. 4 km   23. 0.5 km   24. 6.3 km

Express in kilometres.

25. 8000 m   26. 25 700 m   27. 982 m

28. 46 m   29. 3405 m   30. 206 m

Calculate.

31. $2 \times 6 + 2 \times 3$ 32. $2 \times 9 + 2 \times 4$

33. $2 \times 20 + 2 \times 7$ 34. $2 \times 8 + 2 \times 2$

35. 4×0.7 36. 4×1.2

37. 6×0.8 38. 8×0.7

39. 4×0.03 40. 4×0.9

Simplify.

41. 8^2 42. 3^2 43. 9^2

44. 6^2 45. 2^3 46. 5^3

47. $10^2 - 20$ 48. $4^2 + 6$ 49. $7^2 - 2^2$

Calculate.

50. 26×100 51. 0.5×10

52. 3.4×1000 53. 7.9×100

54. 0.2×1000 55. $12 \div 1000$

56. $47 \div 10$ 57. $326 \div 100$

58. $59.8 \div 100$ 59. $2.73 \div 10$

Investigating Right Triangles

A right triangle has one right angle. The side
opposite the right angle is called the **hypotenuse**.
The other two sides are called the **legs**.

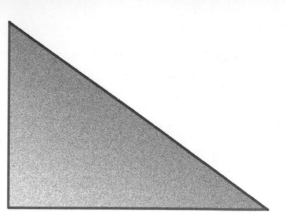

Activity ❶ Areas of Squares on a Grid

The area of a square drawn on a grid can be calculated
by dividing the square into right triangles and, in some
cases, a smaller square. Determine each area by counting
squares on the grid. Compare your method with your classmates'.

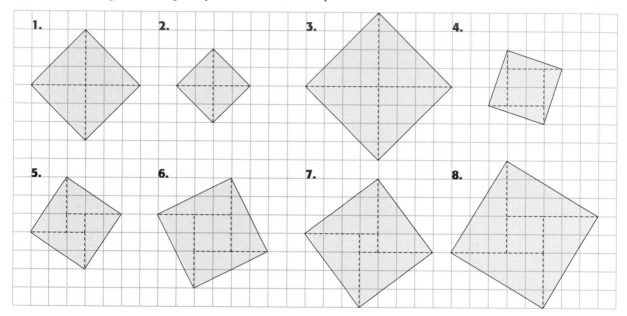

Activity ❷ More Squares on a Grid

Copy the squares onto grid paper. Divide each square into right
triangles and a smaller square. Determine the area of each square
by counting squares on the grid.

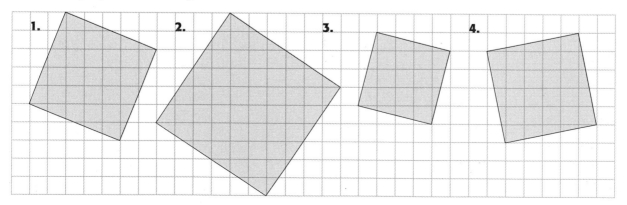

Activity ❸ Squares on the Sides of a Right Triangle

The diagrams show squares on the sides of each triangle. Copy
the table. Count squares on the grid to help complete the table.

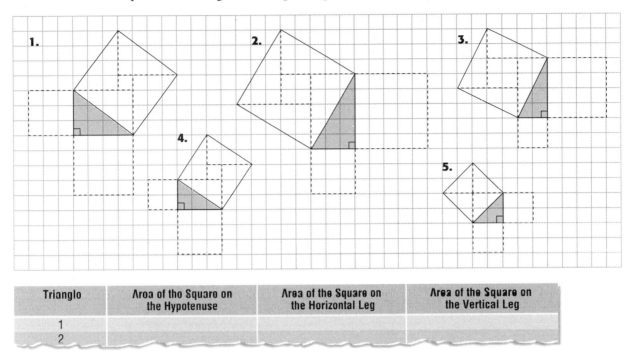

Triangle	Area of the Square on the Hypotenuse	Area of the Square on the Horizontal Leg	Area of the Square on the Vertical Leg
1			
2			

Activity ❹ More Right Triangles

Use the technique from Activity 3 to draw squares on the sides
of these right triangles. Copy and complete the table.

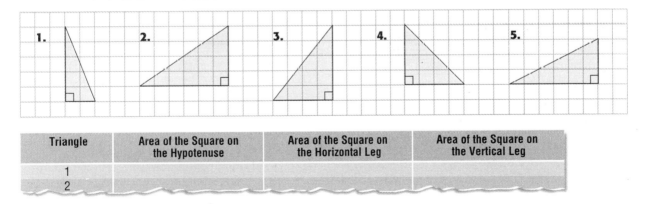

Triangle	Area of the Square on the Hypotenuse	Area of the Square on the Horizontal Leg	Area of the Square on the Vertical Leg
1			
2			

Activity ❺ The Pythagorean Theorem

Describe the relationship between the areas of the squares on
the legs of a right triangle and the area of the square on the
hypotenuse.

7.1 The Pythagorean Theorem

Pythagoras was a very famous Greek mathematician who lived in the sixth century B.C. He and his followers, the Pythagoreans, studied many properties of numbers and geometric figures. The most famous discovery made by Pythagoras was the relationship between the side lengths in right triangles.

Activity: Discover the Relationship

On each geoboard, a triangle has been constructed. The sides have been labelled a, b, and c, where c is the longest side. The squares of the sides of each triangle have also been constructed. Draw a diagram of each figure on grid paper, and find the area of each square. Copy and complete the table.

Triangle	a^2	b^2	c^2	$a^2 + b^2$
1				
2				
3				
4				
5				
6				

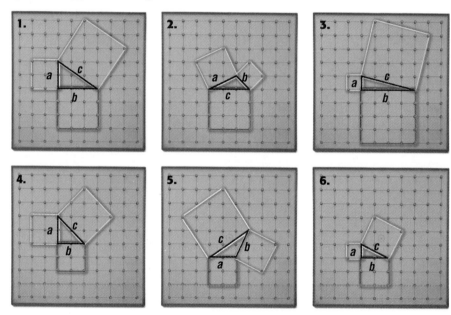

Inquire

1. Which of the 6 triangles are right triangles?

2. In each right triangle, how does the area of the square on the longest side compare with the sum of the areas of the squares on the other 2 sides?

3. Is the relationship you found in question 2 true for the triangles that are not right triangles?

Example

Calculate the length of the unknown side.
If necessary, round to the nearest tenth.

a)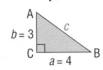

b)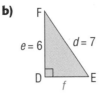

Solution

The Pythagorean Theorem states that in any right triangle,
if c is the length of the hypotenuse, and a and b are the
lengths of the legs, then $a^2 + b^2 = c^2$.

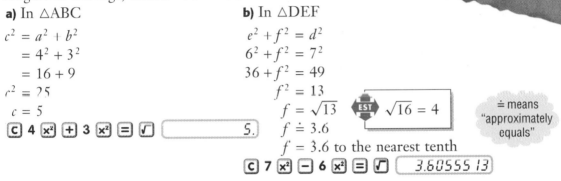

a) In $\triangle ABC$

$$c^2 = a^2 + b^2$$
$$= 4^2 + 3^2$$
$$= 16 + 9$$
$$c^2 = 25$$
$$c = 5$$

C 4 x² + 3 x² = √ [5.]

b) In $\triangle DEF$

$$e^2 + f^2 = d^2$$
$$6^2 + f^2 = 7^2$$
$$36 + f^2 = 49$$
$$f^2 = 13$$
$$f = \sqrt{13}$$
$$f \doteq 3.6$$
$$f = 3.6 \text{ to the nearest tenth}$$

EST $\sqrt{16} = 4$

$\doteq$ means "approximately equals"

C 7 x² − 6 x² = √ [3.6055513]

Practice

*Find the length of the unknown side in each right
triangle. If necessary, round to the nearest tenth.*

1.

2.

3.

4.

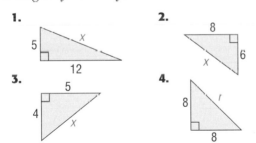

*Find the length of the unknown side in each
triangle. If necessary, round to the nearest tenth.*

5.

6.

7.

8.

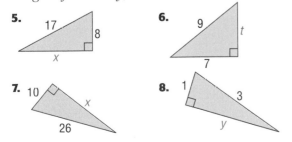

Problems and Applications

9. Use the figure
to answer the
questions.

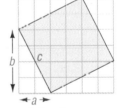

a) What is the area of the large square?
b) What is the area of each triangle?
c) What is the area of the tilted square?
d) What is the relationship between c^2 and $a^2 + b^2$?

10. Which of the following could be the
side lengths in a right triangle?
a) 3 cm, 4 cm, 6 cm
b) 15 m, 17 m, 8 m
c) 13 m, 5 m, 12 m
d) 8 cm, 9 cm, 11 cm

207

7.2 Using the Pythagorean Theorem

Activity: Study the Information

The HMCS *Halifax* left Halifax and sailed east at 25 km/h for 2 h. It then sailed south at 30 km/h for 2 h. The captain wanted to know how far the ship was from Halifax.

Inquire

1. How far did the ship sail east?

2. How far did the ship sail south?

3. Why is ∠HXY a right angle?

4. Write the Pythagorean relationship for △HXY.

5. Find the distance HY to the nearest tenth of a kilometre.

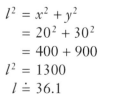 **6. a)** In questions 3 to 5, what assumption have you made about the surface of the Earth?

b) When is it reasonable to make this assumption?

Example

Galleys sailed the Mediterranean in the fifteenth century. They were 40 m long and 10 m wide. There was a 30-m high mast in the middle of each galley. Support ropes ran from the top of the mast to the front, back, and sides of the ship. Find the lengths of the support ropes, to the nearest tenth of a metre.

Solution

Make a diagram. Because the mast was in the middle of the boat, the front and back support ropes were the same length, and so were the 2 side ropes.

For the front and back ropes

$$l^2 = x^2 + y^2$$
$$= 20^2 + 30^2$$
$$= 400 + 900$$
$$l^2 = 1300$$
$$l \doteq 36.1$$

Front and Back Ropes

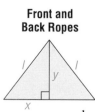

The front and back support ropes were each 36.1 m long, to the nearest tenth of a metre.

For the side ropes

$$s^2 = t^2 + y^2$$
$$= 5^2 + 30^2$$
$$= 25 + 900$$
$$s^2 = 925$$
$$s \doteq 30.4$$

Side Ropes

The side support ropes were each 30.4 m long, to the nearest tenth of a metre.

Practice

Find the length of the third side of each right triangle, to the nearest tenth of a metre.

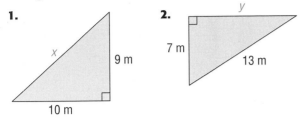

1.

x 9 m
10 m

2.

y
7 m 13 m

Problems and Applications

3. A 7-m ladder is leaning against a wall of a building. The foot of the ladder is 2 m from the base of the building. How far up the wall is the top of the ladder?

4. A ship left Shippegan, New Brunswick, and sailed east at 20 km/h for 2 h, then south at 25 km/h for 1 h. To the nearest tenth of a kilometre, how far was the ship from Shippegan?

5. A camp swimming race starts from the end of a 30-m long pier. The finish point is on the shore 80 m from the foot of the pier. How long is the race, to the nearest metre?

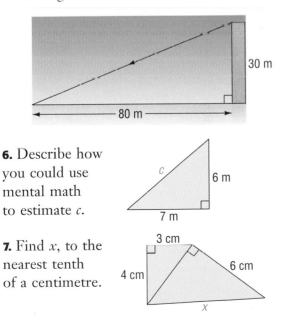

30 m
← 80 m →

6. Describe how you could use mental math to estimate *c*.

c 6 m
7 m

7. Find *x*, to the nearest tenth of a centimetre.

3 cm
4 cm 6 cm
x

8. The base of the Pyramid of Khufu is a square with sides 230 m long. Calculate the length of the diagonal of this square, to the nearest tenth of a metre.

9. An RCMP patrol boat left Long Beach, British Columbia, and sailed west for 2 h at 15 km/h, then north for 2 h at 20 km/h, then east for 1 h at 10 km/h. How far was the patrol boat from Long Beach, to the nearest tenth of a kilometre?

10. Three whole numbers, like 3, 4, and 5, where $3^2 + 4^2 = 5^2$, are called **Pythagorean Triples**. To make Pythagorean Triples, substitute two different whole numbers for *x* and *y* in these expressions.

$a = x^2 - y^2, b = 2xy, c = x^2 + y^2$

Use the whole numbers from 1 to 6 to make sets of Pythagorean Triples. Test each triple to see if it satisfies the equation $a^2 + b^2 = c^2$. Compare your triples with your classmates'.

11. A chessboard has diagonals of length 40 cm. What is the length of each side of the board, to the nearest tenth of a centimetre? Explain your reasoning.

12. Write a problem that can be solved using the Pythagorean Theorem. Have a classmate solve your problem.

LOGIC POWER

There are 6 blocks numbered 1 to 6. They must be put into 2 piles with the same height. A higher number must not be above a lower number in either pile. One way is shown. How many other ways are there?

3	1
4	2
5	6

7.3 Perimeter

Activity: Think About the Process

Jacob was helping to decorate his room. He chose a wallpaper border to go around the top of the painted walls and also around the middle of the walls.

Inquire

1. What measurements did Jacob need before purchasing the border for the top of the walls?

2. Why did the length of the second border differ from the length of the first?

3. What additional measurements were needed to determine the length of the second border?

4. Describe a method Jacob may have used to calculate the total length of wallpaper border needed.

The distance around Jacob's room is called the **perimeter**. To calculate the perimeter of a figure, find the sum of the lengths of all the sides.

Example

Calculate the perimeter of the garden.

Solution

$P = 23 + 11.8 + 16 + 12.5$
$\quad = 63.3$

EST $20 + 10 + 20 + 10 = 60$

The perimeter of the garden is 63.3 m.

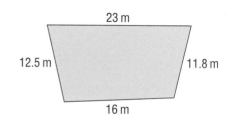

Practice

The distance between points on the grid represents 2 cm. Find the perimeter of each figure.

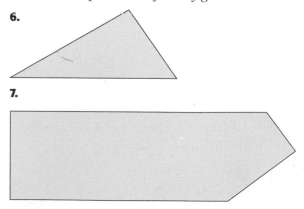

Estimate, then measure each side of the figures. Calculate the perimeter of each figure.

6.

7.

Estimate, then calculate the perimeter of each figure.

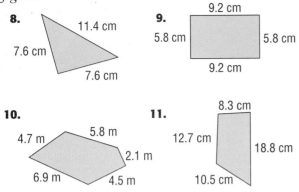

8. 11.4 cm, 7.6 cm, 7.6 cm

9. 9.2 cm, 5.8 cm, 5.8 cm, 9.2 cm

10. 4.7 m, 5.8 m, 2.1 m, 6.9 m, 4.5 m

11. 8.3 cm, 12.7 cm, 18.8 cm, 10.5 cm

Problems and Applications

Calculate each missing length. Check your answer by measuring.

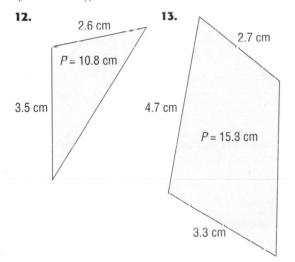

12. 2.6 cm, $P = 10.8$ cm, 3.5 cm

13. 2.7 cm, 4.7 cm, $P = 15.3$ cm, 3.3 cm

14. Describe the method you used to calculate the missing side of each figure in questions 12 and 13.

15. Shona used adhesive tape to seal the package completely around in 2 directions.

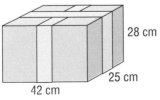

28 cm, 25 cm, 42 cm

What was the smallest length of tape that Shona could have used?

16. Copy and complete the table.

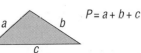

$P = a + b + c$

a	b	c	P
1.5	1.3	1.2	
2.1	1.6	2.5	
3.7		5.6	14.1
6.9	7.2		19.5
	3.7	4.8	13.5
2.4	4.9	5.3	

17. Copy and complete the table.

$P = a + b + c + d$

a	b	c	d	P
1.7	2.1	3.6	2.9	
2.7	5.6		4.5	17.7
	6.2	5.4	6.7	24.1
1.5	2.5	3.2		10
9.7		8.3	9.5	37.9
3.4	2.6	4.5	2.9	

18. A wallpaper border will be put around the walls of the hallway, at the top of the walls.

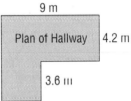

Plan of Hallway — 9 m, 4.2 m, 3.6 m, 3.6 m

a) What length of border will be needed?
b) If the border is sold in 6-m rolls, how many rolls must be purchased?
c) What length of border will be left over?
d) Wallpaper border costs $7.99 for each roll. Find the cost of the border used, excluding the piece left over.

19. The rectangle is made up of 4 different pentominoes. Draw the pentominoes and find the perimeter of each one.

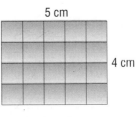

5 cm, 4 cm

7.4 Perimeters of Polygons

Activity: Determine a Formula

Andrew is making jewellery for the craft fair. He will use coloured wire for the outer edges of each piece and a variety of decorative stones for the interiors. Andrew planned the pieces of jewellery using 2-cm lengths for the edges.

Inquire

1. How many lengths of wire are needed for the square? What is the total length of wire needed?

2. Using s for the length of a side, determine a formula to calculate the perimeter of a square.

3. Write a formula for the perimeter of an equilateral triangle.

 **4.** Explain why $P = n \times s$ can be used to calculate the perimeter of any polygon with equal sides, when n represents the number of sides.

5. a) What is the length of Andrew's rectangular piece of jewellery?
b) What is its width?
c) What is its perimeter?

6. Write a formula to calculate the perimeter of a rectangle.

Example

Andrew designed a pin composed of 2 pieces, one rectangular and one a regular hexagon. What is the total length of wire he will need for the outer edges of the pin?

7 cm

1.5 cm

1.5 cm

Solution

For the rectangle
$P = 2 \times l + 2 \times w$
$\quad = 2 \times 7 + 2 \times 1.5$
$\quad = 14 + 3$
$\quad = 17$

For the hexagon
$P = 6 \times s$
$\quad = 6 \times 1.5$
$\quad = 9$

$17 + 9 = 26$

The total length of wire he will need is 26 cm.

Practice

Find the perimeter of each regular polygon.

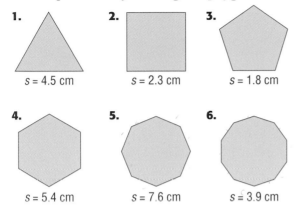

1. $s = 4.5$ cm

2. $s = 2.3$ cm

3. $s = 1.8$ cm

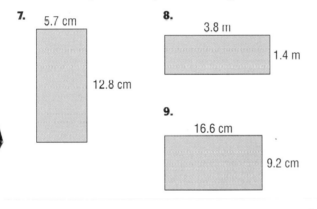

4. $s = 5.4$ cm

5. $s = 7.6$ cm

6. $s = 3.9$ cm

Calculate the perimeter of each rectangle.

7. 5.7 cm · 12.8 cm

8. 3.8 m · 1.4 m

9. 16.6 cm · 9.2 cm

Problems and Applications

10. Janine's construction company was hired to build a wire fence around the community centre's swimming pool. The pool is 55 m by 30 m, with a 2.5-m paved area around it. What is the total length of fencing needed to enclose the pool area?

Find the length of a side of each regular polygon.

11. pentagon, perimeter 22 cm

12. triangle, perimeter 13.2 cm

13. octagon, perimeter 46.4 cm

14. square, perimeter 2.6 m

15. hexagon, perimeter 58.8 cm

16. Sketch and label 3 different rectangles, each with a perimeter of 80 cm.

17. To warm up before a practice, the soccer coach has the team members run around the field 3 times. The length of the field is 100 m and its width is 73 m. How far does each team member run before a practice?

18. Two gardens in the shape of regular triangles are bordered in decorative tile. What is the total length of the tile?

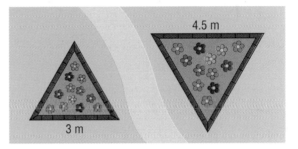

19. Sketch and label all of the regular polygons whose sides are whole numbers of centimetres greater than 3 cm and whose perimeters are 48 cm.

20. Sketch and label all of the rectangles whose sides are whole numbers of centimetres and whose perimeters are 24 cm.

21. In each of the following pairs of regular polygons, the perimeters are equal. How do the side lengths compare in each pair of polygons?
a) square and octagon
b) triangle and nonagon
c) hexagon and triangle
d) dodecagon and hexagon
e) square and dodecagon
f) pentagon and decagon

22. Write a problem that involves the perimeter of a polygon. Have a classmate solve your problem.

Investigating Geometric Constants

Activity ❶

1. Construct a square with each side 4 cm.

2. Draw a diagonal.

3. Measure the diagonal accurately.

4. Divide the perimeter of the square by the length of the diagonal. Note your result.

$$\frac{\text{perimeter}}{\text{diagonal}} = \blacksquare$$

5. Repeat steps 2 through 4 for four different squares.

6. What do you notice about the results?

7. Approximately how many times greater than the diagonal is the perimeter of a square?

Activity ❷

When very accurate measurements are taken, the value of the perimeter, P, of a square divided by its diagonal, d, is a **constant**, k, equal to approximately 2.83.

1. If $\frac{P}{d} = k$, what is the formula for calculating P?

2. What is the formula for calculating d?

3. If the length of a diagonal of a square is known, how would you find the length of each side, s?

4. Calculate the perimeter and the side length of the square for each diagonal. Round answers to the nearest hundredth, if necessary.

a) $d = 10$ cm   **b)** $d = 8$ cm   **c)** $d = 25$ cm

5. Calculate the length of the diagonal from each side length of a square. Round your answers to the nearest hundredth.

a) $s = 5$ cm   **b)** $s = 10$ cm   **c)** $s = 12$ cm

Activity ❸

1. Draw an equilateral triangle with each side 5 cm.

2. Mark the midpoint of one side of the triangle and draw a line from this point to the opposite vertex. This line is called the **median** of the triangle.

3. Measure the median, m, of the triangle accurately.

4. Divide the perimeter of the triangle by the length of the median. Note your result.

5. Repeat steps 2 through 4 for four different equilateral triangles.

6. Does it appear that, in an equilateral triangle, $\frac{P}{m}$ has a constant value? If so, what is that value?

Activity ❹

Investigate geometric constants in other regular polygons.

1. Measure the side and the diagonal or median in each of these polygons.

2. Divide the perimeter by the diagonal or median for each type of polygon. Note your results.

3. Construct regular polygons with sides of different lengths. Divide the perimeter by the median or diagonal for different side lengths of each type of polygon.

4. From your results, does it appear that $\frac{P}{m}$ or $\frac{P}{d}$ has a constant value for each type of regular polygon? If so, what is that value?

5. Are the constant values you found in question 4 grouped around any whole number? If so, what is that number?

215

7.5 Circumference of a Circle

The distance a bicycle travels in one turn of its wheels equals the perimeter or **circumference** of the wheels.

Activity: Discover the Relationship

Draw or trace a circle onto cardboard, then cut it out carefully. Mark a point on the circumference of the circle, then measure the circumference by rolling the circle along a ruler. Fold the circle in half and measure the diameter.

Cut out and measure 4 different circles. Record the measurements in a table. For each set of measurements, divide the circumference by the diameter. Record your answers to the nearest hundredth.

Compare your answers with those of your classmates.

	Circumference	Diameter	$C \div d$
1.			
2.			
3.			
4.			

Inquire

1. Approximately how many times greater than the diameter is the circumference?

2. The constant that represents $C \div d$ in any circle is represented by the Greek letter π. The value of π is approximately 3.14. How close to π were your results?

3. If $C \div d = \pi$, state the formula that can be used to calculate the circumference when the diameter is known.

4. State the formula that can be used to calculate the diameter when the circumference is known.

5. Investigate the origin and the development of the value of π. Write a report of the results of your research.

> π is spelled "pi" and pronounced "pie."
> $\pi = 3.141\ 592\ 653\ldots$
> In this book we use $\pi = 3.14$.

Example

The diameter of a Ferris wheel is 55 m.
What is its circumference?

Solution

$C = \pi \times d$
$ = 3.14 \times 55$
$ = 172.7$

EST $3 \times 60 = 180$

The circumference of the Ferris wheel is 172.7 m.

216

Practice

Round each answer to the nearest hundredth, if necessary.

Measure each radius or diameter and calculate the circumference of each circle.

1.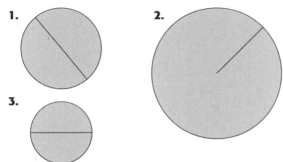

2.

3.

Estimate, then calculate the circumference of each circle.

4. $r = 5.5$ cm

5. $d - 8.35$ cm

6. $d = 15$ cm

7. $r = 2.8$ m

8. $r - 23$ cm

9. $d = 19.2$ cm

Problems and Applications

Estimate, then calculate the perimeter of each figure.

10.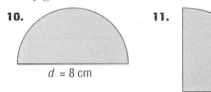

$d = 8$ cm

11.

$r = 12.2$ cm

12. How much longer is the circumference of a quarter than the circumference of a dime?

$d = 23.9$ mm

$d = 18$ mm

13. The diameter of the clock face of Big Ben in London, England, is 7.1 m. What is the circumference of the clock face?

14. Penny-farthing bicycles were popular in Victorian times. A penny-farthing had a large front wheel, radius about 65 cm, and a small back wheel, radius about 25 cm.

a) How many times did the back wheel turn for each turn of the front wheel?

b) How many times did the front wheel turn to travel 1 km?

15. What happens to the circumference of a circle in each of these situations? Use examples to explain your answers.

a) The radius is doubled.

b) The diameter is doubled.

Calculate the perimeter of each figure.

16.

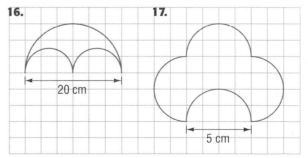

20 cm

17.

5 cm

18. Create a design using circles, semicircles, and quarter circles. Exchange designs with a classmate and calculate the perimeters of each other's designs.

Area

Area is the measure of a surface. Area is expressed in square units.

Activity ❶

Determine the area, in square units, of each figure on the grid.

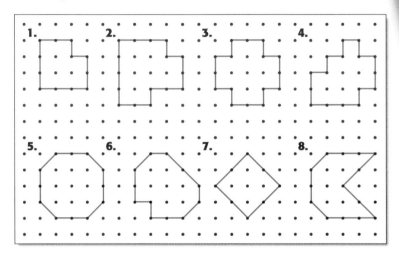

Activity ❷

1. On grid paper, make a region for each of the following.

a) a square with area 16 square units

b) a rectangle with area 18 square units

c) a right triangle with area 6 square units

d) a rectangle with area 12 square units

e) a parallelogram with area 20 square units

f) a right triangle with area 10 square units

2. Compare your results with your classmates'.

a) Which are the same?

b) Which are different?

c) Is it possible to make other regions for the given descriptions?

3. Make all of the possible regions that satisfy each description.

Activity ❸

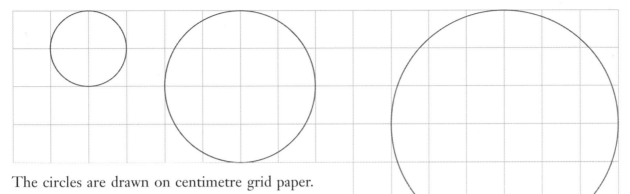

The circles are drawn on centimetre grid paper.

1. What is the radius of each circle?

2. Count squares to estimate the area of each circle. Compare your estimates with the estimates of others in your group. Compare the values given to part squares in your estimates. Decide on a common method.

3. Draw circles with the following radii. Estimate the area of each by counting squares using the group's method. Compare your results with the results of other members of your group.
a) 4 cm   **b)** 1.5 cm   **c)** 6 cm

Activity ❹

When decorating a house, decorators express the areas of walls, windows, and floors in square metres.

1. How many square centimetres are in 1 m²?

2. Complete each statement.
a) 3 m² = ▨ cm²   **b)** 0.01 m² = ▨ cm²
c) 2500 cm² = ▨ m²   **d)** 450 000 cm² = ▨ m²

3. How many math books are needed to cover approximately 1 m²?

4. How many square metres of carpet would be needed to cover your classroom floor?

5. Decorators recommend that curtain material be 3 times as wide as a window. How many square metres of curtain material would be recommended for your classroom windows?

Activity ❺

Areas of land are measured in hectares or square kilometres.

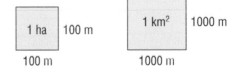

1. How many square metres are in 1 ha? 1 km²?

2. The area of a football field is about 0.5 ha. How large is your school playing field, in hectares?

3. How many times would the floor of your school gymnasium fit into 1 ha?

4. Use an almanac to find areas in square kilometres to help you answer the following.
a) How much bigger is the world's largest lake than Canada's smallest province?
b) How many times bigger than Lake Erie is Victoria Island?

7.6 Area of a Rectangle and Square

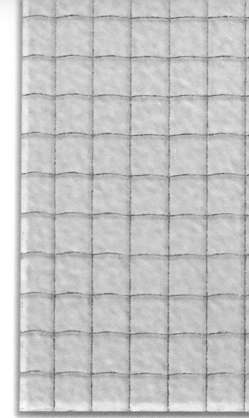

Activity: Discover the Relationship

The rectangular window in the school door is reinforced with wire so that it will not shatter if it is broken. The squares that are formed by the wire each cover 1 cm² of glass.

Inquire

1. The length of the window is 56 cm. How many rows of wire squares are there in the window?

2. The width of the window is 40 cm. How many columns of wire squares are there in the window?

3. What is the total number of squares covering the window?

4. What is the area of the window?

5. If the dimensions of any rectangle are represented by l and w, write a formula for calculating the area of a rectangle.

Activity: Discover the Relationship

There is a small, square window in the door of the boiler room.

Inquire

1. How many rows of wire squares are there in the window?

2. How many columns of wire squares are there?

3. What is the total number of squares covering the window?

4. What is the area of the window?

5. If the side of any square is represented by s, write a formula for calculating the area of a square.

Example

The cost of reinforced window glass is 1.37¢/cm². What is the cost of a window that is 60 cm by 35 cm?

Solution

The window is a rectangle 60 cm by 35 cm.
$A = l \times w$
$\quad = 60 \times 35$
$\quad = 2100$
The area of the window is 2100 cm².
The cost of the glass is 1.37¢/cm².
$1.37 \times 2100 = 2877$¢ or \$28.77
The cost of the window is \$28.77.

Practice

The diagram illustrates the area of a square with side 2.5 cm. Illustrate the areas of squares with the following sides.

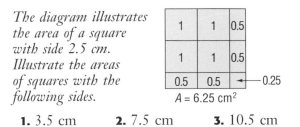

$A = 6.25 \text{ cm}^2$

1. 3.5 cm   **2.** 7.5 cm   **3.** 10.5 cm

Estimate, then calculate the area of each rectangle.

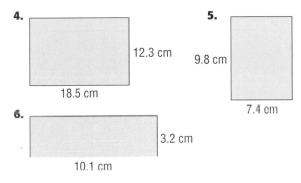

4. 12.3 cm, 18.5 cm

5. 9.8 cm, 7.4 cm

6. 3.2 cm, 10.1 cm

Estimate, then calculate the area of each square with the following sides.

7. 22 cm   **8.** 4.4 cm   **9.** 14.8 cm

Problems and Applications

10. A garden is twice as long as it is wide. Its length is 15 m. What is its area?

11. The perimeter of a square play area is 33.6 m. What is the area?

12. The area of a pathway is 5.46 m². The width is 78 cm. How long is the pathway?

13. One hectare equals 10 000 m². If the dimensions of a 1-ha area are whole numbers of metres, and all angles are right angles, what are the greatest and smallest perimeters?

14. The Imperial Palace in Beijing, China, covers a rectangular area 960 m long and 750 m wide. What area, in hectares, does the palace cover?

15. A tennis court is 23.8 m by 11 m. A tennis club has 3 courts side by side in a fenced area. The courts have 3 m between them and 3 m around the outside.

a) What is the total area of the 3 tennis courts?
b) What are the dimensions of the fenced space?
c) What is the area of the fenced space?
d) Paving costs $45/m². What does it cost to pave the 3 tennis courts?
e) Fencing costs $55/m. What does it cost to fence the 3 tennis courts?

16. Michelle had a valuable stamp mounted and framed. The stamp is 3 cm by 2.5 cm, and the frame is a 9-cm square. What is the area of the background not covered by the stamp?

Stamp reproduced courtesy of Canada Post Corporation

17. What is the greatest number of 2 cm × 3 cm rectangles that can be cut from a 16 cm × 10 cm rectangle? Make a sketch to show where the cuts would be made. Compare your plan with the plans of some classmates.

LOGIC POWER

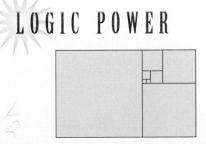

The area of each of the smallest squares is 1 cm². Calculate the area of each of the other squares and the area of the rectangle.

221

7.7 Area of a Parallelogram

The upper and lower rails of the handrail form a
parallelogram with the end posts. Each rail is
the length of the **base** of the parallelogram.
The distance between the rails is the **height**
of the parallelogram.

Activity: Discover the Relationship

Draw a rectangle with length 7 cm and width 5 cm.
Make a non-vertical cut across the rectangle and
fit the 2 pieces together, as shown.

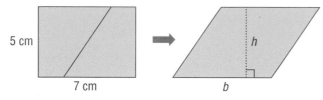

5 cm

7 cm

h

b

Inquire

1. What figure is formed by the 2 pieces of the rectangle?

2. What is the measure of the base of the figure?

3. What is the measure of the height of the figure?

4. What is the relationship of the area of the new figure to
the area of the rectangle?

5. Write a formula for calculating the area of a parallelogram.

Example

A restaurant sign is a rectangle 2.8 m in length and 0.7 m
in width. The name on the restaurant sign is printed on
a parallelogram. The base of the parallelogram
is 2 m and the height is 0.4 m. What area of
the sign is not covered by the parallelogram?

Solution

The sign is a rectangle.

$A = l \times w$

$\quad = 2.8 \times 0.7$

$\quad = 1.96$

For the parallelogram

$A = b \times h$

$\quad = 2 \times 0.4$

$\quad = 0.8$

$A_{\text{rectangle}} - A_{\text{parallelogram}} = 1.96 - 0.8$

$\quad\quad\quad\quad\quad\quad\quad = 1.16$

The area of the sign not covered by the parallelogram is 1.16 m^2.

Practice

1. Measure the necessary dimensions to calculate the area of the following. Explain your method in each case.

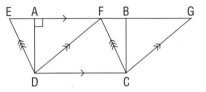

a) rectangle ABCD
b) parallelogram EFCD
c) parallelogram FGCD

Estimate, then calculate the area of each parallelogram.

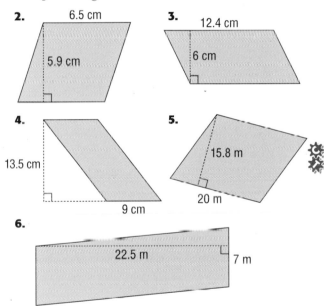

2. 6.5 cm, 5.9 cm

3. 12.4 cm, 6 cm

4. 13.5 cm, 9 cm

5. 15.8 m, 20 m

6. 22.5 m, 7 m

Problems and Applications

7. The area of a parallelogram is 107.5 cm² and the height is 8.6 cm.
a) Write a formula for calculating the base.
b) Calculate the base.

8. The area of a parallelogram is 22.26 cm² and the base is 5.3 cm.
a) Write a formula for calculating the height.
b) Calculate the height.

9. A wallpaper border on top of the baseboard on a flight of stairs is in the shape of a parallelogram. The bottom of the border is 150 cm and the height is 12 cm. What is the area of the border?

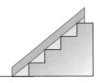

10. In the flag of Trinidad and Tobago, the length of the rectangle is about 4 times the base of the black parallelogram. How do the areas of the rectangle and the parallelogram compare? Explain.

11. The path cuts through a rose garden.

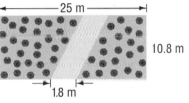

25 m, 10.8 m, 1.8 m

a) What is the area of the path?
b) What area of the garden is planted?

12. a) Copy the trapezoid onto cardboard and cut it out.

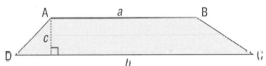

Trace and cut a second identical trapezoid.
b) Fit the 2 figures together along side BC to form a parallelogram. Use a, b, and c to write an expression for the area of the parallelogram.
c) Use a, b, and c to write a formula for the area of the trapezoid.
d) Use your formula to calculate the area of each trapezoid.

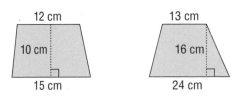

12 cm, 10 cm, 15 cm

13 cm, 16 cm, 24 cm

223

Seven-Point Geometry

The grid has 7 points, 6 in the shape of a regular hexagon and 1 centre point. Copy the 7-point grid several times in your notebook.

Activity ❶ Drawing Polygons

Three of the 19 different polygons that can be made on the 7-point grid are shown.

1. Draw the other 16 polygons. Share your answers with your classmates until you have all 16.

2. Number the polygons from 1 to 19. Work together, so that each group numbers the polygons in the same way. You may want to start with the triangles, then the quadrilaterals, and so on.

Activity ❸ Comparing Sides

There are 3 different lengths that can be drawn on the 7-point grid.

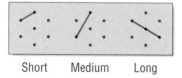

Short   Medium   Long

1. Mark the equal sides on your polygons. Use 1 "tick" for the short length, 2 "ticks" for the medium length, and 3 "ticks" for the long length.

2. Describe each polygon according to the number of equal sides it has. For example:
- All sides have the same length.
- All sides have different lengths.
- Two sides are equal.
- There are two pairs of equal sides.

Activity ❷ Classifying Polygons

1. Name each of the 19 polygons according to the number of sides it has.

2. If you wrap an elastic around a convex polygon, the elastic touches every point of the polygon. If the polygon is concave, the elastic does not touch every point. Classify each of the 19 polygons as either convex or concave.

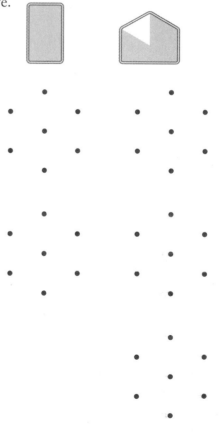

Activity ❹ Comparing Angles

1. Describe each of your 19 polygons according to the numbers of equal angles it has. For example:
- All angles are equal.
- All angles are different.
- Two angles are equal.
- There are two pairs of equal angles.

2. List the types of angles each polygon contains. For example:
- 3 acute angles
- 2 right angles, 2 acute angles, 1 reflex angle

Activity ❺ Finding Angle Measures

1. Find the measure of each angle.

2. Using the results from question 1, find the measure of each interior angle of each of your 19 polygons. For example, for the figure at the right, the angle measures are 60°, 60°, 60°.

Activity ❻ Finding Lines of Symmetry

When a polygon is folded along a line of symmetry, both parts of the polygon match. The polygon at the right has one line of symmetry.

Sort the 19 polygons according to how many lines of symmetry they have.

Activity ❼ Comparing Areas

Let the small equilateral triangle have an area of 1 square unit.

This triangle also has an area of 1 square unit because it is half of 2 small equilateral triangles.

1. Find the area of each of your 19 polygons.

2. Which polygons have the same area?

3. Which polygon has the largest area?

7.8 Area of a Triangle

The office furnishings store sells a triangular insert that connects a main desk to a computer stand. The amount of additional surface the insert provides is the area of the triangle.

Activity: Determine the Relationship

The polygons are formed by elastics on a geoboard.

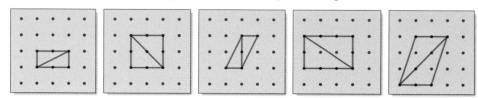

More elastics divide each polygon into 2 equal triangles.

Inquire

1. What is the area in square units of each polygon?

2. Compare each triangle with the polygon from which it is formed.
a) How do their areas compare?
b) How do their bases compare?
c) How do their heights compare?

3. What formula can be used to calculate the area of a triangle?

Example

The sailboat has 2 sails. What is the total area of material in the sails?

Solution

The sails are both triangles.

$A_1 = \frac{1}{2} \times b \times h$

$= \frac{1}{2} \times 10.8 \times 25$

$= 135$

$\boxed{\text{EST} \quad \frac{1}{2} \times 10 \times 30 = 150}$

$A_2 = \frac{1}{2} \times b \times h$

$= \frac{1}{2} \times 8.5 \times 24$

$= 102$

$\boxed{\text{EST} \quad \frac{1}{2} \times 10 \times 20 = 100}$

$135 + 102 = 237$

The total area of material is 237 m^2.

Practice

Determine the area of each shaded triangle.

1. **2.**

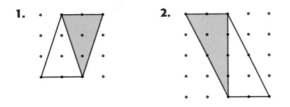

Estimate, then calculate the area of each triangle.

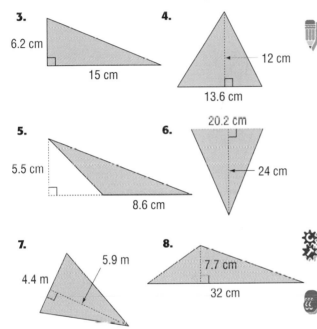

3.
6.2 cm
15 cm

4.
12 cm
13.6 cm

5.
5.5 cm
8.6 cm

6.
20.2 cm
24 cm

7.
5.9 m
4.4 m

8.
7.7 cm
32 cm

Problems and Applications

Calculate the missing value for each triangle.

	Base	Height	Area
9.		3.8	8.55
10.	12.7		82.55
11.	19	8.4	
12.	4.5		10.35
13.	7.6	10.5	
14.		1.8	5.67

15. This section of a patchwork quilt is a 12-cm square with 5 triangles on it. The base of each triangle is 5.2 cm and the height is 3.6 cm.

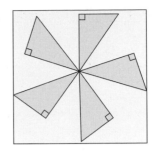

a) What area of fabric is needed for the triangles?

b) What area of the background is visible?

16. Sofia has to mow the following 5 lawns. Which one will take her the longest time? the shortest time? Explain.
- a rectangle 5.2 m by 17.1m
- a square of side 9.1 m
- a trapezoid with bases of 6.8 m and 14.2 m, and a height of 7.3 m
- a parallelogram with base 7.3 m and height 11.5 m
- a triangle with base 12.6 m and height 15.3 m

17. What is the area, to the nearest tenth of a square centimetre, of the largest equilateral triangle that can be drawn on a 5-cm square?

18. a) Work with a partner to make a sketch that shows how the largest possible number of pennants can be cut from 1 m of felt with a width of 90 cm.

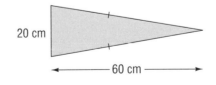

20 cm
60 cm

b) What area of fabric is used for the pennants?

c) What area of fabric is left over?

227

7.9 Area of a Circle

Activity: Study the Diagram

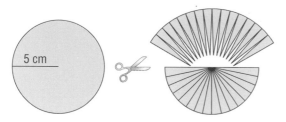 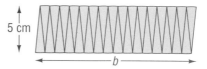

The radius of the circle is 5 cm.
The circumference of the circle is 31.4 cm.

The circle is cut in half, and each half is divided into 16 segments. The segments fit together to form a figure that resembles a parallelogram.

Inquire

1. The base of the parallelogram is formed by half the circumference of the circle. What is the measure of the base of the parallelogram?

2. Why is the height of the parallelogram equal to 5 cm?

3. What is the area of the parallelogram?

4. What is the area of the circle?

5. Explain why the following is true for the area of a circle.

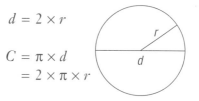

$$d = 2 \times r$$

$$C = \pi \times d$$
$$\quad = 2 \times \pi \times r$$

$$A = b \times h$$
$$\quad = \frac{1}{2} \times C \times r$$
$$\quad = \frac{1}{2} \times 2 \times \pi \times r \times r$$
$$\quad = \pi \times r^2$$

Example

The radius of the dart board at the community centre is 23 cm. What area of the wall is covered by the dart board, to the nearest square centimetre?

Solution

$$A = \pi \times r^2$$
$$\quad = 3.14 \times 23^2 \qquad \boxed{\text{EST}} \quad 3 \times 500 = 1500$$
$$\quad = 3.14 \times 529$$
$$\quad = 1661.06 \qquad \boxed{\text{C}} \; 3.14 \; \boxed{\times} \; 23 \; \boxed{\times} \; 23 \; \boxed{=} \qquad \boxed{1661.06}$$

The area of the wall covered by the dart board is 1661 cm², to the nearest square centimetre.

Practice

Round each answer to the nearest hundredth.

Measure the radius or diameter of each circle and calculate each area.

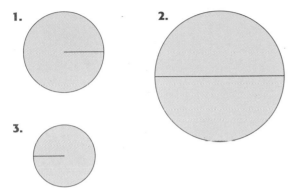

1. **2.**

3.

Estimate, then calculate the area of each circle.

4. $r = 3.8$ cm **5.** $r = 12$ cm

6. $d = 17$ cm **7.** $d = 1.2$ m

8. $r = 21$ cm **9.** $r = 4.6$ m

Problems and Applications

10. The sound waves from a radio station travel approximately 80 km. What is the area of the transmission circle of the station?

11. The world's largest clock face is on a floral clock in Toi, Japan. The clock face is 31 m in diameter. Calculate its area.

Calculate the area of each shaded region.

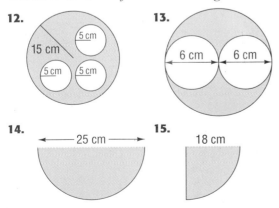

12. 15 cm, 5 cm, 5 cm, 5 cm **13.** 6 cm, 6 cm

14. 25 cm **15.** 18 cm

16. A compact disc has a diameter of 12 cm. The hole in the centre has a diameter of 1.5 cm. What is the area
a) including the hole?
b) excluding the hole?

17. A circular window in a door has a diameter of 32 cm. Its frame is 2 cm wide. What is the total area of the window and its frame?

2 cm
32 cm

18. Oni wants to draw a circle with an area of about 100 cm^2. To what distance should she set her compasses?

19. A decorator table has a diameter of 50 cm and a height of 66 cm. Its circular cover hangs to the floor all around. What is the area of the cover?

50 cm
66 cm

20. Work in a group to predict what happens to the area of a circle in the following cases. Use examples to check your predictions.
a) The diameter is doubled.
b) The radius is tripled.

LOGIC POWER

Jason decided to design a circular medal with an unusual property. He made its area in square centimetres numerically equal to its circumference in centimetres. What was the diameter of Jason's medal?

7.10 Areas of Composite Figures

Composite figures are made up of 2 or more distinct regions.

Activity: Use a Diagram

The plan of a garden shows a circular fountain surrounded by a lawn. To find the area of the lawn, subtract the area of the fountain from the area of the whole garden. The garden can be considered as 3 distinct regions.

$$A_1 = l \times w \qquad A_2 = l \times w \qquad A_3 = \pi \times r^2$$
$$= 8.5 \times 6 \qquad = 14 \times 12 \qquad = 3.14 \times 3 \times 3$$
$$= 51 \qquad = 168 \qquad = 28.26$$

Area of lawn $= A_1 + A_2 - A_3$
$$= 51 + 168 - 28.26$$
$$= 219 - 28.26$$
$$= 190.74$$

EST $50 + 170 - 30 = 190$

The area of the lawn is 190.74 m².

Inquire

1. Copy the diagram. Complete it by adding the dimensions needed to solve the above problem in another way.

2. Solve the problem using this method.

Example

Calculate the area of the rug.

1 m ⎯⎯ 1 m

←⎯ 2.8 m ⎯→

Solution

The rug can be divided into 3 regions.

$$A_1 = \pi \times r^2 \div 2 \qquad A_2 = l \times w \qquad A_3 = \pi \times r^2 \div 2$$
$$= 3.14 \times 1 \times 1 \div 2 \qquad = 2.8 \times 2 \qquad = 3.14 \times 1 \times 1 \div 2$$
$$= 1.57 \qquad = 5.6 \qquad = 1.57$$

Area of rug $= 1.57 + 5.6 + 1.57$
$$= 8.74$$

EST $2 + 6 + 2 = 10$

The area of the rug is 8.74 m².

Practice

Calculate the area of each figure using 2 different methods.

1.

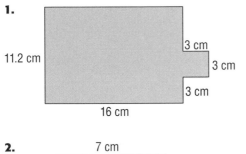

11.2 cm
3 cm
3 cm
3 cm
16 cm

2.

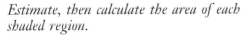

7 cm
4.8 cm
2.4 cm
3 cm
11 cm

Estimate, then calculate the area of each shaded region.

3.

13 m
8 m
15 m

4.

12.5 m
9 m
12.5 m

5.

18 cm
12.5 cm
10.3 cm

6.

1.8 cm   4.5 cm
12.6 cm
4.5 cm   1.8 cm
12.6 cm

7.

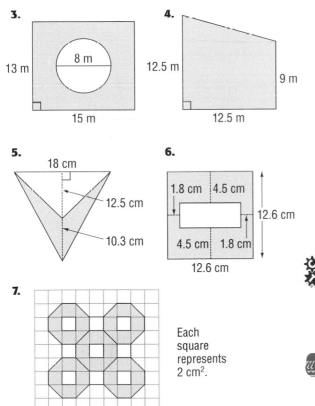

Each square represents 2 cm².

Problems and Applications

8. a) Calculate the area of paving stone needed for the patio shown.

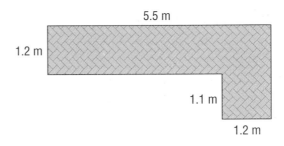

5.5 m
1.2 m
1.1 m
1.2 m

b) Paving costs $42/m². How much does it cost to pave the patio?

9. Ray's Restaurant has a rectangular patio 15.2 m by 5.1 m. There are 4 small trees on the patio. Each is in a circular pot with a diameter of 1 m. What area of the patio is available for seating?

15.2 m
5.1 m

10. a) What area of carpeting is needed to carpet the rectangular living room?

b) Carpeting costs $34.50/m². What does it cost to carpet the room?

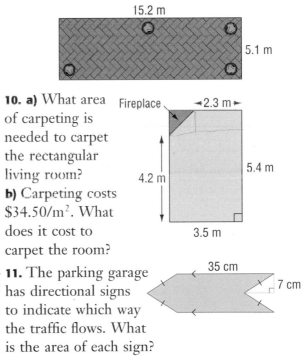

Fireplace   ◄2.3 m►
4.2 m
5.4 m
3.5 m

11. The parking garage has directional signs to indicate which way the traffic flows. What is the area of each sign?

35 cm
7 cm

12. Design a composite figure that includes at least 3 distinct regions. Draw its plan. Ask a classmate to calculate the area of your figure.

7.11 Working with Perimeter and Area

Activity: Solve the Problem

Cans of juice are packed in cases of 24, in 4-by-6 arrays. The diameter of each can is 6.5 cm. The problem is to find how much of the base of the case is not covered by cans.

Inquire

1. If the cans are touching, what is
a) the length of the case?   **b)** the width of the case?

2. What is the area of the base of the case?

3. What is the area of the base of a can?

4. What is the total area of the bases of all the cans?

5. How much of the base of the case is not covered by cans?

Example

Marisa is making a tablecloth for a dining table. The table is 3.2 m long and 1.8 m wide. She wants the cloth to hang 30 cm on all sides.
a) How much material does Marisa need to buy?
b) How much trim will she need to decorate the edges of the cloth?

Recall the steps

Understand the Problem

Solution

Make a diagram.

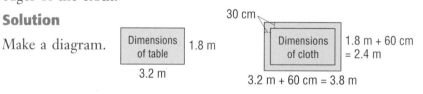

30 cm

| Dimensions of table | 1.8 m |
| Dimensions of cloth | 1.8 m + 60 cm = 2.4 m |

3.2 m

3.2 m + 60 cm = 3.8 m

Think of a Plan

The tablecloth will be a rectangle 3.8 m by 2.4 m.

a) The amount of material needed is the area of the tablecloth.

$A = l \times w$
  $= 3.8 \times 2.4$ EST $4 \times 2.5 = 10$
  $= 9.12$

Marisa needs 9.12 m² of material.

Carry Out the Plan

b) The amount of trim needed is the perimeter of the tablecloth.

$P = 2 \times (l + w)$
  $= 2 \times (3.8 + 2.4)$ EST $4 + 2 = 6$
  $= 2 \times 6.2$ $2 \times 6 = 12$
  $= 12.4$

Marisa needs 12.4 m of trim.
How could you check the answers?

Look Back

Problems and Applications

Round your answers to the nearest hundredth, when necessary.

1. The rectangular table has a semicircular leaf at each end.

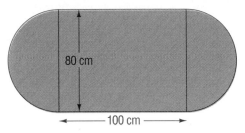

a) What is the total area of the table, in square centimetres?
b) Express the area in square metres.
c) What is the total perimeter of the table, in centimetres?
d) Express the perimeter in metres.

2. Josh and Brenda made pennants to sell at a fund-raiser for the school basketball team.

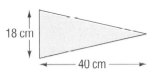

What area of cloth was needed for each pennant?

3. The target is painted on the playground for a game of beanbag toss. The centre circle has a radius of 50 cm. The radius of each circle is

50 cm greater than the one before.
a) Calculate the area and the outside perimeter of each band of colour on the target.
b) If one more band of colour is added, what will be its area?
c) What will be the outside perimeter of the target with the new band of colour?

4. A compact disc has a diameter of 12 cm. It is packaged in a plastic case 14 cm by 12.5 cm.
a) What is the difference between the circumference of the compact disc and the perimeter of the case?
b) What is the difference between the area of the compact disc and the area of the case?

5. The radius of a cylindrical air conditioner in a backyard is 40 cm.
a) What is the length of the sides of the smallest square paving stone that the air conditioner can sit on?
b) What is the area of the paving stone in part a)?

6. A semicircle, with a diameter equal to the side, is drawn on each side of a right triangle.

a) Find the area of each semicircle.
b) What relationship do you notice among the 3 areas?
c) Use 2 more examples to check if this relationship is true for all right triangles.

7. In your group, choose a game that is played on a marked playing area. Use centimetre grid paper to draw a plan of your game surface. Investigate to find the placement and dimensions of the playing lines. Mark them on your plan. Use your plan to write 5 questions involving area and perimeter. Exchange questions with another group, and solve each other's questions.

NUMBER POWER

Find 2 right triangles in which the perimeter is the same number of centimetres as the number of square centimetres in the area.

Using Geometry Software

Complete the following activities with geometry software.
If suitable software is unavailable, use grid paper.

Activity ❶ Areas of Squares and Rectangles

1. Construct all the rectangles with a perimeter of 12 units and whole-number side lengths. (Remember that a square is a rectangle.) Determine the area of each rectangle.

2. Repeat question 1 for all the rectangles with a perimeter of 20 units and whole-number side lengths.

3. From your results in questions 1 and 2, state what happens to the area of a rectangle as it becomes closer to a square.

4. If you used right-angled corners, what is the greatest area you could enclose with 24 m of fencing? Explain.

5. If you used right-angled corners, what is the minimum length of fencing you could use to enclose an area of 64 m²? Explain.

Activity ❷ Areas of Circles and Squares

1. Construct a square with a perimeter of 8 units. Determine its area.

2. Construct a circle with a circumference as close as possible to 8 units. Determine its area.

3. Divide the area of the circle by the area of the square. Round your answer to the nearest hundredth.

4. Repeat questions 1 to 3 for perimeters of 12 units and 16 units.

5. What do you notice about the quotient of the area of a circle divided by the area of a square when their perimeters are equal?

6. If you used a circular fence, what area would you enclose with 24 m of fencing? Compare your answer with the answer to question 4 in Activity 1.

7. If you used a circular fence, what length of fencing would you need to enclose an area of 64 m²? Compare your answer with the answer to question 5 in Activity 1.

8. Most house lots in towns and cities are rectangular. State the advantages and disadvantages of making them circular instead.

Programming Formulas in BASIC

This program calculates the area of a triangle.

```
NEW
10 PRINT "Area of a Triangle"
20 INPUT "The base is";B
30 INPUT "The height is";H
40 A = .5*B*H
50 PRINT "The area is";A"square units."
60 END
```

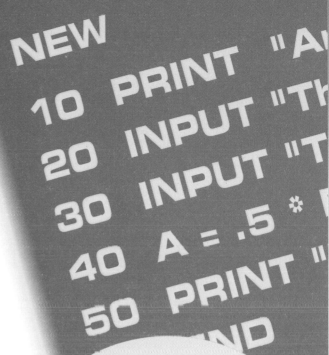

Activity ❶

Use the program to calculate the area of each triangle.

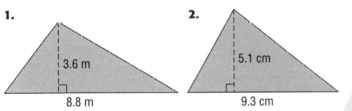

1. 3.6 m / 8.8 m

2. 5.1 cm / 9.3 cm

3. 145 m / 96 m

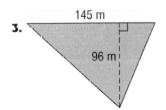

Activity ❷

Modify the program to calculate the following.

1. the area of a rectangle
2. the area of a parallelogram
3. the area of a square
4. the circumference of a circle

Have a classmate test your programs.

Activity ❸

Use your programs to calculate the area of each diagram.

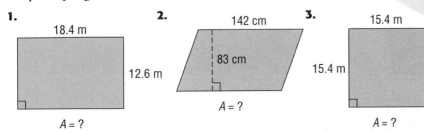

1. 18.4 m / 12.6 m / $A = ?$

2. 142 cm / 83 cm / $A = ?$

3. 15.4 m / 15.4 m / $A = ?$

235

Street Distances

The driving distance or walking distance between two places in a town or city is usually measured in blocks.

The shortest distance between A and B on the street map is 6 blocks.

There are several ways you can walk the 6 blocks from A to B.

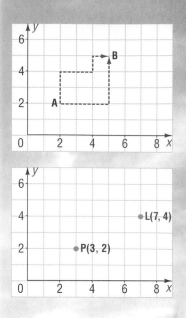

Activity ❶ Locating a Bus Stop

The library is located at (7, 4) and the post office at (3, 2).

1. a) At which corners can a bus stop be located so that the distances from the bus stop to the library and the bus stop to the post office are the same, and the distance to each one is as short as possible?

b) What is the shortest total distance from the bus stop to the library and the bus stop to the post office?

2. At which corners can a bus stop be located so that the shortest distances to the post office and to the library are each 4 blocks?

3. What is the relationship between the shortest total distance found in question 1 b) and the coordinates of the library and the post office?

Activity ❷ Locating a Swimming Pool

An elementary school, a junior high school, and a senior high school are located at E(8, 4), J(3, 2), and S(4, 6).

1. City planners want to build a swimming pool so that the total number of blocks from the pool to each of the schools is as small as possible.

a) What are the coordinates for the location of the pool?

b) What is the distance from the pool to each of the schools?

c) What is the total of the 3 distances in part b)?

d) What is the relationship between the coordinates of the pool found in part a), the coordinates of the 3 schools, and the total distance found in part c)?

2. If the total distance from the pool to the 3 schools can be 10 blocks, what are the coordinates of the possible locations for the pool?

3. a) Find the coordinates of the pool so that the elementary students walk 1 block less than the junior high students, and the junior high students walk 1 block less than the senior high students.

b) How many blocks is it to each school?

Activity ❸ Travelling Downtown

The theatre is located at T(5, 3), the pool at P(8, 5), the library at L(3, 6), and the record store at R(2, 2).

1. If you get a ride downtown, what are the coordinates of the corners at which you could be dropped off, if you want the pool and the library to be the same number of blocks away and the total walking distance to all 4 places to be as short as possible?

2. If you get a ride downtown, what are the coordinates of the corners at which you could be dropped off, if you want the record store and the theatre to be the same number of blocks away and the total walking distance to all 4 places to be as short as possible?

Review

Calculate each unknown length, to the nearest tenth of a centimetre.

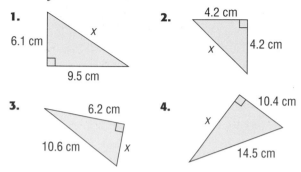

1. 6.1 cm, x, 9.5 cm

2. 4.2 cm, x, 4.2 cm

3. 6.2 cm, 10.6 cm, x

4. 10.4 cm, x, 14.5 cm

5. A ship left Port Alberni, British Columbia, and sailed west for 3 h at 15 km/h, then north for 2 h at 20 km/h. To the nearest tenth of a kilometre, how far was the ship from Port Alberni?

Calculate each perimeter.

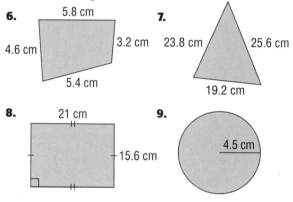

6. 5.8 cm, 4.6 cm, 3.2 cm, 5.4 cm

7. 23.8 cm, 25.6 cm, 19.2 cm

8. 21 cm, 15.6 cm

9. 4.5 cm

Calculate the perimeter of each regular polygon.

10. a pentagon with side 8.6 cm

11. a square with side 12.7 cm

12. an octagon with side 3.15 cm

13. a triangle with side 26.9 cm

14. a hexagon with side 6.6 cm

15. a decagon with side 13.45 cm

16. Sketch and label 2 different rectangles with a perimeter of 64 cm.

17. The length of the minute hand on the clock is 11.5 cm. The hour hand is 9 cm long.

a) What is the circumference of the circle traced by the point of the minute hand in 1 h?

b) What is the circumference of the circle traced by the point of the hour hand in one day?

Determine the area of each figure. The pegs are spaced 1 cm apart.

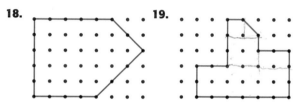

18.

19.

Estimate, then calculate the area of each figure.

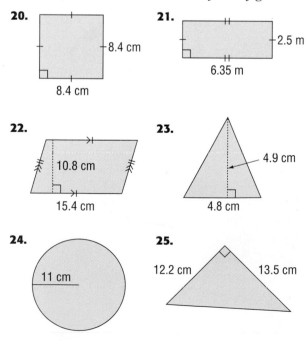

20. 8.4 cm, 8.4 cm

21. 2.5 m, 6.35 m

22. 10.8 cm, 15.4 cm

23. 4.9 cm, 4.8 cm

24. 11 cm

25. 12.2 cm, 13.5 cm

238

Estimate, then calculate the area of each figure.

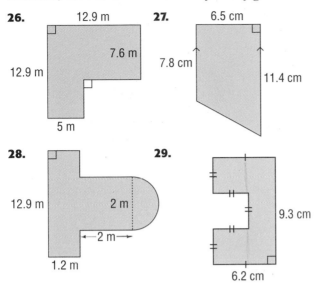

26. 12.9 m, 7.6 m, 12.9 m, 5 m

27. 6.5 cm, 7.8 cm, 11.4 cm

28. 12.9 m, 2 m, 2 m, 1.2 m

29. 9.3 cm, 6.2 cm

In questions 30 and 31, calculate the area of each shaded region.

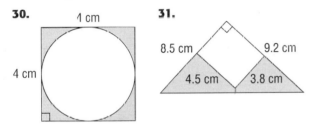

30. 4 cm, 4 cm

31. 8.5 cm, 9.2 cm, 4.5 cm, 3.8 cm

32. a) What is the area of the parking lot?

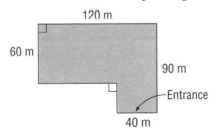

120 m, 60 m, 90 m, Entrance, 40 m

b) How many metres of fencing are needed to surround the parking lot limits, other than the entrance?

33. Find the area of the shape shown at the right.

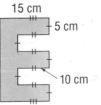

15 cm, 5 cm, 10 cm

Group Decision Making
Making Important Decisions

The science teacher has just given the class a list of 7 questions to study for a test. The teacher said that 4 of the 7 questions will be on the test. Students will be asked to answer any 2 questions.

1. As a class, make sure everyone understands the situation. Your task will be to work in groups to answer the following 4 questions.

a) If you studied answers to 3 of the questions, would you be ready to answer the 2 questions on the test?

b) What is the minimum number of questions you need to study?

c) How would you convince the rest of the class that your answer to question b) is correct?

d) Do you think you should study all 7 questions? Justify your answer.

2. Break into pairs for a 5-min discussion on questions a) and b).

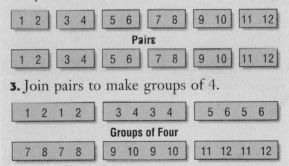

| 1 2 | 3 4 | 5 6 | 7 8 | 9 10 | 11 12 |

Pairs

| 1 2 | 3 4 | 5 6 | 7 8 | 9 10 | 11 12 |

3. Join pairs to make groups of 4.

| 1 2 1 2 | 3 4 3 4 | 5 6 5 6 |

Groups of Four

| 7 8 7 8 | 9 10 9 10 | 11 12 11 12 |

4. In your group of 4, come to an agreement on the answers to questions a) and b).

5. In your group of 4, discuss possible answers to questions c) and d). Present some answers to the class and post others on the board.

Chapter Check

Calculate each unknown length, to the nearest tenth of a centimetre.

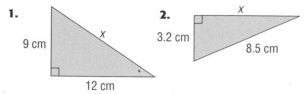

1.

9 cm

x

12 cm

2.

x

3.2 cm

8.5 cm

3. A 10-m ladder is leaning against the side wall of a house. The foot of the ladder is 4 m from the base of the wall. How far up the wall is the top of the ladder, to the nearest tenth of a metre?

Estimate, then calculate the perimeter of each figure.

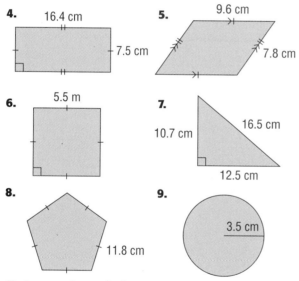

4. 16.4 cm

7.5 cm

5. 9.6 cm

7.8 cm

6. 5.5 m

7. 10.7 cm

16.5 cm

12.5 cm

8. 11.8 cm

9. 3.5 cm

Estimate, then calculate the area of each figure.

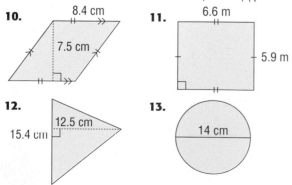

10. 8.4 cm

7.5 cm

11. 6.6 m

5.9 m

12. 12.5 cm

15.4 cm

13. 14 cm

14. Calculate
a) the perimeter of the composite figure
b) the area of the composite figure

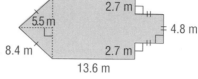

2.7 m

5.5 m

4.8 m

8.4 m

2.7 m

13.6 m

15. The kite is 150 cm long and 90 cm wide. It has a string frame around the outside.

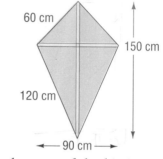

60 cm

150 cm

120 cm

90 cm

a) What is the area of the kite?
b) What is the perimeter of the outside frame?

16. A face-off circle on a hockey rink has a radius of 4.5 m. Calculate the circumference and the area of a face-off circle. Round your answers to the nearest hundredth, if necessary.

17. A soccer goal-mouth is 7.32 m wide and 2.44 m high.

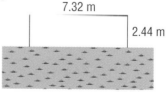

7.32 m

2.44 m

What is the area of the goal-mouth, to the nearest tenth of a square metre?

240

Using the Strategies

1. Find the 2-digit number that is a perfect square and has exactly 9 whole numbers that will divide it evenly.

2. Starting with one cube, the first figure is made by adding a cube to each face. The first figure has 7 cubes. The second figure is made up of 13 cubes. The third figure is made up of 19 cubes.

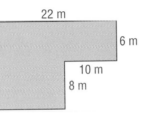

a) How many cubes are in the fourth figure?
b) How many cubes are in the 100th figure? the 3000th figure?

3. The playground is enclosed by a fence with posts 2 m apart. There is a post at each corner.

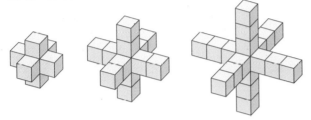

a) What is the total length of the fence?
b) How many posts are there?

4. Place the digits from 1 to 6 in the squares to make a correct multiplication.

5. A store has some bicycles and some tricycles. There are exactly 27 wheels. List the possible combinations of bicycles and tricycles.

6. Pierre owns 6 dogs. Three cans of dog food feed 2 dogs for one day. How many cans of dog food does Pierre need to buy each week?

7. Assume that a race car must slow down at the curves on the track.

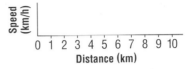

a) Sketch a graph of speed versus distance for 2 laps of the track in the direction shown.

b) Sketch another graph of speed versus distance for 2 laps in the opposite direction.

8. The figure is made up of 6 squares. The total area is 54 m². What is the perimeter of the figure?

9. Irina left for the ski slopes at 06:00 and drove at 80 km/h. Beth left at 07:00 and followed her. Beth drove at 100 km/h. At what time did Beth catch up with Irina?

10. There are 3 monkeys on one side of a river, and 3 tigers on the other. Each group wants to move to the other side of the river. There is one boat that holds no more than 2 animals. At no time can the tigers outnumber the monkeys on one side of the river. How can they switch sides?

DATA BANK

1. What percent of the flying distance from Vancouver to Ottawa is the driving distance from Vancouver to Ottawa? Round your answer to the nearest percent.

2. a) In which month does Regina have the most precipitation?
b) About how much precipitation does Regina have that month?

CHAPTER 8

Surface Area and Volume

Architects must consider many aspects of a building while they design it. These aspects include the volume of the building and the area of the ground floor.

Let 8 interlocking cubes represent a building of a certain volume. Make 8 models to show buildings with equal volumes but 8 different values for the area of the ground floor. Sketch your models and compare your designs with your classmates'.

If you were asked to design the building with the largest possible area of windows, what shape would you make it? Why?

List the factors that you think can affect the shape of a building.

Models in Three Dimensions

Activity ❶

1. a) Cut 2 identical triangles from Bristol board to use as the bases of a prism. Make a small hole in each corner, as shown.

b) Take 3 equal lengths of plastic straw. Thread lengths of yarn or string through each straw, then through the corners of your triangles. Knot each piece of yarn or string at each end.

c) Label your model "TRIANGULAR PRISM."

2. Make models with each of the following shapes as the 2 bases.

a)   **b)**   **c)**

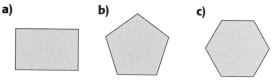

3. Label the models from step 2 as follows.
a) RECTANGULAR PRISM
b) PENTAGONAL PRISM
c) HEXAGONAL PRISM

4. a) Describe the ways in which all 4 of your models are the same.
b) State the part of each model that determines its name.

5. Use Bristol board, plastic straws, and yarn or string to make and label an OCTAGONAL PRISM.

Activity ❷

1. a) Cut a triangle from Bristol board to use as the base of a pyramid. Make a small hole in each corner.
b) Take 3 equal lengths of plastic straw. Thread lengths of yarn or string through each straw, then through the corners of your triangle. Knot each piece of yarn or string at each corner.

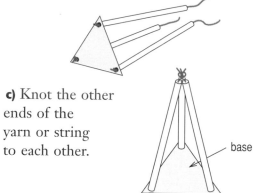

c) Knot the other ends of the yarn or string to each other.

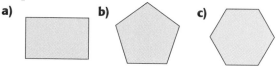

d) Label your model "TRIANGULAR PYRAMID."

2. Make models with each of the following shapes as the base.

a)   **b)**   **c)**

3. Label the models from step 2 as follows.
a) RECTANGULAR PYRAMID
b) PENTAGONAL PYRAMID
c) HEXAGONAL PYRAMID

4. a) Describe the ways in which all 4 of your models are the same.
b) State the part of each model that determines its name.

5. Use Bristol board, plastic straws, and yarn or string to make and label a SQUARE PYRAMID.

Warm Up

Estimate, then calculate the area of each figure. Round each calculated answer to the nearest hundredth, if necessary.

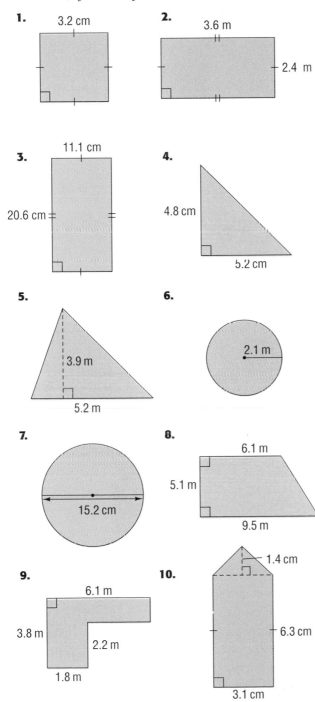

1.
3.2 cm

2.
3.6 m

2.4 m

3.
11.1 cm

20.6 cm

4.
4.8 cm

5.2 cm

5.
3.9 m

5.2 m

6.
2.1 m

7.
15.2 cm

8.
6.1 m

5.1 m

9.5 m

9.
6.1 m

3.8 m

2.2 m

1.8 m

10.
1.4 cm

6.3 cm

3.1 cm

Mental Math

Add.

1. 17 + 14   **2.** 27 + 14

3. 36 + 15   **4.** 46 + 15

5. 55 + 16   **6.** 65 + 16

7. 74 + 17   **8.** 84 + 17

9. 93 + 18   **10.** 23 + 18

Subtract.

11. 60 − 11   **12.** 70 − 11

13. 55 − 12   **14.** 35 − 12

15. 46 − 13   **16.** 76 − 13

17. 78 − 14   **18.** 98 − 14

19. 49 − 15   **20.** 79 − 15

Calculate.

21. 34 + 26 − 10   **22.** 43 − 13 + 27

23. 65 − 15 + 8   **24.** 57 − 17 + 15

25. 41 + 19 − 20   **26.** 56 + 24 − 9

27. 33 − 13 + 21   **28.** 61 + 19 − 40

29. 47 + 23 + 5   **30.** 88 − 28 + 14

Multiply.

31. 3 × 101   **32.** 5 × 101

33. 4 × 202   **34.** 7 × 1001

35. 6 × 202   **36.** 8 × 303

37. 2 × 707   **38.** 3 × 2002

39. 9 × 404   **40.** 8 × 505

Divide.

41. 436 ÷ 4   **42.** 535 ÷ 5

43. 123 ÷ 3   **44.** 186 ÷ 6

45. 749 ÷ 7   **46.** 856 ÷ 8

47. 219 ÷ 3   **48.** 287 ÷ 7

49. 426 ÷ 6   **50.** 945 ÷ 9

8.1 Three-Dimensional Solids

Activity: Study the Shapes

A set of geometric solids includes many different three-dimensional shapes.

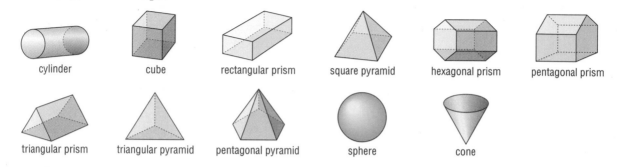

cylinder   cube   rectangular prism   square pyramid   hexagonal prism   pentagonal prism

triangular prism   triangular pyramid   pentagonal pyramid   sphere   cone

Inquire

1. Sort the solids shown into groups. Share with your classmates the criteria you used for sorting.

2. Sort the solids into groups using different criteria. Which solids are grouped together in both of the ways you sorted? Compare your findings with your classmates'.

3. In a set of children's building blocks, there are different numbers of each shape. Which shapes should make up the largest number of blocks? the smallest number of blocks? Explain your answers.

Activity: Use the Definition

A **polyhedron** is a three-dimensional figure with faces that are polygons.

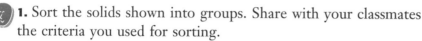

A rectangular prism is an example of a polyhedron.

A square pyramid is also a polyhedron.

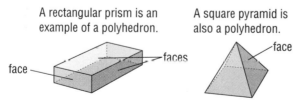

face — faces   — face

Inquire

1. Name the geometric solids at the top of the page that are not polyhedra. Explain why not.

2. List the polyhedra shown at the top of the page. Name the polygons that form the surfaces of each polyhedron and state the number of each polygon needed.

3. State how prisms and pyramids are the same. State how they are different. Compare your conclusions with your classmates'.

Practice

Use the solids shown on the opposite page to list the following.

1. all the solids with more than 4 flat faces

2. all the solids with at least 1 square face

3. all the solids with no flat faces

4. all the solids with no rectangular or square faces

5. all the solids with at least one triangular face

6. The model was built using 3 solids. Name the solids.

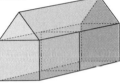

7. Sketch a model of a structure built from at least 3 geometric solids. Name the solids you used.

Problems and Applications

Name the geometric solid suggested by each object.

8.

9.

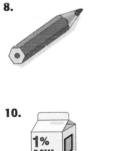

10.

11.

12.

13.

14. a) From the diagrams on the opposite page, describe how a prism is named.
b) Name the faces on an octagonal prism and state how many faces there are of each type.

15. a) From the diagrams on the opposite page, describe how a pyramid is named.
b) Name the faces on a hexagonal pyramid and state how many faces there are of each type.

16. Describe how a prism is like a cylinder. Describe how they are different.

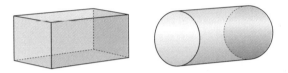

17. How are a pyramid and a cone alike? How are they different?

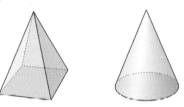

18. Is it possible for a three-dimensional solid to have 2 rectangular faces and 4 square faces? Explain.

19. Name the three-dimensional solids that will roll on a flat surface. Predict the path you think each one will trace. Check your prediction with a classmate, then roll each solid to see if you were correct.

LOGIC POWER

If July 17 falls on a Thursday, on which day of the week will December 31 fall?

8.2 Surface Areas of Polyhedra

Activity: Use a Net

Jocelyn designed and built a trinket box. To calculate how much material she needed to make the box, Jocelyn drew its net and calculated the **surface area**.

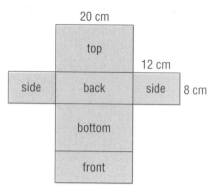

Inquire

1. a) How many different-sized rectangles did the box have?

b) What were the dimensions of each?

c) How many of each of the rectangles were there?

2. a) Describe 2 different methods for calculating the surface area of the box.

b) Use both methods to calculate the surface area of the box.

c) Which method do you prefer? Compare your ideas with your classmates'.

Example

Each edge of the cube is 8.3 cm. What is the surface area of the cube?

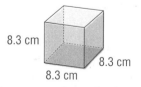

Solution

The cube has 6 square faces.
The area of each face is
$8.3 \times 8.3 = 68.89$

The surface area of the cube is

$6 \times 68.89 = 413.34$

EST
$8 \times 8 = 64$
$6 \times 60 = 360$

The surface area of the cube is 413.34 cm².

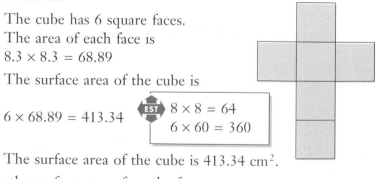

Suggest a formula for calculating the surface area of a cube from the length of an edge.

Practice

Draw the net. Then, estimate and calculate the surface area of each polyhedron.

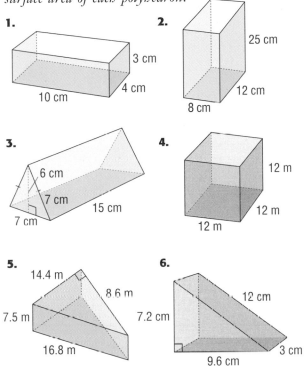

1.
10 cm, 3 cm, 4 cm

2.
25 cm, 12 cm, 8 cm

3.
6 cm, 7 cm, 15 cm, 7 cm

4.
12 m, 12 m, 12 m

5.
14.4 m, 8.6 m, 7.5 m, 16.8 m

6.
12 cm, 7.2 cm, 9.6 cm, 3 cm

Problems and Applications

7. a) The Chans' television was delivered in a cardboard carton. Calculate the minimum amount of cardboard needed to make the carton. What assumptions have you made?

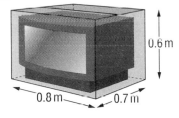

0.6 m, 0.8 m, 0.7 m

b) Estimate the additional amount of cardboard that would actually be used to make the carton. Explain.

8. A highrise office tower is 165 m tall, 85 m long, and 22 m wide. What is the total surface area of the faces and the roof of the tower?

9. The surface area of a rectangular prism is 325 cm^2. The areas of 2 faces are 50 cm^2 each. The areas of 2 other faces are 37.5 cm^2 each. What is the area of each of the two remaining faces?

10. a) Predict which of these solids has the greater surface area. Check your prediction by calculating the surface area of each prism.

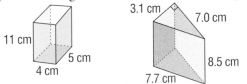

11 cm, 4 cm, 5 cm; 3.1 cm, 7.0 cm, 8.5 cm, 7.7 cm

b) Which prism has the larger surface area? By how much?

11. The surface areas of the rectangular prisms are equal. The missing dimension in each prism is a whole number of centimetres. Find the missing dimensions.

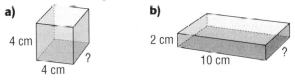

a) 4 cm, 4 cm, ?

b) 2 cm, 10 cm, ?

12. a) A rectangular prism is 30 cm by 12 cm by 6 cm. What is its surface area?

b) Predict which pieces have the greatest and least surface areas when 3 identical prisms are cut in half in the ways shown.

c) Calculate the surface area of each piece to check your prediction.

LOGIC POWER

A car travelled 75 000 km and used 5 tires. Each tire was used for the same distance. For how many kilometres was each tire used?

Estimating and Measuring Volume

Length is the distance between 2 points.
Length has 1 dimension.
Length is measured in linear units.
The length of the line is 3 cm.

_____ 3 cm _____

Area is the measure of a surface.
Area has 2 dimensions.
Area is measured in square units.
The area of the rectangle is 6 cm².

3 cm

2 cm | 6 cm²

Volume is the amount of space filled by an object. Volume has 3 dimensions. Volume is measured in cubic units. The volume of the rectangular prism is 9 cm³.

2 cm
1.5 cm | 9 cm³
3 cm

Activity ❶

A centicube has a volume of 1 cm³. Choose the best estimate for the volume of each of the following. Explain your choice to a classmate.

1 cm
1 cm
1 cm

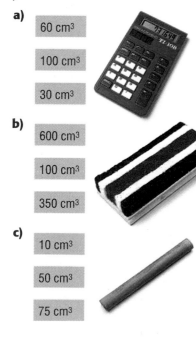

a)
60 cm³
100 cm³
30 cm³

b)
600 cm³
100 cm³
350 cm³

c)
10 cm³
50 cm³
75 cm³

Activity ❷

1. Construct a cube from a net of cardboard, with each face 10 cm by 10 cm.

2. How many centicubes would you need to fill the cube you constructed?

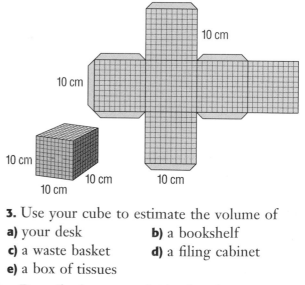

10 cm
10 cm
10 cm
10 cm
10 cm
10 cm
10 cm

3. Use your cube to estimate the volume of
a) your desk   **b)** a bookshelf
c) a waste basket   **d)** a filing cabinet
e) a box of tissues

4. Describe how you obtained each estimate.

5. Compare your estimates with your classmates'.

Activity ❸

Construct each object from centicubes.
Determine the volume of each object.

a)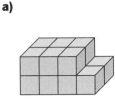

b)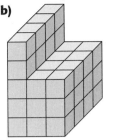

c)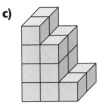

d)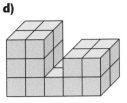

Activity ❹

When you cannot measure the dimensions of an object, you can
measure its volume by finding the volume of water it displaces.

1. Fill an overflow can with water. Place an irregular object, such
as a small stone, in the can. Catch the water the stone displaces
and pour it into a graduated cylinder. Measure the volume of
displaced water to find the volume of the object. For example, if
the stone displaces 8 mL of water, the volume of the stone is 8 cm^3.

2. Estimate, then determine the volumes of several objects by
displacement.

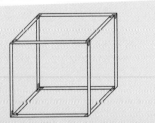

Activity ❺

1. Fasten metre-sticks together with rubber
bands or tape to form a 1-m^3 skeleton.

2. How many centicubes would be needed
to fill the skeleton?

3. Estimate the volume of each of the
following in cubic metres.

a) a teacher's desk   **b)** your classroom
c) a refrigerator   **d)** the gymnasium
e) a school bus

4. Describe how you obtained each estimate.

5. Compare your estimates with your
classmates'.

Activity ❻

1. If you tried to build a cube with a volume
of 1 m^3 from centicubes, how many would
you need?

2. Express in cubic centimetres.
a) 2 m^3 **b)** 3.25 m^3 **c)** 1.4 m^3
d) 0.7 m^3 **e)** 4.38 m^3 **f)** 0.06 m^3

3. Express in cubic metres.
a) 15 000 000 cm^3 **b)** 6000 cm^3
c) 4 500 000 cm^3 **d)** 75 000 cm^3
e) 2800 cm^3 **f)** 930 000 cm^3

8.3 Volumes of Prisms

Many food packages have the shapes of prisms. Different sizes of packages hold different volumes of products.

Activity: Explore with Cubes

In a set of place value blocks, each unit cube is 1 cm on every edge. The volume of the unit cube is 1 cm³. The other blocks in the set are:

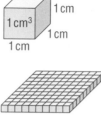

1 cm³ 1 cm 1 cm 1 cm

tens rod   hundreds flat   thousands cube

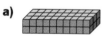

Inquire

1. What are the dimensions of the tens rod? What is its volume?

2. What are the dimensions of the hundreds flat? What is its volume?

3. What are the dimensions of the thousands cube? What is its volume?

4. Suggest a formula that can be used to calculate the volume of a prism. Compare your idea with your classmates'.

5. What is the volume of each of the groups of place value blocks?

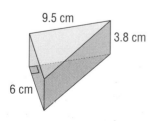

a)   b)   c)

Example

Calculate the volume of the triangular prism.

9.5 cm

3.8 cm

6 cm

Solution

The volume of a prism is the area of the base multiplied by the height of the prism.

$$\text{Area of base} = \frac{1}{2} \times b \times h$$
$$= \frac{1}{2} \times 9.5 \times 6$$
$$= 28.5$$

EST $\frac{1}{2} \times 10 \times 6 = 30$
$30 \times 4 = 120$

$$\text{Volume} = \text{area of base} \times \text{height}$$
$$= 28.5 \times 3.8$$
$$= 108.3$$

The volume of the prism is 108.3 cm³.

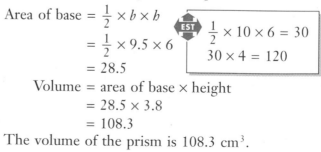

Practice

Estimate, then calculate the volume of each prism.

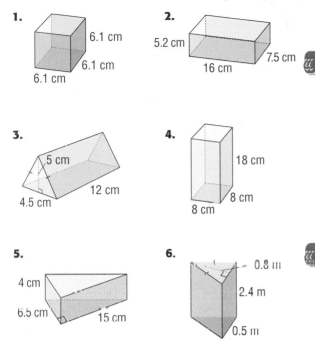

1. 6.1 cm, 6.1 cm, 6.1 cm

2. 5.2 cm, 16 cm, 7.5 cm

3. 5 cm, 12 cm, 4.5 cm

4. 18 cm, 8 cm, 8 cm

5. 4 cm, 6.5 cm, 15 cm

6. 0.8 m, 2.4 m, 0.5 m

Problems and Applications

7. Johann used unit cubes to build larger cubes.
a) What were the volumes of the 4 smallest cubes he could build, excluding the cube made from just 1 unit cube?
b) What was the surface area of each of Johann's cubes?

8. Calculate the volume of the filing cabinet, in cubic metres.

1 m, 60 cm, 45 cm

9. The areas of the faces of the rectangular prism are given. The lengths of the edges are whole numbers. What is the volume of the prism?

20 cm², 15 cm², 12 cm²

10. a) Measure and determine the total volume of the pages in this book, to the nearest cubic centimetre. Exclude the covers.
b) Compare your answer with a classmate's and account for any differences.

11. a) How many different rectangular prisms can you make with 24 unit cubes in each one? Sketch each prism and mark its dimensions.
b) What is the volume of each prism?
c) Predict the order of increasing surface area for the prisms. Compare your prediction with a classmate's.
d) Calculate each surface area to check your prediction.

12. A tent is 4 m long, 3 m wide, and 2 m high.

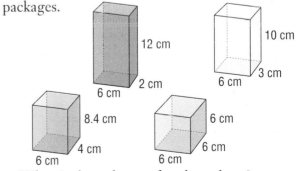

2 m, 3 m, 4 m

a) What is the volume of the tent?
b) How many campers could comfortably sleep in the tent? Give reasons for your answer. Compare your answer with your classmates'.

13. A food company wants to use the smallest amount of material to package a new product. The company is considering 4 possible packages.

12 cm, 6 cm, 2 cm; 10 cm, 6 cm, 3 cm; 8.4 cm, 6 cm, 4 cm; 6 cm, 6 cm, 6 cm

a) What is the volume of each package?
b) What is the surface area of each package?
c) Which package is the most economical for the company to use? Explain. Compare your findings with your classmates'.

8.4 Surface Area and Volume of a Cylinder

Many objects, including hockey pucks and water heaters, are made in the shape of a cylinder.

Activity: Use a Diagram

A juice can is made of 2 circular metal bases and a cardboard tube. The tube can be cut open to form a rectangle.

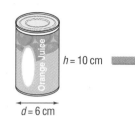

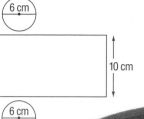

Inquire

1. What measurement of the circle is equal to the length of the cardboard rectangle?

2. Calculate the area of the cardboard rectangle.

3. Calculate the area of each circular base.

4. Calculate the total surface area of the can.

5. State a method for calculating the surface area of a cylinder.

Activity: Use the Relationship

The volume of a cylinder is calculated like the volume of a prism.

V = area of base × height of cylinder

Inquire

1. What formula is used to calculate the area of the base of a cylinder?

2. Write the number sentence needed to calculate the volume of the above juice can.

3. Calculate the volume of the juice can.

Practice

Round each answer to the nearest tenth of a unit.

Estimate, then calculate the surface area and the volume of each cylinder. Use $\pi = 3.14$

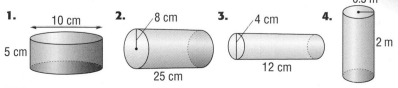

1. 10 cm, 5 cm
2. 8 cm, 25 cm
3. 4 cm, 12 cm
4. 0.5 m, 2 m

254

Problems and Applications

5. The glue stick has a diameter of 3 cm and a height of 10.5 cm. The glue inside has a diameter of 2.5 cm and a height of 9.5 cm. What is the difference between the volume of the container and the volume of the glue?

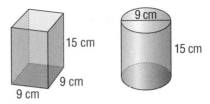

6. The Da Silvas installed a cylindrical water heater with a radius of 30 cm and a height of 120 cm.

a) What is the surface area of the water heater?

b) What is the volume of the water heater?

7. a) Describe a method of measuring, with reasonable accuracy, the diameter and the height of a nickel. What are the diameter and the height?

b) What is the volume of a roll of 40 nickels?

c) What is the minimum surface area of the paper needed to roll a stack of nickels?

8. Copy and complete the chart for 4 cylinders.

Height (cm)	10	10	20	20
Diameter (cm)	3	6	3	6
Volume (cm³)				

a) What happens to the volume of a cylinder when the diameter doubles?

b) What happens to the volume of a cylinder when the height doubles?

c) Predict the volume of a cylinder with a height of 10 cm and a diameter of 12 cm. Calculate to check your prediction.

d) Predict the volume of a cylinder with a height of 20 cm and a diameter of 1.5 cm. Calculate to check your prediction.

9. The side length of the base of the square-based prism equals the diameter of the cylinder. The prism and the cylinder have the same height.

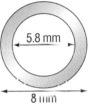

a) Which shape has the greater surface area? By how much is it greater?

b) Which shape has the greater volume? By how much is it greater?

10. The hollow glass tubing used in science laboratories comes in different sizes. A common size has an outer diameter of 8 mm and an inner diameter of 5.8 mm. Calculate the volume of glass in a 100-mm length of this tubing.

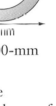

11. Write a problem that requires the calculation of the surface area and volume of a cylinder. Have a classmate solve your problem.

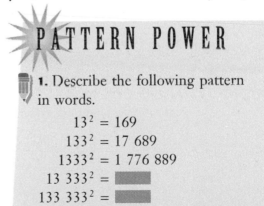

PATTERN POWER

1. Describe the following pattern in words.

$$13^2 = 169$$
$$133^2 = 17\ 689$$
$$1333^2 = 1\ 776\ 889$$
$$13\ 333^2 = \ \rule{1.5cm}{0.3cm}$$
$$133\ 333^2 = \ \rule{1.5cm}{0.3cm}$$

2. Copy and complete the last 2 lines without using a calculator.

Volumes from a Spreadsheet

A spreadsheet can be used to calculate the volume of a rectangular prism. The dimensions of the rectangular prism shown here are 20 cm by 10 cm by 8 cm. Examine the spreadsheet.

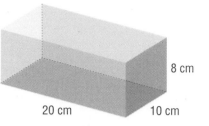

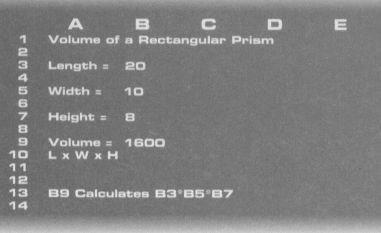

The length is entered into cell B3, the width into cell B5, and the height into cell B7. The formula $V = l \times w \times h$ is entered into cell B9 as +B3*B5*B7. The + sign at the beginning is used to indicate that a formula is being entered. After the formula is entered, the resulting number appears in cell B9.

Activity ❶

1. Set up the spreadsheet on your computer, and use it to determine the volumes of the following rectangular prisms.

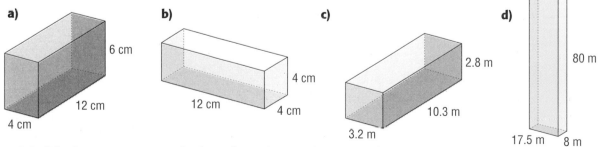

a)   6 cm   12 cm   4 cm

b)   4 cm   12 cm   4 cm

c)   2.8 m   10.3 m   3.2 m

d)   80 m   17.5 m   8 m

2. Modify the program to calculate the volume of a triangular prism. Check that the program works correctly.

A spreadsheet can also be used to see how changes in dimensions affect the volume of a rectangular prism.

Activity ❷

Use this spreadsheet to compare volumes when the length, width, and height of a rectangular prism are changed.

```
        A         B         C         D         E
1   Volume of a Rectangular Prism
2   as Length, Width, and
3   Height Change.
4
5               Original   New
6               Prism      Prism
7
8   Length =    20         10
9
10  Width =     10         5
11
12  Height =    8          4
13
14  Volume =    1600       200
15  L x W x H
16
17
18  B14 Calculates B8*B10*B12
19  C14 Calculates C8*C10*C12
```

We can use a rectangular prism with dimensions 20 cm by 10 cm by 8 cm as the original prism and calculate the new volume as we make changes in the dimensions.

1. Double, triple, and quadruple the length of the original prism. Calculate each new volume.

2. What happens to the volume when the length is doubled, tripled, and quadrupled?

3. Double, triple, and quadruple both the length and width of the original prism, and calculate each new volume.

4. What happens to the volume when both the length and width are doubled, tripled, and quadrupled?

5. What do you think will happen to the volume if all 3 of the original dimensions are doubled, tripled, and quadrupled? Relate your answer to the previous results and explain.

Packing a Rock Band's Equipment

You might not expect to hear terms like "spin," "flip," and "rotate" on a rock-and-roll concert tour, but they are used every time the trucks are loaded and unloaded. Some bands can fit all of their equipment into one truck, but most successful bands use 3 trucks or more. For their 1989 *Steel Wheels* tour, the Rolling Stones used 60 tractor-trailers.

Moving the equipment from one concert to the next is the job of a road manager. A band's equipment must usually be set up and taken down in a single day, several times a week. Speed and efficiency are essential. So, a logical plan must be used to pack the trucks with the lighting pipes or "trusses," the speakers, the parts of the set, and the boxes or "road cases" that hold the equipment.

The road manager's task of fitting the equipment into the smallest possible volume is like solving a three-dimensional jigsaw puzzle. The road manager must take into account the safety of the equipment, the ease of loading and unloading, and the order in which the equipment is needed. For example, there is no point in packing the tools first. At the next stop, the entire truck would have to be unloaded to get the tools before assembly work could begin.

To understand the road manager's task, consider a group with 4 instruments, a low budget, and just one truck to carry its equipment.

Activity ❶ Choosing a Truck

The road manager must decide on the size of truck to rent. If the truck is too small, it will not hold all the equipment. If the truck is too big, it will cost more than necessary to rent and operate. Also, the equipment is more likely to be damaged if there is room for it to roll around in transport.

To choose the truck, the road manager lists the equipment, and records the dimensions of the road cases and the equipment that is not packed in cases. The results are shown in the table.

Department/Equipment		Number of Pieces	Dimensions (cm)			Total Volume (m³)	Code
			l	*w*	*h*		
Lighting	Truss	2	250	45	45	1.01	T2, T5
	L-Shaped Truss	4	250	45	45		T1, T3, T4, T6
	Light Cart*	2	125	65	200		LX1, LX2
	Dimmer Rack*	4	65	50	100		D1, D2, D3, D4
	Cable	2	60	80	80		LX3, LX4
	Chain Motor*	6	80	60	50		CM1–CM6
	Control Board	1	176	25	100		LX0
Sound	Speaker	20	75	60	125		S1–S20
	Amp*	4	60	60	125		A1, A2, A3, A4
	Monitor	3	60	40	75		M1, M2, M3
	Cable	2	70	50	50		S21, S22
	Control Board	1	150	30	150		S0
Set	Set Wagon*	1	175	70	200		SET
Band Equipment	Guitar	6	110	45	15		G1–G6
	Bass Guitar	5	125	50	15		B1–B5
	Keyboard	1	125	50	20		K1
		1	150	65	25		K2
	Drums*	1	150	75	70		DR1
		1	75	50	75		DR2
	Guitar Amp	4	60	50	75		AMP1–AMP4
		2	50	30	60		AMP5–AMP6
	Mic, Stand, etc.*	1	125	60	65		HRD1
	Costumes*	4	60	75	125		C1–C4
	Tools*	1	60	50	100		HRD2

* Indicates that the piece cannot be flipped upside down.

1. a) Copy the table and complete the "Total Volume" column.

b) Add the total volumes to find the volume of equipment that the truck must be able to hold.

2. The table shows the inside dimensions of 3 trucks and the costs of renting from 3 different trucking companies.

Company	Inside Dimensions (m)			Total Volume (m³)	Cost ($/month)
	l	*w*	*h*		
A	7	2.5	2.5		2200.00
B	7.25	2.5	2.75		2400.00
C	8.25	2.5	2.75		2950.00

a) Will the equipment fit into each of the trucks?

b) Which truck do you think the equipment will fit into most economically?

c) The road manager chose to use company B. List some factors, other than volume and cost, that may have influenced this decision.

CONTINUED ▶

Activity ❷ Packing the Truck

The road manager now plans how to pack the truck by flipping, rotating, and rearranging pieces of equipment. Instead of wasting time and energy actually packing the equipment on the truck, the road manager figures out the puzzle with paper and pencil or on a computer.

The road manager's plan for packing the truck is shown in the following overhead view and section views. Note that a code shown in brackets indicates an item that is not visible, because it is underneath or behind another item.

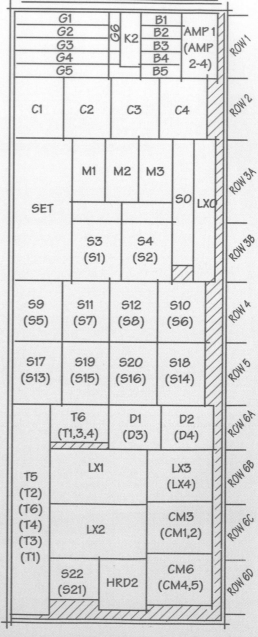

OVERHEAD VIEW OF TRUCK B

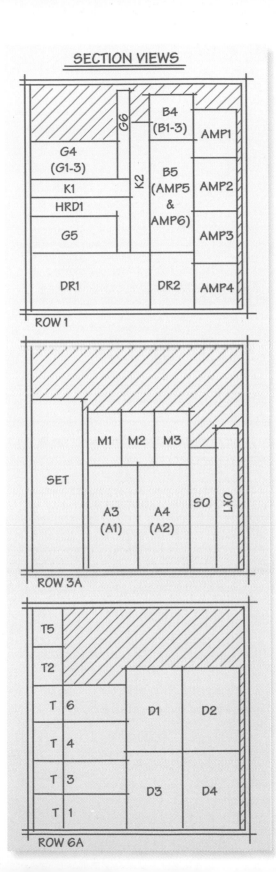

SECTION VIEWS

ROW 1

ROW 3A

ROW 6A

Use the overhead view and section views, and the table you completed in Activity 1, to answer the following questions.

1. How do you know where the back doors of the truck are?

2. a) List the pieces of equipment in row 1.
b) Where are AMP 5 and AMP 6 in relation to B1 to B5?

3. a) What is in row 2?
b) Why is there no section view for this row?

4. a) Why is row 3 divided into row 3A and row 3B?
b) What is in row 3A?

5. What would the overhead view and section views of row 3A look like if the monitors were removed?

6. Why do you need a section view of row 6A?

7. Draw a three-dimensional representation of the following.
a) lighting truss T5
b) lighting truss T6

8. What area of the truck floor is covered by the speakers?

9. What volume of the truck is occupied by the speakers in rows 4 and 5?

10. How far is it from the front of the truck to the front of the row containing the dimmer racks?

11. a) How many different types of transformation can be applied to M2? to HRD2?
b) Why is there a difference?

12. What transformation would have to be applied to trusses 1, 3, 4, and 6 if row 6 were loaded with the chain motors on the driver's side?

261

8.5 Surface Area and Volume of Composite Solids

A **composite solid** is a combination of two or more simple solids.

Activity: Use a Model

Use 1-cm cubes to make the composite solid shown.
Assume that no cubes are missing from the back of the stack.

Inquire

1. Divide this solid into two rectangular prisms. What are the dimensions and the volume of each rectangular prism?

2. What is the total volume of the composite solid?

3. Repeat steps 1 and 2 by dividing the composite solid into two other rectangular prisms.

4. How many faces does the composite solid have? What is the area of each face?

5. What is the surface area of the solid?

Example 1

Find the surface area of this solid.

5 cm
13 cm
10 cm
4 cm
7 cm

Solution

The solid has 6 faces:

10 A_1 13 A_2 7 A_3 7 A_4 10 A_5 13
4   4   5   7   7

Area of each trapezoid, A_1
$= \frac{1}{2} \times (a + b) \times h$
$= \frac{1}{2} \times (10 + 13) \times 4$
$= \frac{1}{2} \times 23 \times 4$
$= 46$

Area of rectangle, A_2
$= 4 \times 7$
$= 28$

Area of rectangle, A_3
$= 5 \times 7$
$= 35$

Area of rectangle, A_4
$= 7 \times 10$
$= 70$

Area of rectangle, A_5
$= 7 \times 13$
$= 91$

Surface area $= 2 \times A_1 + A_2 + A_3 + A_4 + A_5$
$= 2 \times 46 + 28 + 35 + 70 + 91$
$= 316$

The surface area of the solid is 316 cm^2.

Example 2

A square-based prism has a hole 6 cm wide drilled through it. Estimate, then calculate its volume to the nearest 0.1 cm^3.

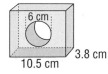

6 cm
3.8 cm
10.5 cm

Solution

The volume of the solid is the volume of a rectangular prism minus the volume of the cylindrical hole.

Volume of prism, V_1
$= l \times w \times h$
$= 10.5 \times 10.5 \times 3.8$
$= 418.95$

EST $10 \times 10 \times 4 = 400$

Volume of cylinder, V_2
$= \pi \times r^2 \times h$
$= 3.14 \times 3^2 \times 3.8$
$= 3.14 \times 9 \times 3.8$
$= 107.388$

EST $3 \times 10 \times 4 = 120$

Volume of the solid, V
$= V_1 - V_2$
$= 418.95 - 107.388$
$= 311.562$

EST $400 - 100 = 300$

The volume of the solid is 311.6 cm^3, to the nearest 0.1 cm^3.

Practice

Each solid is built from 1-cm cubes. Calculate the surface area and the volume.

1.

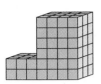

2.

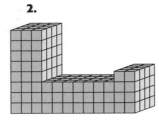

3. The solid is built from 1-cm cubes. The hole passes all the way through. Find the surface area and the volume of the solid.

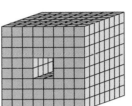

Problems and Applications

Estimate, then calculate the surface area and the volume of each solid. Round each calculated answer to the nearest tenth of a unit, if necessary.

4.

4 cm
3 cm
5 cm
8 cm
6 cm
1 cm
10 cm

5.

20 cm
6 cm
10 cm

6.

11 cm
2 cm
5 cm
22 cm
17 cm

7.

7.2 cm
4.1 cm
8.7 cm
12.4 cm
2.3 cm

8.

12 cm
12 cm
15 cm
10 cm
17 cm

9.

5.6 cm
12.4 cm
4.2 cm
3.6 cm
6.5 cm

10. A metal storage building with no floor has the dimensions shown in the diagram. What is the surface area of the outside of the building?

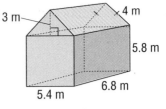

3 m
4 m
5.8 m
6.8 m
5.4 m

11. The podium used for the medal presentations at swimming competitions is made of wood.

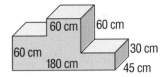

60 cm
60 cm
60 cm
30 cm
180 cm
45 cm

The visible surfaces are painted.

a) What area is painted?

b) If paint costs $5.99/L, and 1 L of paint covers 10 m², what is the cost of painting the podium?

12. This solid is called a ziggurat.

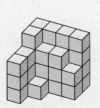

The largest ziggurat in the world is the Ziggurat of Choga Zambil, in Iran. This ziggurat has 5 layers. The dimensions of the bottom layer are 105 m by 105 m. The top layer is 28 m by 28 m, and the total height is 50 m. The heights of the layers are equal. The side lengths of the layers decrease in equal amounts.

a) What is the volume of the ziggurat?

b) What is the surface area of the exposed surfaces of the ziggurat?

LOGIC POWER

Assume that there are no cubes missing from the back of the stack, and each cube represents 1 cm³.

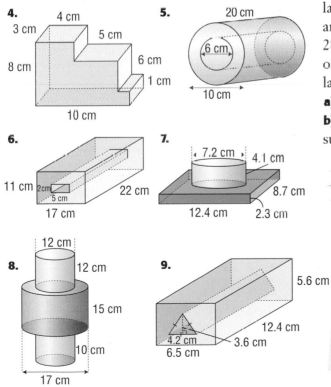

1. What is the volume of the stack?

2. What is the stack's surface area?

263

Review

Round each calculated answer to the nearest tenth, if necessary.

1. Name a three-dimensional solid with
a) 2 triangular faces and 3 rectangular faces
b) 8 vertices   **c)** 15 edges
d) 4 congruent faces

Estimate, then calculate each surface area.

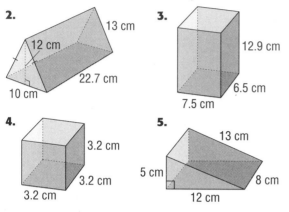

2. 13 cm, 12 cm, 22.7 cm, 10 cm

3. 12.9 cm, 7.5 cm, 6.5 cm

4. 3.2 cm, 3.2 cm, 3.2 cm

5. 13 cm, 5 cm, 8 cm, 12 cm

Estimate, then calculate each volume.

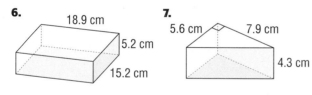

6. 18.9 cm, 5.2 cm, 15.2 cm

7. 5.6 cm, 7.9 cm, 4.3 cm

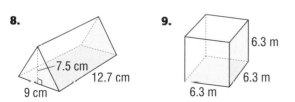

8. 7.5 cm, 12.7 cm, 9 cm

9. 6.3 m, 6.3 m, 6.3 m

Estimate, then calculate the surface area of each cylinder.

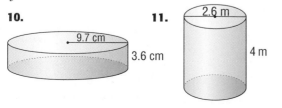

10. 9.7 cm, 3.6 cm

11. 2.6 m, 4 m

Estimate, then calculate the volume of each cylinder.

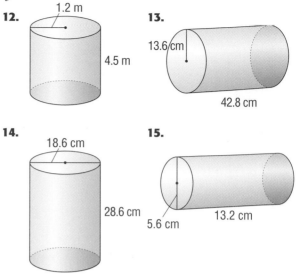

12. 1.2 m, 4.5 m

13. 13.6 cm, 42.8 cm

14. 18.6 cm, 28.6 cm

15. 5.6 cm, 13.2 cm

Estimate, then calculate the volume of each solid.

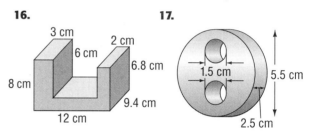

16. 3 cm, 6 cm, 2 cm, 6.8 cm, 8 cm, 9.4 cm, 12 cm

17. 1.5 cm, 5.5 cm, 2.5 cm

Estimate, then calculate the surface area of each solid.

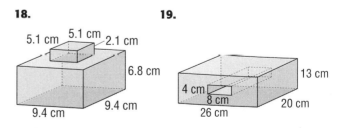

18. 5.1 cm, 5.1 cm, 2.1 cm, 6.8 cm, 9.4 cm, 9.4 cm

19. 13 cm, 4 cm, 8 cm, 20 cm, 26 cm

20. A rectangular box has dimensions 25 cm by 17.5 cm by 20.5 cm.
a) Calculate the surface area of the box.
b) Calculate the volume of the box.

21. The dictionaries are 24 cm high, 18.5 cm wide, and 4.6 cm thick.

They are shipped in cartons of 12. What is the smallest possible volume of a carton?

22. The diagram shows a dumb-bell. Calculate its total surface area.

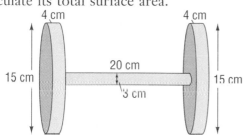

23. The number of windows in the back of a house is the same as the number in the front. There is a window on each side of the house. The windows are all the same size.

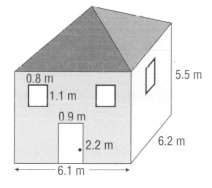

a) Calculate the surface area of the four sides of the house, excluding the windows and the door.

b) Brick costs $55/m² installed. What does it cost to resurface the 4 walls with brick?

24. A video tape box has dimensions 10.4 cm by 18.8 cm by 3.2 cm. What is the total volume of 12 video tapes?

Group Decision Making
Planning a Community

Communities are made up of buildings of many different shapes and sizes. Work in a group to plan and build a model of a community, using your knowledge of three-dimensional shapes.

Home Groups

1. List the buildings that may be found in a community. Include various types of structures from the following categories.

residential	educational
commercial	religious
recreational	governmental
industrial	municipal

2. Work together to plan a small community using a variety of the structures you have listed. Decide which types of buildings you will use and the number of each.

3. On a large piece of cardboard, draw a plan of your community, showing roadways, park areas, and the locations of buildings.

4. Design and build models of your structures using the nets of several three-dimensional shapes.

5. Choose a name for your community and label all the appropriate areas, roadways, and buildings.

6. Compare your community with communities made by other groups. List the three-dimensional structures used in each community.

Chapter Check

Round each calculated answer to the nearest tenth, if necessary.

Name the polygons that form the faces of each polyhedron. State the number of each type.

1. hexagonal prism **2.** cube

Estimate, then calculate each surface area.

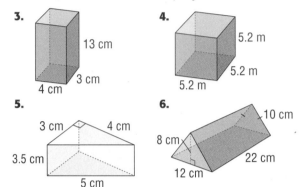

3. 13 cm, 3 cm, 4 cm

4. 5.2 m, 5.2 m, 5.2 m

5. 3 cm, 4 cm, 3.5 cm, 5 cm

6. 10 cm, 8 cm, 22 cm, 12 cm

Estimate, then calculate each volume.

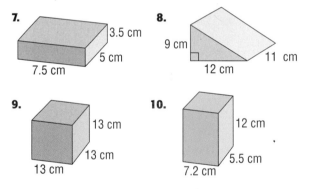

7. 3.5 cm, 5 cm, 7.5 cm

8. 9 cm, 12 cm, 11 cm

9. 13 cm, 13 cm, 13 cm

10. 12 cm, 5.5 cm, 7.2 cm

Estimate, then calculate each surface area.

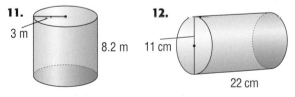

11. 3 m, 8.2 m

12. 11 cm, 22 cm

Estimate, then calculate each volume.

13. 15 cm, 10.5 cm

14. 16 cm, 4.5 cm

15. A rectangular prism is 5.5 cm wide, 3.2 cm high, and 10 cm long. Estimate, then calculate

a) its volume   **b)** its surface area

16. Calculate the surface area of a cylinder with a height of 22 cm and a radius of 8.5 cm.

17. Three cylindrical containers are used to store food. The largest container has a radius of 12 cm and a height of 20 cm. The middle container has a radius of 10 cm and a height of 18 cm. The smallest container has a radius of 8 cm and a height of 16 cm. What is the total volume of the 3 containers?

18. A wedge in the shape of a triangular prism is used to keep a door open. One face of the wedge is a right triangle with a height of 2.5 cm, a hypotenuse of 4.7 cm, and a base of 4 cm. The length of the wedge is 11.5 cm.
a) What is the surface area of the wedge?
b) What is the volume of the wedge?

19. A rectangular box has a length of 15 cm, a width of 8 cm, and a height of 22 cm. It is filled with rice to a height of 18 cm. What is the volume of the rice in the box?

Estimate, then calculate the surface area of each solid.

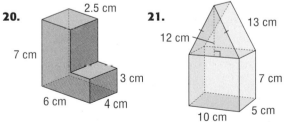

20. 2.5 cm, 7 cm, 3 cm, 6 cm, 4 cm

21. 13 cm, 12 cm, 7 cm, 10 cm, 5 cm

Estimate, then calculate the volume of each solid.

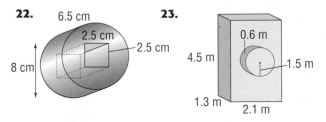

22. 6.5 cm, 2.5 cm, 2.5 cm, 8 cm

23. 0.6 m, 4.5 m, 1.5 m, 1.3 m, 2.1 m

266

Using the Strategies

1. Six triangles are made from wire. Each side of each triangle is 4.5 cm.

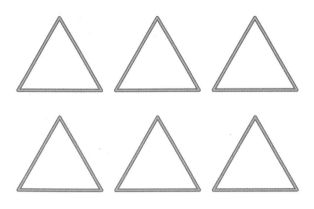

a) What is the perimeter of each triangle?
b) The 6 triangles are used to form a hexagon. What is the perimeter of the hexagon?
c) The 6 triangles are laid side by side to form a parallelogram. Sketch the parallelogram and find its perimeter.
d) Sketch 1 other figure that can be formed from the 6 triangles. Find the perimeter of your figure.

2. What is the smallest whole number that divided by 4 gives a remainder of 3, divided by 3 gives a remainder of 2, and divided by 2 gives a remainder of 1?

3. A pizza ordered by Marc and Pete had a diameter of 30 cm. They ate $\frac{2}{3}$ of the pizza and left 4 pieces. Into how many pieces was the whole pizza cut?

4. The average person uses about 95 L of drinking water each week. How much drinking water is used each week by
a) your family?
b) your class?
c) your school?
d) your community?

5.

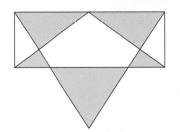

State the number of each polygon that can be found in the diagram.
a) triangles   **b)** rectangles
c) trapezoids   **d)** pentagons
e) other quadrilaterals

6. Mario said to Tara: "Give me $4, so that we will each have the same amount of money." Tara replied to Mario: "No. Give me $4. Then I will have 5 times as much as you." How much money did each of them have?

7. If February 29 falls on a Sunday, on what day of the week will the next February 29 fall?

8. Julia takes trips to deliver flowers from her store. The graph shows Julia's distance from her store on one trip.

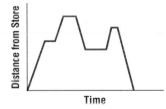

Describe Julia's trip.

DATA BANK

1. How many times larger than Canada's largest island is the world's largest island? Round your answer to the nearest tenth.

2. How many minutes would it take to fly from Victoria to Vancouver at 620 km/h?

Chapter 5

Evaluate for $x = 6$.

1. $x + 5$ **2.** $2x$ **3.** $x - 5$

4. $5 - x$ **5.** $\frac{x}{2}$ **6.** $x^2 - 2$

Evaluate for $x = 3$ and $y = 5$.

7. $x + 2y$ **8.** $3x - y$ **9.** $2(x + y)$

Evaluate for $x = 2$ and $y = -3$.

10. $x + y$ **11.** $3x + 2y$ **12.** $2x - y - 1$

13. a) Copy and complete the table.

Number of Magazines (*n*)	1	2	3	4
Cost, in Dollars (*c*)	4	8		

b) Use the variables to write a formula.
c) Use your formula to find the cost of 25 magazines.
d) How many magazines cost $104?

Copy and complete each table of values. Then, write the ordered pairs.

14.

x	x + 2
0	
1	
2	
3	
4	

15.

x	2x + 1
-2	
-1	
0	
1	
2	

Write 4 ordered pairs for each relation.

16. $x + y = 4$ **17.** $y = 3x + 1$

Plot the points on a grid and join them in order. Identify each figure and find its area and perimeter.

18. M(–1, 4), N(3, 4), P(3, 0), Q(–1, 0)

19. W(–5, 1), X(–5, –3), Y(2, –3), Z(2, 1)

20. C(4, 2), D(4, –2), E(–5, –2), F(–5, 2)

Find 5 ordered pairs that satisfy each relation. Draw each graph.

21. $x + y = 4$ **22.** $y = 2x - 3$

Chapter 6

Describe each equation in words.

1. $m - 4 = 11$ **2.** $3b + 2b = 15$

3. $6x = 48$ **4.** $2a = 9 - a$

Write an equation for each sentence.

5. Six more than a number is ten.

6. One less than a quarter of a number is one.

7. A number plus four times the number is 15.

8. Six less than twice a number is the number.

9. If you multiply a number by five, then add two, the result is seventeen.

Determine whether the number in brackets is a solution of the equation.

10. $a - 4 = 3$ (1)   **11.** $3m - 2 = 13$ (5)

12. $7 = 3 + 2x$ (2)   **13.** $\frac{y}{2} + 4 = 6$ (1)

Solve and check.

14. $4y = 24$ **15.** $22 = m - 3$ **16.** $\frac{w}{5} = 2$

Simplify.

17. $3m - 5m + 2m$ **18.** $11x + 2 - 7x - 5$

Expand.

19. $4(x + 1)$ **20.** $3(2a - 2)$ **21.** $2(4m + 3n)$

Solve and check.

22. $3p - 4 = 5$ **23.** $4x + 7 = 23$

24. $2(x + 5) = 18$ **25.** $11 - 2 = 3(w - 2)$

26. $a + 6 = 2$ **27.** $b - 3 = -5$

28. $\frac{x}{3} + 1.5 = 6$ **29.** $-4 = 1 + 2q$

30. $2p + 1 = 5$ **31.** $y - 3.2 = -5.8$

32. The average life span of an African elephant is 10 years longer than twice the average life span of a polar bear. The average life span of an African elephant is 60 years. What is the average life span of a polar bear?

Chapter 7

Round each calculated answer to the nearest tenth, if necessary.

Calculate the missing length, to the nearest tenth.

1.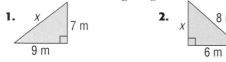

2.

3. Joni has a rectangular garden 20 m by 15 m. She wants to stretch a piece of string from one corner to the corner diagonally opposite. What is the minimum length of string she needs?

Estimate, then calculate the perimeter and the area of each figure.

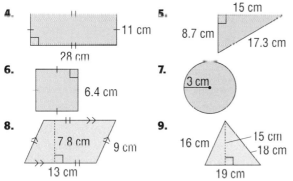

4.   **5.**   **6.**   **7.**

8.   **9.**

10. A hockey puck has a diameter of 7.6 cm.
a) What area of the ice does it cover?
b) What distance does the puck travel if it rolls on its side 8 times?

11. Pauline made a square quilt from 64 identical, square pattern pieces. The quilt has an area of 5.76 m². What is the length of each side of a pattern piece?

Calculate each shaded area.

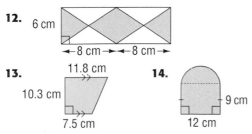

12. 6 cm   8 cm   8 cm

13. 11.8 cm   10.3 cm   7.5 cm

14. 9 cm   12 cm

Chapter 8

Round each calculated answer to the nearest tenth, if necessary.

Estimate, then calculate each surface area.

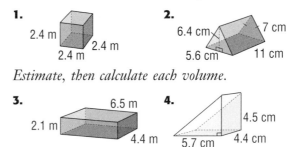

1. 2.4 m   2.4 m   2.4 m

2. 6.4 cm.   7 cm   5.6 cm   11 cm

Estimate, then calculate each volume.

3. 6.5 m   2.1 m   4.4 m

4. 4.5 cm   5.7 cm   4.4 cm

Estimate, then calculate the surface area and volume of each cylinder.

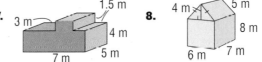

5. 26.5 cm   5.1 cm

6. 22.5 cm   6.4 cm

Estimate, then calculate each surface area and volume.

7. 3 m   1.5 m   4 m   7 m   5 m

8. 4 m   5 m   8 m   6 m   7 m

9. A cylinder has a radius of 5 cm and a height of 20 cm. What is its surface area and volume?

10. A cylindrical plastic tube has an inner diameter of 4 cm and an outer diameter of 6 cm.
a) What volume of plastic is used to make a 12-cm length of the tube?
b) What is the surface area of this piece of tube?

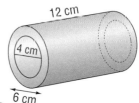

12 cm   4 cm   6 cm

11. Calculate the surface area and volume of this object. The hole passes right through the object.

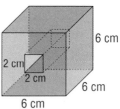

6 cm   2 cm   2 cm   6 cm   6 cm

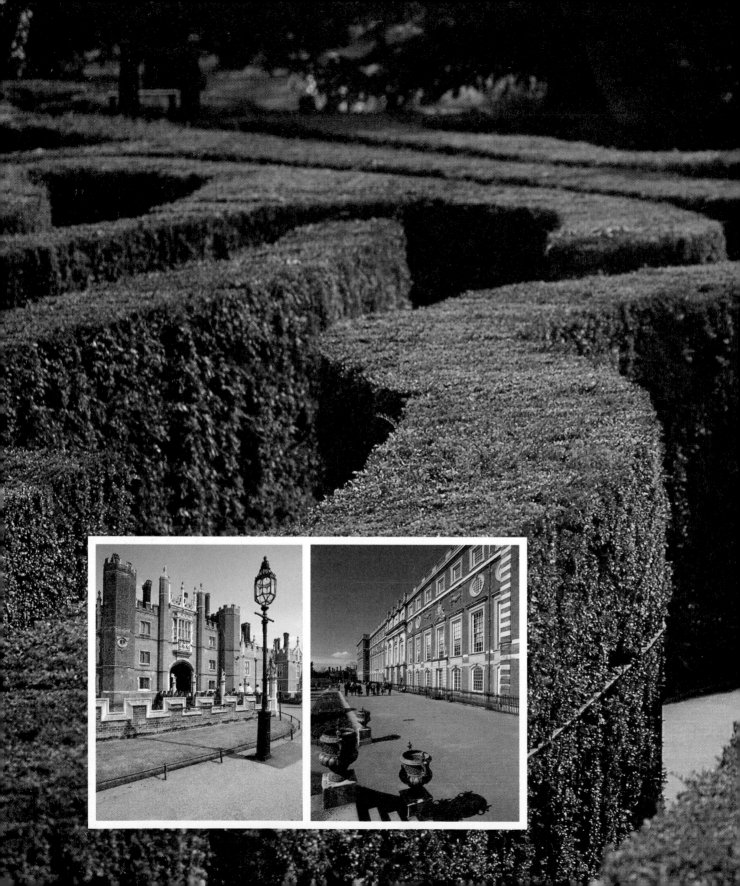

Geometry

Hampton Court is a palace on the River Thames near London, England. King William III's maze at Hampton Court is one of the oldest hedge mazes in England. The drawing shows that the maze is made up of line segments and angles.

The object is to enter the maze at A, make your way to the centre, B, then come back out at A. This is not a difficult challenge if you can see all of the maze.

To get the feeling of wandering among the hedges, cut out a piece of cardboard about 8 cm by 6 cm. Punch a hole in the middle of it, so that the diameter of the hole is about the same as the thickness of a pencil. Now, place the hole over A. Move the hole to the centre of the maze, B, then move it back out to A.

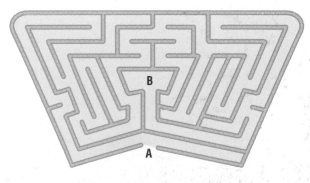

Tangrams

This 7-piece puzzle from China is called a **tangram**. It is a square cut into 7 geometric shapes. Each shape is called a **tan**.

We have labelled the tans with letters.

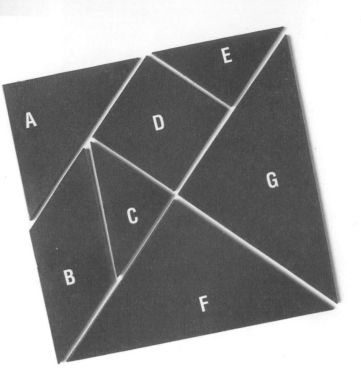

Activity ❶

1. Make the 7 tans out of stiff cardboard or use a plastic tangram set.

2. Identify each tan as a triangle, square, or parallelogram.

3. Which tan exactly matches tan F?

4. Which two tans together match tan D?

5. Which two tans together match tan A?

6. Which two tans together match tan B?

7. Which three tans together match tan F?

Activity ❷

Complete the area sentences.

1. tan A + tan B + tan C + tan D + tan E = tan ▓ + tan ▓

2. tan F + tan G − tan A = tan ▓ + tan ▓ + tan ▓ + tan ▓

3. tan C + tan D + tan E = tan ▓

4. tan A + tan C + tan E = tan ▓

5. tan A − tan E = tan ▓

6. tan F − tan C − tan E = tan ▓

7. tan C + tan D = tan ▓ + tan ▓

Activity ❸

Construct as many of the following figures as you can with up to 7 tans.

1. Squares   **2.** Triangles

3. Rectangles   **4.** Parallelograms

5. Trapezoids

Sketch your solutions in a large chart set up like this one. Be careful! It is impossible to complete all sections of the chart.

272

Activity ④
Use the 7 tans to construct each
of the following figures.

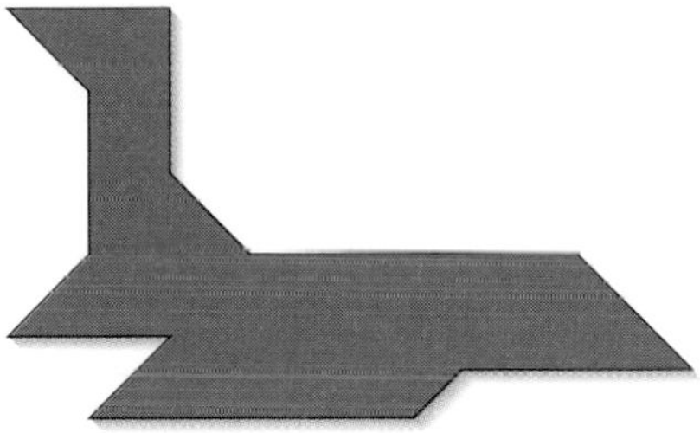

Mental Math			
Add.			
1. $150 + 25$	**2.** $250 + 25$	**3.** $225 + 25 + 25$	**4.** $225 + 50$
5. $250 + 25 + 50$	**6.** $325 + 25 + 50$	**7.** $400 + 25 + 75$	**8.** $450 + 75 + 75$
Subtract			
9. $175 - 25$	**10.** $225 - 50$	**11.** $150 - 75$	**12.** $200 - 75$
13. $300 - 25$	**14.** $200 - 50 - 25$	**15.** $175 - 50 - 50$	**16.** $150 - 25 - 50$
Calculate.			
17. $150 + 75 - 25$	**18.** $200 - 50 + 25$	**19.** $50 + 75 - 100$	**20.** $225 + 50 - 25$
21. $250 - 50 + 25$	**22.** $25 + 50 - 25$	**23.** $75 + 75 - 25$	**24.** $125 - 75 + 50$

Multiply.

25. 3×25	**26.** 25×4	**27.** 6×50	**28.** 8×25	**29.** 75×3
30. 150×2	**31.** 9×25	**32.** 5×50	**33.** 25×7	**34.** 75×6

Divide.

35. $75 \div 3$	**36.** $150 \div 50$	**37.** $125 \div 5$	**38.** $200 \div 8$	**39.** $175 \div 7$
40. $200 \div 4$	**41.** $125 \div 25$	**42.** $250 \div 10$	**43.** $225 \div 9$	**44.** $150 \div 6$

273

9.1 Angle Relationships

Activity: Discover the Relationships

The diagram of Winnipeg International Airport
shows the 3 runways and their numbers. Trace the
diagram and extend runways 36, 07, 13, 18, and
31. Measure each angle and record each measure.

Inquire

1. $\angle a$ and $\angle c$ are called **opposite angles**. Why?

2. Name 3 other pairs of opposite angles.

3. How are the angle measures in a pair of
opposite angles related?

4. Two angles whose sum is 180° are called
supplementary angles. Name the pairs of
supplementary angles.

5. Two angles whose sum is 90° are called
complementary angles. How many pairs
of complementary angles are there?

6. Why are the runways numbered in the
way they are?

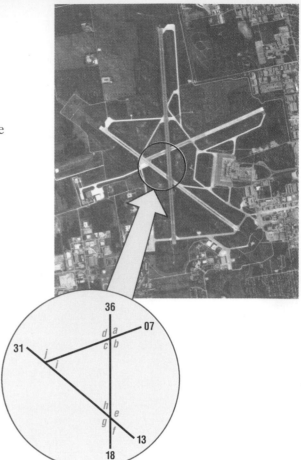

Example

a) Find the measures of the unknown angles.
b) Name a pair of complementary angles.
c) Name a pair of supplementary angles.

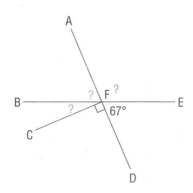

Solution

a) $\angle AFB = \angle EFD$ (opposite angles)
$\angle AFB = 67°$

$\angle EFD + \angle AFE = 180°$ (straight angle)
$67° + \angle AFE = 180°$
$\angle AFE = 113°$

$\angle EFD + \angle CFD + \angle BFC = 180°$ (straight angle)
$67° + 90° + \angle BFC = 180°$
$157° + \angle BFC = 180°$
$\angle BFC = 23°$

b) $\angle AFB + \angle BFC = 67° + 23°$
$= 90°$
$\angle AFB$ and $\angle BFC$ are complementary angles.

c) $\angle DFE + \angle AFE = 67° + 113°$
$= 180°$
$\angle DFE$ and $\angle AFE$ are supplementary angles.

Practice

Find the measure of each unknown angle.

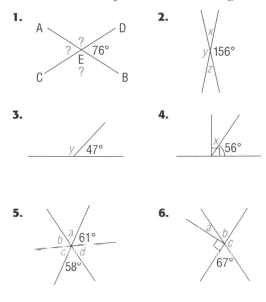

1.

A   D
? 76° E
C   B

2.

x
y 156°
z

3.

y 47°

4.

x 56°

5.

b a 61°
c d
58°

6.

a b
c
67°

Write the measure of the angle that is complementary to each of the following.

7. 35°   **8.** 56°   **9.** 81°

Write the measure of the angle that is supplementary to each of the following.

10. 47°   **11.** 106°   **12.** 157°

State whether each pair of angles is complementary, supplementary, or neither.

13. 34°, 64°   **14.** 133°, 47°

15. 9°, 81°   **16.** 92°, 78°

Problems and Applications

17. When a ray of light is reflected by a mirror, the angle of incidence, i, equals the angle of reflection, r. If $i = 35°$, what is the measure of
a) the complement of i?
b) r?
c) the complement of r?

18. The measure of an angle is 40° more than the measure of its supplement. What is the measure of each angle?

19. The measure of an angle is 10° more than the measure of its complement. What is the measure of each angle?

20. If $\angle M$ and $\angle N$ are supplementary angles, and $\angle M$ and $\angle P$ are complementary angles, what is the relationship between $\angle N$ and $\angle P$?

21. Give examples to show that, when you add the measure of an angle to twice the measure of its complement, the sum is the measure of the angle's supplement.

22. Give examples to show that, when you add the measure of an angle to three times the measure of its complement, the sum equals the sum of the measures of the angle's complement and supplement.

23. Use the figure below to name the following angles. Compare your answers with a classmate's.
a) all right angles
b) all pairs of complementary angles
c) all pairs of supplementary angles

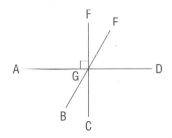

F F
A   G   D
B C

24. Write a question like one of questions 1 to 6. Have a classmate answer your question.

NUMBER POWER

What is the product of all the integers from +50 to −50?

275

9.2 Parallel and Perpendicular Lines

In mathematics, we often use perpendicular and parallel lines.
Perpendicular lines intersect to form right angles.
Parallel lines are lines in the same plane that do not intersect.

$c \perp d$ — $\perp$ means "is perpendicular to"

$a \parallel b$ — $\parallel$ means "is parallel to"

A **transversal** is a line or line segment that crosses 2 or more
lines. When a transversal crosses 2 lines, 8 angles are formed.
$\angle r$ and $\angle u$ are called **alternate angles**. They form a $\angle$ pattern.
$\angle s$ and $\angle t$ are also a pair of alternate angles. They form a $\angle$ pattern.
$\angle s$ and $\angle w$ are called **corresponding angles**. They form an $\vdash$
pattern. Other pairs of corresponding angles are $\angle r$ and $\angle v$
($\dashv$ pattern), $\angle q$ and $\angle u$ ($\vdash$ pattern), and $\angle p$ and $\angle t$ ($\dashv$ pattern).
$\angle s$ and $\angle u$ are called **co-interior angles** or **interior angles on the
same side of the transversal**. They form a $\sqcap$ pattern. $\angle r$ and $\angle t$
are another pair of co-interior angles. They form a $\sqcap$ pattern.
$\angle q$ and $\angle w$ are called **exterior angles on the same side of the transversal**.
They form a $\llcorner$ pattern. $\angle p$ and $\angle v$ are another pair of exterior
angles on the same side of the transversal. They form a $\lrcorner$ pattern.

Activity: Complete the Table

Draw 2 parallel lines on grid paper. Draw a transversal and label
the 8 angles, as shown. Measure the angles and complete the table.

Inquire

$\angle a =$	$\angle b =$	$\angle c =$	$\angle d =$
$\angle e =$	$\angle f =$	$\angle g =$	$\angle h =$

1. a) Name the 2 pairs of alternate angles.
b) How do the measures in each pair compare?

2. a) Name the 4 pairs of corresponding angles.
b) How do the measures in each pair compare?

3. a) Name the 2 pairs of co-interior angles.
b) What is the sum of the measures in each pair?

4. a) Name the 2 pairs of exterior angles on the
same side of the transversal.
b) What is the sum of the measures in each pair?

5. Repeat the Activity and questions 1 to 4 for
a different pair of parallel lines.

6. Copy and complete the statement: When a transversal crosses
2 parallel lines, the alternate angles are ▢ , the corresponding
angles are ▢ , the co-interior angles are ▢ , and the
exterior angles on the same side of the transversal are ▢ .

7. Describe the perpendicular and parallel lines you see in the
photo of the Bank of China building in Hong Kong.

276

Example

Determine the following angle measures.

a) $\angle b$ **b)** $\angle c$ **c)** $\angle d$

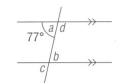

Solution

a) $\angle b = \angle a$ (alternate angles)

    $\angle b = 77°$

b) $\angle c = \angle a$ (corresponding angles)

    $\angle c = 77°$

c) $\angle b + \angle d = 180°$ (co-interior angles)   or $\angle a + \angle d = 180°$ (straight angle)

    $77° + \angle d = 180°$ $77° + \angle d = 180°$

              $\angle d = 103°$ $\angle d = 103°$

Practice

Identify each pair of angles as alternate angles, corresponding angles, co-interior angles, exterior angles on the same side of the transversal, or opposite angles.

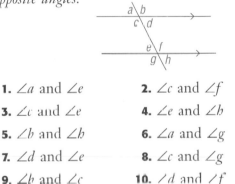

1. $\angle a$ and $\angle e$ **2.** $\angle c$ and $\angle f$

3. $\angle c$ and $\angle e$ **4.** $\angle e$ and $\angle h$

5. $\angle b$ and $\angle h$ **6.** $\angle a$ and $\angle g$

7. $\angle d$ and $\angle e$ **8.** $\angle c$ and $\angle g$

9. $\angle b$ and $\angle c$ **10.** $\angle d$ and $\angle f$

Problems and Applications

Find the missing angle measures. Give reasons for your answers.

11.   **12.**

13.   **14.**

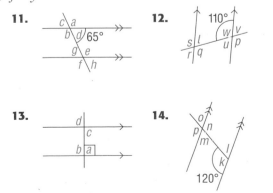

Find the measure of each unknown angle.

15.   **16.**

17.   **18.**

19.   **20.**

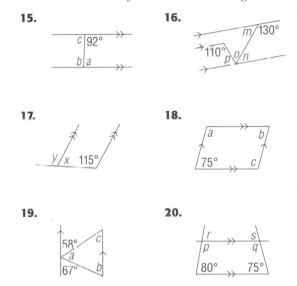

21. If the alternate angles created by 2 parallel lines and a transversal are supplementary, what are their measures? Explain.

22. Work with a partner to list sports playing surfaces that have parallel and perpendicular lines on them. Compare your answers with your classmates'.

23. Write a problem like one of questions 11 to 20. Have a classmate solve your problem.

9.3 Lines of Symmetry

If you fold the drawing of the hawk along the line shown, one half of the hawk exactly matches the other half. The 2 halves are reflection images of each other. The hawk is said to have a **line of symmetry**. The fold line is the line of symmetry.

A figure can have more than 1 line of symmetry. A starfish has 5.

Activity: Draw the Patterns

In each diagram, the 3-by-3 grid has 3 red squares and 6 white squares. Diagram 1 has 1 line of symmetry, and diagram 2 has 2.

A pattern is **symmetrical** if it has at least 1 line of symmetry. Draw the other symmetrical patterns on a 3-by-3 grid using 3 red squares and 6 white squares. Patterns like those shown to the right are considered to be the same.

Diagram 1   Diagram 2

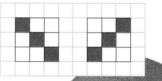

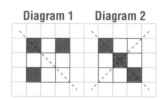

Inquire

1. Compare your patterns with your classmates'. How many different patterns did you find?

2. What is the maximum number of lines of symmetry in any of the patterns?

3. Draw any shape that has 4 lines of symmetry.

4. Draw any shape that has 3 lines of symmetry.

5. Sketch 5 objects in the classroom that have lines of symmetry. Draw the lines of symmetry on your sketches.

Example

How many lines of symmetry does each figure have?

a)

b)

c)

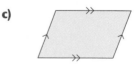

Solution

a) The square has 4.

b) The rectangle has 2.

c) The parallelogram has none. Each diagonal divides it into 2 identical parts, but the parts do not match when the parallelogram is folded along the diagonal.

Practice

Is the red line a line of symmetry? Write "yes" or "no."

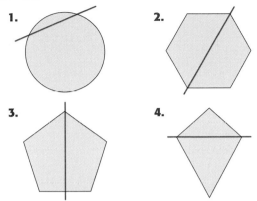

1.

2.

3.

4.

Copy each figure and draw all the lines of symmetry.

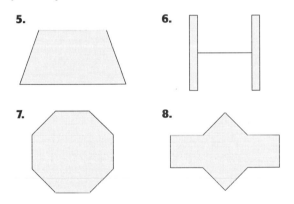

5.

6.

7.

8.

Problems and Applications

Copy each figure onto grid paper. Complete the diagram so that the red line is a line of symmetry.

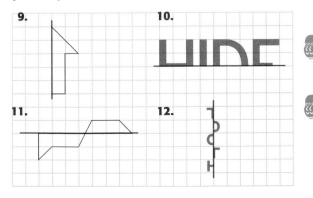

9.

10.

11.

12.

13. Copy each figure onto grid paper. Complete the diagram so that the new figure has
a) 1 line of symmetry   **b)** 2 lines of symmetry

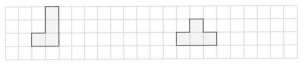

The following symbols are used by meteorologists. Copy the symbols and draw the lines of symmetry.

14. Sleet

15. Snow

16. Haze

17. Overcast

18. Hail Showers

19. Fog

20. This symbol shows that the wind is calm. How many lines of symmetry does it have? Explain.

21. The diagrams show how 4 squares can be coloured on a 3-by-3 grid to give patterns with 1 line of symmetry and 4 lines of symmetry.

Find how many other ways 4 squares can be shaded on a 3-by-3 grid to give patterns that have lines of symmetry.

22. With a classmate, draw 4 signs, symbols, or logos, each having a different number of lines of symmetry.

23. With a classmate, research the shield of each province and territory.
a) Which shields have a line of symmetry?
b) If you ignored the animals, which of the other shields would have a line of symmetry?

279

9.4 Triangles and Angles

Triangles appear in many designs, including the flag of British Columbia. Triangles are classified by the lengths of their sides and the measures of their angles.

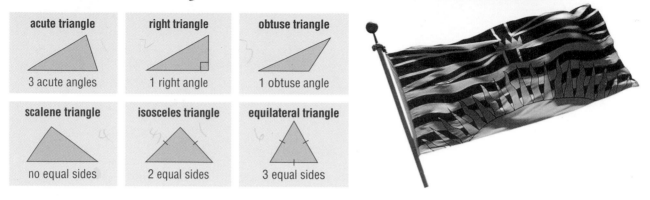

acute triangle	right triangle	obtuse triangle
3 acute angles	1 right angle	1 obtuse angle

scalene triangle	isosceles triangle	equilateral triangle
no equal sides	2 equal sides	3 equal sides

How would you classify the triangles on the flag of British Columbia?

Activity: Use the Definitions

Use a ruler to draw the following triangles. Make each triangle large enough that you can measure its angles with a protractor.

a) a right scalene triangle   **b)** an obtuse isosceles triangle

c) a right isosceles triangle   **d)** an obtuse scalene triangle

e) an acute isosceles triangle

Inquire

1. For each triangle you drew, use a protractor to measure each angle and find the sum of the measures.

2. Draw an acute triangle and cut it out. Tear off the angles and line them up as shown. What is the sum of the measures of the 3 angles?

3. Repeat question 2 for a right triangle and an obtuse triangle.

4. What is the sum of the measures of the interior angles of a triangle?

Example

Calculate the measures of $\angle SRT$ and $\angle WRT$.

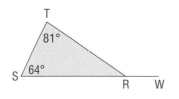

Solution

The sum of the interior angles of a triangle is 180°.

$$\angle S + \angle T + \angle SRT = 180°$$
$$64° + 81° + \angle SRT = 180°$$
$$145° + \angle SRT = 180°$$
$$\angle SRT = 35°$$
$$\angle SRT + \angle WRT = 180° \text{(straight angle)}$$
$$35° + \angle WRT = 180°$$
$$\angle WRT = 145°$$

Practice

Classify each triangle in 2 ways, by its sides and angles.

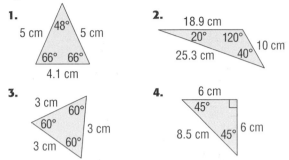

1.
5 cm 48° 5 cm
66° 66°
4.1 cm

2.
18.9 cm
20° 120°
25.3 cm 40° 10 cm

3.
3 cm 60°
60°
3 cm
3 cm 60°

4.
6 cm
45°
8.5 cm 45° 6 cm

Find the measure of the unknown angle.

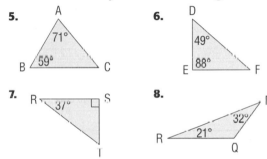

5.
A
71°
B 59° C

6.
D
49°
88°
E F

7.
R 37° S
T

8.
P
32°
R 21°
Q

Problems and Applications

Calculate the missing angle measures.

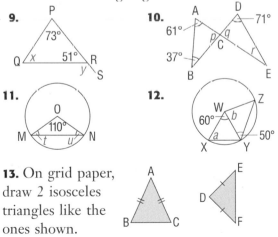

9.
P
73°
Q x 51° R
y S

10.
A D
61° 71°
p q
37° C r
B E

11.
O
110°
M t u N

12.
W Z
60° b
a 50°
X Y

13. On grid paper, draw 2 isosceles triangles like the ones shown.

A
B C

E
D
F

a) Measure the angles. Which angles are equal in each triangle?

b) Describe the relationship between the equal sides and equal angles in each triangle.

14. Find the missing angle measures.

a)
R
x
S 66° y T

b)

X a b Z
50°
Y

15. An **exterior angle** of a triangle is formed when one side of the triangle is extended. In the diagram, ∠c is an exterior angle, and ∠a and ∠b are the two interior angles opposite to ∠c.

b
a c

Draw a diagram like this one and measure angles *a*, *b*, and *c*. How are the angles related? Explain why.

16. Triangles can be classified by the number of lines of symmetry they have. How many lines of symmetry do these triangles have?
a) isosceles **b)** scalene **c)** equilateral

17. State the maximum number of lines of symmetry the following triangles could have. Show your answer with a diagram.
a) right **b)** obtuse **c)** acute

18. A triangle has a perimeter of 12 cm. The length of each side is a whole number of centimetres.
a) How many different triangles can be made?
b) Use the side lengths to classify each triangle.

19. a) Which provinces other than British Columbia have flags that include triangles?
b) With a classmate, find pictures of the flags of the states in the United States. List the flags that include triangles and classify the triangles.

Investigating Quadrilaterals with Geometry Software

A **polygon** is a closed figure made from line segments.
A polygon with 4 sides is called a **quadrilateral**. Some
quadrilaterals have special names.

A **trapezoid** is a
quadrilateral with exactly
2 parallel sides.

A **parallelogram** is a
quadrilateral with
opposite sides parallel.

A **kite** is a quadrilateral with
2 pairs of adjacent sides
equal.

Some parallelograms have special names.

A **rhombus** is a
parallelogram with
4 equal sides.

A **rectangle** is a
parallelogram with 4
right angles.

A **square** is a parallelogram
with 4 equal sides and
4 right angles.

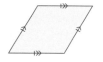

Activity ❶ Angles and Sides

Use geometry software to draw a parallelogram and a rhombus,
like the ones shown. If suitable software is not available, draw
the figures on grid paper. Measure the angles and sides in each
figure. Repeat for a different parallelogram and a different rhombus.

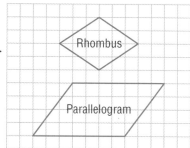

1. How are the opposite angles in a parallelogram related?

2. How are the opposite sides in a parallelogram related?

3. How are the opposite angles in a rhombus related?

Activity ❷ Diagonals

A diagonal is a line segment, other than a side, that joins 2
vertices in a polygon. Use geometry software to draw each figure
and construct its diagonals. Alternatively, copy the figures onto
grid paper and draw the diagonals for each.

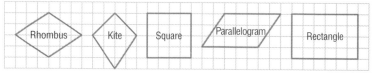

Determine the following.

1. Which quadrilaterals have equal diagonals?

2. Which quadrilaterals have diagonals that meet at right angles?

3. Which quadrilaterals have diagonals that bisect each other?

Activity ❸ Classifying Quadrilaterals

Describe different ways of classifying these quadrilaterals on the basis of

1. the relationships between the angles

2. the relationships between the diagonals

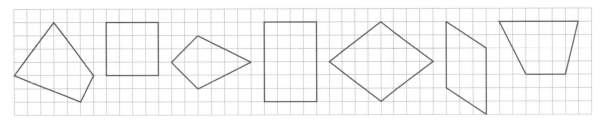

Activity ❹ Missing Measures

Find the missing measures in each figure.

1. Parallelogram

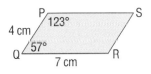

PS = ▨ RS = ▨
∠PSR = ▨ ∠QRS = ▨

2. Square

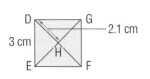

DG = ▨ HF = ▨
GE = ▨ ∠GHF = ▨

3. Kite

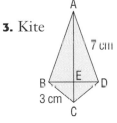

AB = ▨ DC = ▨
∠AED = ▨ ∠DEC = ▨

4. Rectangle

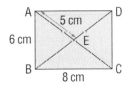

DC = ▨ EC = ▨
AC = ▨ DB = ▨
AD = ▨ BE = ▨

5. Parallelogram

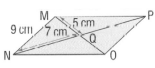

QO = ▨ MO = ▨
PO = ▨ PQ = ▨

6. Rhombus

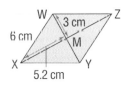

XY = ▨ MY = ▨
XZ = ▨ ∠WMZ = ▨

Activity ❺ Critical Thinking

This diagram illustrates how quadrilaterals are related. Explain the meaning of the diagram.

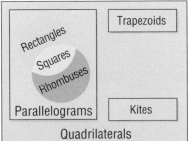

9.5 Polygons

The front, back, and sides of Sudbury's Big Nickel are made up of polygons. A **polygon** is a closed plane figure made up of 3 or more line segments. A polygon is named according to its number of sides. In a **regular polygon**, all the sides are the same length, and all the angles have the same measure. A **diagonal** joins 2 vertices in a polygon and is not a side.

Activity: Use the Table

Draw the following polygons.

a) a quadrilateral with just 1 right angle

b) a pentagon with just 2 acute angles

c) a hexagon with at least 4 right angles

d) an octagon with at least 1 acute angle, 1 right angle, and 1 obtuse angle

e) a polygon with just 2 diagonals

f) a polygon with just 5 diagonals

Inquire

1. Name the polygons that form the front, back, and sides of Sudbury's Big Nickel. Are the polygons regular? Explain.

2. What is the maximum number of diagonals that can be drawn from 1 vertex of each of the following polygons?

a) quadrilateral   **b)** pentagon   **c)** hexagon

3. Use the pattern from question 2 to find the maximum number of diagonals from 1 vertex of these polygons.

a) octagon   **b)** decagon   **c)** dodecagon

Polygon	Sides
Triangle	3
Quadrilateral	4
Pentagon	5
Hexagon	6
Heptagon	7
Octagon	8
Nonagon	9
Decagon	10
Dodecagon	12

The sum of the measures of the interior angles of a triangle is 180°. To find the sum of the interior angles of other polygons, divide the polygon into triangles using all the diagonals from 1 vertex.

 Quadrilateral    Pentagon   Hexagon

2 triangles

Sum = 2 × 180°

= 360°

3 triangles

Sum = 3 × 180°

= 540°

4 triangles

Sum = 4 × 180°

= 720°

The sum of the interior angles of a polygon with n sides is $180° \times (n - 2)$.

Example

Find the measure of each angle in a regular octagon.

Solution

The sum of the interior angles is: $S = 180° \times (8 - 2)$

$= 180° \times 6$

$= 1080°$

There are 8 equal angles. Each angle is $1080° \div 8$ or $135°$.

Practice

Find the sum of the interior angles in each of the following.

1. heptagon   **2.** nonagon

3. decagon   **4.** dodecagon

Find the measure of the unknown angle in each polygon.

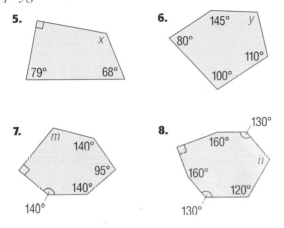

5.

6.

7.

8.

Find the measure of each angle in the following.

9. regular triangle   **10.** regular hexagon

11. regular pentagon   **12.** regular decagon

Problems and Applications

13. What is the common name for a regular quadrilateral?

14. a) How many lines of symmetry are there for a regular hexagon? a regular pentagon?
b) For a regular polygon, how is the number of lines of symmetry related to the number of sides? Test your answer for a regular octagon.

15. Find the measures of the unknown angles in these kites.

a)

b)

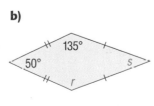

16. An exterior angle of a polygon is formed when one side of the polygon is extended. The diagram shows the 3 exterior angles of an equilateral triangle.

a) What is the measure of each exterior angle?
b) What is the sum of the measures of the 3 exterior angles?
c) Draw any triangle and an exterior angle at each vertex. Measure each exterior angle and find the sum.
d) Draw any quadrilateral and an exterior angle at each vertex. Measure each exterior angle and find the sum.
e) Draw any pentagon and an exterior angle at each vertex. Measure each exterior angle and find the sum.
f) What is the sum of the exterior angles of any polygon?

17. Is it possible for a hexagon to have all 6 sides equal and not be a regular hexagon? Explain.

18. Is it possible for a hexagon to have all 6 angles equal and not be a regular hexagon? Explain.

19. a) If you trace around a one-dollar coin, how many sides does the resulting polygon have?
b) Use your research skills to name a polygon with this number of sides.

20. State an everyday word that has the same prefix as each of the following. Compare your words with your classmates'.

a) triangle   **b)** quadrilateral
c) octagon   **d)** decagon

285

The Golden Ratio

Activity ❶ The Golden Rectangle

The golden rectangle was discovered by the Greeks in the fifth century B.C. Many people find the shape of the rectangle very appealing.

To construct a golden rectangle, follow these steps.

1. Construct square ABCD of side length 4 cm.

2. Find the midpoint of BC and name it E.

3. With centre E and radius ED, draw an arc to intersect the extension of BC at F.

4. Construct a perpendicular to BF at F to meet the extension of AD at G. The rectangle ABFG is a golden rectangle.

5. Measure AG and AB.

6. Use your calculator to divide AG by AB. Write the ratio of AG to AB with the second term equal to 1. The result is an approximation of the golden ratio.

7. The golden rectangle often appears in nature. Verify that the rectangles shown are golden rectangles.

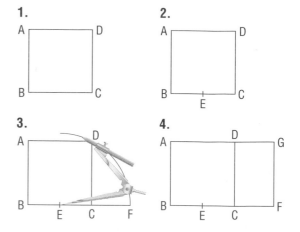

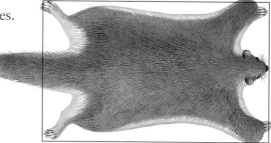

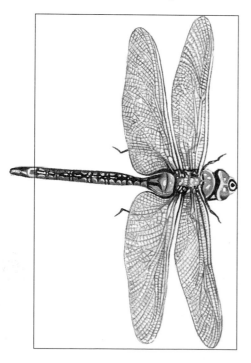

Activity ❷ The Golden Ratio and You

Some people claim that the golden ratio is found in many measurements of the human body. Find the following ratios for each member of your group. Express each ratio with a second term of 1. Are any of the ratios close to the golden ratio?

a) the distance from your shoulder to your fingertips to the distance from your elbow to your fingertips

b) the length of your head to the distance from the top of your ears to your chin

c) the length of your index finger to the length from the second joint to the fingertip

Activity ❸ The Golden Ratio in Art and Architecture

A rectangle whose sides are in the golden ratio is known as a golden rectangle. This picture of the Parthenon in Athens, Greece, shows two of the ways in which the golden rectangle was used in the design.

a) Verify the presence of the golden rectangle in the design of the Parthenon.

b) Determine where the golden rectangle is used in the part of the Legislature Building in Regina, Saskatchewan, shown in the photograph.

c) Use the diagram to describe how Leonardo Da Vinci used the golden rectangle in his portrait of Isabella d'Este.

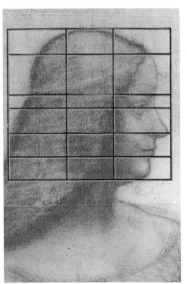

Activity ❹ Researching the Golden Ratio

Use your research skills to find

1. more examples of the golden ratio in art and architecture

2. examples of the golden ratio in nature

9.6 Using Angle Relationships

Activity: Study the Diagram

Around 200 B.C., Eratosthenes used an angle relationship to find the circumference of the Earth. Since the sun is so far away, he assumed that the sun's rays are parallel lines. When the sun was directly overhead at Syene (S), the sun's rays made an angle of about 7° at Alexandria (A), 800 km north of Syene.

A 7° angle is about $\frac{1}{50}$ of a circle. If C is the centre of the Earth, ∠ACS is $\frac{1}{50}$ of a circle because the sun's rays are parallel.

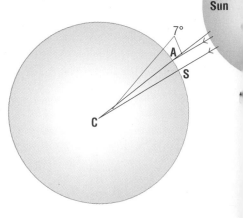

Inquire

1. How do you think Eratosthenes used the information to find the Earth's circumference?

2. How close do you think he came to the actual circumference? Explain.

You have learned the relationships between pairs of lettered angles in diagrams 1 to 4, below. You have also learned the sums of the lettered angles in diagrams 5 and 6.

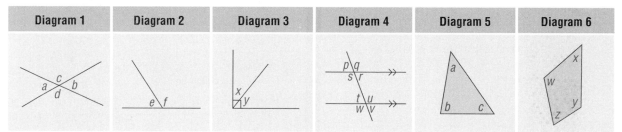

You can apply angle relationships to solve problems.

Example

Find these angle measures and explain your calculations.
a) ∠CGF   **b)** ∠BFG   **c)** ∠BAC

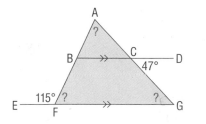

Solution

a) BD || EG, so ∠CGF = ∠DCG (alternate angles)
$$\angle CGF = 47°$$

b) ∠BFG + ∠BFE = 180° (straight angle)
$$\angle BFG + 115° = 180°$$
$$\angle BFG = 65°$$

c) The sum of the interior angles of a triangle is 180°.
$$\angle BAC + \angle BFG + \angle CGF = 180°$$
$$\angle BAC + 65° + 47° = 180°$$
$$\angle BAC + 112° = 180°$$
$$\angle BAC = 68°$$

Practice

Find the unknown angle measures.

1.

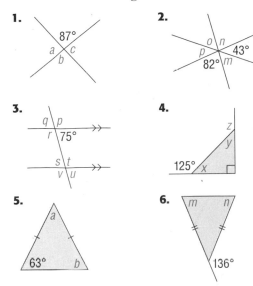

87°
a c
b

2.

o n
p 43°
82° m

3.

q p
r 75°
s t
v u

4.

z
y
125° x

5.

a
63° b

6.

m n
136°

Problems and Applications

Find the unknown angle measures.

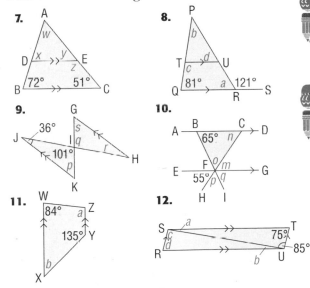

7.

A
w
D x y E
z
B 72° 51° C

8.

P
b
T d U
c
Q 81° a 121° S
R

9.

G
36° s
J I q
101° r H
p
K

10.

A B C D
65° n
E F o m G
55° p q
H I

11.

W
84° a Z
135° Y
b
X

12.

S a T
c 75°
R d 85°
b U

Find the unknown angle measures.

13.

a b d
c
85° 140° 80°

14.

v 30°
y
x z w

15.

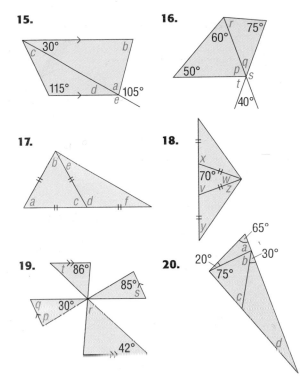

30° b
c
115° d a 105°
e

16.

r 75°
60°
50° q
p s
t
40°

17.

b e
a c d f

18.

x
70° w
v z
y
65°
a 30°
20° b
75°
c
d

19.

t 86°
85°
q 30° s
p r
42°

20.

21. When the sun is overhead in Jamaica, it makes an angle of about 26° in Prince Edward Island. To the nearest 100 km, how far apart are the 2 islands? Explain your method. Compare your result with a classmate's.

22. Write a problem that involves finding at least 3 unknown angles. Check that the problem can be solved, then have a classmate solve it.

PATTERN POWER

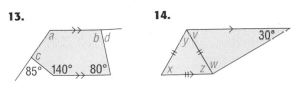

a) Use a calculator to complete the calculations.

$$19^2 = \blacksquare$$
$$199^2 = \blacksquare$$
$$1999^2 = \blacksquare$$

b) Describe the pattern.

c) Use the pattern to predict $19\ 999^2$ and $199\ 999^2$.

Colouring Maps

How many colours do you need to colour the countries on a map? This problem has fascinated mathematicians and geographers for years.

To colour a map correctly, you must use different colours for any two countries that share a border.

Map 1 is coloured correctly. Map 2 is not, because countries A and B share a border and should have different colours.

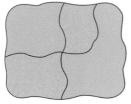 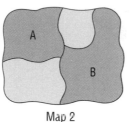

Map 1   Map 2

Activity ❶

1. Copy these straight line maps into your notebook.

2. Colour each map using as few colours as possible. Make sure that regions with shared borders have different colours.

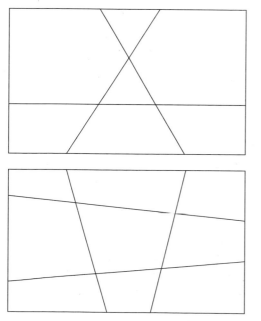

Activity ❷

1. Make up some straight line maps of your own and colour them with as few colours as possible.

2. If you use as few colours as possible, what is the greatest number of colours you ever need for a straight line map?

3. Compare your answer with your classmates'.

Activity ❸

1. Copy these maps into your notebook.

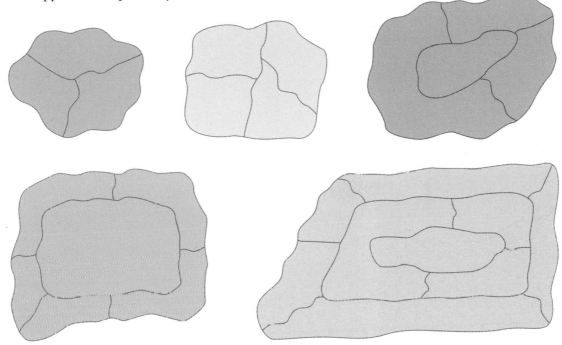

2. Colour each map using as few colours as possible.
Make sure that regions that share borders have different colours.

3. What do you think is the smallest number of colours needed to colour all the maps in an atlas?

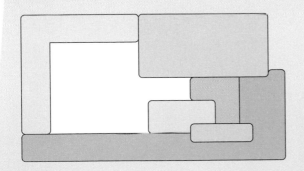

Activity ❹

One area of this map has not been coloured. Four colours have already been used, and it seems that we need a fifth colour to complete the map.

1. Copy the map into your notebook, but omit the present colours.

2. Colour the map with only four colours.

3. Compare your method with your classmates'.

☀ Activity ❺

Test your prediction from question 3 in Activity 3 by colouring a map of North America. Make sure that bordering provinces or states do not have the same colour.

Exploring Skeletons and Shells

Activity ❶

The children's climbing frame is a **skeleton**. The bars outline the **edges** of the polyhedra that form the structure.

1. Name the polyhedra outlined by the bars of the frame.

2. Name 3 other objects that are skeletons of three-dimensional shapes.

3. Design another children's climbing frame using the skeletons of three-dimensional shapes. Sketch your frame and label it with the names of the three-dimensional shapes.

Activity ❷

The skeletons were constructed from Plasticine and 2 different lengths of sticks.

1. Name each three-dimensional shape.

2. The Plasticine joins the sticks at a **vertex**. How many vertices are there on each skeleton?

3. The sticks form the edges of the polyhedra. How many edges are there on each skeleton?

4. Use sticks and Plasticine to construct each polyhedron. State the number of vertices and the number of edges on each one.
a) triangular prism   **b)** cube
c) square pyramid   **d)** hexagonal prism

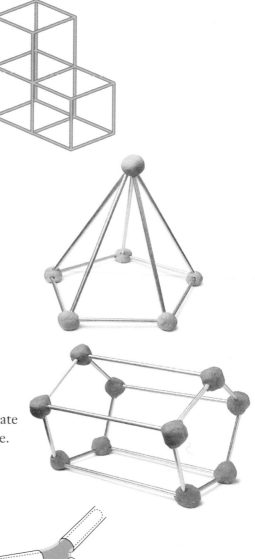

Activity ❸

A polyhedron can be constructed from pieces of straw joined by pieces of pipe cleaner or wire.

1. Construct and identify each polyhedron.

a)   **b)**   **c)**

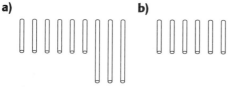

2. Sketch the straws needed to make
a) a pentagonal pyramid
b) a hexagonal prism

Activity ❹

Follow the instructions to construct the **shell** of each polyhedron from cardboard.

1. a) Draw and cut out an equilateral triangle.

b) Fold point A down to the midpoint of BC. The ends of the fold line are called points E and F.

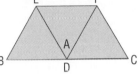

c) Fold point C to point E and point B to point F.

d) Name the polyhedron whose shell can be constructed from the folded triangle.

2. a) Draw a square.

b) Draw congruent squares on each side of the square and cut out the pattern.
c) Cut out and fold the pattern to form the shell of an open cube.
d) Make a sketch to show where you would add a 6th square to the pattern to construct the shell of a closed cube. Check your pattern.

Activity ❺

A pattern that folds to form a polyhedron is called the **net** of the polyhedron.

1. Use solid models of polyhedra. Draw the net of each model by rolling the model on cardboard and tracing the surfaces.

2. a) Compare your nets with your classmates'.
b) Is it possible to have more than one net for a polyhedron?

Activity ❻

1. Which of the nets make the shell of a cylinder?

a) **b)** **c)**

Trace the surfaces of a cylinder to check your answer.

2. Trace a cone to draw its net.

3. What is the shape of the flat face of a cone?

4. What is the shape of the curved surface?

9.7 Solids, Shells, and Skeletons

Activity: Study the Pictures

The pillars in front of the Parthenon in Athens are solids.

The entrance to the Louvre in Paris is a shell.

A hydro tower is a skeleton.

Inquire

1. How are a solid, a shell, and a skeleton the same? How are they different?

2. With a partner, decide whether each of the following is a solid, a shell, or a skeleton.

a) Aztec pyramid **b)** zoo aviary **c)** SkyDome

3. Write a definition describing the characteristics of

a) a solid **b)** a shell **c)** a skeleton

4. List other structures that are examples of solids, shells, and skeletons.

Activity: Use the Diagrams

One face of a pyramid is called a **base**. What shape are the other faces?

A prism has 2 congruent, parallel bases. What shapes can form the other faces?

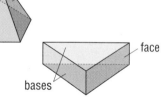

In a shell or solid, the line segment where 2 faces meet is called an **edge**.

In a skeleton, the material used to outline the polyhedron forms the edges.

The point at which edges of a polyhedron meet is called a **vertex**.

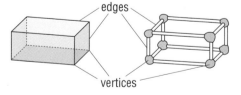

Inquire

1. How many edges does a rectangular prism have?

2. How many vertices does a rectangular prism have?

Practice

In questions 1–6, identify each object as a solid, a shell, or a skeleton.

1.

2.

3.

4.

5.

6.

7. a) Sketch the pieces of glass and metal that are needed to construct a fish tank.

b) Is the tank a solid, a shell, or a skeleton?

State the number of each shape of face needed to make the shell of each polyhedron. Identify the shape of the base in each case.

8. cube

9. pentagonal pyramid

10. triangular prism

11. hexagonal prism

12. square pyramid

13. triangular pyramid

Problems and Applications

14. a) Copy and complete the chart for each polyhedron in questions 8–13.

Polyhedron	Number of Vertices, V	Number of Faces, F	Number of Edges, E

b) Which of the following number sentences represents the formula discovered by the Swiss mathematician Leonhard Euler? This formula works for all polyhedra.

$$V = E - F \qquad E + F = V \qquad V + F - E = 2$$

15. Do some research on Euler's life and write a paragraph about him.

In questions 16–19, work in a group to investigate rigidity in polyhedra.

16. Form a triangle and a square using straws and pipe cleaners.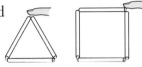

Push down gently on a vertex of the triangle and a vertex of the square. What happens to the shape of each polygon?

17. The triangle is a rigid figure that is used to help make objects stable.

a) Describe how it is used in each of the following.

b) Name 2 other situations where the triangle is used to provide rigidity.

18. Construct each polyhedron using straws and pipe cleaners. Predict which polyhedra you think are rigid, then test each one by pressing gently on a vertex.

a) pentagonal prism   **b)** cube
c) rectangular prism   **d)** triangular prism
e) square pyramid   **f)** hexagonal prism

19. Add straws with pipe cleaners to make non-rigid polyhedra rigid. Experiment to make sure you add as few pieces as possible. Sketch the polyhedra to show where the extra straws were added.

9.8 Nets of Three-Dimensional Shapes

Activity: Study the Figure

The square pyramid is constructed from a building set whose pieces hinge together at the sides.

Inquire

1. Which of the following are nets of the pyramid?

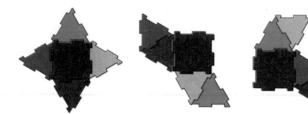

2. Describe a way to determine whether or not an arrangement of shapes is a net.

3. Sketch a different net for the square pyramid. Exchange sketches with a classmate and check that each sketch is a net.

Practice

In questions 1–3, work with a partner and use construction pieces or shapes cut from heavy cardboard to help you. For each polyhedron, state the number and shape of the base(s) and other faces, and draw 2 different nets.

1. triangular prism

2. hexagonal pyramid

3. rectangular prism

Problems and Applications

4. If you cut out and fold a net to make a polyhedron, is the result a solid, a shell, or a skeleton? Explain.

5. a) What polyhedron can be formed from each net?

b) How many edges must be folded to form the polyhedron from each net? How many edges must be sealed?

c) For this polyhedron, is it possible to draw a net that would need a different number of folded and sealed edges?

6. The juice container is a cylinder. Draw the net of the juice container.

7. The gift box is in the shape of a cone. Draw the net that results when the cone is opened and laid flat.

8. The Wilsons bought a new mailbox for their cottage. Draw its net.

9. The construction pieces have been used to form patterns of 6 squares.

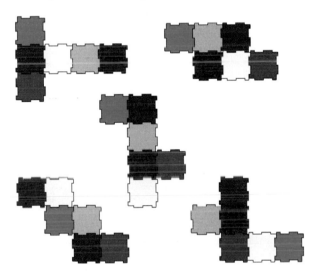

a) Which of the patterns is a net of a cube?
b) For each net, how many edges are folded and how many are sealed to form the cube?
c) A total of 11 patterns of 6 squares can be folded to form a cube. Sketch the patterns that are not shown here.

10. Examine a die to check the numbers of dots on opposite faces. Sketch the net of the die. Mark the dots on the net, so that you could make the die from the net. Compare your net with a classmate's.

11. Tissue boxes come in the shapes of many different rectangular prisms.

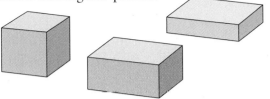

With a classmate, collect several different tissue boxes. Label them A, B, C, and so on. Use a sketch to predict the net for each box. Carefully cut each box and open it to display the net. Compare each of your predictions with the actual net.

LOGIC POWER

A spider is at the vertex S on this wire cube.

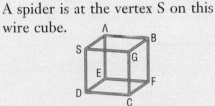

The spider wants to walk to vertex F. To get there, it must follow these rules.

1. The spider can walk only along the edges.

2. The spider can walk along an edge only once.

3. The spider can only go down the vertical edges, never up.

4. The spider can visit any vertex except F more than once. When it gets to F, it must stop.

One way for the spider to make the trip is to go from S to A to B to F. In how many other different ways can the spider make the trip?

The Platonic Solids

Ancient Greek scholars thought that mathematics and science could explain many aspects of the universe. A Greek philosopher, Plato, believed that all things are three-dimensional and are made up of atoms in the shapes of regular polyhedra.

In a **regular polyhedron**, all faces are congruent, regular polygons, and the same number of faces meet at each vertex in exactly the same way.

Plato named 4 of the polyhedra for what were then believed to be the 4 elements of the universe. He believed that the fifth polyhedron represented the universe itself. The 5 regular polyhedra he described are now known as the Platonic solids.

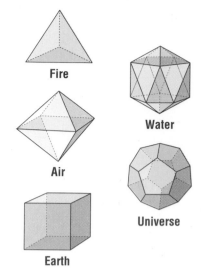

Fire

Water

Air

Universe

Earth

Activity ❶

1. Name the regular polygons that are used to construct each regular polyhedron.

2. Match the correct polyhedron with its name. Find the meaning of each prefix used.

a) cube   **b)** dodecahedron   **c)** tetrahedron
d) icosahedron   **e)** octahedron

3. Suggest another name for the cube, using the appropriate prefix.

4. By what other name do we identify the tetrahedron?

Activity ❷

The following polyhedra have bases that are regular polygons.

Name and describe each polyhedron and state why it is not regular.

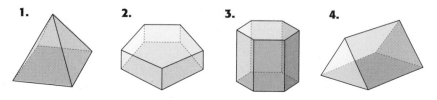

1.   **2.**   **3.**   **4.**

Activity ❸

1. Use grid paper to draw a square. Divide it into 4 smaller squares.

2. Trace the pattern to make 2 copies on stiff cardboard.

3. Cut out one small square from each cardboard piece. Fold each of the resulting shapes so that the cut edges meet. Join the edges with tape.

4. Join the two pieces you have made to form a polyhedron.

5. Name the polyhedron you have constructed. Explain how you know it is regular.

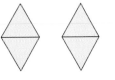

Activity ❹

1. Use triangular dot paper to draw a regular hexagon. Divide it into 6 equilateral triangles.

2. Cut out the hexagon and trace it on stiff cardboard to make 2 copies.

3. For each hexagon, make fold lines on the edges of the triangles. Cut out and discard 2 adjacent triangles. Join the cut edges with tape.

4. How many of these pieces are needed to construct a regular polyhedron?

5. Construct and name the polyhedron.

6. How many triangles meet at a vertex?

7. Describe a way to construct a tetrahedron from these pieces of a hexagon.

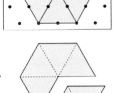

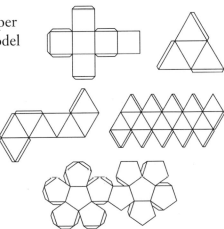

Activity ❺

1. The nets of the 5 regular polyhedra are shown. Use dot paper or templates to draw the nets in various sizes. Construct a model of each polyhedron from brightly coloured cardboard.

2. Copy and complete the chart for the 5 Platonic solids.

Name	Number of Faces	Shape of Faces	Number of Angles at Each Vertex

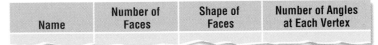

3. Use a set of polyhedra to check whether Euler's formula $V + F = E + 2$ works for each Platonic solid. In this formula, V is the number of vertices, F is the number of faces, and E is the number of edges.

Networks

Network theory was first developed in the eighteenth century by Leonhard Euler. Today, Euler's theories are used to solve communications and scheduling problems.

Activity ❶ Classifying Networks

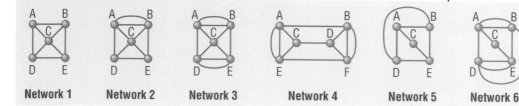

Network 1   Network 2   Network 3   Network 4   Network 5   Network 6

1. Work in groups. Copy the networks onto a piece of paper.

2. Determine whether or not each network is *traceable*. This means that you can trace it in one sweep, without raising your pencil from the paper or copying over a line.

3. Label each network using one of the following descriptions.
a) The network is not traceable, no matter where you start.
b) The network is traceable if you start at vertex ■ or ■.
c) The network is traceable, no matter where you start.

4. Classify each vertex as "even" or "odd," depending on whether an even or odd number of line segments meet at that vertex.

Network	Total Number of Vertices	Number of Odd Vertices	Number of Even Vertices
1			
⋮			
6			

5. You can tell if a network is traceable from the number of odd vertices it has. Use your results from steps 3 and 4 to complete each of the following rules by adding "traceable" or "not traceable."
a) A network with more than 2 odd vertices is ■.
b) A network with 2 odd vertices is ■ if you start at an odd vertex.
c) A network with no odd vertices is ■ from any vertex.

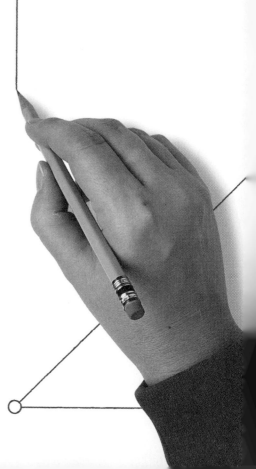

Activity ❷ Designing Networks

1. Determine the number of odd vertices in each of the following networks.

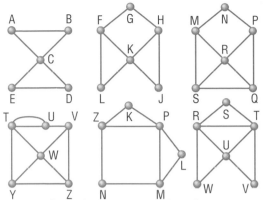

2. Use the rules you completed in step 5 of Activity 1 to predict which of the 6 networks is traceable. Check your predictions.

3. For each network that is not traceable, add as few lines as possible to make it traceable.

4. Design some networks of your own and use them to test the rules.

5. Challenge the members of your group to design one of each of the three kinds of networks described in step 5 of Activity 1.

Activity ❸ The Seven Bridges of Königsberg

Königsberg was a German town built on an island in the middle of a river and was connected to the mainland and both banks of the river by 7 bridges.

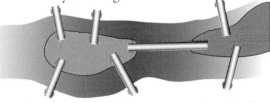

1. Copy or trace the diagram. Decide whether it would be possible to take a bike ride in which you crossed each of the 7 bridges exactly once. Compare your findings with your classmates'.

2. The diagram can be represented by a network.

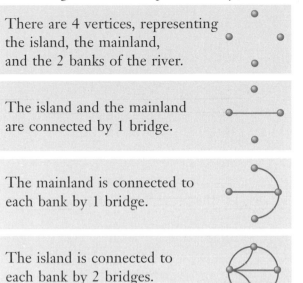

There are 4 vertices, representing the island, the mainland, and the 2 banks of the river.	
The island and the mainland are connected by 1 bridge.	
The mainland is connected to each bank by 1 bridge.	
The island is connected to each bank by 2 bridges.	

a) Is the complete network traceable?

b) What is the minimum number of lines you could add to the network to make it traceable? In how many different ways could you add this number of lines?

c) Use your results from part b) to draw the different ways of adding the minimum number of bridges to the map of Königsberg, so that it would be possible to cycle over each bridge exactly once. Compare your drawings with your classmates'.

Activity ❹ Planning Routes

Each of the following diagrams represents a network of communities. You wish to visit each community on the map at least once and travel along each route only once. For which of the following trips is it possible to

a) visit each community at least once, begin and end in the same community, and travel over each route only once?

b) visit each community at least once, begin and end in different communities, and travel over each route only once?

CONTINUED ▶

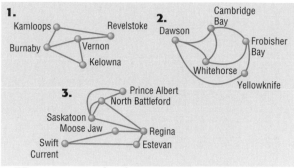

4. Use your results from questions 1 to 3 to complete each of the following rules by adding "the same vertex" or "different vertices."

a) If you trace a network with 2 odd vertices, you begin and end at ▇.

b) If you trace a network with no odd vertices, you begin and end at ▇.

5. Design several networks to test your rules from question 4.

6. Choose 4 or more communities in your province. Connect them with imaginary routes so that you could

a) visit each community at least once, begin and end in the same community, and travel over each route only once

b) visit each community at least once, begin and end in different communities, and travel over each route only once

7. Have a classmate check your routes.

Activity ❺ Travelling Minimum Distances

Covering each route only once means that you travel the minimum distance to visit all the vertices of a network.

There are 2 odd vertices in this network. You can visit each vertex and cover each route only once by starting at either odd vertex (A or C) and ending at the other. The total distance covered is 3 + 4 + 5 + 6 + 7, or 25 units.

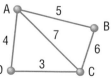

For each of the following networks,
a) what is the total length of all the routes?
b) is it possible to visit each vertex by travelling the distance you calculated in part a)?

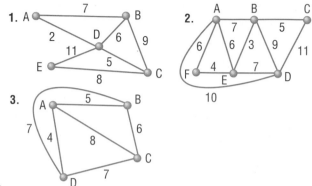

3.

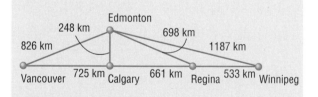

⚙️✏️ **4.** In any of the networks for which it is not possible to cover each route only once, what is the shortest distance you could travel to visit each vertex? Explain.

Activity ❻ Devising an Airline Schedule

The diagram shows some possible airline routes connecting 5 western cities and the flying distances between them.

1. What is the shortest possible distance you could travel to visit each city at least once?

2. To travel the distance you found, where could you start and end your journey?

3. Airline schedules do not always allow you to travel the shortest possible distance on a journey. To understand why, imagine that you are setting up an airline to service the 5 western cities in the diagram. You want to buy as few planes as possible. You need at least one departure from each airport in each 7-h period during the airport's operating hours of 07:00 to 23:00. Assume that your planes average 650 km/h in the air and spend 1 h on the ground between flights.

a) What is the smallest number of planes you can buy? Explain.

b) Work with a classmate. Devise a schedule of arrivals and departures for your planes at each airport.

c) State 3 journeys that you could not complete on direct flights. Use your schedule to suggest the best route for each journey.

Activity ❼ Communication Networks

Some networks include routes that can only be travelled in one direction. The following network of communication lines connects computer terminals. The arrows show the ways information can travel.

Network Administrator

User A   User B   User C

For example, User A can get files or programs from the administrator, but cannot send files to any terminal.

1. Describe what User B can and cannot do.

2. Describe what User C can and cannot do.

3. Describe a way for information to travel
a) from User B to the administrator
b) from User C to User B

Activity ❽ Airline Stopovers

The network shows air travel lines between 4 cities.

Saskatoon
Regina   Winnipeg
Brandon

1. List each city and all the places that can be reached with
a) no stopover

b) exactly one stopover. Include return flights to the same city. For example: Winnipeg to ▇ to Winnipeg.

2. Can you travel from each city to every other city with no stopovers or, at most, 1 stopover?

3. Matrix 1 shows only some of the information from the network in another way.

Matrix 1: No Stopovers

	R	B	S	W
R	0	1	1	1
B	0	0	1	0
S				
W				

See that, from R on the left, there is 1 flight to B, 1 flight to S, and 1 flight to W. There are 0 ways to go from R to R with no stopover. From B, there is only 1 flight to S. Copy and complete the matrix for flights originating in Saskatoon and Winnipeg.

4. Copy and complete the matrix below to show the number of trips with 1 stopover.

Matrix 2: One Stopover

	R	B	S	W
R	2	0	2	1
B	1	0	0	1
S				
W				

5. Copy and complete the matrix to show the number of trips with, at most, 1 stopover.

Matrix 3: No Stopovers or One Stopover

	R	B	S	W
R	2	1	3	2
B	1	0	1	1
S				
W				

6. How are the 3 matrices related?

Review

Find the measure of each unknown angle.

1.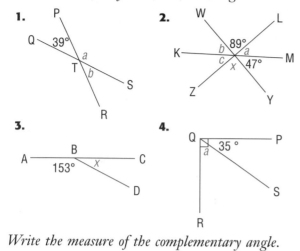

2.

3.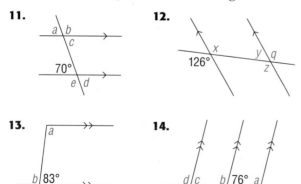

4.

Write the measure of the complementary angle.

5. 35°   **6.** 66°   **7.** 89°

Write the measure of the supplementary angle.

8. 47°   **9.** 102°   **10.** 156°

Find the measure of each unknown angle.

11.

12.

13.

14.

Copy each figure and draw all the lines of symmetry.

15.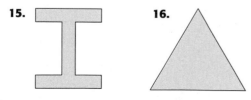

16.

Classify each triangle by sides and by angles.

17.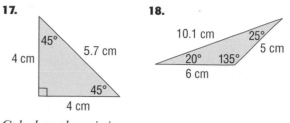

18.

Calculate the missing measures.

19.

20.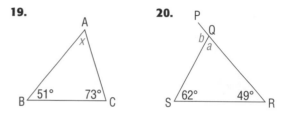

Find the measure of the unknown angle in each polygon.

21.

22.

23.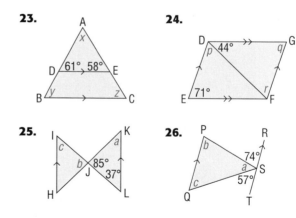

24.

25.

26.

27. Name a three-dimensional solid with each of the following.
a) 2 triangular faces and 3 rectangular faces
b) 4 congruent faces
c) 8 vertices
d) 15 edges

Name each three-dimensional figure and state the number of faces, edges, and vertices for each one.

28.
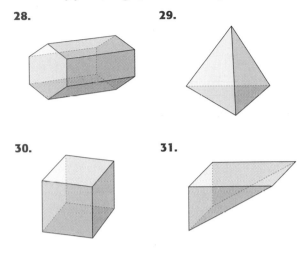

29.

30.

31.

32. A cylinder contains 1 L of water. Is the cylinder a solid, a shell, or a skeleton? Explain.

33. Draw a net for each of the following containers.

a)

b)

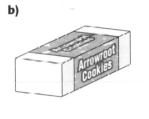

34. The net of a child's cube is shown. Sketch the cube showing
a) the top right view
b) the bottom left view
c) the back view

Use the cat as the front of the cube and the dog as the top.

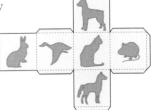

Group Decision Making
Researching Careers of Your Choice

1. Brainstorm as a class the careers you might like to investigate. They might include such careers as archaeologist, astronaut, professional golfer, movie director, astronomer, television news anchor, hotel chef, or university professor. As a class, decide on 6 careers.

2. As a class, list the questions you want to answer about each career. Include a question on how the career makes use of math.

3. Go to home groups.

| 1 | 2 | 3 | 4 | 5 | 6 | | 1 | 2 | 3 | 4 | 5 | 6 |
Home Groups
| 1 | 2 | 3 | 4 | 5 | 6 | | 1 | 2 | 3 | 4 | 5 | 6 |

As a group, decide on a career for each group member to investigate.

4. Form an expert group with students from other home groups who have the same career to research.

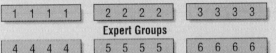

| 1 1 1 1 | 2 2 2 2 | 3 3 3 3 |
Expert Groups
| 4 4 4 4 | 5 5 5 5 | 6 6 6 6 |

In your expert group, decide how to answer the questions about the career. Then, do the research.

5. In your expert group, prepare a class presentation about the career. Relate the format of the presentation to the career. For example, if you researched the career of an astronaut, your presentation might take the form of a trip to the moon.

6. Return to your home group and evaluate the presentations of the expert groups.

Chapter Check

Find the measures of the unknown angles.

1.   **2.**

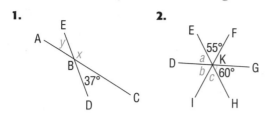

Write the measure of the complementary angle.

3. 44°   **4.** 7°   **5.** 66°

Write the measure of the supplementary angle.

6. 57°   **7.** 101°   **8.** 165°

Copy each figure and draw all the lines of symmetry.

9.   **10.**

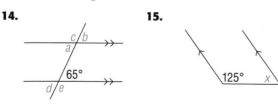

Classify each triangle by sides and by angles.

11.   **12.**

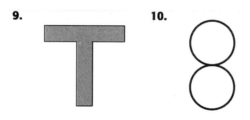

13. What is the measure of each interior angle of a regular dodecagon?

Find the missing measures.

14.   **15.**

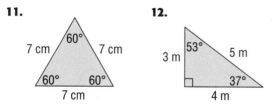

Find the measures of the unknown angles.

16.   **17.**

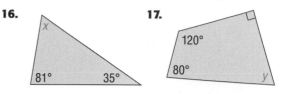

Find the measures of the unknown angles.

18.   **19.**

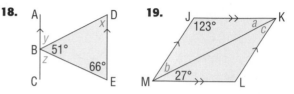

Name each polyhedron, and state its number of faces, edges, and vertices.

20.   **21.**

22.

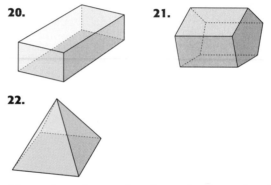

Name the polygons that form the faces of each polyhedron. State the number of each type.

23. hexagonal prism   **24.** cube

Name each three-dimensional shape and draw its net.

25.   **26.**

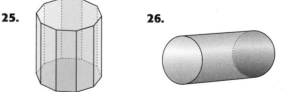

Sketch and name the polyhedron made from each net.

27.   **28.**

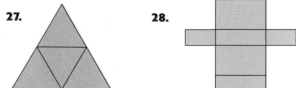

Using the Strategies

1. Find the missing number.

1	3	5	7
3	7	15	27
5	15	37	79
7	27	79	?

2. Three points are marked on the circumference of a circle. If you join each point to every other point, you divide the circle into 4 regions.

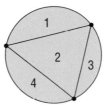

a) Into how many regions do you divide the circle if you start with 4 points?

b) Into how many regions do you divide the circle if you start with 5 points?

3. There are 16 points on the grid. How many squares can be made by joining the points?

```
A   B
C   D   E   F
G   H   I   J
K   L   M   N
    O   P
```

4. Ashir works in the Cookie Loft. A package of oatmeal cookies sells for $1.67, and a package of chocolate chip cookies sells for $1.91. One day, Ashir sold 141 packages of cookies for a total of $255.39. How many packages of each kind of cookie did he sell?

5. If you have 10 coins that total 49¢, what coins do you have?

6. The towns of Acton and Barton are located across from each other on the opposite sides of a lake. Every hour, on the hour, a passenger boat leaves Acton for Barton. It arrives at Barton 1 h later. Sharma left Barton for Acton at 14:15 in her boat. She sailed directly to Acton and arrived at 16:15. How many boats going from Acton to Barton did she meet?

7. One month, John wrote cheques on his bank account for $14.95, $67.80, $21.40, and $114.60. He made one $80.00 withdrawal at the automatic teller. He made two deposits, one for $60.00 and the other for $156.80. At the end of the month, he had $87.88 in his account. How much money was in his account at the start of the month?

8. Maria left the corner grocery store and rode her bicycle 4 blocks north, 3 blocks west, 1 block south, 6 blocks east, 5 blocks south, then 3 blocks east. What is the smallest number of blocks she can ride to get back to the grocery store?

9. Sketch a graph of the number of students in your school gym versus the time of day on a regular Monday.

10. Three students, Tanya, Darrell, and Susan, play in the school band. They play the trumpet, drums, and saxophone. No person's name begins with the same letter as the instrument he or she plays. Susan does not play the trumpet. What instrument does each person play?

DATA BANK

1. Arrange these distances from shortest to longest.

- the driving distance from Edmonton to Victoria
- the length of the South Saskatchewan River
- the flying distance from Toronto to Charlottetown

2. Canada has 9% of the world's fresh water. What percent of the world's fresh water is in Quebec?

CHAPTER 10

Statistics and Probability

A *meteor*, or shooting star, is a small piece of rock or metal that burns up in the Earth's atmosphere. A meteor that strikes the Earth is called a *meteorite*. The best time to see meteors is between midnight and dawn.

Astronomers have collected data about the major annual meteor showers we can see. The names of the showers, the constellations from which they seem to come, and their rates are shown in the table.

Name of Shower	Constellation	Date	Rate (number per hour)	
			Average	Maximum
Quadrantids	Draco	January 4	50	100
Lyrids	Lyra	April 21	5	15
Eta Aquarids	Aquarius	May 4	10	20
Capricornids	Capricornus	July 25	15	30
Delta Aquarids	Aquarius	July 27–29	20	35
Perseids	Perseus	August 12	30	70
Orionids	Orion	October 20–22	15	35
Taurids	Taurus	November 1–4	10	15
Leonids	Leo	November 16	15	20
Geminids	Gemini	December 13	50	80
Ursids	Ursa Minor	December 22	10	15

In which season — fall, winter, spring, or summer — can we see the most meteors?

In which month can we see the most meteors?

How would astronomers collect data about meteor showers?

The Paper-and-Pencil Olympics

Complete the following 4 activities in your group. Decide as a group on the order in which group members will attempt each event. For each event, compare your group's average with the averages of other groups and decide what score best represents your class.

Activity ❶ The 100-m Dash

1. Draw a track with ten 1-cm squares in a row.

2. When it is your turn to be the runner, place a pencil on the start. With your eyes closed, try to put one mark in each square. You score 1 point for each square that contains one and only one mark.

3. Run the race once. Find the average of your group's scores.

Activity ❷ The Hammer Throw

1. Draw a hammer throw area 11 cm long and 1 cm wide, marking every centimetre as shown.

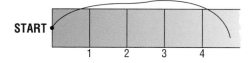

2. When it is your turn to be the thrower, place a pencil on the start and close your eyes. Draw an arc without lifting the pencil. The score on the throw is the farthest score line passed. The score is 0 if the throw does not leave and then reenter the hammer throw area.

3. Throw the hammer once. Find the average of your group's scores.

Activity ❸ The Long Jump

1. Draw a jumping pit 13 cm long and 1.5 cm wide, marking every centimetre as shown.

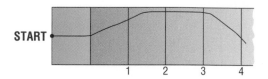

2. When it is your turn to be the jumper, place a pencil on the start and close your eyes. Draw a straight line into the first shaded box, then an arc into the sand pit. The score on a jump is the farthest score line passed. The score is 0 if the jump does not start in the first shaded box or end in the sand pit.

3. Jump twice. Record your better score. Find the average of your group's scores.

Activity ❹ The Javelin

1. Draw a throwing area 11 cm long and 1 cm wide, marking every centimetre as shown.

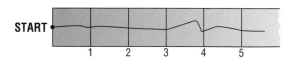

2. When it is your turn to be the thrower, place a pencil on the start and close your eyes. Draw a line, without lifting the pencil. The score on a throw is the farthest score line passed. If any part of the line leaves the throwing area, the score is 0.

3. Take two throws. Record the higher score. Find the average of your group's scores.

Warm Up

Find 25% of each number.

1. 60   **2.** 200   **3.** 500

4. 380   **5.** 164   **6.** 14

Calculate.

7. 72% of 360   **8.** 39% of 360

9. $22\frac{1}{2}$% of 360   **10.** 4% of 360

11. 55% of 360   **12.** 87% of 360

Write each fraction as a decimal. Round your answer to the nearest hundredth, if necessary.

13. $\frac{2}{3}$ **14.** $\frac{3}{8}$ **15.** $\frac{17}{20}$

16. $\frac{32}{36}$ **17.** $\frac{13}{52}$ **18.** $\frac{99}{115}$

Write each fraction as a percent. Round your answer to the nearest tenth of a percent, if necessary.

19. $\frac{2}{5}$ **20.** $\frac{17}{20}$ **21.** $\frac{4}{9}$

22. $\frac{7}{8}$ **23.** $\frac{11}{20}$ **24.** $\frac{5}{12}$

Write each decimal as a percent.

25. 0.8   **26.** 0.43   **27.** 0.551

28. 0.625   **29.** 0.05   **30.** 0.075

What percent is the first number of the second number? Round your answer to the nearest percent.

31. 37, 95   **32.** 52, 114

33. 682, 1250   **34.** 375, 550

35. 198, 1050   **36.** 4690, 5000

Find the average of each pair of numbers.

37. 68, 84   **38.** 49, 71

39. 55, 62   **40.** 27, 34

Mental Math

Calculate.

1. 50% of 200   **2.** 25% of 80

3. 10% of 10   **4.** 50% of 40

5. 25% of 20   **6.** 75% of 200

7. 1% of 100   **8.** 1% of 500

9. 10% of 80   **10.** 25% of 1000

Calculate.

11. 37 + 43 + 50   **12.** 41 − 11 + 16

13. 78 + 22 − 9   **14.** 32 + 56 − 16

15. 21 + 37 + 19   **16.** 54 + 13 − 24

17. 47 − 12 − 17   **18.** 68 + 12 + 4

19. 74 − 11 − 4   **20.** 99 − 83 + 1

Multiply.

21. 4 × 300   **22.** 0.5 × 200

23. 5 × 800   **24.** 7 × 600

25. 0.2 × 700   **26.** 0.3 × 100

27. 0.8 × 900   **28.** 9 × 900

29. 4 × 3000   **30.** 0.2 × 2000

Simplify.

31. 0.7 × 100   **32.** 1.3 × 1000

33. 14 ÷ 100   **34.** 0.6 ÷ 10

35. 0.12 × 1000   **36.** 0.005 × 100

37. 24 ÷ 1000   **38.** 8.8 ÷ 100

Simplify.

39. 4 ÷ 0.1   **40.** 200 × 0.1

41. 300 × 0.01   **42.** 100 ÷ 0.001

43. 1.2 × 0.01   **44.** 1.2 ÷ 0.01

45. 0.2 ÷ 0.1   **46.** 0.2 × 0.1

10.1 Collecting Data

Statistics is the science of collecting and organizing number facts.

Every 10 years, a **census** is conducted in Canada. A census gathers information from an entire population.

To decide how popular a radio station is, a polling company asks *some* listeners which station they listen to. The people asked are called a **sample.** Their responses are used to represent *all* radio listeners, called the **population.**

Activity: Complete the Survey Sheet

Natalia took a survey to find out which 5 activities would be most popular for the Smithville Winter Carnival. She asked a sample of carnival volunteers to choose one favourite activity each.

Copy and complete the survey sheet by writing the sum of the tallies in the frequency column.

Survey Sheet		
Activity	Tally	Frequency
Broomball Tournament	|||| |||| |||| ||||	
Cross-Country Skiing	|||| |||| ||||	
Scavenger Hunt	|||| |||| |||	
Skating Party	|||| |||| |||| |||| |||| |||	
Sleigh Ride	|||| |||| |||| |||| |||| ||||	
Snow Sculpting	|||| |||| |||| |||| |||| ||||		
Snowshoeing	|||| |||| |||| ||||	
Snow Snake Competition	|||| |||| |||| ||||	
Tobogganing	|||| |||| |||| |||| ||||	

Inquire

1. What were the 5 most popular activities?

2. How else might Natalia have decided on the most popular activities?

 3. Why did Natalia survey carnival volunteers, rather than members of the ski club or employees of the skating rink?

A sample for a survey should be a **random sample.** In a random sample, each member of the population has the same chance of being picked. Computers are sometimes used to select random samples.

If each member does not have an equal chance of being picked, the sample is a **biased sample.** A biased sample may give misleading results.

Natalia collected the information by asking people for their opinion. In other words, she conducted a personal survey.

You can also gather information from:
- a telephone survey
- a library
- the Internet and other computer networks
- a mail survey
- an expert
- a data bank
- magazines, books, and newspapers

 Name one advantage and one disadvantage of using each method.

Problems and Applications

1. A survey was conducted to see how people like their eggs. Each person was asked to name one favourite type.

How People Like Their Eggs		
Type	Tally	Frequency
Boiled	卌 卌 卌 II	
Fried	卌 卌 卌 卌 卌 III	
Omelette	IIII	
Poached	II	
Scrambled	卌 卌 卌 卌 卌 卌 IIII	

a) Copy and complete the tally sheet.
b) How many people liked their eggs poached?
c) Which was the most popular type?
d) How many times more people liked scrambled eggs than liked boiled eggs?
e) How many people were surveyed?

2. Terry used an almanac to list the countries that had won at least 3 gold medals in women's Olympic alpine skiing events, up to, and including, the 1994 Winter Olympics. He recorded his results using these abbreviations: A for Austria, C for Canada, F for France, G for Germany (East and/or West), I for Italy, S for Switzerland, and U for the United States of America.

S U A U U S G S G S C A F F A C F S S U
G C G A S U I G A S S A C I A A G U I S

a) Complete a survey sheet for the data.
b) Order the countries that won at least 3 gold medals from most medals won to least medals won.
c) What was the total number of gold medals awarded to these countries?
d) Use your research skills to name the Canadian women who won gold medals.

3. Would the following information come from a census or a sample? Explain.
a) Eight students in a grade 8 class have dogs for pets.

b) There are 4000 maple trees in the forest.
c) There were 500 000 television sets tuned to the Canadian Figure Skating Championships.
d) The population of Snow Valley is 14 764.

4. Suppose you were asked to find out the favourite restaurant in your town and you decided to survey public opinion.
a) Who would make up the population?
b) How would you select a sample so that it was not biased?
c) Describe a sample that would be biased.
d) Suggest a way of finding out the favourite restaurant without asking people's opinions.

5. Work with a classmate and choose a method to gather data on the following. Give reasons for your choices.
a) the names and heights of the 6 tallest mountains in Canada
b) the most popular television program on Thursday evening in your town
c) the most popular home video game in your school
d) the value of an old coin
e) the least popular newspaper cartoon in your community
f) the weather in Miami in February

PATTERN POWER

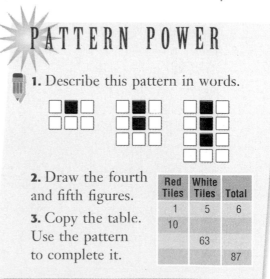

1. Describe this pattern in words.

2. Draw the fourth and fifth figures.

3. Copy the table. Use the pattern to complete it.

Red Tiles	White Tiles	Total
1	5	6
10		
	63	
		87

10.2 Making Predictions

Activity: Study the Information

To predict how much plastic waste was thrown out from lunch during a year, the students from a grade 8 class collected and sorted plastic lunch waste for 5 days. They chose 5 days as a sample to represent the school year.

The table lists the types of waste collected and the number of each item.

Sandwich Bags	937	Juice Containers	379
Straws	174	Pudding Containers	39
Yogurt Containers	29	Spoons	38

Inquire

1. Calculate the average number of each item that would be thrown out each day.

2. Students eat lunch in school about 180 times in a year. Use your answer to question 1 to predict the number of each item thrown out in a year.

3. Why did the students use 5 days as a sample instead of 1 day?

4. Suggest another way of predicting the amount of waste for a year.

Example

There are about 10 000 people 12 years of age or older in Greensville. Francine conducted a survey to predict how often they go to the movies in a year. She chose 50 people for her sample and used a telephone survey. Use the results of Francine's survey to predict how often the people of Greensville go to the movies.

Survey Sheet	
Movies Per Year	**Tally**
0	‖‖ ‖‖ ‖‖ ‖‖ I
1 to 4	‖‖ ‖‖ ‖‖ I
5 to 8	‖‖ I
9 to 12	III
13 or more	IIII

Solution

Total the tallies for each category. Write each total as a percent of the people surveyed.

Movies Per Year	Tally	Frequency	Fraction	Percent
0	‖‖ ‖‖ ‖‖ ‖‖ I	21	$\frac{21}{50}$	42%
1 to 4	‖‖ ‖‖ ‖‖ I	16	$\frac{16}{50}$	32%
5 to 8	‖‖ I	6	$\frac{6}{50}$	12%
9 to 12	III	3	$\frac{3}{50}$	6%
13 or more	IIII	4	$\frac{4}{50}$	8%

Apply the percents to the 10 000 people of Greensville.

Movies Per Year	Percent	Number of People
0	42%	42% of 10 000 = 4200
1 to 4	32%	32% of 10 000 = 3200
5 to 8	12%	12% of 10 000 = 1200
9 to 12	6%	6% of 10 000 = 600
13 or more	8%	8% of 10 000 = 800

Francine predicted that 4200 do not go to the movies, 3200 go 1 to 4 times a year, 1200 go 5 to 8 times, 600 go 9 to 12 times, and 800 go 13 or more times.

Problems and Applications

1. A grade 8 class collected the following lunchroom waste over 5 days.

Fruit scraps: 20 kg
Food scraps: 15 kg
Whole fresh fruit: 10 kg
Non-food waste: 5 kg

The students eat lunch in school about 180 times in a year. Predict the amount of waste for each item in a year.

2. There are 30 000 households in Picton. Two hundred households were surveyed to determine people's favourite shopping days. The table gives the results.

Favourite Shopping Days		
Day	**Frequency**	**Percent**
Monday	8	
Tuesday	10	
Wednesday	24	
Thursday	26	
Friday	34	
Saturday	58	
Sunday	14	
No Preference	26	

a) Copy and complete the table.
b) Use the percents to predict the number of the 30 000 households in which each day is preferred.
c) In how many households is there no preference?

3. There are about 11 000 000 households in Canada. The table shows how many of every 50 households had certain kinds of juice in the refrigerator.

Juices in Refrigerators		
Juice	**Frequency**	**Percent of Households**
Apple	12	
Blended Fruit	9	
Cranberry	6	
Grapefruit	5	
Grape	5	
Orange	28	
Tomato/Vegetable	4	

a) Copy and complete the table.
b) Why do the percents not total 100%?
c) How many Canadian households keep each type of juice in the refrigerator?

4. The table shows some creatures that people fear.

Feared Creatures	
Creature	**Percent**
Beetles	3%
Mice	38%
Wasps/Bees	45%
Worms	2%
Don't Know	12%

a) Predict how many students in your school fear each type of creature.
b) The population of North America is about 300 000 000. About how many North Americans fear each type of creature?

5. A national survey asked 1200 teens aged 13 to 17 which of the following places or events they had attended in the last year. The table gives the result of the survey.

Events That Teenagers Attended	
Place or Event	**Percent Who Attended**
Professional Sports	44%
Art Museum	31%
Other Museum	26%
Rock Concert	28%
Symphony Concert	11%

a) How many of the 1200 teens attended each place or event?
b) Why does the percent column total more than 100%?
c) Survey your class to see how many attended these places or events last year. Compare your class results with the national survey and give reasons for any differences.

6. Decide on a strategy for estimating the number of Canadian households that have dogs or cats for pets.

Surveys

People who design surveys must consider
a) the question(s) they are going to ask
b) the method of asking the question(s)
c) the type of sample they are going to use

Activity ❶ Deciding What to Ask

A **biased answer** is an answer affected by the wording of the question.

1. Each of the following questions is likely to result in a biased answer. Explain why.
a) Would you rather go to beautiful, sunny Florida or to rainy England?
b) Do you agree that John Turner was Canada's best prime minister?
c) Do you think that "junk food" is bad for you?

2. Work with a partner to rewrite each of the above questions so that the answer is less likely to be biased.

Activity ❷ Deciding How to Ask Questions

Mail-in or electronic questionnaires, personal interviews, and telephone interviews are three methods of asking questions.

1. Suppose you design a survey and must choose one of these methods of questioning people. Which method do you think would
a) cost the most? cost the least? Explain.
b) result in the most truthful answers? the least truthful answers? Explain.
c) be the most time-consuming? the least time-consuming? Explain.
d) yield the most replies? the least replies? Explain.
e) yield the most detailed replies? the least detailed replies? Explain.

2. Which method of questioning would you use for each of the following questions? Explain.
a) Which is your favourite television program on a Sunday evening?
b) Have you ever been given too much change in a store and failed to report it?
c) How many telephones do you have in your home?
d) Do you think that convicted criminals should have to compensate their victims?

Activity ❸ Deciding Whom to Ask

These are three of the types of samples you could use in a survey.

In a **random sample**, every person in the population has an equally likely chance of being chosen.

In a **clustered sample**, a specialized group of the population is sampled. For example, if you wish to know the most popular type of hockey stick, you could ask a sample selected randomly from a group of hockey players.

In a **stratified sample**, the population is divided into different groups. Samples are chosen in the same proportion as the numbers in each group. For example, suppose a school has 200 grade 9 students, 150 grade 10 students, and 100 grade 11 students. A stratified sample might include 20 students selected randomly from grade 9, 15 from grade 10, and 10 from grade 11.

Decide which type of sample you would use to survey the following. Explain.

1. the best design for a new national flag

2. the average number of children in a household

3. the favourite colour of Canadians

4. the snacks to sell in the school cafeteria

5. the best baseball glove available

Collecting Data with Computers

Activity ❶ Using the Internet

1. With your classmates, make up a list of questions you would like to include in a survey, to be completed by students in other schools. For example, you might ask
How many hours of homework do you do in a week?
How many pets do you have?
What is your favourite colour?
What is your favourite hobby, and how long do you spend on it in one week?
Input your questions into the computer and include questions about the name and age of the person who responds, and whether the person is male or female.

2. Invite any class on your Internet service to take part in your survey. Include schools across Canada and in other countries.

3. Send your questions to the Internet addresses of those classes that wish to take part in your survey. Ask each class to organize the results of each question in a table and return them within a specified time period, say 2 weeks.

4. Combine the results of all the participants. Organize the information from your survey into categories, based on such information as age, country, and so on.

5. Use your data to answer the questions in your survey. For example:
The average number of hours of homework done by a grade 8 student in Canada is ▇ h. For grade 8 girls, the most popular colour is ▇.

6. Write a report of your conclusions and send it to all of the classes that participated.

7. Share your conclusions with the whole school by setting up a display.

Activity ❷ Information from a Census

Research how Statistics Canada conducts a census.

1. List 3 questions included in the census.

2. Describe the method that people use to enter their responses on the census form.

3. How are the frequencies of the responses tallied?

4. Describe ways in which you think the government can make use of the census results.

Activity ❸ Information from Bar Codes

Research the answers to these questions.

1. What is a bar code?

2. What information does the bar code give?

3. What happens when the bar code of an item is scanned at the check-out counter in a store?

4. What does the store do with the information from the scanner?

How Much History Do Canadians Know?

The Gallup Corporation, a large polling company, gave the following multiple choice history test to a sample of 1016 Canadian adults. For each question, each adult could choose one of the answers provided or could say "don't know."

1. What was the name of Canada's first Prime Minister?

a) W.L. Mackenzie King **b)** Sir Wilfrid Laurier
c) Sir John A. Macdonald **d)** Louis-Joseph Papineau
e) Samuel de Champlain **f)** Sir Robert Borden

2. Who was Canada's longest serving Prime Minister?

a) Sir John A. Macdonald **b)** John Diefenbaker
c) Sir Wilfrid Laurier **d)** Pierre Trudeau
e) W.L. Mackenzie King **f)** Louis St. Laurent

3. Who was the leader of the North-West Rebellion of 1885?

a) Sir John A. Macdonald **b)** William Lyon Mackenzie
c) Gabriel Dumont **d)** Louis-Joseph Papineau
e) Louis Riel **f)** Sir Charles Tupper

4. What year was Confederation?

a) 1776 **b)** 1865
c) 1812 **d)** 1867
e) 1837 **f)** 1885

5. Who was the leader of the English army at the Battle of the Plains of Abraham?

a) Joseph Howe **b)** John Durham
c) Edward Cornwallis **d)** Louis-Joseph de Montcalm
e) James Wolfe **f)** Sir Isaac Brock

6. Who was the leader of the French army at the Battle of the Plains of Abraham?

a) Louis-Joseph de Montcalm **b)** Samuel de Champlain
c) Louis-Joseph Papineau **d)** Jacques Cartier
e) James Wolfe **f)** Louis de Buade Frontenac

The following are the results of the test.

1. What was the name of Canada's first Prime Minister?

2. Who was Canada's longest serving Prime Minister?

3. Who was the leader of the North-West Rebellion of 1885?

4. What year was Confederation?

5. Who was the leader of the English army at the Battle of the Plains of Abraham?

6. Who was the leader of the French army at the Battle of the Plains of Abraham?

Correct Answer	Other Answer	Don't Know
40%	16%	44%
18%	56%	26%
37%	2%	61%
45%	15%	40%
31%	5%	64%
25%	8%	67%

Activity ❶

Have each member of the class try the test. Record the results in a table like the one above. Compare your class results with the results shown in the table.

Activity ❷

The following table shows how the 1016 Canadian adults did by how many questions they answered correctly.

Number of Questions Answered Correctly	Percent of the Canadian Adults Tested
6	5%
5	9%
4	10%
3	13%
2	15%
1	17%

Complete a similar table for your class. Compare your class results with those of the 1016 Canadian adults who took the test.

Activity ❸

1. If 3 questions correct out of 6 is a pass,
a) what percent of the sample of Canadian adults passed?
b) how many of the sample of Canadian adults passed?
c) what percent of your class passed?

2. a) What percent of the sample of Canadian adults did not get any questions correct?
b) What percent of your class did not get any questions correct?

Activity ❹

Is this 6-question test a good measure of Canadians' knowledge of Canada's history? Compare your conclusion and your reasons with your classmates'.

10.3 Reading and Drawing Bar Graphs

Bar graphs are used to compare things.

Activity: Study the Graph

The double bar graph shows how cats and dogs react around strangers.

Inquire

1. What does the vertical axis tell you?

2. Is a dog or cat more likely to be friendly to strangers?

3. About what percent of cats are hostile to strangers?

4. About what percent of dogs are aloof from strangers?

5. How might a statistician collect these data?

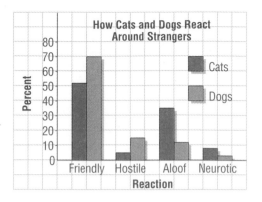

Example

The table gives the average number of hours students spend in class each year in several countries.

Display these data on a bar graph.

Canada	975	China	858
Denmark	1040	France	972
Germany	760	Japan	933
New Zealand	1000	United Kingdom	950

Solution

1. Draw the horizontal axis and decide on the width of the bars. Label the axis.

2. Draw the vertical axis. Since the data go from 760 to 1040, mark the vertical axis from 700 to 1100. Make a break mark at the bottom of the axis to show that the scale between 0 and 700 is not included. Label the axis.

3. Plot the number of hours for each country and draw the bars.

4. Give the graph a title.

Redraw the graph without using a break mark on the vertical axis. Compare the graphs and state the advantages and disadvantages of using the break mark.

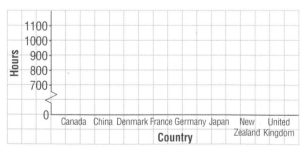

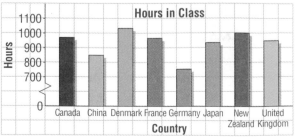

Problems and Applications

1. The horizontal bar graph shows the average distance each person drives a car in a year in each province. To find each figure, the total distance travelled by all the cars in a province is divided by the total population of the province.

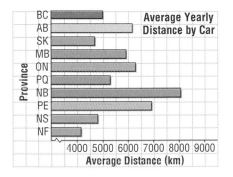

a) In which province is the average distance highest? lowest?

b) About how many more kilometres are driven in Manitoba than in Saskatchewan?

c) In which province is the average distance closest to twice the average distance in Newfoundland?

d) The state of Wyoming has the highest value in North America at 20 600 km per person per year. How much greater is this than the highest value in Canada?

e) List some possible reasons for the differences in the distances.

f) Why are environmentalists interested in these statistics?

2. The table gives the number of people for every automobile in several countries.

Brazil	9.6	Canada	2.2
France	2.4	Japan	3.8
Poland	7.8	Portugal	6.5
U.K.	2.9	U.S.A.	1.7

Display these data on a horizontal bar graph.

3. The table gives percents of the areas of the Great Lakes that lie in Canada and the United States.

Lake	Percent in U.S.A.	Percent in Canada
Erie	50%	50%
Huron	38%	62%
Michigan	100%	0%
Ontario	45%	55%
Superior	65%	35%

Display these data on a double bar graph.

4. The table gives the chief sources of energy for each province by percent of each type used.

Province	Percent of Energy Use		
	Natural Gas	Petroleum	Electricity
DC	31%	42%	25%
AB	49%	33%	16%
SK	48%	36%	14%
MB	37%	38%	23%
ON	36%	33%	21%
PQ	16%	41%	41%
NB	2%	66%	31%
PE	3%	83%	12%
NS	2%	76%	21%
NF	0%	68%	30%

a) Display these data on a triple bar graph.

b) Which provinces use a similar amount and type of energy?

5. With a partner, choose a subject for which you would like to make a comparison. For example, you could choose to compare the favourite rock groups, radio stations, or sports of your classmates.

a) Predict what a bar graph of the comparison would look like.

b) Collect the data and display them on a bar graph.

c) Compare your predicted bar graph with the graph of the data.

10.4 Reading and Drawing Broken-Line Graphs

A broken-line graph is used to show how
something changes over a period of time.

Activity: Study the Graph

The graph shows worldwide whale catches
from 1908 to 1988.

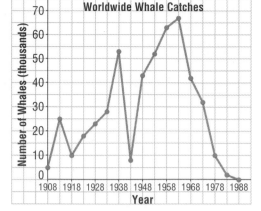

Inquire

1. About how many whales were caught in 1968?

2. In what years were about 10 000 whales caught?

3. In what year do you think the harpoon gun
was invented? Explain.

4. a) In what year was there the greatest number of catches?
b) About how many whales were caught that year?

5. Why did catches drop in 1918 and 1943?

6. Why were there no catches in 1988?

Example

The table gives the areas burned by forest fires in Canada in 7 time periods.

Time Period	1920s	1930s	1940s	1950s	1960s	1970s	1980s
Area (millions of hectares)	13	14	11	9	10	13	24

Display these data on a broken-line graph.

Solution

1. Draw and label the horizontal axis.
Mark the axis from 1920s to 1980s.

2. Draw and label the vertical axis.
Mark the vertical axis from 0 to 24.

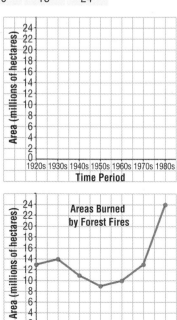

3. Plot the areas burned for different time periods.
Join the points with straight line segments.

4. Give the graph a title.

Why did the area burned by forest fires increase
so much in the 1980s?

Problems and Applications

1. The graph shows music sales in Canada, in millions of units by format, over a 20-year period.

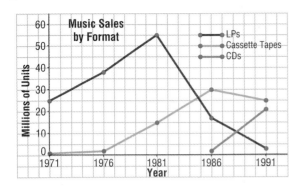

a) About how many LPs were sold in 1981?

b) How many more cassettes than LPs were sold in 1986?

c) What was the difference in CD sales and cassette sales in 1986? in 1991?

d) Which sales showed the greater increase, LPs from 1971 to 1981 or cassettes from 1976 to 1986?

e) Did the total sales of cassettes and CDs in 1991 equal the sales of LPs in 1981? Explain.

2. The table gives the world's population, in billions, from 1900 to 1980 and the United Nation's projected population until 2020.

Year	1900	1920	1940	1960	1980	2000	2020
Population (billions)	1.6	1.9	2.3	3.0	4.4	6.2	7.7

Display these data on a broken-line graph.

3. The table gives the amount of sleep people get each day at different ages.

Age	Newborn	5	10	15
Sleep (h/day)	19	11	8.5	8

Age	20	30	40	50	60
Sleep (h/day)	8	7.5	7	6	5.5

Display these data on a broken-line graph.

4. The table gives the average daily temperature, in degrees Celsius, for each month in Vancouver and Sydney, Australia.

Month	Average Daily Temperature (°C)	
	Vancouver	Sydney
January	2	22
February	3	22
March	5	21
April	9	18
May	12	15
June	15	13
July	18	12
August	17	13
September	13	15
October	9	18
November	5	19
December	2	21

a) Display these data on a double broken-line graph, that is, as two broken-line graphs on the same set of axes.

b) Why might a clothing manufacturer be interested in these data?

5. The table gives the approximate numbers of livestock, in millions, on Canadian farms in different years.

Year	Number of Livestock (millions)		
	Sheep	Cattle	Pigs
1910	3	7	4
1920	3	8	3
1930	4	8	4
1940	2	9	6
1950	2	8	5
1960	1	12	5
1970	1	15	7
1980	1	13	6
1990	2	13	11

Display these data on a triple broken-line graph.

6. With a partner, collect data about the position of a song in the charts over time. Display the data on a broken-line graph.

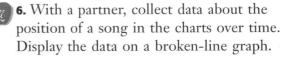

323

10.5 Reading and Drawing Circle Graphs

Activity: Study the Graph

Circle graphs are used to show how something is divided. The circle graph at the right shows what people around the world use for eating.

How People Eat

Hands Alone 8%

Knives, Forks, Spoons 45%

Hands and Knife 11%

Chopsticks 36%

Inquire

1. What is the world's present population to the nearest billion?

2. About how many people in the world use knives, forks, and spoons for eating?

3. About how many people use chopsticks for eating?

4. Do most of the people in the world use a knife?

Example

A survey asked 500 people at what time they usually get out of bed. The results are shown in the table.

Display this information on a circle graph.

Time	Number
Between 05:00 and 06:00	125
Between 06:00 and 07:00	160
Between 07:00 and 08:00	75
Between 08:00 and 09:00	50
Other	90
Total	500

Solution

1. Write each number as a percent of the total.

Between 05:00 and 06:00 $\frac{125}{500} \times 100\% = 25\%$

Between 06:00 and 07:00 $\frac{160}{500} \times 100\% = 32\%$

Between 07:00 and 08:00 $\frac{75}{500} \times 100\% = 15\%$

Between 08:00 and 09:00 $\frac{50}{500} \times 100\% = 10\%$

Other $\frac{90}{500} \times 100\% = 18\%$

2. A circle has 360°. Calculate each percent of a circle. Round to the nearest degree, if necessary.

25% of 360° = 0.25 × 360° = 90°

32% of 360° = 0.32 × 360° $\doteq$ 115°

15% of 360° = 0.15 × 360° = 54°

10% of 360° = 0.1 × 360° = 36°

18% of 360° = 0.18 × 360° $\doteq$ 65°

3. Draw a circle and measure each angle with a protractor. Label each sector with a name and a percent. Give the graph a title.

When People Get Out of Bed

Between 05:00 and 06:00 25%

Other 18%

Between 08:00 and 09:00 10%

Between 07:00 and 08:00 15%

Between 06:00 and 07:00 32%

Problems and Applications

1. North Americans eat, on average, 18 L of frozen desserts a year. The circle graph shows the kinds of frozen desserts.

Frozen Dessert Consumption

Ice Cream 63%
Sherbet 3%
Ice Milk 24%
Yogurt 10%

a) How many litres of ice cream does a person eat?

b) How many litres of sherbet does a person eat?

c) How many litres of frozen yogurt does a person eat?

d) How many litres of ice milk does a person eat?

2. The circle graphs show the results of a survey of 2000 people. The survey asked how many movies the people watch every month and where they watch them.

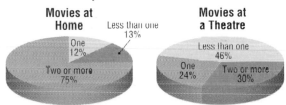

Movies at Home
Less than one 13%
One 12%
Two or more 75%

Movies at a Theatre
Less than one 46%
One 24%
Two or more 30%

a) How many watch 1 movie at home?

b) How many watch 1 movie at a theatre?

c) How many watch 2 or more movies at home?

d) How many watch 2 or more at a theatre?

3. The data show the ways in which our oceans are polluted.

Dumping or from Rivers	54%
Air Pollution	33%
Shipping	12%
Oil, Gas Production	1%

Display these data on a circle graph.

4. The following shows how the average person will spend his or her life.

Activity	Time (years)
Sleeping	24
At Work and School	14
Watching TV	12
Socializing	4
Reading	3
Eating	3
Bathing and Grooming	4
Miscellaneous	11

Display these data on a circle graph.

5. Canada won 6 gold, 6 silver, and 7 bronze medals at the Summer Olympics in Barcelona.

a) Represent these data on a circle graph.

b) Sylvie Frechette won a silver medal for Canada in solo synchronized swimming. A judge's scoring error cost her the gold medal. The error was later corrected, and Sylvie's silver medal was replaced by a gold medal. Correct the data and draw a new circle graph.

6. Choose a subject you would like to display on a circle graph. A possible subject might be: How the broadcast of a sporting event is divided between playing time, announcer talk, and commercials.

a) Predict how the circle graph will look.

b) Collect the data and display them on a circle graph.

c) Compare your graph of the data with your predicted graph.

WORD POWER

Starting with the word PINK, change one letter at a time, forming a new word each time, until you reach the word ROSE. The best solution has the fewest steps.

10.6 Reading and Drawing Pictographs

A graph that uses pictures or symbols to display data is called a pictograph or picture graph.

Activity: Study the Graph

The pictograph shows the number of albums sold for some top-selling Canadian record albums.

Top-Selling Albums	
Rockinghorse, Alannah Myles	⊙ ⊙ (
Reckless, Bryan Adams	⊙ ⊙ ⊙ ⊙ ⊙ ⊙ ⊙ ⊙ ⊙ (
Greatest Hits, Anne Murray	⊙ ⊙ ⊙ ⊙ ⊙ (
Alien Shores, Platinum Blonde	⊙ ⊙ ⊙ ⊙ (
Boy in the Box, Corey Hart	⊙ ⊙ ⊙ ⊙ ⊙ ⊙ ⊙ ⊙ ⊙ (
The Thin Red Line, Glass Tiger	⊙ ⊙ ⊙ ⊙ (

Each ⊙ represents 100 000 albums.

Inquire

1. What were the two best-selling albums? About how many albums were sold of each?

2. About how many of Glass Tiger's *The Thin Red Line* album were sold?

3. About how many of Alannah Myles' *Rockinghorse* album were sold?

4. What is the difference between a pictograph and a bar graph?

5. When would you use a pictograph instead of a bar graph?

Example

A few species of plants and animals have survived from prehistoric times. The table lists some of them and the number of years they have been on Earth.

Display these data on a pictograph.

Species	Millions of Years
Giant Redwood	110
Peripatus (worm)	520
Australian Lungfish	230
Duck-billed Platypus	160
Lingula (sea animal)	570
Tuatara (reptile)	190

Solution

Let the symbol 🐢 represent 100 million years. Round each number to the nearest 50 million years, or half a symbol, to find the number of symbols for each prehistoric survivor.

110	1 symbol
520	5 symbols
230	2.5 symbols
160	1.5 symbols
570	5.5 symbols
190	2 symbols

Draw the graph. Include a title. Also include a key to explain what the symbol represents.

Why would you not use each symbol to represent 10 million years? 500 million years?

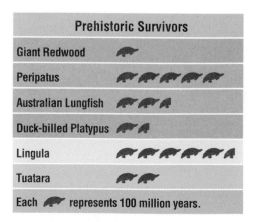

Prehistoric Survivors	
Giant Redwood	🐢
Peripatus	🐢 🐢 🐢 🐢 🐢
Australian Lungfish	🐢 🐢 🐢
Duck-billed Platypus	🐢 🐢
Lingula	🐢 🐢 🐢 🐢 🐢
Tuatara	🐢 🐢

Each 🐢 represents 100 million years.

Problems and Applications

1. The pictograph shows the water used per person per day in the home in several countries.

Water Use Per Person Per Day
Germany
Canada
China
Japan
U.K.
U.S.A.
Each represents 50 L.

a) In which country is the most water used?
b) In which country is the least water used?
c) About how many litres of water does a Canadian use every day?

2. The pictograph shows the number of large dams in Canada by province. Large dams are taller than 10 m.

Canada's Large Dams
Alberta
British Columbia
Manitoba
New Brunswick
Newfoundland
Nova Scotia
Ontario
P.E.I.
Quebec
Saskatchewan
Each represents 20 dams.

a) Which province has the most large dams? About how many does it have?
b) About how many large dams are there in Alberta?
c) Which provinces have about 50% as many large dams as Newfoundland?
d) About how many more large dams are there in British Columbia than in Manitoba?
e) Can you be sure from the pictograph that Prince Edward Island has no large dams? Explain.

3. The table gives the length of railway track, in kilometres, for the 5 countries with the greatest length of railway track.

Country	Length of Railway Track (km)
China	50 000
Canada	67 000
U.S.A.	288 000
Former U.S.S.R.	240 000
India	61 000

Display these data on a pictograph.

4. The table gives the mass, in kilograms, of municipal solid waste generated by each person each year in several countries.

Country	Mass of Municipal Solid Waste (kg)
Canada	612
U.S.A.	546
Australia	695
U.K.	364
Japan	331
Italy	248

a) Display these data on a pictograph.
b) Could you display these data on a bar graph? a broken-line graph? a circle graph? Explain.

5. Choose a subject for which you can collect data from your classmates or other sources and can draw a pictograph.

a) Predict how the pictograph will look.
b) Collect the data and display them on a pictograph in a creative way.
c) Compare the pictograph of your data with your prediction.

NUMBER POWER

a) How many darts are needed to score exactly 100 on the dart board?
b) In how many ways could you score 100 on the dart board with this number of darts?

Graphics Software Packages

Microcomputer systems have four parts.

- The hardware consists of the computer, monitor, keyboard, printer, and other devices.
- The software is a program that tells the computer what to do.
- The data are the facts that people input.
- The manuals give the rules to follow when using the hardware, software, and data.

There are many types of software programs: word processing, spreadsheets, database managers, communications, and graphics. Graphics packages display information visually.

Analytical graphics packages display data on line graphs, circle graphs, and bar graphs.

Presentation graphics packages are used by sales people to make presentations. These packages allow the use of colour, pictures, a three-dimensional look, and other methods a graphic artist might use to show data.

A desktop publishing program lets you combine words and graphics to create professional-looking documents like those you see in magazines.

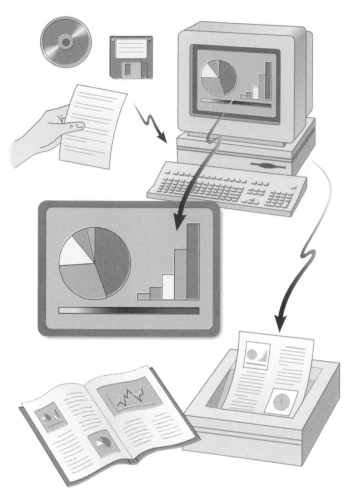

Activity ❶ Television Viewing

A national survey asked 26 000 thirteen-year-olds how many hours a day they spend watching television. The table gives the results.

No time	3%
Up to 1 h	13%
Between 1 h and 2 h	35%
Between 2 h and 3 h	29%
More than 3 h	20%

Use a graphics software package or your own methods to display these data on graphs in different ways. Draw one graph in a creative way, as a graphic artist might.

Activity ❷ Entertainment Spending

The table gives the percent of household entertainment money spent in different ways.

Recreational Equipment, Including Movie Rentals	33%
Electronic Equipment	30%
Admission Fees to Movies, Parks, Concerts	25%
Reading Material	12%

The graph at the right has been drawn using a computer graphics program.

In your group, decide how to display the data in a more appealing and interesting way than the one shown. Draw your graph. Compare your graph with your classmates' graphs.

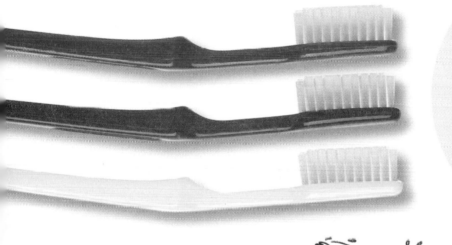

Activity ❸ Toothbrushes

Survey your class to find out what colour of toothbrush each of your classmates uses. Use a graphics software package or your own methods to display the data in an artistic way.

Activity ❹ Physical Recreational Activities

The table gives the percent of Canadians 10 years old and over who participate in these physical recreational activities.

Design and make a one-page document, using graphics and words, to describe the physical recreational activities. In your text, give reasons why some activities are more popular than others. The reasons might include cost, weather, and enjoyment.

Skating	22%
Alpine Skiing	20%
Swimming	42%
Bicycling	39%
Home Exercise	30%
Jogging	19%
Dancing	33%

Misleading Statistics

Activity ❶ Averages

In baseball, a batting average is calculated by dividing the number of hits by the number of times at bat.

1. Terry and Kelly play for the same baseball team. In the first game of a double-header, Terry had 1 hit, a home run, for 1 at bat. Kelly had 3 hits, all singles, for 4 at bats.

a) What batting average did each have for the first game?

b) Who had the better batting average?

2. In the second game, Terry had 2 hits, a double and a triple, for 5 at bats. Kelly had no hits for 1 at bat.

a) What batting average did each have for the second game?

b) Who had the better batting average?

3. Terry said, "The statistics show that I am a better hitter than Kelly." Kelly said, "The statistics show that I am the better hitter."

a) How many hits did each player have in the two games?

b) Calculate each player's batting average for the two games combined.

c) Who had the better batting average?

d) Is batting average the only way to determine if Kelly or Terry is the better hitter?

e) Who do you think is the better hitter? Explain.

Activity ❷ Bar Graphs

There are several ways to present data accurately and still mislead people.

The Sherlock's Home bookstore sold 4000 books in December.

The Mystery Place store sold 2000 books in December.

The graphs show two ways of presenting the data.

1. Are both graphs presenting the data accurately?

2. How is the second graph misleading?

3. The Sherlock's Home bookstore sold twice as many books as the Mystery Place. How many times more sales does the second graph suggest?

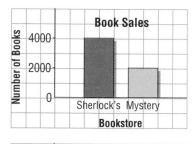

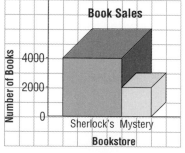

Activity ❸ Polls

Polls are used to get people's opinions. If polls are not random, the results can be misleading.

Suppose the students in your school must decide between a ski trip and a skating trip, and you know that most of them want a skating trip.

1. How could you conduct a poll to show that the students in your school prefer a ski trip?

2. How would you display the results of your poll?

Activity ❹ Line Graphs

The manager of Sherlock's Home bookstore drew this graph to show the owner of the store how sales had increased in 5 weeks.

1. How is the manager trying to mislead the owner with this graph?

2. Draw a broken-line graph to show the increase in sales in a way that is not misleading.

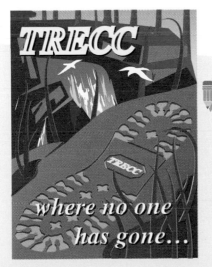

Activity ❺ Advertising

Select two popular products, such as two makes of soft drinks or two makes of shoes. Choose an advertising medium, such as television, radio, or newspapers, where both companies advertise their products.

1. Compare the ways the companies try to get you to buy their products. How are the methods different? How are they the same?

2. Do the companies try to mislead you with their advertisements? If so, how?

10.7 Mean, Median, Mode, and Range

In previous sections, graphs were used to describe and display data. Statisticians are also interested in finding a number to describe the middle or centre of a set of data.

Activity: Examine the Table

It is dangerous for aircraft to fly through thunderstorms, so air traffic controllers keep a careful watch on thunderstorm activity. The table shows the days of thunderstorms per year at airports in some Canadian cities.

Airport	Days of Thunderstorms
Edmonton	27
Halifax	9
Montreal	25
Ottawa	24
Regina	23
St. John's	3
Toronto	27
Vancouver	6
Winnipeg	27

Inquire

1. Rank the data in ascending order, that is, from lowest to highest.

2. a) What is the middle number in the new order?
b) What is the number that occurs most often?
c) Take the average of the numbers in the list.

3. The numbers from question 2 are 3 different ways to describe the centre of a set of data. Compare how effective they are at showing the centre of the data in the table.

4. What is the difference between the highest and lowest values in the data?

The 3 numbers you determined in question 2 above, are known as **measures of central tendency**.

The **mean**, or arithmetic average, is calculated by finding the sum of the data and dividing by the number of pieces of data. It is the most sensitive to changes in the data, because each piece of data helps determine it.

The **median** is the middle value when the data are arranged in numerical order. If the number of pieces of data is even, there are 2 middle values. The median is the arithmetic average of these 2 values. The median is especially useful when there are unusual data that distort the mean.

The **mode** represents popularity. It is the number that occurs most frequently. A set of data may have no mode or more than one mode.

The **range** is not a measure of central tendency. It tells us how spread out the data are. The range is the difference between the highest and lowest values. It does not give any information about the other values.

The mean, median, mode, and range help you analyze data and determine how they are grouped.

Activity: Use the Data

The golf coach asked Carla and Alicia to play 9 holes of golf to decide who would make the golf team. The score card shows the results. Alicia hit her ball into the lake on the fifth hole.

Hole	1	2	3	4	5	6	7	8	9	Total
Carla	6	4	3	7	7	6	3	4	6	46
Alicia	4	4	3	4	15	5	4	3	6	48

Inquire

1. Who won the match?

2. Who won more holes?

3. Calculate the mean score for each player. Round each answer to the nearest tenth.

4. Who had the better mean score?

5. Calculate the median score for each player.

6. Who had the better median score?

7. Determine the mode of each player's scores.

8. Who had the better mode?

9. Who should make the golf team? Explain.

Example

Frank wrote 6 tests when he took his flying course. His results were as follows.

65, 66, 100, 63, 64, 63

a) Find the mean, median, and mode of the data.

b) Which measure of central tendency best represents Frank's knowledge of flying? Explain.

Solution

a) Mean $= \dfrac{65 + 66 + 100 + 63 + 64 + 63}{6}$

$= \dfrac{421}{6}$

$\doteq 70.2$

> **EST** $70 + 70 + 100 + 60 + 60 + 60 = 420$
> $420 \div 6 = 70$

The mean is 70.2 to the nearest tenth.
To find the median, arrange the numbers in order.

63, 63, 64, 65, 66, 100

There are 2 middle numbers, 64 and 65.

The median is $\dfrac{64 + 65}{2}$ or 64.5.

The mode is 63.
So, the mean is about 70.2, the median is 64.5, and the mode is 63.

b) The median value, 64.5, probably best represents Frank's knowledge of flying. The mode is at the low end of the data, and the mean is distorted by Frank's one perfect score.

CONTINUED ▶

Practice

State the measure of central tendency that best describes each of the following.

1. the most requested song on a radio station

2. the test marks 12, 80, 82, 84, 87

3. the most popular baseball cap size

4. the mass of an adult elephant

5. the typical salary paid by a company

6. your bowling ability

Find the mean, median, mode, and range for each set of data.

7. 21, 25, 27, 26, 25

8. 13, 21, 16, 25, 18, 28, 32, 31

9. 8, 16, 28, 41, 16, 11, 8

10. 80, 40, 35, 62, 11, 80

11. 3800, 2700, 1650, 1120, 1360, 4500

Problems and Applications

12. List the following.
a) 5 different numbers with a median of 7
b) 5 different numbers with a mean of 8
c) 6 different numbers with a mean of 9
d) 5 different numbers with a range of 20

13. The list gives the shots on goal for the Hornets in their last 10 games.

$$18 \quad 18 \quad 25 \quad 19 \quad 27$$
$$18 \quad 25 \quad 19 \quad 22 \quad 27$$

a) Find the mean, mode, range, and median.
b) Explain how the following calculates the mean.

$$\frac{3 \times 18 + 2 \times 19 + 22 + 2 \times 25 + 2 \times 27}{10}$$

14. The following list shows the number of years each of Canada's first 23 Governors General served. Find the mean, median, mode, and range.

$$2, 3, 6, 5, 5, 5, 5, 6, 7, 5, 5, 5,$$
$$5, 4, 5, 6, 6, 7, 8, 6, 6, 4, 6$$

15. The table shows the number of provincial parks in each of Canada's provinces.

Province	Number of Provincial Parks
Newfoundland	93
Prince Edward Island	31
Nova Scotia	122
New Brunswick	48
Quebec	50
Ontario	261
Manitoba	147
Saskatchewan	31
Alberta	115
British Columbia	390

a) Determine the mean, median, mode, and range.
b) Does the mode give an accurate indication of the centre of these data? Explain.

16. The mean price of 6 items from a grocery store was $2.15. The mean price of another 10 items from the store was $1.75. What was the mean price of the 16 items?

17. Describe the effect of each change on the mean, median, and mode of this set of numbers.

$$8 \quad 10 \quad 11 \quad 12 \quad 13 \quad 15 \quad 18 \quad 18 \quad 21$$

a) Increase each number in the set by 2.
b) Decrease each number in the set by 3.
c) Double each number.

18. A set of numbers has a range of 20. A second set of numbers has a range of 30. The two sets of numbers are combined into a new set.
a) What is the smallest possible range of the new set? Explain.
b) Can you state a value for the greatest possible range of the new set? Explain.

19. These are Tanya's bowling scores.
145   145   168   170   174   182
a) Does the mode give an accurate indication of how well she bowls? Why?
b) Does the median give a more accurate indication of how well she bowls? Why?

20. The table shows the salaries of all the employees in a small company.

Position	Number	Annual Salary ($)
President	1	100 000
Vice-President	1	60 000
Senior Staff	4	40 000
Junior Staff	2	30 000

a) List all 8 salaries in ascending or descending order. Find the range of the salaries.
b) Find the mean, median, and mode.
c) Which measure of central tendency is closest to the centre of the data? Explain.
d) Drop the highest salary. Find the mean, median, and mode of the remaining 7 salaries.
e) Drop the lowest salary. Find the mean, median, and mode of the remaining 7 salaries.
f) Which measure of central tendency is most affected by the extreme (highest and lowest) salary values?

21. On his first four swimming tests, Lou got marks of 81, 85, 83, and 84. What mark does he need on his next test to have a mean mark of 85?

22. Is each statement always true, sometimes true, or never true? Explain.
a) If a list of numbers has a mode, it is one of the numbers in the list.
b) The median of a list of whole numbers is a whole number.
c) The mean of a list of numbers is one of the numbers in the list.
d) The mean, median, and mode of a list of numbers are not equal.

23. Find six numbers so that the mean is 10, the median is less than 10, and the largest of the six numbers is 25. Compare your numbers with your classmates'.

24. Write the following sets of numbers in ascending order. Compare your answers with a classmate's. Decide whether different answers are possible in each case.
a) 5 numbers with a mean of 15, a median of 12, and a mode of 11
b) 4 numbers with a mean of 12.5, a median of 11.5, and a mode of 10
c) 6 numbers with a mean of 20, a median of 22.5, and no mode
d) 5 numbers whose mean, median, mode, and range all equal 16

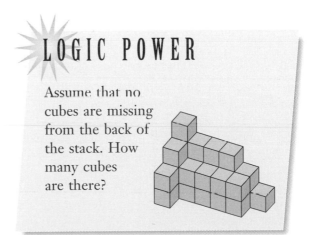

LOGIC POWER

Assume that no cubes are missing from the back of the stack. How many cubes are there?

335

10.8 Stem-and-Leaf Plots

One way of getting a quick picture of a set of data is to use a stem-and-leaf plot.

Activity: Analyze the Data

The following list shows the numbers of games won by the Calgary Flames in their first 21 seasons in the NHL.

25, 30, 34, 35, 34, 34, 41, 35, 39, 29, 32,
34, 41, 40, 46, 48, 54, 42, 46, 31, 43

The first digit of each piece of data is the **stem**, and the second digit is the **leaf.**

First, list the stems, as shown.		Then, record each leaf next to the proper stem.		Finally, arrange the leaves in order from smallest to largest to give a stem-and-leaf plot.	
				Calgary Flames' Wins	
2		2	5 9	2	5 9
3		3	0 4 5 4 4 5 9 2 4 1	3	0 1 2 4 4 4 4 5 5 9
4		4	1 1 0 6 8 2 6 3	4	0 1 1 2 3 6 6 8
5		5	4	5	4

Inquire

1. What is the median of the data?

2. What is the mode?

3. What is the range of these data?

4. In how many seasons did the team win more than 30 games?

Example

The Hartford Whalers and the Winnipeg Jets entered the NHL in 1979–1980. The data show the numbers of games they won in their first 13 seasons.

Hartford
27, 21, 21, 19, 28, 30, 40,
43, 35, 37, 38, 31, 26

Winnipeg
20, 9, 33, 33, 31, 43, 26,
40, 33, 26, 37, 26, 33

a) Draw a back-to-back stem-and-leaf plot for these data.

b) What was the median number of games won by each team?

c) In how many seasons did each team win less than 30 games?

Solution

a) Write the stems in a middle column and then add the leaves.

Arrange the leaves in order, to give a back-to-back stem-and-leaf plot.

Games Won Per Season		
Hartford		Winnipeg
	0	9
9	1	
6 8 1 1 7	2	0 6 6 6
1 8 7 5 0	3	3 3 1 3 7 3
3 0	4	3 0

Games Won Per Season		
Hartford		Winnipeg
	0	9
9	1	
8 7 6 1 1	2	0 6 6 6
8 7 5 1 0	3	1 3 3 3 3 7
3 0	4	0 3

b) The median number of wins for Hartford was 30. The median number of wins for Winnipeg was 33.

c) Hartford won less than 30 games in 6 seasons. Winnipeg won less than 30 games in 5 seasons.

Problems and Applications

1. The heights of the students in a grade 8 class are shown.

Heights of Students (cm)	
15	6 7 8 8 9 9
16	2 3 4 4 5 6 8 9 9
17	0 2 2 4 4 7 8 9
18	0

a) How many students are in the class?
b) What is the median height of the students?
c) What is the mode?
d) What is the range of the data?
e) How many students are taller than 170 cm?

2. The following are the average numbers of days of thunderstorms per year in the provinces and territories.

AB	26	BC	24	MB	26	NB	13
NF	7	NT	12	NS	12	ON	34
PE	11	PQ	27	SK	25	YT	11

a) Display the data on a stem-and-leaf plot.
b) What is the median number of days of thunderstorms?
c) What are the range and the mode?
d) How many provinces or territories have more than 25 days of thunderstorms a year? less than 25?

3. The list shows the numbers of wet days per year for several Canadian cities.

120	137	156	163	166	175	156	148
121	120	162	174	122	143	166	

a) Construct a stem-and-leaf plot.
b) Find the median and the range.
c) How many of the cities have more than 150 wet days a year?
d) How many of the cities have less than 160 wet days a year?

4. The student marks for two first-aid tests are shown.

1st Test	52, 66, 72, 84, 68, 72, 51, 64 54, 81, 84, 67, 70, 73, 60

2nd Test	68, 73, 82, 84, 78, 61, 93, 91 70, 79, 80, 81, 90, 64, 89

a) Display the data on a back-to-back stem-and-leaf plot.
b) How many students wrote each test?
c) What was the median mark for each test?
d) What was the range of marks on each test?
e) How many students scored 70 or higher on the first test? on the second test?
f) How many scored lower than 80 on the first test? on the second test?

10.9 Box-and-Whisker Plots

Kim Campbell was 46 years old when she became Canada's nineteenth Prime Minister.

The mean age of Canada's first 19 Prime Ministers when they began their terms in office was about 55 years. Their ages in ascending order were as follows.

| 39 | 45 | 46 | 46 | 47 | 47 | 48 | 51 | 52 | 54 | 55 | 57 | 60 | 61 | 65 | 66 | 70 | 70 | 74 |

Inquire

1. What is the lowest value in the data?

2. What is the highest value in the data?

3. What is the median value?

4. Consider the 9 values above the median. What is the median of these 9 values?

5. Consider the 9 values below the median. What is the median of these 9 values?

The number you found in question 4 is known as the **upper quartile**. The number you found in question 5 is known as the **lower quartile**. The 5 numbers you found in questions 1–5 are known as a **five-number summary**.

Example 1

a) Use the above data to construct a box-and-whisker plot.
b) About what percent of the values lie in the box? in each whisker?

Solution

a) The 5-number summary is 39, 47, 54, 65, 74. Plot these 5 numbers on a number line. Then, draw vertical line segments through the median and the upper and lower quartiles. Draw a box between the upper and lower quartiles. Draw horizontal segments to the highest and lowest values from the ends of the box. These segments are the whiskers.

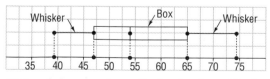

b) About 50% of the numbers lie in the box. Each whisker contains about 25% of the numbers.

338

Example 2

The lengths, in centimetres, of 16 North American sandpipers are given in the table.

a) Display these data in a box-and-whisker plot.

b) Between which 2 values do 50% of the bird lengths occur?

Bird	Length (cm)
Buff-breasted Sandpiper	19
Greater Yellowlegs	35
Hudsonian Godwit	37
Least Sandpiper	14
Lesser Yellowlegs	27
Long-billed Curlew	58
Marbled Godwit	45
Pectoral Sandpiper	23
Purple Sandpiper	22
Sanderling	19
Semipalmated Sandpiper	15
Stilt Sandpiper	20
Upland Sandpiper	29
Western Sandpiper	17
Whimbrel	43
Willet	39

Solution

a) Arrange the data in ascending order.

14, 15, 17, 19, 19, 20, 22, 23, 27, 29, 35, 37, 39, 43, 45, 58

The median is the average of the 2 middle values. $\frac{23 + 27}{2} = 25$

The lower quartile is the average of the 2 middle values below the median. $\frac{19 + 19}{2} = 19$

The upper quartile is the average of the 2 middle values above the median. $\frac{37 + 39}{2} = 38$

The box-and-whisker plot for the data is

b) 50% of the bird lengths lie between 19 cm and 38 cm.

Problems and Applications

1. The number of hours some bands spend practising a new song before they record is shown below.

a) What fraction of the bands spend more than 30 h practising?

b) Within what range of hours do one-half of the bands practise?

c) What fraction of the bands spend less than 45 h practising?

2. a) Draw a box-and-whisker plot to represent the following test scores.

40	47	50	50	50	54	56	56
60	60	62	62	63	65	70	70
72	76	77	80	85	85	95	96

b) Between which 2 test scores do 50% of the scores lie?

c) Between which 2 test scores do the lower 75% of the scores lie?

3. The plots show the math marks for 3 students.

a) One-half of Joan's test scores lie between which 2 values?

b) Which student's test scores are most inconsistent? Explain.

c) What percent of Marie's test scores are above 70%?

4. Measure your pulse rate for 1 min. Plot the results for the whole class in beats per minute

a) on a stem-and-leaf plot

b) on a box-and-whisker plot

10.10 Possible Outcomes

When a hockey team plays a game, there are three possible **outcomes**: they can win, tie, or lose. When you roll a die, there are six possible outcomes or **events**: 1, 2, 3, 4, 5, and 6.

Activity: Complete the List
For each experiment, A, B and C, complete the list of possible outcomes.

Inquire

1. a) One possible outcome in experiment A is "a head and red." List the other possible outcomes in experiment A.

b) How many possible outcomes are there in experiment A?

2. How many possible outcomes are there in experiment B?

3. How many possible outcomes are there in experiment C?

The possible outcomes from an experiment are sometimes called the **sample space.**

Equally likely outcomes have the same chance of occurring.

When you toss a coin, the chances of a head and the chances of a tail are the same, or equally likely.

A **tree diagram** can help you to list the possible outcomes of an experiment.

Example

a) How many possible outcomes are there when you spin the spinner and roll the cube?

b) Are the outcomes equally likely? Explain.

Solution

a) When you spin the spinner, there are 2 possible outcomes: 1 and 2. When you roll the cube, there are 3 possible outcomes: Red, Blue, and Red-Blue.

Spinner	Cube	Outcomes
1	Red	1 and Red
	Blue	1 and Blue
	Red-Blue	1 and Red-Blue
2	Red	2 and Red
	Blue	2 and Blue
	Red-Blue	2 and Red-Blue

There are 6 possible outcomes.

b) The outcomes are not equally likely, because there are 4 ways to get Red-Blue, 1 way to get Red, and 1 way to get Blue.

A Toss a coin and spin the spinner.

Coin	Spinner
Head	Red

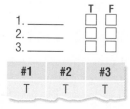

B Toss a dime and a quarter.

Dime	Quarter
T	T

C Answer 3 true or false questions.

	T	F
1. ____	☐	☐
2. ____	☐	☐
3. ____	☐	☐

#1	#2	#3
T	T	T

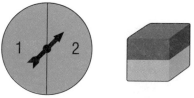

Problems and Applications

In questions 1 to 5, list the possible outcomes of each experiment. If the outcomes are not equally likely, state the most likely outcome.

1. You play a game of tick-tack-toe with a friend.

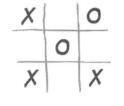

2. You spin the spinner.

3. You draw one tangram piece from a bag.

4. You toss a coin and spin the spinner.

5. You roll a die and spin the spinner.

6. Draw a tree diagram to find the possible outcomes of each of the following.
a) Toss a dime and a nickel, and spin the spinner.

b) Toss a penny, a nickel, and a dime.

7. a) List the possible outcomes when you spin each spinner.

b) One possible outcome is a 1 on the red spinner and a 3 on the blue. The total is 4. What other possible outcomes total 4?
c) How many of the possible outcomes total 5? 3?

8. a) The tetrahedral dice are numbered on the faces using the digits 1, 2, 3, and 4. List the possible outcomes for the face that is down after the red die and the green die are rolled.

b) How many possible outcomes are there?
c) How many possible outcomes total 4?
d) What totals happen most often? In how many ways do they each happen?
e) What totals happen least often?

DESIGN POWER

How many different designs can be made by shading 2 squares on a 3-by-3 grid?

These 4 patterns are considered the same.

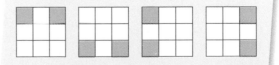

10.11 Probability

Probability is used to study an experiment with several possible outcomes to predict the likelihood of each outcome.

When you toss a coin, there are two possible outcomes. The coin will show a head (H) or a tail (T). If you toss a coin and call "heads," the chance of getting a head is 1 out of 2.

The probability of tossing a head, $P(H) = \frac{1}{2}$

The probability of an event, $P = \dfrac{\text{number of favourable outcomes}}{\text{total number of possible outcomes}}$

Activity: Complete the Tree Diagram

Two lions were born at the zoo each year for two years. Copy and complete the tree diagram to list the possible female (F) and male (M) cubs.

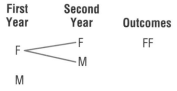

Inquire

1. How many possible outcomes are there?

2. What is the probability of getting 2 female cubs?

3. What is the probability of getting just 1 male cub?

4. What is the probability of getting at least 1 female cub?

The probability of an event can be written in lowest terms, just as fractions can be.

Example 1

Find the probabilities of the following outcomes when you spin the spinner. Write the probabilities as percents.

a) a 3

b) a 5 or a 6

c) an even number

d) a number greater than 7

e) a number from 1 to 10

f) the number 11

Solution

There are 10 equal sectors on the spinner.

a) $P(3) = \frac{1}{10}$ or 10%

b) $P(5 \text{ or } 6) = \frac{2}{10}$ or $\frac{1}{5}$ or 20%

c) $P(\text{even}) = \frac{5}{10}$ or $\frac{1}{2}$ or 50%

d) $P(\text{greater than } 7) = \frac{3}{10}$ or 30%

e) There are 10 numbers from 1 to 10.
$P(1 \text{ to } 10) = \frac{10}{10}$ or 1 or 100%

f) There is no 11.
$P(11) = \frac{0}{10}$ or 0 or 0%

You can see from the example that an *impossible* outcome has a probability of 0, and a *certain* outcome has a probability of 1. Outcomes that are neither impossible nor certain have probabilities between 0 and 1 or 0% and 100%.

You can use probabilities to make predictions.

Example 2

If you rolled a die 200 times, how many 4s would you expect to roll?

Solution

The possible outcomes are 1, 2, 3, 4, 5, and 6. Each of these outcomes is equally likely.

$P(4)$ is $\frac{1}{6}$.

In 200 rolls, the expected number of 4s is $\frac{1}{6} \times 200$ or $33\frac{1}{3}$.

So, the number of 4s you would expect to roll is 33, to the nearest whole number.

Practice

In questions 1 to 4, find the probability of each event.

1. Choose 1 cube from the bag.
a) $P(\text{red})$ **b)** $P(\text{blue})$
c) $P(\text{yellow})$

2. Roll a die.
a) $P(6)$ **b)** $P(3 \text{ or } 4)$ **c)** $P(\text{odd number})$
d) $P(8)$ **e)** $P(\text{number less than 5})$
f) $P(\text{number less than 7})$

3. Spin the spinner.
a) $P(\text{green})$
b) $P(\text{red or yellow})$
c) $P(\text{pink, blue, or green})$
d) $P(\text{white})$

4. Choose a card from a deck of 52 playing cards.
a) $P(\text{black})$ **b)** $P(\text{king})$
c) $P(\text{red queen})$ **d)** $P(\text{face card})$

Problems and Applications

5. The names of the provincial capitals are each written on a card and placed in a bag. If you select 1 card from the bag, what is the probability of selecting
a) a city name with exactly 3 vowels?
b) a city name with at least 4 consonants?
c) a city that is on an island?
d) a city in a province that shares a border with the United States?

6. A bag contains 3 red marbles, 2 orange marbles, 4 blue marbles, and 1 yellow marble. If a marble is pulled from the bag, what is the probability that it is
a) red?   **b)** orange or blue?
c) any colour?   **d)** green?
e) not blue?

7. A bag contains 300 cubes. Marta pulls out 5 cubes from the bag. Four of them are red, and 1 is blue. Predict how many cubes of the following colours are in the bag.
a) red   **b)** blue   **c)** green

8. Raul picks a playing card from a deck of 52 cards 200 times. After each pick, he returns the card to the deck and shuffles the deck. Predict how many times he chooses
a) an ace   **b)** a red queen
c) a club   **d)** a face card

9. A batch of 200 in-line skates has been manufactured. In a sample of 25 skates, 2 have a fault and are rejected.
a) What is the probability that the next skate inspected will be rejected?
b) What is the probability that the next skate inspected will not be rejected?
c) What is the sum of the probabilities in parts a) and b)? What does this sum indicate?
d) Predict how many skates from the whole batch will pass inspection.

Experimental Probability

The probabilities of some outcomes, such as rolling a 5 on a die, can be found mathematically. The probabilities of some other outcomes can be found only by conducting an experiment.

Activity ❶ The Bent Paper Clip

Bend a paper clip like the one shown in the picture.

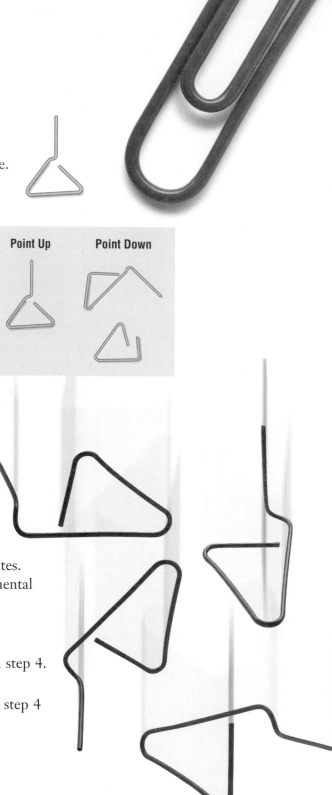

When the paper clip is tossed, it can land in two ways: point up or point down.

1. Estimate the probability of a tossed paper clip landing
a) point up
b) point down

2. Toss a paper clip 20 times and record your results in a table. Use tally marks.

Outcome	Tally
Point Up	
Point Down	

3. Use your results to write the experimental probability of a paper clip landing
a) point up
b) point down

4. Combine your results with those of your classmates. Use the combined results to determine the experimental probability of a paper clip landing
a) point up
b) point down

5. Compare the probabilities found in step 3 and in step 4. Are they different? If they are, explain.

6. Compare the experimental probabilities found in step 4 with the estimated probabilities from step 1.

Activity ❷ The Buffon Needle Experiment

The Buffon needle experiment was performed by Count Buffon in the eighteenth century. To repeat the experiment, work in pairs or in larger groups. Each group will need 10 toothpicks and a large sheet of paper.

1. Draw a set of parallel lines so that each is the length of 2 toothpicks from the next.

2. The experiment involves dropping toothpicks onto the sheet of paper. Predict the probability that a dropped toothpick will
a) touch a line   **b)** not touch a line

3. From a height of at least 0.5 m, drop the 10 toothpicks one at a time onto the paper. Count the toothpicks that touch a line.

4. Repeat step 3 another 9 times. Copy and complete the table.

Trial	1	2	3	4	5	6	7	8	9	10
Toothpicks Touching Lines										
Toothpicks Not Touching Lines										

5. Total the results of the 10 trials. Use the totals to calculate the experimental probability that a dropped toothpick will
a) touch a line   **b)** not touch a line

6. Compare the probabilities from step 5 with your predictions from step 2.

7. Combine your totals from step 5 with the totals obtained by the other groups in the class. Use the combined totals to calculate, to 3 decimal places, the experimental probability that a dropped toothpick will
a) touch a line   **b)** not touch a line

8. Compare the probabilities determined in steps 5 and 7. Which step do you think gives the more reliable values? Explain.

9. Take the reciprocal of the value you found in step 5 a). Round the result to the nearest hundredth.

10. Compare your result from step 9 with the results of other groups. Do the results seem to be close to any value you are familiar with? If so, what is it the value of?

11. Take the reciprocal of the value you found in step 7 a). Does the result confirm the suggestion you made in step 10?

12. Predict the results of step 7 if you drew the parallel lines so that each was only 1 toothpick length from the next. Carry out the experiment to check your predictions.

Activity ❸ Drawing a Line

1. Suppose you closed your eyes and tried to draw, freehand, a 25 cm long straight line. Predict the probability that the length of the line would be
a) < 25 cm   **b)** 25 cm   **c)** > 25 cm

2. Work in groups of about 8. Each try the experiment described in step 1.

3. Measure your line. Record your group's results in a table.

Length of Line (cm)	Tally
< 25	
25	
> 25	

4. Use your group's results to write the experimental probability of drawing a straight line, freehand, with your eyes closed that is
a) < 25 cm   **b)** 25 cm   **c)** > 25 cm

5. Combine the results of all the groups. Use the combined results to find the experimental probability of drawing a straight line, freehand, with your eyes closed that is
a) < 25 cm   **b)** 25 cm   **c)** > 25 cm

6. Compare the probabilities you found in step 5 with your predictions in step 1.

345

Simulations with Random Numbers

Airline pilots train in flight simulators, which act like airplanes. A **simulation** of an experiment acts like the real experiment. One way to complete a simulation is to use random numbers, which can be generated by computers and some calculators.

Activity ❶ Children in Families

1. The tree diagram represents the possible outcomes for the numbers of male and female children in a family with 2 children. What is the probability that both children will be male?

2. Instead of calculating the probability in step 1, you could determine it from a simulation. One way would be to toss 2 coins. If a head represents a male, then tossing 2 heads at the same time represents 2 males.

a) Toss 2 coins 40 times and record the results in a table, like the one shown.

b) Use your results to find the probability that both children will be male.

3. You can also use a table of random numbers to carry out the simulation. Start anywhere in the table and move up or down or left or right in groups of 2. Let the digits 0, 1, 2, 3, and 4 represent a male. Let the digits 5, 6, 7, 8, and 9 represent a female.

a) Choose 40 groups of 2 digits and record the number of males represented by each group of digits. Record your results on a tally sheet.

b) Use your results to determine the probability that both children will be male.

4. Compare your results from steps 1, 2, and 3. Account for any differences.

5. a) Generate your own random number table with a scientific or graphing calculator. Use your table to find the probability that, in a family with 3 children, all 3 are female.

b) Use a tree diagram to determine the probability for part a) and compare it with the result of your simulation.

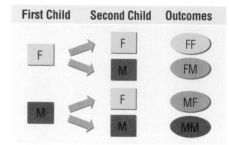

First Child	Second Child	Outcomes
F	F	FF
	M	FM
M	F	MF
	M	MM

Number of Males	Tally	Frequency
0		
1		
2		

Random Number Table

29631	69990	01673	08844	61438	23127
30206	84165	05346	80824	23499	56892
26554	60924	88336	20105	77283	43640
80922	95345	31633	87468	23537	94607
03971	37646	23563	52779	46040	69799
18640	80901	03644	77489	22794	86409
12430	52944	29903	01988	44563	32049
80628	88272	06422	75435	85364	43239
55730	74394	68847	69986	39305	58362
56145	10885	02255	67721	83806	72059
58570	39559	14203	17285	58717	51277
81313	84777	79987	24924	13945	80874

Activity ❷ A Multiple Choice Test

There are 5 true or false questions on a test.
If you guess at each answer, what is the probability
that you will get 3, 4, or 5 questions correct?

1. Simulate the guesses by tossing 5 coins. A head
means a correct answer, and a tail means a wrong
answer. Toss the 5 coins 20 times and record the
results in a table, like the one shown.

2. Another way is to use the random number table
on the previous page. Start anywhere in the table
and use the digits in a group of 5. Let the digits
0, 2, 4, 6, and 8 mean a correct answer. Let the
digits 1, 3, 5, 7, and 9 mean a wrong answer.
Move up or down or left or right in the table
from where you started. Choose 20 sets of 5
digits. Record your results on a tally sheet, like
the one above.

3. Use your results to find the probability of
getting 3, 4, or 5 questions correct.

Number Correct	Tally	Frequency
0		
1		
2		
3		
4		
5		

Activity ❸ Choosing an Option

A record store has a promotion. If you spend $30 in the store,
you have a chance at grab bags. Half the grab bags are empty,
and half of them contain a voucher for a free tape. There are two
ways to take grab bags from the box.

A. You can pick 3 bags.

B. You can keep picking bags until you get an empty one.

Should you choose A or B?

To solve this problem, simulate option A by repeating Activity 2,
above, with 3 coins or random digits instead of 5. Simulate
option B with random digits or by tossing a coin. A head means
the bag has a voucher, and a tail means the bag is empty. The
results for option B may look like this.

1. H H T **2.** T **3.** H H H T **4.** H T **5.** H T **6.** H H H H T

Carry out each simulation 20 times. Compare the results of the
two experiments to decide what option to choose, A or B.

10.12 Independent Events

Activity: Use a Diagram

Use a tree diagram to show all the possible outcomes when a coin is tossed and a die is rolled at the same time.

Inquire

1. How many possible outcomes are there when a coin is tossed and a die is rolled at the same time?

2. State the probability of each outcome in your tree diagram.

3. Use your tree diagram to determine each of the following probabilities.

a) a head and a number less than 7   **b)** a head or a tail and a 5

c) a tail and an even number   **d)** a tail and a number that is not 3

Events are **independent** if each outcome has no effect on the other. The outcome of the toss of a coin does not affect the outcome of the roll of a die. Thus, these outcomes are independent events.

Example 1

A red die and a blue die are rolled at the same time, and the sum is found. Calculate each probability.

a) a sum of 7   **b)** an even sum   **c)** a sum less than 6

Solution

Use a table to construct the sample space.

	Outcome on Red Die					
+	**1**	**2**	**3**	**4**	**5**	**6**
1	2	3	4	5	6	7
2	3	4	5	6	7	8
3	4	5	6	7	8	9
4	5	6	7	8	9	10
5	6	7	8	9	10	11
6	7	8	9	10	11	12

(Outcome on Blue Die)

There are 36 possible outcomes.

a) A sum of 7 occurs 6 times.

$P(\text{sum of 7}) = \frac{6}{36}$
$= \frac{1}{6}$

b) An even sum occurs 18 times.

$P(\text{even sum}) = \frac{18}{36}$
$= \frac{1}{2}$

c) There are 10 sums less than 6.

$P(\text{sum less than 6}) = \frac{10}{36}$
$= \frac{5}{18}$

Example 2

A set of 5 cards has a different vowel written on each card. A card is chosen from a deck of 52 playing cards, and a vowel is chosen from the vowel cards. What is each probability?

a) a black card and an A, $P(B, A)$ **b)** a red card and a vowel, $P(R, V)$

c) a red card and an O or U, $P(R, O \text{ or } U)$

Solution

Use a tree diagram.

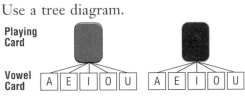

Playing Card

Vowel Card

The sample space is

R, A   R, E   R, I   R, O   R, U
B, A   B, E   B, I   B, O   B, U

There are 10 possible outcomes.

a) There is one outcome B, A. $P(B, A) = \frac{1}{10}$

b) There are five outcomes R, V. $P(R, V) = \frac{5}{10} = \frac{1}{2}$

c) There is one outcome R, O and one outcome R, U.

$$P(R, O \text{ or } U) = \frac{2}{10}$$
$$= \frac{1}{5}$$

Problems and Applications

1. If you toss the coin and spin the spinner, what is each of the following probabilities?

a) a head and red
b) a head and blue
c) a tail and green or red
d) a tail and white
e) a head or a tail and blue

2. Use a tree diagram to show the possible outcomes when you spin the two spinners.

Use your results to find these probabilities.

a) $P(1, \text{red})$ **b)** $P(2, \text{green})$ **c)** $P(5, \text{blue})$
d) $P(\text{even number, green})$
e) $P(\text{number less than 4, red})$
f) $P(\text{number less than 6, red or green})$

3. a) Find the possible outcomes when you spin the red and blue spinners.

b) How many possible outcomes are there?
c) How many outcomes total 6?
d) What is the probability of spinning a total of 6?
e) What is the probability of spinning a total of 4? 9?

4. A playing card pulled from a 52-card deck may belong to one of 4 suits — hearts (H), diamonds (D), spades (S), or clubs (C). Use a tree diagram to find the following probabilities when a card is pulled and a regular die is rolled.

a) $P(H, 1)$ **b)** $P(H \text{ or } D, 2)$
c) $P(C, \text{even number})$ **d)** $P(H, \text{not } 2)$
e) $P(S, \text{number less than } 5)$
f) $P(D \text{ or } C, \text{odd number})$

5. Use a table to show the sample space for the possible sums of the spins on these spinners. Calculate each probability.

a) a sum of 11   **b)** a sum of 2
c) an even sum   **d)** a sum greater than 6
e) a sum of 12   **f)** a sum of 5 or 10

6. A red die is numbered 2, 4, 6, 8, 10, and 12. A blue die is numbered 1, 3, 5, 7, 9, and 11.

a) List all the possible sums of the numbers when the dice are rolled.
b) How many outcomes are there?
c) What is the probability of a sum of 11? a sum of 9? an odd sum? an even sum?

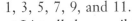

7. Write a probability problem that uses one die and one spinner. Have a classmate solve your problem.

349

Review

1. Barry conducted a survey to find out which of the following team nicknames grade 8 students like most: Bears, Lions, Tigers, Eagles, or Wolves. Each student was limited to one choice.

Survey Sheet		
Nickname	**Tally**	**Frequency**
Bears	₩ ₩ ₩ II	
Lions	IIII	
Tigers	₩ ₩ ₩ ₩ IIII	
Eagles	₩ ₩ ₩ ₩ I	
Wolves	₩ ₩ IIII	

a) Copy and complete the survey sheet.
b) How many students chose Bears?
c) List the choices from most popular to least popular.
d) How many students were surveyed?

2. The bar graph shows how much hot water is used for activities in the home.

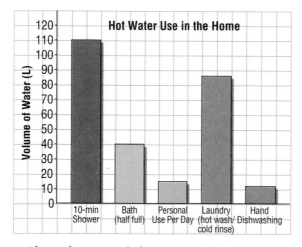

a) About how much hot water is used for a bath if the tub is half full?
b) About how much hot water is used for a 10-min shower? a 2-min shower?
c) Which activity uses about 7 times more hot water than hand dishwashing?

3. The table gives the average daily temperature, in degrees Celsius, for each month in Casablanca, Morocco, and Vienna, Austria.

Average Daily Temperature (°C)					
	Casablanca	**Vienna**		**Casablanca**	**Vienna**
January	12	0	July	22	20
February	13	1	August	23	19
March	14	5	September	22	16
April	16	10	October	20	10
May	18	15	November	16	5
June	20	18	December	13	1

Display these data on a double broken-line graph.

4. The breakdown of residential energy use is as shown.

Space Heating	67%
Water Heating	17%
Appliances	14%
Lighting	2%

Display these data on a circle graph.

5. Find the mean, median, mode, and range of these data: 83, 82, 83, 85, 83, 82.

6. List the following.
a) five different numbers with a median of 8
b) six different numbers with a mean of 7
c) six different numbers with a median of 10

7. The numbers of games won by the Vancouver Canucks in their first 23 seasons are given below.

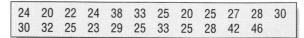

24	20	22	24	38	33	25	20	25	27	28	30
30	32	25	23	29	25	33	25	28	42	46	

a) Construct a stem-and-leaf plot for these data.
b) Find the median, mode, and range.

8. The wingspans, in centimetres, of 60 large owls and 60 small owls are shown on the box-and-whisker plot.

| 20 | 40 | 60 | 80 | 100 | 120 | 140 | 160 |
Owls' Wingspans (cm)

a) What is the median wingspan for each type of owl?

b) How many large owls have wingspans between 100 cm and 130 cm?

c) How many small owls have wingspans between 35 cm and 50 cm?

d) About how many small owls have wingspans less than 35 cm?

e) About how many large owls have wingspans greater than 130 cm?

9. Spin the spinner. Calculate each probability.

a) P(red)

b) P(blue)

c) P(blue or green)

d) P(yellow)

e) P(white)

10. If you roll a die 150 times, how many times do you think an outcome less than 3 will occur?

11. Use a tree diagram to find each of the following probabilities when you spin the spinner and roll the die.

a) P(green, 2)

b) P(green or blue, 4)

c) P(red, odd number)

d) P(white, 6)

e) P(yellow or blue, 3 or 4)

f) P(blue, not 5)

Group Decision Making
Reducing Waste

Many Canadians are making an effort to reduce waste. The list shows some types of waste and the percent of waste they make up.

Type of Waste	Percent
Mixed Paper (magazines, junk mail, phone books, grocery bags)	20%
Newspaper	15%
Cardboard Boxes	3%
Glass Bottles and Jars	9%
Metals (aluminum cans and foil, tin/steel cans)	5%
Plastic	5%
Yard Waste	25%
Food Scraps	10%

1. Brainstorm as a class the places where waste occurs. Include your school cafeteria, school grounds, home, parks, food stores, and shopping malls.

2. Decide as a class which one of the places each home group will investigate.

3. Go to home groups and list the ways waste can be reduced in your chosen place for four of the categories of waste listed.

| 1 2 3 4 5 6 | 1 2 3 4 5 6 |

Home Groups

| 1 2 3 4 5 6 | 1 2 3 4 5 6 |

4. Prepare a presentation for the class on the ways waste can be reduced. Be creative.

5. As a class, decide what steps you and your classmates can take to reduce waste.

Chapter Check

1. The circle graph shows the population distribution in Canada's four westernmost provinces.

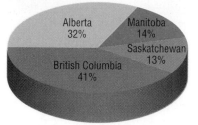

Alberta 32%
Manitoba 14%
Saskatchewan 13%
British Columbia 41%

a) In which two provinces are the populations about equal?

b) Which two provinces, together, account for about three-quarters of the population?

c) The total population of these four provinces is about 8 000 000. About how many people live in Alberta?

2. The table gives the percent of colds that start on each day of the week for teenagers. Display these data on a broken-line graph.

Sun	16%	Mon	17%	Tues	14%	Wed	13%
Thurs	12%	Fri	13%	Sat	15%		

3. Find the mean, median, mode, and range of each set of data.

a) 29, 22, 23, 31, 30, 22, 25

b) 70, 91, 85, 75, 80, 76

c) 7, 10, 9, 7, 10, 9, 1, 9

4. Marks for a math test are shown.

> 88, 83, 80, 73, 90, 90, 77, 86, 92, 94,
> 73, 80, 89, 93, 85, 82, 78, 91, 88, 92, 89

a) Display the data on a stem-and-leaf plot.

b) What are the median mark and the range of marks?

5. Alice Munro is a famous Canadian writer. Suppose you write each letter of her name on a different card, place the cards in a bag, and draw one card from the bag. Write the following probabilities as percents.

a) $P(C)$

b) $P(M$ or $N)$

c) $P(\text{vowel})$

d) $P(\text{consonant})$

e) $P(L, M,$ or $N)$

f) $P(\text{not } L, M,$ or $N)$

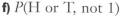

6. When a coin is tossed and a die is rolled, what are the following probabilities?

a) $P(H, 4)$

b) $P(T, 3$ or $6)$

c) $P(H$ or $T, 2)$

d) $P(H$ or $T, 9)$

e) $P(T, \text{odd number})$

f) $P(H$ or $T, \text{not } 1)$

BUREAU OF STATISTICS

PROBABLE ENTRANCE

PROBABLE EXIT

©1993 Tribune Media Services, Inc. All Rights Reserved

Reprinted with permission—The Toronto Star Syndicate. Copyright: Tribune Media Services.

Using the Strategies

1. What is the smallest number of cubes that can be used to build a tower with 8 layers and a different number of cubes in each layer?

2. What percent of students in your school are in grade 8?

3. The playground is enclosed by a fence with posts 2 m apart. There is a post at each corner.

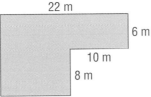

a) What is the total length of the fence?
b) How many posts are there?

4. How many times do you use the digit 3 if you count by tens from 0 to 500?

5. Barry put $\frac{1}{3}$ of his babysitting money into the bank. He spent $\frac{1}{4}$ of it on a cassette tape, and he had $13.00 left. How much did he earn babysitting?

6. The length of a rectangle is 3 times its width. The perimeter is 52 cm.
a) What are the dimensions of the rectangle?
b) What is its area?

7. Petra has the same number of nickels, dimes, and quarters. She has $3.20 altogether. How many of each type of coin does she have?

8. How often does February 29 fall on a Monday?

9. How many diagonals does a regular octagon have?

10. The square of a whole number equals the cube of half the number. What is the number?

11. Straws can be used to represent the sides and a diagonal of a square.

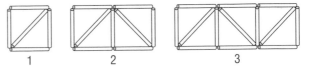

How many straws will be needed for the tenth figure?

12. Alina jogs at a steady pace around an oval track from the starting point shown.

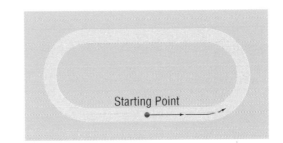

Starting Point

Sketch a graph of her distance from the starting point versus time for one complete circuit of the track.

13. a) Use the clues to help you find the Mystery Number.
b) Make up a set of clues for another Mystery Number. Ask a classmate to find the number.

Mystery Number
1. Between 10^2 and 10^3.
2. Sum of digits 10.
3. Prime factors 5 and 13.
4. All digits prime.

DATA BANK

1. Which Canadian waterfall is closest to one-third the height of Della Falls?

2. The lowest wind chill temperature recorded on Prince Edward Island occurred when the air temperature was −32°C and the wind speed was 37 km/h. Estimate the wind chill temperature.

Chapter 9

Find the missing measures.

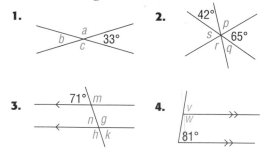

1.

2. 42° p s 65° r q

3. 71° m n g h k

4. v w 81°

Copy each figure and draw its lines of symmetry.

5.

6.

Find the missing measures.

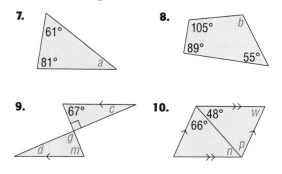

7. 61° 81° a

8. 105° b 89° 55°

9. 67° c g d m

10. 48° w 66° n p

a) *Name the polyhedron formed from each net.*
b) *Is the pohyhedron formed a solid, shell, or skeleton? Explain.*
c) *State the number of faces, edges, and vertices for each polyhedron.*

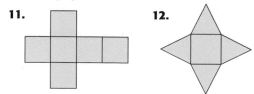

11.

12.

13. Draw the net of a triangular prism.

Chapter 10

1. A recent survey gave this information on how teenagers describe their environmental education.

Need More	75%
Need Less	5%
Right Amount	20%

Out of 200 teenagers chosen at random, predict how many would say they needed more environmental education.

2. The table gives the approximate distribution of blood in the body during relaxation.

Brain	13%
Liver	27%
Kidneys	17%
Muscles	14%
Rest of Body	29%

Display this information on a circle graph.

3. The ranges of some aircraft are shown in the table. Represent the data on
a) a bar graph   **b)** a pictograph

Aircraft	Range (km)
L-1011	8850
B-767	9500
B-727	4340
B-747	6600
DC-9	2400

4. These are the speeds, in kilometres per hour, of 15 go-carts after the first lap of a race.

30, 35, 41, 40, 39, 29, 28, 36,
44, 40, 33, 29, 37, 42, 46

a) Find the mean, median, mode, and range.
b) Display the data on a stem-and-leaf plot.
c) Display the data on a box-and-whisker plot.

5. A coin is tossed and a die is rolled. Calculate each probability.
a) a 6 and a head
b) an even number and a head
c) a number greater than 4 and a tail

Evaluate.

1. $(2^2)^3$ **2.** $(4^2)^2$ **3.** $(3^2)^4$

Write each number in standard form.

4. 10^{-2} **5.** $\dfrac{1}{10^3}$ **6.** -10^5

Evaluate.

7. $2^3 \times 2 \times 2^2$ **8.** $5^4 \div 5^2$

Write each number in scientific notation.

9. 42 000 000   **10.** 0.0062

11. 25 700   **12.** 0.000 005 4

Write each number in standard form.

13. 1.02×10^4 **14.** 3.6×10^5

15. 8.2×10^{-3} **16.** 4.6×10^{-5}

Use a number line to arrange the rational numbers in the order from least to greatest.

17. $0.52,\ 0.025,\ 5\frac{1}{2},\ 3.125,\ -1\frac{1}{4},\ -1.12$

18. $\frac{1}{5},\ -\frac{3}{5},\ -0.2,\ 1.5,\ 4,\ 1\frac{1}{4}$

Write as a percent.

19. 0.62 **20.** 1.45 **21.** 0.275

22. $\frac{3}{5}$ **23.** $1\frac{1}{4}$ **24.** $\frac{16}{20}$

25. $2{:}5$ **26.** $3{:}2$ **27.** $4{:}25$

Write as a decimal.

28. 22.5% **29.** 150% **30.** $6\frac{3}{4}\%$

31. 20% **32.** 68% **33.** 95%

Evaluate.

34. $\sqrt{289}$ **35.** $\sqrt{1.96}$

Calculate.

36. $\frac{5}{7} + \frac{3}{7}$ **37.** $\frac{3}{4} + \frac{5}{12}$ **38.** $2\frac{1}{2} + 1\frac{5}{6}$

39. $\frac{7}{9} - \frac{5}{9}$ **40.** $\frac{4}{5} - \frac{1}{2}$ **41.** $3\frac{2}{3} - 1\frac{1}{2}$

42. $\frac{2}{5}$ of 15 **43.** $\frac{7}{8} \times \frac{2}{3}$ **44.** $\frac{5}{8} \times 1\frac{1}{5}$

45. $1\frac{1}{4} \div \frac{1}{2}$ **46.** $1\frac{1}{6} \div 2\frac{1}{3}$ **47.** $2\frac{2}{5} \div \frac{2}{5}$

48. Write the reciprocal of $1\frac{1}{4}$.

Calculate.

49. 4.1×0.8 **50.** -2.4×0.6

51. $6 \div 2.5$ **52.** $0.312 \div (-0.52)$

53. $4.7 + (-2.5)$ **54.** $-1.25 + (-0.75)$

55. $3.125 - 0.217$ **56.** $-11.4 \div 3.8$

57. Write 2 ratios equivalent to 4:7.

Find the unknown value.

58. $\frac{3}{2} = \frac{x}{8}$ **59.** $\frac{y}{5} = \frac{12}{10}$ **60.** $\frac{1}{m} = \frac{7}{56}$

Find the unknown values.

61. $15{:}18{:}k = 5{:}n{:}2$ **62.** $66{:}36{:}30 = q{:}6{:}p$

63. A pack of 12 bottles of juice costs $3.48. How much do 7 bottles of juice cost?

Find the unit price of each item. Round each answer to the nearest tenth of a cent, if necessary.

64. 3 kg of potatoes for $2.99

65. 5 lightbulbs for $4.49

66. Vancouver's Port Mann bridge has a main span 366 m in length. A model of the bridge is built to a scale of 1:2000. What is the length, in centimetres, of the main span in the model?

67. The flying distance from Calgary to Victoria is 725 km. These cities are 14.5 cm apart on a map. What is the scale of the map?

Estimate, then calculate.

68. What is 17% of 200?

69. What percent is 54 of 216?

70. What is $85\frac{1}{2}\%$ of 76?

71. 75% of a number is 375. What is the number?

CONTINUED ➤

72. The regular price of a ski jacket is $249.95. A store advertises 20% off.
a) What is the sale price of the ski jacket?
b) What is the total cost of the jacket, including GST and PST in your province?

73. Phillipe works in a sports store and earns $13.50/h, plus 2% commission on his sales. One week, Phillipe worked 32 h and had sales of $5500. Find his earnings for that week.

74. What percent of 2.5 is 0.82?

75. What percent of 16 is 20?

76. If 35% of a number is 49, what is the number?

77. If 2.24 is 7% of a number, what is the number?

78. Elk Island, Mount Revelstoke, and Pacific Rim national parks are all in Western Canada. The area of Mount Revelstoke national park is 52% of the area of Pacific Rim national park. The area of Elk Island national park is 75% of the area of Mount Revelstoke national park. If the area of Pacific Rim national park is 500 km², find the area of
a) Mount Revelstoke national park
b) Elk Island national park

Evaluate for x = 5.

79. $5 - x$ **80.** $x - 3$ **81.** $x + 5$

82. $x + 1$ **83.** $-3x$ **84.** x^2

Evaluate for x = 3 and y = −2.

85. $2x + 3y$ **86.** $3(x + y)$

87. $x - 2y$ **88.** $3x + y$

89. $5x - 4y$ **90.** $x^2 + y^2$

91. a) Copy and complete the table for a boat travelling at 15 km/h.

Time (h)	Distance (km)
1	
2	
3	
4	

b) Write the results from the table as ordered pairs.
c) Let *d* represent the distance in kilometres, and *t* represent the time, in hours. Write an equation in the form $d = \blacksquare \times t$.
d) Use your equation to find the distance travelled in 5 h; 8 h; 3.5 h.

Use each of the following equations.
a) *Describe the relation in words.*
b) *Copy and complete the table of values.*
c) *Write the ordered pairs.*

92. $x + y = 7$ **93.** $y = x - 4$ **94.** $y = 3x$

x	y	x	y	x	y
2		2		2	
1		1		1	
0		0		0	
−1		−1		−1	
−2		−2		−2	

95. For the equation $y = 2x - 1$, find the missing value in each ordered pair.
a) $(1, \blacksquare)$ **b)** $(-4, \blacksquare)$ **c)** $(\blacksquare, 3)$
d) $(\blacksquare, 0)$ **e)** $(2, \blacksquare)$ **f)** $(\blacksquare, 5)$

Write 5 ordered pairs for each relation.

96. $x + y = 5$ **97.** $x - y = 3$

98. $y = x + 1$ **99.** $y = x - 2$

100. $y = 2x - 2$ **101.** $y = 3x - 5$

Write an equation for each relation.

102.

x	y
1	4
2	3
3	2
4	1
5	0

103.

x	y
4	5
5	4
6	3
7	2
8	1

Plot the points on a grid and join them in order. Identify each figure.

104. M(−1, 4), N(3, 4), P(3, 0), Q(−1, 0)
105. W(−5, 1), X(−5, −3), Y(2, −3), Z(2, 1)

Find 5 ordered pairs that satisfy each relation. Draw each graph.

106. $x + y = 4$ **107.** $y = 2x - 3$

Describe each equation in words.

108. $m - 2 = 3$ **109.** $3y + 2 = 8$

110. $\frac{x}{3} = 2$ **111.** $3y = y + 5$

Write an equation for each sentence.

112. Four more than a number is seventeen.

113. Three times a number is two more than twice the number.

114. One sixth of a number is three.

115. A number increased by ten is half the number.

Solve and check.

116. $y - 2 = 6$ **117.** $m + 5 = 9$

118. $a + 4 = 2$ **119.** $m - 3 = -4$

120. $1.5 + z = 3$ **121.** $4.6 = d - 3.2$

Solve and check.

122. $2x = 8$ **123.** $\frac{a}{3} = 7$

124. $3y = 7$ **125.** $2z = -4$

126. $\frac{x}{3} = 1.2$ **127.** $\frac{x}{4} = -1$

Simplify.

128. $-2x + 3x + x$ **129.** $y + 2y + 2 - 3y + 5$

Expand.

130. $4(x + 1)$ **131.** $-2(3x + 1)$

Solve and check.

132. $2m + 1 = 5$ **133.** $3x - 2 = 4$

134. $5 = 4y + 1$ **135.** $\frac{t}{3} - 1 = 2$

136. $4 = \frac{k}{2} + 3$ **137.** $2(c + 1) = 6$

Solve and check.

138. $2x - 1 = 3x + 5$ **139.** $2(x + 1) = -2$

140. The average mass of a white-tailed deer is 8 kg more than five times the average mass of a baboon The average mass of a white-tailed deer is 98 kg. What is the average mass of a baboon?

141. One less than three times the width of a rectangle is the length of the rectangle. The length is 14 cm. What is the width?

142. The average depth of the Black Sea is 653 m more than the average depth of the Red Sea. The average depth of the Black Sea is 1191 m. What is the average depth of the Red Sea?

Find the missing length, to the nearest tenth of a centimetre.

143.   **144.**

145. Abdul wants to construct a new rectangular garden bed 2.5 m by 1.5 m.
a) What will the length of the diagonal be, to the nearest tenth of a metre?
b) What length of fencing will he need to enclose the garden?

Calculate the perimeter of each figure.

146.   **147.**

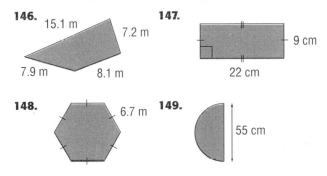

148.   **149.**

150. The diameter of the wheels of a bicycle is 53 cm. What distance does the bicycle cover for each complete turn of the wheels?

CONTINUED

Estimate, then calculate the area of each figure. Round each calculated answer to the nearest tenth, if necessary.

151.

152.

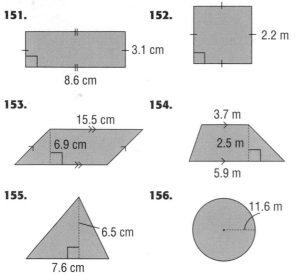

3.1 cm
8.6 cm

2.2 m

153.

15.5 cm
6.9 cm

154.

3.7 m
2.5 m
5.9 m

155.

6.5 cm
7.6 cm

156.

11.6 m

Calculate the perimeter and area of each shape. Round each answer to the nearest tenth, if necessary.

157.

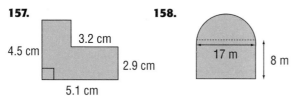

3.2 cm
4.5 cm
2.9 cm
5.1 cm

158.

17 m
8 m

Estimate, then calculate the surface area of each polyhedron. Round each calculated answer to the nearest tenth, if necessary.

159.

3.2 m   2.5 m
7.5 m

160.

1.7 m   3.0 m
1.6 m
2.5 m

Estimate, then calculate the volume of each prism. Round your answers to the nearest tenth, if necessary.

161.

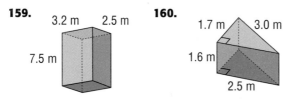

7.1 cm
7.1 cm
7.1 cm

162.

14.2 cm
13.6 cm
18.5 cm

Estimate, then calculate the surface area and the volume of each cylinder. Round each calculated answer to the nearest tenth, if necessary.

163.

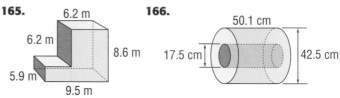

8 cm
22 cm

164.

7.5 m
6.3 m

Estimate, then calculate the surface area and the volume of each solid.

165.

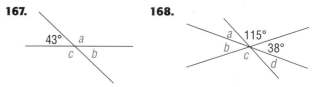

6.2 m
6.2 m
8.6 m
5.9 m
9.5 m

166.

50.1 cm
17.5 cm
42.5 cm

Find the missing measures.

167.

43°   *a*
c   *b*

168.

a   115°
b   38°
c   *d*

Write the measure of the complementary angle.

169. 5°   **170.** 80°   **171.** 35°

Write the measure of the supplementary angle.

172. 125°   **173.** 15°   **174.** 65°

Copy each figure and draw its lines of symmetry.

175.

176.

M

Find the missing angle measures.

177.

88°
a   46°

178.

116°
a
145°   50°

179.

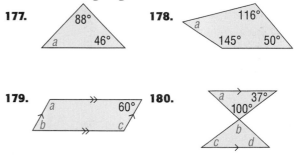

a   60°
b   *c*

180.

a   37°
100°
b
c   *d*

Identify the faces of the following solids.

181. square pyramid

182. triangular prism

Identify each of the following shapes.

183.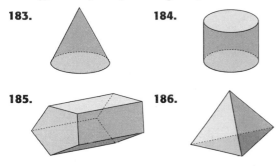

184.

185.

186.

187. Draw the net of a rectangular prism.

188. The table shows the world's 8 longest tunnels for road traffic.

Tunnel	Length (km)
Brooklyn-Battery (U.S.A.)	3.4
Great St. Bernard (Switzerland-Italy)	5.5
Lincoln (U.S.A.)	4.0
Mt. Blanc (France-Italy)	12.1
Mt. Ena (Japan)	8.5
Mount Royal (Canada)	5.1
Queensway Road (U.K.)	3.5
St. Gotthard (Switzerland)	16.4

a) Represent the data on a bar graph.
b) Which tunnel is 1.5 times longer than the Brooklyn-Battery Tunnel?

189. The table shows the number of species of different types of birds that breed in Canada. Use the data to draw a circle graph.

Type of Bird	Breeding Species in Canada
Ducks	36
Birds of Prey	19
Shorebirds	71
Owls	14
Perching Birds	180
Other	80

190. The table shows the approximate circulations of 6 magazines in Canada.

Magazine	Circulation
Canadian Geographic	250 000
Chatelaine	890 000
Equinox	170 000
L'Actualité	225 000
Maclean's	565 000
Westworld	825 000

a) Display the data on a pictograph.
b) Which two magazines have a combined circulation that is closest to *Westworld*'s?
c) Find the range of the data.

191. Write 6 numbers with a mean of 12, a mode of 11, and a median of 12.

192. The following speeds, in kilometres per hour, were measured for cars passing through a 50 km/h zone.
44, 50, 52, 63, 46, 50, 54, 56, 59, 63, 56, 39, 44, 45, 51
a) Display the data on a stem-and-leaf plot.
b) What is the median speed?

193. Draw a box-and-whisker plot to represent the following driving test scores.
85, 86, 60, 55, 73, 75, 81, 83, 84, 98, 56, 64, 68, 66, 88, 90, 92

194. a) List the possible outcomes when you spin the green and yellow spinners.
b) What is the probability of spinning a total of 4? 6? 7?

195. You spin the spinner and choose a card from a deck of playing cards. Find each probability.
a) a 5 and a black card
b) an even number and a diamond
c) a number and a card
d) a 0 and a red card

FLYING DISTANCES BETWEEN CANADIAN CITIES

From	To	(km)
Calgary	Edmonton	248
	Montreal	3003
	Ottawa	2877
	Regina	661
	Saskatoon	520
	Toronto	2686
	Vancouver	685
	Victoria	725
	Winnipeg	1191
Charlottetown	Ottawa	976
	Toronto	1326
Edmonton	Calgary	248
	Ottawa	2848
	Regina	698
	Saskatoon	484
	Toronto	2687
	Vancouver	826
	Winnipeg	1187
Halifax	Montreal	803
	Ottawa	958
	Saint John	192
	St. John's	880
	Sydney	306
	Toronto	1287
Montreal	Calgary	3003
	Fredericton	562
	Halifax	803
	Moncton	707
	Ottawa	151
	Saint John	614
	St. John's	1618
	Toronto	508
	Vancouver	3679
	Winnipeg	1816

From	To	(km)
Ottawa	Calgary	2877
	Charlottetown	976
	Edmonton	2848
	Halifax	958
	Montreal	151
	Toronto	363
	Vancouver	3550
	Winnipeg	1687
Regina	Calgary	661
	Edmonton	698
	Saskatoon	239
	Toronto	2026
	Vancouver	1330
	Winnipeg	533
St. John's	Halifax	880
	Montreal	1618
	Toronto	2122
Toronto	Calgary	2686
	Charlottetown	1326
	Edmonton	2687
	Halifax	1287
	Montreal	508
	Ottawa	363
	Regina	2026
	St. John's	2122
	Vancouver	3342
	Windsor	314
	Winnipeg	1502
Victoria	Calgary	725
	Vancouver	62
Windsor	Toronto	314
Winnipeg	Calgary	1191
	Edmonton	1187
	Montreal	1816
	Ottawa	1687
	Regina	533
	Saskatoon	707
	Toronto	1502
	Vancouver	1862

DRIVING DISTANCES BETWEEN CANADIAN CITIES (km)

From \ To	Edmonton	Halifax	Montreal	Ottawa	Quebec City	Regina	Saint John	St. John's	Saskatoon	Toronto	Vancouver	Victoria	Whitehorse	Winnipeg
Calgary	299	4973	3743	3553	4014	764	4664	6334	620	3434	1057	1162	2385	1336
Edmonton		5013	3764	3574	4035	785	4704	6367	528	3455	1244	1349	2086	1357
Halifax			1249	1439	982	4228	309	1503	4485	1788	6050	6154	7099	3656
Montreal				190	270	2979	940	2602	3236	539	4801	4905	5850	2408
Ottawa					460	2789	1130	2792	3046	399	4611	4715	5660	2218
Quebec City						3249	673	2363	3507	809	5071	5176	6120	2678
Regina							3919	5581	257	2670	1822	1926	2871	571
Saint John								1727	4176	1479	5741	5845	6790	3347
St. John's									5839	3141	7403	7775	8452	5010
Saskatoon										2927	1677	1782	2614	829
Toronto											4492	4596	5528	2099
Vancouver												105	2697	2232
Victoria													2802	2337
Whitehorse														3524

PLANETS: DISTANCES, ORBITS, MOONS

Mercury

Distance from the sun: 58 000 000 km

Time to orbit sun: 88 d

Number of moons: 0

Venus

Distance from the sun: 108 000 000 km

Time to orbit sun: 225 d

Number of moons: 0

Earth

Distance from the sun: 150 000 000 km

Time to orbit sun: 1 year

Number of moons: 1

Mars

Distance from the sun: 228 000 000 km

Time to orbit sun: 687 d

Number of moons: 2

Jupiter

Distance from the sun: 779 000 000 km

Time to orbit sun: 12 years

Number of moons: 16

Saturn

Distance from the sun: 1 425 000 000 km

Time to orbit sun: 29.5 years

Number of moons: 18

Uranus

Distance from the sun: 2 870 000 000 km

Time to orbit sun: 84 years

Number of moons: 15

Neptune

Distance from the sun: 4 497 000 000 km

Time to orbit sun: 165 years

Number of moons: 8

Pluto

Distance from the sun: 5 866 000 000 km

Time to orbit sun: 248 years

Number of moons: 1

WIND CHILL CHART

Wind Speed	Thermometer Reading (degrees Celsius)														
	4	2	−1	−4	−7	−9	−12	−15	−18	−21	−23	−26	−29	−32	−34
Calm	4	2	−1	−4	−7	−9	−12	−15	−18	−21	−23	−26	−29	−32	−34
8 km/h	3	1	−3	−6	−9	−11	−14	−17	−21	−24	−26	−29	−32	−36	−37
16 km/h	−2	−6	−9	−13	−17	−19	−23	−26	−30	−33	−36	−39	−43	−47	−50
24 km/h	−6	−9	−12	−17	−21	−24	−28	−32	−36	−40	−43	−46	−51	−54	−57
32 km/h	−8	−11	−16	−20	−23	−27	−31	−36	−40	−43	−47	−51	−56	−60	−63
40 km/h	−9	−14	−18	−22	−26	−30	−34	−38	−43	−47	−50	−55	−59	−64	−67
48 km/h	−11	−15	−19	−24	−28	−32	−36	−41	−45	−49	−53	−57	−61	−66	−70
56 km/h	−12	−16	−20	−25	−29	−33	−37	−42	−47	−51	−55	−58	−64	−68	−72
64 km/h	−13	−17	−21	−26	−30	−34	−38	−43	−48	−52	−56	−60	−66	−70	−74

Legend: Cold   Very Cold   Bitterly Cold   Extremely Cold

CANADA'S LONGEST RIVERS

River	Length (km)
Mackenzie	4241
Yukon	3185
St. Lawrence	3058
Nelson	2575
Columbia	2000
Saskatchewan	1939
Peace	1923
Churchill (Manitoba)	1609
South Saskatchewan	1392
Fraser	1370

WORLD'S LARGEST ISLANDS

Island	Area (km^2)
Greenland	2 175 600
New Guinea	792 540
Borneo	725 459
Madagascar	587 044
Baffin	507 454
Sumatra	427 350
Honshu	227 415
Great Britain	218 078
Victoria	217 291
Ellesmere	196 237

CANADA'S FRESH WATER

Province/ Territory	Percent of Canada's Fresh Water (nearest percent)
Alberta	2%
British Columbia	2%
Manitoba	13%
New Brunswick	0%
Newfoundland	5%
Northwest Territories	18%
Nova Scotia	0%
Ontario	24%
Prince Edward Island	0%
Quebec	24%
Saskatchewan	11%
Yukon Territory	1%

CANADA'S TALLEST WATERFALLS

Waterfall	Vertical Drop (m)
Della Falls	440
Takakkaw Falls	254
Hunlen Falls	253
Panther Falls	183
Helmcken Falls	137
Bridal Veil Falls	122
Virginia Falls	90
Chute Montmorency	84
Chute Ouiatchouan	79
Churchill Falls	75

CANADIAN WEATHER DATA

Average Monthly High and Low Temperatures

The temperature is represented by a vertical bar. The top of the bar represents the average daily high temperature for that month. The bottom of the bar represents the average daily low temperature for that month. The horizontal line represents the average annual temperature.

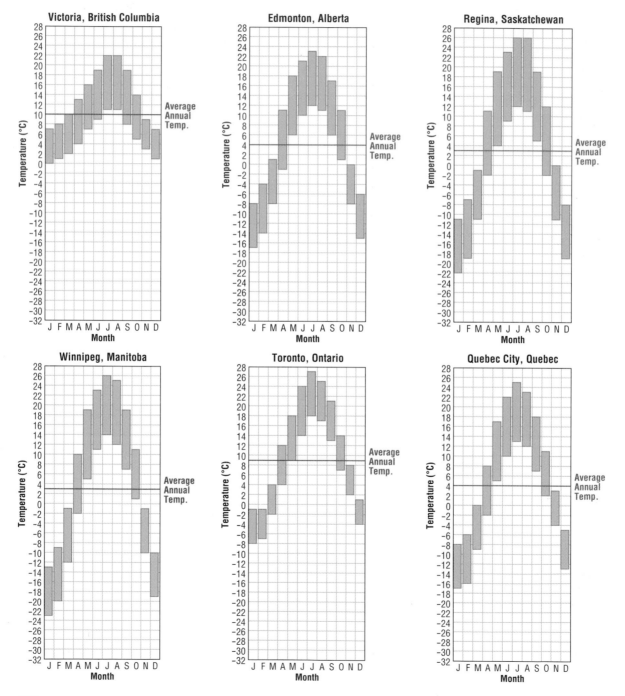

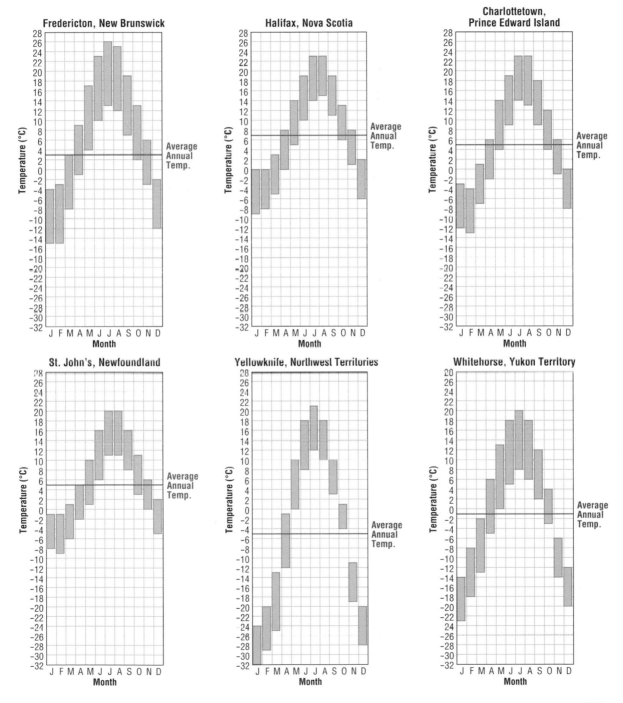

CANADIAN WEATHER DATA

Average Monthly Precipitation

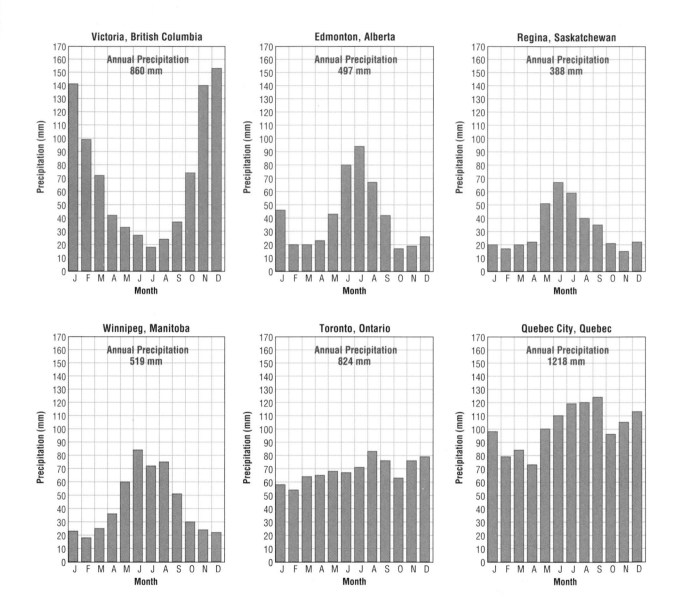

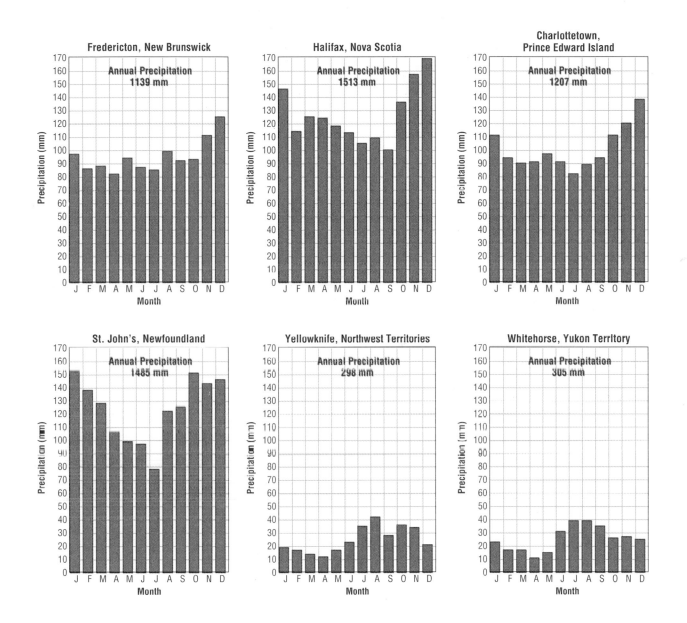

Fredericton, New Brunswick
Annual Precipitation 1139 mm

Halifax, Nova Scotia
Annual Precipitation 1513 mm

Charlottetown, Prince Edward Island
Annual Precipitation 1207 mm

St. John's, Newfoundland
Annual Precipitation 1485 mm

Yellowknife, Northwest Territories
Annual Precipitation 298 mm

Whitehorse, Yukon Territory
Annual Precipitation 305 mm

Answers

Exploring Math

Problem Solving p. xi

1. 127   **2.** Answers may vary. 5, 6, 7, 8; 1, 2, 3, 4, 9, 10, 11, 12   **3.** Answers may vary. Labelling the cells of the grid as on a spreadsheet, colour the cells as follows: A1–red, A2–green, A3–red, B1–green, B2–blue, B3–blue, C1–blue, C2–red, C3–green   **4.** 19 others   **5.** at the service centre

Communication p. xii

Activity 1:   **1. a)** D   **b)** B   **c)** > means "greater than"; < means "less than"   **Activity 2:**   **1.** 40
2. rectangle (includes square), certain trapezoids
3. 49, 64, 81, 100, 121, 144   **4.** triangular pyramid
5. 1:2, 0.5, 50% (many other ways are possible)
6. 1, 36; 2, 18; 3, 12; 4, 9; 6, 6

Reasoning p. xiii

Activity 1:   **1.** 25, 225, 625, 1225, 2025, 3025, 4225, 5625, 7225, 9025   **3.** The last 2 digits of each product are 25. The first digits are obtained by multiplying the digit preceding the ones digit by the same digits plus one.   **4. a)** 22 500   **b)** 202 500
c) 15 625   **d)** 38 025   **Activity 2:** 8 tiles by 6 tiles or 12 tiles by 5 tiles

Connections p. xiv

Activity 1:   **1. a)** 80 cm   **b)** 85 cm   **c)** 89 cm
Activity 2:   **1. a)** $\frac{1}{4}$ note   **b)** $\frac{1}{2}$ note   **c)** whole
note   **2. a)** $\frac{1}{4}$ note   **b)** $\frac{1}{4}$ note   **3.** 4   **Activity 3:**
1. a) rectangle, circle   **b)** rectangle, kite, or rhombus
c) rectangle, trapezoid   **d)** triangle, trapezoid, pentagon

Number and Number Relationships p. xv

Activity 1:   **1.** Each of large bedroom, kitchen, and living room: $\frac{1}{5}$; each small bedroom: $\frac{3}{25}$; bathroom: $\frac{1}{10}$; hallway: $\frac{3}{50}$ **2.** 20%, 12%, 10%, 6%
3. 0.2, 0.12, 0.1, 0.06   **5.** no   **Activity 2: a)** Start time: 08:00; Stop times: 10:00, 13:00, 16:00; Arrival time: 19:00   **b)** 550 km   **c)** 50 km/h, 100 km/h

Number Systems and Number Theory p. xvi

Activity 1:   **1.** 1, 2, 3, 4, 5, 6   **2.** Add 1 to the last odd number and divide the total by 2.   **3. a)** 45
b) 76   **c)** 105   **4.** 1, 4, 9, 16   **5.** Multiply the number of odd numbers by itself.   **6. a)** 2401
b) 3364   **c)** 12 769   **7. a)** 27   **b)** 146   **Activity 2:**
1. 2, 3, 4, 6, 8, 12, 24   **2.** 12, 8, 6, 4, 3, 2, 1; Chantal always gets one extra pencil.

Computation and Estimation p. xvii

Activity 1:   **1.** 87   **2.** 88   **3.** 151   **4.** 161
5. 765   **6.** 961   **7.** 15.5   **8.** 146.9   **Activity 2:**
1. 195   **2.** 938   **3.** 729   **4.** 595   **5.** 477   **6.** 282
7. 5.1   **8.** $0.83   **Activity 3:**   **1.** $7.50   **2.** $4.25
3. $3.03   **4.** $5.68   **5.** $2.31   **6.** $6.48   **7.** $12.45
8. $15.26

Patterns and Functions p. xviii

Activity 1:   **1.** 8   **2. a)** 16   **b)** 24   **c)** 36   **d)** 48
3. 11   **Activity 2:**   **1.** 1×1, 6; 2×2, 24; 3×3, 54; 4×4, 96; 5×5, 150; 6×6, 216   **2.** The number of small cube faces showing is 6 times the product of the dimensions of the face of the large cube.   **3.** 600

Algebra p. xix

Activity 1:   **1.** Use dimensions 1 by 7, 2 by 6, and 3 by 5.   **2.** Use 2 rectangles of dimension 1 by 4 connected along the edge of length 4.   **3.** Use 3 rectangles of dimension 1 by 2 or rectangles of dimensions 1 by 1, 1 by 2, and 1 by 3, connected in series along the edge of length 1.   **Activity 2:**
1. 2, 1; 6, 3; 8, 4   **2. a)** 1, 2; 2, 4; 3, 6   **b)** 1, 3; 2, 6; 3, 9   **c)** 1, 0; 2, 2; 3, 4   **d)** 1, 1; 2, 3; 3, 5   **e)** 0, 4; 1, 3; 2, 2   **Activity 3:**   **1. a)** 4   **b)** 5   **c)** 8   **2. a)** 9
b) 4   **c)** 3   **3. a)** $n + 3 = 8$, 5   **b)** $4 \times n = 12$, 3
c) $n - 7 = 4$, 11

Statistics p. xx

Activity 2:   **1.** Certain sums should occur more frequently than others. For example, a sum of 9 should occur most frequently since there are 10 possible combinations of the last 2 digits that will yield this sum.

Probability p. xxi

Activity 1:   **1.** since there is 1 tile numbered with a 3, and 10 is the total number of tiles   **2.** $\frac{1}{2}$ **3.** $\frac{1}{2}$
4. $\frac{4}{10}$

Chapter 1

Getting Started pp. 2–3

Activity 4: **1.** false **2.** true **3.** false **4.** true
5. false **6.** true **7.** false **Activity 5:**
2. a) 16.7 min **b)** 2.8 h **c)** 1 day 3.8 h **Activity 6:**
1. a) 11 days, 13 h, 46.7 min **b)** 1.9 **c)** unlikely
(about 114 years old) **Mental Math** **1.** 86 **2.** 158
3. 118 **4.** 132 **5.** 200 **6.** 323 **7.** 125 **8.** 187
9. 163 **10.** 256 **11.** 126 **12.** 155 **13.** 328
14. 201 **15.** 327 **16.** 22 **17.** 109 **18.** 44 **19.** 542
20. 91 **21.** 463 **22.** 687 **23.** 339 **24.** 189 **25.** 92
26. 432 **27.** 985 **28.** 471 **29.** 24 **30.** 72 **31.** 240
32. 360 **33.** 810 **34.** 600 **35.** 7200 **36.** 105
37. 319 **38.** 440 **39.** 147 **40.** 198 **41.** 192
42. 133 **43.** 420 **44.** 207 **45.** 80 **46.** 900 **47.** 40
48. 9 **49.** 60 **50.** 15 **51.** 800 **52.** 10 **53.** 50
54. 12 **55.** 90 **56.** 12 **57.** 15 **58.** 32

Section 1.1 pp. 5–6

Practice **1.** 2, 5, 32 **2.** 4, 3, 64 **3.** 5, 2, 25
4. 6, 1, 6 **5.** 7, 3, 343 **6.** 3^5 **7.** 10^8 **8.** 5^5 **9.** 2^{10}
10. 2^5 **11.** 2^1 **12.** 2^7 **13.** 2^8 **14.** 2^{10} **15.** 2^3
Problems and Applications **16.** 2^7 **17.** 3^5 **18.** 5^1
19. 2^1 **20.** 1^9 **21.** 1^3 **22.** 5^3 **23.** 7^3 **24.** 5^7
25. 2^3 **26.** 6^4 **27.** 4^6 **28.** 2^8 **29.** 5^3 **30.** 4^7
31. 10^8 **32.** 16 **33.** 81 **34.** 1 000 000 **35.** 256
36. 1 **37.** 729 **38. a)** 1000 **b)** 10^{30} kg **39.** 1024
40. 29 days **41.** 1 000 000 000 000, one trillion
42. 1 **43. a)** 81, 243, 729; 16, 32, 64; 64, 256, 1024;
1000, 10 000, 100 000 **b)** 3^0, 3^1, 3^2, 3^3, 3^4, 3^5, 3^6;
2^0, 2^1, 2^2, 2^3, 2^4, 2^5, 2^6; 4^0, 4^1, 4^2, 4^3, 4^4, 4^5;
10^0, 10^1, 10^2, 10^3, 10^4, 10^5 **c)** 3^0, 2^0, 4^0, 10^0 **d)** 1

Section 1.2 p. 7

Practice **1.** 10^5 **2.** 10^7 **3.** 10^{-5} **4.** 10^{-7} **5.** 10^{-5}
6. 10^{-9} **7.** 10 000 **8.** 100 000 **9.** 0.0001 **10.** 0.1
11. 0.000 000 001 **12.** 10 **Problems and
Applications** **13.** 10^{-3} **14.** < **15.** < **16.** > **17.** =
18. > **19.** = **20. a)** 1000 **b)** 1000

Section 1.3 p. 9

Problems and Applications **1.** 21, 25, 29
2. 53, 46, 39 **3.** 30, 25, 19 **4.** 48, 96, 192
5. m, p, s **6.** o, u, b **7.** 17, 27 **8.** 18, 29
9. 14, 18, 13 **10.** 8, 11, 45 **11.** 1, 5, 10, 10, 5, 1;
1, 6, 15, 20, 15, 6, 1; 1, 7, 21, 35, 35, 21, 7, 1;
1, 8, 28, 56, 70, 56, 28, 8, 1 **12. a)** 15, 21
b) Multiply the number of rays by one less than
the number of rays, and divide by 2 to get the

number of angles. **13. a)** 64, 144, 625 **b)** The kth
figure has $k \times k$ triangles. **14. a)** 42, 420, 10 100
b) The sum of the first k even numbers is $k \times (k + 1)$.
15. a) twice the first plus the second **b)** 13, 2, 7
16. a) twice the sum of the first and the second
b) 24, 9, 5

Section 1.4 p. 10

Practice **1.** 3 **2.** 5 **3.** 6 **4.** 7 **5.** 4 **6.** 6
7. 2.8 **8.** 3.6 **9.** 1.2 **10.** 6.3 **11.** 9.45 **12.** 7
13. 4.3×10^4 **14.** 8.25×10^5 **15.** 1.5×10^6
16. 9×10^3 **17.** 3.6×10^7 **18.** 9.8×10^2
19. 8.45×10^3 **20.** 3.4×10^5 **21.** 1.0×10^4
Problems and Applications **22.** 58 000
23. 90 000 000 **24.** 425 000 **25.** 1700 **26.** 600
27. 263 000 000 **28.** 7 500 000 **29.** 5 450 000 000
30. 6.5×10^5 km^2 **31.** 2.1×10^8 to 1.4×10^8
32. a) 3.43×10^2 km **b)** 3.43×10^5 m **33. a)** 17.2×10^4 **b)** 4.92×10^5 **c)** 4.3×10^5 **d)** 5.994×10^9

Section 1.5 p. 11

Practice **1.** -2 **2.** -5 **3.** -1 **4.** -3 **5.** -4 **6.** -6
7. -7 **8.** 4.6 **9.** 5.3 **10.** 2.4 **11.** 9.9 **12.** 7.3
13. 4 **14.** 8.7 **15.** 4.6×10^{-4} **16.** 3×10^{-6}
17. 1.24×10^{-2} **18.** 7.8×10^{-5} **19.** 1×10^{-4}
20. 2.7×10^{-7} **Problems and Applications**
21. 0.000 58 **22.** 0.0203 **23.** 0.000 000 007 96
24. 0.000 000 45 **25.** 0.000 010 3 **26.** 0.003 45
27. 5×10^{-3} mm **28.** 1.8×10^{-3}% **29.** 1.9×10^{-2}
30. 3.7×10^{-1} **31.** 3.36×10^{-3} **32.** 2.356×10^{-3}
33. 9.23×10^{-6} **34.** 1.748×10^{-8}

Section 1.6 pp. 16–17

Practice **1.** rational **2.** rational **3.** rational
4. undefined **5.** rational **6.** rational **7.** rational
8. irrational **9.** irrational **10.** rational **11.** rational
12. undefined **13.** $\frac{2}{-5}$ **14.** $\frac{7}{1}$ **15.** $\frac{6}{-12}$ **16.** $\frac{8}{3}$
17. $\frac{3}{-4}$ **18.** $\frac{5}{-1}$ **19.** $\frac{-2}{3}$ **20.** $\frac{2}{5}$ **21.** $\frac{1}{2}$ **22.** $\frac{-1}{2}$
23. $\frac{-1}{4}$ **24.** -7 **25.** $\frac{-6}{7}$ **26.** $\frac{-4}{5}$ **27.** $\frac{-1}{3}$ **28.** $\frac{4}{5}$
29. $\frac{11}{4}$ **30.** $\frac{2}{5}$ **31.** $\frac{-7}{1}$ **32.** $\frac{-6}{5}$ **33.** $\frac{-7}{2}$ **34.** $\frac{9}{4}$
35. $\frac{-3}{10}$ **36.** $\frac{-2}{3}$ **37.** $\frac{3}{4}$ **38.** $\frac{8}{3}$ **39.** $\frac{-3}{4}$ **40.** $\frac{-4}{-5}$
41. < **42.** < **43.** = **44.** > **45.** > **46.** <
47. 2, $1\frac{2}{5}$, $\frac{4}{5}$, $\frac{-7}{-10}$, $\frac{1}{2}$, 0, -0.5 **48.** $\frac{9}{4}$, $1\frac{7}{8}$, $\frac{11}{6}$, $1\frac{2}{3}$,
$1\frac{1}{2}$, $\frac{5}{4}$ **49.** $\frac{11}{9}$, $\frac{-11}{-9}$, $\frac{4}{-3}$, $\frac{-5}{3}$ or $\frac{-11}{-9}$, $\frac{11}{9}$, $\frac{4}{-3}$, $\frac{-5}{3}$
50. $\frac{9}{2}$, $\frac{7}{4}$, -0.75, -2, -2.6, -3, $-3\frac{1}{2}$ **Problems
and Applications** **51. a)** $\frac{1}{6}$ **b)** $\frac{-4}{2}$ **c)** $\frac{1}{-16}$
52. $\frac{2}{1}$ **53. a)** $\frac{5}{3}$ **b)** $\frac{4}{3}$ **c)** $\frac{3}{4}$ **d)** $\frac{5}{4}$ **e)** $\frac{1}{1}$ **f)** $\frac{3}{2}$ **g)** $\frac{7}{4}$

h) $\frac{2}{1}$ **54. a)** $\frac{2}{1}, \frac{7}{4}, \frac{5}{3}, \frac{3}{2}, \frac{4}{3}, \frac{5}{4}, \frac{1}{1}, \frac{3}{4}$ **b)** Gander
55. Elephants: $\frac{-2}{9}$, Monkeys: $\frac{1}{1}$, Giraffes: $\frac{5}{14}$,
Rhinoceros: $\frac{-2}{3}$, Hyenas: $\frac{0}{1}$ **56.** $\frac{10}{7}$ **57.** No;
opposite of $\frac{-3}{4}$ is $\frac{3}{4}$.   **59. a)** sometimes true
b) sometimes true   **c)** always true   **d)** always true
e) sometimes true

Section 1.7 p. 19

Problems and Applications   **1.** length of
the Mackenzie River   **2.** −32°C with a wind
speed of 40 km/h   **3.** 2.1 h   **4.** 501 km   **5.** 61
6. approximately 16:21   **7.** 3   **8.** 4.15 years
9. 19:00 Friday   **10.** 31 250   **11. a)** Saturday at
approximately 14:00   **b)** a stopover on the way from
Edmonton to Winnipeg

Section 1.8 pp. 20–21

Practice   **1.** 3:2:2   **2.** 2:3:7   **3.** 2:5:3   **4.** 5:2:7
5. 4:8:3   **6.** 4:6:9   **Problems and Applications**
7. 3:4:5   **8.** 13:12:11   **9. a)** 1:1   **b)** 13:16   **c)** 8:7
d) 13:7:16   **10. a)** 3:1   **b)** 2:3   **c)** 6:2:3   **11. a)** 5:3
b) 2:3   **c)** 4:15   **d)** 3:2   **e)** 2:3:5   **f)** 10:6:15
12. a) 6:5:3   **b)** 12:25:30   **c)** because each number in
the ratio in part a) must be multiplied by a different
number to obtain the ratio in part b)   **13. a)** 4:3
b) 8:1   **c)** 1:5   **d)** 2:1   **e)** 5:15:2   **f)** 4:7:1   **14.** The
term is a multiple of the prime number.

Learning Together pp. 22–23

Activity 2:   **1. b)** 25%   **2.** 25%   **4. b)** 12.5%
c) shade 37.5 squares from the hundred grid,
62.5 squares from the hundred grid, 87.5 squares
from the hundred grid   **Activity 3:**   **1.** 130%
Activity 4:   **1.** $\frac{1}{2}$, 50%   **2.** $\frac{1}{4}$, 25%   **3.** $\frac{3}{4}$, 75%
4. $\frac{1}{4}$, 25%   **5.** $\frac{1}{2}$, 50%   **6.** 1, 100%   **7.** $\frac{3}{4}$, 75%
8. $\frac{1}{2}$, 50%   **Activity 5:**   **1.** $\frac{8}{25}$, 32%   **2.** $\frac{7}{20}$, 35%
3. $\frac{3}{4}$, 75%   **4.** $\frac{3}{10}$, 30%   **5.** $\frac{6}{25}$, 24%   **6.** $\frac{11}{20}$, 55%
7. $\frac{1}{4}$, 25%   **8.** $\frac{7}{10}$, 70%   **9.** $\frac{1}{2}$, 50%   **10.** $\frac{13}{25}$, 52%

Section 1.9 p. 25

Practice   **1.** 40%   **2.** 52%   **3.** 20%   **4.** 34%
5. 62.5%   **6.** 60%   **7.** 66.7%   **8.** 75%   **9.** 25%
10. 20%   **11.** 37.5%, 40%, 33.3%, 25%, 75%, 80%
15. Estimates may vary.   **a)** 32%   **b)** 50%   **16.** 15, 15
17. 140, 140   **18.** 44, 88   **19.** 11, 44   **20.** 41, 164
21. 71, 35.5   **22.** 70%   **23.** 2%   **24.** 96%   **25.** 45%

26. 75%   **27.** 33.3%   **28.** 125%   **29.** 100%
30. 37.5%   **31.** $\frac{4}{5}$, 80%   **32.** $\frac{3}{4}$, 75%   **33.** $\frac{1}{2}$, 50%
34. $\frac{5}{3}$, 166.7%   **35.** $\frac{3}{8}$, 37.5%   **36.** $\frac{1}{5}$, 20%
Problems and Applications   **37.** 85%   **38.** 133.3%
39. 36%   **41. a)** 88%

Section 1.10 p. 27

Practice   **1.** 40%   **2.** 25%   **3.** 37.5%   **4.** 24%
5. 110%   **6.** 20%   **7.** 12.5%   **8.** 9.8%   **9.** 67.5%
10. 33.3%   **11.** 18.2%   **12.** 50%   **13.** 57.1%
14. 5.5%   **15.** 180%   **16.** 0.18   **17.** 0.859
18. 0.0675   **19.** 0.03   **20.** 0.333   **21.** 0.05   **22.** <
23. <   **24.** >   **25.** <   **26.** =   **27.** >   **Problems and**
Applications   **28.** 2%   **29.** 262%, $\frac{131}{50}$
30. 0.44, 44%   **31.** $\frac{3}{25}$, 12%   **32.** $\frac{4}{25}$, 0.16
33. 0.2, 20%   **34.** $\frac{2}{25}$, 8%   **35. a)** $0.\overline{142857}$ **b)** 14%
36. a) 50%, 80%, 60%   **b)** 1, 2.8, 3.4   **37.** 200%

Learning Together p. 28

Activity 1:   **1.** 3 units   **2.** $3 \times 3 = 9$ **3.** 3
4. a) 4 units, $4 \times 4 = 16$, 4   **b)** 5 units, $5 \times 5 = 25$, 5
Activity 2:   **1.** 3   **2.** 3.5   **3.** 3.5   **4.** 12.25, no
5. a) 4.5   **b)** 2.5   **c)** 5.5   **d)** 6.5   **Activity 3:**
1. 4 by 4, 2   **2.** divide by 4   **3.** 4.25   **4.** 4.25
5. a) 2.25   **b)** 2.75   **c)** 4.75   **d)** 6.25   **7. a)** 3.33
b) 3.66   **c)** 5.2   **d)** 6.17

Section 1.11 p. 31

Practice   **1.** 12   **2.** 20   **3.** 16   **4.** 25   **5.** 2.2
6. 0.9   **7.** 1.3   **8.** 0.5   **9–14.** Answers may vary.
9. 50   **10.** 130   **11.** 20   **12.** 90   **13.** 3   **14.** 10
15. 7, 8   **16.** 5, 6   **17.** 4, 5   **18.** 6, 7   **19.** 8, 9
20. 10, 11   **21.** 10, 9.6   **22.** 30, 28.3   **23.** 30, 31.6
24. 3, 3.2   **25.** 1, 0.9   **26.** 0.3, 0.3   **Problems**
and Applications   **27. a)** 1, 4, 9, 16, 25, 36, 49,
64, 81, 100, 121, 144, 169, 196, 225, 256, 289,
324, 361, 400   **b)** The last digit of a perfect square
must be 0, 1, 4, 5, 6, or 9.   **c)** 961, 3481, 2025,
1296   **28. a)** 75 km   **b)** 1241 km   **c)** 272   **29.** 9 cm,
4.5 cm   **30. a)** 18 cm², 32 cm²   **b)** 4.2 cm, 5.7 cm
31. a) sometimes true   **b)** always true   **c)** sometimes
true   **d)** sometimes true (when $n = 4$)   **e)** sometimes
true (when $n = 0$)

Connecting Math and Geography p. 33

Activity 1:   **1. Part 1:** 64 days, **Part 2:** 96 days,
Part 3: 86 days, **Part 4:** 68 days   **2.** 207   **3.** 107
Activity 2:   **1. a) Part 1:** 104.4 km/day, **Part 2:**
61.8 km/day, **Part 3:** 50 km/day, **Part 4:** 35.1 km/day

b) 57.2 km/day   **2. a)** downstream   **b)** Mackenzie's rate: 120 km/day; Students' rate: 104 km/day
3. Both rates are 35 km/day.   **Activity 3:**
1. 3240 strokes   **2.** 1714 h   **3.** 5 553 360 strokes

Section 1.12 p. 35

Problems and Applications   1. $266 570
2. $217.25   **3.** $790.25   **4.** $710   **5.** 1819
6. 14.5 m   **7.** cash, by $18.85   **8.** $4.40, assuming 8 h/week   **9.** 32 per year, assuming a uniform distribution   **10.** 450 000   **11.** $10   **12.** $605

Review pp. 36–37

1. 64   **2.** 625   **3.** 144   **4.** 2025   **5.** $3^4, 10^2, 5^3$
6. $4^3, 2^6, 11^2$ or $2^6, 4^3, 11^2$ **7.** 5^6 **8.** 3^6 **9.** 2^3
10. 2.4×10^4 **11.** 3.6×10^5 **12.** 5.8×10^6
13. 26 000   **14.** 83 100 000   **15.** 170 000
16. 6.3×10^{-3} **17.** 5.2×10^{-5} **18.** 4.7×10^{-2}
19. 4.6×10^{-8} **20.** 0.0043   **21.** 0.000 008 902
22. 0.0002   **23.** 0.000 051 3   **24.** $\frac{3}{5}$ **25.** $-\frac{14}{5}$
26. $-\frac{17}{10}$ **27.** $\frac{5}{3}$ **28.** $-175, -99.2, 50.2, 101.9, 155.7$
29. $-1.5, -0.91, 0, \frac{5}{4}, 1\frac{5}{6}, 2.9, 15.8$ **30.** 5.1
31. 1:4:5   **32.** 10:1:5   **34.** 1:3   **35.** 1:1
36. 1:2   **37.** 8:1   **38.** 4:1   **39.** 5:1   **40.** 2:5:1
41. 4:6:3   **42.** 6:3:8   **45.** Estimates may vary.
a) 35%   **b)** 55%   **46.** 0.2   **47.** 1.68   **48.** 0.358
49. 0.005   **50.** $\frac{1}{10}$ **51.** $\frac{3}{5}$ **52.** $\frac{1}{8}$ **53.** $\frac{47}{25}$ **54.** $\frac{3}{500}$
55. $\frac{1}{50}$ **56.** 40%   **57.** 55%   **58.** $104.1\overline{6}$ **59.** 175%
60. 83%   **61.** 1.5%   **62.** 187.5%   **63.** 132%
64. 66.7%   **65.** 44.4%   **66.** 155.6%   **67.** 11
68. 0.7   **69.** 30   **70.** 0.2   **71.** 21   **72.** 1.4
73–75. Estimates may vary.   **73.** 12.2   **74.** 2.9
75. 41.2   **76. a)** 1×10^{-6} s   **b)** 60×10^6 microseconds
c) 6×10^7 microseconds   **77.** 25.9 km   **78.** 10^{18} km
79. a) 9:10   **b)** 10:13:9   **80.** 81, 243, 729   **81.** 16, 8, 4   **82.** 82, 89, 96   **83.** 54, 43, 32

Chapter Check p. 38

1. $4^5, 1024$ **2.** $10^6, 1 000 000$ **3.** $2^9, 512$ **4.** $3^4, 81$
5. $6^3, 216$ **6.** 5.2×10^4 **7.** 2.7×10^5 **8.** 6.15×10^6
9. 5.8×10^{-2} **10.** 7×10^{-5} **11.** 1.13×10^{-3}
12. 2700   **13.** 79 000   **14.** 16 500 000   **15.** 0.032
16. 0.000 006 13   **17.** 0.000 028   **18.** $-5, -3.022, -0.5, \frac{3}{4}, 1.11, 1\frac{1}{2}, 5.01$ **19.** 1:3   **20.** 2:1   **21.** 1:2:3
22. 1:3   **23.** 1:1   **24.** 25%   **25.** 60%   **26.** 41%
27. 50%   **28.** 60%   **29.** 125%   **30.** 4%   **31.** 9.5%
32. 255%   **33.** 12.5%   **34.** $0.45, \frac{9}{20}$ **35.** $0.625, \frac{5}{8}$
36. $1.2, \frac{6}{5}$ **37.** $0.005, \frac{1}{200}$ **38–43.** Estimates may

vary.   **38.** 80%   **39.** 25%   **40.** 16   **41.** 2.5   **42.** 9.4
43. 0.4   **44.** 64   **45.** 10^{12} greater   **46.** 1.5×10^5 kg
47. 1000^3 **48. a)** 2:1   **b)** 3:8   **c)** 8:6:3

Using the Strategies p. 39

1. a) 31, 37, 43   **b)** 32, 64, 128   **c)** 77, 78, 73
d) j, l, n   **e)** si, se, ei   **f)** 53, 49, 46   **2. b)** The differences between consecutive pairs of triangular numbers start at 2 and increase by 1 each time.
c) 1, 3, 6, 10, 15, 21, 28, 36, 45, 55, 66, 78, 91, 105, 120   **d)** 4   **e)** 9   **f)** 16   **g)** sequence of perfect squares
3. a) 64   **b)** 169   **c)** 2601   **d)** 3025   **5.** $647.50
6. a) 3 times the difference of the first and the second   **b)** 21, 2, 7   **7. a)** 720 km   **b)** 40 km   **Data Bank   1.** Mackenzie and Nelson   **2.** approximately 3.6 h   **3.** Jupiter

Chapter 2

Getting Started pp. 42–43

Activity 1:   **1.** $\frac{1}{6}$ **2.** $\frac{3}{6}, \frac{1}{2}$ **3.** trapezoid   **4.** $\frac{1}{3}$
5. $\frac{2}{3}$ **6.** 4   **7.** $\frac{4}{6}, \frac{2}{3}$ **Activity 2:**   **1. a)** $\frac{1}{2}$ **b)** $\frac{1}{3}$
c) $\frac{2}{3}$ **d)** $\frac{2}{3}$ **e)** $\frac{5}{6}$ **f)** $\frac{5}{6}$ **3. a)** $1\frac{1}{6}$ **b)** $2\frac{1}{2}$ **c)** $2\frac{5}{6}$ **d)** $1\frac{2}{3}$
Warm Up   1. 87, 612, 315   **2.** 5, 7   **3.** 2, 3
4. 3, 7   **5.** 2   **6.** 3, 17   **7.** 2, 3   **8.** 2   **9.** 1   **10.** 5
11. 3   **12.** 8   **13.** 1   **14.** 6   **15.** 4   **16.** 8, 16, 24, 32, 40   **17.** 6, 12, 18, 24, 30   **18.** 2, 4, 6, 8, 10
19. 4, 8, 12, 16, 20   **20.** 12, 24   **21.** 16, 32   **22.** 12
23. 24   **24.** A: $\frac{1}{8}$, B: $\frac{1}{2}$, C: $\frac{5}{8}$, D: $\frac{3}{4}$ **25.** $\frac{8}{1}$ **26.** $2\frac{1}{2}$, $1\frac{4}{5}, 3\frac{1}{4}, 6\frac{2}{3}$ **27.** $\frac{4}{3}$ **28.** 1   **29.** $\frac{1}{2}$ **30.** 0   **31.** 1
32. 2   **33.** 3   **34.** 5   **35.** 1   **Mental Math   1.** 1
2. $\frac{4}{5}$ **3.** 1   **4.** 1   **5.** $5\frac{1}{4}$ **6.** $3\frac{1}{2}$ **7.** $4\frac{3}{5}$ **8.** 4   **9.** 2
10. 2   **11.** 3   **12.** 1   **13.** 2   **14.** 2   **15.** $\frac{1}{3}$ **16.** $\frac{1}{2}$
17. 1   **18.** $\frac{12}{5}$ **19.** $2\frac{2}{5}$ **20.** $\frac{1}{2}$ **21.** 10   **22.** 8   **23.** 9
24. 8   **25.** 5   **26.** 3   **27.** 7   **28.** 15   **29.** 14   **30.** 17
31. 17   **32.** 11   **33.** 4   **34.** 9   **35.** 8   **36.** 16   **37.** 25
38. 36

Section 2.1 p. 45

Problems and Applications   1. 151   **2.** 201
3. Determine the length of time to read 10 pages, then multiply that result by 21.   **4.** 45   **5.** 132
6. 212   **7.** Answers may vary.   **a)** Count the number of breaths in 1 min. Then, multiply by 10 080, the number of minutes in a week.   **8.** 0.000 000 005
10. 3825   **11.** 83   **12. a)** 1   **b)** 1

Learning Together pp. 46–47

Activity 2: **1.** 3, $\frac{3}{6} = \frac{1}{2}$ **2.** 4, $\frac{4}{12} = \frac{1}{3}$ **3.** Answers may vary. **a)** $\frac{2}{6}, \frac{3}{9}; \frac{1}{3} = \frac{2}{6}, \frac{1}{3} = \frac{3}{9}, \frac{2}{6} = \frac{3}{9}$ **b)** $\frac{2}{8}, \frac{3}{12}$; $\frac{1}{4} = \frac{2}{8}, \frac{1}{4} = \frac{3}{12}, \frac{2}{8} = \frac{3}{12}$ **c)** $\frac{6}{8}, \frac{9}{12}$; $\frac{3}{4} = \frac{6}{8}, \frac{3}{4} = \frac{9}{12}$, $\frac{6}{8} = \frac{9}{12}$ **d)** $\frac{2}{4}, \frac{1}{2}$; $\frac{4}{8} = \frac{2}{4}, \frac{4}{8} = \frac{1}{2}, \frac{2}{4} = \frac{1}{2}$ **e)** $\frac{2}{3}, \frac{8}{12}$; $\frac{4}{6} = \frac{2}{3}, \frac{4}{6} = \frac{8}{12}, \frac{2}{3} = \frac{8}{12}$ **Activity 3:** **2. a)** $\frac{4}{5}$ **b)** $\frac{7}{8}$ **c)** $\frac{7}{10}$ **d)** $\frac{7}{12}$ **4. a)** $\frac{5}{8}$ **b)** $\frac{9}{10}$ **c)** $\frac{7}{8}$ **d)** $\frac{9}{12}$ **Activity 4:** **2. a)** $\frac{2}{6}$ **b)** $\frac{4}{10}$ **c)** $\frac{2}{5}$ **d)** $\frac{6}{12}$ **4. a)** $\frac{3}{8}$ **b)** $\frac{3}{10}$ **c)** $\frac{8}{12}$ **d)** $\frac{7}{12}$ **Activity 5:** **1.** $\frac{4}{8}, \frac{4}{6}$ **2.** $\frac{1}{2}, \frac{2}{3}$ **3. a)** $\frac{3}{5}$ **b)** $\frac{5}{6}$ **c)** $\frac{1}{2}$

Section 2.2 p. 49

Practice **1.** $\frac{1}{4} + \frac{1}{2} = \frac{3}{4}$ **2.** $\frac{1}{4} + \frac{5}{8} = \frac{7}{8}$ **3.** $\frac{6}{8} + 1\frac{2}{3} = 2\frac{5}{12}$ **4.** $\frac{3}{5}$ **5.** 1 **6.** $\frac{2}{3}$ **7.** $1\frac{1}{2}$ **8.** $1\frac{1}{4}$ **9.** $1\frac{2}{9}$ **10.** $\frac{2}{3}$ **11.** $\frac{11}{12}$ **12.** $\frac{11}{12}$ **13.** $1\frac{1}{8}$ **14–27.** Estimates may vary. **14.** $2\frac{1}{2}$ **15.** 4 **16.** 6 **17.** $6\frac{2}{5}$ **18.** $1\frac{3}{4}$ **19.** $3\frac{5}{8}$ **20.** $4\frac{1}{10}$ **21.** $3\frac{5}{6}$ **22.** $8\frac{4}{15}$ **23.** $3\frac{7}{12}$ **24.** $1\frac{1}{2}$ **25.** $1\frac{5}{8}$ **26.** $2\frac{9}{14}$ **27.** $6\frac{3}{4}$ **Problems and Applications** **28.** $\frac{1}{2}$ **29.** $\frac{7}{8}$ **30.** $\frac{17}{20}$ **31.** no; $\frac{1}{3} + \frac{1}{4} + \frac{1}{2} = 1\frac{1}{12}$ **32.** $3\frac{1}{4}$ **33.** Answers may vary. **a)** $\frac{1}{3}, \frac{1}{6}; \frac{1}{10}, \frac{2}{5}$ **b)** $\frac{2}{3}, \frac{5}{6}; \frac{4}{5}, \frac{7}{10}$

Section 2.3 p. 51

Practice **1.** $\frac{1}{12}$ **2.** $\frac{1}{2}$ **3.** $\frac{1}{3}$ **4.** $\frac{1}{4}$ **5.** $\frac{1}{8}$ **6.** $\frac{3}{10}$ **7.** $\frac{1}{2}$ **8.** $\frac{1}{6}$ **9.** $\frac{1}{3}$ **10.** $\frac{1}{12}$ **11–22.** Estimates may vary. **11.** $2\frac{2}{5}$ **12.** $4\frac{1}{4}$ **13.** $4\frac{1}{2}$ **14.** $1\frac{1}{3}$ **15.** $2\frac{1}{4}$ **16.** $1\frac{1}{8}$ **17.** $1\frac{2}{3}$ **18.** $2\frac{3}{4}$ **19.** $1\frac{1}{6}$ **20.** $2\frac{3}{10}$ **21.** $\frac{7}{12}$ **22.** $1\frac{11}{12}$ **Problems and Applications** **23.** $\frac{1}{20}$ **24. a)** Subtract $\frac{2}{3}$ from both sides. **b)** $1\frac{1}{6}$ **25.** $\frac{2}{5}$ **26.** $1\frac{5}{12}$ **27.** $1\frac{1}{8}$ **28.** $3\frac{1}{12}$ **29. a)** Carol **b)** $\frac{1}{12}$ lap **30.** $\$3\frac{3}{4}$ **31.** $\frac{5}{12}$ **32.** Answers may vary. **a)** $\frac{9}{20}, \frac{1}{5}; \frac{7}{12}, \frac{1}{3}$ **b)** $\frac{17}{24}, \frac{1}{3}; \frac{7}{8}, \frac{1}{2}$ **c)** $\frac{5}{6}, \frac{1}{3}; \frac{13}{18}, \frac{2}{9}$

Section 2.4 p. 53

Problems and Applications **1.** Avenue B and 2nd Street **2.** 1901 **3.** 06:25 **4.** 46 **5.** 36 **6.** 22 **7.** 16 **8.** $30 824.60 **9.** $206.66 **10.** 18:35 **11.** $25 000

Learning Together pp. 54–55

Activity 2: **1.** $\frac{3}{8}$ **2.** $\frac{4}{9}$ **3.** $\frac{3}{16}$ **4.** $\frac{2}{12}$ **5.** $\frac{1}{12}$ **6.** $\frac{2}{9}$ **7.** no **Activity 3:** **1.** $\frac{4}{6}$ **2.** $\frac{3}{4}$ **3.** $1\frac{3}{12}$ **Activity 4:** **1.** 1 **2.** 1 **3.** 1 **4.** a fraction and its reciprocal

Section 2.5 p. 57

Practice **1.** $\frac{1}{8}$ **2.** $\frac{2}{9}$ **3.** $\frac{3}{10}$ **4.** $\frac{1}{12}$ **5.** $\frac{2}{15}$ **6.** $\frac{3}{8}$ **7.** $\frac{5}{12}$ **8.** $\frac{1}{2}$ **9.** $\frac{5}{8}$ **10.** $\frac{1}{8}$ **11.** $\frac{1}{2}$ **12.** 4 **13–21.** Estimates may vary. **13.** $\frac{9}{2}$ **14.** 9 **15.** $\frac{13}{2}$ **16.** $\frac{20}{3}$ **17.** $\frac{7}{12}$ **18.** $\frac{9}{16}$ **19.** 3 **20.** $\frac{55}{6}$ **21.** $\frac{25}{9}$ **22.** $\frac{4}{15}$ **23.** $\frac{5}{12}$ **24.** $\frac{7}{8}$ **25.** 11 **26.** 4 **27.** $\frac{1}{3}$ **28.** $\frac{5}{3}$ **29.** $\frac{4}{5}$ **30.** $\frac{9}{2}$ **31.** $\frac{2}{7}$ **32.** $\frac{3}{7}$ **33.** $\frac{8}{15}$ **Problems and Applications** **34.** $\frac{5}{24}$ **35.** 170 **36.** $\frac{1}{9}$ **37.** 54 **38.** 2 **39. a)** $10\frac{1}{2}$ **b)** 45 **c)** $\frac{3}{4}$ **40.** No; the reciprocal must be less than 1.

Section 2.6 p. 59

Practice **1.** $\frac{1}{2}$ **2.** 4 **3.** 4 **4.** $1\frac{1}{2}$ **5.** $\frac{3}{4}$ **6.** $1\frac{1}{9}$ **7.** 6 **8.** 9 **9.** $\frac{1}{6}$ **10.** 5 **11.** 11 **12.** $\frac{9}{20}$ **13.** $\frac{1}{3}$ **14.** $1\frac{1}{2}$ **15.** $1\frac{5}{6}$ **Problems and Applications** **16.** 8 **17.** $\frac{3}{10}$ **18.** 13 **19.** 40 **20.** 40 W **21.** 80 years **22.** because $2\frac{3}{4}$ is closer to 3 than to 2 **23.** larger; since you multiply by the reciprocal, which is larger than 1 **24. a)** 2, 2, 2, $\frac{1}{4}$, $1\frac{1}{2}$, $1\frac{1}{4}$, $\frac{1}{2}$ **b)** the same denominator **c)** 2, 2, 2, $\frac{1}{4}$, $1\frac{1}{2}$, $1\frac{1}{4}$, $\frac{1}{2}$ **e)** $1\frac{1}{2}$, $1\frac{1}{4}$, $2\frac{1}{2}$, 8, $2\frac{1}{2}$, $1\frac{7}{8}$

Technology p. 62

Activity 1: **1.** yes **2. a)** $\frac{13}{20}$, 0.65 **b)** $2\frac{1}{4}$, 2.25 **c)** $\frac{1}{2}$, 0.5 **d)** $\frac{5}{12}$, 0.41$\overline{6}$ **e)** $\frac{1}{3}$, 0.$\overline{3}$ **f)** $1\frac{7}{8}$, 1.875 **g)** $\frac{5}{6}$, 0.8$\overline{3}$ **h)** 3, 3 **i)** 10 , 10 **j)** $\frac{1}{2}$, 0.5 **Activity 2:** Answers may vary. **1. a)** 1.018 75 **b)** C ⎀ 1 + 3 ÷ 4 ⎀ ÷ ⎀ 5 ÷ 8 ⎀ = **c)** C 5 ÷ 8 = M+ C 1 + 3 ÷ 4 = ÷ MRC = **2. a)** 0.85, $\frac{17}{20}$ **b)** 2.15, $2\frac{3}{20}$ **c)** 0.5, $\frac{1}{2}$ **d)** 0.875, $\frac{7}{8}$ **e)** 0.$\overline{4}$, $\frac{4}{9}$ **f)** 3.9375, $3\frac{15}{16}$ **g)** 2.$\overline{8}$, $2\frac{8}{9}$ **h)** 0.$\overline{36}$, $\frac{4}{11}$ **i)** 0.30$\overline{5}$, $\frac{11}{36}$ **j)** 0.8$\overline{3}$, $\frac{5}{6}$

Section 2.7 pp. 64–65

Practice **1.** $\frac{1}{2} \times \frac{2}{3} = \frac{1}{3}$ **2.** $\frac{1}{2} \times \frac{1}{2} = \frac{1}{4}$ **3.** $\frac{3}{4} \times \frac{1}{2} = \frac{3}{8}$
4. 9 **5.** −21 **6.** 12 **7.** −9 **8.** −0.15 **9.** −0.15
10. 1 **11.** $\frac{1}{16}$ **12.** −0.075 **13.** −0.375 **14.** $1\frac{4}{5}$
15. 0.525 **16.** $\frac{1}{4}$ **17.** 0 **18.** $4\frac{7}{8}$ **19.** −1.875
20. 2.505 **21.** −0.875 **22.** $4\frac{3}{8}$ **23.** 10 **24. a)** 0.3
b) −0.45 **c)** −0.225 **Problems and Applications**
25. 140 **26.** 37.375 km **27.** −6.5°C **28.** 546 h
29. 15 000 **30. a)** 0.5 million **31. a)** never true
b) always true **c)** sometimes true

Section 2.8 pp. 67–68

Practice **1.** $\frac{1}{2} \div 2 = \frac{1}{4}$ **2.** $\frac{2}{3} \div 4 = \frac{1}{6}$ **3.** 2 **4.** 2
5. −0.2 **6.** 2 **7.** 4 **8.** 2 **9.** $\frac{3}{5}$ **10.** $\frac{2}{7}$ **11.** $\frac{1}{3}$
12. $\frac{4}{7}$ **13.** none **14.** $\frac{5}{11}$ **15.** negative **16.** positive
17. positive **18.** negative **19.** positive **20.** negative
21. $\frac{3}{4} \div \frac{1}{2} = \frac{3}{2}$ **22.** $1\frac{3}{4} \div \frac{1}{4} = 7$ **23.** $\frac{2}{3} \div \frac{1}{3} = 2$
24. 5 **25.** 3.5 **26.** −42 **27.** −125 **28.** undefined
29. 1 **30.** $4\frac{2}{3}$ **31.** −0.4375 **32.** 2.25 **33.** −39.75
Problems and Applications **34.** 5 **35.** 92 km/h
36. a) $2.03 **b)** $506.89 **37.** about 125 **38.** 11
39. $\frac{1}{16}$ **40.** 8 L **41.** 260 **42.** $16 600 **43.** −1
44. Answers may vary. **a)** $\frac{5}{2}$, 2 **b)** $-\frac{1}{8}, \frac{1}{4}$ **c)** $11\frac{1}{4}, 2\frac{1}{4}$

Section 2.9 pp. 70 71

Practice **1.** 10 **2.** 8 **3.** 12 **4.** 4 **5.** 1 **6.** 3
7. 3 **8.** 1 **9.** 7 **10.** true **11** false **12.** false
13. true **14.** $\frac{25}{12}$ **15.** 3.75 **16.** $\frac{10}{9}$ **17.** $\frac{3}{10}$
18. −0.92 **19.** $\frac{7}{20}$ **20.** −1.1 **21.** $1\frac{9}{16}$ **22.** $2\frac{2}{9}$
23. −0.04 **24.** 9.88 **25.** $\frac{83}{100}$ **26.** $\frac{99}{100}$ **27.** −14.56
28. −6.45 **29.** −0.66 **30.** 3.75 **31.** 1.73
Problems and Applications **32.** −1.9°C **33.** −1.5
34. $\frac{3}{4}$ **35.** $\frac{5}{8}$, $315 **36.** 1 min 27.66 s **37.** $\frac{1}{5}$
38. a) opposites **b)** both equal 0 **39. a)** sometimes
b) sometimes **c)** sometimes **40.** Answers may vary.
a) $-\frac{7}{10}, \frac{1}{10}$ **b)** $-\frac{1}{4}, -\frac{5}{8}, -\frac{11}{8}$ **c)** $\frac{11}{8}, \frac{3}{4}$

Section 2.10 p. 73

Problems and Applications **2. a)** that she will
be required to pay $2000 as a first year student
b) fees may increase **3. a)** 11, 13, 15 **b)** 10, 6, 2
c) 81, 243, 729 **d)** 32, 16, 8 **e)** 16, 22, 29 **f)** 11,
10, 13 **g)** j, o, m **4. a)** 3 **b)** not required to stop
5. a) He would score 10 points per game, on average.

b) not necessarily **6. a)** 3.5 h **b)** constant speed of
80 km/h **7. a)** 12 school days **8. a)** He would sell
8000 cards per month, on average. **b)** Some months
are better than others for selling cards. **10. a)** 30 s
b) constant rate of decrease **c)** no

Review pp. 74–75

1. Answers may vary. $\frac{6}{8}, \frac{12}{16}, \frac{9}{12}$ **2.** 5 **3.** 1 **4.** 20
5–18. Estimates may vary. **5.** $\frac{1}{2}$ **6.** $\frac{5}{8}$ **7.** $2\frac{1}{2}$
8. 5 **9.** $3\frac{1}{3}$ **10.** $7\frac{1}{6}$ **11.** $2\frac{7}{8}$ **12.** $4\frac{3}{5}$ **13.** $\frac{1}{3}$ **14.** $\frac{1}{6}$
15. $\frac{2}{3}$ **16.** $\frac{9}{10}$ **17.** $\frac{13}{20}$ **18.** $\frac{1}{8}$ **19.** $\frac{3}{8}$ **20.** $1\frac{1}{6}$ **21.** $\frac{2}{3}$
22. 3 **23–28.** Estimates may vary. **23.** 10 **24.** $\frac{3}{16}$
25. 2 **26.** $\frac{2}{5}$ **27.** $1\frac{1}{9}$ **28.** $6\frac{1}{2}$ **29.** 2 **30.** $\frac{8}{3}$ **31.** $\frac{1}{3}$
32. $\frac{3}{16}$ **33–38.** Estimates may vary. **33.** $1\frac{1}{2}$ **34.** $\frac{1}{3}$
35. $\frac{1}{4}$ **36.** $1\frac{3}{8}$ **37.** $1\frac{5}{8}$ **38.** $\frac{6}{11}$ **39.** 3.5 **40.** 0.1875
41. 5.79 **42.** $\frac{6}{7}$ **43.** 9 **44.** 3.316 **45.** 0.3 **46.** 0.333
47. 1.8 **48.** −3.5 **49.** 5.4 **50.** −6.5 **51. a)** 0.4
b) −0.2 **c)** −0.7 **d)** 1.6 **e)** 1.3 **f)** 1.3 **52.** $1\frac{7}{12}$
53. $\frac{1}{50}$ **54.** 2 **55.** $4\frac{1}{2}$ h **56.** $\frac{7}{8}$ **57.** $\frac{3}{4}$ **58.** $\frac{2}{5}$
59. 450 cm **60.** 425 kg **61. a)** $70.13 **b)** $114.69
c) $173.05 **62. a)** 26.25 cm² **b)** 6.76 m² **63.** 63.125
64. a) no: activities add up to a 25 h day **b)** yes

Chapter Check p. 76

1. Answers may vary. $\frac{4}{6}, \frac{8}{12}$ **2.** $1\frac{1}{5}$ **3.** $1\frac{1}{3}$ **4.** $3\frac{1}{2}$
5. $6\frac{1}{4}$ **6.** $\frac{1}{3}$ **7.** $\frac{1}{3}$ **8.** $\frac{7}{12}$ **9.** $2\frac{7}{12}$ **10.** 6 **11.** $\frac{1}{6}$
12. $\frac{1}{6}$ **13.** $1\frac{5}{6}$ **14.** 3, $\frac{5}{11}$ **15.** 2 **16.** $1\frac{1}{2}$ **17.** 10
18. $1\frac{5}{9}$ **19.** 0.994 **20.** −0.36 **21.** 8 **22.** 19
23. −4.975 **24.** 1.715 **25.** −5.368 **26.** 217.495
27. 3.45 **28.** −8 **29.** −7.6 **30.** 2.1 **31.** 0.3
32. −0.375 **33.** $3.20 **34. a)** $7.39 **b)** $12.61
35. $\frac{19}{20}$ **36. a)** $1683.00 **b)** $49.50 **c)** $1633.50
37. $\frac{3}{5}$ **38.** 20 years

Using the Strategies p. 77

1. 67, 69, 71 **2.** 72, 67, 68 **3.** v, u, t **4.** ev, fu, gt
5. j, j, a **6. a)** 21 **b)** 1001, 15 001 **7.** 10 kiwis,
5 pineapples, 6 bananas **9.** Answers vary depending
on climate assumptions. **10.** $471 526.25 **11.** $74
12. 8 years **13. a)** 6 **b)** 24 **14.** 57 weeks, 1 day
16. 131 **Data Bank** **1.** 15:00 on a Tuesday
2. via Calgary is shorter by 95 km

33. 72   **34.** 28   **35.** 24 310 km²   **36.** $13.20, $6.80, $6.00, $9.20, $4.80   **37.** $28.50, $28.50, $38.00

Section 4.3 p. 118

Practice Estimates may vary.   **1.** 25%   **2.** 33%   **3.** 80%   **4.** 40   **5.** 60   **6.** $20   **7.** $10   **8.** 90%   **9.** 75%   **10.** 67%   **11.** 50%   **Problems and Applications**   **12.** 60%   **13.** $6   **14.** $2.40   **15.** $1.50   **16.** $18   **17.** $3   **18.** $4.50   **19.** 42 000   **20.** 150

Section 4.4 p. 119

Problems and Applications   Estimates may vary.   **1.** $8, $7.99   **2.** $1, $1.13   **3.** $36, $35.20   **4.** $42, $41.97   **5.** $120, $119.99   **6.** $2, $1.88   **7.** $1200, $1205.55   **8.** $25.50, $25.46   **9.** $360, $359.60   **10.** yes   **11.** $36

Section 4.5 p. 120

Problems and Applications   Estimates for GST only. Estimates may vary.   **1.** $7   **2.** $1.40   **3.** $2100   **4.** $4.20   **5–10.** Answers for GST only.   **5.** $106.95   **6.** $2192.43   **7.** $23.27   **8.** $8.45   **9.** $115.56   **10.** $192.60

Section 4.6 p. 121

Problems and Applications   **1. a)** $4800   **b)** $1800   **c)** $1132.50   **d)** $1406.25   **2. a)** $200   **b)** $155   **c)** $317.50   **d)** $199.80   **3.** $513.90   **4.** $790.74   **5.** $3358.71

Section 4.7 p. 123

Problems and Applications   **1.** Robert   **2.** Ana: 6, Brenda: 8, Carlos: 7, Devon: 4   **3.** Mary: art, Harminder: math, Allison: history   **4.** Tessa: 7, Yuri: 8, Jennifer: 9   **5.** 44   **6.** Shelly, Francine, Donna   **7.** 7   **8.** Manitoba, British Columbia, Prince Edward Island, Alberta   **9.** Aaron: Inca Room, Jessica: Dinosaur Room, Stephanie: Aztec Room, Roberto: Egyptian Room   **10.** 8

Technology pp. 124–125

Activity 1:   **2. a)** trapezoid   **b)** rectangular prism

Section 4.8 p. 127

Practice   **1.** 80%   **2.** 57%   **3.** 51.5%   **4.** 167%   **5.** 2%   **6.** 240%   **7.** 30.2%   **8.** 99.9%   **9.** 0.7%   **10.** 80%   **11.** 30%   **12.** 65%   **13.** 32%   **14.** 100%

15. 125%   **16.** 22%   **17.** 30%   **18.** 37.5%   **19.** 66.7%   **20.** 57.1%   **21.** 55.6%   **22.** 16.7%   **23.** 136.4%   **24.** 107.7%   **25.** 12.5%   **26.** 60%   **27.** 87.5%   **28.** 133.3%   **29.** 68.6%   **30.** 15%   **Problems and Applications**   **31. a)** 40%   **b)** 87.5%   **32. a)** 80%   **b)** 20%   **33.** 47.4%   **34.** 30%   **35. a)** 20%   **b)** 120%   **36.** 91%

Section 4.9 p. 129

Practice   **1.** 4   **2.** 3   **3.** 2   **4.** 6.1   **5.** 500   **6.** 2600   **7.** 820   **8.** 2970   **9.** 5, 500   **10.** 5, 500   **11.** 4, 400   **12.** 200   **13.** 300   **14.** 600   **15.** 40   **16.** 700   **17.** 12   **18.** 800   **19.** 90   **Problems and Applications**   **20.** $23 000   **21.** 493 000 000 km²   **22.** 10 000   **23.** $350   **24. a)** 60   **b)** 30

Section 4.10 p. 130

Problems and Applications   **1.** $48, $848   **2.** $140, $1140   **3.** $390, $2390   **4.** $205, $5205   **5.** $2700, $10 200   **6.** $2250, $12 250   **7.** $1449, $5949   **8.** $351, $9351   **9.** $1720   **10.** $5250, $110 250; $110 250, 5%, $5512.50, $115 762.50; $115 762.50, 5%, $5788.13, $121 550.63; $121 550.63, 5%, $6077.53, $127 628.16

Connecting Math and Geology p. 131

Activity 1:   **1.** New Brunswick, Nova Scotia, Prince Edward Island   **3.** 20°N, 90°W

Section 4.11 p. 133

Problems and Applications   **1. a)** $112.50   **b)** $101.25   **c)** 67.5%   **d)** $48.75   **e)** 32.5%   **2. a)** 3000 km   **b)** 4200 km   **c)** 210%   **3. a)** $1500   **b)** $6000   **c)** $7500   **d)** 5%   **4.** no   **5.** Answers may vary.   **a)** 150%, 120%   **b)** 120%, 120%, 125%

Section 4.12 p. 135

Problems and Applications   **1. a)** 176 m   **b)** Michigan   **c)** 1.66   **2.** 18   **3.** $9   **4.** 14:00   **5.** Aces: 2, 1, and 1, 5 points; Bisons: 3, 1, and 0, 6 points; Chargers: 0, 3, 1, 1 point   **6.** $20

Connecting Math and the Environment pp. 136–137

Activity 2:   **1.** Afghanistan, 1.1%; Greece, 0.6%; Iran, 1.1%; Israel, 0.2%; Italy, 0.3%; Mongolia, 11.1%; Poland, 1%; Spain, 0.8%; Scandinavia, 0.1%; Former U.S.S.R., 77.8%   **2.** 1800   **3.** 27 000   **Activity 3:** Answers may vary.

Review pp. 138–139

Estimates will vary. **1.** $60 **2.** $32 **3.** $40
4. $0.25 **5.** $9.75 **6.** $87 **7.** $3.24 **8.** $387.50
9. $123 **10.** $576 **11.** $21.55 **12.** $4.56
13. $1.06 **14.** $1.71 **15.** $2 **16.** $11 **17.** $37
18. $37 **19.** $60.38 **20.** $7.56 **21.** $207
22. $3.40 **23.** $87.50 **24.** $135 **25.** $325
26. $875 **27.** 62.5% **28.** 5% **29.** 28.6%
30. 250% **31.** 40 **32.** 212.5 **33.** 180 **34. a)** 40%
b) 60% **c)** 75% **35.** 544 m **36.** 5.4 kg **37.** 85.4%
38. 53% **39.** 10 cm **40.** 33.5% **41. a)** 20%
b) 120% **42.** $2.25, $20.25 **43.** $23.85, $135.15
44. $20, $59.99 **45.** $29.25, $204.75 **46–55.** PST
will vary. **46.** GST: $4.41 **47.** GST: $6.65
48. GST: $90.93 **49.** GST: $66.50 **50–55.** Answers
for GST only. **50.** $4.27 **51.** $6.41 **52.** $38.50
53. $1710.93 **54.** $319.93 **55.** $31.30 **56.** $2340
57. $217 **58. a)** 88.55 cm **b)** 126.5% **c)** 26.5%

Chapter Check p. 140

1. 48% **2.** 175% **3.** 18.2% **4.** 0.4% **5.** 142.9%
6. 14.3% **7.** 3 **8.** 27.6 **9.** 10 **10.** 7.5 **11.** 66
12. 1.44 **13.** 83.3% **14.** 156.25% **15.** 14%
16. 200 **17.** 28 **18.** 200 000 **19.** $10 **20.** $577.80
21. Answer for GST only. $267.50 **22.** $700
23. $149.25

Using the Strategies p. 141

1. 9, 2, 7; 4, 6, 8; 5, 10, 3 **2. a)** 9 **c)** 18 **e)** 36
3. a) 875.2 **b)** 2.578 **c)** 8.752 **d)** 87.52 **e)** 875.2
4. a) 22.68, 2.7 **b)** 32.76, 5.2 **c)** 91.35, 12.6 **5.** 18,
54, or −18, −54 **6.** It equals the number of playing
cards in a full deck of 52. **7.** 168 cm **8. a)** 20, 16,
28, 20 **b)** 68, 40 **9.** 38 **Data Bank** **1.** Halifax
b) 100 mm

Cumulative Review, Chapters 1–4
pp. 142–143

Chapter 1: **1.** 7.152, 15.072, 15.271, 909.001,
1275 **2.** 8456, 25 048, 26 584, 52 846, 1 000 001
3. 625 **4.** 64 **5.** 4096 **6.** 3^5 **7.** 6^2 **8.** 4^3
9. 0.01 **10.** −1000 **11.** 10 000 000 **12.** 2.8×10^7
13. 8×10^{-4} **14.** 1.56×10^5 **15.** 820 000
16. 0.000 002 7 **17.** 0.000 529 **18.** $\frac{7}{2}$ **19.** $\frac{4}{5}$
20. $-\frac{19}{10}$ **21.** $\frac{2}{5}$ **22.** 2 to 1 **23.** 2:3:5 **26.** 46%
27. 68% **28.** 60% **29.** 250% **30.** 60% **31.** 7%
32. 235% **33.** 150% **34.** 45.2% **35.** 37.5%
36. 33.3% **37.** 120% **38.** 0.536 **39.** 0.045
40. 1.45 **41.** 0.0025 **42.** 19 **43.** 1.5 **Chapter 2:**

1. $\frac{1}{2}$ **2.** $\frac{9}{10}$ **3.** $1\frac{5}{12}$ **4.** $2\frac{3}{4}$ **5.** $2\frac{5}{6}$ **6.** $5\frac{1}{3}$ **7.** $\frac{2}{5}$
8. $\frac{3}{8}$ **9.** $\frac{1}{12}$ **10.** $1\frac{1}{4}$ **11.** $1\frac{1}{2}$ **12.** $\frac{9}{10}$ **13.** $\frac{1}{3}$ **14.** $\frac{1}{2}$
15. $\frac{3}{8}$ **16.** $\frac{3}{8}$ **17.** $3\frac{1}{5}$ **18.** $3\frac{1}{3}$ **19.** 6 **20.** $\frac{1}{2}$ **21.** $2\frac{2}{5}$
22. $\frac{3}{4}$ **23.** $1\frac{7}{9}$ **24.** $2\frac{1}{12}$ **25.** −9.25 **26.** 0.8625
27. 4.1 **28.** −300 **29.** 8 **30.** −4.6 **31.** −0.75
32. 3.28 **33.** −0.2 **34.** 38.27 **35.** 20 000
36. 2.5°C **37.** 4 **Chapter 3:** **1.** Answers may
vary. 6:10, 9:15, 12:20 **2.** 5 **3.** 2 **4.** 5 **5.** 7, 12
6. 15, 18 **7.** Claudia **8.** 21 **9.** 42 yellow cubes
and 21 green cubes are left in the jar **10.** $2.25
11. $4.33/L **12.** $0.1625/pencil **13.** 590 g
14. 2.8 m **15.** 6 cm **16.** 4.69 m/s **Chapter 4:**
1. 73.5 **2.** 3.6 **3.** 11 **4.** 1.25 **5.** 400 **6.** 240
7. 240 **8.** 4000 **9.** 90 **10.** 990 **11.** 64%
12. 200% **13.** 20% **14.** $62.40 **15.** $604.50
16. Answer for GST only $89.88 **17.** $6553.99
18. about 574 194 km² **19.** 221 cm

Chapter 5

Getting Started pp. 146–147

Activity 1: **1.** 4, 5, 6; 11, 12, 13; 18, 19, 20
2. 5, 6, 7; 12, 13, 14; 19, 20, 21 **3.** 9, 10, 11; 16,
17, 18; 23, 24, 25 **4.** 14, 15, 16; 21, 22, 23; 28, 29,
30 **Activity 2:** **1.** 30 **2.** 30 **3.** 30 **4.** three
times the middle number **5.** yes **6.** The square
centres around the number obtained by dividing the
sum by three. **Activity 3:** **1.** 68 **2.** four times
the middle number **3.** The square centres around
the number 19. **Activity 4:** **1.** 117 **2.** nine
times the middle number **3.** yes **4.** The square
centres around the number 18. **Activity 5:** **1.** 87
2. three times the sum of the middle dates **3.** three
times the sum of the middle dates **4.** 11, 12, 18,
19, 25, 26 **5.** 42, 43, 49, 50, 56, 57 **Activity 6:**
1. 159 **2.** three times the sum of the middle dates
3. 9, 10, 11, 16, 17, 18 **4.** 45, 46, 47, 52, 53, 54
Mental Math **1.** 3, 6, 9, 12, 15, 18, 21, 24 **2.** 5,
10, 15, 20, 25 **3.** 4, 8, 12, 16, 20, 24 **4.** 6, 12,
18, 24, 30, 36 **5.** 7, 14, 21, 28, 35, 42, 49 **6.** 8,
16, 24, 32, 40 **7.** 9, 18, 27, 36, 45, 54, 63 **8.** 11,
22, 33, 44, 55, 66 **9.** 1, 2, 4 **10.** 1, 2, 3, 6 **11.** 1,
7 **12.** 1, 2, 4, 8 **13.** 1, 2, 5, 10 **14.** 1, 2, 4, 5, 10,
20 **15.** 1, 2, 3, 4, 6, 8, 12, 24 **16.** 1, 17 **17.** 1,
2, 4, 8, 16 **18.** 1, 2, 3, 4, 6, 9, 12, 18, 36 **19.** 9
20. 16 **21.** 36 **22.** 27 **23.** 16 **24.** 1 **25.** 1000
26. 125 **27.** 32 **28.** 9 **29.** 10 **30.** 14 **31.** 20
32. 36 **33.** 7 **34.** 3 **35.** 3 **36.** 1

Learning Together pp. 148–149

Activity 1: **1. a)** 8 **b)** 0 **c)** 0 **d)** 0 **2. a)** 8 **b)** 12 **c)** 6 **d)** 1 **3. a)** 8 **b)** 24 **c)** 24 **d)** 8 **4. a)** 8 **b)** 36 **c)** 54 **d)** 27 **5. a)** 8, 0, 0, 0; 8, 12, 6, 1; 8, 24, 24, 8; 8, 36, 54, 27 **b)** 8, 48, 96, 64 **c)** 8, 60, 150, 125 **Activity 2:** **1. b)** 1, 6, 11, 16, 21, 26 **c)** The number of cubes is equal to 5 times the diagram number minus 4. **d)** 46 **e)** 30 **2. b)** 15 cylinders on the bottom row and 14 cylinders on the top row **c)** 29 **d)** 120 **e)** No stack has an even number of pipes. **3. a)** 3, 8; 4, 10; 5, 12; 6, 14; 7, 16; 8, 18 **b)** The number of seats is two more than twice the number of tables. **c)** 42 **d)** 15 tables **4. b)** by rows: 5, 20, 45, 80, 225; 12, 24, 36, 48, 60 **c)** 5 times the square of the diagram number **d)** 12 times the diagram number **e)** 96 **f)** 405

Connecting Math and Logic pp. 150–151

Activity 1: 2, 2, 4, 4, 6, 6, 8, 8, 10, 10 **1.** The number of squares passed through is one more than the second dimension if the second dimension is odd, and equal to the second dimension if the second dimension is even. **2.** 12, 12, 14, 14 **3.** 26, 32 **4.** a number of squares equal to the second dimension **5. a)** 50 **b)** 88 **c)** 2000 **6.** a number of squares equal to one more than the second dimension **7. a)** 54 **b)** 100 **c)** 2014 **8. a)** 19, 20 **b)** 125, 126 **c)** 209, 210 **Activity 2:** 3, 4, 3, 6, 7, 6, 9, 10, 9 **1.** a number of squares equal to the second dimension **2. a)** 36 **b)** 45 **c)** 3000 **3.** 333 or 331 **4.** a number of squares equal to two more than the second dimension **5. a)** 30 **b)** 46 **c)** 2002 **6.** 77 **Activity 3:** **1.** If the second dimension is odd, the number of squares equals the second dimension plus 3. If the second dimension is even but not a multiple of 4, the number of squares equals the second dimension plus 2. If the second dimension is a multiple of 4, the number of squares equals the second dimension. **3. a)** 44 **b)** 58 **c)** 44

Section 5.1 p. 153

Practice **1.** $l + 7$ **2.** $3h - 4$ **3.** $2h + 4w$ **4.** $5d - 2c$ **5.** two times h plus four **6.** three times w minus six **7.** two times l plus three times w minus one **8.** two times d minus three times c plus six **9.** 6 **10.** 12 **11.** 6 **12.** 6 **13.** 14 **14.** 28 **15.** 1 **16.** 50 **17.** 12 **18.** 28 **19.** 8 **20.** 0 **21.** 6 **22.** 26 **23.** 14 **24.** 22 **25.** 6 **26.** 15 **27.** 2 **28.** 4 **29.** 3 **30.** 6 **31.** 12 **32.** 5 **33.** 1 **34.** 13 **35.** 7 **36.** 2 **37.** 5 **38.** 6 **39.** 11 **40.** 0 **41.** 9 **42.** 2 **43.** 4.6 **44.** 1.8 **45.** 6 **46.** 6.8 **47.** 14.2 **48.** 9.2

49. −4 **50.** −5 **51.** 3 **52.** −13 **53.** −1 **54.** 10 **55.** −5 **56.** −13 **57.** 0 **58.** −15 **Problems and Applications** **59.** $814 **60.** 97, 60, 102, 24, 104, 99, 101 **62. a)** 31 **b)** 10 **c)** −2 **63. a)** 0, 1, 2 **b)** 0, 1, 2, 3

Section 5.2 p. 155

Practice **1.** 16, 20, 24; $y = 4x$ **2.** 14, 16, 18; $t = s + 5$ **3.** 36, 45, 54; $w = 9h$ **4.** 126, 168; $c = 21n$ **5. a)** 54 m^2 **b)** 6 m **c)** 3 m **6. a)** 36 m **b)** 17 m **c)** 20 m **Problems and Applications** **7. a)** 10, 18, 26, 34, 42 **b)** 8 **c)** 50, 58 **d)** $P = 8n + 2$ **8. a)** 3, 4, 5, 6, 7, 8 **b)** $P = n + 2$ **c)** 32 **d)** 40 **9. a)** 8, 12, 16, 20, 24, 28 **b)** $P = 4n + 4$ **c)** 64 **d)** 21

Section 5.3 pp. 157–158

Practice **1. a)** The sum of the x and y values is six. **b)** 3, 4, 5, 6, 7 **c)** (3, 3), (2, 4), (1, 5), (0, 6), (−1, 7) **2. a)** The sum of the x and y values is two. **b)** 0, 1, 2, 3, 4 **c)** (2, 0), (1, 1), (0, 2), (−1, 3), (−2, 4) **3. a)** The x value less the y value is two. **b)** 4, 3, 2, 1, 0 **c)** (6, 4), (5, 3), (4, 2), (3, 1), (2, 0) **4. a)** The x value less the y value is zero. **b)** 3, 2, 1, 0, −1 **c)** (3, 3), (2, 2), (1, 1), (0, 0), (−1, −1) **5. a)** 6 **b)** 2 **c)** 7 **d)** 9 **e)** 10 **f)** 12 **g)** 11 **h)** 16 **6. a)** 5 **b)** 1 **c)** 4 **d)** 8 **e)** −2 **f)** −1 **7. a)** The value of y is the value of x, plus 3. **b)** 5, 4, 3, 2, 1 **c)** (2, 5), (1, 4), (0, 3), (−1, 2), (−2, 1) **8. a)** The value of y is the value of x, less 1. **b)** 2, 1, 0, −1, −2 **c)** (3, 2), (2, 1), (1, 0), (0, −1), (−1, −2) **9. a)** The value of y is two times the value of x, plus 1. **b)** 5, 3, 1, −1, −3 **c)** (2, 5), (1, 3), (0, 1), (−1, −1), (−2, −3) **10. a)** The value of y is three times the value of x, less 2. **b)** 4, 1, −2, −5, −8 **c)** (2, 4), (1, 1), (0, −2), (−1, −5), (−2, −8) **11. a)** 4 **b)** 5 **c)** 1 **d)** 2 **e)** 3 **f)** −2 **12. a)** 1 **b)** 3 **c)** −3 **d)** −4 **e)** 8 **f)** 3 **13–16.** Answers may vary. **13.** (−2, 7), (−1, 6), (0, 5), (1, 4), (2, 3) **14.** (−2, −5), (−1, −4), (0, −3), (1, −2), (2, −1) **15.** (−2, 2), (−1, 3), (0, 4), (1, 5), (2, 6) **16.** (−2, −2), (−1, 0), (0, 2), (1, 4), (2, 6) **Problems and Applications** **17.** $x + y = 7$ **18.** $x − y = 4$ **19.** $y = x + 1$ **20.** $y = x − 2$ **21–23.** Answers may vary. **21.** (−2, 2), (−1, 3), (0, 4), (1, 5), (2, 6) **22.** (−4, −2), (−2, −1), (0, 0), (2, 1), (4, 2) **23.** (4, −2), (5, −1), (6, 0), (7, 1), (8, 2) **24. a)** 15, 30, 45, 60 **b)** The distance increases by 15 each second. **c)** 75 m, 90 m **d)** (1, 15), (2, 30), (3, 45), (4, 60) **e)** The distance, in metres, is fifteen times the time, in seconds. **f)** $d = 15 \times t$ **g)** 180 m, 750 m **h)** 5.4 km **i)** 54 km/h **25. a)** 4, 6, 8, 10, 12 **b)** The perimeter increases by 2 each time. **c)** 14, 16

d) (1, 4), (2, 6), (3, 8), (4, 10), (5, 12) **e)** The perimeter is two times the number of squares, plus 2. **f)** $P = 2 \times n + 2$ **g)** 28, 50, 602

Section 5.4 p. 159

Practice **1.** A(5, 1), B(2, 3), C(6, 0), D(4, 6), F(5, 2), G(0, 3), H(2, 5), I(3, 0), J(3, 2), K(7, 2), L(6, 4), M(8, 1), N(1, 6), P(1, 1), Q(0, 5), R(4, 4), S(8, 6) **Problems and Applications** **2.** square, 25 **3.** rectangle, 20 **4.** rectangle, 24 **5.** rectangle, 20 **6. b)** pentagon **7. b)** 10, 6 **c)** 20, 24 **d)** Perimeter is doubled; area is quadrupled. **8. b)** (8, 5) **c)** 18, 18 **9.** Answers will vary.

Section 5.5 p. 161

Practice **1.** A(4, 2), B(–3, 3), C(–5, –2), D(3, –2), E(2, 0), F(–3, 0), G(–2, –2), H(0, –1), I(0, 3), J(2, –3), K(–5, 2) **2.** A **3.** H **4.** E **5.** F **6.** I **7.** C **8.** G **9.** D **10.** B **11.** J **12.** K **13.** L **Problems and Applications** **14.** GRID **15.** square, 9 **16.** rectangle, 60 **17.** square, 16 **18.** rectangle, 72 **19. b)** D(5, 1), D(–3, 1), and D(7, 7) **20. b)** (3, 1) **c)** behind

Section 5.6 p. 163

Practice **1.** The sum of the x and y values is three. **2.** The y value is the x value, less 1. **3.** The y value is two times the x value. **4–13.** Answers may vary. **4.** (2, 5), (1, 6), (0, 7), (–1, 8), (–2, 9) **5.** (2, 4), (1, 5), (0, 6), (–1, 7), (–2, 8) **6.** (2, 1), (1, 0), (0, –1), (–1, –2), (–2, –3) **7.** (2, 2), (1, 1), (0, 0), (–1, –1), (–2, –2) **8.** (2, 2), (1, –1), (0, 0), (–1, 1), (–2, 2) **9.** (2, 4), (1, 3), (0, 2), (–1, 1), (–2, 0) **10.** (2, 6), (1, 5), (0, 4), (–1, 3), (–2, 2) **11.** (2, 0), (1, –1), (0, –2), (–1, –3), (–2, –4) **12.** (2, 5), (1, 3), (0, 1), (–1, –1), (–2, –3) **13.** (2, 2), (1, –1), (0, –4), (–1, –7), (–2, –10) **Problems and Applications** **14. a)** 12, (1, 12); 6, (2, 6); 4, (3, 4); 3, (4, 3); 2, (6, 2); 1, (12, 1) **c)** half of the perimeter of the rectangle **d)** 4 cm by 3 cm **15–16.** Answers may vary. **15.** (3, –2), (3, –1), (3, 0), (3, 1), (3, 2); a vertical line **16.** (–2, –3), (–1, –3), (0, –3), (1, –3), (2, –3); a horizontal line **17. a)** (1, 6), (2, 7), (3, 8), (4, 9), (5, 10), (6, 11), (7, 12), (8, 13), (9, 14), (10, 15) **b)** (1, 2), (2, 4), (3, 6), (4, 8), (5, 10), (6, 12), (7, 14), (8, 16), (9, 18), (10, 20) **d)** 5; 6, 7, 8, 9, or 10 mugs; 1, 2, 3, or 4 mugs **18. a)** 22, (1, 22); 20, (2, 20); 18, (3, 18); 16, (4, 16); 14, (5, 14); 12, (6, 12); 10, (7, 10); 8 (8, 8); 6, (9, 6); 4, (10, 4); 2, (11, 2) **c)** the area of the rectangular lot **d)** 12 m by 6 m

Technology pp. 164–165

Activity 1: **1. a)** D3 **b)** F2 **c)** B5 **d)** A1
Activity 2: **1.** 1 **2.** Add the number in cell B2 to 7 and leave the result in cell A2. **3.** By rows: 8, 1, 6; 3, 5, 7; 4, 9, 2 **4.** Put the sum of the upward diagonal entries A4, B3, and C2 into cell D1. Put the sum of the row entries A2, B2, and C2 into cell D2. Put the sum of the row entries A3, B3, and C3 into cell D3. Put the sum of the row entries A4, B4, and C4 into cell D4. Put the sum of the downward diagonal entries A2, B3, and C4 into cell D5. All sums are 15. **5.** Put the sum of the column entries A2, A3, and A4 into cell A5. Put the sum of the column entries B2, B3, and B4 into cell B5. Put the sum of the column entries C2, C3, and C4 into cell C5. All sums are 15. **6.** because the columns, rows, and diagonals sum to the same number **7.** The resulting squares are magic squares. **Activity 3:** **1.** E1:@SUM[A5, B4, C3, D2]; E2:@SUM[A2..D2]; E3:@SUM[A3..D3]; E4:@SUM[A4..D4]; E5:@SUM[A5..D5]; E6:@SUM[A2, B3, C4, D5]; A6:@SUM[A2..A5]; B6:@SUM[B2..B5]; C6:@SUM[C2..C5]; D6:@SUM[D2..D5] **2.** 34

Review pp. 166–167

1. $a - 7$ **2.** $4s + 3t$ **3.** three times w plus two **4.** two times w divided by 3 **5.** five times a plus b minus 3 **6.** 1 **7.** 3 **8.** 34 **9.** 16 **10.** 1 **11.** 5 **12.** 12 **13. a)** 4, 14; 5, 17; 6, 20 **b)** $3n + 2$ **c)** 62 **d)** 33 **15. a)** 4 **b)** 0 **c)** 3 **d)** 5 **e)** 7 **f)** 6 **g)** 6 **h)** 7 **16. a)** The x value plus the y value equals 8. **b)** 4, 5, 6, 7, 8 **c)** (4, 4), (3, 5), (2, 6), (1, 7), (0, 8) **17. a)** The value of y is the value of x, plus 5. **b)** 7, 6, 5, 4, 3 **c)** (2, 7), (1, 6), (0, 5), (–1, 4), (–2, 3) **18. a)** 8 **b)** 9 **c)** –4 **d)** –6 **e)** 3 **f)** –10 **19–24.** Answers may vary. **19.** (2, 2), (1, 3), (0, 4), (–1, 5), (–2, 6) **20.** (2, 1), (3, 2), (4, 3), (5, 4), (–1, –2) **21.** (0, 3), (1, 4), (2, 5), (3, 6), (4, 7) **22.** (0, –4), (1, –3), (2, –2), (3, –1), (4, 0) **23.** (0, 5), (1, 7), (2, 9), (3, 11), (–1, 3) **24.** (0, –1), (1, 2), (2, 5), (3, 8), (4, 11) **25.** $x + y = 8$ **26.** $y = x - 2$ **27.** $y = x + 2$ **28. a)** 140, 210, 280 **b)** 350 km , 420 km **c)** add 70 to the previous value **d)** (1, 70), (2, 140), (3, 210), (4, 280) **e)** distance is equal to seventy times the time **f)** $D = 70 \times t$ **29.** A **30.** C **31.** E **32.** G **33.** I **34.** K **35.** H **36.** J **37.** L **38.** F **39.** D **40.** B **41. b)** AB, HI, FG, LM **c)** The x- and y-coordinates of the first ordered pair are the opposites of the x- and y-coordinates of the second ordered pair. **42.** rectangle, 15 **43.** square, 9 **44.** trapezoid **45.** parallelogram **46–51.** Answers may vary. **46.** (0, 7), (1, 6), (2, 5), (3, 4), (4, 3)

47. (0, –2), (1, –1), (2, 0), (3, 1), (4, 2) **48.** (0, 3), (1, 4), (2, 5), (3, 6), (4, 7) **49.** (0, –4), (1, –3), (2, –2), (3, –1), (4, 0) **50.** (0, 3), (1, 5), (2, 7), (3, 9), (–1, 1) **51.** (0, –1), (1, 2), (2, 5), (3, 8), (–1, –4)

Chapter Check p. 168

1. 13 **2.** 4 **3.** 16 **4. a)** 36 m **b)** 9 m **c)** 7 m **5. b)** 6, 8, 10, 12, 14 **c)** The perimeter is twice the diagram number, plus four. **d)** 20 **e)** 10 **6. a)** the x value plus the y value equals 6 **b)** 2, 3, 4, 5, 6 **c)** (4, 2), (3, 3), (2, 4), (1, 5), (0, 6) **7. a)** twice the x value plus 5 equals the y value **b)** 9, 7, 5, 3, 1 **c)** (2, 9), (1, 7), (0, 5), (–1, 3), (–2, 1) **8.** $x + y = 5$ **9.** $y = x + 2$ **10. a)** 60, 90, 120 **b)** add 30 to the previous value **c)** $150, $180 **d)** (1, 30), (2, 60), (3, 90), (4, 120) **e)** The cost is thirty times the number of T-shirts. **f)** $C = 30 \times n$ **g)** $360, $1500 **11.** A(4, 2), B(–2, 4), C(–5, –4), D(2, –5), E(3, 0), F(–5, 1), G(–3, 0), H(0, –3), I(–2, –3), J(4, –3), K(0, 3) **12.** rectangle, 12 **13.** square, 16 **14–15.** Answers may vary. **14.** (0, 7), (1, 6), (2, 5), (3, 4), (4, 3) **15.** (0, 1), (1, 3), (2, 5), (–1, –1), (–2, –3)

Using the Strategies p. 169

1. 4 **2.** 8 **3.** 21 **4.** 1 block west and 2 blocks north or 1 block north, 1 block west, and 1 block north or 2 blocks north and 1 block west **5. a)** Beth **b)** Bob **c)** Svend and Li-Ying **d)** Li-Ying and Bob **7.** $\frac{1}{3} + \frac{2}{4}$ **8.** 64 cm^2 **9.** 1, 4, 9, 121, 484 **Data Bank** **1.** $1\frac{1}{14}$ or $\frac{15}{14}$ **2.** Manitoba, Saskatchewan, Newfoundland, Northwest Territories, Yukon

Chapter 6

Getting Started pp. 172–173

Activity 1: **1. a)** 3 g **b)** 6 g **2.** 15, 21, 18, 24, 30, 36 **Activity 2:** row 1: 5, 5, 5, 5; row 2: 1, 2, 3, 4; row 3: 4, 3, 2, 1 **Activity 3:** **1. a)** 4 g **b)** 2 g **c)** 4 g **Order of Operations** **1.** 11 **2.** 13 **3.** 21 **4.** 25 **5.** 3.4 **6.** 1 **7.** 1 **8.** 1.2 **9.** 6.5 **10.** 1.2 **11.** 5 **12.** 5 **13.** 11 **14.** 1 **15.** 46 **16.** 66 **17.** $(3 + 5) \times 3$ **18.** $(2 + 4) \times 4$ **19.** $12 \times (8 - 6)$ **20.** $4 + 5 \times (7 - 3)$ **21.** $2 \times (10 + 2)$ **22.** $6 \times (4 + 4) \div 2$ **23.** 24 **24.** 20 **25.** 18 **26.** 20 **27.** 7 **28.** 30 **29.** 9.9 **30.** 5 **31.** 5 **32.** 39.4 **33.** $4 + 5 \times 2 + 1$ **34.** $3 \times 4 + 7 - 4$ **35.** $5 \times 2 + 6 - 1$ **36.** $36 \div 9 + 6 + 5$ **37.** $4 + 3 \times 4 - 1$ **38.** $6 \times 6 \div 3 + 3$ **39.** $5 \times 5 - 3 \times 3 - 1$ **40.** $18 - 8 + 3 + 1 \times 2$ **Mental Math** **1.** 55 **2.** 145 **3.** 630 **4.** 650 **5.** 400

6. 500 **7.** 600 **8.** 1350 **9.** 50 **10.** 140 **11.** 120 **12.** 110 **13.** 100 **14.** 75 **15.** 410 **16.** 400 **17.** 310 **18.** 410 **19.** 130 **20.** 120 **21.** 48 **22.** 480 **23.** 50 **24.** 100 **25.** 500 **26.** 1000 **27.** 4700 **28.** 47 000 **29.** 400 **30.** 40 000 **31.** 5 **32.** 500 **33.** 50 **34.** 5 **35.** 350 **36.** 7 **37.** 720 **38.** 6000 **39.** 1000 **40.** 6 **41.** 4 **42.** 3 **43.** 5 **44.** 1 **45.** 1 **46.** 6 **47.** 2 **48.** 1 **49.** 2 **50.** 3.7 **51.** 4.35 **52.** 63.3 **53.** 63.37 **54.** 0.525 **55.** 0.0525 **56.** 755 **57.** 75 500

Section 6.1 p. 175

Practice **1.** five less than x is seven **2.** eleven is equal to two more than y **3.** two times m is eight **4.** n divided by four is three **5.** three more than m is equal to m less than seven **6.** two plus three times t is five **7.** half of w plus one third of w is twenty-five **8.** two less than one third of a is equal to four less than a **9.** $n + 4 = 19$ **10.** $n - 3 = 9$ **11.** $4n = 12$ **12.** $12 - n = 4$ **13.** $\frac{n}{4} = 3$ **14.** $4n + 3 = 11$ **15.** $5(n + 3) = 23$ **16.** $4(n - 3) = 12$ **17.** $2n + 5 = 15$ **18.** $2n - 4 = 50$ **19.** $2n - 2 = 12$ **20.** $\frac{a}{3} - 2 = 3$ **21.** $l + 4 = 11$ **22.** $5w = 60$ **23.** $p - 6 = 40$ **24.** $3A - 12 = 10$ **25.** $\frac{n}{6} = 2$ **26.** $2n + 1 = 7$ **Problems and Applications** **27.** $a + 3 = 16$ **28.** $n - 10 = 15$ **29.** $\frac{t}{2} = 1$ **30.** $2r = 50$ **31.** $2s + 2 = 26$ **32.** $4t = 80$ **33.** $2m + 250 = 1596$ **34.** $2t + 2.50 = 17.50$ **35.** $0.05n = 0.5$

Section 6.2 p. 177

Practice **1.** yes **2.** yes **3.** yes **4.** yes **5.** no **6.** yes **7.** no **8.** no **9.** 4 **10.** 7 **11.** 9 **12.** 5 **13.** 25 **14.** 16 **15.** 12 **16.** 21 **17.** 7 **18.** 9 **19.** 12 **20.** 6 **21.** 7 **22.** 8 **23.** 49 **24.** 20 **25.** 10 **26.** 40 **27.** 32 **28.** 24 **29.** 7 **30.** 7 **31.** 7 **32.** 20 **33.** 2 **34.** 7 **35.** 4 **36.** 3 **37.** 3 **38.** 6 **39.** 15 **40.** 12 **Problems and Applications** **41–44.** Answers may vary. **41.** $x + 5 = 7$ **42.** $x + 6 = 9$ **43.** $6x = 30$ **44.** $\frac{x}{2} = 5$ **45.** $n + 5 = 20$; 15 **46.** $n - 150 = 30$; 180

Learning Together pp. 178–179

Activity 1: **1. a)** $2x$ **b)** $4x + 1$ **c)** $x^2 + 2x$ **d)** $x^2 + 2$ **e)** $2x^2 + x + 4$ **f)** $3x^2 + 2x + 5$ **Activity 2:** **1. a)** $-2x$ **b)** $-4x - 4$ **c)** $-x^2 - 1$ **d)** $-3x^2 - 4x - 4$ **Activity 3:** **1.** x; $-2x^2$; $x^2 - 2x$; $-x + 4$ **2. a)** 2 small white squares **b)** 2 long white **c)** 1 long green, 2 small red squares **d)** 1 large white square, 2 long green, 1 small white square

Section 6.3 p. 181

Practice **1.** 8 **2.** 7 **3.** 5 **4.** 1 **5.** 3 **6.** 4
7. −5 **8.** −8 **9.** −2 **10.** −15 **11.** −7 **12.** −7 **13.** 9
14. 8 **15.** 5 **16.** 10 **17.** 12 **18.** 20 **19.** 15 **20.** 4
21. 15 **22.** 8 **23.** 19 **24.** 13 **25.** 10 **26.** 12
27. 18 **28.** 16 **29.** 8.2 **30.** 11.5 **31.** 2.7 **32.** 5.2
33. 13.2 **34.** 9.1 **35.** 5.5 **36.** 1.3 **37.** 7.9 **38.** 5.7
39. 3 **40.** 3 **41.** 2.2 **42.** 0.5 **Problems and
Applications** **43.** $16 **44.** 7 **45.** 32 **46.** 35°C
47–48. Answers may vary. **47.** $x − 6 = 0, x − 3 = 3$
48. $x + 15 = 23, x + 8 = 16$ **49.** no change **50.** −3
51. −4 **52.** −3 **53.** −3 **54.** −5 **55.** −1 **56.** −4
57. −1

Section 6.4 p. 182

Practice **1.** 3 **2.** 5 **3.** 7 **4.** 4 **5.** 9 **6.** 10
7. 15 **8.** 3 **9.** 6 **10.** 2 **11.** 1 **12.** 9 **13.** 12
14. 4 **15.** 5 **16.** 2 **17.** 3 **18.** 4 **19.** 4 **20.** 3
21. 4 **22.** 2.5 **23.** 1.2 **24.** 0.9 **25.** 0.5 **26.** 20
27. 40 **28.** 2 **29.** 3 **30.** 6 **31.** 200 **Problems
and Applications** **32.** 17 cm **33.** Answers may
vary. $3x = 9, 7x = 21$ **34.** −2 **35.** −4 **36.** −3 **37.** 4

Section 6.5 p. 183

Practice **1.** 3 **2.** 2 **3.** 5 **4.** 4 **5.** 7 **6.** 6
7. 32 **8.** 16 **9.** 18 **10.** 6 **11.** 25 **12.** 0 **13.** 49
14. 8 **15.** 27 **16.** 6 **17.** 8 **18.** 0 **19.** 6.2 **20.** 0.8
21. 3.6 **22.** 3.5 **23.** 66.6 **24.** 0 **Problems and
Applications** **25.** 64 **26.** Answers may vary. $\frac{x}{7} = 1$,
$\frac{x}{14} = 0.5$ **27.** the equation $0 = 0$ **28.** −8 **29.** −3
30. −20 **31.** 15 **32.** −10 **33.** −3

Section 6.6 p. 186

Practice **1.** $8x$ **2.** $3a^2$ **3.** $9t$ **4.** $8w$ **5.** 0
6. $5y$ **7.** $13a + 6$ **8.** $10x + 7x^2$ **9.** $9b + 9$ **10.** 0
11. $2a + 2b$ **12.** $8y$ **Problems and Applications**
13. $7t + 2w$; 20 **14.** $6w + 2t$; 22 **15.** w; 3
16. $−t − w$; −5 **17. a)** $4t + 6s$ **b)** 360 m
18. Answers may vary. $6x + 2y − 4x + y, x + y + x + 2y$

Section 6.7 p. 187

Practice **1.** $2x + 10$ **2.** $3b + 9$ **3.** $6y − 6$
4. $5t − 15$ **5.** $7m + 7$ **6.** $4a − 28$ **7.** $16 + 4m$
8. $8x − 32$ **9.** $21 + 7t$ **10.** $6x + 8$ **11.** $8y + 4$
12. $12m − 9$ **13.** $25t − 10$ **14.** $6 + 12x$
15. $28w − 49$ **16.** $6x + 4y$ **17.** $12a + 15b$
18. $−9m + 6n$ **19.** $−15s + 5t$ **20.** $6x + 12y + 3$
21. $2a + 2b + 2$ **22.** $12c − 8d + 20$ **23.** $5x − 15 + 20y$
24. $−12 − 18x − 6y$ **25.** $−2 + 2x + 2y$ **Problems**

and Applications **26.** 33, 33 **27.** 3, 3 **28.** 380
29. 840 **30.** 1480 **31.** 1100 **32.** 820 **33.** 990

Section 6.8 p. 189

Practice **1.** 2 **2.** 3 **3.** 4 **4.** 1 **5.** 4 **6.** 3
7. 2 **8.** 2 **9.** 3 **10.** 3 **11.** 3 **12.** 2 **13.** 5
14. 2 **15.** 1 **16.** 3 **17.** 5 **18.** 5 **19.** 2 **20.** 2
21. 0.4 **22.** 1.1 **23.** 2 **24.** 6 **25.** 4 **26.** 20 **27.** 5
28. 6 **29.** 3 **30.** 1 **31.** 3 **32.** 2 **33.** 3 **34.** 4
35. 2 **36.** 6 **37.** 4 **38.** 3 **39.** 9 **40.** 8 **41.** 2
42. 5 **Problems and Applications** **43.** 10 kg
44. 201 km **45.** Answers may vary. $2x + 3 = 9$

Section 6.9 p. 191

Problems and Applications **1.** 16 **2.** 20 **3.** 81
full time, 27 part time **4.** 7, 8, 9 **5.** horse: 12 m,
lion: 2 m **6.** $125 **7.** Canada: 10 million square
kilometres, Russia: 17 million square kilometres
8. a) 17, 19, 21 **b)** two more than the previous value,
starting with 15 **c)** $s = 13 + 2n$ **d)** 33 **e)** 20

Section 6.10 p. 193

Practice **1.** −3 **2.** −2 **3.** −4 **4.** −7 **5.** −5 **6.** −3
7. −3 **8.** −6 **9.** −12 **10.** −21 **11.** −1 **12.** $−\frac{1}{2}$
13. −2 **14.** −4 **15.** 0 **16.** −3 **17.** $\frac{3}{4}$ **18.** $−1\frac{1}{2}$
19. −2 **20.** −3 **21.** −7 **22.** $2\frac{1}{2}$ **23.** 1 **24.** −5
25. −3 **26.** −2 **27.** −3 **28.** $1\frac{2}{5}$ **29.** −4 **30.** −2
31. −8 **32.** −3 **33.** 1 **34.** −2 **35.** −4 **36.** −2
37. −7 **38.** −4 **39.** −6.6 **40.** 3.2 **Problems and
Applications** **41.** 2 or 2 **42.** 3 or 3 **43.** 5 or −5
44. 4 or −4 **45.** −8 **46.** $−2\frac{2}{5}$ **47.** 4 **48.** 2 **49.** 4
50. $3t + 19 = −170$; −63°C

Connecting Math and the Environment
pp. 194–195

Activity 1: **1.** Caspian, Siberian, South China,
Bengal, Indo-Chinese, Sumatran, Javan, Bali **2.** 8
3. 3 **4.** 37.5% **Activity 2:** **1. a)** 6200 **b)** 6.2%
c) 69% **2. a)** 4195 **b)** 4.2% **3.** about 40%

Review pp. 196–197

1. two more than x is equal to five **2.** three times x
equals twelve **3.** one fourth of b is three **4.** three
minus two times x is equal to one **5.** $2x − 7 = 12$
6. $2x − 10 = 26$ **7.** $\frac{b}{5} + 9 = 2b$ **8.** yes **9.** no
10. no **11.** yes **12.** yes **13.** yes **14.** no **15.** yes
20. 4 **21.** 4 **22.** 10 **23.** 6 **24.** 6 **25.** 10 **26.** 2.7
27. 7.1 **28.** $8x$ **29.** $3a$ **30.** $−5w$ **31.** $5b − 5$

32. $3n + 1$ **33.** $3 + 6k$ **34.** $4x + 4$ **35.** $6a - 6$
36. $8m + 6n$ **37.** $-12s + 6t$ **38.** $-6p - 3q$
39. $-2x - 8y$ **40.** 4   **41.** 3   **42.** 2   **43.** 5   **44.** 2
45. 3   **46.** 2.4   **47.** 1.3   **48.** 4   **49.** 12   **50.** -3
51. -4 **52.** -2 **53.** -3 **54.** -6 **55.** -8 **56.** -3
57. -1 **58.** 9   **59.** -7 **60.** -1.1 **61.** 1.1   **62.** 0.9
63. -4.8 **64.** $\frac{3}{4}$ **65.** $-1\frac{1}{5}$ **66.** -2.0 **67.** 0.6
68. -3.8 **69.** $\frac{1}{2}$ **70.** 12   **71.** Canada: 7 and Italy:
14   **72.** 18   **73.** 90 m   **74.** 205 m   **75.** 16 km/h
76. 15   **77.** $-7.1°$C   **78.** white-tailed deer: 48 km/h,
elk: 72 km/h   **79.** 40 kg

Chapter Check p. 198

1. two more than y is seven   **2.** one more than twice
x is five   **3.** one half of m is seventeen   **4.** $x + 8 = 15$
5. $\frac{c}{2} = 12$ **6.** $2m - 5 = 1$ **10.** 5   **11.** 12   **12.** 8
13. 4   **14.** 3   **15.** 6   **16.** 1.2   **17.** $\frac{1}{5}$ **18.** -4 **19.** -4
20. 5.1   **21.** -2.8 **22.** 4   **23.** -2 **24.** -0.5 **25.** -7
26. $5y$ **27.** $8t + 2$ **28.** $3n - 6$ **29.** $6x + 8y$ **30.** $59 = 2 + H$ **31.** $17   **32.** 3   **33.** 6   **34.** $-63°$C   **35.** 12.5 h

Using the Strategies p. 199

1. 8 days   **2.** 180 km/h   **3.** $1.50   **4.** 95 km/h
5. 54   **6. b)** 1, 3, 6, 10, 15; 4, 8, 12, 16, 20
d) 6:21, 24; 7:28, 28   **7.** 10   **8.** Amanda: swimming;
Brittany: biking; Christopher: tennis; Dalil: jogging
9. a) 150 m   **b)** 100 m   **c)** Jordan   **Data Bank**
1. a) Victoria   **b)** Quebec   **2. a)** 69 L   **b)** 157 L
c) 174 L   **d)** 326 L

Chapter 7

Getting Started pp. 202–203

Activity 1:   **1. a)** 1000   **b)** 0.001   **c)** 100   **d)** 0.01
e) 0.001   **f)** 1000   **g)** 10   **h)** 0.1   **2. a)** hundredth
b) thousandth   **c)** thousand   **Warm Up**   **1.** 4020.5
2. 16.44   **3.** 0.587   **4.** 6835   **5.** 92.63   **6.** one
hundred twelve and seven tenths   **7.** two thousand
thirty-six and eight hundredths   **8.** fifty-nine
and six thousandths   **9.** three hundred forty-five
thousandths   **10.** three and sixty-two hundredths
11. seventy-five thousand two hundred sixty-four and
nine tenths   **12.** 14.7   **13.** 425   **14.** 8.43   **15.** 9570
16. 55.0   **17.** 56.8   **18.** 4503   **19.** 36   **20.** 845.57
21. 0.0273   **22.** 1.86   **23.** 4.652   **24.** 0.5209
25. 0.0276   **26.** 3.8165   **27.** 0.562 19   **28.** 0.026
29. 780   **30.** 193.5   **31.** 246 115   **32.** 4206
33. 65.75   **34.** 148.68   **35.** 58.4   **36.** 39.44
37. 184.75   **38.** 39.25   **39.** 325.68   **40.** 69.7

Mental Math   **1.** 50 mm   **2.** 160 mm   **3.** 2 mm
4. 2000 mm   **5.** 300 mm   **6.** 1160 mm   **7.** 400 cm
8. 2500 cm   **9.** 170 cm   **10.** 80 cm   **11.** 3.6 cm
12. 11.2 cm   **13.** 2.4 m   **14.** 5.16 m   **15.** 0.24 m
16. 0.09 m   **17.** 13.5 m   **18.** 9.05 m   **19.** 1.5 m
20. 0.625 m   **21.** 0.052 m   **22.** 4000 m   **23.** 500 m
24. 6300 m   **25.** 8 km   **26.** 25.7 km   **27.** 0.982 km
28. 0.046 km   **29.** 3.405 km   **30.** 0.206 km   **31.** 18
32. 26   **33.** 54   **34.** 20   **35.** 2.8   **36.** 4.8   **37.** 4.8
38. 5.6   **39.** 0.12   **40.** 3.6   **41.** 64   **42.** 9   **43.** 81
44. 36   **45.** 8   **46.** 125   **47.** 80   **48.** 22   **49.** 45
50. 2600   **51.** 5   **52.** 3400   **53.** 790   **54.** 200
55. 0.012   **56.** 4.7   **57.** 3.26   **58.** 0.598   **59.** 0.273

Learning Together pp. 204–205

Activity 1:   **1.** 18   **2.** 8   **3.** 32   **4.** 10   **5.** 13
6. 20   **7.** 25   **8.** 34   **Activity 2:**   **1.** 29   **2.** 52
3. 17   **4.** 26   **Activity 3:**   **1.** 25, 16, 9   **2.** 34,
9, 25   **3.** 20, 4, 16   **4.** 13, 9, 4   **5.** 8, 4, 4
Activity 4:   **1.** 29, 4, 25   **2.** 52, 36, 16   **3.** 41, 16,
25   **4.** 32, 16, 16   **5.** 45, 36, 9   **Activity 5:** The
sum of the areas of the squares on the legs equals
the area of the square on the hypotenuse.

Section 7.1 p. 207

Practice   **1.** 13   **2.** 10   **3.** 6.4   **4.** 11.3   **5.** 15
6. 5.7   **7.** 24   **8.** 2.8   **Problems and Applications**
9. a) 36   **b)** 4   **c)** 20   **d)** equal   **10.** b and c

Section 7.2 p. 209

Practice   **1.** 13.5 m   **2.** 11.0 m   **Problems and
Applications**   **3.** 6.7 m   **4.** 47.2 km   **5.** 85 m
7. 7.8 cm   **8.** 325.3 m   **9.** 44.7 km   **10.** 3, 4, 5;
6, 8, 10; 5, 12, 13; 8, 15, 17; 12, 16, 20; 7, 24, 25;
10, 24, 26; 20, 21, 29; 16, 30, 34; 9, 40, 41; 12, 35,
37; 24, 32, 40; 27, 36, 45; 20, 48, 52; 11, 60, 61
11. 28.3 cm

Section 7.3 pp. 210–211

Practice   **1.** 32 cm   **2.** 36 cm   **3.** 40 cm   **4.** 56 cm
5. 40 cm   **6.** 10.2 cm   **7.** 18.5 cm   **8.** 26.6 cm
9. 30 cm   **10.** 24 m   **11.** 50.3 cm   **Problems and
Applications**   **12.** 4.7 cm   **13.** 4.6 cm   **15.** 246 cm
16. 4, 6.2, 4.8, 5.4, 5, 12.6   **17.** 10.3, 4.9, 5.8, 2.8,
10.4, 13.4   **18. a)** 33.6 m   **b)** 6   **c)** 2.4 m   **d)** $44.74
19. 10 cm, 12 cm, 12 cm, 12 cm

Section 7.4 p. 213

Practice   **1.** 13.5 cm   **2.** 9.2 cm   **3.** 9.0 cm
4. 32.4 cm   **5.** 60.8 cm   **6.** 39.0 cm   **7.** 37.0 cm

8. 10.4 m　**9.** 51.6 cm　**Problems and Applications**　**10.** 190 m　**11.** 4.4 cm　**12.** 4.4 cm　**13.** 5.8 cm　**14.** 0.65 m　**15.** 9.8 cm　**17.** 1038 m　**18.** 22.5 m　**21. a)** The side length of the square is 2 times that of the octagon.　**b)** The side length of the triangle is 3 times that of the nonagon.　**c)** The side length of the triangle is 2 times that of the hexagon.　**d)** The side length of the hexagon is 2 times that of the dodecagon.　**e)** The side length of the square is 3 times that of the dodecagon.　**f)** The side length of the pentagon is 2 times that of the dodecagon.

Learning Together pp. 214–215

Activity 1:　**3.** 5.7 cm　**4.** 2.83　**7.** 2.83　**Activity 2:**　**1.** $P = k \times d$　**2.** $d = \frac{P}{k}$　**3.** $s = \frac{k \times d}{4}$　**4. a)** 28.3 cm, 7.08 cm　**b)** 22.64 cm, 5.66 cm　**c)** 70.75 cm, 17.69 cm　**5. a)** 7.07 cm　**b)** 14.13 cm　**c)** 16.96 cm　**Activity 3:**　**3.** 4.3 cm　**4.** 3.46　**6.** 3.46　**Activity 4:**　**4.** pentagon: 3.25, hexagon: 3, octagon: 3.06　**5.** 3

Section 7.5 p. 217

Practice　**1.** 2.1 cm, 6.59 cm　**2.** 1.7 cm, 10.68 cm　**3.** 1.6 cm, 5.02 cm　**4–9.** Estimates may vary.　**4.** 36 cm, 34.54 cm　**5.** 24 cm, 26.22 cm　**6.** 48 cm, 47.1 cm　**7.** 18 m, 17.58 m　**8.** 120 cm, 144.44 cm　**9.** 60 cm, 60.29 cm　**Problems and Applications**　**10.** 20 cm, 20.56 cm　**11.** 42 cm, 43.55 cm　**12.** 18.53 mm　**13.** 22.29 m　**14. a)** 2.6　**b)** 245　**15. a)** doubled　**b)** doubled　**16.** 62.8 cm　**17.** 31.4 cm

Learning Together pp. 218–219

Activity 1:　**1.** 8　**2.** 13　**3.** 12　**4.** 11　**5.** 14　**6.** 12　**7.** 8　**8.** 11　**Activity 3:**　**1.** 1 cm, 2 cm, 3 cm　**Activity 4:**　**1.** 10 000 cm²　**2. a)** 30 000　**b)** 100　**c)** 0.25　**d)** 45　**Activity 5:**　**1.** 10 000 m², 1 000 000 m²

Section 7.6 p. 221

Practice　**1.** 12.25 cm²　**2.** 56.25 cm²　**3.** 110.25 cm²　**4–9.** Estimates may vary.　**4.** 228 cm², 227.55 cm²　**5.** 70 cm², 72.52 cm²　**6.** 30 cm², 32.32 cm²　**7.** 400 cm², 484 cm²　**8.** 16 cm², 19.36 cm²　**9.** 225 cm², 219.04 cm²　**Problems and Applications**　**10.** 112.5 m²　**11.** 70.56 m²　**12.** 7 m　**13.** 20 002 m, 400 m　**14.** 72 ha　**15. a)** 785.4 m²　**b)** 45 m by 29.8 m　**c)** 1341 m²　**d)** $35 343　**e)** $8228　**16.** 73.5 cm²　**17.** 26

Section 7.7 p. 223

Practice　**1. a)** 3.36 cm²　**b)** 3.36 cm²　**c)** 3.36 cm²　**2–6.** Estimates may vary.　**2.** 42 cm², 38.35 cm²　**3.** 72 cm², 74.4 cm²　**4.** 126 cm², 121.5 cm²　**5.** 320 m², 316 m²　**6.** 161 m², 157.5 m²　**Problems and Applications**　**7. a)** $b = \frac{A}{h}$　**b)** 12.5 cm　**8. a)** $h = \frac{A}{b}$　**b)** 4.2 cm　**9.** 1800 cm²　**10.** The rectangle has an area 4 times that of the parallelogram.　**11. a)** 19.44 m²　**b)** 250.56 m²　**12. b)** $A = c \times (a + b)$　**c)** $A = \frac{c \times (a + b)}{2}$　**d)** 135 cm², 296 cm²

Learning Together pp. 224–225

Activity 5:　**1.** 60°, 120°, 90°, 30°, 300°, 120°　**Activity 7:**　**1.** In square units; 2 have area 1, 3 have area 2, 6 have area 3, 5 have area 4, 2 have area 5, 1 has area 6.　**3.** regular hexagon

Section 7.8 p. 227

Practice　**1.** 3　**2.** 4　**3–8.** Estimates may vary.　**3.** 45 cm², 46.5 cm²　**4.** 84 cm², 81.6 cm²　**5.** 24 cm², 23.65 cm²　**6.** 240 cm², 242.4 cm²　**7.** 12 m², 12.98 m²　**8.** 128 cm², 123.2 cm²　**Problems and Applications**　**9.** 4.5　**10.** 13　**11.** 79.8　**12.** 4.6　**13.** 39.9　**14.** 6.3　**15. a)** 46.8 cm²　**b)** 97.2 cm²　**16.** triangle: largest area; trapezoid: smallest area　**17.** 11.6 cm²　**18. a)** 12　**b)** 7200 cm²　**c)** 1800 cm²

Section 7.9 p. 229

Practice　**1.** 1 cm, 3.14 cm²　**2.** 3.5 cm, 9.62 cm²　**3.** 0.8 cm, 2.01 cm²　**4–9.** Estimates may vary.　**4.** 48 cm², 45.34 cm²　**5.** 432 cm², 452.16 cm²　**6.** 192 cm², 226.87 cm²　**7.** 1.1 cm², 1.13 m²　**8.** 1200 cm², 1384.74 cm²　**9.** 75 m², 66.44 m²　**Problems and Applications**　**10.** 20 096 km²　**11.** 754.39 m²　**12.** 471 cm²　**13.** 56.52 cm²　**14.** 245.31 cm²　**15.** 254.34 cm²　**16. a)** 113.04 cm²　**b)** 111.27 cm²　**17.** 1017.36 cm²　**18.** 5.6 cm　**19.** 26 002.34 cm²　**20. a)** area increases by a factor of 4　**b)** area increases by a factor of 9

Section 7.10 p. 231

Practice　**1.** 188.2 cm²　**2.** 50.4 cm²　**3–7.** Estimates may vary.　**3.** 150 m², 144.76 m²　**4.** 126 m², 134.375 m²　**5.** 90 cm², 92.7 cm²　**6.** 133 cm², 126.36 cm²　**7.** 60 cm², 60 cm²　**Problems and Applications**　**8. a)** 7.92 m²　**b)** $332.64　**9.** 74.38 m²　**10. a)** 18.18 m²　**b)** $627.21　**11.** 490 cm²

Section 7.11 p. 233

Problems and Applications **1. a)** 13 024 cm^2
b) 1.3024 m^2 **c)** 451.2 cm **d)** 4.512 m **2.** 360 cm^2
3. a) 7850 cm^2, 314 cm; 23 550 cm^2, 628 cm;
39 250 cm^2, 942 cm; 54 950 cm^2, 1256 cm;
70 650 cm^2, 1570 cm **b)** 86 350 cm^2 **c)** 1884 cm
4. a) 15.32 cm **b)** 61.96 cm^2 **5. a)** 80 cm
b) 6400 cm^2 **6. a)** 3.5325 cm^2, 6.28 cm^2, 9.8125 cm^2
b) The sum of the two smaller areas equals the larger
area. **c)** yes

Technology p. 234

Activity 1: **1.** 5, 8, 9 **2.** 9, 16, 21, 24, 25 **3.** It
approaches the largest area. **4.** 36 m^2 **5.** 32 m
Activity 2: **1.** 4 **2.** 5.09 **3.** 1.27 **4.** 9, 11.46,
1.27; 16, 20.37, 1.27 **5.** always 1.27 **6.** 45.8 m^2
7. 28.3 m

Technology p. 235

Activity 1: **1.** 15.84 m^2 **2.** 23.72 cm^2 **3.** 6960 m^2
Activity 3: **1.** 231.84 m^2 **2.** 11 786 cm^2
3. 237.16 m^2

Connecting Math and City Planning
pp. 236–237

Activity 1: **1. a)** (4, 4), (5, 3), (6, 2) **b)** 6 blocks
2. (4, 5), (6, 1) **3.** The shortest total distance equals
the sum of the difference in the *x*-coordinates and
the difference in the *y*-coordinates. **Activity 2:**
1. a) (4, 4) **b)** elementary: 4 blocks; junior high:
3 blocks; senior high: 2 blocks **c)** 9 blocks **d)** The
sum of the differences in the *x*- and *y*-coordinates
for the pool and each of the schools gives a result of
9. $(4 - 4) + (6 - 4) + (8 - 4) + (4 - 4) + (4 - 3) +$
$(4 - 2) = 9$ **2.** (5, 4), (3, 4), (4, 5), (4, 3) **3. a)** (6, 3)
b) elementary: 3 blocks; junior high: 4 blocks; senior
high: 5 blocks **Activity 3:** **1.** (5, 3), (5, 4), (5, 5)
2. (3, 3), (3, 4), (3, 5)

Review pp. 238–239

1. 11.3 cm **2.** 5.9 cm **3.** 8.6 cm **4.** 10.1 cm
5. 60.2 km **6.** 19 cm **7.** 68.6 cm **8.** 73.2 cm
9. 28.26 cm **10.** 43 cm **11.** 50.8 cm **12.** 25.2 cm
13. 80.7 cm **14.** 39.6 cm **15.** 134.5 cm
17. a) 72.22 cm **b)** 113.04 cm **18.** 28.5 cm^2
19. 19.5 cm^2 **20–29.** Estimates may vary.
20. 64 cm^2, 70.56 cm^2 **21.** 18 m^2, 15.875 m^2
22. 165 cm^2, 166.32 cm^2 **23.** 12.5 cm^2, 11.76 cm^2
24. 363 cm^2, 379.94 cm^2 **25.** 84 cm^2, 82.35 cm^2
26. 129 m^2, 124.54 m^2 **27.** 57 cm^2, 62.4 cm^2

28. 20 m^2, 21.05 m^2 **29.** 45 cm^2, 48.05 cm^2
30. 3.44 cm^2 **31.** 22 cm^2 **32. a)** 8400 m^2 **b)** 380 m
33. 275 cm^2

Chapter Check p. 240

1. 15 cm **2.** 7.9 cm **3.** 9.2 m **4–13.** Estimates
may vary. **4.** 46 cm, 47.8 cm **5.** 36 cm, 34.8 cm
6. 20 m, 22 m **7.** 39 cm, 39.7 cm **8.** 60 cm, 59 cm
9. 21 cm, 21.98 cm **10.** 56 cm^2, 63 cm^2 **11.** 42 m^2,
38.94 m^2 **12.** 84 cm^2, 96.25 cm^2 **13.** 147 cm^2,
153.86 cm^2 **14. a)** 63.8 m **b)** 189.81 m^2
15. a) 6750 cm^2 **b)** 360 cm **16.** 28.26 m, 63.59 m^2
17. 17.9 m^2

Using the Strategies p. 241

1. 36 **2. a)** 25 **b)** 601, 18 001 **3. a)** 72 m **b)** 36
4. $54 \times 3 = 162$ **5.** 12, 1; 9, 3; 6, 5; 3, 7; 0, 9 **6.** 63
8. 42 m **9.** 11:00 **10.** Begin on the side with the
3 tigers. Take 2 tigers to the other side and return
with 1 monkey. Then take the empty boat to the
other side and return with 2 monkeys. Then take
the tiger to the other side. **Data Bank** **1.** 130%
2. a) June **b)** 67 mm

Chapter 8

Getting Started pp. 244–245

Activity 1: **4. a)** 2 congruent bases joined by
rectangles **b)** base **Activity 2:** **4. a)** Triangular
faces meet at a vertex. **b)** base **Warm Up** **1–10.**
Estimates may vary. **1.** 9 cm^2, 10.24 cm^2 **2.** 8 m^2,
8.64 m^2 **3.** 210 cm^2, 228.66 cm^2 **4.** 12 cm^2,
12.48 cm^2 **5.** 10 m^2, 10.14 m^2 **6.** 12 m^2, 13.85 m^2
7. 169 cm^2, 181.37 cm^2 **8.** 37.5 m^2, 39.78 m^2
9. 16 m^2, 13.72 m^2 **10.** 20 cm^2, 21.7 cm^2 **Mental
Math** **1.** 31 **2.** 41 **3.** 51 **4.** 61 **5.** 71 **6.** 81
7. 91 **8.** 101 **9.** 111 **10.** 41 **11.** 49 **12.** 59
13. 43 **14.** 23 **15.** 33 **16.** 63 **17.** 64 **18.** 84
19. 34 **20.** 64 **21.** 50 **22.** 57 **23.** 58 **24.** 55
25. 40 **26.** 71 **27.** 41 **28.** 40 **29.** 75 **30.** 74
31. 303 **32.** 505 **33.** 808 **34.** 7007 **35.** 1212
36. 2424 **37.** 1414 **38.** 6006 **39.** 3636 **40.** 4040
41. 109 **42.** 107 **43.** 41 **44.** 31 **45.** 107
46. 107 **47.** 73 **48.** 41 **49.** 71 **50.** 105

Section 8.1 p. 247

Practice **1.** cube, rectangular prism, square
pyramid, hexagonal prism, pentagonal prism,
triangular prism, pentagonal pyramid **2.** cube,

square pyramid   **3.** sphere   **4.** cylinder, triangular pyramid, pentagonal pyramid, sphere, cone   **5.** square pyramid, triangular prism, triangular pyramid, pentagonal pyramid   **6.** 2 rectangular prisms, 1 triangular prism   **Problems and Applications**   **8.** hexagonal prism   **9.** cone   **10.** pentagonal prism   **11.** rectangular prism   **12.** cylinder   **13.** triangular prism   **14. a)** by the number of sides of the congruent polygons forming the ends   **b)** 2 octagons, 8 rectangles   **15. a)** by the number of sides of the polygon forming the base   **b)** 1 hexagon, 6 triangles   **16.** Both have congruent and parallel ends. The cylinder has a curved lateral surface instead of polygons.   **17.** Both have a single base with the lateral surfaces meeting at a point. The cone has a curved lateral surface.   **18.** no   **19.** cone, cylinder, sphere

Section 8.2 p. 249

Practice   **1–6.** Estimates may vary.   **1.** 164 cm^2 **2.** 1192 cm^2 **3.** 357 cm^2 **4.** 864 m^2 **5.** 422.34 m^2 **6.** 155.52 cm^2 **Problems and Applications**   **7. a)** 2.92 m^2; assuming carton dimensions of 0.8 m by 0.7 m by 0.6 m   **8.** 37 180 m^2 **9.** 75 cm^2 **10. a)** 238 cm^2, 173 cm^2 **b)** rectangular prism by 65 cm^2 **11.** Answers may vary.   **a)** 5 cm   **b)** 3 cm   **12. a)** 1224 cm^2 **c)** 684 cm^2, 792 cm^2, 972 cm^2

Learning Together pp. 250–251

Activity 1:   **a)** 100 cm^3 **b)** 350 cm^3 **c)** 10 cm^3 **Activity 2:**   **2.** 1000   **Activity 3: a)** 14 cm^3 **b)** 44 cm^3 **c)** 16 cm^3 **d)** 22 cm^3 **Activity 5:**   **2.** 1 000 000   **Activity 6:**   **1.** 1 000 000   **2. a)** 2 000 000 cm^3 **b)** 3 250 000 cm^3 **c)** 1 400 000 cm^3 **d)** 700 000 cm^3 **e)** 4 380 000 cm^3 **f)** 60 000 cm^3 **3. a)** 15 m^3 **b)** 0.006 m^3 **c)** 4.5 m^3 **d)** 0.075 m^3 **e)** 0.0028 m^3 **f)** 0.93 m^3

Section 8.3 p. 253

Practice   **1–6.** Estimates may vary.   **1.** 216 cm^3, 226.981 cm^3 **2.** 560 cm^3, 624 cm^3 **3.** 120 cm^3, 135 cm^3 **4.** 1280 cm^3, 1152 cm^3 **5.** 180 cm^3, 195 cm^3 **6.** 1 m^3, 0.48 m^3 **Problems and Applications**   **7. a)** 8, 27, 64, 125   **b)** 24, 54, 96, 150   **8.** 0.27 m^3 **9.** 60 cm^3 **11. a)** 6   **b)** 24 unit^3 **d)** 52, 56, 68, 70, 76, 98   **12. a)** 12 m^3 **13. a)** 144 cm^3, 180 cm^3, 201.6 cm^3, 216 cm^3 **b)** 216 cm^2 for each   **c)** The 6 cm by 6 cm by 6 cm package yields the largest volume per unit surface area.

Section 8.4 pp. 254–255

Practice   **1–4.** Estimates may vary.   **1.** 307 cm^2, 314 cm^2; 375 cm^3, 392.5 cm^3 **2.** 1610 cm^2, 1657.9 cm^2; 4800 cm^3, 5024 cm^3 **3.** 168 cm^2, 175.8 cm^2; 144 cm^3, 150.7 cm^3 **4.** 7.5 m^2, 7.9 m^2; 1.5 m^3, 1.6 m^3 **Problems and Applications**   **5.** 27.6 cm^3 **6. a)** 28 260 cm^2 **b)** 339 120 cm^3 **7. a)** diameter: 2 cm, height: 0.18 cm   **b)** 22.6 cm^3 **c)** 51.5 cm^2 **8.** 70.65, 282.6, 141.3, 565.2   **a)** the volume quadruples   **b)** the volume doubles   **c)** 1130.4 cm^3 **d)** 35.3 cm^3 **9. a)** square-based prism by 150.9 cm^2 **b)** square-based prism by 261.2 cm^3 **10.** 2383.3 mm^3

Technology pp. 256–257

Activity 1:   **1. a)** 288 cm^3 **b)** 192 cm^3 **c)** 92.288 m^3 **d)** 11 200 m^3 **Activity 2:**   **1.** 3200 cm^3, 4800 cm^3, 6400 cm^3 **2.** doubles; triples; quadruples   **3.** 6400 cm^3, 14 400 cm^3, 25 600 cm^3 **4.** The volume is 4 times, 9 times, and 16 times the original volume.   **5.** The volume is 8 times, 27 times, and 64 times the original volume.

Section 8.5 p. 263

Practice   **1.** 138 cm^2, 90 cm^3 **2.** 274 cm^2, 212 cm^3 **3.** 440 cm^2, 480 cm^3 **Problems and Applications**   **4.** 244 cm^2, 244 cm^2; 204 cm^3, 204 cm^3 **5.** 1056 cm^2, 1105.3 cm^2; 960 cm^3, 1004.8 cm^3 **6.** 1880 cm^2, 1894 cm^2; 3780 cm^3, 3894 cm^3 **7.** 408 cm^2, 405.5 cm^2; 432 cm^3, 415 cm^3 **8.** 2100 cm^2, 2083.1 cm^2; 4800 cm^3, 5889.9 cm^3 **9.** 534 cm^2, 514 cm^2; 400 cm^3, 357.6 cm^3 **10.** 212.1 m^2 **11. a)** 37 800 cm^2 **b)** $5.99   **12. a)** 258 168.75 m^3 **b)** 24 325 m^2

Review pp. 264–265

1. a) triangular prism   **b)** cube   **c)** pentagonal prism   **d)** rectangular prism   **2–19.** Estimates may vary.   **2.** 850 cm^2, 937.2 cm^2 **3.** 450 cm^2, 458.7 cm^2 **4.** 54 cm^2, 61.4 cm^2 **5.** 300 cm^2, 300 cm^2 **6.** 1500 cm^3, 1493.9 cm^3 **7.** 96 cm^3, 95.1 cm^3 **8.** 400 cm^3, 428.6 cm^3 **9.** 216 cm^3, 250.0 cm^3 **10.** 840 cm^2, 810.2 cm^2 **11.** 45 m^2, 43.3 m^2 **12.** 15 m^3, 20.3 m^3 **13.** 24 000 cm^3, 24 857.1 cm^3 **14.** 7200 cm^3, 7767.1 cm^3 **15.** 400 cm^3, 325.0 cm^3 **16.** 500 cm^3, 485.04 cm^3 **17.** 60 cm^3, 50.5 cm^3 **18.** 472 cm^2, 475.2 cm^2 **19.** 2600 cm^2, 2652 cm^2 **20. a)** 2617.5 cm^2 **b)** 8968.8 cm^3 **21.** 24 508.8 cm^3 **22.** 1163.4 cm^2 **23. a)** 128.04 m^2 **b)** $7042.20   **24.** 7508 cm^3

Chapter Check p. 266

1. 2 hexagons, 6 rectangles **2.** 6 squares
3–15. Estimates may vary. **3.** 200 cm^2, 206 cm^2
4. 150 m^2, 162.2 m^2 **5.** 60 cm^2, 54 cm^2 **6.** 800 cm^2, 800 cm^2 **7.** 105 cm^3, 131.3 cm^3 **8.** 600 cm^3, 594 cm^3 **9.** 2000 cm^3, 2197 cm^3 **10.** 420 cm^3, 475.2 cm^3 **11.** 200 m^2, 211.0 m^2 **12.** 900 cm^2, 949.9 cm^2 **13.** 1800 cm^3, 1854.6 cm^3 **14.** 960 cm^3, 1017.4 cm^3 **15. a)** 180 cm^3, 176 cm^3 **b)** 210 cm^2, 209.2 cm^2 **16.** 1628.1 cm^2
17. 17 910.6 cm^3 **18. a)** 138.8 cm^2 **b)** 57.5 cm^3
19. 2160 cm^3 **20–23.** Estimates may vary.
20. 160 cm^2, 160 cm^2 **21.** 510 cm^2, 510 cm^2
22. 260 cm^3, 285.9 cm^3 **23.** 13 m^3, 16.5 m^3

Using the Strategies p. 267

1. a) 13.5 cm **b)** 27 cm **c)** 36 cm **2.** 11 **3.** 12
5. a) 13 **b)** 1 **c)** 5 **d)** 11 **6.** Mario: $8, Tara: $16
7. Friday **Data Bank 1.** 4.3 **2.** 6 min

Cumulative Review Chapters 5–8
pp. 268–269

Chapter 5: 1. 11 **2.** 12 **3.** 1 **4.** −1 **5.** 3
6. 34 **7.** 13 **8.** 4 **9.** 16 **10.** −1 **11.** 0 **12.** 6
13. a) 12, 16 **b)** $4n = c$ **c)** $100 **d)** 26 **14.** 2, 3, 4, 5, 6; (0, 2), (1, 3), (2, 4), (3, 5), (4, 6) **15.** −3, −1, 1, 3, 5; (−2, −3), (−1, −1), (0, 1), (1, 3), (2, 5)
16–17. Answers may vary. **16.** (0, 4), (1, 3), (8, −4), (−5, 9) **17.** (0, 1), (1, 4), (−4, −11), (−2, −5) **18.** square, 16, 16 **19.** rectangle, 28, 22 **20.** rectangle, 36, 26 **21.** (0, 4), (1, 3), (−4, 8), (4, 0), (−3, 7) **22.** (0, −3), (1, −1), (2, 1), (−3, −9), (5, 7) **Chapter 6: 1.** four less than m is eleven **2.** two times b added to three times b is fifteen **3.** six times x is forty-eight **4.** a less than nine is twice a **5.** $x + 6 = 10$ **6.** $\frac{x}{4} - 1 = 1$
7. $n + 4n = 15$ **8.** $2m - 6 = m$ **9.** $5p + 2 = 17$
10. no **11.** yes **12.** yes **13.** no **14.** 6 **15.** 25
16. 10 **17.** 0 **18.** $4x - 3$ **19.** $4x + 4$ **20.** $6a - 6$
21. $8m + 6n$ **22.** 3 **23.** 4 **24.** 4 **25.** 5 **26.** −4
27. −2 **28.** 13.5 **29.** $-\frac{5}{2}$ **30.** 2 **31.** −2.6 **32.** 25 years **Chapter 7: 1.** 11.4 m **2.** 5.3 m **3.** 25 m
4–9. Estimates will vary. **4.** 78 cm, 78 cm; 300 cm^2, 308 cm^2 **5.** 41 cm, 41 cm; 75 cm^2, 65.3 cm^2
6. 26 cm, 25.6 cm; 42 cm^2, 41.0 cm^2 **7.** 18 cm, 18.8 cm; 27 cm^2, 28.3 cm^2 **8.** 44 cm, 44 cm; 100 cm^2, 101.4 cm^2 **9.** 55 cm, 53 cm; 200 cm^2, 142.5 cm^2 **10. a)** 45.3 cm^2 **b)** 190.9 cm^2 **11.** 0.3 m
12. 48 cm^2 **13.** 99.4 cm^2 **14.** 164.5 cm^2
Chapter 8: 1–8. Estimates will vary. **1.** 36 m^2, 34.6 m^2 **2.** 250 cm^2, 251.4 cm^2 **3.** 56 m^3, 60.1 m^3

4. 60 cm^3, 56.4 cm^3 **5.** 1200 cm^2, 1526.9 cm^2; 3000 cm^3, 2811.5 cm^3 **6.** 1200 cm^2, 1161.5 cm^2; 3000 cm^3, 2893.8 cm^3 **7.** 188.5 m^2, 158.75 m^3
8. 344 m^2, 344 m^2; 400 m^3, 420 m^3 **9.** 785 cm^2, 1570 cm^3 **10. a)** 188.4 cm^3 **b)** 408.2 cm^2
11. 256 cm^2, 192 cm^3

Chapter 9

Getting Started pp. 272–273

Activity 1: 2. A C, E, F, and G are triangles; B is a parallelogram; D is a square. **3.** G
4. C, E **5.** C, E **6.** C, E **7.** A, C, E; B, C, E; D, C, E **Activity 2: 1.** F, G **2.** B, C, D, E
3. F or G **4.** F or G **5.** C **6.** A, B, or D
7. A, E or B, E **Mental Math 1.** 175 **2.** 275
3. 275 **4.** 275 **5.** 325 **6.** 400 **7.** 500 **8.** 600
9. 150 **10.** 175 **11.** 75 **12.** 125 **13.** 275
14. 125 **15.** 75 **16.** 75 **17.** 200 **18.** 175 **19.** 25
20. 250 **21.** 225 **22.** 50 **23.** 125 **24.** 100
25. 75 **26.** 100 **27.** 300 **28.** 200 **29.** 225
30. 300 **31.** 225 **32.** 250 **33.** 175 **34.** 450
35. 25 **36.** 3 **37.** 25 **38.** 25 **39.** 25 **40.** 50
41. 5 **42.** 25 **43.** 25 **44.** 25

Section 9.1 p. 275

Practice 1. ∠AEC = 76°, ∠AED = 104°, ∠CEB = 104° **2.** ∠x = 24°, ∠y = 156°, ∠z = 24°
3. ∠y = 133° **4.** ∠x = 34° **5.** ∠a = 58°, ∠b = 61°, ∠c = 61°, ∠d = 61° **6.** ∠a = 23°, ∠b = 67°, ∠c = 113°
7. 55° **8.** 34° **9.** 9° **10.** 133° **11.** 74° **12.** 23°
13. neither **14.** supplementary **15.** complementary
16. neither **Problems and Applications 17. a)** 55°
b) 35° **18.** 110°, 70° **19.** 50°, 40° **20.** ∠N − ∠P = 90°
23. a) ∠AGF, ∠FGD, ∠DGC, ∠CGA **b)** ∠FGE, ∠EGD; ∠AGB, ∠BGC **c)** ∠AGF, ∠FGD; ∠FGE, ∠EGC; ∠EGD, ∠DGB; ∠FGD, ∠DGC; ∠DGC, ∠CGA; ∠DGB, ∠BGA; ∠CGB, ∠BGF; ∠BGA, ∠AGE; ∠AGE, ∠EGD; ∠EGC, ∠CGB; ∠CGA, ∠AGF; ∠BGF, ∠FGE

Section 9.2 p. 277

Practice 1. corresponding **2.** alternate
3. co-interior **4.** opposite **5.** exterior
6. exterior **7.** alternate **8.** corresponding
9. opposite **10.** co-interior **Problems and Applications 11.** ∠a = 115°, ∠b = 115°, ∠c = 65°, ∠e = 115°, ∠f = 115°, ∠g = 65°, ∠h = 65°
12. ∠q = 110°, ∠r = 70°, ∠s = 110°, ∠t = 70°,

$\angle u = 70°$, $\angle v = 70°$, $\angle p = 110°$ **13.** $\angle a = 90°$, $\angle b = 90°$, $\angle c = 90°$, $\angle d = 90°$ **14.** $\angle l = 60°$, $\angle m = 60°$, $\angle n = 120°$, $\angle o = 60°$, $\angle p = 120°$ **15.** $\angle a = 88°$, $\angle b = 92°$, $\angle c = 88°$ **16.** $\angle m = 50°$, $\angle n = 50°$, $\angle o = 60°$, $\angle p = 70°$ **17.** $\angle x = 65°$, $\angle y = 115°$ **18.** $\angle a = 105°$, $\angle b = 75°$, $\angle c = 105°$ **19.** $\angle a = 55°$, $\angle b = 67°$, $\angle c = 58°$ **20.** $\angle p = 100°$, $\angle q = 105°$, $\angle r = 80°$, $\angle s = 75°$ **21.** 90°; alternate angles are equal

Section 9.3 p. 279

Practice **1.** no **2.** yes **3.** yes **4.** no **Problems and Applications** **20.** infinitely many; every diameter line is a line of symmetry

Section 9.4 p. 281

Practice **1.** isosceles, acute **2.** scalene, obtuse **3.** equilateral, acute **4.** isosceles, right **5.** 50° **6.** 43° **7.** 53° **8.** 127° **Problems and Applications** **9.** $\angle x = 56°$, $\angle y = 129°$ **10.** $\angle p = 82°$, $\angle q = 82°$, $\angle r = 27°$ **11.** $\angle t = 35°$, $\angle u = 35°$ **12.** $\angle a = 60°$, $\angle b = 80°$ **13. a)** $\angle B$, $\angle C$; $\angle E$, $\angle F$ **b)** angles opposite equal sides are equal **14. a)** $\angle x = 48°$, $\angle y = 66°$ **b)** $\angle a = 65°$, $\angle b = 65°$ **15.** $\angle c = \angle a + \angle b$ **16. a)** 1 **b)** none **c)** 3 **17. a)** 1 **b)** 1 **c)** 3 **18. a)** 3 **b)** 3 cm, 4 cm, 5 cm: scalene; 2 cm, 5 cm, 5 cm: isosceles; 4 cm, 4 cm, 4 cm: equilateral

Technology pp. 282–283

Activity 1: **1.** equal **2.** equal **3.** equal **Activity 2:** **1.** square, rectangle **2.** rhombus, kite, square **3.** rhombus, square, parallelogram, rectangle **Activity 4:** **1.** PS = 7 cm, RS = 4 cm, $\angle$PSR = 57°, $\angle$QRS = 123° **2.** DG = 3 cm, HF = 2.1 cm, GE = 4.2 cm, $\angle$GHF = 90° **3.** AB = 7 cm, DC = 3 cm, $\angle$AED = 90°, $\angle$DEC = 90° **4.** DC = 6 cm, EC = 5 cm, AC = 10 cm, DB = 10 cm, AD = 8 cm, BE = 5 cm **5.** QO = 5 cm, MO = 10 cm, PO = 9 cm, PQ = 7 cm **6.** XY = 6 cm, MY = 3 cm, XZ = 10.4 cm, $\angle$WMZ = 90°

Section 9.5 p. 285

Practice **1.** 900° **2.** 1260° **3.** 1440° **4.** 1800° **5.** 123° **6.** 105° **7.** 115° **8.** 110° **9.** 60° **10.** 120° **11.** 108° **12.** 144° **Problems and Applications** **13.** square **14. a)** 6, 5 **b)** equal **15. a)** $\angle x = 120°$, $\angle y = 120°$ **b)** $\angle r = 135°$, $\angle s = 40°$ **16. a)** 120° **b)** 360° **c)** sum: 360° **d)** sum: 360° **e)** sum: 360° **f)** 360° **17.** yes **18.** yes **19. a)** 11 sides **b)** hendecagon

Section 9.6 p. 289

Practice **1.** $\angle a = 93°$, $\angle b = 87°$, $\angle c = 93°$ **2.** $\angle m = 55°$, $\angle n = 82°$, $\angle o = 55°$, $\angle p = 43°$ **3.** $\angle p = 105°$, $\angle q = 75°$, $\angle r = 105°$, $\angle s = 75°$, $\angle t = 105°$, $\angle u = 75°$, $\angle v = 105°$ **4.** $\angle x = 55°$, $\angle y = 35°$, $\angle z = 145°$ **5.** $\angle a = 54°$, $\angle b = 63°$ **6.** $\angle m = 68°$, $\angle n = 68°$ **Problems and Applications** **7.** $\angle w = 57°$, $\angle x = 72°$, $\angle y = 51°$, $\angle z = 129°$ **8.** $\angle a = 59°$, $\angle b = 40°$, $\angle c = 99°$, $\angle d = 59°$ **9.** $\angle p = 43°$, $\angle q = 101°$, $\angle r = 36°$, $\angle s = 43°$ **10.** $\angle m = 55°$, $\angle n = 55°$, $\angle o = 60°$, $\angle p = 60°$, $\angle q = 65°$ **11.** $\angle a = 96°$, $\angle b = 45°$ **12.** $\angle a = 20°$, $\angle b = 20°$, $\angle c = 85°$, $\angle d = 75°$ **13.** $\angle a = 125°$, $\angle b = 100°$, $\angle c = 95°$, $\angle d = 80°$ **14.** $\angle v = 60°$, $\angle w = 90°$, $\angle x = 60°$, $\angle y = 60°$, $\angle z = 60°$ **15.** $\angle a = 75°$, $\angle b = 75°$, $\angle c = 35°$, $\angle d = 30°$, $\angle e = 150°$ **16.** $\angle p = 70°$, $\angle q = 40°$, $\angle r = 65°$, $\angle s = 140°$, $\angle t = 70°$ **17.** $\angle a = 60°$, $\angle b = 60°$, $\angle c = 60°$, $\angle d = 120°$, $\angle e = 30°$, $\angle f = 30°$ **18.** $\angle v = 70°$, $\angle w = 40°$, $\angle x = 110°$, $\angle y = 35°$, $\angle z = 35°$ **19.** $\angle p = 85°$, $\angle q = 65°$, $\angle r = 52°$, $\angle s = 65°$, $\angle t = 42°$ **20.** $\angle a = 95°$, $\angle b = 55°$, $\angle c = 50°$, $\angle d = 20°$

Learning Together pp. 292–293

Activity 1: **1.** cubes **Activity 2:** **1.** pentagonal pyramid, pentagonal prism **2.** 6, 10 **3.** 10, 15 **4. a)** 6, 9 **b)** 8, 12 **c)** 5, 8 **d)** 12, 18 **Activity 3:** **1. a)** triangular prism **b)** triangular pyramid **c)** rectangular prism **Activity 4:** **1. d)** triangular pyramid **Activity 5:** **2. b)** yes **Activity 6:** **1.** a and c **3.** circle **4.** sector of a circle

Section 9.7 p. 295

Practice **1.** shell **2.** solid **3.** shell **4.** shell **5.** shell **6.** solid **7. b)** shell **8.** base: square; 6 squares **9.** base: pentagon; 1 pentagon, 5 triangles **10.** base: triangle; 2 triangles, 3 rectangles **11.** base: hexagon; 2 hexagons, 6 rectangles **12.** base: square; 1 square, 4 triangles **13.** base: triangle; 4 triangles **Problems and Applications** **14. a)** 8, 6, 12; 6, 6, 10; 6, 5, 9; 12, 8, 18; 5, 5, 8; 4, 4, 6 **b)** $V + F - E = 2$

Section 9.8 pp. 296–297

Practice **1.** 2 triangular bases; 3 rectangular faces **2.** 1 hexagonal base; 6 triangular faces **3.** 2 rectangular bases; 4 other rectangles **Problems and Applications** **4.** shell **5. a)** triangular pyramid **b)** 3, 3 **c)** no **9. a)** top left, middle, and bottom left only **b)** 5 and 7, in each case

Connecting Math and History pp. 298–299

Activity 1: **1.** Fire: triangles; Universe: pentagons; Air: triangles; Water: triangles; Earth: squares
2. a) Earth **b)** Universe **c)** Fire **d)** Water **e)** Air; tetra - four, octa - eight, dodeca - twelve, icosa - twenty **3.** hexahedron **4.** triangular pyramid
Activity 2: **1.** square pyramid; consists of both triangles and a square **2.** pentagonal prism; consists of both pentagons and rectangles **3.** hexagonal prism; consists of both hexagons and rectangles
4. triangular prism; consists of both triangles and rectangles **Activity 3:** **5.** cube; all faces are congruent **Activity 4:** **4.** 2 **5.** octahedron **6.** 4
Activity 5: **2.** cube, 6, square, 3; tetrahedron, 4, triangular, 3; octahedron, 8, triangular, 4; dodecahedron, 12, pentagonal, 3; icosahedron, 20, triangular, 5

Connecting Math and Communications pp. 300–303

Activity 1: **3.** 1a, 2b (if start at vertex D or E), 3c, 4b (if start at vertex C or D), 5a, 6c **4.** 1, 5, 4, 1; 2, 5, 2, 3; 3, 5, 0, 5; 4, 6, 2, 4; 5, 5, 4, 1; 6, 5, 0, 5 **5. a)** not traceable **b)** traceable **c)** traceable
Activity 2: **1.** 0, 2, 4, 4, 2, 0 **2.** traceable, traceable, not traceable, not traceable, traceable, traceable **Activity 3:** **2. a)** not traceable **b)** 2, 2 ways **Activity 4:** **1.** a **2.** neither **3.** b
4. a) different places **b)** the same place **Activity 5:** **1. a)** 48 units **b)** yes **2. a)** 68 units **b)** yes **3. a)** 37 units **b)** no **Activity 6:** **1.** 2745 km **2.** Start: Winnipeg, End: Edmonton **Activity 7:** **1.** can obtain files from the administrator and can send files to User C; cannot receive files from User A **2.** can obtain files from User B and from the administrator and can send files to the administrator; cannot receive files from User A **3. a)** via User C **b)** via the administrator **Activity 8:** **1. a)** Regina to Brandon, Saskatoon, Winnipeg; Brandon to Saskatoon; Saskatoon to Regina, Winnipeg; Winnipeg to Regina, Saskatoon **b)** Regina to Saskatoon to Regina, Regina to Winnipeg to Regina, Regina to Brandon to Saskatoon, Regina to Winnipeg to Saskatoon, Regina to Saskatoon to Winnipeg, Brandon to Saskatoon to Regina, Brandon to Saskatoon to Winnipeg, Saskatoon to Winnipeg to Saskatoon, Saskatoon to Regina to Saskatoon, Saskatoon to Winnipeg to Regina, Saskatoon to Regina to Winnipeg, Saskatoon to Regina to Brandon, Winnipeg to Saskatoon to Winnipeg, Winnipeg to Regina to Winnipeg, Winnipeg to Regina to Brandon, Winnipeg to Saskatoon to Regina, Winnipeg to Regina to Saskatoon **2.** No, you cannot go from Brandon to Brandon with at most one stopover. **3.** 1, 0, 0, 1; 1, 0, 1, 0 **4.** 1, 1, 2, 1; 1, 1, 1, 2 **5.** 2, 1, 2, 2; 2, 1, 2, 2 **6.** Matrix 3 is the sum of matrices 1 and 2.

Review pp. 304–305

1. $\angle a = 141°$, $\angle b = 39°$ **2.** $\angle a = 44°$, $\angle b = 47°$, $\angle c = 44°$, $\angle x = 89°$ **3.** 27° **4.** 55° **5.** 55° **6.** 24°
7. 1° **8.** 133° **9.** 78° **10.** 24° **11.** $\angle a = 70°$, $\angle b = 110°$, $\angle c = 70°$, $\angle d = 70°$, $\angle e = 110°$
12. $\angle q = 126°$, $\angle x = 126°$, $\angle y = 54°$, $\angle z = 126°$
13. $\angle a = 97°$, $\angle b = 97°$ **14.** $\angle a = 104°$, $\angle b = 104°$, $\angle c = 76°$, $\angle d = 104°$ **17.** isosceles, right
18. scalene, obtuse **19.** 56° **20.** $\angle a = 69°$, $\angle b = 111°$
21. 41° **22.** 139° **23.** $\angle x = 61°$, $\angle y = 61°$, $\angle z = 58°$
24. $\angle p = 65°$, $\angle q = 71°$, $\angle r = 65°$ **25.** $\angle a = 58°$, $\angle b = 85°$, $\angle c = 37°$ **26.** $\angle a = 49°$, $\angle b = 74°$, $\angle c = 57°$
27. a) triangular prism **b)** square pyramid **c)** cube **d)** pentagonal prism **28.** hexagonal prism, 8, 18, 12
29. triangular pyramid, 4, 6, 4 **30.** cube, 6, 12, 8
31. triangular prism, 5, 9, 6 **32.** shell

Chapter Check p. 306

1. $\angle x = 143°$, $\angle y = 37°$ **2.** $\angle a = 60°$, $\angle b = 65°$, $\angle c = 55°$ **3.** 46° **4.** 83° **5.** 24° **6.** 123° **7.** 79°
8. 15° **11.** equilateral, acute **12.** scalene, right
13. 150° **14.** $\angle a = 65°$, $\angle b = 65°$, $\angle c = 115°$, $\angle d = 65°$, $\angle e = 115°$ **15.** 55° **16.** 64° **17.** 70° **18.** $\angle x = 63°$, $\angle y = 63°$, $\angle z = 66°$ **19.** $\angle a = 27°$, $\angle b = 30°$, $\angle c = 30°$
20. rectangular prism, 6, 12, 8 **21.** pentagonal prism, 7, 15, 10 **22.** square pyramid, 5, 8, 5 **23.** 2 hexagons, 6 rectangles **24.** 6 squares
25. decagonal prism **26.** cylinder **27.** triangular pyramid **28.** rectangular prism

Using the Strategies p. 307

1. 195 **2. a)** 8 **b)** 16 **3.** 18 **4.** 58 oatmeal, 83 chocolate chip **5.** Answers may vary. 3 dimes, 3 nickels, 4 pennies **6.** 3 **7.** $169.83 **8.** 8
9. Tanya: saxophone; Darrell: trumpet; Susan: drums
Data Bank **1.** flying distance from Toronto to Charlottetown, driving distance from Edmonton to Victoria, length of South Saskatchewan River **2.** about 2.2%

Chapter 10

Getting Started pp. 310–311

Warm Up **1.** 15 **2.** 50 **3.** 125 **4.** 95 **5.** 41
6. 3.5 **7.** 259.2 **8.** 140.4 **9.** 81 **10.** 14.4
11. 198 **12.** 313.2 **13.** 0.67 **14.** 0.375 **15.** 0.85
16. 0.89 **17.** 0.25 **18.** 0.86 **19.** 40% **20.** 85%
21. 44.4% **22.** 87.5% **23.** 55% **24.** 41.7%
25. 80% **26.** 43% **27.** 55.1% **28.** 62.5% **29.** 5%
30. 7.5% **31.** 39% **32.** 46% **33.** 55% **34.** 68%
35. 19% **36.** 94% **37.** 76 **38.** 60 **39.** 58.5
40. 30.5 **Mental Math** **1.** 100 **2.** 20 **3.** 1
4. 20 **5.** 5 **6.** 150 **7.** 1 **8.** 5 **9.** 8 **10.** 250
11. 130 **12.** 46 **13.** 91 **14.** 72 **15.** 77 **16.** 43
17. 18 **18.** 84 **19.** 59 **20.** 17 **21.** 1200 **22.** 100
23. 4000 **24.** 4200 **25.** 140 **26.** 120 **27.** 720
28. 8100 **29.** 12 000 **30.** 400 **31.** 70 **32.** 1300
33. 0.14 **34.** 0.06 **35.** 120 **36.** 0.5 **37.** 0.024
38. 0.088 **39.** 40 **40.** 20 **41.** 3 **42.** 100 000
43. 0.012 **44.** 120 **45.** 2 **46.** 0.02

Section 10.1 p. 313

Problems and Applications **1. a)** 17, 28, 4, 2, 34
b) 2 **c)** scrambled **d)** 2 **e)** 85 **2. b)** Switzerland,
Austria, Germany and United States of America,
Canada, France and Italy **c)** 40: Austria: 8; Canada:
4; France: 3; Germany: 6; Italy: 3; Switzerland: 10;
United States of America: 6 **3. a)** census **b)** sample
c) sample **d)** census

Section 10.2 p. 315

Problems and Applications **1.** Fruit scraps:
720 kg; Food scraps: 540 kg; Whole fresh fruit:
360 kg; Non-food waste: 180 kg **2. a)** 4%, 5%,
12%, 13%, 17%, 29%, 7%, 13% **b)** Monday:
1200; Tuesday: 1500; Wednesday: 3600; Thursday:
3900; Friday: 5100; Saturday: 8700; Sunday:
2100 **c)** 3900 **3. a)** 24%, 18%, 12%, 10%, 10%,
56%, 8% **b)** A household may have more than
one kind of juice in the refrigerator. **c)** Apple:
2 640 000; Blended Fruit: 1 980 000; Cranberry:
1 320 000; Grapefruit: 1 100 000; Grape: 1 100 000;
Orange: 6 160 000; Tomato/Vegetable: 880 000
4. b) Beetles: 9 000 000; Mice: 114 000 000;
Wasps/Bees: 135 000 000; Worms: 6 000 000
5. a) Professional Sports: 528; Art Museum: 372;
Other Museum: 312; Rock Concert: 336; Symphony
Concert: 132 **b)** A person may have attended more
than one event.

Connecting Math and Canadian History
p. 319

Activity 3: **1. a)** 37% **b)** 376 **2. a)** 31%

Section 10.3 p. 321

Problems and Applications **1. a)** New Brunswick,
Newfoundland **b)** 1250 km **c)** New Brunswick
d) 12 500 km **4.** Alberta and Saskatchewan, Manitoba,
Ontario and British Columbia, New Brunswick and
Newfoundland, Prince Edward Island and Nova Scotia

Section 10.4 p. 323

Problems and Applications **1. a)** 55 000 000
b) 13 000 000 **c)** 29 000 000, 5 000 000 **d)** LPs
from 1971 to 1981 **e)** no; 10 000 000 less

Section 10.5 p. 325

Problems and Applications **1. a)** 11.34 L **b)** 0.54 L
c) 1.8 L **d)** 4.32 L **2. a)** 240 **b)** 480 **c)** 1500 **d)** 600

Section 10.6 p. 327

Problems and Applications **1. a)** U.S.A. **b)** China
c) 525 L **2. a)** Quebec, 190 **b)** 50 **c)** Nova Scotia
and Saskatchewan **d)** 60 **e)** No, though it should
have fewer than ten. **4. b)** A bar graph may be
used. The data is not suited for a broken-line graph
since comparisons are not being made over time.
A circle graph may be used, with the full circle
representing the total mass of waste.

Learning Together pp. 330–331

Activity 1: **1. a)** Terry: 1.000, Kelly: 0.750
b) Terry **2. a)** Terry: 0.400, Kelly: 0.000 **b)** Terry
3. a) 3 **b)** Terry: 0.500, Kelly: 0.600 **c)** Kelly **d)** No
Activity 2: **1.** no **2.** 8 times more **Activity 3:**
1. Poll the members of the ski club. **Activity 4:**
1. The break mark on the vertical axis allows an
exaggerated vertical scale.

Section 10.7 pp. 334–335

Practice **1.** mode **2.** median **3.** mode **4.** mean
5. median **6.** mean **7.** 24.8, 25, 25, 6 **8.** 23,
23, no mode, 19 **9.** 18.3, 16, 8 and 16, 33
10. 51.3, 51, 80, 69 **11.** 2522, 2175, no mode,
3380 **Problems and Applications** Answers may
vary. **12. a)** 2, 6, 7, 8, 9 **b)** 2, 6, 7, 8, 17 **c)** 2, 6,
7, 8, 14, 17 **13. a)** 21.8, 18, 9, 20.5 **b)** Each shot
total is weighted according to the number of times
it occurred. **14.** 5.3, 5, 5, 6 **15. a)** 128.8, 104,

31, 359 **b)** no, too low **16.** $1.90 **17. a)** mean increased by 2, median increased by 2, mode increased by 2 **b)** mean decreased by 3, median decreased by 3, mode decreased by 3 **c)** mean is doubled, median is doubled, mode is doubled **18. a)** 30 **b)** no **19. a)** no; too low **b)** yes; more representative **20. a)** $70 000 **b)** $47 500, $40 000, $40 000 **c)** median or mode **d)** $40 000, $40 000, $40 000 **e)** $50 000, $40 000, $40 000 **f)** mean **21.** 92 **22. a)** always true **b)** sometimes true **c)** sometimes true **d)** sometimes true **23.** Answers may vary. 4, 5, 6, 8, 12, 25 **24. a)** 11, 11, 12, 15, 26; other lists are possible **b)** 10, 10, 13, 17; only possibility **c)** 3, 19, 20, 25, 26, 27; other lists are possible **d)** 8, 16, 16, 16, 24; other lists are possible

Section 10.8 p. 337

Problems and Applications **1. a)** 25 **b)** 168 cm **c)** 172 cm **d)** 24 cm **e)** 9 **2. b)** 18.5 **c)** 27; 11, 12, and 26 **d)** 4, 7 **3. b)** 156, 55 **c)** 8 **d)** 9 **4. b)** 15 **c)** 1st test: 68; 2nd test: 80 **d)** 1st test: 33, 2nd test: 32 **e)** 1st test: 7, 2nd test: 12 **f)** 1st test: 12, 2nd test: 7

Section 10.9 p. 339

Problems and Applications **1. a)** $\frac{1}{2}$ **b)** 20 h–45 h **c)** $\frac{3}{4}$ **2. b)** 56 and 76 **c)** 40 and 76 **3. a)** 60 and 70 **b)** Carlos **c)** 25%

Section 10.10 p. 341

Problems and Applications **1.** win, lose, tie; tie is most likely **2.** red, blue, green, yellow **3.** large triangle, medium triangle, small triangle, square, parallelogram; large triangle is most likely **4.** head, red; tail, red; head, yellow; tail, yellow; head, blue; tail, blue; head, green; tail, green **5.** 1, black; 2, black; 3, black; 4, black; 5, black; 6, black; 1, yellow; 2, yellow; 3, yellow; 4, yellow; 5, yellow; 6, yellow; yellow on spinner is most likely **6. a)** H, H, red; H, T, red; T, H, red; T, T, red; H, H, blue; H, T, blue; T, H, blue; T, T, blue; H, H, green; H, T, green; T, H, green; T, T, green **b)** H, H, H; H, H, T; H, T, H; T, H, H; T, T, H; T, H, T; H, T, T; T, T, T **7. a)** 1 red, 1 blue; 1 red, 2 blue; 1 red, 3 blue; 2 red, 1 blue; 2 red, 2 blue; 2 red, 3 blue; 3 red, 1 blue; 3 red, 2 blue; 3 red, 3 blue **b)** 2 red, 2 blue and 3 red, 1 blue **c)** 2; 2 **8. a)** 1 red, 1 green; 1 red, 2 green; 1 red, 3 green; 1 red, 4 green; 2 red, 1 green; 2 red, 2 green; 2 red, 3 green; 2 red, 4 green; 3 red, 1 green; 3 red, 2 green; 3 red, 3 green; 3 red, 4 green;

4 red, 1 green; 4 red, 2 green; 4 red, 3 green; 4 red, 4 green **b)** 16 **c)** 3 **d)** 5; 4 ways **e)** 2 and 8

Section 10.11 p. 343

Practice **1. a)** $\frac{1}{2}$ **b)** $\frac{1}{8}$ **c)** $\frac{3}{8}$ **2. a)** $\frac{1}{6}$ **b)** $\frac{1}{3}$ **c)** $\frac{1}{2}$ **d)** 0 **e)** $\frac{2}{3}$ **f)** 1 **3. a)** $\frac{1}{5}$ **b)** $\frac{2}{5}$ **c)** $\frac{3}{5}$ **d)** 0 **4. a)** $\frac{1}{2}$ **b)** $\frac{1}{13}$ **c)** $\frac{1}{26}$ **d)** $\frac{3}{13}$ **Problems and Applications** **5. a)** $\frac{3}{5}$ **b)** $\frac{4}{5}$ **c)** $\frac{3}{10}$ **d)** $\frac{7}{10}$ **6. a)** $\frac{3}{10}$ **b)** $\frac{3}{5}$ **c)** 1 **d)** 0 **e)** $\frac{3}{5}$ **7. a)** 240 **b)** 60 **c)** 0 **8. a)** 15 **b)** 8 **c)** 50 **d)** 46 **9. a)** 8% **b)** 92% **c)** 100% **d)** 184

Technology pp. 346–347

Activity 1: **1.** $\frac{1}{4}$

Section 10.12 p. 349

Problems and Applications **1. a)** $\frac{1}{4}$ **b)** $\frac{1}{8}$ **c)** $\frac{3}{8}$ **d)** 0 **e)** $\frac{1}{4}$ **2. a)** 10% **b)** 10% **c)** 0% **d)** 20% **e)** 30% **f)** 100% **3. a)** 1 on red, 1 on blue; 1 on red, 2 on blue; 1 on red, 3 on blue; 1 on red, 4 on blue; 2 on red, 1 on blue; 2 on red, 2 on blue; 2 on red, 3 on blue; 2 on red, 4 on blue; 3 on red, 1 on blue; 3 on red, 2 on blue; 3 on red, 3 on blue; 3 on red, 4 on blue **b)** 12 **c)** 2 **d)** $\frac{1}{6}$ **e)** $\frac{1}{4}$, 0 **4. a)** $\frac{1}{24}$ **b)** $\frac{1}{12}$ **c)** $\frac{1}{8}$ **d)** $\frac{5}{24}$ **e)** $\frac{1}{6}$ **f)** $\frac{1}{4}$ **5. a)** $\frac{1}{24}$ **b)** $\frac{1}{16}$ **c)** $\frac{1}{2}$ **d)** $\frac{23}{48}$ **e)** 0 **f)** $\frac{3}{16}$ **6. a)** 3, 5, 7, 9, 11, 13, 15, 17, 19, 21, 23 **b)** 36 **c)** $\frac{5}{36}$, $\frac{1}{9}$, 1, 0

Review pp. 350–351

1. a) 17, 4, 24, 21, 14 **b)** 17 **c)** Tigers, Eagles, Bears, Wolves, Lions **d)** 80 **2. a)** 40 L **b)** 110 L, 22 L **c)** Laundry **5.** 83, 83, 83, 3 **6.** Answers may vary. **a)** 1, 5, 8, 9, 12 **b)** 1, 5, 6, 7, 8, 15 **c)** 1, 4, 8, 12, 13, 15 **7. b)** median: 27, mode: 25, range: 26 **8. a)** 110 cm, 40 cm **b)** 30 **c)** 30 **d)** 15 **e)** 15 **9. a)** $\frac{3}{8}$ **b)** $\frac{1}{4}$ **c)** $\frac{3}{8}$ **d)** $\frac{1}{4}$ **e)** 0 **10.** 50 **11. a)** $\frac{1}{24}$ **b)** $\frac{1}{12}$ **c)** $\frac{1}{8}$ **d)** 0 **e)** $\frac{1}{6}$ **f)** $\frac{5}{24}$

Chapter Check p. 352

1. a) Saskatchewan and Manitoba **b)** Alberta and British Columbia **c)** 2 560 000 **3. a)** 26, 25, 22, 9 **b)** 79.5, 78, no mode, 21 **c)** 7.75, 9, 9, 9 **4. b)** 88, 21 **5. a)** 10% **b)** 20% **c)** 50% **d)** 50% **e)** 30% **f)** 70% **6. a)** $\frac{1}{12}$ **b)** $\frac{1}{6}$ **c)** $\frac{1}{6}$ **d)** 0 **e)** $\frac{1}{4}$ **f)** $\frac{5}{6}$

Using the Strategies p. 353

1. 36 **3. a)** 72 m **b)** 36 **4.** 15 **5.** $31.20
6. a) 19.5 cm by 6.5 cm **b)** 126.75 cm^2 **7.** 8
8. every 28 years **9.** 20 **10.** 0 or 8 **11.** 41
13. a) 325 **Data Bank** **1.** Helmcken Falls
2. −62°C

Cumulative Review, Chapters 9–10 p. 354

Chapter 9: **1.** $\angle a = 147°$, $\angle b = 33°$, $\angle c = 147°$
2. $\angle p = 73°$, $\angle q = 42°$, $\angle r = 73°$, $\angle s = 65°$
3. $\angle g = 109°$, $\angle h = 109°$, $\angle k = 71°$, $\angle m = 109°$,
$\angle n = 71°$ **4.** $\angle v = 81°$, $\angle w = 99°$ **7.** 38° **8.** 111°
9. $\angle c = 23°$, $\angle d = 23°$, $\angle g = 90°$, $\angle m = 67°$
10. $\angle n = 48°$, $\angle p = 66°$, $\angle w = 66°$ **11. a)** cube
b) shell **c)** 6, 12, 8 **12. a)** square pyramid **b)** shell
c) 5, 8, 5 **Chapter 10:** **1.** 150 **4. a)** 36.6, 37, 29
and 40, 18 **5. a)** $\frac{1}{12}$ **b)** $\frac{1}{4}$ **c)** $\frac{1}{6}$

Cumulative Review, Chapters 1–10
pp. 355–359

1. 64 **2.** 256 **3.** 6561 **4.** 0.01 **5.** 0.001
6. −100 000 **7.** 64 **8.** 25 **9.** 4.2×10^7
10. 6.2×10^{-3} **11.** 2.57×10^4 **12.** 5.4×10^{-6}
13. 10 200 **14.** 360 000 **15.** 0.0082 **16.** 0.000 046
17. $-1\frac{1}{4}$, −1.12, 0.025, 0.52, 3.125, $5\frac{1}{2}$ **18.** $-\frac{3}{5}$, −0.2,
$\frac{1}{5}$, $1\frac{1}{4}$, 1.5, 4 **19.** 62% **20.** 145% **21.** 27.5%
22. 60% **23.** 125% **24.** 80% **25.** 40%
26. 150% **27.** 16% **28.** 0.225 **29.** 1.5 **30.** 0.0675
31. 0.2 **32.** 0.68 **33.** 0.95 **34.** 17 **35.** 1.4
36. $1\frac{1}{7}$ **37.** $1\frac{1}{6}$ **38.** $4\frac{1}{3}$ **39.** $\frac{2}{9}$ **40.** $\frac{3}{10}$ **41.** $2\frac{1}{6}$
42. 6 **43.** $\frac{7}{12}$ **44.** $\frac{3}{4}$ **45.** $2\frac{1}{2}$ **46.** $\frac{1}{2}$ **47.** 6
48. $\frac{4}{5}$ **49.** 3.28 **50.** −1.44 **51.** 2.4 **52.** −0.6
53. 2.2 **54.** −2 **55.** 2.908 **56.** −3 **57.** 8:14, 20:35
58. 12 **59.** 6 **60.** 8 **61.** 6, 6 **62.** 11, 5 **63.** $2.03
64. $0.997/kg **65.** $0.898/bulb **66.** 18.3 cm
67. 1:5 000 000 **68–71.** Estimates may vary.
68. 34, 34 **69.** 25%, 25% **70.** 72, 64.98 **71.** 500,
500 **72. a)** $199.96 **b)** GST only: $213.96
73. $542.00 **74.** 32.8% **75.** 125% **76.** 140
77. 32 **78. a)** 260 km^2 **b)** 195 km^2 **79.** 0 **80.** 2
81. 10 **82.** 6 **83.** −15 **84.** 25 **85.** 0 **86.** 3 **87.** 7
88. 7 **89.** 23 **90.** 13 **91. a)** 15, 30, 45, 60
b) (1, 15), (2, 30), (3, 45), (4, 60) **c)** $d = 15 \times t$
d) 75 km, 120 km, 52.5 km **92. a)** the sum of x
and y is seven **b)** 5, 6, 7, 8, 9 **c)** (2, 5), (1, 6), (0, 7),
(−1, 8), (−2, 9) **93. a)** y equals four less than x **b)** −2,
−3, −4, −5, −6 **c)** (2, −2), (1, −3), (0, −4), (−1, −5),
(−2, −6) **94. a)** y equals three times x **b)** 6, 3, 0,
−3, −6 **c)** (2, 6), (1, 3), (0, 0), (−1, −3), (−2, −6)

95. a) 1 **b)** −9 **c)** 2 **d)** $\frac{1}{2}$ **e)** 3 **f)** 3 **96–101.** Answers
may vary. **96.** (0, 5), (1, 4), (−1, 6), (3, 2), (−5, 10)
97. (−5, −8), (5, 2), (3, 0), (0, −3), (1, −2) **98.** (0, 1),
(1, 2), (2, 3), (−1, 0), (−2, −1) **99.** (0, −2), (1, −1),
(−1, −3), (−2, −4), (2, 0) **100.** (0, −2), (1, 0),
(−1, −4), (2, 2), (−2, −6) **101.** (0, −5), (1, −2), (2, 1),
(−1, −8), (−2, −11) **102.** $y = -x + 5$ **103.** $y = -x + 9$
104. square **105.** rectangle **106–107.** Answers
may vary. **106.** (0, 4), (1, 3), (2, 2), (−1, 5), (−5, 9)
107. (0, −3), (−1, −5), (1, −1), (3, 3), (−4, −11)
108. two less than a number is three **109.** two
more than three times a number is eight **110.** one
third of a number is two **111.** five more than a
number is three times the number **112.** $4 + x = 17$
113. $3x = 2 + 2x$ **114.** $\frac{x}{6} = 3$ **115.** $x + 10 = \frac{x}{2}$ **116.** 8
117. 4 **118.** −2 **119.** −1 **120.** 1.5 **121.** 7.8 **122.** 4
123. 21 **124.** 2.33 **125.** −2 **126.** 3.6 **127.** −4
128. $2x$ **129.** 7 **130.** $4x + 4$ **131.** $-6x - 2$ **132.** 2
133. 2 **134.** 1 **135.** 9 **136.** 2 **137.** 2 **138.** −6
139. −2 **140.** 18 kg **141.** 5 cm **142.** 538 m
143. 5.7 cm **144.** 9.8 cm **145. a)** 2.9 m
b) 8 m **146.** 38.3 m **147.** 62 cm **148.** 40.2 m
149. 141.35 cm **150.** 166.4 cm **151–156.** Estimates
may vary. **151.** 27 cm^2, 26.7 cm^2 **152.** 4 m^2, 4.8 m^2
153. 112 cm^2, 106.95 cm^2 **154.** 15 m^2, 12 m^2
155. 28 cm^2, 24.7 cm^2 **156.** 432 m^2, 422.5 m^2
157. 19.2 cm, 17.8 cm^2 **158.** 59.7 m, 249.5 m^2
159–166. Estimates may vary. **159.** 114 m^2, 101.5 m^2
160. 22 m^2, 15.77 m^2 **161.** 343 cm^3, 357.9 cm^3
162. 1400 cm^3, 1786.4 cm^3 **163.** 1500 cm^2,
1507.2 cm^2; 4200 cm^3, 4421.1 cm^3 **164.** 200 m^2,
210.7 m^2; 240 m^3, 233.7 m^3 **165.** 400 m^2, 336.1 m^2;
360 m^3, 361.3 m^3 **166.** 10 600 cm^2, 11 793.8 cm^2;
45 000 cm^3, 58 992.8 cm^3 **167.** $\angle a = \angle c = 137°$,
$\angle b = 43°$ **168.** $\angle a = \angle d = 27°$, $\angle b = 38°$, $\angle c = 115°$
169. 85° **170.** 10° **171.** 55° **172.** 55° **173.** 165°
174. 115° **177.** 46° **178.** 49° **179.** $\angle a = 120°$,
$\angle c = 120°$, $\angle b = 60°$ **180.** $\angle a = \angle d = 43°$, $\angle b = 100°$,
$\angle c = 37°$ **181.** triangle, square **182.** rectangle,
triangle **183.** cone **184.** cylinder **185.** pentagonal
prism **186.** triangular pyramid **188. b)** Mount
Royal **190. b)** Maclean's and Canadian Geographic
c) 720 000 **192. b)** 51 km/h **194. a)** (1G, 1Y),
(1G, 2Y), (1G, 3Y), (2G, 1Y), (2G, 2Y), (2G, 3Y),
(3G, 1Y), (3G, 2Y), (3G, 3Y) **b)** $\frac{1}{3}$, $\frac{1}{9}$, 0 **195. a)** $\frac{1}{8}$
b) $\frac{1}{8}$ **c)** 1 **d)** 0

Glossary

A

Acute Angle An angle whose measure is less than 90°.

Acute Triangle A triangle with all 3 angles less than 90°.

Alternate Angles Two angles formed by two lines and a transversal. The angles are on opposite sides of the transversal in a Z or S pattern.

Amount The total of the principal and the interest for a deposit or loan.

Angle The figure formed by 2 rays or 2 line segments with a common endpoint.

Area The number of square units needed to cover a surface.

Average The mean of a set of numbers, found by dividing the sum of the numbers by the number of numbers.

Axes The intersecting number lines on a graph.

B

Bar Graph A graph that uses bars to represent data visually.

Base (of a polygon) Any side of a polygon.

Base (of a power) The number used as a factor for repeated multiplication. In 6^3, the base is 6.

BASIC A computer programming language.

Biased Answer An answer affected by the wording of the question.

Biased Sample A sample in which each member of the population does not have an equal chance of being selected.

Broken-Line Graph A graph that represents data with line segments joined end to end.

C

Capacity The greatest volume that a container can hold, usually measured in litres or millilitres.

Cell A rectangular entry in a computer spreadsheet.

Census A survey in which data are collected from every member of a population.

Chord A line segment that joins 2 points on the circumference of a circle.

Circle Graph A graph that uses sectors of a circle to show how data are divided into parts.

Circumference The perimeter of a circle.

Closing Price The price of one share of stock at the time when the stock market closes for the day.

Clustered Sample A sample from a specialized group of the population.

Co-interior Angles Two angles formed by 2 lines and a transversal. Co-interior angles are on the same side of the transversal in a $\sqsubset$ or $\sqsupset$ pattern.

Commission A percent of the cost of goods sold.

Common Denominator A number that is a common multiple of the denominators of a set of fractions. The common denominator of $\frac{1}{2}$ and $\frac{1}{3}$ is 6.

Common Factor A number that is a factor of two or more numbers. The common factor of 6 and 9 is 3.

Common Multiple A number that is a multiple of two or more numbers. Common multiples of 6 and 10 are 30, 60, 90, and so on.

Complementary Angles Two angles whose sum is 90°.

Composite Figures Figures made up of 2 or more distinct regions.

Composite Number A number that has more than 2 different factors. $6 = 1 \times 2 \times 3$

Composite Solid A combination of two or more simple solids.

Computer Spreadsheet A computer program that stores information in cells and uses formulas to perform a variety of computations.

Congruent Figures Figures with the same size and shape.

Consecutive Numbers Numbers that differ by 1. Examples are 7, 8, and 9.

Coordinate Plane The 2-dimensional or (x, y) plane. Also known as the Cartesian plane.

Coordinates An ordered pair, (x, y), that locates a point on a coordinate plane.

Corresponding Angles Angles that have the same relative positions in geometric figures.

Corresponding Angles (from 2 lines and a transversal) Two angles that form an $\vdash$, $\dashv$, $\vdash$, $\dashv$ pattern.

Corresponding Sides Sides that have the same relative positions in geometric figures.

Cube A polyhedron with 6 congruent square faces.

Cylinder A solid whose base and top are two equal, parallel circles. A glue stick is an example.

D

Data Facts or information.

Database An organized and sorted list of information.

Decagon A polygon with 10 sides.

Degree The unit for measuring angles. $1° = \frac{1}{360}$ of a complete turn.

Denominator The number of equal parts in a whole or a group. In $\frac{3}{4}$ the denominator is 4.

Diagonal A line segment joining 2 non-adjacent vertices in a polygon.

Diameter A chord that passes through the centre of a circle.

Dilatation A transformation that changes the size of an object.

Discount An amount deducted from the price of an item.

Divisible A number is divisible by another number when the remainder is zero.

Dodecagon A polygon with 12 sides.

E

Edge The straight line formed where 2 faces of a polyhedron meet.

Enlargement A dilatation for which the image is larger than the original figure.

Equation A number sentence that contains the symbol =.

Equilateral Triangle A triangle with all sides equal.

Equivalent Fractions Fractions, such as $\frac{1}{3}$, $\frac{2}{6}$, and $\frac{3}{9}$, that represent the same part of a whole or a group.

Equivalent Ratios Ratios, such as 1:3, 2:6, and 3:9, that represent the same fractional number or amount.

Estimate An approximate value.

Event Any possible outcome of an experiment in probability.

Expanded Form The way in which numbers are written to show the total value of each digit. $235 = 2 \times 100 + 3 \times 10 + 5 \times 1$

Exponent The raised number used in a power to show the number of repeated multiplications of the base. In 4^2, the exponent is 2.

Exponential Form A shorthand method for writing numbers expressed as repeated multiplications. $81 = 3 \times 3 \times 3 \times 3 = 3^4$

Expression A mathematical phrase made up of numbers and variables, connected by operators.

Exterior Angle of a Polygon An angle formed by one extended side of a polygon and the other side at the same vertex.

F

Face A plane surface of a polyhedron.

Factors The numbers multiplied to give a specific product.

Flow Chart An organized diagram that displays the steps in the solution to a problem.

Formula An equation that shows how quantities are related.

Fraction A number that describes part of a whole or part of a group.

Frequency The number of times an item or event occurs.

Frequency Table A table that uses tallies to count data.

G

Graph A representation of data in a pictorial form.

Greatest Common Factor (GCF) The largest factor that two or more numbers have in common. The GCF of 8, 12, and 24 is 4.

Grid A pattern of dots or lines.

H

Height The perpendicular distance from a vertex of a polygon to the opposite side.

Hexagon A polygon with 6 sides.

Hypotenuse The side opposite the right angle in a right triangle.

I

Image The figure produced by a transformation.

Improper Fraction A fraction whose numerator is greater than its denominator.

Independent Events Events in which the outcome of one event has no effect on the outcome of another event.

Inequality The statement that one expression is greater than, less than, or not equal to another expression.

Integers Numbers in the sequence ..., -3, -2, -1, 0, 1, 2, 3, ...

Intersecting Lines Two lines that cross each other at 1 point.

Irrational Number A number such as $\sqrt{2}$ that cannot be written as the quotient of two integers. It is a non-repeating and non-terminating decimal.

Isosceles Right Triangle A triangle with one 90° angle and 2 equal sides.

Isosceles Triangle A triangle with 2 equal sides.

K

Key Digit The digit to the right of the place value to which a number is being rounded.

Kite A quadrilateral with 2 pairs of adjacent sides equal.

L

Like Terms Terms such as x and $4x$ with the same variable.

Line A set of points that contains no endpoints.

Line of Symmetry A mirror line that reflects an object onto itself.

Line Segment A part of a line. A line segment has 2 endpoints.

Lowest Common Denominator (LCD) The lowest multiple shared by two or more denominators. The LCD of $\frac{1}{8}$ and $\frac{1}{6}$ is 24.

Lowest Terms A way of writing a fraction so that the numerator and denominator have no common factors other than 1.

M

Mapping A correspondence of points between an object and its image.

Mass The amount of matter in an object. Mass is usually measured in grams or kilograms.

Matrix A matrix is composed of a rectangular assembly of numbers, in rows and columns.

Mean The sum of the numbers divided by the number of numbers in a set.

Median The middle number in a set of numbers arranged in order. If there is an even number of numbers, the median is the average of the 2 middle numbers.

Midpoint The point that divides a line segment into 2 equal parts.

Mixed Number A number that is the sum of a whole number and a fraction. An example is $3\frac{1}{6}$.

Mode The number that occurs most frequently in a set of data. In 1, 2, 2, 6, 6, 6, the mode is 6.

Multiples Repeated additions within a group. For example, 5, 10, 15, and 20 are multiples of 5.

N

Natural Numbers Numbers in the sequence 1, 2, 3, 4, 5, … .

Net A pattern used to construct a polyhedron.

Nonagon A polygon with 9 sides.

Non-repeating Decimal A decimal in which a digit or digits do no repeat.

Non-terminating Decimal A decimal that continues without end, such as 0.3333…

Numerator The number of equal parts being considered in a whole or a group. In the fraction $\frac{3}{4}$, the numerator is 3.

O

Obtuse Angle An angle whose measure is more than 90° but less than 180°.

Obtuse Triangle A triangle with 1 obtuse angle.

Octagon A polygon with 8 sides.

Opening Price The price of one share of stock at the time when the stock market opens for the day.

Opposite Angles The equal angles formed by 2 intersecting lines.

Order of Operations The rules to be followed when simplifying expressions: **B**rackets, **E**xponents, **D**ivision and **M**ultiplication, **A**ddition and **S**ubtraction.

Ordered Pair A pair of numbers, (x, y), indicating the x- and y-coordinates of a point on a coordinate plane.

Origin The intersection of the horizontal and vertical axes on a graph. The origin has coordinates (0, 0).

Outcome The result of an experiment.

P

Parallel Lines Lines in the same plane that never meet.

Parallelogram A quadrilateral with opposite sides parallel and equal in length.

Pentagon A polygon with 5 sides.

Percent A fraction or ratio in which the denominator is 100.

Perfect Square A number that has a whole number as its principal square root.

Perimeter The distance around a polygon.

Perpendicular Lines Two lines that intersect at a 90° angle.

Perspective The different views of an object; for example, top, bottom, side, front.

Pi (π) The quotient that results when the circumference of a circle is divided by its diameter.

Pictograph A graph that uses pictures or symbols to represent similar data.

Poll A survey used to get people's opinions.

Polygon A closed figure formed by 3 or more line segments.

Polyhedron A 3-dimensional figure with polygons as faces.

Population The entire set of items from which data can be taken.

Power A number, such as 3^4, written in exponential form.

Prime Factorization A composite number expressed as a product of its prime factors. $30 = 2 \times 3 \times 5$

Prime Number A number with exactly 2 different factors, 1 and itself. $3 = 1 \times 3$

Principal An amount of money deposited or borrowed.

Principal Square Root The positive square root of a number.

Prism A polyhedron with 2 parallel and congruent bases in the shape of polygons. The other faces are parallelograms.

Probability The ratio of the number of ways an outcome can occur to the total number of possible outcomes.

Program A set of instructions that a computer carries out in order.

Proper Fraction A fraction whose numerator is smaller than its denominator.

Proportion An equation, such as $\frac{3}{4} = \frac{6}{8}$, which states that 2 ratios are equal.

Pyramid A polyhedron with 1 base and the same number of triangular faces as there are sides on the base.

Pythagorean Theorem The area of the square drawn on the hypotenuse of a right triangle is equal to the sum of the areas of the squares drawn on the other 2 sides.

Q

Quadrant One of the 4 regions formed in the coordinate plane by the intersection of the x-axis and the y-axis.

Quadrilateral A polygon with 4 sides.

Quotient A number resulting from a division.

R

Radius The length of the line segment that joins the centre of a circle and a point on the circumference.

Random Sample A sample in which each member of the population has an equal chance of being selected.

Range The difference between the highest and lowest numbers in a set.

Rate A comparison of 2 measurements with different units, such as $\frac{9 \text{ m}}{2 \text{ s}}$.

Ratio A comparison of numbers, such as 4:5 or $\frac{4}{5}$.

Rational Number A number that can be expressed as the quotient of 2 integers.

Ray A part of a line. A ray contains 1 endpoint.

Real Numbers All rational and irrational numbers.

Reciprocals Two numbers whose product is 1.

Rectangle A quadrilateral with opposite sides parallel and equal in length, and with four 90° angles.

Rectangular Prism A prism whose bases are congruent rectangles.

Reduction A dilatation for which the image is smaller than the original figure.

Reflection A flip transformation of an object in a mirror line or reflection line.

Reflex Angle An angle whose measure is more than 180° but less than 360°.

Regular Polygon A closed figure with all sides equal and all angles equal.

Regular Polyhedron A 3-dimensional figure with identical regular polygons as faces.

Relation A set of ordered pairs.

Repeating Decimal A decimal in which a digit or digits repeat without end. $\frac{9}{11} = 0.818181...$ or $0.\overline{81}$

Rhombus A quadrilateral with opposite sides parallel and all 4 sides equal.

Right Angle An angle whose measure is 90°.

Right Triangle A triangle with 1 right angle.

S

Sample A selection from a population.

Sample Space The possible outcomes from an experiment.

Scale Drawing An accurate drawing that is either an enlargement or a reduction of an actual object.

Scalene Right Triangle A triangle with one 90° angle and no sides equal.

Scalene Triangle A triangle with no sides equal.

Scientific Notation A short-form notation that involves decimals and powers of ten. $849\,000 = 8.49 \times 10^5$

Semicircle Half of a circle.

Shell A 3-dimensional object whose interior is empty.

Skeleton A representation of the edges of a polyhedron.

Solid A 3-dimensional object whose interior is completely filled.

Solution A number that replaces a variable to make an equation true.

Solving by Inspection Mentally solving an equation or problem.

Square A quadrilateral with 4 equal sides and 4 right angles.

Square Root of a Number A number that multiplies itself to give the number. $8 \times 8 = 64$, so 8 is a square root of 64.

Standard Form The way in which numbers are usually written. Examples are 2.345 and 678 000.

Stem-and-Leaf Plot Numbers tabulated so that the last digit is the leaf, and the digit or digits in front of it are the stem.

Straight Angle An angle whose measure is 180°.

Stratified Sample The population is divided into different groups. Samples are chosen in the same proportion as the numbers in each group.

Supplementary Angles Two angles whose sum is 180°.

Surface Area The sum of the areas of the faces of a 3-dimensional figure.

Survey A sampling of information.

T

Tan Each shape in a tangram.

Tangram A square puzzle cut into seven geometric shapes.

Terminating Decimal A decimal, such as 3.154, whose digits terminate.

Transformation A mapping of points of a plane onto points of the same plane.

Transversal A line that intersects 2 lines in the same plane at 2 distinct points.

Trapezoid A quadrilateral with exactly 2 parallel sides.

Tree Diagram A diagram that shows the possible outcomes of consecutive events.

Triangle A polygon with 3 sides.

U

Unit Rate A comparison of 2 measurements in which the second term is 1, for example, $\frac{3 \text{ m}}{1 \text{ s}}$ or 3 m/s.

Unlike Terms Terms, such as $2x$, $3x^2$, and $2y$, with different variables.

V

Variable A letter or symbol used to represent a number.

Vertex The common endpoint of 2 rays or line segments.

Volume The number of cubic units contained in a space.

W

Whole Numbers Numbers in the sequence 0, 1, 2, 3, 4, 5, ...

X

x-axis The horizontal number line in the Cartesian coordinate system.

x-coordinate The first number in an ordered pair.

Y

y-axis The vertical number line in the Cartesian coordinate system.

y-coordinate The second number in an ordered pair.

Index

square roots, 29
Standard form of numbers, 4, 7, 10, 11
Statistics, xx, 312
  biased answer, 316
  biased sample, 312
  census, 312
  clustered sample, 316
  mean, 332
  measures of central tendency, 332
  median, 332
  misleading, 330
  mode, 332
  population, 312
  random sample, 312, 316
  range, 332
  sample, 312
  stratified sample, 316
  surveys, 316
Stem-and-leaf plots, 336
Straight angle, 274
Stratified sample, 316
Substitution, 152
  algebraic expressions, 152
  terms, 152
Subtraction
  fractions, 47, 50
  numbers, 69–70
  rational numbers, 69–70
Supplementary angles, 274
Surface area, 243, 250
  composite solid, 262
  cylinder, 254
  polyhedron, 248
  solids, 262
Surveys
  biased answer, 316
  clustered sample, 316
  random sample, 316
  stratified sample, 316
Symmetry
  line, 225, 278
  patterns, 278
  polygons, 225

T

Tangram, 201, 272
Technology. *See also* Calculators, Computer spreadsheets, Geometry software, Graphics software, Spreadsheets
  computer spreadsheets and exchange rates, 94–95
  formulas in BASIC, 235
  fractions and calculators, 62
  geometry software, 282–283
  graphics software, 328–329
  information superhighway, 184–185
  multi-purpose vehicle, 12–13
  simulations with random numbers, 346–347
  theatrical sets, 124–125
  volumes, 256–257
Terminating decimals, 14
Terms, 152
  algebraic expressions, 152
  like, 186
  lowest, 47
  substitution, 152
  unlike, 186
Transversal, 276
Trapezoid, 282, 283
  angles, 282
  sides, 282
Tree diagram, 340, 342–343, 348
Triangles, 284
  acute, 280
  angles, 280
  area, 226
  equilateral, 280
  exterior angle, 281
  interior angles, 280
  isosceles, 280
  median, 215
  obtuse, 280
  perimeter, 212
  right, 204, 280
  scalene, 280
Triangular prism, 244, 246
Triangular pyramid, 244, 246
Trinomial, 153

U

Unit price, 92
Unit rate, 92

V

Variable, 152
  expression, 152
  isolation of, 188
Vertex
  diagonal, 284
  networks, 300, 301
  shell, 294
  skeleton, 292, 294
  solid, 294
Volume, 234
  composite solid, 262
  cylinder, 254
  estimation, 250–251
  measuring, 250–251
  prism, 252
  solids, 262
  spreadsheet, 256

W

Whole numbers, 15
Word power
  doublets, 73, 117, 325

X

x-axis, 159
x-coordinate, 159

Y

y-axis, 159
y-coordinate, 159

Text Credits

22 Tribune Media Services; **108** Tribune Media Services; **140** United Feature Syndicate; **198** Tribune Media Services

Photo Credits

iii, iv, v Ian Crysler; **vi** Susan Ashukian; **vii** Ian Crysler; **xii top right** Mike and Moppet Reed/Animals, Animals, **centre, bottom right** ZEFA/Masterfile; **xiii** Susan Ashukian; **xiv** Ian Crysler; **xvi, xvii, xviii–xx** Dan Paul; **xxii top** © 1994 M.C. Escher/Cordon Art, Baarn, Holland. all rights reserved, **bottom** Canadian Olympic Association; **xxiii** Dan Paul; **1** Dan Paul (photo manipulation by Jun Park); **2 left** Dan Paul, **right** Bill Ivy; **4 top right** Electra/First Light, **bottom right** First Light/Dennis Kunkel; **8** Dan Paul; **10** NASA, **11** Science VU-IBMRL/Visuals Unlimited; **14 top** Tourism Nova Scotia, Bill Brooks/Masterfile, Barrett & MacKay, Calgary Convention & Visitors Bureau, Barrett & MacKay/Masterfile; **19** NASA; **20 top** Susan Ashukian; **23** Ian Crysler; **24** Dale Sanders/Masterfile; **26** Susan Ashukian; **29 left** Dan Paul; **30** Canadian Sport Images/Ted Grant; **32 top** National Gallery Of Canada, Ottawa; **33–35** Dan Paul; **41 left** Courtesy of Linda Weilgart, **right** Courtesy of Hal Whitehead; **44** Mark Tomalty/Masterfile; **49** Susan Ashukian; **52 bottom** Calgary Convention & Visitors Bureau; **54** Susan Ashukian; **55** Joe Lepiano; **57** Ralph A. Clevenger/First Light; **58** Susan Ashukian; **60** Ian Crysler; **71** Canadian Sport Images/Mike Ridewood; **72** Dan Paul; **78 79** J.A Kraulis/Masterfile; **81** Boden/Ledingham/Masterfile; **82** Dan Paul; **86–87** Susan Ashukian; **88** Ian Crysler; **90** Adrian Dorst; **91, 92** Susan Ashukian; **94** Joe Lepiano; **95 top, bottom right** Susan Ashukian, **bottom right** Joe Lepiano; **97 top** Dawn Goss/First Light, **bottom** Tom Thomson Photography; **102 top** John Reader/Science Photo Library, **bottom** From © Oxford University Press, Leakey and Harris. Laetoli, 1987. Reprinted by permission of Oxford University Press; **103** John Reader/Science Photo Library; **104** © 1994 Christine Chew/Neo-Sport Photography; **110–111** Michael Melford/Image Bank; **114** Susan Ashukian; **116** Kerry Hayes; **118** Canapress Photo; **119** Susan Ashukian; **120–121** Dan Paul; **127** New Paramount/National Archives of Canada/PA127295; **128** Susan Ashukian; **130** Bank of Canada; **131 top** Geological Survey of Canada, **bottom** Dale Wilson/First Light; **132** Greg Holman; **135** Marineland, Niagara Falls, Canada; **136** Norman Lightfoot/Ivy Images; **150–151** Dan Paul; **152** Susan Ashukian; **156** Barrett & MacKay/Masterfile; **162** Dan Paul; **164** Ian Crysler; **165** Joe Lepiano; **170–171** Springer/Bettmann Film Archive; **174** The Bettmann Archive; **178** Ian Crysler; **179** Susan Ashukian; **190 left** Daryl Benson/Masterfile, **right** Peter Griffith/Masterfile; **194–195** Mike Dobel/Masterfile; **195 map** Copyright © 1994 by The New York Times Company, Reprinted by permission; **200–201** Susan Ashukian (photo manipulation by Pronk&Associates); **206** Artbase Inc.; **208 top** Canapress, **bottom** The Bettmann Archive; **210, 212** Susan Ashukian; **214–215** Ian Crysler; **216 top** Susan Ashukian, **bottom** Roy Ooms/Masterfile; **218 top, 220** Susan Ashukian; **221** Stamp reproduced courtesy of Canada Post Corporation; **222, 225** Ian Crysler; **226, 228, 232** Susan Ashukian; **234** Ian Crysler; **242–243** Ken Davies/Masterfile; **246** Susan Ashukian; **248** Ian Crysler; **250–251** Dan Paul; **252, 254** Susan Ashukian; **257** Ian Crysler; **259, 260 top** Susan Ashukian; **270–271** British Tourist Authority; **272** Dan Paul; **274** Transport Canada: Winnipeg International Airport; **276** Leslie E. Robertson Associates; **278 bottom** Bill Ivy; **280 top** Thomas Kitchen/First Light, **bottom** Dan Paul; **284** Science North, Sudbury; **287 top** Vic Thomasson/Tony Stone Images, **bottom left** Saskatchewan Tourism Authority, **bottom right** Photographie Giraudon, Pairs; **292, 293** Dan Paul; **294 right** Bettmann Archive, **centre** Dallas & John Heaton/First Image, **left** Canapress/Uniphoto; **296 right** Joe Lepiano; **298** The Bettmann Archive; **299** Susan Ashukian; **300** Dan Paul (photo manipulation by Jun Park); **310** Pronk&Associates; **314** Joe Lepiano; **318** Canapress Photo Services; **319** The Public Archives of Canada/C-86515; **324 top** Susan Ashukian; **326** Canapress Photo Services/Hans Deryk; **333** Colin Erricson; **336** National Hockey League; **338** Canapress Photo Service/Tom Hanson; **344, 347** Susan Ashukian; **352 top** Neil Graham, **bottom** Tribune Media Services

Illustration Credits

xi Michael Herman; **xii left** Margo Davies Leclair/Visual Sense Illustration; **xxi** Michael Herman; **12–13** Ian Phillips; **15** Mike Herman; **18, 29 right** Jun Park; **32 map** Stephen Harris; **40** Margo Stahl; **41** Margo Stahl, **graph** The Globe & Mail; **48, 50** Stephen Harris; **52 top** Stephen Harris; **56** Pronk&Associates; **59** Bernadette Lau; **62** Pronk&Associates; **63** Jun Park; **66** Michael Herman; **78 chart** © John Bianchi; **80** Pronk&Associates; **96** Margo Davies Leclair/Visual Sense Illustration; **98 bottom** Bernadette Lau, **top right** Margo Davies Leclair/Visual Sense Illustration; **99** Bernadette Lau; **100** Jun Park; **101** From "A Roman Apartment Complex" by Donald J. Watts and Carol Martin Watts.

Copyright © 1986 by Scientific American, Inc. All
rights reserved; **106** Bernadette Lau; **122** Bill Suddick;
124–125 Ted Nasmith; **126 top** Ted Nasmith, **bottom**
Michel Garneau; **133** Jun Park; **134** Susan Ashukian; **137**
Stephen Harris; **144–145** Ian Phillips/Joe Lepiano; **147**
Dave Whamond; **154** Michael Herman; **160**, **176** Margo
Davies Leclair/Visual Sense Illustration; **184–185** Ian
Phillips; **186** Michael Herman; **218 bottom** Michael
Herman; **230** Michael Herman; **235** Margo Davies
Leclair/Visual Sense Illustrations; **236–237** Michael
Herman; **247**, **249** Margo Davies Leclair/Visual Sense
Illustration; **258** Martha Newbigging; **260 right**, **261**
Margo Davies Leclair/Visual Sense Illustration; **278 top**
Bernadette Lau; **286** Bernadette Lau; **290** James Laish;
295 Margo Davies Leclair/Visual Sense Illustration; **296**
left and **right bottom** Margo Davies Leclair/Visual
Sense Illustration; **308–309** Ted Nasmith; **312** Michael
Herman; **317** Ian Phillips; **320** Michel Garneau; **322**
Bernadette Lau; **324 bottom** Michel Garneau; **328**
top Margo Davies Leclair/Visual Sense Illustration,
bottom Pronk&Associates; **329 top** Pronk&Associates,
centre Susan Ashukian, **bottom** Michel Garneau; **330**
Dave McKay; **331 top** Michel Garneau, **centre** Susan
Ashukian, **bottom** Dave McKay; **332** Andrew Plewes; **342**
Pronk&Associates

WINDSOR SECONDARY SCHOOL
931 BROADVIEW DRIVE
NORTH VANCOUVER, BC V7H 2E9

011215